Published by
The Kabbalah Centre International Inc.

155 E. 48th St., New York, NY 10017
1062 S. Robertson Blvd., Los Angeles, CA 90035

Director Rav Berg

First Printing 2001

Revised Edition 2003

Printed in USA

ISBN: 1-57189-198-6

בזכות רבי שמעון בר יוחאי
והזהר הקדוש

להורי

יוסף בן מרים ואברהם
שמחה בת קלרה ואברהם

לבריאות, אושר, שמחה והצלחה כלכלית - נצחיים
שנזכה לחצות את גבולות ההגיון, שנדע להבדיל בין טוב לרע
שנזכה לכח לעזור לנו ולאחרים

לחיים טובים וארוכים
לאחיי

דוד, רינת ושמואל

אושר, שלווה ומציאת הזיווג המתאים

שאזכה לשלמות עם עצמי ומעשיי, שאדע להעניק אהבה אינסופית. להגשמת חלומותיי ויעודי בחיים, מציאת הזיווג הנכון והקמת בית בישראל. שלעולם לא אדע פחד, למען הפצת הקבלה והזהר הקדוש, לחיבור לכח של בילע המות לנצח ותחיית המתים, ביחד עם הרב וקרן וכל הסניפים בעולם.

״משום שעתידים ישראל לטעום מעץ החיים
שהוא ספר הזהר הזה, יצאו בו
מן הגלות ברחמים״

אור בת יוסף ושמחה

לעילוי נשמת

אהרון בן מסלי

אבי

לב בן יעקב

סבתי

שנדל בת אברהם

ת.נ.צ.ב.ה.

להבדיל, לחיים טובים וארוכים, לבריאות,
פרנסה והצלחה, לגדילה רוחנית וחיבור אינסופי לאור

לבעלי

שמואל בן זינאידה ושמעון

הבנות

נחמה בת שמואל

מרים בת אהרון

לאימי

לריסה בת שנדל ורומן

לאחותי

נטלי בת לייב ולריסה

שבזכות רבי שמעון בר יוחאי וספר הזהר הקדוש
יתגלה המשיח במהרה בימינו, אמן

מוהש

תודה לזהר הקדוש
ולספר פנחס בפרט
שריפא אותי ממחלת נפש קשה, כרונית וחשוכת מרפא.

אני מקדיש דף זה לקהילת נפגעי הנפש
המיוחדת והמקסימה באשר היא.

עוצמתה האדירה של אנרגית הזהר
טמונה בעדינותה וברכותה.
היפתחו אליה וקבלוה באהבה והרבה רצון.

בני האנוש, החי, הצומח, הדומם
והיקום כולו עשויים מאבק נוצץ של אהבה.
האור הוא האהבה והאהבה היא האור.

תאהבו את עצמכם ואת הסובב לכם.
זוהי הדרך להרפא.

אפשר

אוהב אתכם
שחר יהלום

״פותח את ידך ומשביע לכל חי רצון״

שבזכות הפצת הזהר הקדוש נזכה לפתוח את ידינו
לנתינה והשפעה אין סופית
ושיתקיים הפסוק
״וייתן לך האלקים מטל השמים
ומשמני הארץ ורוב דגן ותירוש...״

לחיים ארוכים, אור ובריאות

ישראל יעקב רז

פנינה רז

תמר ודוד זדרמן ומשפחתם

ארז ואורנה רז ומשפחתם

ניר ונעה רז ומשפחתם

צפורה וייס

ורד רז למציאת הזיווג המתאים

שזכות ספר הזהר יגן עליהם כל ימי חייהם
ויאיר דרכם עם כל עם ישראל, אמן.

לעילוי נשמת

מרדכי דוד רסלר נלב״ע ל׳ ניסן תשל״ט

מרים רסלר נלב״ע כ״ט כסלו תשמ״ו

בצלאל וייס נלב״ע א׳ אדר תש״ס

שנשמתם תהא צרורה בצרור החיים

לדיאן

Diane

שזכותו של ספר הזהר

וחכמת הקבלה

יגנו עליה.

שהאור והברכה יביאו הצלחה בעסקים

ושתזכה, בזכות זו, למצוא בן זוג אמיתי

בקרוב וביחד יחיו חיי אור ואושר

ויזכו להפיץ את האור לעולם

May the light of the Zohar
bring peace, harmony and joy
to

Greg Oyster

and his son

Cyrrus Oyster

for finding a soulmate, protection,
love and success.

For the entire family

Frank and Carol Oyster
Rima, Stacy and Dennis
Mathew, Nicolas, Bobby
Amanda and Xavier

May immortality bring peace on earth
for all of mankind.

To the Rav and Karen
Thank you for sharing the Light.
May the Light of the Zohar
open the hearts of the people
of the world and fill them with love
and may my family and friends
be blessed with good health,
sustenance and spiritual wisdom.

פלורנס בת גון ופלורנס גירדנו

New York

APPLYING THE POWER OF THE ZOHAR

The Zohar is a book of great mystical power and wisdom. It is Universally recognized as the definitive work on the Kabbalah – and it is also so Much more.

The Zohar is a wellspring of spiritual energy, a fountainhead of metaphysical power that not only reveals and explains, but literally brings blessing, protection, and well-being into the lives of all those who read or peruse its sacred texts. All that is required is worthy desire, the certainty of a trusting heart, and an open and receptive mind. Unlike other books, including the great spiritual texts of other traditions, The Zohar is written in a kind of code, through which metaphors, parables, and cryptic language at first conceal but ultimately reveal the forces of creation.

As electrical current is concealed in wire and cable before disclosing itself as an illuminated light bulb, the spiritual Light of the Creator is wrapped in allegory and symbolism throughout the Aramaic text of the Zohar. And while many books contain information and knowledge, the Zohar both expresses and embodies spiritual Light. The very letters on its pages have the power to bring spiritual wisdom and positive energy into every area of our lives.

As we visually scan the Aramaic texts and study the accompanying insights that appear in English, spiritual power is summoned from above – and worlds tremble as Light is sent forth in response.

It's primary purpose is not only to help us acquire wisdom, but to draw Light from the Upper Worlds and to bring sanctification into our lives. Indeed, the book itself is the most powerful of all tools for cleansing the soul and connecting to the Light of the Creator. As you open these pages, therefore, do not make understanding in the conventional sense your primary goal.

Although you may not have a knowledge of Aramaic, look first at the Aramaic text before reading the English. Do not be discouraged by difficulties with comprehension. Instead, open your heart to the spiritual transformation the Zohar is offering you.

Ultimately, the Zohar is an instrument for refining the individual soul – for removing darkness from the earth – and for bringing well being and blessing to our fellow man.

Its purpose is not only to make us intellectually wise, but to make us spiritually pure.

Torah

Also known as the Five Books of Moses, the Torah is considered to be the physical body of learning, whereas the Zohar is the internal soul. The literal stories of the Torah conceal countless hidden secrets. The Zohar is the Light that illuminates all of the Torah's sublime mysteries.

Beresheet	Genesis
Shemot	Exodus
Vayikra	Leviticus
Bemidbar	Numbers
Devarim	Deuteronomy

Prophets

Amos	Amos
Chagai	Haggai
Chavakuk	Habakkuk
Hoshea	Hosea
Malachi	Malachi
Melachim	Kings
Michah	Micah
Nachum	Nahum
Ovadyah	Obadiah
Shmuel	Samuel
Shoftim	Judges
Tzefanyah	Zephaniah
Yechezkel	Ezekiel
Yehoshua	Joshua
Yeshayah	Isaiah
Yirmeyah	Jeremiah
Yoel	Joel
Yonah	Jonah
Zecharyah	Zechariah

Writings

Daniel	Daniel
Divrei Hayamim	Chronicles
Eicha	Lamentations
Ester	Esther
Ezra	Ezra
Nechemiah	Nehemiah
Iyov	Job
Kohelet	Ecclesiastes
Mishlei	Proverbs
Rut	Ruth
Sir Hashirim	Songs of Songs
Tehilim	Psalms

The Ten Sfirot – Emanations

To conceal the blinding *Light* of the Upper World, and thus create a tiny point into which our universe would be born, ten *curtains* were fabricated. These ten *curtains* are called Ten Sfirot. Each successive Sfirah further reduces the emanation of *Light*, gradually dimming its brilliance to a level almost devoid of *Light* – our physical world known as *Malchut*. The only remnant of Light remaining in this darkened universe is a *pilot light* which sustains our existence. This Light is the life force of a human being and the force that gives birth to stars, sustains suns and sets everything from swirling galaxies to busy ant hills in motion. Moreover, the Ten Sfirot act like a prism, refracting the Light into many *colors* giving rise to the diversity of life and matter in our world.

The Ten Sfirot are as follows:

Keter	Crown
Chochmah	Wisdom
Binah	Understanding
Da'at	Knowledge
Zeir Anpin	Small Face,
	(includes the next six Sfirot):
Chesed	Mercy (Chassadim - plural)
Gvurah	Judgment (Gvurot - Plural)
Tiferet	Splendor
Netzach	Victory (Eternity)
Hod	Glory
Yesod	Foundation
Malchut	Kingdom

The Partzufim - Spiritual forms

One complete structure of the Ten Sfirot creates a *Partzuf* or Spiritual Form. Together, these forces are the building blocks of all reality. As water and sand combine to create cement, the Ten Sfirot combine to produce a Spiritual Form

[Partzuf]. Each of the Spiritual Forms below are therefore composed of one set of Ten Sfirot.

These Spiritual Forms are called:

Atik	Ancient
Atik Yomin	Ancient of Days
Atika Kadisha	Holy Ancient
Atik of Atikin	Anceint of Ancients
Aba	Father
Arich Anpin	Long Face
Ima	Mother
Nukva	Female
Tevunah	Intelligence
Yisrael Saba	Israel Grandfather
Zachar	Male

These names are not meant to be understood literally. Each represents a unique spiritual force and building block, producing a substructure and foundation for all the worlds make up reality.

The Five Worlds

All of the above Spiritual Forms *[Partzufim]* create one spiritual world. There are Five Worlds in total that compose all reality, therefore, five sets of the above Spiritual Forms are required.

Our physical world corresponds to the world of: Asiyah – Action

Adam Kadmon	Primordial Man
Atzilut	Emanation
Briyah	Creation
Yetzirah	Formation
Asiyah	Action

The Five Levels of the soul

Nefesh	First, Lowest level of Soul
Ruach	Second level of Soul
Neshamah	Third level of Soul
Chayah	Fourth level of Soul
Yechidah	Highest, fifth level of Soul

Names of God

As a single ray of white sunlight contains the seven colors of the spectrum, the one Light of the Creator embodies many diverse spiritual forces. These different forces are called *Names of God.* Each Name denotes a specific attribute and spiritual power. The Hebrew letters that compose these Names are the interface by which these varied Forces act upon our physical world. The most common Name of God is the Tetragrammaton (the four letters, *Yud Hei Vav Hei* יהוה.) Because of the enormous power that the Tetragrammaton transmits, we do not utter it aloud. When speaking of the Tetragrammaton, we use the term *Hashem* which means, *The Name.*

Adonai, El, Elohim, Hashem, Shadai, Eheyeh, Tzevaot, Yud Hei Vav Hei

People

Er	The son of Noach
Rabbi Elazar	The son of Rabbi Shimon bar Yochai
Rabbi Shimon bar Yochai	Author of the Zohar
Shem, Cham, Yefet	Noach's children
Shet	Seth
Ya'akov	Jacob
Yishai	Jesse (King David's father)
Yitzchak	Isaac
Yosef	Joseph
Yitro	Jethro
Yehuda	Judah

Angels

Angels are distinct energy components, part of a vast communication network running through the upper worlds. Each unique Angel is responsible for transmitting various forces of influence into our physical universe.

Adriel, Ahinael, Dumah (name of Angel in charge of the dead), Gabriel, Kadshiel, Kedumiel, Metatron, Michael, Rachmiel,

Raphael, Tahariel, Uriel

Nations

Nations actually represent the inner attributes and character traits of our individual self. The nation of Amalek refers to the doubt and uncertainty that dwells within us when we face hardship and obstacles. Moab represents the dual nature of man. Nefilim refers to the sparks of Light that we have defiled through our impure actions, and to the negative forces that lurk within the human soul as a result of our own wrongful deeds.

Amalek, Moab, Nefilim

General

Aba	Father Refers to the male principle and positive force in our universe. Correlates to the proton in an atom.
Arvit	The Evening prayer
Chayot	Animals
Chupah	Canopy (wedding ceremony)
Et	The
Avadon	Hell
Gehenom	Hell
Sheol	Hell The place a soul goes for purification upon leaving this world.
Ima	Mother The female principle and minus force in our universe. Correlates to the electron in an atom.
Kiddush	Blessing over the wine
Klipah	Shell (negativity)
Klipot	Shells (Plural)
Kriat Sh'ma	The Reading of the Sh'ma
Mashiach	Messiah
Minchah	The Afternoon prayer
Mishnah	Study
Mochin	Brain, Spiritual levels of Light
Moed	A designated time or holiday
Negev	The south of Israel
Nukva	Female
Partzuf	Face
Shacharit	The Morning prayer
Shamayim	Heavens (sky)
Shechinah	The Divine presence, The female aspect of the Creator
Tefilin	Phylacteries
The Dinur river	The river of fire
Tzadik	Righteous person
Zion	Another name for Jerusalem
Yisrael	The land of Israel The nation of Israel or an individual Israelite
Zohar	Splendor

The Hebrew vowels

Chirik אִ, Cholam אוֹ אֹ, Kamatz אָ, Patach אַ, Segol אֶ, Sh'va אְ, Shuruk אוּ אֻ, Tzere אֵ.

The Twelve Tribes

Asher, Dan, Ephraim, Gad, Issachar, Judah, Levi, Menasheh, Naphtali, Reuben, Shimon, Zebulun

Jewish Holidays

Rosh Hashanah	The Jewish New Year
Yom Kippur	Day of Atonement
Sukkot	Holiday of the Booths
Shmini Atzeret	The day of Convocation
Simchat Torah	Holiday on which we dance with the Torah
Pesach	Passover
Shavout	Holiday of the Weeks

כרך כב

פרשת ואתחנן, עקב, שופטים,
כי תצא, וילך, האזינו

Vol. XXII

Vaetchanan, Ekev, Shoftim
Ki Tetze, Vayelech, Ha'azinu

A Prayer from The Ari

To be recited before the study of the Zohar

Ruler of the universe, and Master of all masters, The Father of mercy and forgiveness, we thank You, our God and the God of our fathers, by bowing down and kneeling, that You brought us closer to Your Torah and Your holy work, and You enable us to take part in the secrets of Your holy Torah. How worthy are we that You grant us with such big favor, that is the reason we plead before You, that You will forgive and acquit all our sins, and that they should not bring separation between You and us.

And may it be your will before You, our God and the God of our fathers, that You will awaken and prepare our hearts to love and revere You, and may You listen to our utterances, and open our closed heart to the hidden studies of Your Torah, and may our study be pleasant before Your Place of Honor, as the aroma of sweet incense, and may You emanate to us Light from the source of our soul to all of our being. And, may the sparks of your holy servants, through which you revealed Your wisdom to the world, shine.

May their merit and the merit of their fathers, and the merit of their Torah, and holiness, support us so we shall not stumble through our study. And by their merit enlighten our eyes in our learning as it stated by King David, The Sweet Singer of Israel: "Open my eyes, so that I will see wonders from Your Torah" (Tehilim 119:18). Because from His mouth God gives wisdom and understanding.

"May the utterances of my mouth and the thoughts of my heart find favor before You, God, my Strength and my Redeemer" (Tehilim 19:15).

VAETCHANAN

Name of Articles

1. "but you shall meditate therein day and night"

A Synopsis

Rabbi Yosi emphasizes the deep importance of meditating constantly on the Torah. He says that people must accept upon themselves the yoke of the kingdom of heaven when they go to sleep since everyone tastes death at night.

1. וָאֶתְחַנַּן אֶל יְיָ׳ בָּעֵת הַהִיא לֵאמֹר. אֲדֹנָ״י יֱדֹוִ״ד אַתָּה הַחִלּוֹתָ לְהַרְאוֹת אֶת עַבְדְּךָ וְגוֹ׳. ר׳ יוֹסֵי פָּתַח, וַיַּסֵּב חִזְקִיָּהוּ פָּנָיו אֶל הַקִּיר וַיִּתְפַּלֵּל אֶל יְיָ׳. ת״ח, כַּמָּה הוּא חֵילָא תַּקִּיפָא דְּאוֹרַיְיתָא, וְכַמָּה הוּא עִלָּאָה עַל כֹּלָּא. דְּכָל מַאן דְּאִשְׁתְּדַל בְּאוֹרַיְיתָא, לָא דָּחִיל מֵעִלָּאֵי וְתַתָּאֵי. וְלָא דָּחִיל מֵעַרְעוּרִין בִּישִׁין דְּעָלְמָא. בְּגִין דְּאִיהוּ אָחִיד בְּאִילָנָא דְּחַיֵּי, וְאָכִיל מִנֵּיהּ בְּכָל יוֹמָא.

1. "And I besought Hashem at that time, saying, Adonai Elohim, You began to show Your servant" (Devarim 3:23-24). Rabbi Yosi opened with, "Then Hezekiah turned his face toward the wall, and prayed to Hashem" (Yeshayah 38:2). Come and see how powerful is the force of the Torah and how superior it is to anything else. For whoever is occupied with the Torah does not fear the higher or lower beings, nor fear evil incidents in the work, because he is attached to the Tree of Life, WHICH IS THE TORAH, and eats from it daily.

2. דְּהָא אוֹרַיְיתָא אוֹלִיף לֵיהּ לְב״נ, לְמֵיהַךְ בְּאֹרַח קְשׁוֹט. אוֹלִיף לֵיהּ עֵיטָא הֵיךְ יְתוּב קַמֵּי מָארֵיהּ. וַאֲפִילּוּ יִתְגְּזָר עָלֵיהּ מוֹתָא, כֹּלָּא יִתְבַּטַּל וְיִסְתַּלַּק מִנֵּיהּ, וְלָא שַׁרְיָא עֲלוֹי. וְע״ד בָּעֵי לְאִשְׁתַּדְּלָא בְּאוֹרַיְיתָא יְמָמָא וְלֵילֵי, וְלָא יִתְעֲדֵי מִנַּהּ, הה״ד וְהָגִיתָ בּוֹ יוֹמָם וָלַיְלָה. וְאִי אַעְדֵּי מִינֵּיהּ אוֹרַיְיתָא, אוֹ אִתְפְּרַשׁ מִנַּהּ, כְּאִלּוּ אִתְפְּרַשׁ מִן חַיֵּי.

2. For the Torah teaches man to walk the path of truth and gives him counsel how to repent before his Master. Even when he is sentenced to death, everything is repealed and gone from him, not to rest upon him. Therefore he should be occupied with the Torah day and night and not move from it. This is the meaning of, "but you shall meditate therein day and night" (Yehoshua 1:8). If he removed the Torah from himself or separates from it, it is as if he separated from life.

3. ת״ח, עֵיטָא דְּב״נ כַּד אִיהוּ סָלִיק בְּלֵילְיָא עַל עַרְסֵיהּ, בָּעֵי לְקַבְּלָא עָלֵיהּ עוֹל מַלְכוּתָא דִּלְעֵילָּא, בְּלִבָּא שְׁלִים. וּלְאַקְדְּמֵי לְמִימְסַר גַּבֵּיהּ פִּקְדוֹנָא דְּנַפְשֵׁיהּ. וְהָא אוּקְמוּהָ, בְּגִין דְּכָל עָלְמָא טַעֲמִין טַעֲמָא דְּמוֹתָא, דְּהָא אִילָנָא דְּמוֹתָא שַׁרְיָא בְּעָלְמָא, וְכָל רוּחֵי דִּבְנֵי נָשָׁא נָפְקִין, וְסַלְּקִין וְאִתְטַמְּרָן גַּבֵּיהּ. וּבְגִין דְּאִינּוּן בְּפִקְדוֹנָא, כֻּלְּהוּ תַּיְיבִין לְאַתְרַיְיהוּ.

3. Come and see, there is advice for man. When he climbs into his bed at night, he should accept upon himself the yoke of the kingdom of heaven wholeheartedly and hasten to give Him the deposit of his Nefesh. It was explained that this is since every man tastes AT NIGHT the taste of death, because the tree of death rests upon the world, WHICH IS MALCHUT. And all the spirits of people come out, rise and hide in it, IN MALCHUT. Since they are GIVEN as a deposit, they all return LATER to their place.

2. Midnight

A Synopsis

Rabbi Yosi speaks about the obligation that people have to study the Torah at night and to cleanse themselves and go to prayer in the morning. He says that every word that a man utters during his prayers rises up and splits the firmaments.

4. ת״ח, כַּד אִתְּעַר רוּחַ צָפוֹן בְּפַלְגוּת לֵילְיָא, וְכָרוֹזָא נָפִיק. וְקוּדְשָׁא בְּרִיךְ הוּא אָתֵי לְגִנְתָּא דְּעֵדֶן לְאִשְׁתַּעְשְׁעָא בְּרוּחֵיהוֹן דְּצַדִּיקַיָּיא, כְּדֵין מִתְעָרֵי כָּל בְּנֵי מַטְרוֹנִיתָא, וְכָל בְּנֵי הֵיכָלָא, לְשַׁבְּחָא לֵיהּ לְמַלְכָּא קַדִּישָׁא. וּכְדֵין כָּל אִינּוּן פִּקְדוֹנִין דְּרוּחִין דְּאִתְמַסְּרָן בִּידָהּ, כֻּלְּהוּ אָתִיב לְמָארֵיהוֹן. וְרוּבָּא דִּבְנֵי עָלְמָא מִתְעָרִין בְּהַהִיא שַׁעֲתָא, וְהָא פִּקְדוֹנֵיהּ דְּכֻלְּהוּ אָתִיב לְגַבַּיְיהוּ.

4. Come and see, when the north wind awakens at midnight, the crier comes out and the Holy One, blessed be He, comes to the Garden of Eden to be delighted in the spirits of the righteous, and all the members of the Queen's household and all the members of the chamber are roused to praise the Holy King, ZEIR ANPIN. Then the deposits of the spirits handed to her, TO MALCHUT, are all returned to their owners. Most people awaken from their sleep at that time, and their deposits are returned to them all.

5. אִינּוּן דִּבְנֵי הֵיכָלָא עִלָּאָה קַיְימֵי בְּקִיּוּמַיְיהוּ, מִתְעָרֵי מִשְׁתַּדְּלֵי בְּתוּשְׁבַּחְתָּא דְּאוֹרַיְיתָא, וּמִשְׁתַּתְּפֵי בִּכְנֶסֶת יִשְׂרָאֵל, עַד דְּנָהִיר יְמָמָא. כַּד אָתֵי צַפְרָא, הִיא, וְכָל בְּנֵי הֵיכָלָא דְּמַלְכָּא כֻּלְּהוּ אַתְיָין לְגַבֵּי מַלְכָּא קַדִּישָׁא, וְאִינּוּן אִקְרוּן בְּנִין דְּמַלְכָּא וּמַטְרוֹנִיתָא. וְהָא אוּקְמוּהָ.

5. The members of the highest chamber, WHO SERVE HASHEM, take resolve and awaken to be occupied with the praises of the Torah. They join the Congregation of Yisrael, WHICH IS MALCHUT, until daylight. When morning comes, he, together with all the members of the King's chamber, comes to the Holy King, ZEIR ANPIN. They are called the children of the King and Queen. This was already explained.

6. כַּד אָתֵי צַפְרָא, בָּעֵי לְנַקָּאָה גַּרְמֵיהּ בְּכֹלָּא, וּלְמֵיזַן זַיְינֵיהּ, לְאִשְׁתַּדְּלָא עִם מַלְכָּא קַדִּישָׁא, דְּהָא בְּלֵילְיָא אִשְׁתְּדַל בְּמַטְרוֹנִיתָא. הַשְׁתָּא אַתְיָא עִם מַטְרוֹנִיתָא, לְזַוְּוגָא לָהּ עִם מַלְכָּא.

6. When morning comes, one should clean himself in every respect, THE CLEANLINESS OF BOTH BODY AND SOUL, put on his arms, NAMELY THE TZITZIT AND TEFILIN, and endeavor by the Holy King, ZEIR ANPIN, since at night he endeavored by the Queen. Now IN THE MORNING he comes with the Queen to join her to the King.

7. אָתֵי לְבֵי כְּנִישְׁתָּא, מַדְכֵּי גַּרְמֵיהּ בְּקָרְבְּנִין, מְשַׁבַּח בְּתוּשְׁבְּחַתְּיְיהוּ דְּדָוִד מַלְכָּא. אָחִיד תְּפִלִּין בְּרֵישֵׁיהּ, וְצִיצִית בְּגַדְפֵיהּ, אוֹמֵר תְּהִלָּה לְדָוִד. וְהָא אוּקְמוּהָ, צַלֵּי צְלוֹתָא קַמֵּי מָארֵיהּ, בִּצְלוֹתָא בָּעֵי לְמֵיקַם, כְּגַוְונָא דְּמַלְאֲכֵי עִלָּאֵי, לְאִתְחַבְּרָא בַּהֲדַיְיהוּ, דְּאִינּוּן אִקְרוּן הָעוֹמְדִים, כד״א, וְנָתַתִּי לְךָ מַהְלְכִים בֵּין הָעוֹמְדִים. וּלְכַוְּונָא רְעוּתֵיהּ קַמֵּי מָארֵיהּ, וְיִתְבַּע בָּעוּתֵיהּ.

7. He comes to the synagogue, cleanses himself by reciting the offerings, and sings the praises of King David. Fastened with Tefilin on his head and Tzitzit at the corners of his garment, he recites "A praise of David" (Tehilim 145). It was explained that he who prays before his Master should stand when praying like the supernal angels and join those who are called 'those who stand by', as written, "I will give you access among these who stand by" (Zecharyah 3:7). IT BEHOOVES HIM to concentrate his will before his Master and submit his petition.

8. ת״ח, בְּשַׁעֲתָא דְּב״נ קָאִים בְּפַלְגּוּת לֵילְיָא מֵעַרְסֵיהּ, לְאִשְׁתַּדְּלָא בְּאוֹרַיְיתָא, כָּרוֹזָא קָארֵי עָלֵיהּ וְאָמַר, הִנֵּה בָּרֲכוּ אֶת יְיָ׳ כָּל עַבְדֵי יְיָ׳ הָעוֹמְדִים בְּבֵית יְיָ׳ בַּלֵּילוֹת. הַשְׁתָּא כַּד אִיהוּ קָאִים בִּצְלוֹתָא קַמֵּי מָארֵיהּ, הַהוּא כָּרוֹזָא קָארֵי עָלֵיהּ וְאָמַר, וְנָתַתִּי לְךָ מַהְלְכִים בֵּין הָעוֹמְדִים הָאֵלֶּה.

8. Come and see, when man rises at midnight from his bed to be occupied with the Torah, a crier announces over him, saying, "Behold, bless Hashem, all you servants of Hashem, who stand by night in the house of Hashem" (Tehilim 134:1). Now IN THE MORNING, when he stands in prayer before his Master, the crier proclaims about him saying, "I will give you access among these who stand by."

9. בָּתַר דִּמְסַיֵּים צְלוֹתָא בִּרְעוּ קַמֵּי מָארֵיהּ, הָא אוּקְמוּהָ, דְּבָעֵי לְמִימְסַר נַפְשֵׁיהּ בִּרְעוּתָא דְּלִבָּא, לְהַהוּא אֲתָר דְּאִצְטְרִיךְ. וְכַמָּה עֵיטִין אִית לֵיהּ לְבַר נָשׁ בְּכֹלָּא. וּבְשַׁעֲתָא דִּצְלוֹתָא קַיְּימָא, כָּל אִינּוּן מִלִּין דְּאַפִּיק בַּר נָשׁ מִפּוּמֵיהּ בְּהַהִיא צְלוֹתָא, כֻּלְּהוּ סַלְּקִין לְעֵילָּא, וּבָקְעִין אֲוִירִין וּרְקִיעִין, עַד דְּמָטוּ לְהַהוּא אֲתָר דְּמָטוּ וּמִתְעַטְּרוּ בְּרֵישָׁא דְּמַלְכָּא, וְעָבֵיד מִנַּיְיהוּ עֲטָרָה. וְהָא אוּקְמוּהָ חַבְרַיָּיא, צְלוֹתָא דְּבָעֵי ב"נ לְקוּדְשָׁא בְּרִיךְ הוּא, לְכַוְּונָא דִּיהֵא צְלוֹתָא תַּחֲנוּנִים. מְנָלָן. מִמֹּשֶׁה, דִּכְתִּיב וָאֶתְחַנַּן אֶל יְיָ'. דָּא אִיהוּ צְלוֹתָא מְעַלְיָא.

9. After finishing his prayer favorably before his Master, it was explained that it behooves him to deliver his soul with a willing heart to the required place, NAMELY MALCHUT. Man has many counsels about anything. When he is in prayer, all the words a man utters in his mouth in that prayer rise up and cleave airs and firmaments until they reach wherever they reach. They are adorned on the head of the King, who turns them into a diadem. The friends explained that when a man asks the Holy One, blessed be He in his prayer, he should meditate for it to be a prayer of supplication. Whence do we know that? From Moses, as written, "And I besought Hashem" (Devarim 3:23). Such is a goodly prayer.

3. One should cover one's eyes so as not to behold the Shechinah

A Synopsis

We hear from Rabbi Yosi that Rav Hamnuna Saba said anyone who does not keep his eyes lowered or closed during prayer will not see the light of the Shechinah when he dies, nor will he die by a kiss. Whoever stands in prayer should first praise God and then offer his own prayer, and his prayer should unify night and day.

10. ת״ח, מַאן דְּקָאִים בִּצְלוֹתָא, בָּעֵי לְכַוְּונָא רַגְלוֹי, וְאוּקְמוּהָ. וּבָעֵי לְחַפְּיָא רֵישֵׁיהּ, כְּמַאן דְּקָאִים קַמֵּי מַלְכָּא. וּבָעֵי לְמִכְסְיָיה עֵינוֹי, בְּגִין דְּלָא יִסְתָּכַּל בִּשְׁכִינְתָּא. וּבְסִפְרָא דְּרַב הַמְנוּנָא סָבָא אָמַר, מַאן דְּפָקַח עֵינוֹי בְּשַׁעֲתָא דִּצְלוֹתָא, אוֹ דְּלָא מָאִיךְ עֵינוֹי בְּאַרְעָא, אַקְדִּים עָלֵיהּ מַלְאַךְ הַמָּוֶת, וְכַד תִּיפּוּק נַפְשֵׁיהּ, לָא יִסְתָּכַּל בִּנְהִירוּ דִּשְׁכִינְתָּא, וְלָא יָמוּת בִּנְשִׁיקָה. מַאן דִּמְזַלְזֵל בִּשְׁכִינְתָּא מִתְזַלְזֵל הוּא בְּהַהוּא שַׁעֲתָא דְּאִצְטְרִיךְ בֵּיהּ, הה״ד, כִּי מְכַבְּדַי אֲכַבֵּד וּבוֹזַי יֵקָלּוּ.

10. Come and see, whoever stands in prayer should straighten his legs, which has already been explained. He should cover his head as one standing before the king and cover his eyes so as not to behold the Shechinah. In his book Rav Hamnuna Saba said, Whoever opens his eyes during prayer or does not lower his eyes to the ground, the Angel of Death comes to him earlier. When his soul goes out, WHEN HE DEPARTS FROM THE WORLD, he will not see the light of the Shechinah nor die by a kiss. Whoever treats the Shechinah lightly is treated lightly when he needs Her. This is the meaning of, "for them that honor Me I will honor, and they that despise Me shall be lightly esteemed" (I Shmuel 2:30).

11. הַאי מַאן דְּאִסְתָּכַּל בִּשְׁכִינְתָּא, בְּשַׁעֲתָא דְּאִיהוּ מְצַלֵּי. וְהֵיךְ יָכִיל לְאִסְתַּכְּלָא בִּשְׁכִינְתָּא. אֶלָּא לְינְדַע דְּוַדַּאי שְׁכִינְתָּא קַיְּימָא קַמֵּיהּ, הה״ד, וַיַּסֵּב חִזְקִיָּהוּ פָּנָיו אֶל הַקִּיר, דְּתַמָּן שָׁארִי שְׁכִינְתָּא. בג״כ לָא בַּעְיָא לְמֶהֱוֵי חוֹצֵץ בֵּינוֹ וּבֵין הַקִּיר, וְאוּקְמוּהָ.

11. YOU TALK ABOUT he who beholds the Shechinah when he prays, yet how can he look at the Shechinah? AND HE ANSWERS, It means knowing the Shechinah is surely before him WHEN HE PRAYS. HENCE HE MUST NOT OPEN HIS EYES. This is the meaning of, "Then Hezekiah turned his face toward the wall" (Yeshayah 38:2), where the Shechinah rested. For that reason there must be nothing between him and the wall WHEN HE PRAYS. This has already been explained.

12. מַאן דְּקָאֵים בִּצְלוֹתָא, בָּעֵי לְסַדְּרָא שְׁבָחָא דְּמָארֵיהּ בְּקַדְמֵיתָא, וּלְבָתַר יִתְבַּע בָּעוּתֵיהּ. דְּהָא מֹשֶׁה הָכִי אָמַר בְּקַדְמֵיתָא, אַתָּה הַחִלּוֹתָ וְגוֹ'. וּלְבַסּוֹף אֶעְבְּרָה וְגוֹ'. ר' יְהוּדָה אָמַר, מַאי שְׁנָא הָכָא דִּכְתִּיב אֲדֹנָ"י בְּקַדְמֵיתָא, בְּאָלֶ"ף דָּלֶ"ת נוּ"ן יוֹ"ד, וּלְבַסּוֹף ידו"ד, וְקָרֵינָן אֱלֹהִ"ים. אֶלָּא סִדּוּרָא הָכִי הוּא מִתַּתָּא לְעֵילָּא, וּלְאַכְלְלָא מִדַּת יוֹם בְּלַיְלָה, וּמִדַּת לַיְלָה בְּיוֹם וּלְזַוְּוגָא כֹּלָּא כַּחֲדָא כַּדְקָא יָאוּת.

12. Whoever stands in prayer should first arrange the praise of his Master and then recite his own prayer. For this is what Moses said first, "You have begun..." (Devarim 3:23), and at last HE RECITED HIS PRAYER, "I pray You, let me go over..." (Ibid. 25). Rabbi Yehuda said, What is the difference here in first saying Adonai spelled Aleph Dalet Nun Yud and then Yud Hei Vav Hei, which we pronounce Elohim, NAMELY "ADONAI ELOHIM, YOU HAVE BEGUN..." HE ANSWERS, The order is so, from below upwards, SINCE ADONAI IS MALCHUT AND YUD HEI VAV HEI IS ZEIR ANPIN. HE SAID IT SO in order to include the quality of day with night and the quality of night with day and unify everything together properly. THE QUALITY OF DAY IS ZEIR ANPIN AND THE QUALITY OF NIGHT IS MALCHUT.

4. "You have begun to show..."

A Synopsis

Rabbi Yosi says that Moses was in a sense a beginning in the world, encompassing all the children of Yisrael, the Torah, the Tabernacle, the priests and Levites, the twelve tribes with their princes and the seventy members of the Sanhedrin; he was absolutely perfect, and attained what no one else ever did. As Moses was the beginning, King Messiah is the ending, because when he comes there will be perfection in the world. Rabbi Chiya talks about how Moses was told to prepare Joshua to succeed him, as the moon cannot shine until the sun departs. Rabbi Yosi tells us that although all the other nations of the world were given to appointed ministers, Yisrael was kept by God Himself as His own special portion, and He gave them the great gift of the Torah.

13. אַתָּה הַחִלּוֹתָ לְהַרְאוֹת אֶת עַבְדְּךָ. מַאי שֵׁירוּתָא הָכָא. אֶלָּא וַדַּאי מֹשֶׁה שֵׁירוּתָא הֲוָה בְּעָלְמָא, לְמֶהֱוֵי שְׁלִים בְּכֹלָּא. וְאִי תֵּימָא יַעֲקֹב שְׁלִים הֲוָה, וְאִילָנָא אִשְׁתְּלִים לְתַתָּא כְּגַוְונָא דִּלְעֵילָּא. הָכִי הוּא וַדַּאי, אֲבָל מַה דַּהֲוָה לְמֹשֶׁה, לָא הֲוָה לְב"נ אַחֲרָא, דְּהָא אִתְעֲטָּר בִּשְׁלִימוּ יַתִּיר, בְּכַמָּה אֲלַף וְרִבְבָן מִיִּשְׂרָאֵל, בְּאוֹרַיְיתָא, בְּמַשְׁכְּנָא, בְּכֹהֲנִין, בְּלֵיוָאֵי, בִּתְרֵיסַר שְׁבָטִין, רַבְרְבִין מְמָנָן עָלַיְיהוּ, בְּשַׁבְעִין סַנְהֶדְרִין. הוּא אִשְׁתְּלִים בְּגוּפָא שְׁלִים. אַהֲרֹן לִימִינָא, נַחְשׁוֹן לִשְׂמָאלָא, הוּא בֵּינַיְיהוּ.

13. "You have begun to show Your servant" (Devarim 3:23). HE ASKS, What manner of a beginning is here, IN SAYING, "YOU HAVE BEGUN?" AND HE ANSWERS, Surely Moses was a beginning in the world, in being absolutely perfect. You may say that Jacob was perfect PRIOR TO MOSES. For the tree, ZEIR ANPIN, was perfected through him below as it was above, BECAUSE HE HAD TWELVE SONS THAT CORRESPOND TO THE TWELVE BORDERS OF ZEIR ANPIN AND SEVENTY SOULS THAT CORRESPOND TO THE SEVENTY BRANCHES IN THE SUPERNAL TREE, ZEIR ANPIN. It is surely so. But Moses attained what no one else did, by being more completely bedecked with many thousands and tens of thousands of people of Yisrael, with the Torah, with the Tabernacle, with the priests and Levites, with the twelve tribes, WITH TWELVE princes appointed over them, with the seventy members of the Sanhedrin. He was completed in a whole body, THE SECRET OF TIFERET THAT INCLUDES RIGHT AND LEFT. For Aaron was to his right, Nachshon to his left and he was between them.

14. בְּגִין כַּךְ אֶת גָּדְלְךָ, מִימִינָא, דָּא אַהֲרֹן. וְאֶת יָדְךָ הַחֲזָקָה, מִשְּׂמָאלָא, דָּא נַחְשׁוֹן. וְהָא אִתְּמַר. בג״כ מֹשֶׁה שֵׁירוּתָא בְּעָלְמָא הֲוָה. וְאִי תֵּימָא מַאן הֲוָה סִיּוּמָא. סִיּוּמָא מַלְכָּא מְשִׁיחָא הוּא, דְּהָא כְּדֵין יִשְׁתְּכַּח שְׁלִימוּ בְּעָלְמָא, מַה דְּלָא הֲוָה כֵּן לְדָרֵי דָּרִין. בְּהַהוּא זִמְנָא יִשְׁתְּכַּח שְׁלִימוּ לְעֵילָּא וְתַתָּא, וְיֵהוֹן עָלְמִין כֻּלְּהוּ בְּזִוּוּגָא חַד, כְּדֵין כְּתִיב בַּיּוֹם הַהוּא יִהְיֶה יְיָ׳ אֶחָד וּשְׁמוֹ אֶחָד.

14. For that reason IT IS WRITTEN, "YOU HAVE BEGUN TO SHOW YOUR SERVANT Your greatness," NAMELY from the right, Aaron; "and Your mighty hand" (Ibid.), NAMELY from the left, which is Nachshon. We already learned that. It was Moses therefore who was a beginning in the world, AND NOT JACOB. You may ask who was the ending. AND HE ANSWERS, King Messiah is the ending, because then there will be perfection in the world, which was not the case for generations. At that time perfection will abide above and below, and all the worlds will be united as one. Then it is written, "on that day Hashem shall be one, and His name One" (Zecharyah 14:9).

15. וַיֹּאמֶר יְיָ׳ אֵלַי רַב לָךְ אַל תּוֹסֶף וְגוֹ׳. אָמַר ר׳ חִיָּיא, א״ל קוּדְשָׁא בְּרִיךְ הוּא לְמֹשֶׁה, מֹשֶׁה, רַב לָךְ דְּאִזְדַּוְּוגַת בִּשְׁכִינְתָּא, מִכָּאן וּלְהָלְאָה אַל תּוֹסֶף, רַבִּי יִצְחָק אָמַר, רַב לָךְ בִּנְהִירוּ דְּשִׁמְשָׁא דַּהֲוָה גַּבָּךְ, אַל תּוֹסֶף, דְּהָא זִמְנָא דְּסִיהֲרָא מָטָא, וְסִיהֲרָא לָא יָכִיל לְאַנְהָרָא, עַד דְּיִתְכְּנִישׁ שִׁמְשָׁא. אֲבָל וְצַו אֶת יְהוֹשֻׁעַ וְחַזְּקֵהוּ וְאַמְּצֵהוּ. אַנְתְּ דְּהוּא שִׁמְשָׁא, בָּעֵי לְאַנְהָרָא לְסִיהֲרָא, וְהָא אִתְּמַר.

15. "And Hashem said to me, Let it suffice you; speak no more..." (Devarim 3:26). Rabbi Chiya said, The Holy One, blessed be He, said to Moses: 'Moses, "Let it suffice you" to have joined the Shechinah. From now on, "speak no more." Rabbi Yitzchak said, "Let it suffice you," the light of the sun that was with you; "no more" because the time for the moon has come, WHICH IS JOSHUA, and the moon cannot shine until the sun is gathered.

"But charge Joshua, and encourage him, and strengthen him" (Ibid. 28). You, who are the sun, should illuminate the moon. We have already learned this.

16. וְאַתֶּם הַדְּבֵקִים בַּיְיָ' אֱלֹהֵיכֶם וְגוֹ'. ר' יוֹסֵי אָמַר אַשְׁרֵי הָעָם שֶׁכָּכָה לוֹ וְגוֹ'. זַכָּאָה עַמָּא, דְּקוּדְשָׁא בְּרִיךְ הוּא בָּחַר בְּהוּ מִכָּל עַמִּין עכו"ם, וְסָלִיק לוֹן לְעַדְבֵיהּ, וּבָרִיךְ לוֹן בְּבִרְכָתָא דִּילֵיהּ בְּבִרְכָתָא דִּשְׁמֵיהּ, הֲדָא הוּא דִּכְתִּיב כִּי הֵם זֶרַע בֵּרַךְ יְיָ', בֵּרַךְ יְיָ' מַמָּשׁ.

16. "But you that did cleave to Hashem your Elohim" (Devarim 4:4). Rabbi Yosi said, "Happy is that people, that is in such a case" (Tehilim 144:15). Happy is the people whom the Holy One, blessed be He, has chosen above all heathen peoples and raised to His lot, and blessed them with His blessing, with His name's blessing. This is the meaning of, "they are the seed which Hashem has blessed" (Yeshayah 61:9), Hashem has actually blessed, NAMELY, THE BLESSING OF HIS NAME.

17. תָּא חֲזִי, כָּל שְׁאַר עַמִּין דְּעָלְמָא, יָהַב לוֹן קוּדְשָׁא בְּרִיךְ הוּא לְרַבְרְבֵי מְמַנָּן, דְּשַׁלְטִין עֲלַיְיהוּ. וְיִשְׂרָאֵל אָחִיד לוֹן קוּדְשָׁא בְּרִיךְ הוּא לְעַדְבֵיהּ, לְחוּלָקֵיהּ, לְאִתְאַחֲדָא בֵּיהּ מַמָּשׁ. וְיָהִיב לוֹן אוֹרַיְיתָא קַדִּישָׁא, בְּגִין לְאִתְאַחֲדָא בִּשְׁמֵיהּ, וְע"ד וְאַתֶּם הַדְּבֵקִים בַּיְיָ', וְלָא בִּמְמָנָא אַחֲרָא כִּשְׁאַר עַמִּין, וְהָא אוֹקְמוּהָ בְּכַמָּה אֲתָר.

17. Come and see, the Holy One, blessed be He, gave all the rest of the nations in the world to the appointed ministers that rule over them. As for Yisrael, the Holy One, blessed be He, held to them for His lot and portion, to actually unite with them. And He gave them the holy Torah in order to unite with His name. Hence, "you that did cleave to Hashem," and not to any other minister as the other nations. This has been explained in different places.

5. "the voice of the words"

A Synopsis

The rabbis examine the scripture that tells of Moses' admonitions to Yisrael where he reminds them that God spoke to them out of the midst of the fire and that they heard the voice of the words. The people heard the words but saw no form, and we learn that "a form" is an inner voice, namely Binah. Rabbi Elazar talks about the second Torah, Deuteronomy, that Moses spoke himself. He analyzes all the voices, the inner voice, the outer voice and the voice of the words, and the words and the speech that came out and spoke from within the fire. We learn that Yisrael did not want to hear directly from God but only through Moses; this weakened the power of Moses and the power of Malchut. Lastly Rabbi Elazar says that if a person does a wicked deed but has no evil intention he is not punished.

18. וַיְדַבֵּר יְיָ׳ אֲלֵיכֶם מִתּוֹךְ הָאֵשׁ קוֹל דְּבָרִים אַתֶּם שׁוֹמְעִים וְגוֹ׳. א״ר אֶלְעָזָר, הַאי קְרָא אִית לְאִסְתַּכְּלָא בֵּיהּ, קוֹל דְּבָרִים, מַאי קוֹל דְּבָרִים. אֶלָּא קוֹל דְּאִקְרֵי דִּבּוּר, דְּכָל דִּבּוּרָא בֵּיהּ תַּלְיָא. וְע״ד כְּתִיב, וַיְדַבֵּר ה׳ אֲלֵיכֶם, דְּהָא דִּבּוּר בַּאֲתָר דָּא תַּלְיָא, לְהַאי אִקְרֵי קוֹל דְּבָרִים.

18. "And Hashem spoke to you out of the midst of the fire. You heard the voice of the words..." (Devarim 4:12). Rabbi Elazar said, We have to examine this verse. IT SAYS "the voice of the words." What does that mean? AND HE ANSWERS that IT MEANS voice is considered speech, since every speech comes from it. THE VOICE IS ZEIR ANPIN AND SPEECH IS MALCHUT, BUT SINCE WORDS COME FROM VOICE, MALCHUT IS CALLED "THE VOICE OF THE WORDS." Hence it is written, "And Hashem spoke to you OUT OF THE MIDST OF THE FIRE," since speech comes from that place, MALCHUT THAT IS CALLED FIRE. And it, MALCHUT, is called "the voice of the words."

19. אַתֶּם שׁוֹמְעִים, דִּשְׁמִיעָה לָא תַּלְיָא אֶלָּא בְּהַאי. בְּגִין דִּשְׁמִיעָה בְּדִבּוּר תַּלְיָא. וּבג״כ אַתֶּם שׁוֹמְעִים. וְהָא אוֹקְמוּהָ, וְרָצַע אֲדוֹנָיו אֶת אָזְנוֹ בַּמַּרְצֵעַ, בְּגִין דְּפָגִים אַתְרָא דְּאִקְרֵי שְׁמִיעָה, וְהוּא דִּבּוּר וְהוּא שְׁמִיעָה.

19. "You heard," since hearing depends on it, ON MALCHUT, since hearing comes from speech. Hence IT IS WRITTEN, "You heard." This has already been explained. "and his master shall bore his ear through with an awl" (Shemot 21:6), because he blemished that place called hearing, which means both words and hearing.

20. קוֹל דְּבָרִים אַתֶּם שׁוֹמְעִים וּתְמוּנָה אֵינְכֶם רוֹאִים. מַאי וּתְמוּנָה. כד"א וּתְמוּנַת יְיָ' יַבִּיט. ד"א וּתְמוּנָה, דָּא קוֹל פְּנִימָאָה, דְּלָא הֲוָה מִתְחֲזֵי כְּלַל. זוּלָתִי קוֹל, דָּא קוֹל אַחֲרָא דְּקָאַמְרָן. וּתְמוּנָה, אֲמַאי אִקְרֵי הָכִי. בְּגִין דְּכָל תִּקוּנָא דְּגוּפָא מִינֵּיהּ נָפְקָא.

20. "You heard the voice of the words, but saw no form." HE ASKS, What is a form, AND ANSWERS, It resembles "and the similitude of Hashem does he behold" (Bemidbar 12:8), WHICH IS MALCHUT. THIS WAS SAID TO PRAISE MOSES, WHO USED TO LOOK AT THE SHINING MIRROR, WHICH IS ZEIR ANPIN, AND HENCE, "THE SIMILITUDE OF HASHEM DOES HE BEHOLD," WHICH IS MALCHUT THAT REVEALS YUD HEI VAV HEI. According to another explanation, "a form" is an inner voice, NAMELY BINAH, which was not visible at all, NOT EVEN TO MOSES; "only a voice" (Devarim 4:12) refers to another EXTERNAL voice, as we said, NAMELY MALCHUT CALLED "THE VOICE OF THE WORDS." And why is BINAH called a form (or: 'similitude')? HE ANSWERS, Because it manifests the body, WHICH IS ZEIR ANPIN CALLED BODY, THAT IS, THE FORM OF THE SIX EXTREMITIES, THE TWELVE BORDERS AND SEVENTY BRANCHES, ETC. which comes out from it, FROM BINAH.

21. וְאִי תֵּימָא אַחֲרָא אִקְרֵי הָכִי נָמֵי. אִין. דְּהַאי אַחֲרָא תִּקוּנָא דִּלְתַתָּא מִינֵּיהּ נָפְקָא, וּבג"כ, ה' עִלָּאָה ה' תַּתָּאָה, ה' עִלָּאָה, קוֹל גָּדוֹל וְלָא יָסָף, דְּלָא פַּסְקֵי מַבּוּעֵי לְעָלְמִין, וְכָל אִינּוּן קוֹלוֹת תַּמָּן אִשְׁתְּכָחוּ כַּד אִתְיְיהִיבַת אוֹרַיְיתָא לְיִשְׂרָאֵל. וְכֹלָּא נָפְקָא מֵהַהוּא קוֹל פְּנִימָאָה דְּכֹלָּא, בְּגִין דְּבֵיהּ תַּלְיָא מִלְּתָא.

21. You may argue that another, NAMELY MALCHUT, is also named thus, A FORM. WHY IS IT CALLED A FORM? HE ANSWERS, It is so, for the other one IS ALSO CALLED A FORM, BECAUSE the lower manifestations IN

BRIYAH, YETZIRAH AND ASIYAH emerge from it. For that reason BINAH AND MALCHUT ARE CALLED supernal Hei and lower Hei BECAUSE THEY ARE EQUAL. The supernal Hei IS THE SECRET OF, "a great voice which was not heard again" (Devarim 5:19), since its founts never stop flowing, BECAUSE IT IS WITH ABA, CHOCHMAH, IN A NEVER-ENDING UNION. All these voices were there when the Torah was given to Yisrael, THE SECRET OF THE SEVEN VOICES OF ZEIR ANPIN. They all came out from the inner voice above all, WHICH IS BINAH, since everything is suspended from it AS THEY EMANATED FROM BINAH.

22. הַאי דְּאִקְרֵי מִשְׁנֵה תּוֹרָה, מֹשֶׁה מִפִּי עַצְמוֹ אֲמָרָן. וְהָא אוֹקִימְנָא מִלָּה. אֲמַאי הָכִי. אֶלָּא חָכְמָה עִלָּאָה, כְּלָלָא דְּאוֹרַיְיתָא אִתְקְרֵי, וּמִנָּהּ נָפְקָא כֹּלָּא, בְּהַהוּא קוֹל פְּנִימָאָה. לְבָתַר מִתְיַשְּׁבָא כֹּלָּא וְאִתְאֲחָד, בַּאֲתָר דְּאִקְרֵי עֵץ הַחַיִּים, וּבֵיהּ תַּלְיָא כְּלַל וּפְרָט, תּוֹרָה שֶׁבִּכְתָּב ושבע״פ, וְהוּא אִקְרֵי תּוֹרָה וּמִשְׁנֵה תּוֹרָה. בְּקַדְמֵיתָא גְּבוּרָה דְּלָא פָּסַק, וְהַשְׁתָּא כֹּלָּא כַּחֲדָא. בג״כ הָכָא בְּאִלֵּין י׳ הַדִּבְּרוֹת, כֹּלָּא רָשִׁים בְּוָא״ו, וְלֹא תִּנְאָף, וְלֹא תִּגְנוֹב, וְלֹא תַעֲנֶה, וְלֹא תַחְמוֹד, וְלֹא תִתְאַוֶּה, וְהָא אוֹקְמוּהָ.

22. Moses spoke from himself the words of Deuteronomy (lit. 'the second Torah'). This has already been explained. HE ASKS why it is so AND ANSWERS, Supernal Chochmah is called the embodiment of the Torah, from which everything comes out into the inner voice, WHICH IS BINAH. Afterwards, everything is settled and becomes attached to the place called the Tree of Life, WHICH IS ZEIR ANPIN CALLED MOSES. The general and the particular come from it, namely the Written Torah, WHICH IS ZEIR ANPIN CALLED GENERAL, and the Oral Torah, WHICH IS MALCHUT CALLED PARTICULAR. They are also called the Torah and the second Torah. ZEIR ANPIN IS CALLED TORAH AND MALCHUT IS CALLED THE SECOND TORAH. IT WAS THEREFORE SAID THAT MOSES, WHO IS ZEIR ANPIN, SPOKE THE SECOND TORAH, WHICH IS MALCHUT, FROM HIMSELF, NAMELY, IT EMANATED FROM MOSES. At first, THE FIRST SET OF TEN COMMANDMENTS CAME OUT from uninterrupted Gvurah, NAMELY FROM BINAH, OF WHICH IT IS SAID, "A GREAT VOICE WHICH WAS NOT HEARD AGAIN." Now, WITH THE SECOND SET OF TEN COMMANDMENTS IN THE SECOND TORAH THEY CAME OUT all together, THAT IS, FROM ZEIR ANPIN

AND MALCHUT, ACCORDING TO THE PRINCIPLE THAT MOSES, ZEIR ANPIN, SPOKE THEM FROM HIMSELF. For that reason, all these ten commandments are spelled with Vav, in, "neither (Heb. *ve*) shall you commit adultery. Neither shall you steal. Neither shall you bear... Neither shall you covet...neither shall you desire" (Ibid. 17-18), AS VAV INDICATES ZEIR ANPIN.

23. אָמַר ר׳ יוֹסֵי, מַאי וְלֹא תִתְאַוֶּה, כֵּיוָן דִּכְתִּיב וְלֹא תַחְמוֹד, דְּהָא בְּהַאי סַגֵּי. א״ל, זַכָּאִין אִינּוּן מָארֵי קְשׁוֹט, חֲמִידָה חַד דַּרְגָּא. תַּאֲוָה דַּרְגָּא אַחֲרָא. חֲמִידָה: דְּאִי יָכִיל, אָזִיל לְמֵיסַב דִּילֵיהּ בְּגִין הַהִיא חֲמִידָה דְּנָקַט, אָזִיל לְמֶעְבַּד עוֹבָדָא. תַּאֲוָה: לָאו הָכִי, דְּהָא אֲפִילּוּ דְּלָא יִנְקוּט אוֹרְחָא לְמֵהַךְ אֲבַתְרֵיהּ, וְהָא אוּקְמוּהָ חַבְרַיָּיא.

23. Rabbi Yosi said, What is meant by, "neither shall you desire"? "Neither shall you covet" should suffice. He said to him, Blessed are the truly righteous. Coveting is one grade, desire another. Coveting MEANS that if he can, he will grab her, for the coveting that took him over will cause him to act. Desire is not so. Even when he will not take to following her, IT IS STILL CONSIDERED DESIRE. This has already been explained.

24. א״ל רַבִּי יוֹסֵי, אֲמַאי לָא כְּתִיב וְלֹא תִרְצַח, כְּהָנֵי אַחֲרִינֵי. א״ל בְּגִין דְּדַרְגָּא דְּדִינָא בִּגְבוּרָה תַּלְיָא, וְלָא בַּאֲתָר דְּרַחֲמֵי, בג״כ לֹא תִרְצַח לָא כְּתִיב בֵּיהּ וָא״ו. וּבְגִין דִּבְעָיָין ה׳ וָוִין אִתּוֹסָף וָא״ו וְלֹא תִתְאַוֶּה, דְּהָא בְּלֹא תִרְצַח לָא בָּעֵי לְמִשְׁרֵי וָא״ו, וְאִתּוֹסַף הָכָא.

24. Rabbi Yosi said to him, Why is not it written, 'Neither shall you murder' SPELLED WITH VAV like the others? He said to him, For the level OF MURDER is Judgment and comes from Gvurah THROUGH THE LEFT COLUMN instead of from the place of Mercy, WHICH IS ZEIR ANPIN CALLED VAV. Hence "You shall not murder" (Ibid. 17) is without Vav. Since five Vavs are needed, CORRESPONDING TO CHESED, GVURAH, TIFERET, NETZACH AND HOD, Vav was added to "shall you covet," since in "You shall not murder" no Vav should dwell BECAUSE IT IS IN GVURAH. HENCE Vav was added here.

25. שָׁמַע ר׳ פִּנְחָס דְּיָתִיב אֲבַתְרֵיהּ, וּנְשָׁקֵיהּ. בָּכָה וְחָיִיךְ. אָמַר גּוּר אַרְיֵה, לֵית מַאן דְּקָאִים קַמַּיְיהוּ, מַאן יָכִיל לְקַיְּימָא קַמֵּיהּ וַאֲבוּהָ בְּעָלְמָא. זַכָּאָה חוּלָקֵיהוֹן דְּצַדִּיקַיָּיא, וְזַכָּאָה חוּלָקִי בְּהַאי עָלְמָא, וּבְעָלְמָא דְּאָתֵי, דְּזָכֵינָא לְהַאי. עַל דָּא כְּתִיב, יִרְאוּ צַדִּיקִים וְיִשְׂמָחוּ.

25. Rabbi Pinchas, who sat behind RABBI ELAZAR, heard it. He kissed him, wept and laughed. He said OF RABBI ELAZAR, Who can stand before him and his father in the world! Happy is the lot of the righteous, and happy is my own lot in this world and in the World to Come to have merited it. Of this it is written, "The righteous see it, and are glad" (Iyov 22:19).

26. ר׳ אֶלְעָזָר פָּתַח וְאָמַר, קְרַב אַתָּה וּשֲׁמָע וְגוֹ׳. ת״ח, בְּשַׁעֲתָא דְּאִתְיְיהִיבַת אוֹרַיְיתָא לְיִשְׂרָאֵל, כֻּלְּהוֹן קוֹלוֹת אִשְׁתְּכָחוּ. וְקוּדְשָׁא בְּרִיךְ הוּא יָתִיב עַל כּוּרְסַיָּיא, וְדָא מִגּוֹ דְּדָא אִתְחֲזֵי, וּמִלּוּלָא דְּדָא נָפִיק מִגּוֹ עִלָּאָה דְּעָלֵיהּ, וְדָא הוּא רָזָא דִּכְתִּיב, פָּנִים בְּפָנִים דִּבֶּר יְיָ׳ עִמָּכֶם בָּהָר מִתּוֹךְ הָאֵשׁ, דְּמִלּוּלָא נָפְקָא, וּמַלִּיל מִגּוֹ אֶשָּׁא וְשַׁלְהוֹבָא, דְּדָחֵי לֵיהּ לְבַר, בִּדְפִיקוּ דְּרוּחָא וּמַיָּיא, דְּיָהֲבִין חֵילָא. דְּאֶשָּׁא וְרוּחָא וּמַיָּיא, מִגּוֹ שׁוֹפָר, דְּאִיהוּ כָּלִיל לְכֻלְּהוּ נָפִיק. וְיִשְׂרָאֵל אִתְרַחִיקוּ מִדְּחִילוּ דָּא.

26. Rabbi Elazar opened with, "Go you near, and hear..." (Devarim 5:24). Come and see, when the Torah was given to Yisrael, all voices were present, NAMELY, FROM BINAH, ZEIR ANPIN AND MALCHUT. BINAH IS CALLED AN INNER VOICE, ZEIR ANPIN AN OUTER VOICE AND MALCHUT THE VOICE OF THE WORDS. The Holy One, blessed be He, sat on the throne, WHICH IS MALCHUT, and one was visible from within another – ZEIR ANPIN WAS SEEN FROM WITHIN MALCHUT. The words of the one, MALCHUT, came from within that which was above it, ZEIR ANPIN. This is the secret of the verse, "Hashem talked with you face to face in the mountain out of the midst of the fire" (Devarim 5:4), AS ZEIR ANPIN AND MALCHUT WERE FACE TO FACE. And speech came out and spoke from within the fire and the flame, WHICH ARE THE LEFT COLUMN that pushed the speech out OF ZEIR ANPIN by striking of wind and water, WHICH ARE the CENTRAL AND RIGHT COLUMNS that empower THE LEFT, SO THAT SPEECH, WHICH IS MALCHUT, COMES OUT FROM ALL THREE COLUMNS

OF ZEIR ANPIN. For fire, wind and water, THE THREE COLUMNS OF ZEIR ANPIN, came out of the Shofar, BINAH, as it, BINAH, includes them all. Yisrael kept away from this awe.

27. ובג״כ, וְאַתְּ תְּדַבֵּר אֵלֵינוּ, לָא בָּעֵינָן בְּתוּקְפָּא עִלָּאָה דִּלְעֵילָּא, אֶלָּא מֵאֲתָר דְּנוּקְבָּא וְלָא יַתִּיר, וְאַתְּ תְּדַבֵּר אֵלֵינוּ וְגוֹ׳. אָמַר מֹשֶׁה וַדַּאי חֲלַשְׁתּוּן חֵילָא דִּילִי, חֲלַשְׁתּוּן חֵילָא אַחֲרָא, דְּאִלְמָלֵא לָא אִתְרַחֲקוּ יִשְׂרָאֵל, וְיִשְׁמְעוּן כָּל הַהִיא מִלָּה כַּד בְּקַדְמֵיתָא, לָא הֲוָה יָכִיל עָלְמָא לְמֶהֱוֵי חָרִיב לְבָתַר, וְאִינּוּן הֲווֹ קַיְימִין לְדָרֵי דָּרִין.

27. Because of that, BECAUSE OF THAT AWE, YISRAEL SAID TO MOSES, "and speak to us" (Ibid. 24), SAYING, we do not want this lofty force from above, NAMELY FROM ZEIR ANPIN, but from the place of the Female, MALCHUT, and no further. THIS IS THE MEANING OF, "and speak to us," WITH A FEMININE SUFFIX. Moses said TO THEM, You have surely weakened my power and weakened another power OF MALCHUT, for had not Yisrael distanced themselves, they would have heard all those words FROM ZEIR ANPIN as before, the world would not have been destroyed and Yisrael would have lived for generations.

28. דְּהָא בְּשַׁעְתָּא קַדְמֵיתָא מִיתוּ. מ״ט. בְּגִין דְּהָכִי אִצְטְרִיךְ, דְּהָא אִילָנָא דְּמוֹתָא גָּרִים. לְבָתַר דְּחַיִּיוּ וְקָמוּ וְקָא סָגוּ, וּבָעָא קוּדְשָׁא בְּרִיךְ הוּא לְאַעֲלָא לוֹן לְאִילָנָא דְּחַיֵּי, דְּקָאֵים עַל הַהוּא אִילָנָא דְּמוֹתָא, בְּגִין לְמֶהֱוֵי קַיְימִין לְעָלְמִין, אִתְרַחַק וְלָא בָּעוֹן, כְּדֵין אִתְחֲלָשׁ חֵילָא דְּמֹשֶׁה עֲלַיְיהוּ, וְאִתְחַלָּשׁ חֵילָא אַחֲרָא. אָמַר קוּדְשָׁא בְּרִיךְ הוּא, אֲנָא בָּעֵינָא לְקַיְימָא לְכוּ בַּאֲתָר עִלָּאָה, וּלְאִתְדַּבְּקָא בַּחַיִּים, אַתּוּן בָּעִיתוּן אֲתָר דְּנוּקְבָא שַׁרְיָא. וּבג״כ, לֵךְ אֱמוֹר לָהֶם וְגוֹ׳. כָּל חַד יְהַךְ לְנוּקְבֵיהּ, וְיִתְיַחֵד בָּהּ.

28. The first time, AFTER HEARING THE FIRST WORDS, they died. The reason is that it had to be so, since the tree of death, MALCHUT, brought it upon them. Later they were resurrected, rose and grew BY RECEIVING MOCHIN OF GREATNESS. The Holy One, blessed be He, wanted to bring them into the Tree of Life, ZEIR ANPIN, that is situated above that tree of death, so they will live forever. But they distanced themselves and refused AS MENTIONED. Then the power of Moses who was above them weakened, and another power OF MALCHUT weakened. The Holy One, blessed be He, said, 'I desire to uphold you in a supernal place, that you shall cleave to life, yet you wish the place where the Nukva dwells. For that reason, "Go say to them, Return again to your tents" (Ibid. 27), each one will go to his wife and mate with her', BECAUSE THEY DESCENDED TO THE WORLD OF THE FEMALE.

29. וְעִם כָּל דָּא, כֵּיוָן דְּיִשְׂרָאֵל לָא עָבְדוּ, אֶלָּא בִּדְחִילוּ עִלָּאָה דַּהֲוָה עֲלַיְיהוּ, לָא אִתְּמַר עֲלַיְיהוּ, אֶלָּא מִי יִתֵּן וְהָיָה לְבָבָם זֶה לָהֶם וְגוֹ'. מִכָּאן אוֹלִיפְנָא, כָּל מַאן דְּעָבֵיד מִלָּה, וְלִבָּא וּרְעוּתֵיהּ לָא שַׁוֵּי לְסִטְרָא בִּישָׁא, אע"ג דְּאִיהוּ בִּישׁ, הוֹאִיל וְלָא עָבֵיד בִּרְעוּתָא, עוֹנְשָׁא לָא שַׁרְיָא עָלֵיהּ. וְלָא כבּ"נ אַחֲרָא. וְקוּדְשָׁא בְּרִיךְ הוּא לָא דָּאִין לֵיהּ לְבִישׁ.

29. Nevertheless, since Yisrael did it only because of the highest awe that rested upon them, it did not say of them but, "O that there were such a heart in them, that they would fear Me" (Ibid. 26). From this we learned that whoever does something but does not concentrate in his mind and wish on the Evil Side, even though it is evil, since he did not do it on purpose there is no punishment for him, and he is not like another WHO DOES IT PURPOSELY. And the Holy One, blessed be He, does not sentence him for evil.

6. “But as for you, stand here by Me”

A Synopsis

First we hear about the great qualities of Moses. Then Rabbi Yehuda says that if people are travelling on the road in fear of thieves, the best protection is the study of Torah because this brings the Shechinah to join them.

30. וְאַתָּה פֹּה עֲמוֹד עִמָּדִי. מֵהָכָא, אִתְפְּרַשׁ מִכֹּל וָכֹל, מְאִתְּתֵיהּ, וְאִתְדַּבָּק וְאִסְתַּלָּק בַּאֲתָר אַחֲרָא דִּדְכוּרָא, וְלָא בְּנוּקְבָּא. זַכָּאָה חוּלָקָא דְּמֹשֶׁה נְבִיאָה מְהֵימָנָא, דְּזָכָה לְדַרְגִּין עִלָּאִין, מַה דְּלָא זָכָה ב"נ אָחֳרָא לְעָלְמִין. עַל דָּא כְּתִיב, טוֹב לִפְנֵי הָאֱלֹהִים יִמָּלֵט מִמֶּנָּה. מַאי טוֹב. דָּא מֹשֶׁה. דִּכְתִּיב כִּי טוֹב הוּא. וּבְגִין דַּהֲוָה טָב, סָלִיק לְדַרְגָּא אַחֲרָא עִלָּאָה. וְע"ד כְּתִיב, כִּי הַמָּקוֹם אֲשֶׁר אַתָּה עוֹמֵד עָלָיו אַדְמַת קֹדֶשׁ הוּא, עוֹמֵד עָלָיו דַּיְיקָא. מ"ט. בְּגִין כִּי טוֹב הוּא, וְטוֹב הוּא דְּכוּרָא.

30. “But as for you, stand here by Me” (Devarim 5:28): from this WE UNDERSTAND that he totally separated from his wife, and cleaved and rose to another place of THE WORLD OF the male, instead of the female. Happy is the lot of Moses, the faithful prophet, who attained the highest grades, such as no other man ever attained. Of that it is written, “he who pleases (lit. ‘good before’) Elohim shall escape from her” (Kohelet 7:26). What is “good”? It is Moses, of whom it is written, “he was a goodly child” (Shemot 2:2). Since he was good, he rose to another high level, THE GRADE OF ZEIR ANPIN, and therefore it is written, “for the place on which you stand is holy ground” (Shemot 3:5). “you stand” is precise. The reason STANDING IS MENTIONED is because it is good, and good is the male, WHICH IS YESOD OF ZEIR ANPIN, AND STANDING PERTAINS TO THE MALE.

31. וְאִי תֵּימָא, דְּהָא אָמַר רַבִּי יְהוּדָה, הָא דָּוִד דִּכְתִּיב בֵּיהּ טוֹב, כד"א וְטוֹב רֹאִי, אֲמַאי לָא הֲוָה יַתִּיר. א"ל וְטוֹב רֹאִי כְּתִיב. טוֹב רֹאִי, דָּא דְּאִיהוּ חֵיזוּ לְאִסְתַּכְּלָא, הָכִי הֲוָה דָּוִד. טוֹב רֹאִי, הֲוָה טוֹב דְּאִיהוּ חֵיזוּ. וּבְמֹשֶׁה כְּתִיב טוֹב הוּא מַמָּשׁ, וְהָכָא טוֹב רֹאִי. וְעִם כָּל דָּא, בְּתַרְוַויְיהוּ הֲוָה אָחִיד, דְּהָא דָּא בְּדָא אָחִיד. וּמֹשֶׁה לְבָתַר דַּהֲוָה טַב, סָלִיק לְמֶהֱוֵי גּוּפָא אִישׁ. אִישׁ הָאֱלֹהִים, וְהָאִישׁ מֹשֶׁה עָנָו מְאֹד.

31. You may say that Rabbi Yehuda said that 'good' is said of David, as written, "good looking" (I Shmuel 16:12), which means that as the mirror (Heb. *mar'ah*) in which to look, WHICH IS THE SECRET OF MALCHUT CALLED MIRROR, was good, so David was good looking (Heb. *mar'eh*). Of Moses it is written, "a goodly child," namely, he himself. But here IT ONLY SAYS "and good looking." Nevertheless, DAVID was attached to both, NAMELY TO YESOD CALLED GOOD AND TO MALCHUT CALLED MIRROR, since the one is attached to the other. FOR YESOD AND MALCHUT ARE ALWAYS MUTUALLY ATTACHED, ONLY HE WAS MAINLY OF MALCHUT AND REMAINED THERE. Moses, since he was good, BEING YESOD OF ZEIR ANPIN, rose to be THE ASPECT OF the body, WHICH IS ZEIR ANPIN HIMSELF, CALLED man, as written, "the man of Elohim" (Devarim 33:1), and "Now the man Moses was very meek" (Bemidbar 12:3).

32. אָמַר רַבִּי יְהוּדָה, בְּכָל עוֹבָדוֹי, בָּעֵי ב״נ לְשַׁוָּאָה לָקֳבְלֵיהּ לְקוּדְשָׁא בְּרִיךְ הוּא, וְהָא אוֹקִימְנָא מִלָּה. רַבִּי יְהוּדָה לְטַעְמֵיהּ, דְּא״ר יְהוּדָה, הַאי מַאן דְּאָזִיל בְּאָרְחָא, יְכַוֵּין לִתְלַת מִלִּין, וְעֵילָּא מִנְּהוֹן צְלוֹתָא, וְאע״ג דִּצְלוֹתָא יַתִּיר עִלָּאָה מִכֹּלָּא, תְּרֵי חַבְרֵי אוֹ תְּלָתָא דְּלָעָאן בְּמִלֵּי דְּאוֹרַיְיתָא. דְּהָא לָא מִסְתָּפֵי, בְּגִין דִּשְׁכִינְתָּא אִשְׁתַּתְּפָא בַּהֲדַיְיהוּ.

32. Rabbi Yehuda said, In all his deeds, man has to set the Holy One, blessed be He, before him, as we already explained. Rabbi Yehuda followed his own reasoning, saying that whoever walks on the road AND FEARS ROBBERS should meditate on three things, A GIFT, A PRAYER AND WAR, LIKE JACOB WHEN HE FEARED ESAU. The most valuable is prayer. And even though prayer is more VALUABLE, two or three friends studying the words of the Torah is even more valuable, because they do not fear ROBBERS, because the Shechinah is joined to them BECAUSE THEY ARE OCCUPIED IN THE TORAH.

7. “Coats of skin”

A Synopsis

Rabbi Elazar and Rabbi Chiya discuss whether Adam and Eve had coats of skin before they sinned, and we learn that at first the man and woman were clothed in the likeness of above, surrounded by celestial light. Only after their sin were they reduced to the clothing of skin that comes from the lower world. In the future God will open the eyes of those who were unwise so that they will have supernal wisdom. Next the rabbis are followed by two robbers, who are suddenly killed by two wild animals.

33. ר׳ אֶלְעָזָר וְר׳ חִיָּיא הֲווֹ אַזְלֵי בְּאָרְחָא, א״ר אֶלְעָזָר כְּתִיב, וַיַּעַשׂ יְיָ׳ אֱלֹהִים לְאָדָם וּלְאִשְׁתּוֹ כָּתְנוֹת עוֹר. וְכִי עַד הַשְׁתָּא פְּשִׁיטֵי הֲווֹ מֵהַהוּא עוֹר. אִין. אֶלָּא מָאנֵי לְבוּשֵׁי יְקַר הֲווֹ. א״ל ר׳ חִיָּיא, אִי הָכִי לָא אִתְחָזוּן לְהוּ אֲפִילּוּ כָּתְנוֹת עוֹר. וְכִי תֵּימָא דְּעַד לָא חָאבוּ אַלְבִּישׁוּ לְהוּ, לָא. אֶלָּא לְבָתַר דְּחָבוּ כְּתִיב, וַיַּעַשׂ יְיָ׳ אֱלֹהִים לְאָדָם וּלְאִשְׁתּוֹ כָּתְנוֹת עוֹר וַיַּלְבִּישֵׁם וְגוֹ׳.

33. Rabbi Elazar and Rabbi Chiya were walking on the way. Rabbi Elazar said, It is written, “For the man and for his wife did Hashem Elohim make coats of skin” (Beresheet 3:21). Were they divested of that skin until then? HE ANSWERS, Yes, SINCE UNTIL THAT TIME THEY DID NOT HAVE THESE COATS OF SKIN, which were precious garments. Rabbi Chiya said to him, In that case, they were not even worthy of coats of skin, SINCE THEY SINNED BY THE TREE OF KNOWLEDGE OF GOOD AND EVIL. You may say that before they sinned, He clothed them WITH COATS OF SKIN, yet it is not so. Only after they sinned, it is written, “For the man and for his wife did Hashem Elohim make coats of skin, and clothed them.”

34. א״ל, הָכִי הוּא וַדַּאי, בְּקַדְמֵיתָא הֲווֹ כְּגַוְונָא דִּלְעֵילָּא, וּמִתְפַּשְׁטָן מִן גְּוָונֵי דִּלְתַתָּא, וַהֲוָה נְהוֹרָא דִּלְעֵילָּא אַסְחַר עֲלַיְיהוּ. וּלְבָתַר דְּחָבוּ, אַהֲדָר לוֹן בִּגְוָונֵי דְּהַאי עָלְמָא, וְאַעְבַּר מִנַּיְיהוּ גַּוְונֵי דִּלְעֵילָּא. מַה כְּתִיב. וַיַּעַשׂ יְיָ׳ אֱלֹהִים לְאָדָם וּלְאִשְׁתּוֹ כָּתְנוֹת עוֹר וַיַּלְבִּישֵׁם מִגַּוְונָא דְּהַאי עָלְמָא. כְּתִיב וְאֶת אַהֲרֹן וְאֶת בָּנָיו תַּקְרִיב וְהִלְבַּשְׁתָּם כָּתְנוֹת,

הָתָם כְּגַוְונָא דִּלְעֵילָּא. הָכָא כְּגַוְונָא דִּלְתַתָּא. הָתָם כְּתְנוֹת שֵׁשׁ, הָכָא כָּתְנוֹת עוֹר. וְאע״ג דְּאִיהוּ הָכִי, שַׁפִּירָא דְּאִינּוּן לְבוּשִׁין סָלִיק עַל כֹּלָּא.

34. He said to him, It is surely so THAT IT OCCURRED AFTER THE SIN, only at first THEY WERE CLOTHED in the likeness of above, NAMELY WITH THE SUPERNAL SPLENDOR OF ZEIR ANPIN and were divested of the lower hues OF THIS WORLD, and the celestial light surrounded them. After they sinned, He returned them to the colors of this world, and removed from them the supernal colors THEY HAD FROM ZEIR ANPIN. It is written, "For the man also and for his wife did Hashem Elohim make coats of skin, and clothed them" as in this world. It is written, "And you shall bring his sons, and put coats upon them" (Shemot 29:9). In the latter verse, it bore resemblance to the supernal, NAMELY THE LIGHT OF ZEIR ANPIN, while here, REGARDING THE COATS OF SKIN OF ADAM, they bore resemblance to the lower. FOR THAT REASON they are called linen (Heb. *shesh*) coats THAT ALLUDES TO ZEIR ANPIN THAT IS CALLED SIX (HEB. *SHESH*), AFTER THE SIX EXTREMITIES. In this verse there are coats of skin, WHICH PERTAIN TO MALCHUT THAT IS CALLED SKIN, WHICH BEARS THE ASPECT OF THIS WORLD. Even though it is so, the beauty of these garments surpassed everything.

35. וַתִּפָּקַחְנָה עֵינֵי שְׁנֵיהֶם בְּטִיפְסָא דְּהַאי עָלְמָא, מַה דְּלָא הֲוָה קוֹדֶם, דַּהֲווֹ מַשְׁגִּחִין וּפַקְחִין לְעֵילָּא. לְזִמְנָא דְּאָתֵי כְּתִיב, וְהוֹלַכְתִּי עִוְרִים בְּדֶרֶךְ לֹא יָדָעוּ וְגוֹ׳. זַמִּין קוּדְשָׁא בְּרִיךְ הוּא לְאַפְקְחָא עַיְינִין דְּלָא חַכִּימִין, וּלְאִסְתַּכְּלָא בְּחָכְמְתָא עִלָּאָה, וּלְאִתְדַּבְּקָא בְּמַאי דְּלָא אִתְדָּבְקוּ בְּהַאי עָלְמָא, בְּגִין דְּיִנְדְּעוּן לְמָארֵיהוֹן. זַכָּאִין אִינּוּן צַדִּיקַיָּא, דְּיִזְכּוּן לְהַהִיא חָכְמְתָא, דְּלָאו חָכְמְתָא כְּהַהִיא חָכְמְתָא, וְלָאו יְדִיעָה כְּהַהִיא יְדִיעָה, וְלָאו דְּבֵקוּתָא כְּהַהִיא דְּבֵקוּתָא.

35. "And the eyes of them both were opened" (Beresheet 3:7), which means THEIR EYES OPENED to the mold of this world, NAMELY TO THE REGULAR MODEL OF THIS WORLD, which was not the case before when they were above, observing with open eyes, in the supernal world. In the future to come, it is written, "And I will bring the blind by a way that they knew not..." (Yeshayah 42:16). For the Holy One, blessed be He, will open eyes that were unwise so they will behold supernal wisdom and attain what they did not attain in this world so as to recognize their Master. Happy are the righteous that will attain this wisdom, since there is no wisdom as that wisdom, nor is there knowing such as that knowing.

36. עַד דַּהֲווֹ אַזְלֵי, חָזוּ אִינּוּן לִסְטִים אָזְלֵי בַּתְרַיְיהוּ, לְאַקְפְּחָא לוֹן. אִסְתָּכַּל בְּהוּ ר׳ אֶלְעָזָר, אָתוּ תְּרֵין חֵיוָן בָּרָא וְקַטְלֵי לוֹן. אָמַר ר׳ אֶלְעָזָר, בְּרִיךְ רַחֲמָנָא דְּשֵׁיזְבָן, קָרָא עֲלַיְיהוּ, בְּלֶכְתְּךָ לֹא יֵצַר צַעֲדֶךָ וְאִם תָּרוּץ לֹא תִכָּשֵׁל, וּכְתִיב כִּי מַלְאָכָיו יְצַוֶּה לָּךְ וְגוֹ׳. וּכְתִיב כִּי בִי חָשַׁק וַאֲפַלְּטֵהוּ.

36. While they were walking they saw robbers following them to rob them. Rabbi Elazar looked at them, and two wild animals came and killed them. Rabbi Elazar said, Blessed is the Merciful who saved us. He recited about them, "When you go, your steps shall not be confined; and when you run, you shall not stumble" (Mishlei 4:12), and, "Because he has set his delight upon Me, therefore will I deliver him" (Tehilim 91:14).

8. The four paragraphs of the Tefilin

A Synopsis

Rabbi Elazar tells of the supernal source of the four Mochin in the head of Zeir Anpin that correspond to the four paragraphs in the four compartments of the Tefilin. The rabbis talk about the whole flow of mercy and supernal light; the Holy Name Yud Hei Vav Hei and the various Sfirot are brought in to illuminate the discussion. We learn about the four pillars of the Chariot, that are the three Patriarchs and David. Rabbi Yitzchak says that God will not enter celestial Jerusalem until His people enter terrestrial Jerusalem. He also talks about testimony, that is the flowing of the illumination of Chochmah from supernal Eden.

37. תָּאנָא בְּרָזָא עִלָּאָה בְּסִפְרָא דִּצְנִיעוּתָא, ג׳ חֲלָלִין דְּאַתְוָון רְשִׁימִין, אִתְגַּלְיָין בָּהּ בְּגוּלְגַּלְתָּא דִּזְעֵיר אַנְפִּין. וְתָנֵינָן, ג׳ מוֹחֵי אִינּוּן, דִּסְתִימוּ בְּאִינּוּן חֲלָלִין. וּמְשֵׁירוּתָא דְּמוֹחָא עִלָּאָה סְתִימָאָה דְּעַתִּיקָא קַדִּישָׁא דְּאִתְמְשִׁיךְ בְּהַהוּא ז״א, אִשְׁתְּכָחוּ ד׳ מוֹחֵי. וְאִלֵּין ד׳ מוֹחִין, מִשְׁתַּכְּחִין וּמִתְפָּשְׁטִין בְּכָל גּוּפָא וְאִינּוּן ד׳ רִיהֲטֵי, דְּאַרְבַּע בָּתֵּי דִּתְפִילִין, דְּאָנַח קוּדְשָׁא בְּרִיךְ הוּא.

37. We learned from a supernal mystery in the Concealed Book that there are three cavities of engraved letters, WHICH ARE YUD HEI VAV OF YUD HEI VAV HEI, seen in the skull of Zeir Anpin. And we learned that there are three parts of the brain (Mochin), CHOCHMAH, BINAH AND DA'AT, which are hidden in these cavities. THE CAVITIES ARE VESSELS AND THE LOBES OF THE BRAIN ARE THE LIGHTS THAT ARE CLOTHED IN THEM. From the top of the highest concealed brain of Atika Kadisha that flows into the Mochin of that Zeir Anpin, there are four Mochin, CHOCHMAH, BINAH, THE RIGHT SIDE OF DA'AT, WHICH IS TIFERET, AND THE LEFT SIDE OF DA'AT, WHICH IS MALCHUT. These four Mochin ARE IN THE HEAD OF ZEIR ANPIN AND expand throughout the body. These are the four paragraphs in the four compartments of the Tefilin, which the Holy One, blessed be He, puts on.

38. וּבג״כ בָּעֵי בַּר נָשׁ לַאֲנָחָא בְּכָל יוֹמָא, בְּגִין דְּאִינּוּן שְׁמָא קַדִּישָׁא עִלָּאָה בְּאַתְווֹי רְשִׁימָן, דִּכְתִּיב וְרָאוּ כָּל עַמֵּי הָאָרֶץ כִּי שֵׁם יְיָ׳ נִקְרָא

עָלֶיךָ. וּתְנָן, שֵׁם יְיָ׳ מַמָּשׁ, וְאִלֵּין תְּפִלִּין דְּרֵישָׁא.

38. One should put on TEFILIN every day, because they are the supernal Holy Name of engraved letters, YUD HEI VAV HEI, NAMELY THE FOUR MOCHIN, as written, "And all people of the earth shall see that you are called by the name of Hashem" (Devarim 28:10). We learned this is the actual name of Hashem. These are the head Tefilin.

39. ר׳ יִצְחָק אָמַר, הֲדָא הוּא דִּכְתִּיב, קַדֶּשׁ לִי כָל בְּכוֹר, דָּא הִיא כִּתְרָא דְּכָלִיל וְאַסְתִּים כָּל אִינּוּן אַחֲרָנִין. מְשִׁיכוּתָא דִּלְעֵילָּא סְתִימָא בֵּיהּ. וְדָא אִקְרֵי פֶּטֶר כָּל רֶחֶם, פְּתִיחוּתָא דְּכָל מְשִׁיכוּתָא דְּרַחֲמֵי, וּנְהִירוּ דִּלְעֵילָּא.

39. Rabbi Yitzchak said, This is what is meant by the verse, "Sanctify to Me (Heb. *kadesh li*) all the firstborn" (Shemot 13:2). This is the Sfirah that includes and conceals all the others, NAMELY, CHOCHMAH THAT INCLUDES INSIDE ITSELF ALL THE SFIROT. The drawing OF LIGHT from above is hidden within it. It is called "whatever opens the womb" (Ibid.), because it opens the whole flow of mercy and supernal light.

40. אָמַר ר״ש, וְסָתִים בְּיוּ״ד דִּשְׁמָא קַדִּישָׁא. וְדָא חַד בֵּיתָא דִּתְפִלִּין, דְּהוּא קַדֶּשׁ לִי כָל בְּכוֹר סְתָם. מוֹחָא עִלָּאָה, חָכְמָה.

40. Rabbi Shimon said, THIS SFIRAH OF CHOCHMAH is hidden in the Yud of the Holy Name YUD HEI VAV HEI. It is one compartment of the Tefilin, which is "Sanctify to Me all the firstborn." Unspecific FIRSTBORN relates to the supernal part of the brain, Chochmah.

41. בֵּיתָא תִּנְיָינָא, וְהָיָה כִּי יְבִיאֲךָ יְיָ׳. א״ר יְהוּדָה מוֹחָא דִּתַרְעוֹי נָפְקִין לַחַמְשִׁין תַּרְעִין. תַּרְעִין סַגִּיאִין, וְאִינּוּן לָקֳבֵל זִמְנִין סַגִּיאִין דִּכְתִּיב אֲשֶׁר הוֹצֵאתִיךָ מֵאֶרֶץ מִצְרַיִם. הוֹצִיאֲךָ יְיָ׳ מִמִּצְרַיִם. וְאִדְכַּר זִמְנִין סַגִּיאִין דּוּכְרָנָא דְּמִצְרַיִם. וְאִינּוּן חַמְשִׁין לָקֳבֵל חַמְשִׁין.

41. The second compartment OF THE TEFILIN is, "And it shall be, when Hashem your Elohim shall bring you (Heb. *vehayah ki yeviacha*)" (Devarim 6:10). Rabbi Yehuda said, This is the part of the brain the gates of which become fifty gates, NAMELY BINAH, WHICH EXPANDS INTO THE FIFTY GATES OF BINAH. These many gates correspond to the many mentions of the phrases, "who have brought you out of the land of Egypt," and "brought you forth out of Egypt." The memory of the exodus from Egypt is mentioned many times in the Torah, fifty TIMES that correspond to the fifty GATES OF BINAH. FOR THE EXODUS FROM EGYPT CAME THROUGH THE ILLUMINATION OF BINAH. THEY ARE THEREFORE FIFTY, TO CORRESPOND TO ITS FIFTY GATES.

42. וְתָנֵינָן בְּסִפְרָא דְּרַב הַמְנוּנָא סָבָא, דְּאָמַר תַּרְעִין סַגִּיאִין דִּלְעֵילָּא וְתַתָּא, תָּבַר קוּדְשָׁא בְּרִיךְ הוּא, דַּהֲווֹ סְתִימִין וּמִתְקַטְרִין בְּשַׁלְשְׁלֵיהוֹן, בְּגִין לְאַפָּקָא לְהוּ לְיִשְׂרָאֵל. דְּהָא מֵאִלֵּין תַּרְעִין דְּהַהוּא מוֹחָא, מִתְפַּתְּחֵי וּמִשְׁתְּרוּ כָּל שְׁאַר תַּרְעִין. וְאִלְמָלֵא דְּאִתְעָרוּ וְאִתְפְּתָחוּ אִינּוּן תַּרְעִין דְּהַאי מוֹחָא, לָא הֲווֹ מִתְפַּתְּחִין אִינּוּן אַחֲרָנִין לְמֶעְבַּד דִּינָא, וּלְאַפָּקָא לוֹן לְיִשְׂרָאֵל מִן עַבְדוּתָא.

42. We learned from the book of Rav Hamnuna Saba, who said that the Holy One, blessed be He, broke many upper and lower gates that were bound by chains, in order to bring Yisrael out of Egypt. For through these gates of the brain lobe OF BINAH the other BLOCKED gates were opened and loosened. Had not the gates of the brain lobe OF BINAH opened and aroused, the other BLOCKED gates would not have opened to execute punishment AGAINST EGYPT to bring Yisrael out of slavery. FOR THAT REASON THE EXODUS FROM EGYPT WAS MENTIONED FIFTY TIMES, WHICH OCCURRED BY MEANS OF THE FIFTY GATES OF BINAH.

43. וְכֹלָּא סָתִים בְּהַאי דְּאִקְרֵי אִימָּא עִלָּאָה, דְּמִנָּהּ אִתְּעַר חֵילָא לְאִימָּא תַּתָּאָה. וּמַאי אִיהוּ. דִּכְתִּיב בָּהּ וּלְאֻמִּי אֵלַי הַאֲזִינוּ. אַל תִּקְרֵי לְאוּמִּי, אֶלָּא לְאִמִּי. דְּלָא זָז קוּדְשָׁא בְּרִיךְ הוּא מֵחַבְּבָהּ לִכְנֶסֶת יִשְׂרָאֵל, עַד דִּקְרָאָהּ אִמִּי. וְהַאי נָפְקָא מֵאִימָּא עִלָּאָה, דְּהִיא בֵּיתָא תִּנְיָינָא, דְּאִקְרֵי ה׳ דִּשְׁמָא קַדִּישָׁא, דְּאִתְפַּתְּחָא לְחַמְשִׁין תַּרְעִין. וּמֵהַאי נָפַק רוּחָא לְחַד נוּקְבָּא דְּפַרְדַּשְׁקָא דְּחוֹטָמָא.

43. Everything is concealed inside this BRAIN OF BINAH, which is called supernal Ima, from which power was roused for lower Ima, WHICH IS MALCHUT. What is that? It is that of which is written, "and give ear to Me, O My nation (Heb. *le'umi*)" (Yeshayah 51:4), which should be pronounced '*le'imi* (Eng. 'to my mother'), rather than le'umi. For the Holy One, blessed be He cherished the Congregation of Yisrael, WHICH IS MALCHUT, to the extent of calling her 'My mother', SO MALCHUT RECEIVED THE LIGHTS OF SUPERNAL IMA. For these LIGHTS come out of supernal Ima, which is the second compartment OF THE TEFILIN, which is called Hei of the Holy Name YUD HEI VAV HEI that opened into fifty gates. From this part of the brain a wind goes out to a nostril in the window of the nose of Zeir Anpin.

44. וְתָנֵינָן, יוֹבְלָא דְּנָפְקִין בֵּיהּ עַבְדִּין לְחֵירוּ, בְּהַאי מוֹחָא אִתְאֲחָד. וְאִינּוּן חַמְשִׁין שְׁנִין דְּיוֹבְלָא. וְאִינּוּן חַמְשִׁין יוֹמִין דְּחוּשְׁבָּנָא דְּעוֹמֶר, בֵּיהּ אִתְאֲחָדוּ. דִּבְהוּ נַיְיחִין רוּחֵי דְּעַבְדִּין, וּמַפְּקֵי רוּחֵיהוֹן לְנַיְיחָא. כְּמָה דִּכְתִּיב, בְּיוֹם הָנִיחַ יְיָ׳ לְךָ מֵעָצְבְּךָ וּמִרָגְזֶךָ וּמִן הָעֲבוֹדָה וְגוֹ׳. וּבְגִין כַּךְ, ה׳ נַיְיחָא דְּרוּחָא, וּלְאַפָּקָא רוּחָא לְחֵירוּ. וְהַאי בֵּיתָא יְצִיאַת מִצְרַיִם בָּהּ תַּלְיָיא, וּבְאָת ה׳ דִּשְׁמָא קַדִּישָׁא, כְּמָה דְּאִתְמַר. ע״כ כְּלָלָא דְּי״ה דִּשְׁמָא קַדִּישָׁא.

44. We learned that the Jubilee, in which slaves are freed, is united with this brain lobe OF BINAH. THE FIFTY GATES OF BINAH are the fifty years of the Jubilee, and the fifty days of the counting of the Omer unite WITH THE BRAIN LOBE OF BINAH, in which the spirits of the slaves rest, and their spirit achieves FREEDOM AND rest, as written, "the day that Hashem shall give you rest from your sorrow, and from your fear, and from the hard bondage..." (Yeshayah 14:3). For that reason, FIRST Hei OF YUD HEI VAV HEI, WHICH IS BINAH, rests the spirit and liberates the spirit. The exodus from Egypt comes out from the SECOND compartment OF THE TEFILIN and the FIRST Hei of the Holy Name, as we learned. Up to here, THE FIRST TWO COMPARTMENTS OF THE TEFILIN all is about Yud Hei of the Holy Name.

45. ת״ח, מִסִּטְרָא דְּאַבָּא נָפִיק חֶסֶד. מִסִּטְרָא דְּאִמָּא נָפִיק גְּבוּרָה. וְכֹלָּא אָחִיד קוּדְשָׁא בְּרִיךְ הוּא, וּמִתְעַטָּר בְּהוּ, אָת וָא״ו.

45. Come and see, from the aspect of Aba, WHICH IS CHOCHMAH, Chesed emerges, and from the aspect of Ima, WHICH IS BINAH, Gvurah comes out. The Holy One, blessed be He, WHO IS ZEIR ANPIN, is attached to them all and is adorned with them, being the letter Vav, FOR ZEIR ANPIN IS THE CENTRAL COLUMN THAT COMPREHENDS THE RIGHT AND THE LEFT, WHICH ARE ABA AND CHESED TO THE RIGHT AND IMA AND GVURAH TO THE LEFT.

46. בֵּיתָא תְּלִיתָאָה שְׁמַע יִשְׂרָאֵל יִשְׂרָאֵל סָבָא. וְאָהַבְתָּ אֵת יְיָ׳ אֱלֹהֶיךָ. תָּאנָא ר״ש, דָּא הוּא רָזָא עִלָּאָה, דְּיִשְׂרָאֵל עִלָּאָה אִתְעֲטָר בְּסִטְרָא דְּאַבָּא. וּמַאי אִיהוּ. אַבְרָהָם. וְאִתְעֲטָר בְּסִטְרָא דְּאִימָּא. וּמַאי אִיהוּ. יִצְחָק.

46. The third compartment OF THE TEFILIN IS "Hear O Yisrael (Heb. *Sh'ma Yisrael*)" (Devarim 6:4), which is Yisrael Saba, TOGETHER WITH "And you shall love Hashem your Elohim" (Ibid. 5). Rabbi Shimon taught, this is a high mystery that the supernal Yisrael, WHICH IS ZEIR ANPIN, was adorned with the aspect of Aba. This is Abraham. Adorned with the aspect of Ima it is Isaac.

47. תָּנֵינָן, וְאָהַבְתָּ מַאן דְּרָחִים לֵיהּ לְמַלְכָּא, עָבֵיד יַתִּיר טִיבוּ חֶסֶד עִם כֹּלָּא. וְחֶסֶד יַתִּירָא, הַהוּא דְּאִקְרֵי חֶסֶד דֶּאֱמֶת, דְּלָא בָּעֵי אֲגָר עָלֵיהּ, אֶלָּא בְּגִין רְחִימוּתָא דְּמַלְכָּא, דְּרָחִים לֵיהּ יַתִּיר, וּבִרְחִימוּתָא דְּמַלְכָּא תַּלְיָא חֶסֶד. וְע״ד אִקְרֵי אַבְרָהָם אוֹהֲבִי. וּבְגִין דְּרָחִים לֵיהּ יַתִּיר, אַסְגֵּי חֶסֶד בְּעָלְמָא. וְע״ד, הָכָא וְאָהַבְתָּ. וּבִרְחִימוּתָא תַּלְיָא חֶסֶד, וְדָא הִיא בֵּיתָא תְּלִיתָאָה.

47. We learned about, "And you shall love" that he who loves the King does much kindness (Chesed), BY BEING KIND to everyone. This type of kindness is called an act of true kindness, not wishing for reward FOR ONE'S DEEDS, but acting so for the love one bears for the King. HENCE Chesed comes out of the love for the King. Abraham was called My beloved because for his love for Him he did much kindness in the world. Hence it is written here, IN THE THIRD COMPARTMENT OF THE TEFILIN, WHICH IS CHESED, "And you shall love," BECAUSE Chesed comes from love. This is the third compartment OF THE TEFILIN.

48. בֵּיתָא רְבִיעָאָה, וְהָיָה אִם שָׁמוֹעַ. הִשָּׁמְרוּ לָכֶם. וְחָרָה אַף יְיָ'. גְּבוּרָה תַּקִּיפָא, וְדִינָא קַשְׁיָא הִיא, וְנַפְקַת מִסִּטְרָא דְּאִימָּא עִלָּאָה. וְתָנֵינָן, אע"ג דְּלֵית הִיא דִּינָא, מִסִּטְרָהָא נָפְקָא דִּינָא, גְּבוּרָה עִלָּאָה. וְאִי תֵּימָא, וְהָיָה אִם שָׁמוֹעַ דְּלָאו הִיא דִּינָא. לֵית כִּתְרָא מִכָּל כִּתְרֵי מַלְכָּא, דְּלָא יִתְכְּלִיל דִּינָא וְרַחֲמֵי, כ"ש גְּבוּרָה דְּאִתְכְּלִיל טַב וּבִישׁ.

48. The fourth compartment OF THE TEFILIN IS "And it shall come to pass, if you hearken (Heb. *vehayah im shamo'a*)... Hashem's anger be inflamed..." (Devarim 11:13-17), WHICH IS ALL AN INDICATION OF harsh Judgment. And harsh Judgment emerges from the aspect of supernal Ima. We learned that though IMA is not of Judgment, Judgment, which is supernal Gvurah, comes out of its aspect. You may say that, "And it shall come to pass, if you hearken" is not Judgment, BECAUSE THE PARAGRAPH ALSO SAYS, "I WILL GIVE YOU THE RAIN OF YOUR LAND IN ITS DUE SEASON…THAT YOU MAY EAT AND BE FULL." HE ANSWERS, Among all the Sfirot of the King there is none that is not including both Judgment and Mercy, and Gvurah more than the others, in which both good and evil are included. HENCE GOOD THINGS ARE WRITTEN IN THE PARAGRAPH OF, "AND IT SHALL COME TO PASS, IF YOU HEARKEN," BUT IN GENERAL, IT IS HARSH JUDGMENT.

49. וְאִלֵּין אַרְבָּעָה נָטִיל לוֹן וָא"ו, וְאִתְעֲטַר בְּהוּ. וְאִלֵּין אִינּוּן תְּפִלִּין דְּאָנַח קוּדְשָׁא בְּרִיךְ הוּא. תָּנֵינָן, הַאי וָא"ו סָלִיק וְאִתְעֲטַר בְּעִטְרוֹי, וְאָחִיד לְהַאי וּלְהַאי, וְאִתְעֲטַר בְּכֻלְּהוּ, וְע"ד וָא"ו, אֶמְצָעִיתָא דְּכֹלָּא, דְּעֵילָּא וְתַתָּא, לְאַחֲזָאָה חָכְמְתָא שְׁלֵימָתָא מִכָּל סִטְרוֹי.

49. The Vav, WHICH IS ZEIR Anpin, receives these four PASSAGES, WHICH ARE CHOCHMAH, BINAH, THE RIGHT SIDE OF DA'AT AND THE LEFT SIDE OF DA'AT, and adorns itself with them, WHICH MEANS THEY BECOME ITS MOCHIN. These are the Tefilin the Holy One, blessed be He, puts on. We learned that this Vav, ZEIR ANPIN, rises TO BINAH, which is adorned with its crowns and one is attached to the other, NAMELY, ITS RIGHT COLUMN, ITS CHOCHMAH AND ITS LEFT COLUMN, ITS BINAH. It is adorned with them all. Vav, ZEIR ANPIN, is therefore in the center of everything, above and below, to display the completion of Chochmah in every direction.

50. תָּאנֵי ר׳ אַבָּא, כְּתִיב רַק בַּאֲבוֹתֶיךָ חָשַׁק יְיָ׳. מִכָּאן אר״ש, אֲבָהָתָא אִינּוּן רְתִיכָא קַדִּישָׁא עִלָּאָה, וּכְתִיב חָשַׁק יְיָ׳. ת״ח, כְּמָה דְּאִית רְתִיכָא קַדִּישָׁא לְתַתָּא, כַּךְ אִית רְתִיכָא קַדִּישָׁא לְעֵילָּא. וּמַאי נִיהוּ, הָא דְּאַמָרָן, רְתִיכָא קַדִּישָׁא כֹּלָּא אִקְרֵי, וְכֹלָּא אִתְקַשַּׁר דָּא בְּדָא, וְאִתְעָבֵיד כֹּלָּא חַד.

50. Rabbi Aba taught, it is written, "Only Hashem took delight in your fathers" (Devarim 10:15). From this Rabbi Shimon deduced that the fathers are the holy supernal Chariot, as is also written, "Hashem took delight." Come and see, just as there is a holy Chariot below IN MALCHUT, WHICH IS FROM THE CHEST BELOW OF ZEIR ANPIN there is a holy Chariot above, FROM THE CHEST UP OF ZEIR ANPIN. Who are they? They are those we mentioned, THE FATHERS CALLED CHESED, GVURAH AND TIFERET. The whole is called a holy Chariot, because everything is interconnected and becomes one.

51. רַק בַּאֲבוֹתֶיךָ תְּלָתָא, וּרְתִיכָא אַרְבְּעָה, ד׳ מְנָלָן. דִּכְתִּיב וַיִּבְחַר בְּזַרְעָם אַחֲרֵיהֶם. מַאי מַשְׁמַע. לְאַכְלְלָא בְּהוּ דָּוִד מַלְכָּא, דְּאִיהוּ רְבִיעָאָה, לְאִתְתַּקְנָא בִּרְתִיכָא קַדִּישָׁא. דְּתָנֵינָן, אֲבָהָתָא תִּקּוּנָא וּשְׁלֵימוּתָא דְּכֹלָּא, וְגוּפָא בְּהוּ אִשְׁתַּכְלָל וְאִתְבְּנֵי, וּבְהוּ אִתְאֲחִיד. אָתָא דָּוִד מַלְכָּא, וְשַׁכְלִיל כֹּלָּא, וְאַתְקִין גּוּפָא, וְאַשְׁלְמֵיהּ בְּהוּ. וא״ר יִצְחָק, כְּמָה דְּזָכוּ אֲבָהָתָא לְאִתְעַטְּרָא בִּרְתִיכָא קַדִּישָׁא, כַּךְ זָכָה דָּוִד לְאִתְתַּקְנָא בְּסַמְכָא רְבִיעָאָה דִּרְתִיכָא.

51. "ONLY HASHEM TOOK DELIGHT IN your fathers," WHO YOU SAID WERE A CHARIOT, ARE BUT three, yet a Chariot consists of four. Whence do we get a fourth? AND HE ANSWERS, From the verse, "and He chose their seed after them" (Ibid.). HE ASKS what it means AND ANSWERS THAT THE PURPOSE OF THE VERSE IS to include King David with the Patriarchs, being the fourth to be established in a holy Chariot. For we learned that the Patriarchs establish and perfect everything. They are the body, NAMELY

CHESED, GVURAH AND TIFERET THAT ARE CALLED BODY. By them THE BODY is completed and built and to them it is attached, NAMELY, THE BODY, ZEIR ANPIN, IS MOSTLY CHESED, GVURAH AND TIFERET IN HIM, WHICH ARE ABOVE THE CHEST AND ARE CALLED THE PATRIARCHS. King David came and perfected everything. He established the body and perfected it through them, BY BECOMING A FOURTH, THE SECRET OF MALCHUT THAT PERFECTS ZEIR ANPIN THAT IS CALLED BODY. Rabbi Yitzchak said, Just as the Patriarchs merited to be adorned with a holy Chariot, so did David merit to be established as a fourth pillar of the Chariot.

52. א״ר יְהוּדָה, כְּתִיב בֵּיהּ בְּדָוִד, וְהוּא אַדְמוֹנִי עִם יְפֵה עֵינַיִם וְטוֹב רֹאִי. מַאי טַעֲמָא אַדְמוֹנִי. מִשּׁוּם דְּחוּלָקָא דְּעַדְבֵיהּ גַּרְמָא לֵיהּ. אַדְמוֹנִי דִּינָא וַדַּאי. עִם יְפֵה עֵינַיִם, דִּינָא בְּרַחֲמֵי. כְּמָה דִּכְתִּיב חַסְדֵּי דָּוִד הַנֶּאֱמָנִים.

52. Rabbi Yehuda said, It is written of David, "Now he was ruddy, with fine eyes, and good looking" (I Shmuel 16:12). What is the reason HE IS CALLED ruddy? Because the portion of his lot brought it on him, SINCE BEING A CHARIOT TO MALCHUT, HE WAS OF THE ASPECT OF JUDGMENT LIKE MALCHUT. Ruddy is certainly of Judgment; "with fine eyes" means Judgment included Mercy, as written, "the sure loving promises of David" (Yeshayah 55:3).

53. א״ר יִצְחָק, חַסְדֵּי דָּוִד, בְּאַתְרֵיהּ אוּקִימְנָא. אֶלָּא וְהוּא אַדְמוֹנִי, כִּדְאַמָרָן. עִם יְפֵה עֵינַיִם, אִלֵּין אֲבָהָתָא. ת״ח, יְרוּשָׁלַיִם וְצִיּוֹן, דִּינָא וְרַחֲמֵי. ואע״פ כֵּן כְּתִיב, עִיר דָּוִד הִיא צִיּוֹן. וּכְתִּיב בְּקִרְבְּךָ קָדוֹשׁ וְלֹא אָבֹא בְּעִיר, נִשְׁבַּע קוּדְשָׁא בְּרִיךְ הוּא שֶׁלֹּא יִכָּנֵס בִּירוּשָׁלַם שֶׁל מַעֲלָה וְכוּ׳. אֵימָתַי. א״ר יְהוּדָה, כַּד אִתְהַדָּר מַלְכוּ בֵּית דָּוִד לְאַתְרֵיהּ לְתַתָּא.

53. Rabbi Yitzchak said, We explained about "the sure loving promises (Chassadim) of David" in its place. THEY DO NOT ALLUDE TO THE INCLUSION OF JUDGMENT WITH CHESED. But "Now he was ruddy" MEANS as we said THAT HE IS JUDGMENT; "with fine eyes" refers to the

Patriarchs, CHESED, GVURAH AND TIFERET THAT SHINE IN THE THREE COLORS OF THE EYE. Come and see, Jerusalem and Zion are Judgment and Mercy, yet it is written, "the city of David, which is Zion" (I Melachim 8:1), WHICH INDICATES THAT JUDGMENT COMPREHENDS MERCY. It is also written, "the Holy One is in the midst of you, and I will not come into the city" (Hoshea 11:9), WHICH HAS BEEN SAID TO INDICATE THAT the Holy One, blessed be He, will not enter celestial Jerusalem UNTIL YISRAEL WILL ENTER TERRESTRIAL JERUSALEM. HE ASKS WHEN THIS WILL TAKE PLACE. Rabbi Yehuda said, When the kingdom of David would return to its place below, THE HOLY ONE, BLESSED BE HE, WOULD ENTER CELESTIAL JERUSALEM.

54. רַבִּי יִצְחָק אָמַר, ש׳ דִּרְשִׁימָא בִּתְלַת קִשְׁרֵי, ש׳ דְּאַרְבַּע קִשְׁרִין, רְמִיזָא הִיא לִתְלָתָא, וּרְמִיזָא לְאַרְבְּעָה. תְּלַת הָא דְּאַמָרָן. אַרְבְּעָה, לְמֶהֱוֵי רְתִיכָא קַדִּישָׁא כַּחֲדָא. דְּהָא הוּא כְּלָלָא דְּתִקּוּנָא עִלָּאָה. וּמֵהָכָא, מִתְפָּרְשָׁן וְאִתְמַשְׁכָן תַּתָּאֵי בְּאָרְחַיְיהוּ, בִּרְצוּעֵיהוֹן. דְּתַלְיָין בְּהָנֵי שַׂעֲרֵי דְּרֵישָׁא, דְּתַלְיָין בְּהוּ, וְאִתְמַשְׁכָן מִנַּיְיהוּ כָּל אִינּוּן אַחֲרָנִין, עַד דְּאִתְקַשְׁרָן בְּאַתְרַיְיהוּ.

54. Rabbi Yitzchak said, There is a Shin with three knots, THAT IS, THREE HEADS, and a Shin with four knots, NAMELY FOUR HEADS. It alludes to three and alludes to four. We spoke of the three, NAMELY THE THREE PATRIARCHS, CHESED, GVURAH AND TIFERET. The four INCLUDE MALCHUT AS WELL to form a holy Chariot together, for MALCHUT is the inclusion of the supernal establishment, SINCE MALCHUT COMPLETES ZEIR ANPIN. From here the lower grades spread and flow by their ways and straps. They come out of the hairs on the head, suspended from them as all these other grades come down from them, until they are tied in their place.

55. תָּנֵינָן, ו׳ נָטִיל אִינּוּן עִלָּאֵי דְּאַמָרָן, וְאִלֵּין תְּפִלִּין דְּאָנַח קוּדְשָׁא בְּרִיךְ הוּא. בְּגִין כַּךְ בָּעֵי בַּר נָשׁ לְאִתְפָּאֲרָא בְּהוּ, עָלֵיהּ כְּתִיב וְרָאוּ כָּל עַמֵּי הָאָרֶץ כִּי שֵׁם יְיָ׳ נִקְרָא עָלֶיךָ, שֵׁם יְיָ׳ מַמָּשׁ. וְאִלֵּין אִינּוּן תְּפִלִּין דְּרֵישָׁא, תְּפִלִּין דִּדְרוֹעָא הִיא שְׂמָאלָא, דְּאִקְרֵי עֹז, וְיָרְתָא מֵעֹז, הה״ד וְהָיָה לְאוֹת עַל יָדְכָה בְּהֵ״א, וְהִיא הֵ״א דְּאוֹקִימְנָא. זַכָּאָה חוּלָקֵהוֹן

דְּיִשְׂרָאֵל. וְע״ד, הֵ״א בַּתְרָאָה נַטְלָא תְּפִלִּין, דְּהִיא שְׂמָאלָא.

55. We learned that Vav, ZEIR ANPIN, receives these supernal MOCHIN, CHOCHMAH, BINAH AND DA'AT we mentioned, which are the Tefilin the Holy One, blessed be He, dons. For that reason, one should be glorified in them, BECAUSE TEFILIN ARE CALLED GLORY. Of them it is written, "And all people of the earth shall see that you are called by the name of Hashem" (Devarim 28:10), the actual name of Hashem, THE MOCHIN CHOCHMAH AND BINAH, YUD-HEI, AND THE RIGHT AND LEFT OF DA'AT, WHICH ARE VAV-HEI. These are the head Tefilin. The hand Tefilin are the left, called strength, ACCORDING TO THE SECRET MEANING OF, "HASHEM HAS SWORN BY HIS RIGHT HAND, AND BY THE ARM OF HIS STRENGTH" (YESHAYAH 62:8). THE RIGHT HAND IS THE TORAH AND THE ARM OF HIS STRENGTH IS THE TEFILIN. MALCHUT receives from the strength, THE SECRET OF THE LEFT COLUMN. This is why, "And it shall be for a sign to you upon your hand (Heb. *yadechah*)" (Shemot 13:9) is spelled with EXTRA Hei. This is the Hei we discussed, NAMELY MALCHUT. Happy is the portion of Yisrael. Hence the last Hei, MALCHUT, receives the Tefilin, being left BECAUSE MALCHUT IS BUILT BY THE LEFT COLUMN. HENCE SHE RECEIVES THE TEFILIN ON THE LEFT ARM.

.56 לְמַאן אִינּוּן אִלֵּין אַרְבְּעָה, דְּאִינּוּן חַד גּוּפָא, וְע״ד כְּלִילָן בְּחַד, וּמַאן אִינּוּן. תִּפְאֶרֶת נֶצַח הוֹד יְסוֹד. וְהִיא הֵ״א דְּיָדְכָה, וְכֻלְּהוּ אֲחִידָא בָּהּ, בְּגִין לְאִתְבָּרְכָא מִנַּיְיהוּ, וּכְלִילָא מִכֻּלְּהוּ.

56. HE ASKS, Who are these four PASSAGES for, which are one body, for which reason they are included in one compartment, and what are they? HE ANSWERS, They are Tiferet, Netzach, Hod and Yesod, NAMELY THE FOUR SFIROT FROM THE CHEST AND LOWER OF ZEIR ANPIN. They are the Hei in '*yadechah*', WHICH IS MALCHUT. For they all, ALL FOUR SFIROT, TIFERET, NETZACH, HOD AND YESOD FROM THE CHEST LOWER are attached TO MALCHUT so she would be blessed by them. HENCE she includes all four SFIROT FROM THE CHEST AND LOWER OF ZEIR ANPIN.

.57 א״ר חִיָּיא, אִי הָכִי הָא כְּתִיב וְרָאִיתָ אֶת אֲחוֹרָי, וְתָנֵינָן דָּא קֶשֶׁר שֶׁל תְּפִלִּין. אָמַר לֵיהּ הָא אוֹקְמוּהָ, וְשַׁפִּיר הוּא, וְכֹלָּא בְּרִירָא דְּמִלָּה.

וְע״ד מֵהַאי תַּלְיָיא רְצוּעָה חַד לְתַתָּא, דְּהָא מִנָּהּ תַּלְיָין תַּתָּאֵי, וְאִתְּזָנוּ מִנָּהּ. וְע״ד אִיתְקְרֵי אוֹת. כד״א זֹאת אוֹת הַבְּרִית. וּכְתִיב וְהָיָה לְאוֹת עַל יָדְכָה בְּה׳ וְהָא אוּקְמוּהָ.

57. Rabbi Chiya said, Yet it is written, "and you shall see My back" (Shemot 33:23). We also learned it is the knot of Tefilin. He said to him, We have already explained and it is fine and clarifies the matter. Hence from this HAND TEFILIN one strap hangs down, WHICH INDICATES the lower beings are suspended from it and nourish from it. Hence it is called a sign, BECAUSE IT IS ATTACHED TO YESOD. This is the meaning of, "This is the token of the covenant" (Beresheet 9:17). It is also written, "And it shall be for a sign to you upon your hand (Heb. *yadechah*)" with EXTRA Hei, which has already been explained.

58. שְׁמַע יִשְׂרָאֵל. א״ר יֵיסָא, יִשְׂרָאֵל סָבָא. ר׳ יִצְחָק אָמַר ע׳ רַבְרְבָא, לְאַכְלְלָא שַׁבְעִין שְׁמָהָן, סַהֲדוּתָא דְּכֹלָּא שְׁמַע יִשְׂרָאֵל, כְּמָה דִּכְתִּיב, שִׁמְעוּ שָׁמַיִם. וּכְתִיב הַאֲזִינוּ הַשָּׁמַיִם. אוּף הָכָא שְׁמַע יִשְׂרָאֵל. וְכֹלָּא חַד מִלָּה הוּא.

58. Rabbi Yesa says that "Hear (*Sh'ma*), O Yisrael" (Devarim 6:4) is Yisrael Saba. Rabbi Yitzchak said that the large Ayin IN SH'MA includes seventy names, THE SECRET OF THE NAME OF 72 NAMES: THE SEVENTY NAMES PLUS THE TWO WITNESSES. It is overall testimony, NAMELY THE FLOWING OF THE ILLUMINATION OF CHOCHMAH from SUPERNAL EDEN, CALLED TESTIMONY. "Hear O Yisrael" resembles the words, "Hear, heavens" (Yeshayah 1:2) and, "Give ear, O heavens" (Devarim 32:1), WHICH MEANS THEY SHOULD BE WITNESSES. Here too, "Hear, O Yisrael" INDICATES TO MOCHIN OF TESTIMONY. It all pertains to the same issue.

59. יְדֹוָ״ד: רֵישָׁא דְּכֹלָּא, בִּנְהִירוּ דְּעַתִּיקָא קַדִּישָׁא. וְהַאי הוּא דְּאִקְרֵי אָ״ב. אֱלֹהֵינוּ: עֲמִיקְתָא דְּנַחֲלִין וּמַבּוּעִין, דְּנָפְקִין וְנַגְדִּין לְכֹלָּא. יְדֹוָ״ד: גּוּפָא דְּאִילָנָא שְׁלִימוּ דְּשָׁרָשִׁין. אֶחָד: כְּנֶסֶת יִשְׂרָאֵל. וְכֹלָּא חַד שְׁלֵימוּתָא, וְאִתְקְשַׁר דָּא בְּדָא, וְלָא אִשְׁתְּכַח פְּרוּדָא, אֶלָּא כֹּלָּא חַד.

59. AFTER EXPLAINING "HEAR, O YISRAEL" HE GOES ON TO INTERPRET THE OTHER WORDS IN THE VERSE. Hashem is the highest of all in the illumination of Atika Kadisha, WHICH IS Chochmah. It is called father, NAMELY ABA. "our Elohim" is the depths of the rivers and streams FROM WHENCE they emerge and flow on everything, NAMELY BINAH, FROM WHICH MALE, FEMALE AND ALL LOWER BEINGS RECEIVE, AND WHICH IS CALLED IMA. The SECOND Yud Hei Vav Hei is the trunk of the tree, NAMELY ZEIR ANPIN, which is the whole of the roots, BEING THE CENTRAL COLUMN THAT INCLUDES CHOCHMAH AND BINAH, WHICH ARE "HASHEM OUR ELOHIM." "One" is the Congregation of Yisrael, NAMELY MALCHUT, and everything, ALL THESE SFIROT, make one wholeness and are interconnected. There is no division BETWEEN THEM, but all is one.

60. תָּנֵי ר׳ יִצְחָק, רְתִיכָא קַדִּישָׁא עִלָּאָה, אַרְבַּע בָּתֵּי דִּתְפִלִּין דְּאָנַח ו׳. כְּמָה דְּאִתְּמַר. רְתִיכָא קַדִּישָׁא אָחֳרָא, אַרְבַּע אַחֲרָנִין דִּכְלִילָן בְּחַד, דְּאָנַח ה׳ בַּתְרָאָה כְּמָה דְּאוֹקְמוּהָ.

60. Rabbi Yitzchak taught that the supernal holy Chariot, CHOCHMAH AND BINAH, TIFERET AND MALCHUT, are the four compartments of the Tefilin that Vav puts on, WHICH IS ZEIR ANPIN, as we learned. Another holy Chariot, TIFERET, NETZACH, HOD AND YESOD are the four other PASSAGES included in one COMPARTMENT, WHICH ARE THE TEFILIN the last Hei OF YUD HEI VAV HEI puts on, WHICH IS MALCHUT, as we explained.

9. Upper union and lower union

A Synopsis

We are told that the purpose of the recital of the Sh'ma is to unify the name of God. The unification perfects the ministers and officers of 248 worlds, all called body parts. We hear about the 613 commandments in the lilies and the secret of "the apple tree among the trees of the wood."

רעיא מהימנא

61. שְׁמַע יִשְׂרָאֵל יְיָ' אֱלֹהֵינוּ יְיָ' אֶחָד, פִּקּוּדָא דָּא, לְיַחֲדָא שְׁמֵיהּ דְּקוּדְשָׁא בְּרִיךְ הוּא בְּכָל יוֹמָא, דְּהָא כְּמָה דִּמְיַיחֲדֵי שְׁמָא דְּקוּדְשָׁא בְּרִיךְ הוּא לְתַתָּא, הָכִי אִתְיַיחָד שְׁמֵיהּ לְעֵילָּא. אִשְׁתְּכַח קוּדְשָׁא בְּרִיךְ הוּא יְחִידָאי עֵילָּא וְתַתָּא. מַאן דִּמְיַיחֵד שְׁמֵיהּ דְּקוּדְשָׁא בְּרִיךְ הוּא, יְשַׁוֵּי לִבֵּיהּ וּרְעוּתֵיהּ בְּהַהוּא יִחוּדָא דְּקָאַמְרָן, וִיחַבֵּר כָּל שַׁיְיפוֹי בְּהוּא יִחוּדָא לְמֶהֱוֵי כֻּלְּהוּ אֶחָד. כְּמָה דְּשַׁוֵּי כָּל שַׁיְיפוֹי בְּרָזָא דְּחָד, הָכִי לְעֵילָּא מְחַבֵּר כָּל שַׁיְיפִין עִלָּאִין בְּהַהוּא יִחוּדָא, לְמֶהֱוֵי כֻּלְּהוּ חַד.

Ra'aya Meheimna (the Faithful Shepherd)

61. "Hear, O Yisrael, Hashem our Elohim; Hashem is one" (Devarim 6:4). The commandment is to declare the unity of the name of the Holy One, blessed be He, below; for as the name of the Holy One, blessed be He, is unified below, so it is unified above. Thus the Holy One, blessed be He, is one and only above and below. Whoever declares the unity of the name of the Holy One, blessed be He, should direct his attention and will to the meditation (lit. 'unification') we mentioned, NAMELY UNITE HIS NAME BELOW, and connect all His limbs, NAMELY THE SFIROT by means of the meditation so that they will all become one. For as one arranges all the limbs OF THE NAME according to a mystery below, so one connects all the supernal limbs by means of that meditation so they will all become one.

62. בְּשַׁעֲתָא דְּאָתֵי ב"נ לְיַיחֲדָא שְׁמָא דְּקוּדְשָׁא בְּרִיךְ הוּא, כָּל חֵילֵי שְׁמַיָּא כֻּלְּהוּ, קַיְימִין שׁוּרִין, בְּגִין לְאִתְתַּקְנָא וּלְאִתְכַּלְּלָא כֻּלְּהוּ בְּהַהוּא יִחוּדָא, לְמֵיקָם בְּרָזָא דְּחָד בְּיִחוּדָא חֲדָא. כֻּלְּהוּ מִתְתַּקְּנָן

בְּתִקּוּנֵיהוֹן כַּדְקָא יָאוּת. בְּהַאי שַׁעֲתָא קַיְימָא חַד מְמָנָא שַׁמָּשָׁא, דְּקַיְימָא תְּחוֹת רמ"ח עָלְמִין, וְכֻלְּהוּ אִקְרוּן שַׁיְיפִין דְּגוּפָא. וְדָא אִקְרֵי הלני"ו, קַיְימָא מְחַכָּה לְהַהוּא יִחוּדָא, וְדָא אִיהוּ מְלַקֵּט שׁוֹשַׁנִּים, כד"א וְלִלְקוֹט שׁוֹשַׁנִּים. דְּאִינּוּן שַׁיְיפִין דְּגוּפָא.

62. When man is about to unite the name of the Holy One, blessed be He, all the hosts of heaven stand in rows so as to be established and reach perfection by means of that meditation, to be founded by one mystery and meditation. They are all properly established BY THAT MEDITATION. At that time, there is a minister and officer situated under 248 worlds, all called body parts. This OFFICER is called Halanu, and stands awaiting that unification. He is the gatherer of lilies, as written, "to gather lilies" (Shir Hashirim 6:2), which are the body parts.

63. שַׁיְיפִין עִלָּאִין לָקִיט לוֹן שְׁמָא עִלָּאָה, בְּרָזָא דְּיִחוּדָא דְּקָא אִתְיָיחָד בְּרָזָא דְּמ"ב שְׁמָהָן. וְלָקִיט כָּל אִינּוּן שׁוֹשַׁנִּים עִלָּאִין, וְשַׁמָּשָׁא דָּא לָקִיט כָּל אִינּוּן תַּתָּאִין, דִּי כֻּלְּהוּ מְמָנָן בִּכְלָלָא דְּע"ב שְׁמָהָן, וְאִתְלְקִיטוּ כֻּלְּהוּ בְּהַהוּא יִחוּדָא, וְאִתְעֲבֵידוּ כֻּלְּהוּ גּוּפָא חֲדָא. בְּרָזָא חֲדָא. וְהַהוּא יִחוּדָא סַלְּקָא, וְקָא מְיַיחֵד כֹּלָּא בִּתְרֵין סִטְרִין בְּיִחוּדָא חֲדָא. בְּהַהוּא שַׁעֲתָא מִתְלַקְּטִין שַׁיְיפִין כֻּלְּהוּ, וּמִתְחַבְּרָן בְּחִבּוּרָא חֲדָא, לְמֶהֱוֵי כֻּלְּהוּ בְּרָזָא דְּחָד, עֵילָּא וְתַתָּא, בְּרָזָא דַּיְדֹוָד אֶחָד וּשְׁמוֹ אֶחָד.

63. The Supernal Name gathers the supernal body parts according to the meditation that is unified by means of the 42 names. It gathers all those supernal lilies. This officer gathers all the lower, which are all ministers, into 72 names. They are all gathered by that meditation and all become one body, according to the same mystery. That meditation rises and unites everything in the two sides into one unity. At that time all body parts are gathered and connected into one, so they will all be according to the same meaning above and below, according to the secret of, "Hashem shall be one, and His name One" (Zecharyah 14:9).

64. וְע"ד מַאֲרִיכִין בְּאֶחָד, בִּתְרֵי אַתְוָון. לְמִלְקַט שׁוֹשַׁנִּים, לְאִתְיַיחֲדָא

בְּרָזָא דְּאֶחָד בְּיִחוּדָא שְׁלִים. כֵּיוָן דְּאִתְיַיחֲדָן שַׁיְיפִין כֻּלְּהוּ, בְּרָזָא חֲדָא דְּיִחוּדָא חֲדָא, כְּדֵין אִתְקְרֵי כֹּלָּא קָרְבָּן שְׁלִים. וְעַל רָזָא דָּא, אָעִיל לֵיהּ קוּדְשָׁא בְּרִיךְ הוּא בג״ע לְאָדָם קַדְמָאָה, כְּמָה דִּכְתִּיב לְעָבְדָהּ וּלְשָׁמְרָהּ. וְתָנֵינָן, דְּאִלֵּין אִינּוּן קָרְבְּנִין תְּרֵין, רָזָא דַּיְדֹוָד אֶחָד וּשְׁמוֹ אֶחָד. דְּאִינּוּן קָרְבְּנִין כְּתִיב, וְלִלְקוֹט שׁוֹשַׁנִּים. אִלֵּין שַׁיְיפִין דִּתְרֵין סִטְרִין, דְּאִינּוּן חַד.

64. For that reason in the word '*Echad* (Eng. 'one')' the pronunciation of two letters Chet and Dalet is lengthened, to gather lilies so as to be united by means of the same mystery by the complete meditation. Once all body parts are united according to the same secret of the same meditation, everything is considered a peace (or: 'whole') offering. For that secret reason the Holy One, blessed be He, entered Adam into the Garden of Eden, as written, "to till it and to keep it" (Beresheet 2:15). We learned that these are the two offerings, according to the secret of, "Hashem shall be one, and His name One." For in reference to these offerings it is written, "to gather lilies." These are the body parts of the two sides that are one.

65. שׁוֹשַׁנִּים רָזָא אִיהוּ. דְּכַד מִתְחַבְּרָן כָּל אִינּוּן שַׁיְיפִין כַּחֲדָא, לְמֶהֱוֵי כֻּלְּהוּ בְּיִחוּדָא חֲדָא, רָזָא דְּקָרְבָּן, כְּדֵין מִתְעַטֵּר קוּדְשָׁא בְּרִיךְ הוּא בַּעֲטָרָה בְּרֵישָׁא דְּכֶתֶם פָּז, לְמֶהֱוֵי בִּיקָרוֹי מִתְעַטְּרָא. וְרָזָא דָּא הֲוֵי דִּכְתִּיב שׁוֹשַׁנִּים, רָזָא דְּכָל אִינּוּן שַׁיְיפִין דְּעֵילָּא וְתַתָּא. וְרָזָא דְּהַהוּא פָּז, עִטּוּרָא דְּמִתְעַטְּרָא וְסַלְקָא מִבֵּינַיְיהוּ, וְכֹלָּא אִיהוּ בֵּיהּ.

65. The lilies are a mystery. When these body parts are connected together so as to be all one by means of one meditation according to the secret of the offering, the Holy One, blessed be He, is adorned with a crown of fine gold, so as to be adorned with His honor. This is the meaning behind the word lilies, which are the secret of all the body parts above and below. The secret of that gold is that it is a crown that is adorned and rises from among them. There is everything in them, IN THE LILIES.

66. בְּהָנֵי שׁוֹשַׁנִּים אִית בָּהּ שִׁית מְאָה וּתְלֵיסָר פִּקּוּדִין, דְּאִינּוּן שַׁיְיפִין דִּתְרֵין סִטְרִין, רָזָא דַּיְדֹוָד אֶחָד וּשְׁמוֹ אֶחָד. וְאִית בֵּיהּ סְלִיקוּ דְּהַהוּא

פָּז, דְּקָא סָלִיק מִבֵּינַיְיהוּ. וּבְכָל אֲתָר דְּאִינּוּן מִשְׁתַּכְּחִין, הַהוּא סְלִיקוּ עִלָּאָה אִשְׁתְּכַח מִבֵּינַיְיהוּ לְאִסְתַּלְקָא. וְרָזָא דָּא תַּפּוּחַ בַּעֲצֵי הַיַּעַר. וְשׁוֹשַׁנָּה בֵּין הַחוֹחִים. דָּא וְדָא אִצְטְרִיךְ לְאִסְתַּלְקָא כַּחֲדָא בְּיִחוּדָא שְׁלִים. זַכָּאָה אִיהוּ מַאן דְּקָרִיב קָרְבְּנִין אִלֵּין, וַדַּאי לְרַעֲוָא לֵיהּ בְּהַאי עָלְמָא וּבְעָלְמָא דְּאָתֵי.

66. There are 613 commandments in these lilies, which are the body parts of the two sides, according to the secret of, "Hashem shall be one, and His name One." Among them is the ascent of that gold that rises from among them. Wherever they are, THAT IS, THE UNIFICATION OF THE BODY PARTS OF BOTH SIDES, that supernal ascent of THE CROWN OF gold rises from among them. This is the secret of "the apple tree among the trees of the wood" (Shir Hashirim 2:3), and, "the lily among thorns" (Ibid. 2), as both the one and the other should rise as one by the complete meditation. Happy is he who sacrifices these offerings, NAMELY, PERFORMS THESE MEDITATIONS. Surely, it is favorable to him both in this world and the World to Come.

10. Awe

A Synopsis

The Faithful Shepherd says that it is a commandment to be in awe of God in a general way, but that one should also be in awe of Him in particular; this means that he should feel awe out of love, that is the base and foundation of the love of God.

67. פִּקּוּדָא לְיִרְאָה בְּאֹרַח כְּלָל, וּבְאֹרַח פְּרָט. וְהָא יִרְאָה אוֹקִימְנָא, בְּגִין דְּאִית עָלֵיהּ דְּב״נ לְדַחֲלָא מִקַּמֵּי קוּדְשָׁא בְּרִיךְ הוּא תָּדִיר. כד״א, לְיִרְאָה אֶת הַשֵּׁם הַנִּכְבָּד וְהַנּוֹרָא הַזֶּה אֵת יְיָ׳ אֱלֹהֶיךָ. וּבְגִין יִרְאָה דָּא, יִסְתְּמַר בְּאָרְחוֹי. וְיִרְאָה, אֲתָר הוּא דְּאִקְרֵי יִרְאָה, בְּגִין דְּתַמָּן שַׁרְיָא דַּחֲלָא דְּקוּדְשָׁא בְּרִיךְ הוּא, אִיהוּ יִרְאַת יְיָ׳ לְדַחֲלָא מִנֵּיהּ, וְדָא אִיהוּ רָזָא דִּכְתִּיב, וּמִמִּקְדָּשִׁי תִּירָאוּ בְּהַאי יִרְאָה שַׁרְיָא פּוּלְסָא דְּנוּרָא, לְאַלְקָאָה לוֹן לְחַיָּיבַיָּא, דְּלָא נַטְרִין פִּקּוּדֵי אוֹרַיְיתָא וְע״ד בְּאֹרַח כְּלַל, אִית לְדַחֲלָא.

67. It is a commandment to be in awe of the Holy One, blessed be He, in general and in particular. HE EXPLAINS, we explained awe TO MEAN that man should be always in awe of the Holy One, blessed be He, as written, "that you may fear this glorious and fearful name, Hashem your Elohim" (Devarim 28:58). Awe is a place called awe, NAMELY MALCHUT, since there the awe of the Holy One, blessed be He LIES. It is CALLED the awe of Hashem BECAUSE ONE SHOULD BE in awe of Him. This is the secret of the verse, "and reverence My sanctuary" (Vayikra 19:30). For in this awe, MALCHUT, a baton of fire dwells that strikes the evil who do not observe the commandments of the Torah SINCE PUNISHMENTS COME FROM MALCHUT. Hence one should be in awe in general, NAMELY FEAR OF PUNISHMENT.

68. וּבָתַר בְּאֹרַח פְּרָט, כַּד יָדַע ב״נ מַאן אִיהִי יִרְאַת יְיָ׳, וְדָא אִיהוּ דַּחֲלָא דַּחֲבִיבוּתָא, דְּאִיהִי עִיקָּר וִיסוֹדָא לְמִרְחַם לֵיהּ לְקוּדְשָׁא בְּרִיךְ הוּא. הַאי יִרְאָה עָבֵיד לְנַטְרָא כָּל פִּקּוּדוֹי דְּאוֹרַיְיתָא, לְמֶהֱוֵי ב״נ עֶבֶד נֶאֱמָן לְגַבֵּי קוּדְשָׁא בְּרִיךְ הוּא כַּדְקָא יָאוּת.

68. Then ONE SHOULD BE IN AWE OF HIM in particular, namely, when man knows what the awe of Hashem is, BY ATTAINING THE QUALITY OF MALCHUT HERSELF. This is awe out of love, which is the base and foundation of the love of the Holy One, blessed be He. This awe causes one to observe all the commandments of the Torah, so man will be a faithful servant of the Holy One, blessed be He, as is proper.

11. Love

A Synopsis

Moses now says that it is a commandment to love. He tells us that whoever loves God maintains ten sayings and passes ten tests. We hear about great love and everlasting love, and that the two are one without division. The Faithful Shepherd asserts that love surpasses every other kind of worship there is in the whole world.

69. פִּקּוּדָא לְאַהֲבָה, וְהָא אוֹקִימְנָא רְחִימוּ דְּקוּדְשָׁא בְּרִיךְ הוּא, דְּבָעֵי ב"נ לְרַחֲמָא לֵיהּ רְחִימוּ סַגֵּי כְּאַבְרָהָם, דְּרָחִים לֵיהּ לְקוּדְשָׁא בְּרִיךְ הוּא בְּכַמָּה רְחִימוּ, וּמָסַר גּוּפֵיהּ וְנַפְשֵׁיהּ לְגַבֵּיהּ. מִכָּאן אוֹלִיפְנָא, מַאן דְּרָחִים לֵיהּ לְקוּדְשָׁא בְּרִיךְ הוּא, אִיהוּ מְקַיֵּים עֲשַׂר אֲמִירָן עֵילָּא וְתַתָּא. וְע"ד כָּל אִינּוּן עֶשֶׂר נִסְיוֹנֵי דְּאִתְנַסָּא אַבְרָהָם, וְקָאֵים בְּכֻלְּהוּ לָקֳבֵל עֲשַׂר אֲמִירָן, כָּל נִסְיוֹנָא אֲמִירָא הִיא, וְאִתְנָסָּא בְּהַהוּא אֲמִירָא, וְקָאֵים בֵּיהּ.

69. It is a commandment to love. We explained that the love for the Holy One, blessed be He, MEANS that man should love Him with great love as did Abraham, who loved the Holy One, blessed be He, with great love and risked his body and soul for His sake. From this we derived that whoever loves the Holy One, blessed be He, maintains ten sayings, NAMELY TEN SFIROT, above and below. Hence all these ten tests Abraham underwent and withstood correspond to the ten sayings, since every test is one saying, NAMELY ONE SFIRAH. And he was tested by that saying and withstood it.

70. וְע"ד אִינּוּן עֶשֶׂר נִסְיוֹנֵי, וְכֻלְּהוּ קָאֵים בְּהוּ אַבְרָהָם, בְּגִין דְּאִתְקְשַׁר וְאִתְדַּבָּק בִּימִינָא דְּקוּדְשָׁא בְּרִיךְ הוּא, דְּאִיהִי אַהֲבָה רַבָּה. מ"ט אִיקְרֵי אַהֲבָה רַבָּה. בְּגִין מַאן דְּקָאֵים בְּהַאי אַהֲבָה, אִתְקְשַׁר בְּעָלְמָא עִלָּאָה. אַהֲבַת עוֹלָם, דָּא רָזָא דְּעָלְמָא תַּתָּאָה, דְּאִתְקְשַׁר בֵּיהּ רְחִימוּ דִּילֵיהּ, וְכֹלָּא רָזָא חֲדָא, בְּלָא פֵּרוּדָא, וְהָא אִתְּמַר רָזָא דְּאַהֲבָה, רְחִימוּ דָּא סָלִיק עַל כָּל פּוּלְחָנִין דְּעָלְמָא, בְּהַאי אִתְיְיקַר שְׁמֵיהּ דְּקוּדְשָׁא בְּרִיךְ הוּא יַתִּיר מִכֹּלָּא, וְאִתְבְּרַךְ. בְּרִיךְ הוּא לְעָלַם וּלְעָלְמֵי עָלְמִין, וְרָזָא דְּאַהֲבָה אִתְּמַר.

70. There are therefore ten tests THAT CORRESPOND TO THE TEN SFIROT, and Abraham withstood them all, because he was attached and cleaved to the right hand of the Holy One, blessed be He that is called great love, NAMELY CHESED OF ZEIR ANPIN. It is called great love because whoever is in that state of love is attached to the supernal world, ZEIR ANPIN. Everlasting love is the secret of the lower world, NAMELY MALCHUT, to which the love of the Holy One, blessed be He, is attached. Everything, GREAT LOVE AND EVERLASTING LOVE, is the same mystery without division BETWEEN THEM. We have now learned the mystery of love that love surpasses every kind of worship in the world. By love the name of the Holy One, blessed be He, is honored above everything, and is blessed. Blessed be He forever and ever. This is the clarification of the secret of love.

71. פִּקּוּדָא לְמִקְרֵי קְרִיאַת שְׁמַע ב׳ זִמְנִין בְּכָל יוֹמָא חַד, לָקֳבֵל דַּרְגָּא דִּימָמָא. וְחַד, לָקֳבֵל דַּרְגָּא דְּלֵילְיָא. וּלְאַכְלְלָא בִּימָמָא דַּרְגָּא דְּלֵילְיָא, וּלְאַכְלְלָא בְּלֵילְיָא דַּרְגָּא דִּימָמָא, וְהָא אִתְּמַר. וְע״ד תְּרֵין זִמְנִין בְּכָל יוֹמָא, חַד בִּימָמָא וְחַד בְּלֵילְיָא.

71. It is a commandment to recite the Sh'ma twice every day, once to correspond to the grade of day, WHICH IS ZEIR ANPIN, and once to correspond to the grade of night, WHICH IS MALCHUT, so as to include the grade of night in day and the grade of day in the night. We have already learned this. We therefore need to do this twice daily, once during the day and once at night.

12. The Mezuzah

A Synopsis

We are told that affixing a Mezuzah at the door ensures that God will guard the inhabitants when they enter and leave. Another reason for the Mezuzah is that it reminds people of God so they remember to do His will. We hear how the evil demon that stands near the door is distracted so he can not do any harm.

72. פִּקּוּדָא לְמִקְבַּע ב״נ מְזוּזָה לְתַרְעֵיהּ, לְמֶהֱוֵי כָּל ב״נ נָטִיר מֵעִם קוּדְשָׁא בְּרִיךְ הוּא, כַּד נָפִיק וְכַד עָיֵיל. וְרָזָא יְיָ׳ יִשְׁמָר צֵאתְךָ וּבֹאֶךָ מֵעַתָּה וְעַד עוֹלָם. בְּגִין דְּרָזָא דִּמְזוּזָה אִיהוּ קָאִים תָּדִיר לְפִתְחָא. וְדָא אִיהוּ פִּתְחָא דִּלְעֵילָּא, וְדָא אִיהוּ דַּרְגָּא דְּאִקְרֵי שׁוֹמֵר, לְאִשְׁתַּכְּחָא בִּנְטִירוּ.

72. It is a commandment that man should fix a Mezuzah at his door, so that everyone will be guarded by the Holy One, blessed be He, upon leaving THE HOUSE and entering THE HOUSE. This is the secret of, "Hashem shall preserve your going out and your coming in from this time forth, and for evermore" (Tehilim 121:8). For the secret of the Mezuzah always rests at the door, which is the entrance to the higher, BEING MALCHUT, THE ENTRANCE TO ZEIR ANPIN, ACCORDING TO THE SECRET OF, "THIS IS THE GATE OF HASHEM" (TEHILIM 118:20). This grade is called guardian, so one is guarded.

73. דְּב״נ לָאו אִיהוּ נָטִיר, בַּר נְטִירוּ דְּקוּדְשָׁא בְּרִיךְ הוּא, דְּאִיהוּ נָטִיר תָּדִיר, וְקָאִים לְפִתְחָא, וּב״נ לְגוֹ. וְתוּ, דְּלָא יִנְשֵׁי ב״נ דּוּכְרָנָא דְּקוּדְשָׁא בְּרִיךְ הוּא לְעָלְמִין. וְדָא אִיהוּ כְּגַוְונָא דְּצִיצִית, כד״א וּרְאִיתֶם אוֹתוֹ וּזְכַרְתֶּם אֶת וְגוֹ׳. כֵּיוָן דְּחָמֵי בַּר נָשׁ לְהַאי דּוּכְרָנָא, אִדְכַּר בְּגַרְמֵיהּ לְמֶעְבַּד פִּקּוּדָא דְּמָארֵיהּ. וְרָזָא דִּמְהֵימְנוּתָא, מְזוּזָה כְּלָלָא דְּכַר וְנוּקְבָא כַּחֲדָא.

73. For man is not guarded except by the Holy One, blessed be He, who constantly guards and is present at the door TO THE HOUSE, while one is inside THE HOUSE. Another REASON FOR THE MEZUZAH is that one must never forget the memory of the Holy One, blessed be He. This REASON is like the Tzitzit, as said, "that you may look upon it, and remember" (Bemidbar 15:39). When one sees that reminder, he is reminded to do his Master's bidding. The secret of Faith is that the Mezuzah includes a male and a female together.

74. בְּסִפְרָא דִּשְׁלֹמֹה, סָמִיךְ לְפִתְחָא, לָקֳבֵל תְּרֵין דַּרְגִּין, אִזְדְּמַן חַד שֵׁידָא וְאִית לֵיהּ רְשׁוּ לְחַבְּלָא. וְאִיהוּ קָאֵים לִסְטַר שְׂמָאלָא. זָקִיף ב"נ עֵינוֹי, חָמֵי לֵיהּ לְרָזָא דִּשְׁמָא דְּמָארֵיהּ, וְאִדְכַּר לֵיהּ, וְלָא יָכִיל לֵיהּ לְאַבְאָשָׁא. וְאִי תֵּימָא, אִי הָכִי כִּי נָפִיק ב"נ מִתַּרְעֵיהּ לְבַר, הָא הַהוּא שֵׁידָא קָאֵים לִימִינֵיהּ, וּמְזוּזָה לִשְׂמָאלֵיהּ, וְהֵאַיךְ אִתְנְטִיר ב"נ, אִי אִיהוּ שָׁארֵי לִשְׂמָאלֵיהּ.

74. In the book of Solomon IT IS WRITTEN: near the entrance, against the two grades, comes a certain demon that has permission to harm. It stands at the left side OF THE DOOR. Man lifts up his eyes, sees the secret of his master's Name IN THE MEZUZAH AT THE RIGHT SIDE OF THE DOOR and remembers it, and THE DEMON cannot harm. You may say that if this is so, IT IS TRUE WHEN ONE COMES INTO THE HOUSE. BUT when leaving the door OF THE HOUSE outside, the demon TO THE LEFT SIDE OF THE DOOR is at the right side OF THE MAN and the Mezuzah to his left. How is man guarded then, if THE MEZUZAH is to his left?

75. אֶלָּא כָּל מַה דְּעָבֵיד קוּדְשָׁא בְּרִיךְ הוּא, כָּל מִלָּה וּמִלָּה אִתְמְשַׁךְ בָּתַר זִינֵיהּ. בְּבַר נָשׁ קַיְימִין תְּרֵין דַּרְגִּין, חַד מִימִינָא, וְחַד מִשְּׂמָאלָא. הַהוּא דִּימִינָא אִקְרֵי יצה"ט, וְהַהוּא דִּשְׂמָאלָא אִקְרֵי יֵצֶר הָרָע. כֵּיוָן דְּנָפַק בַּר נָשׁ מִתַּרְעָא דְּבֵיתֵיהּ, הַהוּא שֵׁידָא זָקִיף עֵינוֹי, וְחָמֵי לְיֵצֶר הָרָע, דְּשָׁארֵי לִשְׂמָאלָא, אִתְמְשַׁךְ לְהַהוּא סִטְרָא וְאִתְעֲדֵי מִימִינָא. וּבְהַהוּא סִטְרָא, קָאֵים שְׁמָא דְּמָארֵיהּ, וְלָא יָכִיל לְקָרְבָא וּלְאַבְאָשָׁא לֵיהּ, וְנָפִיק ב"נ וְאִשְׁתְּזִיב מִנֵּיהּ. כַּד עָיֵיל, הָא שְׁמָא קַדִּישָׁא לִימִינָא קָאֵים, וְלָא יָכִיל לְקַטְרְגָא בַּהֲדֵיהּ.

75. AND HE ANSWERS, All that the Holy One, blessed be He, does, follows its own kind. There are two grades to man, one to his right and one to his left. The one to the right is called the Good Inclination and the one to the left is called the Evil Inclination. When one goes out of his house's door, that demon lifts up its eyes and sees the Evil Inclination dwelling at the left side. It is attracted to that side WHERE THE EVIL INCLINATION ABIDES, NAMELY THE LEFT, and is removed from the right. Then at the LEFT side rests his master's Name, NAMELY THE MEZUZAH, and it cannot approach him to cause him harm and that man goes out and is saved from it. Upon coming INTO THE HOUSE the Holy Name IN THE MEZUZAH is to his right, AND THUS THE RIGHT OVERPOWERS THE LEFT, and it cannot prosecute him.

76. וְע״ד אִצְטְרִיךְ ב״נ, דְּלָא יַעֲבִיד טִנּוּפָא וְלִכְלוּכָא בְּתַרְעָא דְּבֵיתֵיהּ, וְלָא יוֹשִׁיד מַיִין עֲכוּרִין. חַד, דְּלָא יַעֲבִיד קְלָנָא לְגַבֵּי שְׁמָא דְּמָארֵיהּ. וְחַד, דְּאִית לֵיהּ רְשׁוּ לְהַהוּא מְחַבְּלָא לְחַבְּלָא. וּבְג״כ יִזְדַּהַר ב״נ מֵהַאי, וְיִזְדְּהַר ב״נ דְּלָא יִמְנַע מִתַּרְעָא דְּבֵיתֵיהּ שְׁמָא דְּמָארֵיהּ.

76. One must therefore be careful not to soil the door to his house with filth and refuse, or spill dirty water FOR TWO REASONS; the one is not to desecrate his Master's Name IN THE MEZUZAH and the other is that then that fiend, NAMELY THE DEMON, has permission to cause harm. For that reason man must be careful about it and take care not to push away his Master's Name from the door to his house.

77. וְכַד בַּר נָשׁ אַתְקִין מְזוּזָה לְפִתְחֵיהּ, כַּד עָיֵיל הַהוּא ב״נ, הַהוּא יֵצֶר הָרָע וְהַהוּא שֵׁידָא בְּעַל כָּרְחַיְיהוּ נַטְרֵי לֵיהּ, וְאַמְרֵי זֶה הַשַּׁעַר לַיְיָ׳ צַדִּיקִים יָבֹאוּ בוֹ. וְכַד לָא קָאֵים מְזוּזָה לְפִתְחֵיהּ דְּב״נ, יֵצֶר הָרָע וְהַהוּא שֵׁידָא מִתְתַּקְּנִין כַּחֲדָא, שַׁוּוּ יְדַיְיהוּ עַל רֵישֵׁיהּ בְּזִמְנָא דְּעָיֵיל, פַּתְחֵי וְאַמְרֵי, וַוי לֵיהּ לִפְלַנְיָא, דְּהָא נָפַק מֵרְשׁוּתָא דְּמָארֵיהּ, מֵהַהוּא זִמְנָא קָאֵים בְּלָא נְטִירוּ, דְּלֵית מַאן דְּנָטִיר עָלֵיהּ, רַחֲמָנָא לִישֵׁזְבָן.

77. When man fixes a Mezuzah at his door, when he enters his house, the Evil Inclination and the demon guard him in spite of themselves and say, "this is the gate of Hashem, into which the righteous shall enter" (Tehilim 118:20). When there is no Mezuzah at a man's entrance, the Evil Inclination and that demon GROW STRONG AND come together and place their hands on his head when he enters and begin to say, Woe to so-and-so who went out of his Master's domain. From that time ON he is not guarded and there is no one to guard him. May the Merciful One save us.

13. Sh'ma and 'Blessed be the name of the glory of His kingdom forever and ever'

A Synopsis

This section talks about the unification of the two names Yud Hei Vav Hei and Elohim, the first by the meditation "Sh'ma Yisrael" and the second by the meditation beginning "Blessed be the name." This concept is applied also to the Torah, that consists of the Written Torah and the Oral Torah, the first being general and the second being particular. The unification spoken of here pertains to the Torah, to the names of God, to the above and the below, to Zeir Anpin and Malchut, to 'remember' and 'keep', to night and day and to right and left; it is the unification of everything. Finally we are told how the Tefilin relate to this topic.

78. שְׁמַע יִשְׂרָאֵל יְיָ׳ אֱלֹהֵינוּ יְיָ׳ אֶחָד, דָּא אִיהוּ יִחוּדָא חַד. בָּרוּךְ שֵׁם כְּבוֹד מַלְכוּתוֹ לְעוֹלָם וָעֶד, הָא יִחוּדָא אַחֲרָא, לְמֶהֱוֵי שְׁמֵיהּ רָזָא חַד. וְרָזָא דָּא, יְיָ׳ הוּא הָאֱלֹהִים, דָּא כְּתִיב, כַּד אִינוּן בְּיִחוּדָא חַד.

78. "Hear (Sh'ma), O Yisrael, Hashem our Elohim, Hashem is one" (Devarim 6:4) is one meditation (lit. 'unification'), and 'Blessed be the name of the glory of His kingdom forever and ever' is another meditation, so that His Name, WHICH IS MALCHUT CALLED NAME, should be of the same secret. According to this secret of "Hashem, He is the Elohim" (I Melachim 18:39), YUD HEI VAV HEI, WHICH IS ZEIR ANPIN, IS MALCHUT CALLED ELOHIM. This is written WHEN ZEIR ANPIN AND MALCHUT are unified together. HENCE, "SH'MA YISRAEL" IS THE SECRET OF YUD HEI VAV HEI, AND, 'BLESSED BE THE NAME OF THE GLORY OF HIS KINGDOM FOREVER AND EVER' IS THE ELOHIM.

79. וְאִי תֵּימָא, אִי הָכִי כְּגַוְונָא דִּכְתִּיב יְיָ׳ אֶחָד וּשְׁמוֹ אֶחָד, לָאו אִיהִי יְיָ׳ הוּא הָאֱלֹהִים, דְּאִי כְּתִיב יְיָ׳ וּשְׁמוֹ הוּא אֶחָד, הֲוֵינָא אַמְרֵי הָכִי, לָא כְּתִיב אֶלָּא יְיָ׳ אֶחָד וּשְׁמוֹ אֶחָד, וְאִצְטְרִיךְ לוֹמַר בְּגַוְונָא דָּא, יְיָ׳ הוּא הָאֱלֹהִים הוּא, וְיִתְחֲזֵי יְיָ׳ אֶחָד וּשְׁמוֹ אֶחָד.

79. You may say that in that case THE MEDITATION OF SH'MA AND 'BLESSED BE...' resembles the verse, "Hashem shall be one, and His name One" (Zecharyah 14:9), which is not equal to, "Hashem, He is the Elohim."

For had it been written, 'Hashem and His name shall be one' we would say so THAT IT EQUALS, "HASHEM, HE IS THE ELOHIM," BUT it is not written so but, "Hashem shall be one, and His name One." IN THAT CASE it should have said thus: 'Hashem is, the Elohim is', and it would equal, "Hashem shall be one, and His name One." BUT SINCE IT IS NOT WRITTEN SO, BUT, "HASHEM, HE IS THE ELOHIM" IT IS NOT SIMILAR TO, "HASHEM SHALL BE ONE, AND HIS NAME ONE." HOW CAN WE CLAIM THAT THE MEDITATION OF "SH'MA" AND 'BLESSED BE...', WHICH ARE TWO MEDITATIONS, LIKE "HASHEM SHALL BE ONE, AND HIS NAME ONE," IS EQUAL TO, "HASHEM, HE IS THE ELOHIM"?

80. אֶלָּא כֹּלָּא חַד, דְּכַד אִתְאַחֲדָן תְּרֵין שְׁמָהָן אִלֵּין, דָּא בְּיִחוּדָא חַד, וְדָא בְּיִחוּדָא חַד, כְּדֵין תְּרֵין שְׁמָהָן אִלֵּין אִתְעֲבִידוּ חַד, וְאִתְכְּלִילָן דָּא בְּדָא, וַהֲוֵי כֹּלָּא שְׁמָא שְׁלִים בְּיִחוּדָא חֲדָא, וּכְדֵין יְיָ׳ הוּא הָאֱלֹהִים, דְּהָא כְּדֵין אִתְכְּלִיל כֹּלָּא דָּא בְּדָא לְמֶהֱוֵי חַד, וְעַד דְּאִתְיַיחֲדוּ כָּל חַד דָּא בִּלְחוֹדוֹי וְדָא בִּלְחוֹדוֹי, לָא אִתְכְּלִילוּ דָּא בְּדָא, לְמֶהֱוֵי כֹּלָּא חַד.

80. HE ANSWERS, Everything is one; THE MEDITATION OF "SH'MA" AND 'BLESSED BE...', THE SECRET OF "HASHEM SHALL BE ONE" IN "SH'MA" AND "HIS NAME ONE" IN 'BLESSED BE...' ARE ONE WITH "HASHEM, HE IS THE ELOHIM." For when these two names are unified – YUD HEI VAV HEI, WHICH IS ZEIR ANPIN, TOGETHER WITH ELOHIM, WHICH IS MALCHUT, the one by one meditation, WITH THE MEDITATION OF "SH'MA YISRAEL," and the other by another meditation, NAMELY THE MEDITATION OF, 'BLESSED BE...', or when the two names become one and are mutually included in each other and everything becomes one complete name, then IT IS WRITTEN, "Hashem, He is the Elohim." For then everything is included in each other to be one. But before they are unified each on its own, they cannot be mutually included to be all one, IN SUCH A WAY THAT "HASHEM SHALL BE ONE, AND HIS NAME ONE" IS NOT EQUAL TO "HASHEM, HE IS THE ELOHIM," BUT THE LATTER IS THE RESULT OF THE FORMER, AS EXPLAINED.

81. כְּלָלָא דְּכָל אוֹרַיְיתָא, הָכִי הוּא וַדַּאי, דְּהָא אוֹרַיְיתָא אִיהִי תּוֹרָה שֶׁבִּכְתָב, וְאִיהִי תּוֹרָה שֶׁבְּעַל פֶּה. תּוֹרָה שֶׁבִּכְתָב, דָּא הוּא דִּכְתִיב יְיָ׳.

תּוֹרָה שֶׁבְּעַל פֶּה, דִּכְתִּיב הָאֱלֹהִים. וּבְגִין דְּאוֹרַיְיתָא אִיהִי רָזָא דִּשְׁמָא קַדִּישָׁא, אִקְרֵי הָכִי.

81. The generality of the whole Torah, NAMELY THE WRITTEN TORAH AND THE ORAL TORAH TOGETHER, is surely that way, for the Torah is the Written Torah and is the Oral Torah. The Written Torah is as written, "Hashem," NAMELY ZEIR ANPIN; the Oral Torah is as written, "the Elohim," WHICH IS MALCHUT. Since the Torah is the secret of the Holy Name it is therefore called thus, THE ONE IS CALLED YUD HEI VAV HEI AND THE OTHER THE ELOHIM.

82. תּוֹרָה שֶׁבִּכְתָב וְתוֹרָה שֶׁבְּעַל פֶּה, דָּא כְּלָל, וְדָא פְּרָט. כְּלַל אִצְטְרִיךְ לִפְרָט, וּפְרָט אִצְטְרִיךְ לִכְלָל, וְאִתְיַיחֲדוּ דָּא בְּדָא, וַהֲוֵי כֹּלָּא חַד. וְע״ד כְּלָלָא דְּאוֹרַיְיתָא, אִיהוּ כְּלָלָא דִּלְעֵילָּא וְתַתָּא, בְּגִין דִּשְׁמָא דָּא לְעֵילָּא, וּשְׁמָא דָּא לְתַתָּא. דָּא רָזָא דְּעָלְמָא עִלָּאָה. וְדָא רָזָא דְּעָלְמָא תַּתָּאָה. וְע״ד כְּתִיב אַתָּה הָרְאֵתָ לָדַעַת כִּי יְיָ׳ הוּא הָאֱלֹהִים, דָּא כְּלָלָא דְּכֹלָּא, וְכָל דָּא דְּאָמָרָן, אִצְטְרִיךְ ב״נ לְמִנְדַּע בְּהַאי עָלְמָא.

82. The Written Torah and the Oral Torah, the one is general and the other particular. THE WRITTEN TORAH IS GENERAL, NAMELY ZEIR ANPIN, WHILE THE ORAL TORAH IS PARTICULAR, NAMELY MALCHUT. The general needs the particular and the particular needs the general. THE ONE CANNOT REACH PERFECTION WITHOUT THE OTHER UNTIL THE TWO ARE JOINED, they unite with each other and everything becomes one. Therefore the generality of the whole Torah is the generality above, ZEIR ANPIN, and the generality below, MALCHUT, since that name exists above and that name exists below. The one, THE WRITTEN TORAH, is the secret of the supernal world, ZEIR ANPIN, and the other, THE ORAL TORAH, is the secret of the lower world, MALCHUT. Hence it is written, "To you it was shown, that you might know that Hashem He is the Elohim" (Devarim 4:35), WHERE BOTH ARE ONE. This includes everything, ALL WORLDS. All that we said one should know in this world.

83. וְאִי תֵּימָא, פִּקּוּדֵי אוֹרַיְיתָא אָן אִינּוּן הָכָא, בִּכְלָלָא דָּא. אֶלָּא דָּא אִיהוּ זָכוֹר. וְדָא אִיהוּ שָׁמוֹר. וְכָל פִּקּוּדֵי אוֹרַיְיתָא בְּהָנֵי כְּלִילָן, בְּרָזָא

13. Sh'ma and 'Blessed be the name of the glory of His kingdom forever and ever'

דְּזָכוֹר, וּבְרָזָא דְּשָׁמוֹר, וְכֹלָּא אִיהוּ חַד.

83. You may ask where the commandments of the Torah are in this inclusion, WHETHER "HASHEM, HE IS THE ELOHIM," INCLUDES EVERYTHING. HE ANSWERS, The one, YUD HEI VAV HEI, is 'remember', while the other, THE ELOHIM, is 'keep'. All the commandments of the Torah are included in these in the mystery of 'remember' and the mystery of 'keep'. 'REMEMBER' INCLUDES THE 248 POSITIVE COMMANDMENTS AND 'KEEP' INCLUDES THE 365 NEGATIVE COMMANDMENTS, and everything is one.

84. פָּתַח ר׳ יוֹסִי וְאָמַר, הָא דִּתְנֵינָן צְלוֹתָא דְּעַרְבִית חוֹבָה אִיהוּ, וַדַּאי בְּגִין דְּק״ש דְּעַרְבִית חוֹבָה, וְקוּדְשָׁא בְּרִיךְ הוּא אִתְיָיחָד בְּלֵילְיָא, כְּמָה דְּאִתְיָיחַד בִּימָמָא. וּמִדַּת לַיְלָה אִתְכְּלִיל בִּימָמָא, וּמִדַּת יְמָמָא אִתְכְּלִיל בְּלֵילְיָא, וְאִתְעָבֵיד יִחוּדָא. וּמַאן דְּאָמַר רְשׁוּת, בְּגִין אֵימוּרִין וּפְדָרִין דְּמִתְעַכְּלֵי בְּלֵילְיָא. וְהָא אוֹקִימְנָא.

84. Rabbi Yosi opened with, The fact that we learned that Arvit (the evening prayer) is obligatory is surely so, because the Holy One, blessed be He, is unified at night THROUGH THE THE SH'MA READING, just as He is unified during the day. The quality of night is included in day and the quality of day is included in night, and unification takes place. Whoever says it is optional, it is BECAUSE THE PRAYER WAS COMPOSED to correspond to the portions of the sacrifices and the fatty parts that are consumed AND BURNED at night, WHICH ARE NOT OBLIGATORY. FOR SHACHARIT (THE MORNING PRAYER) AND MINCHAH (THE AFTERNOON PRAYER) CORRESPOND TO THE TWO DAILY OFFERINGS, WHICH ARE OBLIGATORY, BUT THE EVENING PRAYER CORRESPONDS TO THE PORTIONS OF THE SACRIFICES, ETC., WHICH ARE OPTIONAL. We have already explained it.

85. דִּכְתִּיב וְאָהַבְתָּ אֶת יְיָ׳ אֱלֹהֶיךָ, הַאי קְרָא אוֹקִימְנָא, וְאוֹקְמוּהָ חַבְרַיָּיא. אֲבָל אִית לְשָׁאֲלָא, אִי בְּהַאי יִחוּדָא דִּשְׁמַע יִשְׂרָאֵל, אִתְכְּלִיל

כֹּלָּא, יְמִינָא וּשְׂמָאלָא, אֲמַאי כְּתִיב לְבָתַר וְאָהַבְתָּ, וְהָיָה אִם שָׁמוֹעַ, דְּהָא בְּיִחוּדָא אִתְכְּלִילוּ. אֶלָּא הָתָם בִּכְלָל. הָכָא בִּפְרָט. וְהָכִי אִצְטְרִיךְ.

85. It is written, "And you shall love (Heb. *ve'ahavta*) Hashem your Elohim" (Devarim 6:5). We have explained this verse, and so did the friends. But we should ask: if everything, right and left, is included in this meditation of "Sh'ma Yisrael," why it is then written, "And you shall love," WHICH IS THE RIGHT, and, "And it shall come to pass, if you hearken (Heb. *vehayah im shamo'a*)" (Devarim 11:13-17), WHICH IS LEFT, if they were already included in the meditation OF THE SH'MA READING? AND HE ANSWERS, There, IN THE SH'MA READING, it is part of the general, WHERE THE RIGHT AND LEFT OF DA'AT WERE COMPREHENDED INTO A GENERAL PRINCIPLE, and here it is of the particular: AT FIRST IT IS WRITTEN, "AND YOU SHALL LOVE" IN ITSELF, WHICH IS CHESED, AND THEN "AND IT SHALL COME TO PASS, IF YOU HEARKEN," WHICH IS GVURAH. And so it should be.

86. וּבְרָזָא דְּיִחוּדָא דְּהָא אִתְעָרְנָא בֵּיהּ, יִחוּדָא אִיהוּ כְּגַוְונָא דִּתְפִלִּין דְּרֵישָׁא, וּתְפִילִּין דִּדְרוֹעָא, בִּתְפִילִּין דְּרֵישָׁא ד' פַּרְשִׁיָּין, וְהָא אִתְּמַר. וְהָכָא ג' שְׁמָהָן אִינּוּן. הָתָם אַרְבַּע פַּרְשִׁיָּין, וְכָל חַד וְחַד בִּלְחוֹדוֹי. וְהָכָא ג' שְׁמָהָן, מַה בֵּין הַאי לְהַאי.

86. In the secret of the meditation we remarked on, the meditation OF THE SH'MA READING is like THE MEDITATION OF the head Tefilin and the hand Tefilin. In the head Tefilin there are four passages, which we have already learned, and here IN THE SH'MA READING there are three names, YUD HEI VAV HEI, OUR ELOHIM, YUD HEI VAV HEI. There, there are four passages, each on its own, and here there are only three names. What is the difference between them?

14. The four passages of the head and hand Tefilin

A Synopsis

We learn how there can be four passages in the Tefilin yet only three names in the the Sh'ma reading. The numerology of the 25 letters in the Sh'ma, the 24 letters in the unification that begins with "Blessed be the name," the 49 gates of Binah and the 25 things used to complete the building of the tabernacle are all explained in detail.

Rabbi Aba asks Rabbi Shimon about the leather straps of the Tefilin, comparing it to skin. Rabbi Shimon gives him an explanation, and then says that when a person studies the Torah all night and then puts on the Tefilin in the morning, when he goes out of his house wearing the Tzitzit and passing the Mezuzah on his doorpost, then he is escorted by four holy angels that go with him to the synagogue. We are also told about the artistic work of people who create the Tefilin, the Tzitzit, and the Mezuzah. Rabbi Shimon closes by saying that if people really knew the Torah they would know that there isn't a single letter or word of it that does not contain supernal secrets.

87. אֶלָּא אִינוּן אַרְבַּע פַּרְשִׁיָּין הָא אִתְּעֲרוּ בְּהוּ, חַד נְקוּדָה קַדְמָאָה. וְחַד רָזָא דְּעָלְמָא דְּאָתֵי. וְחַד יְמִינָא וְחַד שְׂמָאלָא. אִלֵּין רָזָא דִּתְפִילִּין דְּרֵישָׁא. וְהָכָא בְּרָזָא דָּא, יִחוּדָא דָּא תְּלַת שְׁמָהָן עִלָּאִין, אִינּוּן כְּגַוְונָא דְּאִינּוּן אַרְבַּע פָּרְשִׁיָּין. יְיָ' קַדְמָאָה, דָּא נְקוּדָה עִלָּאָה, רֵאשִׁיתָא דְּכֹלָּא. אֱלֹהֵינוּ, רָזָא דְּעָלְמָא דְּאָתֵי. יְיָ' בַּתְרָאָה, כְּלָלָא דִּימִינָא וּשְׂמָאלָא כַּחֲדָא, בִּכְלָלָא חֲדָא וְאִלֵּין אִינּוּן תְּפִלָּה דְּרֵישָׁא, וְדָא אִיהוּ יִחוּדָא קַדְמָאָה.

87. HE ANSWERS, It has been remarked about these four passages that one, NAMELY, "SANCTIFY (HEB. *KADESH LI*)" (SHEMOT 13:2), is the first point, NAMELY YUD OF YUD HEI VAV HEI, WHICH IS CHOCHMAH. One, NAMELY, "AND IT SHALL BE, WHEN HASHEM YOUR ELOHIM SHALL BRING YOU (HEB. *VEHAYAH KI YEVIACHA*)" (DEVARIM 6:10), is the secret of the World to Come, WHICH IS BINAH. One, NAMELY "HEAR (HEB. *SH'MA*)" (DEVARIM 6:4) is the right side OF DA'AT, and one, WHICH IS, "AND IT SHALL COME TO PASS, IF YOU HEARKEN (HEB. *VEHAYAH IM SHAMO'A*)" (DEVARIM 11:13-17), is the left side OF DA'AT. They are the secret of the head Tefilin. Here, in this secret OF THE SH'MA READING, this unification of the three supernal names, YUD HEI VAV HEI, OUR ELOHIM, YUD HEI VAV HEI, resemble the four passages OF THE TEFILIN. The first Yud Hei Vav Hei is the supernal point, the beginning of everything, NAMELY CHOCHMAH. Our Elohim is the secret of the World to Come, NAMELY BINAH. The last Yud Hei Vav Hei is the entirety of right and left OF DA'AT together as one whole. These are THE ORDER OF the head Tefilin, and the first meditation OF THE SH'MA READING.

88. תְּפִלִּין דִּדְרוֹעָא, כְּלָלָא דְּכָל הָנֵי כַּחֲדָא, וְדָא אִיהוּ רָזָא, בָּרוּךְ שֵׁם כְּבוֹד מַלְכוּתוֹ לְעוֹלָם וָעֶד. הָכָא כְּלָלָא דְּאִינּוּן תְּפִלִּין דְּרֵישָׁא, דְּאִתְכְּלִילוּ גוֹ תְּפִלִּין דִּדְרוֹעָא.

88. The hand Tefilin are the entirety of these FOUR PASSAGES together, NAMELY IN ONE COMPARTMENT, and this is the secret OF THE SECOND UNIFICATION IN THE SH'MA READING, WHICH IS 'Blessed be the name of the glory of His kingdom forever and ever'. Here IN THE SECOND UNIFICATION is the whole of THE FOUR PASSAGES OF the head Tefilin comprehended in the hand Tefilin IN ONE COMPARTMENT. THAT MEANS THAT THE UNIFICATION OF 'BLESSED BE...' RESEMBLES THE UNIFICATION OF THE FOUR PASSAGES OF THE HAND TEFILIN.

89. וְרָזָא דָּא, בָּרוּךְ: דָּא רָזָא דִּנְקוּדָה עִלָּאָה, דְּאִיהוּ בָּרוּךְ, דְּכָל בִּרְכָאן נַבְעִין מִתַּמָּן. וְאִי תֵּימָא, עָלְמָא דְּאָתֵי אִקְרֵי בָּרוּךְ. לָאו הָכִי. דְּהָא נְקוּדָה עִלָּאָה אִיהוּ דְּכַר, עָלְמָא דְּאָתֵי נוּקְבָא, אִיהוּ בָּרוּךְ, וְאִיהִי בְּרָכָה, בָּרוּךְ דְּכַר, בְּרָכָה נוּקְבָא. וְע"ד בָּרוּךְ אִיהוּ נְקוּדָה עִלָּאָה. שֵׁם: דָּא עָלְמָא דְּאָתֵי, דְּאִיהוּ שֵׁם גָּדוֹל. כד"א וּמַה תַּעֲשֵׂה לְשִׁמְךָ הַגָּדוֹל. כְּבוֹד: דָּא כְּבוֹד עִלָּאָה, דְּאִיהוּ יְמִינָא וּשְׂמָאלָא, וְכֻלְּהוּ כְּלִילָן בְּהַאי תְּפִלָּה שֶׁל יַד, דְּאִיהוּ מַלְכוּתוֹ. וְנָטִיל כֹּלָּא בְּגַוֵּיהּ, וּבְהַאי אִתְכְּלִילָן בְּהַאי מַלְכוּת, עָלְמִין כֻּלְּהוּ, לְמֵיזַן לוֹן, וּלְסַפְּקָא לוֹן, בִּכְמָּה דְּאִצְטְרִיכוּ.

89. This secret is as follows: 'Blessed' is the secret of the supernal point, WHICH IS CHOCHMAH, which is blessed because all blessings flow from there. You may argue that the World to Come is called 'Blessed', WHICH IS

BINAH. This is not so, because the supernal point, CHOCHMAH, is male and the World to Come, BINAH, is female, and hence he, THE MALE, is called 'Blessed', and she, THE FEMALE, is called a blessing. Blessed is masculine and Blessing is feminine, and therefore 'Blessed' is the supernal point, NAMELY CHOCHMAH. 'Name' is the World to Come, NAMELY BINAH, which is a great name, as written, "and what will You do for Your great name" (Yehoshua 7:9). 'Glory' is the supernal glory, NAMELY DA'AT, which is right and left OF DA'AT, which are all included in the hand Tefilin, NAMELY IN MALCHUT, which is THE SECRET OF THE WORD 'His kingdom'. Malchut receives everything within her, and thus all the worlds were comprised to be nourished and fed in what they need, WHICH IS THE MEANING OF 'FOREVER AND EVER'. FOR 'EVER (HEB. *VA'ED*)' MEANS FOOD AS IN, "IN THE MORNING HE SHALL DEVOUR THE PREY (HEB. *AD*)" (BERESHEET 49:27). 'FOREVER (LIT. 'FOR THE WORLD') AND EVER' MEANS THAT MALCHUT FEEDS THE WHOLE WORLD.

90. וְדָא אִיהוּ יִחוּדָא דִּתְפִלִּין דְּרֵישָׁא וּתְפִלִּין דִּדְרוֹעָא, כְּגַוְונָא דְּרָזָא דְּיִחוּדָא דִּתְפִלִּין, הָכִי הוּא יִחוּדָא דְּכֹלָּא. וְדָא אִיהוּ בְּרִירוּ דְּמִלָּה. וְהָא סָדַּרְנָא יִחוּדָא דָּא קַמֵּי בּוּצִינָא קַדִּישָׁא, וְאָמַר לִי דְּהָא בְּד׳ גַּוְונִין אִתְסָדַּר יִחוּדָא, וְדָא בְּרִירָא דְּכֻלְּהוּ. וְהָכִי אִיהוּ וַדַּאי, וְכֻלְּהוּ רָזָא דְּיִחוּדָא, אֲבָל סִדּוּרָא דִּתְפִלִּין, דָּא הוּא יִחוּדָא עִלָּאָה כַּדְקָא יָאוּת.

90. This is ALSO the unification of the head Tefilin and the hand Tefilin, since just like the secret of the unification of the Tefilin so is the unification of everything. This clarifies the matter. And this way have I arranged this meditation before the Holy Luminary RABBI SHIMON and he told me that this meditation OF THE SH'MA READING is arranged in four manners, and that this order is the clearest of them all. The secret of unification exists in them all, NAMELY IN THE SH'MA READING AND OTHER THINGS, but the order of the Tefilin is a proper supernal meditation.

91. וּמִגּוֹ דְּאִתְכְּלִילוּ יְמִינָא וּשְׂמָאלָא בְּרָזָא דִּשְׁמָא חַד בְּאֹרַח כְּלָל, אִצְטְרִיךְ לְבָתַר לְאַפָּקָא לוֹן. בְּאֹרַח פְּרָט, אֲבָל לָאו בְּאֹרַח יִחוּדָא, דְּהָא יִחוּדָא בְּקְרָאֵי קַדְמָאֵי אִיהוּ, לְמֶהֱוֵי יְיָ׳ אֶחָד, בִּתְפִלִּין דְּרֵישָׁא. וּשְׁמוֹ אֶחָד, בִּתְפִלִּין דִּדְרוֹעָא. וַהֲוֵי כֹּלָּא חַד. כֵּיוָן דְּיִחוּדָא אִתְסָדַּר כֹּלָּא

בִּכְלָלָא, מֵרֵישָׁא דִּנְקוּדָה עִלָּאָה, אִצְטְרִיךְ לְבָתַר לְאִתְעַטְּרָא מֵרֵישָׁא דִּנְהוֹרָא קַדְמָאָה, דְּאִיהוּ רֵישָׁא דְּכֹלָּא.

91. And since the right and left OF DA'AT is included in the secret of the same name IN THE SH'MA READING, NAMELY IN THE LAST YUD HEI VAV HEI, in a general way, one should utter them after in a particular manner, NAMELY, "AND YOU SHALL LOVE (HEB. *VE'AHAVTA*)" (DEVARIM 6:5), "AND IT SHALL COME TO PASS, IF YOU HEARKEN (HEB. *VEHAYAH IM SHAMO'A*)," EACH ON ITS OWN, but not by way of unification, because unification was already performed in the earlier verses, "HEAR (HEB. *SH'MA*), AND 'BLESSED BE...', so that "Hashem shall be one" in the head Tefilin, and "His name SHALL BE One" in the hand Tefilin, WHICH IS THE UNIFICATION OF 'BLESSED BE...' and everything became one. Once the unification is arranged in its entirety from the top of the supernal point, one should then adorn it from the top of the primordial light, which is the top of everything, NAMELY KETER.

92. גָּלִיף וְאַתְקִין מֹשֶׁה, כ״ה אַתְוָון בְּרָזָא דִּפְסוּקָא דְּיִחוּדָא, דִּכְתִּיב שְׁמַע יִשְׂרָאֵל יְיָ׳ אֱלֹהֵינוּ יְיָ׳ אֶחָד. וְאִינּוּן כ״ה אַתְוָון גְּלִיפִין, מְחַקְּקִין בְּרָזָא דִּלְעֵילָּא. יַעֲקֹב בָּעָא לְאַתְקְנָא לְתַתָּא, בְּרָזָא דְּיִחוּדָא, וְאַתְקִין בְּכ״ד אַתְוָון, וְאִינּוּן בשכמל״ו. וְלָא אַשְׁלִים לְכ״ה אַתְוָון, בְּגִין דְּעַד לָא אִתְתְּקַן מַשְׁכְּנָא. כֵּיוָן דְּאִתְתְּקַן מַשְׁכְּנָא, וְאִשְׁתְּלִים מִלָּה דַּהֲוָה נָפִיק מִנֵּיהּ, כַּד אִשְׁתְּלִים, לָא מַלִּיל אֶלָּא בְּכ״ה אַתְוָון, לְאַחֲזָאָה דְּהָא אִשְׁתְּלִים דָּא, כְּגַוְונָא דִּלְעֵילָּא, דִּכְתִּיב וַיְדַבֵּר יְיָ׳ אֵלָיו מֵאֹהֶל מוֹעֵד לֵאמֹר, הָא כ״ה אַתְוָון.

92. Moses engraved and composed 25 letters by means of the unification of the verse that says, "Hear, O Yisrael, Hashem our Elohim; Hashem is one" (Devarim 6:4). There are 25 engraved letters, engraved by the supernal secret, NAMELY THE SECRET OF ZEIR ANPIN, SINCE 25 INDICATES THE 22 LETTERS OF THE TORAH, AND THE TORAH, THE PROPHETS AND THE WRITINGS, WHICH ARE THE THREE COLUMNS, AS SHALL BE WRITTEN. Jacob wanted to compose below, IN MALCHUT, by the secret of unification, and composed it with 24 letters, which are 'Blessed be the name of the glory of His kingdom forever and ever', WHICH JACOB COMPOSED, AND WHICH

IS SPELLED WITH 24 LETTERS, but he did not complete it to 25 letters because DURING HIS TIME the tabernacle, WHICH CORRESPONDS TO MALCHUT, was not yet built. Once the tabernacle was built and that from which the tabernacle was drawn was completed, after its completion He spoke with him only with 25 letters to indicate that this, MALCHUT, was completed like the supernal, LIKE ZEIR ANPIN THAT HAS 25 LETTERS, as written, "and spoke to him out of the Tent of Meeting, saying" (Vayikra 1:1). Here THERE ARE 25 letters.

93. וְע"ד כ"ה זִינִין, לְאַשְׁלְמָא תִּקּוּנָא דְּמַקְדְּשָׁא, וְכָל הָנֵי אַתְוָון אוֹקִימְנָא בְּאִינּוּן אַתְוָון גְּלִיפִין דְּאוֹלִיפְנָא מִמַּר. וּבְגִין דְּמַשְׁכְּנָא אִשְׁתְּלִים בְּרָזִין אִלֵּין, אִקְרֵי כ"ה, בְּיִחוּדָא דִּשְׁלִימוּ דְּמַשְׁכְּנָא. וְע"ד וַחֲסִידֶיךָ יְבָרְכוּכָה כְּתִיב, רָזָא דִּשְׁלִימוּ דְּכָל מַשְׁכְּנָא, וְתִקּוּנָא דִּילֵיהּ.

93. Hence 25 different things are used to complete the building of the tabernacle, THE THIRTEEN KINDS OF GOLD, SILVER, ETC., AND THE TWELVE STONES IN THE BREASTPLATE. We learned all these letters when studying the engraved letters we learned from our master. Since the tabernacle was completed by these secrets OF 25 LETTERS, the tabernacle, NAMELY MALCHUT, is therefore called BY THE NAME '*kah*' (= 25), WHICH INDICATES the unification of completion in the tabernacle, WHICH IS MALCHUT. Hence it is written, "and Your pious ones shall bless You (Heb. *yevarchuchah*)" (Tehilim 145:10), WHICH IS SPELLED AS 'shall bless (Heb. *yevarchu kah)*', which is the secret of the completion of the tabernacle and the building of it.

94. כ"ה: לָקֳבֵל כ"ב אַתְוָון, וְתוֹרָה וּנְבִיאִים וּכְתוּבִים, דְּאִינּוּן כְּלָלָא חֲדָא, רָזָא חֲדָא. בְּשַׁעֲתָא דְּיִשְׂרָאֵל קָא מְיַחֲדֵי יִחוּדָא בְּהַאי קְרָא, בְּרָזָא דְּכ"ה אַתְוָון, דְּאִינּוּן שְׁמַע יִשְׂרָאֵל יְיָ' אֱלֹהֵינוּ יְיָ' אֶחָד, וּבשכמל"ו, דְּאִינּוּן כ"ד אַתְוָון, וִיכַוֵּין כָּל חַד בְּהוּ, כֻּלְּהוּ אַתְוָון מִתְחַבְּרָן כַּחֲדָא, וְסַלְּקִין לְחִבּוּרָא חַד, תֵּשַׁע וְאַרְבָּעִים תַּרְעִין, בְּרָזָא דְּיוֹבְלָא. וּכְדֵין אִצְטְרִיךְ לְסַלְּקָא וָעֶד, לָא יַתִּיר. וּכְדֵין אִתְפְּתָחוּ תַּרְעִין, וְחָשִׁיב קוּדְשָׁא בְּרִיךְ הוּא לְהַהוּא ב"נ, כְּאִילּוּ קִיֵּים אוֹרַיְיתָא כֻּלָּהּ, דְּאִיהִי אַתְיָא בְּמ"ט פָּנִים בְּכֹלָּא.

94. 25 stands for the 22 letters and the Torah, the Prophets and the Writings, AS 3 PLUS 22 EQUAL 25. They are one whole, one mystery. When Yisrael perform this unification according to the secret of the 25 letters in this verse, which are, "Hear, O Yisrael, Hashem our Elohim; Hashem is one," and THE UNIFICATION OF 'Blessed be the name of the glory of His kingdom forever and ever', which has 24 letters, and when one directs his attention to each of them, all letters join together and amount to a single connection, which are 49 words that correspond to the 49 gates in the secret of Jubilee, WHICH IS BINAH. One then should continue THE UNIFICATION TO THE WORD 'EVER' but no more, SINCE IN THE WORD 'EVER' THE RECKONING REACHES 49. Then the 49 gates OF BINAH open and the Holy One, blessed be He, considers that man as if he maintained the whole Torah that comes all in 49 manners.

95. וְע"ד אִצְטְרִיךְ לְכַוְּונָא רְעוּתָא בְּכ"ה וּבְאַרְבָּע וְעֶשְׂרִין, לְסַלְּקָא לוֹן בִּרְעוּתָא דְּלִבָּא, בְּתֵשַׁע וְאַרְבְּעִין תַּרְעִין דְּקַאמְרָן, כֵּיוָן דְּאִתְכַּוַּון בְּהַאי, יִתְכַּוָּון בְּהַהוּא יִחוּדָא דְּאָמַר מַר, שְׁמַע יִשְׂרָאֵל וְגו' בָּרוּךְ שֵׁם כְּבוֹד מַלְכוּתוֹ לְעוֹלָם וָעֶד, כְּלָלָא דְּכָל אוֹרַיְיתָא כֹּלָּא. זַכָּאָה חוּלָקֵיהּ מַאן דְּיִתְכַּוֵּין בְּהוּ, וַדַּאי כְּלָלָא אִיהוּ דְּכָל אוֹרַיְיתָא דְּעֵילָּא וְתַתָּא. וְדָא אִיהוּ רָזָא דְּאָדָם, שְׁלִימוּ דִּדְכַר וְנוּקְבָּא, וְרָזָא דְּכָל מְהֵימְנוּתָא.

עד כאן רעיא מהימנא

95. One should therefore direct one's will to the 25 LETTERS OF THE SH'MA and the 24 OF 'BLESSED BE...', and elevate them with the desire of the heart by the 49 gates OF BINAH that we mentioned. After meditating on that, one should meditate on the unification our master spoke of, that, "Hear, O Yisrael...," and 'Blessed be the name of the glory of His kingdom forever and ever', are the entirety of the whole Torah. Happy is the lot of he who meditates on them. Surely it is the entirety of the whole Torah that is above, WHICH IS ZEIR ANPIN, and below, WHICH IS MALCHUT. This is the secret of Adam, which is the perfection of male and female, NAMELY THE PERFECTION OF ZEIR ANPIN AND MALCHUT. THIS UNIFICATION IS the secret of the whole Faith.

End of Ra'aya Meheimna (the Faithful Shepherd)

96. רַבִּי אַבָּא שָׁלַח לֵיהּ לְרַ׳ שִׁמְעוֹן וְאָמַר לֵיהּ, הַאי דְּאוֹקְמֵיהּ מַר בַּתְּפִלִּין דְּמָארֵי עָלְמָא, ד׳ פָּרְשִׁיָּין אִינּוּן קוּדְשָׁא דְּקוּדְשִׁין, שַׁפִּיר. מִשְׁכָא דְּעַל תְּפִילִּין, וְאִינּוּן רְצוּעִין אִקְרוּ קְדוּשָׁה אַסְמַכְתָּא מְנָלָן. שָׁלַח לֵיהּ וַיַּעַשׂ יְיָ׳ אֱלֹהִים לְאָדָם וּלְאִשְׁתּוֹ וְגוֹ׳ דַּיְיקָא, וְהָכִי אוֹקְמֵיהּ רַב הַמְנוּנָא סָבָא. וְאִלֵּין אִינּוּן דְּרֵישָׁא, וּדְרוֹעָא יָדְכָה בְּהֵ״א, וְהָא אוֹקְמוּהָ.

96. Rabbi Aba sent to Rabbi Shimon, saying to him: That which you, our master, explained about the Tefilin of the Master of the universe that the four passages are the holy of holies, NAMELY CHOCHMAH AND BINAH, AND TIFERET AND MALCHUT OF DA'AT, is good. Whence do we deduce the leather on the Tefilin and the straps that are considered holiness? He sent to him: "For the man also and for his wife did Hashem Elohim make coats of skin..." (Beresheet 3:21). LEATHER is precise, NAMELY MALCHUT THAT IS CALLED SKIN. This is the way Rav Hamnuna Saba explained it. These belong to the head, AS THE FOUR PASSAGES ARE THE FOUR MOCHIN OF ZEIR ANPIN AND THE LEATHER IS MALCHUT OF ZEIR ANPIN. In the hand TEFILIN "upon your hand (Heb. *yadechah*)" (Shemot 13:9) is spelled with Hei TO INDICATE THAT THE FOUR PORTIONS ARE THE MOCHIN OF HEI, WHICH IS MALCHUT. This has already been explained.

97. אר״ש, אִית מַאן דְּמַתְנֵי בְּהַאי גַּוְונָא, וְהָיָה דְּרוֹעָא שְׂמָאלָא דְּקוּדְשָׁא בְּרִיךְ הוּא, וְאִקְרֵי גְּבוּרָה אִי הָכִי לָא אִשְׁתַּאֲרָן בְּרֵישָׁא אֶלָּא תְּלַת. וְאִינּוּן אַרְבַּע. אֲבָל תְּרֵין רְתִיכִין קַדִּישִׁין אִינּוּן, דָּא אִתְקְשַׁר בְּלִבָּא. וְדָא אִתְקְשַׁר בְּמוֹחָא. וְלִבָּא וּמוֹחָא, אִתְקְשַׁר דָּא בְּדָא. וְזִווּגָא חַד לְהוּ, וְשַׁפִּיר קָאַמְרוּ חַבְרַיָּיא. וְהָיָה לְאוֹת עַל יָדְכָה, כְּמָה דְּאִתְּמַר, וְלָא אִקְרֵי אֶלָּא אוֹת.

97. Rabbi Shimon said, Some teach it this way: "And it shall come to pass, if you hearken," is the left arm of the Holy One, blessed be He, and is considered the Sfirah of Gvurah. In that case only three PASSAGES are left in the head: "SANCTIFY TO ME ALL THE FIRSTBORN," "AND IT SHALL COME TO PASS, IF YOU HEARKEN," AND "HEAR O YISRAEL" (DEVARIM 6:4), WHICH ARE CHOCHMAH, BINAH, AND THE RIGHT OF DA'AT. THE

FOURTH LOBE OF THE BRAIN, WHICH IS THE LEFT SIDE OF DA'AT, IS MISSING. YOU CLAIM THAT, "AND IT SHALL COME TO PASS..." IS IN THE SFIRAH OF GVURAH, WHICH IS IN THE BODY, yet there are four LOBES OF THE BRAIN IN THE HEAD. But there are two holy Chariots OF CHOCHMAH, BINAH, TIFERET AND MALCHUT; the one OF THE HAND TEFILIN is connected to the heart, WHICH IS MALCHUT, and the other OF THE HEAD TEFILIN is connected to the brain, WHICH IS ZEIR ANPIN. THUS THE FOURTH PASSAGE OF THE HEAD TEFILIN IS ALSO IN THE BRAIN, NAMELY THE LEFT SIDE OF DA'AT, AND NOT IN THE BODY. The heart and the brain, WHICH ARE ZEIR ANPIN AND MALCHUT, are connected to each other into one union. The friends have spoken well that "And it shall be for a sign to you upon your hand" REFERS TO MALCHUT, as we learned that MALCHUT is only called a sign, SINCE THE HAND TEFILIN ARE THE MOCHIN OF MALCHUT.

98. אָמַר ר"ש, בְּשַׁעֲתָא דְּב"נ אַקְדִּים בְּפַלְגּוּת לֵילְיָא, וְקָם וְאִשְׁתָּדַּל בְּאוֹרַיְיתָא, עַד דְּנָהִיר צַפְרָא. בְּצַפְרָא אֲנָח תְּפִילִּין בְּרֵישֵׁיהּ, וּתְפִילִּין בִּרְשִׁימָא קַדִּישָׁא בִּדְרוֹעֵיהּ, וְאִתְעַטָּף בְּעִטּוּפָא דְּמִצְוָה, וְאָתֵי לְנָפְקָא מִתַּרְעָא דְּבֵיתֵיהּ, אִעֲרַע בִּמְזוּזָה, רְשִׁימָא דִּשְׁמָא קַדִּישָׁא בְּתַרְעָא דְּבֵיתֵיהּ, אַרְבַּע מַלְאָכִין קַדִּישִׁין מִזְדַּוְּוגִין עִמֵּיהּ וְנָפְקִין עִמֵּיהּ מִתַּרְעָא דְּבֵיתֵיהּ, וְאוֹזְפֵי לֵיהּ לְבֵי כְּנִישְׁתָּא, וּמַכְרְזֵי קַמֵּיהּ, הָבוּ יְקָרָא לְדִיוּקְנָא דְּמַלְכָּא קַדִּישָׁא, הָבוּ יְקָרָא לִבְרֵיהּ דְּמַלְכָּא, לְפַרְצוּפָא יְקָרָא דְּמַלְכָּא, רוּחָא קַדִּישָׁא שַׁרְיָא עָלֵיהּ, אַכְרִיז וְאָמַר יִשְׂרָאֵל אֲשֶׁר בְּךָ אֶתְפָּאַר.

98. Rabbi Shimon said, When man prods himself to rise at midnight and studies the Torah until day breaks, and in the morning puts on Tefilin on the head and Tefilin on the holy sign, NAMELY TEFILIN OF MALCHUT, on the arm, and when he wraps himself with a Tzitzit and is about to go out the entrance to his house, he meets the Mezuzah, which is the imprint of the Holy Name, WHICH IS MALCHUT, at the gate to his house; THEN four holy angels join him and go out with him from the door of his house and escort him to the synagogue. They declare before him, give honor to the image of the Holy King, give honor to the son of the King, to the countenance of the King. The Holy Spirit dwells on him, and declares, saying, "Yisrael, in whom I will be glorified" (Yeshayah 49:3).

99. כְּדֵין הַהוּא רוּחָא קַדִּישָׁא סַלְקָא לְעֵילָּא, וְאַסְהִיד עָלֵיהּ קָמֵי מַלְכָּא קַדִּישָׁא, כְּדֵין פָּקִיד מַלְכָּא עִלָּאָה, לְמִכְתַּב קַמֵּיהּ כָּל אִינּוּן בְּנֵי הֵיכָלֵיהּ, כָּל אִינּוּן דְּאִשְׁתְּמוֹדְעָן קַמֵּיהּ, הה"ד וַיִּכָּתֵב סֵפֶר זִכָּרוֹן לְפָנָיו לְיִרְאֵי יְיָ׳ וּלְחוֹשְׁבֵי שְׁמוֹ. מַאי וּלְחוֹשְׁבֵי שְׁמוֹ. כד"א וְחוֹשְׁבֵי מַחֲשָׁבוֹת, אִינּוּן דְּעַבְדִּין לִשְׁמֵיהּ, אוּמָנוּתָא בְּכֹלָּא, אוּמָנוּתָא דִּתְפִילִּין, בְּבָתֵּיהוֹן בִּרְצוּעֵיהוֹן וּכְתִיבַתְהוֹן. אוּמָנוּתָא דְּצִיצִית, בְּחוּטֵיהוֹן בְּחוּטָא דִּתְכֶלְתָּא. אוּמָנוּתָא דִּמְזוּזָה. וְאִלֵּין אִינּוּן חוֹשְׁבֵי שְׁמוֹ. וּכְתִיב וְחוֹשְׁבֵי מַחֲשָׁבוֹת.

99. That Holy Spirit then rises up and testifies before the Holy King. The supernal King then commands to write before Him all His household members, all those known before Him. This is the meaning of, "and a book of remembrance was written before Him for those who feared Hashem, and took heed of His name" (Malachi 3:16). Who are those who "took heed (Heb. *choshvei*) of His name"? They are as those in, "and those who devise (Heb. *choshvei*) artistic work" (Shemot 35:35). HERE TOO, those who do for His name works of art in any way – the art of the Tefilin, their compartment and straps and writing them, the art of the Tzitzit (Eng. 'the fringes'), their threads, the blue thread, and the art of the Mezuzah. These are those who "took heed of His name," as in "devise artistic work."

100. וְלֹא עוֹד אֶלָּא דְּקוּדְשָׁא בְּרִיךְ הוּא מִשְׁתַּבַּח בֵּיהּ, וּמַכְרִיז עָלֵיהּ בְּכֻלְּהוּ עָלְמִין, חָמוּ מַה בְּרָיָה עַבְדֵּית בְּעוֹלָמִי. וּמַאן דְּיֵיעוּל קַמֵּיהּ לְבֵי כְּנִישְׁתָּא, כַּד נָפִיק מִתַּרְעֵיהּ, וְלָא תְּפִילִּין בְּרֵישֵׁיהּ וְצִיצִית בִּלְבוּשֵׁיהּ, וְאוֹמֵר אֶשְׁתַּחֲוֶה אֶל הֵיכַל קָדְשְׁךָ בְּיִרְאָתֶךָ. קוּדְשָׁא בְּרִיךְ הוּא אָמַר, אָן הוּא מוֹרָאִי, הָא סָהִיד סַהֲדוּתָא דְּשִׁקְרָא.

100. Moreover, the Holy One, blessed be He, praises Himself with him and declares about him throughout the worlds, 'see what My son has achieved in My world'. Whoever enters before Him into the synagogue after leaving his door without Tefilin on his head and Tzitzit on his garment, yet says, "and in the fear of You I will worship towards Your Temple" (Tehilim 5:8), the Holy One, blessed be He, says, 'Where is the fear of Me? He bears false testimony'.

101. א״ר יוֹסִי, זַכָּאָה חוּלָקֵיהּ דְּמֹשֶׁה, דְּהָכָא אָמַר אֱלֹהֵינוּ. דְּא״ר שִׁמְעוֹן, מֹשֶׁה בְּדַרְגָּא עִלָּאָה יַתִּיר אִתְאֲחָד, עַל שְׁאַר נְבִיאֵי מְהֵימְנֵי. וְא״ר שִׁמְעוֹן, אִלְמָלֵא הֲווּ יַדְעֵי בְּנֵי נָשָׁא מִלִּין דְּאוֹרַיְיתָא, לִינְדְּעוּן דְּהָא לֵית שׁוּם מִלָּה בְּאוֹרַיְיתָא, אוֹ אָת בְּאוֹרַיְיתָא, דְּלָא אִית בָּהּ רָזִין עִלָּאִין וְיַקִּירִין.

101. Happy is the lot of Moses, who said here, IN "SH'MA YISRAEL," Our Elohim. For Rabbi Shimon said, Moses was attached to a higher grade than the rest of the faithful prophets. Rabbi Shimon also said, If men knew the words of the Torah, they would know that there is not a word or a letter in the Torah that does not contain supernal precious secrets.

15. Our Elohim, your Elohim

A Synopsis

Rabbi Shimon talks about the voice of Moses, that is the voice to which he is attached. He explains the difference between the curses that Moses uttered in Leviticus and those in Deuteronomy. We hear that God gave the commandments to Yisrael so that they would be saved from the prosecutors.

102. ת״ח, כְּתִיב, מֹשֶׁה יְדַבֵּר וְהָאֱלֹהִים יַעֲנֶנּוּ בְקוֹל. וְתָנֵינָן, מַאי בְּקוֹל. בְּקוֹלוֹ שֶׁל מֹשֶׁה. וְשַׁפִּיר הוּא, בְּקוֹלוֹ שֶׁל מֹשֶׁה דַּיְיקָא, בְּהַהוּא קוֹל דְּאִיהוּ אָחִיד בֵּיהּ, עַל כָּל שְׁאַר נְבִיאִין. וּבְגִין דְּאִיהוּ אִתְאֲחִיד עַל כֻּלְּהוּ, בְּהַהוּא קוֹל, דַּרְגָּא עִלָּאָה, הֲוָה אָמַר לְהוּ לְיִשְׂרָאֵל, יְיָ׳ אֱלֹהֶיךָ, אִיהוּ דַּרְגָּא דְּאִקְרֵי שְׁכִינְתָּא, דְּשַׁרְיָיא בְּגַוַּויְיהוּ. זַכָּאָה חוּלָקֵיהּ.

102. Come and see, it is written, "Moses speaks, and Elohim answers him by a voice" (Shemot 19:19). We learned that "by a voice" refers to the voice of Moses. This is good, and the voice of Moses is precise, namely, the voice to which he is attached, WHICH IS ZEIR ANPIN, BY WHICH HE SURPASSES above all the other prophets, WHO ARE ATTACHED ONLY TO MALCHUT AND NOT TO ZEIR ANPIN. Since he is attached TO THAT VOICE, WHICH IS ZEIR ANPIN more than all the others, by that voice, which is the supernal grade, he said to Yisrael, 'Hashem your Elohim', which is a grade called the Shechinah that dwells within YISRAEL, WHICH IS BELOW THE GRADE OF ZEIR ANPIN, TO WHICH MOSES IS ATTACHED. Happy is his lot.

103. וְאר״ש, תָּנֵינָן, קְלָלוֹת שבת״כ, מֹשֶׁה מִפִּי הַגְּבוּרָה אֲמָרָן. וְשֶׁבְּמִשְׁנֵה תּוֹרָה, מֹשֶׁה מִפִּי עַצְמוֹ אֲמָרָן. מַאי מִפִּי עַצְמוֹ. וְכִי ס״ד דַּאֲפִילּוּ אָת זְעֵירָא בְּאוֹרַיְיתָא, מֹשֶׁה אָמַר לֵיהּ מִגַּרְמֵיהּ.

103. Rabbi Shimon also said, We learned that Moses uttered the curses in Leviticus, IN THE BOOK OF VAYIKRA, from the mouth of Gvurah, WHICH IS BINAH THAT IS CALLED SUPERNAL GVURAH. Those IN DEUTERONOMY he uttered with his own mouth. Could you possibly imagine that Moses would speak even a small letter in the Torah from himself?

104. אֶלָּא שַׁפִּיר הוּא, וְהָא אִתְעַרְנָא, מֵעַצְמוֹ לָא תָּנֵינָן, אֶלָּא מִפִּי עַצְמוֹ. וּמַאי אִיהוּ. הַהוּא קוֹל דְּאִיהוּ אָחִיד בֵּיהּ. וְע״ד, הַלָּלוּ מִפִּי הַגְּבוּרָה. וְהַלָּלוּ מִפִּי עַצְמוֹ. מִפִּי הַהוּא דַּרְגָּא דְּאִתְקְשַׁר בֵּיהּ עַל שְׁאַר נְבִיאֵי מְהֵימְנֵי. וְעַל דָּא, בְּכָל אֲתַר אֱלֹהֶיךָ, וְהָכָא אֱלֹהֵינוּ.

104. AND HE ANSWERS, This is good, and we remarked that we did not learn it as from himself but as from his own mouth. What does this mean? It is that voice to which Moses was attached, NAMELY ZEIR ANPIN. Hence these IN LEVITICUS were from the mouth of Gvurah, WHICH IS BINAH THAT IS CALLED SUPERNAL GVURAH, while those IN DEUTERONOMY were from his own mouth, namely from the mouth of the grade to which Moses was attached more than all the faithful prophets, WHICH IS THE GRADE OF ZEIR ANPIN. Hence it is always SAID 'your Elohim', SINCE IT ALLUDES TO MALCHUT THAT IS BELOW ZEIR ANPIN; but here, IN "SH'MA YISRAEL" IT IS SAID "our Elohim," SINCE IT ALLUDES TO BINAH THAT IS ABOVE ZEIR ANPIN, TO WHICH MOSES IS ATTACHED.

105. ת״ח, כַּמָּה אִית לְהוּ לִבְנֵי נָשָׁא לְאִסְתַּמְּרָא אוֹרְחַיְיהוּ, בְּגִין דְּיִשְׁתַּדְּלוּן בְּפֻלְחָנָא דְּמָארֵיהוֹן, וְיִזְכּוּן לְחַיֵּי עָלְמִין. תְּחוֹת כּוּרְסְיָיא דְּמַלְכָּא קַדִּישָׁא, אִית מָדוֹרִין עִלָּאִין. וּבְהַהוּא אֲתַר דְּכוּרְסְיָיא, מְזוּזָה אִתְקְשַׁר, לְאִשְׁתְּזָבָא מִכַּמָּה מָארֵי דִּינִין, דִּזְמִינִין לְאַתְּעָרָא בְּהוּ בִּבְנֵי נָשָׁא, בְּהַהוּא עָלְמָא. כְּגַוְונָא דָּא עָבִיד קוּדְשָׁא בְּרִיךְ הוּא לְיִשְׂרָאֵל, וְיָהַב לְהוּ פִּקּוּדֵי אוֹרַיְיתָא, בְּגִין דְּיִשְׁתַּדְּלוּן בָּהּ וְיִשְׁתֵּזְבוּן בְּהַאי עָלְמָא, מִכַּמָּה מָארֵי דִּינִין, מִכַּמָּה מְקַטְרְגֵי, דְּאִזְדַּמְּנוּן בְּהוּ בִּבְנֵי נָשָׁא בְּכָל יוֹמָא.

105. Come and see how much people should guard their ways so that they will be occupied with the worship of their Master and merit everlasting life. Underneath the throne of the Holy King, WHICH IS MALCHUT, there are supernal compartments. And to that place of the throne, WHICH IS MALCHUT, the Mezuzah is connected to save man from many Judgments, the purpose of which is to awaken people through them. Similarly the Holy One, blessed be He, did to Yisrael by giving them the commandments of the Torah, so they will endeavor in them and be saved in this world from many prosecutors and those that bring charges who meet people daily.

16. Waste water before the door

A Synopsis

Rabbi Chiya tells us that people must not spill waste water between the doorposts because a demon lies there and sees everything that is done in the house, and the waste water will give him permission to cause harm. We are told about the role of the Mezuzah, and Rabbi Chiya says that wherever the Holy Name abides people are safe from the accusations of the evil ones.

106. ר׳ חִיָּיא אָמַר, הַאי מַאן דְּבָעֵי דְּיִסְתָּמַר אוֹרְחוֹי, לָא יֶעְבַּר עַל מַיָּיא דְּאוֹשְׁדִין קַמֵּי פִּתְחָא. בְּגִין דְּתַמָּן שָׁרֵי חַד שֵׁידָא, וְהוּא בֵּין תְּרֵין דָּשִׁין דְּפִתְחָא, וְאַנְפּוֹי לָקֳבְלֵיהּ דְּפִתְחָא, וְאִסְתָּכֵי כָּל מַה דְּעַבְדִין בְּבֵיתָא, וְלָא לִבְעֵי לֵיהּ לֶאֱנוֹשׁ דְּיִשְׁדֵּי מַיָּיא בֵּין תְּרֵי תַּרְעֵי. ר׳ יִצְחָק אָמַר, מַיִין צְלִילָן לֵית לָן בָּהּ. וְהוּא דְּלָא יוֹשִׁיט לוֹן אֹרַח קְלָנָא. מַאי טַעֲמָא. בְּגִין דְּאִית לֵיהּ רְשׁוּ לְנַזְקָא. וְלָא עוֹד אֶלָּא דְּיֶהְדַּר רֵישֵׁיהּ לָקֳבְלֵי בֵּיתָא, וּבְכָל מַה דְּאִסְתְּכַל אִתְלַטְיָיא.

106. Rabbi Chiya said, Whoever wishes to observe his ways must not pass waste water before the door, because a certain demon lies there between the two doorposts facing the door. It sees whatever is done in the house. HENCE one must not spill water between the two doorposts. Rabbi Yitzchak said, Clean water is not forbidden, but it must not be spilled with contempt. The reason is that it, THE DEMON, has permission to cause harm. Moreover, it turns its head towards the house and whatever it beholds becomes cursed.

107. תְּלַת מְאָה וְשִׁתִּין וְחָמֵשׁ, כְּחוּשְׁבַּן יְמֵי שַׁתָּא, אִית לֵיהּ שַׁמָּשִׁין, דְּהוּא שַׁלִּיט עֲלַיְיהוּ, וְכֻלְּהוּ נָפְקִין עִם ב״נ, כַּד נָפִיק מִתַּרְעָא דְּבֵיתֵיהּ. א״ר אֶלְעָזָר, כָּל דָּא בָּעֵי קוּדְשָׁא בְּרִיךְ הוּא לְנַטְרָא לוֹן לְיִשְׂרָאֵל, וְאַתְקִין שְׁמֵיהּ קַדִּישָׁא לְעֵילָּא, דְּאִיהוּ אוֹרַיְיתָא, וְאוֹרַיְיתָא כֹּלָּא חַד שְׁמָא קַדִּישָׁא אִיהוּ, וּמַאן דְּאִשְׁתְּדַל בְּאוֹרַיְיתָא, אִשְׁתַּדַּל בִּשְׁמֵיהּ.

107. It, THE DEMON, has 365 officers, as the number of the days in the year, and it rules over them. They all go out with a man when he goes out the door of his house. Rabbi Elazar said, All this transpires because the Holy

One, blessed be He, wished to guard Yisrael and composed His Holy Name above, which is the Torah. The whole Torah is one Holy Name, and whoever is occupied with the Torah is occupied with His Name.

108. ת״ח, בָּעֵי ב״נ בְּפִתְחָא דְּבֵיתָא לְרַשְׁמָא שְׁמָא קַדִּישָׁא, דְּאִיהוּ מְהֵימְנוּתָא דְּכֹלָּא. דְּהָא בְּכָל אֲתָר דִּשְׁמָא קַדִּישָׁא אִשְׁתְּכַח זִינִין בִּישִׁין לָא מִשְׁתַּכְּחֵי תַּמָּן, וְלָא יַכְלִין לְקַטְרְגָא לֵיהּ לְב״נ, כְּמָה דִּכְתִּיב לֹא תְאוּנֶּה אֵלֶיךָ רָעָה וְגוֹ׳.

108. Come and see, man should imprint the Holy Name, which is the universal Faith, on the door of his house, for wherever the Holy Name abides there are no evil species and they cannot bring charges against him, as written, "No evil shall befall you…" (Tehilim 91:10).

109. אֲתָר דְּפִתְחָא דְּבֵיתָא שַׁרְיָא כְּגַוְונָא דִּלְעֵילָּא אֲתָר דְּפִתְחָא דְּבֵיתָא עִלָּאָה שַׁרְיָא, מְזוּזָא אִקְרֵי. דְּהוּא תִּקּוּנָא דְּבֵיתָא, וּפִתְחָא דְּבֵיתָא. מֵהַהִיא מְזוּזָה עַרְקִין מָארֵי נִימוּסִין, מָארֵי דְּדִינִין קַמֵּיהּ לָא מִשְׁתַּכְּחִין. וְקָבֵל דָּא לְתַתָּא, כַּד ב״נ אַתְקִין מְזוּזָה לְפִתְחָא דְּבֵיתָא, וְהַאי שְׁמָא קַדִּישָׁא רָשִׁים בְּאַתווֹי, הַאי ב״נ אִתְעֲטָּר בְּעִטְרוֹי דְּמָארֵיהּ, וְלָא קְרָבִין לְפִתְחָא דְּבֵיתֵיהּ זִינִין בִּישִׁין, וְלָא מִשְׁתַּכְּחֵי תַּמָּן.

109. The place where the door of the house lies is a reflection of the higher. The place where the supernal door of the house lies is called a Mezuzah, which brings the house and the door of the house to completion. The litigants flee that Mezuzah, and the prosecutors cannot dwell before it. Correspondingly below, when a man fixes a Mezuzah at the door of his house, and this Holy Name SHADAI is imprinted with its letters, that man is adorned with his Master's crowns and the evil species do not come near the door of his house or rest there.

110. ר׳ אַבָּא הֲוָה אָתֵי מִלְּמֵחֱמֵי לְר״ש, פָּגַע בֵּיהּ ר׳ יִצְחָק, אָמַר לֵיהּ מֵאָן אָתֵי, מָארֵיהּ דִּנְהוֹרָא, גְּבָר דְּאִתְדַּבָּק בְּנוּרָא דְּאַכְלָא כָּל יוֹמָא, הָא נְהוֹרָא עִמֵּיהּ שָׁרֵי. אָמַר לֵיהּ, תָּנֵינָן דְּחִיּוּבָא עָלֵיהּ דְּב״נ, לְקַבְּלָא

אַפֵּי שְׁכִינְתָּא, בְּכָל רֵישׁ יַרְחֵי וְשַׁבְּתֵי. וּמַאן אִיהוּ. רַבֵּיהּ. כ״ש בּוּצִינָא עִלָּאָה קַדִּישָׁא, דְּכָל בְּנֵי עָלְמָא בָּעָאן לְקַבְּלָא אַנְפּוֹי. א״ר יִצְחָק, אַהֲדַרְנָא עִמָּךְ, וְאַקְבֵּל אַנְפֵּי שְׁכִינְתָּא, וְאַטְעַם מֵאִינּוּן מִלִּין עִלָּאִין, דְּאַטְעֲמַת קַמֵּיהּ.

110. Rabbi Aba came from seeing Rabbi Shimon when Rabbi Yitzchak met him. He said to him, Whence do you come, man of light? A man who cleaves daily to a consuming fire, light dwells with him, AND HE NEED NOT SEEK ANYONE. He said to him, We learned that man is obligated to welcome the Shechinah every first day of the month and every Shabbat. What is that? It is one's Rabbi, and all the more so the holy supernal Luminary, RABBI SHIMON, whom the whole world should welcome. Rabbi Yitzchak said, Let me return with you TO RABBI SHIMON and welcome the Shechinah and taste from those lofty matters you tasted before him.

17. "O You who dwell in the heavens"

A Synopsis

Rabbi Shimon explains the inner meaning of the 123rd psalm, telling us that as the author is not mentioned it is the holy spirit; the holy spirit is speaking about Yisrael in exile. Rabbi Shimon and Rabbi Yitzchak and Rabbi Aba discuss the Mezuzah again, and then the marks by which Yisrael are recognized as the children of God.

111. פָּתַח ר׳ אַבָּא וְאָמַר, שִׁיר הַמַּעֲלוֹת אֵלֶיךָ נָשָׂאתִי אֶת עֵינַי הַיּוֹשְׁבִי בַּשָּׁמַיִם. שִׁיר דָּא לָא כְּתִיב מַאן אֲמָרוֹ. אֶלָּא בְּכָל אֲתָר דְּאִיהוּ סָתִים, רוּחַ הַקֹּדֶשׁ אֲמָרוֹ עָלַיְיהוּ דְּיִשְׂרָאֵל בְּגָלוּתָא. הַיּוֹשְׁבִי בַּשָּׁמַיִם, הַיּוֹשֵׁב מִבָּעֵי לֵיהּ, מַאי הַיּוֹשְׁבִי.

111. Rabbi Aba opened with, "A song of ascent. To You I lift up my eyes, O You who dwell in the heavens" (Tehilim 123:1). It is not written who recited this song. But wherever the place is undisclosed, AND THE AUTHOR IS NOT MENTIONED, it is the Holy Spirit, WHICH IS MALCHUT, that said it about Yisrael in exile. "You who dwell (Heb. *hayoshvi*)" should have used the more common form 'hayoshev'. Why does it use "hayoshvi"?

112. אֶלָּא אוֹקִימְנָא, מַאן דְּבָעֵי לְצַלָּאָה צְלוֹתֵיהּ קַמֵּי מַלְכָּא קַדִּישָׁא, בָּעֵי לְמִבְעֵי מֵעֲמִיקְתָא דְּכֹלָּא, לְאַרְקָא בִּרְכָאן לְתַתָּא, כְּמָה דִּכְתִּיב שִׁיר הַמַּעֲלוֹת מִמַּעֲמַקִּים קְרָאתִיךָ יְיָ׳. וְהַאי יוֹ״ד יַתִּיר, עֲמִיקְתָא דְּכֹלָּא הִיא, וּבְהַאי בָּעֵי לְמִבְעֵי בָּעוּתֵיהּ, לְאַרְקָא בִּרְכָאן לְהַהוּא אֲתָר דְּאִקְרֵי שָׁמַיִם, לְאַתְזְנָא מִנֵּיהּ כֹּלָּא, וְע״ד הַיּוֹשְׁבִי בַּשָּׁמַיִם, בַּשָּׁמַיִם מַמָּשׁ, דְּכַד אִינּוּן בִּרְכָאן נְגִידוּ וְאִתְמְשָׁכוּ מֵהַהוּא אֲתָר עוּמְקָא דְּכֹלָּא, וְאִתְיַשְּׁבָן בַּאֲתָר דְּאִקְרֵי שָׁמַיִם, כְּדֵין בִּרְכָאן מִשְׁתַּכְּחֵי בְּעִלָּאֵי וְתַתָּאֵי.

112. AND HE ANSWERS, We have explained that whoever wishes to say his prayer before the Holy King should ask the deepest, NAMELY BINAH, to bestow blessings downwards, as written, "A song of ascent. Out of the depths I have cried to You, Hashem" (Tehilim 130:1). That extra Yud IN "HAYOSHVI" is the deepest of all, BINAH, and is the one from which he should request to pour blessings to that place called heaven, WHICH IS ZEIR

ANPIN, so that everything will be sustained by it. Hence it is written, "who dwell in the heavens," NAMELY IN ZEIR ANPIN THAT IS CALLED HEAVEN, since when the blessings pour and come out of that deepest place, WHICH IS BINAH, and settle in the place called heaven, NAMELY IN ZEIR ANPIN, there are blessings in the higher and lower.

113. כְּעֵינֵי עֲבָדִים אֶל יַד אֲדוֹנֵיהֶם, מַאי כְּעֵינֵי עֲבָדִים. אִלֵּין אִינּוּן שְׁאַר רַבְרְבֵי עַמִּין, דְּלָא אִתְּזָנוּ אֶלָּא מִשְּׁיוּרָא נוֹפָא דְּאִילָנָא, דְּיִשְׂרָאֵל מִתְדַּבְּקֵי בֵּיהּ. וְכַד יִשְׂרָאֵל נַטְלִין בִּרְכָאן מֵהַהוּא אֲתָר, כֻּלְּהוּ מִתְבָּרְכָן מִיִּשְׂרָאֵל.

113. "as the eyes of servants look to the hand of their masters" (Tehilim 123:2). HE ASKS, What are the eyes of servants, AND ANSWERS, They are the other ministers of the nations, WHICH ARE THE SEVENTY SUPERNAL MINISTERS, which are nourished only from the residue of the boughs of the tree, WHICH IS ZEIR ANPIN, to which Yisrael cleave. When Yisrael receive blessings from that place, everyone is blessed from Yisrael.

114. כְּעֵינֵי שִׁפְחָה אֶל יַד גְּבִירְתָּהּ, דָּא הִיא שִׁפְחָה דְּאוֹקִימְנָא, דְּקָטִיל קוּדְשָׁא בְּרִיךְ הוּא חֵילָא דִּילָהּ בְּמִצְרַיִם, דְּהָא לֵית חֵילָא דִּידָהּ, אֶלָּא כַּד אִתְנְגִיד מִתַּמְצִית דְּהַאי אֶרֶץ יִשְׂרָאֵל. וְאֶרֶץ יִשְׂרָאֵל גְּבִרְתָּהּ אִקְרֵי. וְעַל הַאי כְּתִיב, תַּחַת שָׁלֹשׁ רָגְזָה אֶרֶץ. מַאן אֶרֶץ. דָּא אֶרֶץ יִשְׂרָאֵל, כְּמָה דְּאִתְּמַר. תַּחַת עֶבֶד כִּי יִמְלוֹךְ, אִלֵּין אִינּוּן עֲבָדִים דְּקָאַמְרָן. כַּד אִתְיְהִיב שֻׁלְטָנוּתָא לְחַד מִנַּיְיהוּ. וְדָא הוּא דִּכְתִּיב, אֲשֶׁר הוֹצֵאתִיךָ מֵאֶרֶץ מִצְרַיִם מִבֵּית עֲבָדִים. שִׁפְחָה כִּי תִירַשׁ גְּבִירְתָּהּ דָּא הִיא שִׁפְחָה דְּקָאַמְרָן.

114. "and as the eyes of a maid to the hand of her mistress" (Ibid.) refers to the maid we mentioned, whose power the Holy One, blessed be He, slew in Egypt, NAMELY THE VERSE, "THE FIRSTBORN OF THE MAIDSERVANT" (SHEMOT 11:5). For she has power only when it comes from the residue OF BOUNTY of the land of Yisrael, WHICH IS MALCHUT. The land of Yisrael is called her mistress, THE MISTRESS OF THE MAID. Of this it is written, “For three things the earth is disquieted” (Mishlei 30:21). The earth is the land of Yisrael, WHICH IS MALCHUT, as we learned. “a slave when he becomes king” (Ibid. 22) refers to the servants we mentioned, THE SEVENTY MINISTERS OF THE NATIONS. THIS WAS SAID when power was given to one of them. This is the meaning of, “who have brought you out of the land of Egypt, out of the house of bondage” (Shemot 20:2), NAMELY FROM THE ENSLAVEMENT TO THE MINISTERS OF THE NATIONS. “a handmaid that is heir to her mistress” (Mishlei 30:23) refers to the maid we spoke of, OF WHOM IT SAYS, “THE FIRSTBORN OF THE MAIDSERVANT.”

115. ת״ח, מִסִּטְרָא דְּהַאי שִׁפְחָה, נַפְקֵי כַּמָּה גַּרְדִּינֵי טְהִירִין, מְקַטְרְגִין לְקַבְלַיְיהוּ דְּיִשְׂרָאֵל, וּלְקַטְרְגָא לוֹן. וְקוּדְשָׁא בְּרִיךְ הוּא עָבֵיד לְהוּ לְיִשְׂרָאֵל נְטִירוּ, כְּאַבָּא דְּבָעֵי לְנַטְרָא לִבְרֵיהּ מִן כֹּלָּא. אָמַר קוּדְשָׁא בְּרִיךְ הוּא לְיִשְׂרָאֵל, כַּמָּה מְקַטְרְגִין זְמִינִין לְקַבְלַיְיכוּ, אִשְׁתְּדָלוּ בְּפוּלְחָנִי, וַאֲנָא אֶהֱא נָטִיר לְכוּ לְבַר. וְאַתּוּן תֶּהֱווֹן זְמִינִין בְּבָתֵּיכוֹן מִלְּגוֹ, וְנַיְימֵי בְּעַרְסֵיכוֹן, וַאֲנָא אֶהֱא נָטִיר לְכוּ לְבַר, וְסוּחֲרָנֵי עַרְסַיְיכוּ.

115. Come and see, many litigant spirits came out of the aspect of that maid, which denounce Yisrael and COME TO prosecute them. And the Holy One, blessed be He, guards Yisrael like a father who wishes to guard his child from all THINGS. The Holy One, blessed be He, said to Yisrael, ‘Many prosecutors are ready against you. Be occupied in My worship and I shall guard you from outside. You shall be encased in your houses from within and sleep on your beds, and I shall guard you from outside and around your beds’.

116. ות״ח, בְּשַׁעֲתָא דְּאִינּוּן זִינִין בִּישִׁין קָרִיבִין לְפִתְחָא דְּב״נ זַקְפָן רֵישָׁא, וּמִסְתַּכְּלָן בִּשְׁמָא קַדִּישָׁא דְּאִתְחָזֵי לְבַר, דְּאִיהוּ שַׁדַּי, דְּמִתְעַטָּר בְּעִטְרוֹי, שְׁמָא דָּא שַׁלִּיט עַל כֻּלְּהוּ, מִנֵּיהּ דַּחֲלִין וְעַרְקִין, וְלָא קָרְבִין לְפִתְחָא דְּב״נ.

116. Come and see, when these evil species approach a man’s door, they lift up their heads and behold the Holy Name that is seen from outside, which is Shadai, decorated with its crowns. This name has power over them all, and they fear it and flee and do not approach man’s door.

117. א״ל רַבִּי יִצְחָק, אִי הָכִי, יִרְשׁוֹם ב״נ שְׁמָא דָּא בְּפִתְחָא דְּבֵיתָא, וְלָא יַתִּיר, אֲמַאי כָּל פַּרְשְׁתָּא. אָמַר לֵיהּ שַׁפִּיר הוּא, דְּהָא שְׁמָא דָּא לָא אִתְעֲטָּר, אֶלָּא בְּאִינּוּן אַתְוָון כֻּלְּהוּ, רְשִׁימִין בִּרְשִׁימָא דְּמַלְכָּא, וְכַד אַכְתָּב כָּל פַּרְשְׁתָּא, כְּדֵין שְׁמָא דָּא מִתְעֲטָּר בְּעִטְרוֹי וְנָפִיק מַלְכָּא בְּכָל חֵילוֹי, כֻּלְּהוּ רְשִׁימִין בִּרְשִׁימָא דְּמַלְכָּא, כְּדֵין דַּחֲלִין מִנֵּיהּ, וְעַרְקִין מִקַּמֵּיהּ.

117. Rabbi Yitzchak said, In that case man should mark that name, SHADAI, at the door of the house and no more. Why THE NEED for the whole passage IN THE MEZUZAH? He said to him, This is well, for that name, SHADAI, WHICH IS YESOD, is adorned only with all the letters that are marked with the King's mark, NAMELY, THAT ARE WRITTEN IN THE MEZUZAH. When the whole passage is written, that name is adorned with its crowns and the King, ZEIR ANPIN, comes out with all His armies, all imprinted with the King's mark, WHICH IS MALCHUT. Then they all fear it and flee from it.

118. ת״ח, וְהָיָה שְׁמָא קַדִּישָׁא, מִתַּתָּא לְעֵילָּא. וְעַל דָּא, שַׁדַּי אִתְרְשִׁים מִלְּבַר, לָקֳבְלֵי שְׁמָא דָּא. וְהָיָ״ה מִלְּגַו, שַׁדַּ״י מִלְּבַר. לְמֶהֱוֵי נָטִיר ב״נ מִכָּל סִטְרִין מִלְּגָאו וּמִלְּבַר. א״ר אַבָּא, כַּמָּה חַיָּילִין קַדִּישִׁין זְמִינִין בְּהַהִיא שַׁעֲתָא דְּאָנַח ב״נ מְזוּזָה לְתַרְעֵיהּ, כֻּלְּהוּ מַכְרְזֵי וְאַמְרֵי זֶה הַשַּׁעַר לַיְיָ׳ וְגוֹ׳.

118. Come and see, in "And it shall come to pass, if you hearken (Heb. *vehayah im shamo'a*)" (Devarim 11:13-17), *vehayah* is a Holy Name, YUD HEI VAV HEI, from below upwards, BECAUSE IT IS SPELLED VAV-HEI FIRST AND THEN YUD-HEI. For that reason the name Shadai is written on the outside against that name. THE NAME Vehayah is on the inside and Shadai is on the outside so one would be guarded from all sides, from within and from without. Rabbi Aba said, Many holy hosts stand ready at that time when a man fixes a Mezuzah at his door. They all declare, saying, "this is the gate of Hashem…" (Tehilim 118:20).

119. זַכָּאָה חוּלָקֵהוֹן דְּיִשְׂרָאֵל, כְּדֵין אִשְׁתְּמוֹדְעָן יִשְׂרָאֵל דְּאִינּוּן בְּנֵי מַלְכָּא קַדִּישָׁא, דְּהָא כֻּלְּהוּ אִתְרְשִׁימוּ מִנֵּיהּ. אִתְרְשִׁימוּ בְּגוּפַיְיהוּ,

בִּרְשִׁימָא קַדִּישָׁא. אִתְרְשִׁימוּ בִּלְבוּשַׁיְיהוּ, בְּעִטּוּפַיְיהוּ דְּמִצְוָה. אִתְרְשִׁימוּ בְּרֵישַׁיְיהוּ, בְּבָתֵּי דִּתְפִילֵי, בִּשְׁמָא דְּמָארֵיהוֹן. אִתְרְשִׁימוּ בִּידַיְיהוּ, בִּרְצוּעֵי דִּקְדוּשָּׁא. אִתְרְשִׁימוּ בִּמְסָאנַיְיהוּ, בִּמְסָאנָא דְּמִצְוָה. אִתְרְשִׁימוּ לְבַר, בִּזְרִיעָה בַּחֲצָדָא. אִתְרְשִׁימוּ בְּבָתֵּיהוֹן, בִּמְזוּזָה דְּפִתְחָא. בְּכֹלָּא רְשִׁימִין דְּאִינּוּן בְּנֵי מַלְכָּא עִלָּאָה, זַכָּאָה חוּלָקֵהוֹן.

119. Happy is the lot of Yisrael, for Yisrael are then recognized as the children of the Holy King, since they are all marked by Him, marked in their body with the holy imprint OF CIRCUMCISION, marked in their clothing by a Tzitzit. They are marked on their head with the compartments of the Tefilin, which are their Master's Name, and marked on their hands with the straps of holiness. They are marked in their shoes by a precept fulfilling shoes, NAMELY, OF THE PASCAL SACRIFICE, AS WRITTEN, "YOUR SHOES ON YOUR FEET" (SHEMOT 12:11), AND THE CHALITZAH. They are marked in the field by sowing and harvesting, marked in their houses with the Mezuzah on the doorpost. In every thing they are marked as the supernal King's children. Happy is their portion.

18. "they have forsaken Me"

A Synopsis

Rabbi Aba talks about people who are false to the sign of the holy imprint. He says that the idol worshipping nations are broken cisterns but that Yisrael is a well, from which living waters are drawn. Anyone who is false to the holy imprint prevents the well from being blessed. We hear that only a virgin is blessed with seven blessings.

120. עַד דַּהֲווֹ אָזְלֵי, אָמַר רַבִּי אַבָּא, מַאי דִּכְתִּיב אוֹתִי עָזְבוּ מְקוֹר מַיִם חַיִּים לַחְצוֹב לָהֶם בֹּארוֹת וְגוֹ'. אוֹתִי עָזְבוּ, דָּא הוּא מַאן דִּמְשַׁקֵּר בְּאָת רְשִׁימָא קַדִּישָׁא. וּבְמָּה מְשַׁקֵּר בֵּיהּ. דְּעָיֵיל לֵיהּ בִּרְשׁוּתָא אַחֲרָא, כד"א וּבָעַל בַּת אֵל נֵכָר, דְּאִקְרֵי בּוֹרוֹת נִשְׁבָּרִים. דְּהָא עַמִּין עוֹבְדֵי עכו"ם אִקְרוּ בּוֹרוֹת נִשְׁבָּרִים.

120. While they were walking Rabbi Aba said, In the verse, "they have forsaken Me, the fountain of living waters, and have hewn them out cisterns…" (Yirmeyah 2:13), "they have forsaken Me" refers to he who is false to the sign of the holy imprint. How is he false to it? By placing it in the domain of another, as written, "and has married the daughter of a strange El" (Malachi 2:11), who are called broken cisterns. For the idol worshiping nations are called broken cisterns.

121. וּדְיִשְׂרָאֵל, אִקְרֵי בְּאֵר מְקוֹר מַיִם חַיִּים, דָּא רְשׁוּתָא קַדִּישָׁא, מְהֵימְנוּתָא קַדִּישָׁא. וְאִקְרֵי בְּאֵר מַבּוּעֵי דְּמַיִין צְלִילָן, נָפְקִין וְנַזְלִין מִנָּהּ, כד"א וְנוֹזְלִים מִן לְבָנוֹן. וְנוֹזְלִים מִתּוֹךְ בְּאֵרֶךָ. וּכְתִיב מַעְיַן גַּנִּים בְּאֵר מַיִם חַיִּים. סִטְרָא אַחֲרָא אִקְרֵי בּוֹרוֹת נִשְׁבָּרִים. אֲשֶׁר לֹא יָכִילוּ הַמָּיִם.

121. That of Yisrael, WHICH IS MALCHUT, is called a well, "the fountain of living waters." This is the holy domain of the holy Faith, WHICH IS MALCHUT that is called a well of springs of clear water that comes out and pours from it, as written, "and streams from Lebanon" (Shir Hashirim 4:15), AND ALSO, "running waters out of your own well" (Mishlei 5:15), and, "a fountain of gardens, a well of living waters" (Shir Hashirim 4:15). The Other Side is called, "broken cisterns, that can hold no water" (Yirmeyah 2:13).

122. ת״ח, נַהֲרָא דְּנָגִיד וְנָפִיק, אַשְׁקֵי לְכָל גִּינְתָּא, וְרַוֵּי לְכָל אֲתָר וַאֲתָר, כְּמָה דְּאוֹקִימְנָא, עַד דְּמָלֵי לְהַהוּא אֲתָר בְּגִנְתָּא, דְּאִקְרֵי בְּאֵר מַיִם חַיִּים. וּמִתַּמָּן אִתְּזָנוּ עִלָּאִין וְתַתָּאִין, כד״א וּמִשָּׁם יִפָּרֵד.

122. Come and see, the river that flows and comes out, WHICH IS YESOD, waters the whole garden, MALCHUT, and waters each and every place, as we explained, until it fills the place of the garden that is called a well of living water, WHICH IS YESOD OF MALCHUT, whence the higher and lower are nourished, as written, "and from thence it was parted…" (Beresheet 2:10).

123. וְכָל אִינּוּן סִטְרִין דִּסְטָר שְׂמָאלָא, לָא מִשְׁתַּקְיָין מֵהַהוּא נְבִיעוּ דְּמַיִין נְבִיעִין, בְּגִין דְּאִינּוּן מִסִּטְרָא דִּשְׁאַר עַמִּין, וְאִקְרוּ בּוֹרוֹת נִשְׁבָּרִים. וּמַאן דִּמְשַׁקֵּר בִּרְשִׁימָא קַדִּישָׁא בְּהַהוּא סִטְרָא, אִתְדְּבַק בְּבוֹרוֹת נִשְׁבָּרִים אֲשֶׁר לֹא יָכִילוּ הַמָּיִם, וְלָא עַיְילֵי לְתַמָּן. וְהַהוּא דְּזָכֵי לְנַטְרָא לֵיהּ, זָכֵי לְאִתְשַׁקְיָיא מֵהַהוּא נְבִיעוּ דְּנַחֲלָא בְּעָלְמָא דְּאָתֵי, וְזָכֵי דְּאִתְמְלֵי הַהוּא בְּאֵר עִלָּאָה, לְנַגְּדָא בִּרְכָאן לְעֵילָּא וְתַתָּא. זַכָּאָה אִיהוּ בְּעָלְמָא דֵּין, וּבְעָלְמָא דְּאָתֵי, עַל דָּא כְּתִיב, וְהָיִיתָ כְּגַן רָוֶה וּכְמוֹצָא מַיִם אֲשֶׁר לֹא יְכַזְּבוּ מֵימָיו.

123. None of the aspects of the left side are watered from that spring of gushing water, because they are from the aspect of the other nations and are called broken cisterns. Whoever is false to the holy imprint by that side cleaves to "broken cisterns, that can hold no water," because it does not flow in there. Whoever merits to keep it deserves to be watered by the stream of the river in the World to Come and merits that the supernal well will be filled and blessings will be drawn above and below. Happy is he in this world and in the World to Come. Of this it is written, "and you shall be like a watered garden, and like a spring of water, whose waters fail not" (Yeshayah 58:11).

124. וַוי לְמַאן דִּמְשַׁקֵּר בִּרְשִׁימָא קַדִּישָׁא, דְּהָא מְשַׁקֵּר בִּשְׁמָא עִלָּאָה. וְלֹא. עוֹד, אֶלָּא דְּגָרִים לְהַאי בְּאֵר דְּלָא אִתְבָּרְכָא, וְקָרֵינָן עָלֵיהּ כִּי הוֹצִיא שֵׁם רָע עַל בְּתוּלַת יִשְׂרָאֵל. בְּתוּלַת יִשְׂרָאֵל דַּיְיקָא. וְאוֹקְמֵיהּ

רַבִּי שִׁמְעוֹן בְּאַתְרֵיהּ, מַאן דְּשַׁוֵּי תִּסְקוֹפֵי מִלִּין עַל אִנְתְּתֵיהּ קַדְמִיתָא, וְאַפִּיק עֲלָהּ שׁוּם בִּישׁ, כְּמָה דְּאַפִּיק לְעֵילָּא, דִּכְתִּיב כִּי הוֹצִיא שֵׁם רָע עַל בְּתוּלַת יִשְׂרָאֵל סְתָם.

124. Woe to him who is false to the holy imprint, because he is false to the Supernal Name. Moreover, he causes that well, MALCHUT, not to be blessed. He is called, “he has brought out an evil name upon a virgin of Yisrael” (Devarim 22:19). “A virgin of Yisrael” is precise, THAT IS, MALCHUT THAT IS CALLED THE VIRGIN OF YISRAEL, BECAUSE SHE ALWAYS REVERTS TO BEING A VIRGIN. Rabbi Shimon explained in its place that whoever lays accusing speeches against his first wife and brings out an evil name against her IS LIKE one who brings out an evil name against the higher, MALCHUT, as written, “he has brought out an evil name upon a virgin of Yisrael” unspecified, WHICH REFERS TO MALCHUT.

125. וְאַזְלָא הָא, כִּי הָא דְּאָמַר רַבִּי חִיָּיא אָמַר רַבִּי יוֹסִי, בְּתוּלָה יָרְתָא שֶׁבַע בְּרָכוֹת, דְּאִתְבָּרְכָא בְּשֶׁבַע, בְּגִין דִּבְתוּלַת יִשְׂרָאֵל יָרְתָא שֶׁבַע בִּרְכָן, וְעַל דָּא אִתְקְרֵי בַּת שֶׁבַע.

125. This follows the interpretation of Rabbi Chiya in the name of Rabbi Yosi that a virgin receives seven blessings, because she is blessed by seven SFIROT, since the virgin of Yisrael, WHICH IS MALCHUT, inherits seven blessings, WHICH ARE THE SECRET OF SEVEN SFIROT. She is therefore called the daughter of seven.

126. וְאִנְתְּתָא אַחֲרָא, מַאן בִּרְכָאן דִּילָהּ. בִּרְכָתָא דְּבֹעַז וְרוּת, כד"א, וַיֹּאמְרוּ כָּל הָעָם אֲשֶׁר בַּשַּׁעַר וְהַזְּקֵנִים עֵדִים יִתֵּן יְיָ' אֶת וְגוֹ', דְּוַדַּאי בְּתוּלָה בְּז' אִתְבָּרְכָא, וְלָא אִתְּתָא אַחֲרָא בְּרָזָא דָּא. כֵּיוָן דְּמָטוּ בַּחֲקָל חַד, חָמוּ אִילָנִין, יָתְבוּ תְּחוֹתַיְיהוּ. אָמַר רַבִּי אַבָּא, הָא צָחוּתָא דְּמִלֵּי דְּאוֹרַיְיתָא. נֵיתִיב.

126. HE ASKS, And another woman, NAMELY A WIDOW OR A DIVORCEE, WHO REMARRIES, from whence come her blessings? AND HE ANSWERS, From the blessings of Boaz and Ruth, as written, “And all the people that were in the gate, and the elders, said, We are witnesses. Hashem make..." (Rut 4:11). For surely ONLY a virgin is blessed with seven blessings, and no other woman is in that secret. When they reached a certain field they saw trees and sat under them. Rabbi Aba said, HERE is clarity for words of Torah. Let us sit down.

19. “they shall come who were lost in the land of Assyria”

A Synopsis

We are told of the day when the Shofar will be blown and all the children of Yisrael who were lost, who lost their faith, will come again to worship God on the holy mountain at Jerusalem.

127. פָּתַח וְאָמַר, וְהָיָה בַּיּוֹם הַהוּא יִתָּקַע בְּשׁוֹפָר גָּדוֹל וּבָאוּ הָאוֹבְדִים בְּאֶרֶץ אַשּׁוּר וְהַנִּדָּחִים בְּאֶרֶץ מִצְרָיִם וְגוֹ׳. וְהָיָה בְּיוֹם הַהוּא, מַאן בַּיּוֹם הַהוּא. אֶלָּא הַהוּא יוֹמָא דְּאִתְיְדַע לְקוּדְשָׁא בְּרִיךְ הוּא כד״א וְהָיָה יוֹם אֶחָד הוּא יִוָּדַע לַיְיָ׳. תּוּ, בַּיּוֹם הַהוּא, כד״א בְּיוֹם בֹּא גוֹג עַל אַדְמַת יִשְׂרָאֵל.

127. He opened with the verse, “And it shall come to pass on that day, that a great Shofar shall be blown, and they shall come who were lost in the land of Assyria, and the outcasts in the land of Egypt…” (Yeshayah 27:13). “And it shall come to pass on that day”: what is that day? AND HE ANSWERS, It is that day known to the Holy One, blessed be He, as written, “one particular day which shall be known as Hashem’s” (Zecharyah 14:7). “on that day” is as in, “on that day, when Gog shall come against the land of Yisrael” (Yechezkel 38:18).

128. יִתָּקַע בְּשׁוֹפָר גָּדוֹל. מַה לָּן בֵּיהּ, אִי הוּא רַב אוֹ זְעֵיר. אֶלָּא הַהוּא שׁוֹפָר עִלָּאָה, דְּבֵיהּ נָפְקִין עַבְדִּין לְחֵירוּ תָּדִיר, וְהַאי אִיהוּ יוֹבְלָא, דְּיוֹבְלָא עִלָּאָה וְרַבְרְבָא הוּא. וְכַד הַאי אִתְּעַר, כָּל חֵירוּ דְּעָלְמִין מִתְעָרִין בֵּיהּ, וְהַהוּא אִקְרֵי שׁוֹפָר גָּדוֹל.

128. “a great Shofar shall be blown”: HE ASKS, What difference does it make to us whether it is a great or small SHOFAR? AND HE ANSWERS, It is a supernal Shofar, by which slaves are always freed. This is Jubilee, NAMELY BINAH, which is a supernal and great Jubilee. When it is aroused TO BESTOW PLENTY, every kind of freedom of the worlds is aroused through it. And it is called a great Shofar.

129. וּבָאוּ הָאוֹבְדִים בְּאֶרֶץ אַשּׁוּר. הָאֲבוּדִים מִבָּעֵי לֵיהּ, אוֹ הַנֶּאֱבָדִים,

מַאי הָאוֹבְדִים. הָאוֹבְדִים מַמָּשׁ, בְּגִין דְּאִינּוּן בְּאַרְעָא אַחֲרָא, וּמַאן דְּשָׁארֵי בְּאַרְעָא אַחֲרָא, יָנִיק מֵרְשׁוּתָא אַחֲרָא וּכְאִלּוּ לָא שַׁרְיָא בִּמְהֵימְנוּתָא, בג״כ אוֹבְדִים אִקְרוּן. אוֹבְדִים אִינּוּן בְּכָל סִטְרִין, דְּכַד יִשְׂרָאֵל שַׁרְיָין בְּאַרְעָא קַדִּישָׁא, זַכָּאִין, זַכָּאִין תָּדִיר בְּכֹלָּא, זַכָּאן לְעֵילָּא וְתַתָּא.

129. "and they shall come who were lost (lit. 'they who lose') in the land of Assyria." HE ASKS, It should have said, 'they who were lost' or 'they who are lost'. What is meant by, "they who lose"? HE ANSWERS, It is they who actually lose, because they are in another land, and whoever dwells in another land is nourished by another domain and it is as if he does not live in Faith. This is why they are called they who lose, SINCE THEY LOST THEIR FAITH. They lose in every direction, ABOVE AND BELOW, since when Yisrael dwell in the Holy Land, they are righteous and always merit everything, THE PLENTY OF ZEIR ANPIN above and THE PLENTY OF MALCHUT below, BUT WHEN THEY ARE OUT OF THE HOLY LAND THEY LOSE ALL THAT.

130. ד״א וּבָאוּ הָאוֹבְדִים, מַאן אִינּוּן. אִלֵּין צַדִּיק וּכְנֶסֶת יִשְׂרָאֵל. דְּאִקְרוּן אוֹבְדִים. מְנָלָן. כְּנֶסֶת יִשְׂרָאֵל, דִּכְתִּיב עַל מַה אָבְדָה הָאָרֶץ, אֲבוּדָה אוֹ נֶאֱבֶדֶת לָא כְּתִיב, אֶלָּא אָבְדָה הָאָרֶץ, דָּא כְּנֶסֶת יִשְׂרָאֵל. צַדִּיק, דִּכְתִּיב הַצַּדִּיק אָבָד, אָבוּד אוֹ נֶאֱבַד לָא כְּתִיב, אֶלָּא אָבָד, וְהָא אוּקְמוּהָ.

130. According to another explanation, "they shall come who lose" are the Righteous, YESOD, and the Congregation of Yisrael, WHICH IS MALCHUT, who are called 'they who lose'. Whence do we derive this? It is written of the Congregation of Yisrael, "why does the land perish (or: 'lose')" (Yirmeyah 9:11), NAMELY MALCHUT THAT IS CALLED LAND. It is not written that it is lost or was lost, but that the land, which is the Congregation of Yisrael, loses. It is written of the Righteous, "The righteous perishes (or: 'loses')" (Yeshayah 57:1). HENCE THE RIGHTEOUS AND THE CONGREGATION OF YISRAEL ARE CALLED THEY WHO LOSE, as we explained.

131. וְאִי תֵּימָא, וּבָאוּ, מֵאָן אֲתָר אַתְיָין אִלֵּין אוֹבְדִים. אֶלָּא, כְּנֶסֶת יִשְׂרָאֵל מִן גָּלוּתָא. צַדִּיק, כְּמָה דְּאוֹקְמוּהָ, דִּכְתִּיב בְּשׁוּב יְיָ׳ אֶת שִׁיבַת צִיּוֹן, בְּגִין דְּיֵיתוּב לְאַתְרֵיהּ, וְיֵיתֵי לְאִתְחַבְּרָא בִּכְנֶסֶת יִשְׂרָאֵל. וְעַל דָּא, וּבָאוּ הָאוֹבְדִים בְּאֶרֶץ אַשּׁוּר. וְהִשְׁתַּחֲווּ לַיְיָ׳ בְּהַר הַקֹּדֶשׁ בִּירוּשָׁלָיִם, מַאי קָא מַיְירֵי. אֶלָּא מִלָּה דָּא דְּהַנִּדָּחִים בְּאֶרֶץ מִצְרָיִם, כִּבְיָכוֹל, יִשְׂרָאֵל לָא יִפְקוּן מִן גָּלוּתָא, אֶלָּא בִּשְׁכִינְתָּא, כְּמָה דְּאוֹקְמוּהָ, וְאִינּוּן נִדָּחִים הִשְׁתַּחֲווּ לַיְיָ׳.

131. You may ask in reference to "shall come," where they who lose come from, THE RIGHTEOUS AND THE CONGREGATION OF YISRAEL, WHICH ARE YESOD AND MALCHUT. AND HE ANSWERS, The Congregation of Yisrael COMES from exile. The Righteous, as we explained in relation to the verse, "When Hashem brought back the captivity of Zion" (Tehilim 126:1), IS YESOD CALLED ZION, so it shall return to its place and come to JOIN the Congregation of Yisrael. Hence, "they shall come who were lost in the land of Assyria." HE ASKS, What is meant by, "and shall worship Hashem on the holy mountain at Jerusalem" (Yeshayah 27:13), IF THEY WHO LOSE ARE YESOD AND MALCHUT? AND HE ANSWERS, This phrase, "AND SHALL WORSHIP...," REFERS TO "the outcasts in the land of Egypt," WHO SHALL WORSHIP HASHEM, since Yisrael do not come out of exile except with the Shechinah so to speak, as we explained. These outcasts shall worship Hashem, WHICH IS THE SHECHINAH.

20. "Hashem shall preserve your going out and your coming in"

A Synopsis

Rabbi Aba explains what is meant by the title verse, and he talks again about the importance of the Mezuzah in protecting people from evil.

132. תּוּ אָמַר רַבִּי אַבָּא, כְּתִיב, יְיָ׳ יִשְׁמוֹר צֵאתְךָ וּבוֹאֶךָ מֵעַתָּה וְעַד עוֹלָם. יִשְׁמָר צֵאתְךָ תִּינַח. אֶלָּא וּבוֹאֶךָ, מַאי קָא מַיְירֵי, דְּהָא מַאן דְּעָאל לְבֵיתֵיהּ לָא מִסְתָּפֵי. אֶלָּא הַאי ב״נ דְּשַׁוֵּי רְשִׁימָא קַדִּישָׁא לְבֵיתֵיהּ, בְּמִלִּין דִּשְׁמָא עִלָּאָה, הַאי אִתְנְטִיר מִכֹּלָּא. כַּד נָפִיק הַהוּא דְּמָדוֹרֵיהּ לְתַרְעָא דְּבֵיתֵיהּ, זָקִיף וְחָמֵי רְשִׁימָא קַדִּישָׁא, וְעַיְין בְּפִתְחֵיהּ. כַּד נָפִיק ב״נ, הוּא אוֹזִיף לֵיהּ, וְנָטִיר לֵיהּ. כַּד עָיֵיל לְבֵיתֵיהּ, הוּא אַכְרִיז קַמֵּיהּ, אִזְדָּהֲרוּ בִּיקָרָא דְּדִיּוּקְנָא דְּמַלְכָּא קַדִּישָׁא. וְכָל דָּא, בְּגִין הַהוּא רְשִׁימָא דִּשְׁמָא קַדִּישָׁא, דְּאִתְרְשִׁים בְּתַרְעֵיהּ.

132. Rabbi Aba continued, It is written, "Hashem shall preserve your going out and your coming in from this time forth, and for evermore" (Tehilim 121:8). HE ASKS, "preserve your going out" is correct, but what is meant by, "your coming in"? For whoever enters his house is not afraid AND NEEDS NOT BE KEPT. HE ANSWERS, The man who places the holy mark in his house with the words of the Supernal Name, NAMELY THE MEZUZAH, is protected from everything. When that man goes out of his apartment to the gate of his house, he lifts up his eyes, sees the holy mark and looks at the gate. When he leaves, it escorts and guards him. When that man enters, it pronounced before him, Take care of the honor of the King's image. All this because of that mark of the Holy Name that is marked on his door.

133. וְלָאו דַּי לֵיהּ לְב״נ דְּאִתְנְטַר בְּבֵיתֵיהּ, אֶלָּא קוּדְשָׁא בְּרִיךְ הוּא נָטִיר לֵיהּ כַּד עָיֵיל, וְכַד נָפִיק. דִּכְתִּיב, יְיָ׳ יִשְׁמָר צֵאתְךָ וּבוֹאֶךָ מֵעַתָּה וְעַד עוֹלָם. זַכָּאִין אִינּוּן יִשְׂרָאֵל בְּהַאי עָלְמָא, וּבְעָלְמָא דְּאָתֵי.

133. Not only is a man kept in his house, the Holy One, blessed be He, keeps him when he comes in and goes out, as written, "Hashem shall preserve your going out and your coming in." Happy are Yisrael in this world and in the World to Come.

134. ת״ח, הַאי רוּחָא בִּישָׁא דְּשַׁארֵי בֵּין תַּרְעֵי. וַוי לֵיהּ לְב״נ, דְּלָא יָדַע לְאִזְדַּהֲרָא מִנֵּיהּ, וְלָא רָשִׁים לְפִתְחָא דְּבֵיתֵיהּ שְׁמָא עִלָּאָה קַדִּישָׁא, דִּישְׁתְּכַח עִמֵּיהּ. דְּהָא אִית לֵיהּ תְּלַת מְאָה וְשִׁתִּין וְחָמֵשׁ שַׁמָּשִׁין בִּישִׁין מְקַטְרְגִין, כָּל חַד מְשַׁמֵּשׁ יוֹמֵיהּ, וְכֻלְּהוּ מִשְׁתַּכְּחֵי עִמֵּיהּ כָּל יוֹמֵי שַׁתָּא, וּמְקַטְרְגֵי בֵּיהּ לְעֵילָּא וְתַתָּא. וְכֻלְּהוּ מִשְׁתַּכְּחֵי בֵּיהּ בִּימָמָא וּבְלֵילְיָא. בִּימָמָא, לְקַטְרְגָא לֵיהּ. בְּלֵילְיָא, לְצַעֲרָא לֵיהּ בְּחֶלְמֵיהּ.

134. Come and see, woe to the man who does not know how to beware of the evil spirit that lies between the doorposts, and does not mark the gate to his house with a holy Supernal Name, NAMELY THE MEZUZAH, to be with him. For that evil spirit has 365 evil prosecuting officers IN THE 365 DAYS OF THE YEAR; each serves on its day. They are all present with him, WITH THAT MAN, throughout the days of the year and denounce him above and below. They are all with him day and night. They prosecute him by day and by night distress him in his dreams.

135. כַּד נָפִיק לְקַטְרְגָא לֵיהּ, כַּד עָאל, שַׁוְּוֹין יְדַיְיהוּ עֲלֵיהּ דִּכְתְפֵּיהּ, וְאַמְרִין לֵיהּ, וַוי לֵיהּ לִפְלַנְיָא דְּנָפַק מֵרְשׁוּתָא דְּמָארֵיהּ. וַוי לֵיהּ לִפְלַנְיָא בְּהַאי עָלְמָא, וּבְעָלְמָא דְּאָתֵי. בג״כ בָּעְאן בְּנֵי מְהֵימְנוּתָא, לְמֶהֱוֵי רְשִׁימִין בְּכֹלָּא, לְמֶהֱוֵי רְשִׁימִין בִּרְשִׁימָא דְּמָארֵיהוֹן, לְאִזְדַּעְזְעָא מִנַּיְיהוּ כָּל סִטְרִין זִינִין בִּישִׁין, לְמֶהֱוֵי נְטִירִין בְּהַאי עָלְמָא, וּבְעָלְמָא דְּאָתֵי. זַכָּאִין חוּלָקֵהוֹן דְּיִשְׂרָאֵל, עֲלַיְיהוּ כְּתִיב וְעַמֵּךְ כֻּלָּם צַדִּיקִים לְעוֹלָם יִירְשׁוּ אָרֶץ וְגוֹ׳.

135. When it is about to denounce him when he enters HIS HOUSE, they put their hands on his shoulders and say to him, Woe to so-and-so who left his Master's domain. Woe to so-and-so in this world and in the World to Come. For that reason the faithful should be marked in every way, marked with their Master's imprint, NAMELY WITH THE PRECEPT, so every aspect of evil species shall fear them and so they will be kept in this world and in the World to Come. Happy is the lot of Yisrael. It is written of them, "Your people also shall be all righteous. They shall inherit the land for ever" (Yeshayah 60:21).

21. "And you shall love Hashem your Elohim"

A Synopsis

Rabbi Yosi talks about the pleasure that God takes in the children of Yisrael when they are in their own land, and the anguish He feels when they are in exile. Rabbi Yosi emphasizes that there is no worship like the love of God. Rabbi Aba concurs, saying that love is the essence of the Torah. He says that you must love God with both your good and your evil heart and with your good and your evil soul. Rabbi Aba gives the example of Abraham, who gave up his own wishes, his son, his wife and his money for the love of God; this is why he was given the crown of Chesed, and why all the worlds were blessed for his sake. Rabbi Yosi tells the rabbis that the righteous have many dwellings in the world beyond, and the highest of all is for those who are connected to the love of God, and their chamber is connected to the highest chamber, that is called Love. Everything is called love and therefore whoever loves God is connected to that love.

136. וְאָהַבְתָּ אֵת יְיָ' אֱלֹהֶיךָ. רַבִּי יוֹסִי פָּתַח, וְעַתָּה מַה לִּי פֹה נְאֻם יְיָ' כִּי לֻקַּח עַמִּי חִנָּם וְגוֹ'. ת"ח, רְחִימוּתָא דְקוּדְשָׁא בְּרִיךְ הוּא בְּיִשְׂרָאֵל אע"ג דְּחוֹבַיְיהוּ גָּרְמוּ לְאִסְתַּלְּקָא מִבֵּינַיְיהוּ, וְאִתְבַּדָּרוּ בֵּינֵי עַמְמַיָּא, הוּא תָּבַע עֶלְבּוֹנָא דִּלְהוֹן. וְת"ח, בְּשַׁעֲתָא דְּיִשְׂרָאֵל שָׁרָאן בְּאַרְעֲהוֹן, קוּדְשָׁא בְּרִיךְ הוּא מִשְׁתַּעֲשָׁע בְּגִנְתֵּיהּ, וְקָרִיב לְגַבַּיְיהוּ דְּיִשְׂרָאֵל, וְשָׁמַע קָלֵיהוֹן, וְאִשְׁתְּבַח בְּהוּ.

136. "And you shall love Hashem your Elohim" (Devarim 6:5). Rabbi Yosi opened, "Now therefore, what have I here, says Hashem, that My people is taken away for naught..." (Yeshayah 52:5). Come and see the love of the Holy One, blessed be He, for Yisrael. Even though transgressions caused His departure from among them and they dispersed among the nations, He demands satisfaction for their insult. Come and see, when Yisrael live in their land and the Holy One, blessed be He, takes delight in His garden, MALCHUT, and comes near Yisrael, and hears their voices, He praises Himself with them.

137. כֵּיוָן דְּגַרְמוּ חוֹבַיְיהוּ, וְאִתְגְּלֵי יִשְׂרָאֵל מֵאַרְעָא קַדִּישָׁא, קוּדְשָׁא בְּרִיךְ הוּא לָא עָאל בְּגִנְתֵּיהּ, וְלָא מִשְׁתַּעֲשָׁע בֵּיהּ. וְלָא עוֹד, אֶלָּא

דְּאִיהוּ צָוַוח וְאָמַר, וְעַתָּה מַה לִּי פֹה נְאֻם יְיָ׳, וּכְתִיב הָתָם פֹּה אֵשֵׁב כִּי אִוִּיתִיהָ. כִּי לֻקַּח עַמִּי חִנָּם, כְּמָה דְּאַתְּ אָמֵר, חִנָּם נִמְכַּרְתֶּם.

137. When their transgressions caused Yisrael to become exiled from the Holy Land, the Holy One, blessed be He, does not enter His garden, MALCHUT, and takes no delight in it. Moreover, He cries out and says, "Now therefore, what have I here, says Hashem." It is written elsewhere, "here will I dwell; for I have desired it" (Tehilim 132:14). AS "HERE" IN THE LATTER IS THE SHECHINAH, SO "HERE" IN THE FORMER IS THE SHECHINAH. "My people is taken away for naught" is the same as, "You were sold for naught" (Yeshayah 52:3).

138. וּמֵהַהוּא יוֹמָא דְּאִתְגְּלִיאוּ יִשְׂרָאֵל מֵאַרְעֲהוֹן, לָא אִשְׁתְּכַח חֶדְוָותָא קָמֵיהּ קוּדְשָׁא בְּרִיךְ הוּא. הה״ד, אַלְבִּישׁ שָׁמַיִם קַדְרוּת וְשַׂק אָשִׂים כְּסוּתָם. וְכָל דָּא, בְּגִין רְחִימוּתָא דִּלְהוֹן, דְּרָחִים לוֹן קוּדְשָׁא בְּרִיךְ הוּא, כְּמָה דְּאַתְּ אָמֵר, אָהַבְתִּי אֶתְכֶם אָמַר יְיָ׳. וְעַל דָּא וְאָהַבְתָּ אֵת יְיָ׳ אֱלֹהֶיךָ. וְאָהַבְתָּ: דְּבָעֵי בַּר נָשׁ לְאִתְקַשְּׁרָא בֵּיהּ בִּרְחִימוּתָא עִלָּאָה, דְּכָל פּוּלְחָנָא דְּבָעֵי ב״נ לְמִפְלַח לְקוּדְשָׁא בְּרִיךְ הוּא, דְּיִפְלַח בִּרְחִימוּ. דְּלֵית לָךְ פּוּלְחָנָא, כְּמוֹ רְחִימוּתָא דְּקוּדְשָׁא בְּרִיךְ הוּא. ר׳ אַבָּא אָמַר, הָנֵי מִלֵּי כְּלָלָא דְּאוֹרַיְיתָא אִינּוּן, בְּגִין דַּעֲשַׂר אֲמִירָן דְּאוֹרַיְיתָא, הָכָא אִתְכְּלִילוּ, וְהָא אוֹקְמוּהָ חַבְרַיָּיא.

138. Ever since the day Yisrael were exiled from their country there is no joy before the Holy One, blessed be He. This is the meaning of, "I clothe the heavens with blackness, and I make sackcloth their covering" (Yeshayah 50:3). All this is for the love the Holy One, blessed be He, has for them, as written, "I have loved you, says Hashem" (Malachi 1:2). Hence, "And you shall love Hashem your Elohim." "And you shall love" MEANS that man should be connected to Him with supernal love that at every worship man should serve the Holy One, blessed be He; let him perform it with love. For there is no worship like the love for the Holy One, blessed be He. Rabbi Aba said, These things, NAMELY LOVE, are the essence of the Torah, since the Ten Commandments are included here. The friends have already explained it.

139. ת״ח, לֵית לָךְ מִלָּה בַּחֲבִיבוּתָא קַמֵּי קוּדְשָׁא בְּרִיךְ הוּא, כְּמַאן דְּרָחִים לֵיהּ כַּדְּקָא יָאוּת. וּמַה הוּא. כְּמָה דִּכְתִּיב, בְּכָל לְבָבְךָ. בְּכָל, מַאי קָא מַיְירֵי, בִּלְבָבְךָ מִבָּעֵי לֵיהּ. בְּנַפְשְׁךָ, בִּמְאֹדֶךָ, מַהוּ בְּכָל לְבָבְךָ. אֶלָּא לְאַכְלְלָא תְּרֵין לִבִּין, חַד טַב וְחַד בִּישׁ. בְּכָל נַפְשְׁךָ: חַד טַב, וְחַד בִּישׁ. בְּכָל מְאֹדֶךָ, דָּא לָא אַתְיָא לִדְרָשָׁא. א״ר אֶלְעָזָר, וַאֲפִילּוּ הַאי לִדְרָשָׁא הוּא. מ״ט. בֵּין דְּנָפַל לֵיהּ מָמוֹנָא מִירוּתָא, אוֹ מִסִּטְרָא אַחֲרָא, אוֹ בֵּין דְּאִיהוּ רָוַוח לֵיהּ, וְעַ״ד כְּתִיב בְּכָל מְאֹדֶךָ.

139. Come and see, nothing is more precious before the Holy One, blessed be He, than he who loves Him properly. This accords with the verse, "with all your heart" (Devarim 6:5). What is meant by "all"? It should have said, 'with your heart' AND ALSO 'with your soul, and with your might'. What is, "with all your heart"? AND HE ANSWERS, Its purpose is to include two hearts, a good one and an evil. "With all your soul" (Ibid.) IS WITH TWO SOULS, a good one and an evil. "With all your might" (Ibid.) IS LITERAL AND needs no interpreting. Rabbi Elazar said, Even this needs interpreting. The reason is that whether he receives money as an inheritance or from another source, or whether he earns it, it is written of it, "with all your might."

140. א״ר אַבָּא, אַהַדְרְנָא לַקְּרָא וְאָהַבְתָּ. מַאן דְּרָחִים לְקוּדְשָׁא בְּרִיךְ הוּא, אִתְעַטָּר בְּחֶסֶד מִכָּל סִטְרִין, וְעָבֵיד חֶסֶד בְּכֹלָּא, וְלָא חָיֵיס עַל גּוּפֵיהּ וְעַל מָמוֹנֵיהּ. מְנָלָן. מֵאַבְרָהָם. כְּמָה דְּאִתְּמַר, דְּהָא לָא חָס בִּרְחִימוּתָא דְּמָארֵיהּ, עַל לִבֵּיהּ, וְעַל נַפְשֵׁיהּ, וְעַל מָמוֹנֵיהּ.

140. Rabbi Aba said, Let us return to the verse, "And you shall love." Whoever loves the Holy One, blessed be He, is adorned with Chesed on every direction, does kindness with everyone, and cares not for his body or money. We derive that from Abraham, as we learned, who, for love of his Master had no pity on his own heart, soul or money.

141. עַל לִבֵּיהּ לָא אַשְׁגַּח, עַל רְעוּתָא דִּילֵיהּ, בְּגִין רְחִימוּתָא דְּמָארֵיהּ. עַל נַפְשֵׁיהּ, דְּלָא חָס עַל בְּרֵיהּ, וְעַל אִתְּתֵיהּ, בְּגִין רְחִימוּתָא דְּמָארֵיהּ.

עַל מָמוֹנֵיהּ, דַּהֲוָה קָאֵים בְּפָרָשַׁת אָרְחִין, וְאַתְקִין מְזוֹנֵי לְכָל עָלְמָא. בג"כ, אִתְעֲטָּר בְּעִטְרָא דְּחֶסֶד. כְּמָה דִּכְתִּיב, חֶסֶד לְאַבְרָהָם. וּמַאן דְּאִתְקְשַׁר בִּרְחִימוּתָא דְּמָארֵיהּ, זָכָה לְהַאי. וְלֹא עוֹד, אֶלָּא דְּעָלְמִין כֻּלְּהוּ מִתְבָּרְכָן בְּגִינֵיהּ. הה"ד, וַחֲסִידֶיךָ יְבָרְכוּכָה, אַל תִּקְרֵי יְבָרְכוּכָה, אֶלָּא יְבָרְכוּ כ"ה.

141. HE EXPLAINS HIS WORDS: his own heart means that ABRAHAM did not pay attention to his own wishes for love of his Master; his soul means that he had no pity on his son and his wife for love of his Master; his money means that he used to stand at the crossroads and prepare nourishment for the whole world. For that reason he was adorned with a crown of kindness, NAMELY THE SFIRAH OF CHESED, as written, "loyal love (Heb. *Chesed*) to Abraham" (Michah 7:20). Whoever is connected to the love for his Master merits that. Moreover, all the worlds are blessed for his sake. This is the meaning of, "and Your pious ones shall bless You (Heb. *yevarchuchah*)" (Tehilim 145:10). Do not pronounce it as "shall bless You," but 'shall bless (Heb. *yevarchu*) *koh*'. THIS MEANS THAT THE PIOUS ONES (HEB. *CHASSIDIM*), NAMELY THOSE WHO ATTAINED THE SFIRAH OF CHESED, SHALL BLESS THE SHECHINAH CALLED '*KOH*'. THUS EVEN THE SHECHINAH IS BLESSED FOR THEIR SAKES.

142. יוֹמָא חַד, הֲוָה חָלַשׁ רַבִּי יוֹסִי, עָאל לְגַבֵּיהּ, ר' אַבָּא וְר' יְהוּדָה וְר' יִצְחָק, חָמוּ לֵיהּ, דַּהֲוָה נָפִיל עַל אַנְפּוֹי, וְנָאִים. יָתְבוּ. כַּד אִתְּעַר, חָמוּ לֵיהּ לְאַנְפּוֹי דְּחַיְיכִין. א"ל ר' אַבָּא, מִלָּה חַדְתָּא חֲמֵיתָא. א"ל וַדַּאי, דְּהַשְׁתָּא סַלְקָא נַפְשִׁי, וְחָמֵית יְקָרָא, מֵאִינּוּן דְּמָסְרוּ גַּרְמַיְיהוּ עַל קְדוּשָּׁה דְּמָארֵיהוֹן, דַּהֲווֹ עָאלִין בִּתְלֵיסַר נַהֲרֵי דְּאֲפַרְסְמוֹנָא דַּכְיָא. וְקוּדְשָׁא בְּרִיךְ הוּא מִשְׁתַּעֲשַׁע בְּהוּ. וַחֲמֵינָא מַה דְּלָא יָהֲבוּ לִי רְשׁוּתָא לְמֵימַר. וְשָׁאִילְנָא לוֹן, אֲמֵינָא, הַאי יְקָרָא דְּמַאן הוּא. אָמְרוּ לִי, מֵאִינּוּן דִּרְחִימוּ לְמָארֵיהוֹן בְּהַהוּא עָלְמָא. וּמִמָּה דְּחָמֵית נַפְשָׁאי וְלִבָּאי אִתְנְהִיר, וְעַל דָּא אַנְפָּאי חַיְיכִין.

142. One day Rabbi Yosi was ill. Rabbi Aba and Rabbi Yehuda visited him. They saw him prostrated on his face, sleeping. When he awoke FROM HIS

SLEEP, they saw his face smiling. Rabbi Aba said to him, You have seen something new. He said to them, Indeed, for my soul rose and saw the glory of those who suffered martyrdom for the sanctity of their Master going into thirteen rivers of pure balsam and the Holy One, blessed be He, taking delight in them. I saw what I was given no permission to relate. I asked them saying, Whose glory is this, and they told me it is that of those who loved their Master in that world, NAMELY THIS WORLD. From what my soul has seen, my heart is illuminated. Hence my face is smiling.

143. א״ל ר׳ אַבָּא, זַכָּאָה חוּלָקָךְ, אֲבָל אוֹרַיְיתָא אַסְהִיד בְּהוּ, דִּכְתִּיב עַיִן לָא רָאָתָה אֱלֹהִים זוּלָתְךָ יַעֲשֶׂה לִמְחַכֵּה לוֹ. א״ל ר׳ יְהוּדָה, הָא שָׁאִילוּ חַבְרַיָּיא, דָּא דִּכְתִּיב יַעֲשֶׂה, תַּעֲשֶׂה מִבָּעֵי לֵיהּ.

143. Rabbi Aba said, Happy is your portion. Yet the Torah bears witness to them, as written, "neither has the eye seen, that an Elohim, beside You, should do such a thing for him that waits for Him" (Yeshayah 64:3). Rabbi Yehuda said to him, The friends have enquired why it is written, "should do" in the third person, instead of the second, THOUGH IT IS WRITTEN, "BESIDE YOU" IN THE SECOND PERSON.

144. א״ל, הָא אִתְּמַר. אֲבָל רָזָא דְּמִלָּה, הַיְינוּ דִּכְתִּיב לַחֲזוֹת בְּנֹעַם יְיָ׳ וּלְבַקֵּר בְּהֵיכָלוֹ. וְאוֹקְמוּהָ, נֹעַם יְיָ׳, הַהוּא דְּאַתְיָא מֵעַתִּיקָא קַדִּישָׁא, דְּקוּדְשָׁא בְּרִיךְ הוּא מִשְׁתַּעֲשָׁע בֵּיהּ. דְּהָא הַהוּא נֹעַם מֵעַתִּיקָא נָפְקָא. וּלְבַקֵּר בְּהֵיכָלוֹ, בְּהֵיכָלָא עִילָּאָה עַל כֹּלָּא. אוּף הָכָא עַיִן לֹא רָאָתָה אֱלֹהִים זוּלָתְךָ יַעֲשֶׂה, מַאן, הַהוּא עַתִּיקָא סְתִימָא דְּכֹלָּא, דְּהָא בֵּיהּ תַּלְיָא, א״ל וַדַּאי הָכִי הוּא. זַכָּאָה חוּלָקֵהוֹן דְּאִינוּן, דִּרְחִימוּתָא דְּמָארֵיהוֹן מִתְדַּבְּקָן בְּהוּ, לְאִלֵּין לֵית שִׁעוּרָא לְחוּלָקֵהוֹן בְּהַהוּא עָלְמָא.

144. He said to him, We have learned that, yet its secret is the words, "to behold the beauty of Hashem, and to inquire in His temple" (Tehilim 27:4). We have explained that "the beauty of Hashem" is THE PLENTY coming from Atika Kadisha, WHICH IS KETER, in which the Holy One, blessed be He, takes delight. For that beauty comes out of Atika. "to inquire in His temple” refers to the highest temple, BINAH. Here too, “neither has the eye seen, that an Elohim, beside You, should do.” Who SHALL DO? That most hidden Atika, for that PLENTY comes from it. HENCE “SHOULD DO” IS WRITTEN IN THE THIRD PERSON. He said to him, It is surely so. Happy is the portion of those whose Master’s love cleaves to them. Their portion in that world is immeasurable.

145. אָמַר ר׳ יִצְחָק, כַּמָּה מָדוֹרִין עַל מָדוֹרִין אִית לְהוּ לְצַדִּיקַיָּיא בְּהַהוּא עָלְמָא, וּמָדוֹרָא עִלָּאָה דְּכֹלָּא, אִינּוּן דִּרְחִימוּתָא דְּמָארֵיהוֹן אִתְקְשַׁר בְּהוּ, דְּהָא מָדוֹרֵיהוֹן אִתְקְשַׁר בְּהֵיכָלָא דְּסָלִיק עַל כֹּלָּא. מ״ט, בְּגִין דְּקוּדְשָׁא בְּרִיךְ הוּא בְּהַאי אִתְעַטָּר.

145. The righteous have many dwellings upon dwellings in that world, and the highest apartment is for those to whom the love of their Master is connected, for their dwelling is connected to the chamber that surpasses everything. The reason is that the Holy One, blessed be He is adorned with it, WITH LOVE.

146. ת״ח, הֵיכָלָא דָּא, אַהֲבָה אִתְקְרֵי, וּבְגִין אַהֲבָה קַיְימָא כֹּלָּא. כְּמָה דִּכְתִּיב, מַיִם רַבִּים לֹא יוּכְלוּ לְכַבּוֹת אֶת הָאַהֲבָה. וְכֹלָּא בִּרְחִימוּתָא קַיְימָא, דְּהָא שְׁמָא קַדִּישָׁא הָכִי אִשְׁתְּכַח דְּהָא אוּקְמוּהָ, י׳ לָא מִתְפְּרַשׁ קוֹצָא דִּלְעֵילָּא מִן י׳ לְעָלְמִין. דְּהָא בִּרְחִימוּתָא שַׁרְיָא עֲלֵיהּ, וְלָא מִתְפְּרַשׁ מִנֵּיהּ לְעָלְמִין. ה׳, הָא אוּקְמוּהָ, דְּיוֹד לָא מִתְפְּרַשׁ מִנָּהּ, וְאִשְׁתְּכָחוּ כַּחֲדָא בַּחֲבִיבוּתָא, לָא אִתְפָּרְשָׁן דָּא מִן דָּא. כְּגַוְונָא דָּא ה׳ וְהָא אִתְּמַר, כְּמָה דִּכְתִּיב, וְנָהָר יוֹצֵא מֵעֵדֶן, יוֹצֵא תָּדִיר לְעָלְמִין, בַּחֲבִיבוּתָא אִתְדַּבְּקָן.

146. Come and see, this HIGHEST chamber is called love, and everything is based on love, as written, “Many waters cannot quench love” (Shir Hashirim 8:7). Everything is based on love, because the Holy Name, YUD HEI VAV HEI, is this way. For we have explained that Yud OF YUD HEI VAV HEI, WHICH IS CHOCHMAH, its higher tip, WHICH IS KETER, is never separated from it, since KETER rests on it with love and never separates from it. As for Hei OF YUD HEI VAV HEI, WHICH IS BINAH, it has been explained that Yud, WHICH IS CHOCHMAH, never separates from it and they are together lovingly, NOT separated from each other. Such is Hei OF YUD HEI VAV HEI, as we learned that it accords with the words, "And a river went out of Eden" (Beresheet 2:10). THE RIVER IS BINAH AND EDEN IS CHOCHMAH. BINAH always comes out OF CHOCHMAH, and they cleave always with love.

147. ו״ה כַּד אִתְדַּבְּקָן דָּא בְּדָא, אִתְדַּבְּקָן בַּחֲבִיבוּתָא כַּחֲדָא, חָתָן בְּכַלָּה, דְּאָרְחַיְיהוּ תָּדִיר בַּחֲבִיבוּתָא אִשְׁתְּכַח. י׳ בְּה׳, ה׳ עִם ו׳, ו׳ עִם ה׳. וְדָא בְּדָא אִתְקְשַׁר בַּחֲבִיבוּתָא. וְכֹלָּא אַהֲבָה אִקְרֵי. וְע״ד מַאן דְּרָחִים לְמַלְכָּא, הָא אִתְקְשַׁר בְּהַהוּא אַהֲבָה. וּבג״כ, וְאָהַבְתָּ אֵת יְיָ׳ אֱלֹהֶיךָ.

147. When Vav-Hei, WHICH ARE ZEIR ANPIN AND MALCHUT, cleave to each other with love together, a groom with a bride, who are customarily always in love, then Yud is with Hei, Hei with Vav, and Vav is with LAST Hei, mutually attached with love. Everything is called love and therefore whoever loves the King is connected to that love. Hence, "And you shall love Hashem your Elohim."

22. "All my bones shall say"

A Synopsis

Rabbi Yitzchak talks about the psalms of David, and tells us that at the time of the redemption God will fix each person's bones and draw them into place. He also says that the Evil Inclination is as hard as a rock, but the Good Inclination is flesh, as we read in, "and I will take away the stony heart and I will give you a heart of flesh."

148. וְהָיוּ הַדְּבָרִים הָאֵלֶּה וְגוֹ'. ר' יִצְחָק פָּתַח, כָּל עַצְמוֹתַי תֹּאמַרְנָה יְיָ' מִי כָמוֹךָ מַצִּיל עָנִי מֵחָזָק מִמֶּנּוּ וְעָנִי וְאֶבְיוֹן מִגּוֹזְלוֹ. הַאי קְרָא דָּוִד אַמְרֵיהּ בְּרוּחָא דְקוּדְשָׁא, כָּל עַצְמוֹתַי תֹּאמַרְנָה, וְכִי מַאן חָמָא, גַּרְמֵי דְּאָמְרוּ שִׁירָתָא. אֶלָּא הַאי קְרָא, בְּזִמְנָא דְקוּדְשָׁא בְּרִיךְ הוּא זַמִּין לְאַחֲיָיא מֵתַיָּיא, וְזַמִּין קוּדְשָׁא בְּרִיךְ הוּא לְאַתְקְנָא גַּרְמֵי, וּלְקָרְבָא כָּל חַד וְחַד לְאַתְרַיְיהוּ, דִּכְתִּיב וַתִּקְרְבוּ עֲצָמוֹת עֶצֶם אֶל עַצְמוֹ. וּכְתִיב וְעַצְמוֹתֶיךָ יַחֲלִיץ. כְּדֵין זְמִינִין אִינּוּן לְמֵימַר שִׁירָתָא.

148. "And these words…" (Devarim 6:6). Rabbi Yitzchak opened, "All my bones shall say, Hashem, who is like You, who delivers the poor from him that is too strong for him, and the poor and the needy from him that robs him?" (Tehilim 35:10). David said that verse by the Holy Spirit. HE ASKS, "All my bones shall say": who has seen bones reciting poetry? AND HE ANSWERS, This verse WAS SAID of the time the Holy One, blessed be He, will resurrect the dead. And the Holy One, blessed be He, will fix the bones and draw each to its place, as written, "and the bones came together, bone to its bone" (Yechezkel 37:7), and, "and make strong your bones" (Yeshayah 58:11). Then YISRAEL will recite poetry.

149. מַאי שִׁירָתָא אַמְרֵי. יְיָ' מִי כָמוֹךָ וְדָא שִׁירָתָא מְעַלְיָיא, מִמַּה דְּאָמְרוּ יִשְׂרָאֵל עַל יַמָּא, דְּהָא אִינּוּן לָא אַדְכְּרוּ שְׁמָא קַדִּישָׁא, אֶלָּא בָּתַר תְּלַת מִלִּין, דִּכְתִּיב מִי כָמוֹכָה בָּאֵלִים יְיָ'. וְהָכָא אִינּוּן מַקְדְּמֵי לִשְׁמָא קַדִּישָׁא, דִּכְתִּיב יְיָ' מִי כָמוֹךָ. מַצִּיל עָנִי מֵחָזָק מִמֶּנּוּ, דָּא יֵצֶר טוֹב, מִיֵּצֶר רָע. בְּגִין דְּיִצה"ר תַּקִּיף הוּא כְּאַבְנָא. כְּמָה דִּכְתִּיב וַהֲסִירוֹתִי אֶת לֵב הָאֶבֶן. ויצ"ט הוּא בִּשְׂרָא, דִּכְתִּיב וְנָתַתִּי לָכֶם לֵב בָּשָׂר.

149. HE ASKS, What kind of poetry will they recite, AND ANSWERS, "Hashem, who is like You." This poetry is more valuable than the one Yisrael recited by the sea, because they mentioned the Holy Name only after three words, as written, "Who is like You, Hashem, among the Elim" (Shemot 15:11). But here they put the Holy Name first, as written, "Hashem, who is like You." "who delivers the poor from him that is too strong for him" refers to the Good Inclination, WHO DELIVERS HIM from the Evil Inclination, since the Evil Inclination is hard as a rock, as written, "and I will take away the stony heart" (Yechezkel 36:26). And the Good Inclination is flesh, as written, "and I will give you a heart of flesh" (Ibid.).

23. At first the Evil Inclination is like a guest

A Synopsis

Rabbi Chiya talks about the way the Evil Inclination insinuates its way into a person's life until it becomes his master. He says that one must constantly keep the words of Torah in his heart because it is thus that the Evil Inclination can be conquered.

150. ת״ח, יֵצֶר הָרָע לְמָה הוּא דוֹמֶה. בְּשַׁעֲתָא דְּאָתֵי לְאִזְדַּוְּוגָא בב״נ, הוּא כְּפַרְזְלָא, עַד דְּעָאלִין לֵיהּ בְּנוּרָא. בָּתַר דְּיִתְחַמֵּם אִתְהַדָּר כֹּלָּא כְּנוּרָא.

150. Come and see what the Evil Inclination is like. When it comes to join man, it is like iron before it is put into the fire. After it is heated the whole of it again becomes like fire.

151. רַבִּי חִיָּיא אָמַר, יֵצֶר הָרָע כַּד אָתֵי לְאִזְדַּוְּוגָא בֵּיהּ לְב״נ, דָּמֵי לְב״נ דְּקָרִיב לְפִתְחָא, וְחָמֵי דְּלָא אִית מַאן דְּמָחֵי בִּידֵיהּ. עָאל לְבֵיתָא, וְאִתְעָבֵיד לֵיהּ אֹרֵחַ. חָמָא דְּלָא אִית מַאן דְּמְחֵי בִּידֵיהּ, וְיֵיזִיל לֵיהּ לְאָרְחֵיהּ. כֵּיוָן דְּעָיֵיל לְבֵיתָא, וְלָא אִית דְּיִמְחֵי בִּידֵיהּ, אִתְמְנָא עָלֵיהּ וְאִתְעָבֵיד מָארֵיהּ דְּבֵיתָא עַד דְּיִשְׁתְּכַח דְּכָל בֵּיתָא קָאֵים בִּרְשׁוּתֵיהּ.

151. Rabbi Chiya said, When the Evil Inclination comes to join man, it is like a man who approaches the gate and sees there is no one AT HOME to detain him. It enters the house and becomes a guest, seeing there is no one to prevent it to send it on its way. Once it entered the house and no one prevents it, it is in charge over the house and becomes the landlord, so that the whole house is at its disposal.

152. מַאן אוֹלִיפְנָא. מִפַּרְשְׁתָּא דְּדָוִד אוֹלִיפְנָא. מַה כְּתִיב, וַיָּבֹא הֵלֶךְ לְאִישׁ הֶעָשִׁיר, הֵלֶךְ דְּקָרִיב לְפִתְחָא, וְלָא בָּעֵי לְאִתְעַכְּבָא תַּמָּן, אֶלָּא לְמֵהַךְ לְאָרְחֵיהּ. כַּךְ הוּא יֵצֶר הָרָע, כְּמָה דְּמִקְרַב לְבֵיתָא, מִתְקָרֵב גַּבֵּי דְּב״נ, אִתְּעַר עָלֵיהּ בְּחוֹבָא זְעֵיר, דָּא הוּא אוֹרֵחַ עֲרָאִי. חָמֵי דְּלֵית דְּמְחֵי בִּידֵיהּ, מַה כְּתִיב, לַעֲשׂוֹת לָאוֹרֵחַ הַבָּא אֵלָיו, אִתְעָבֵיד לֵיהּ

אוֹרֵחַ אַכְסְנַאי בְּבֵיתָא, אִתְּעַר עָלֵיהּ בְּחוֹבוֹי יַתִּיר, יוֹמָא חַד, אוֹ תְּרֵין יוֹמִין, כְּהַאי אוֹרֵחַ דְּשָׁרָאן לֵיהּ בְּבֵיתָא, יוֹמָא חֲדָא, אוֹ ב׳ יוֹמִין, כֵּיוָן דְּחָמֵי דְּלֵית מַאן דְּמָחֵי בִּידֵיהּ, מַה כְּתִיב, וַיַּעַשׂ לְאִישׁ הַבָּא אֵלָיו, אִתְעֲבִיד מָארֵי דְּבֵיתָא, כד״א הָאִישׁ אֲדוֹנֵי הָאָרֶץ. אִישׁ נָעֳמִי. כָּךְ הוּא יֵצֶר הָרָע, אִתְעֲבִיד לָקֳבְלֵיהּ דְּב״נ אִישׁ, בַּעַל הַבַּיִת, הָא אִתְקְשַׁר ב״נ בְּפוּלְחָנֵיהּ, וְהוּא עָבִיד בֵּיהּ רְעוּתֵיהּ.

152. Whence do I learn that? I learn it from the passage about David. It is written, "and there came a traveler to the rich man" (II Shmuel 12:4). A traveler means he approaches the gate yet does not want to stay there but go on his way. Such is the Evil Inclination AT FIRST, which, like one approaching the house, it approaches man and rouses him to sin a little, only by coincidence. When it sees no one prevents it, it is written, "to prepare it for the wayfaring man (or: 'guest') that was come to him" (Ibid.). Now he becomes a guest who stays at the house, which means it rouses him to sin more for a day or two like a guest that is kept at home for a day or two. When it sees no one prevents it, it is written, "prepared it for the man that was come to him" (Ibid.), because it became the landlord, as written, "The man, who is the lord of the land" (Beresheet 42:30), and, "Naomi's husband (lit. 'man')" (Rut 1:3). Such is the Evil Inclination, who has become a man, landlord over that man who was attached to serve it, and THE EVIL INCLINATION does with him as it pleases.

153. וע״ד בָּעֵי ב״נ לְשַׁוָּאָה מִלִּין דְּאוֹרַיְיתָא עָלֵיהּ תָּדִיר, בְּגִין דְּיִהֵא הַהוּא יצה״ר תָּבִיר בְּהוּ, דְּלֵית לֵיהּ מְקַטְרֵג לְיֵצֶר הָרָע, בַּר מִלֵּי דְּאוֹרַיְיתָא. וְע״ד כְּתִיב, וְהָיוּ הַדְּבָרִים הָאֵלֶּה וְגו׳, עַל לְבָבֶךָ, עַל תְּרֵי יְצָרֶיךָ, יֵצֶר הַטּוֹב אִתְעֲטָר בְּהוּ, וְיֵצֶר הָרָע אִתְכַּפְיָא בְּהוּ. א״ר יְהוּדָה, יֵצֶר הַטּוֹב, מַה בָּעֵי מִלֵּי דְּאוֹרַיְיתָא. א״ל, יֵצֶר הַטּוֹב אִתְעֲטָר בְּהוּ. וְיֵצֶר הָרָע, כֵּיוָן דְּחָמֵי ב״נ לָא תָּב, וְלָא בָּעֵי לְאִשְׁתַּדְּלָא בְּאוֹרַיְיתָא, כְּדֵין הוּא סָלִיק לְעֵילָּא, וְאוֹלִיף עָלֵיהּ חוֹבָה, הה״ד וּכְסִילִים מֵרִים קָלוֹן.

153. One must therefore constantly place upon oneself words of Torah, so that the Evil Inclination will be broken by them, for the Evil Inclination has no greater enemy than words of Torah. Hence it is written, "And these words…shall be in your heart" (Devarim 6:6). "Your heart" means your two inclinations, since the Good Inclination is adorned with them and the Evil Inclination is subdued by them. Rabbi Yehuda said, What does the Good Inclination need words of Torah for? He said to him, The Good Inclination is adorned with them, and the Evil Inclination, when it sees that the man does not repent and does not care to study Torah, it rises up and speaks ill of him. This is the meaning of, "but fools shall get (or: 'raise') shame" (Mishlei 3:35).

24. The Ten Commandments are indicated in the passage of the Sh'ma reading

A Synopsis

Rabbi Shimon lists the ten commandments in Devarim chapter six, that correspond to the Ten Commandments that Moses gave. He says that everyone who recites them fully twice a day is blessed.

154. כַּד אָתָא ר"ש, אָמַר, הָא וַדַּאי פַּרְשְׁתָּא דְּק"ש רְמִיזָא בֵּיהּ י' אֲמִירָן כְּמָה דְּאוּקְמוּהָ, וְהָכִי הוּא וַדַּאי. וְהָיוּ הַדְּבָרִים הָאֵלֶּה, כְּלָלָא דְּעֶשֶׂר אֲמִירָן אִינּוּן. ובג"כ י' פִּקּוּדִין אִית הָכָא, לָקֳבֵל י' פִּקּוּדִין דְּאוֹרַיְיתָא. וּמַאן אִינּוּן. וְשִׁנַּנְתָּם לְבָנֶיךָ. וְדִבַּרְתָּ בָּם. בְּשִׁבְתְּךָ בְּבֵיתֶךָ. וּבְלֶכְתְּךָ בַדֶּרֶךְ. וּבְשָׁכְבְּךָ. וּבְקוּמֶךָ. וּקְשַׁרְתָּם לְאוֹת עַל יָדֶךָ. וְהָיוּ לְטוֹטָפוֹת בֵּין עֵינֶיךָ. וּכְתַבְתָּם עַל מְזוּזוֹת בֵּיתֶךָ. וּבִשְׁעָרֶיךָ. הָא י', לָקֳבֵל י' אֲמִירָן. וְע"ד פָּרְשִׁיָּין אִלֵּין כְּלַל רַב אִינּוּן בְּאוֹרַיְיתָא, זַכָּאָה חוּלָקֵיהּ, מַאן דְּאַשְׁלִים לֵיהּ בְּכָל יוֹמָא תְּרֵי זִמְנֵי, דְּהָא אִתְקַדָּשׁ בְּפוּמֵיהּ שְׁמָא קַדִּישָׁא, כַּדְקָא יָאוּת.

154. When Rabbi Shimon came he said, Surely the Ten Commandments are indicated in the passage of the Sh'ma reading, as has been explained. It is surely so. "And these words" (Devarim 6:6) are the essence of the Ten Commandments. Hence there are ten commandments here that correspond to the Ten Commandments in the Torah. They are, "and you shall teach them diligently to your children 1), and shall talk of them 2), when you sit in your house 3), and when you walk by the way 4), and when you lie down 5), and when you rise up 6). And you shall bind them for a sign upon your arm 7), and they shall be as frontlets between your eyes 8). And you shall write them upon the doorposts of your house 9), and on your gates 10)" (Devarim 6:7-9). So here are ten that correspond to the Ten Commandments. Therefore these passages are a great rule in the Torah. Happy is the portion of he who recites them fully twice a day, since the Holy Name is properly sanctified by his mouth.

25. "for He is your life, and the length of your days"

A Synopsis

The rabbis talk about the critical importance of studying and adhering to the Torah.

155. ר׳ אַחָא, הֲוָה קָאֵים עִמֵּיהּ דר׳ אֶלְעָזָר, לֵילְיָא חַד, בָּתַר פַּלְגּוּת לֵילְיָא, וַהֲווֹ מִשְׁתַּדְּלֵי בְּאוֹרַיְיתָא. פָּתַח ר׳ אֶלְעָזָר, וְאָמַר, כִּי הוּא חַיֶּיךָ וְאוֹרֶךְ יָמֶיךָ וְגוֹ׳. ת״ח, עַל כָּל פִּקּוּדִין דְּגָזַר קוּדְשָׁא בְּרִיךְ הוּא כַּד עָאלוּ לְאַרְעָא דְּיִשְׂרָאֵל, גְּזֵרָה דְּאוֹרַיְיתָא הֲוָה. מַאי טַעֲמָא, בְּגִין דִּשְׁכִינְתָּא לָא מִתְיַישְׁבָא בְּאַרְעָא, אֶלָּא בְּאוֹרַיְיתָא. וְלָא מִתְיַישְׁבָא לְעֵילָּא, אֶלָּא בְּאוֹרַיְיתָא.

155. Rabbi Acha was with Rabbi Elazar one night after midnight and they were occupied with the Torah. Rabbi Elazar opened with, "for He is your life, and the length of your days..." (Devarim 30:20). Above all the precepts the Holy One, blessed be He, decrees when they entered the land of Yisrael, was the decree OF THE STUDY of Torah. The reason is that the Shechinah settles in the land solely with Torah. Nor does it settle above save with Torah, WHICH IS ZEIR ANPIN.

156. דְּהָכִי אָמַר אַבָּא, תּוֹרָה שבע״פ לָא אִשְׁתְּמוֹדָע, אֶלָּא בְּגִין תּוֹרָה שֶׁבִּכְתָב. שְׁכִינְתָּא לָא מִתְיַישְׁבָא לְעֵילָּא אֶלָּא עִם תּוֹרָה דִּלְתַתָּא. דְּכָל זִמְנָא דְּאוֹרַיְיתָא אִשְׁתְּכַח עִמֵּיהּ, יַכְלָא לְמֵיקַם בְּעָלְמָא. הה״ד, כִּי הוּא חַיֶּיךָ וְאוֹרֶךְ יָמֶיךָ לָשֶׁבֶת עַל הָאֲדָמָה. עַל הָאֲדָמָה סְתָם. וְאִי לָאו דְּאַפְסִיק מִלֵּי דְּאוֹרַיְיתָא לָא יַכְלָא לְמֵיקָם. דִּכְתִּיב, עַל מָה אָבְדָה הָאָרֶץ. וּכְתִיב, וַיֹּאמֶר יְיָ׳ עַל עָזְבָם אֶת תּוֹרָתִי.

156. For thus did my father say, NAMELY RABBI SHIMON: The Oral Torah, MALCHUT, is known only through the Written Torah, WHICH IS ZEIR ANPIN. The Shechinah does not settle above except through the Torah STUDIED below. As long as the Torah is with Her, the Shechinah can be present in the world. This is the meaning of, "for He is your life, and the length of your days that you may dwell in the land." The land in general IS

MALCHUT. But if it is not so, but the study of Torah IS NEGLECTED, it cannot survive, as written, "why does the land perish... And Hashem says, Because they have forsaken My Torah" (Yirmeyah 9:11-12).

157. עַד דַּהֲווֹ יָתְבֵי, מָאִיךְ ר׳ שִׁמְעוֹן רֵישֵׁיהּ, אָמַר וַדַּאי הָכִי הוּא וְדָא הוּא רָזָא דְּאַשְׁכַּחְנָא בְּסִפְרָא דְּרַב הַמְנוּנָא סָבָא, וְאוֹקִים קְרָא דָּא, בְּרָזָא דִּכְנֶסֶת יִשְׂרָאֵל, דִּכְתִּיב שְׁאֵרָהּ כְּסוּתָהּ וְעוֹנָתָהּ לֹא יִגְרָע. וְאִי אִתְמְנָעוּ מִנָּהּ, מָה כְּתִיב, וְיָצְאָה חִנָּם אֵין כָּסֶף. כד״א, אֵי זֶה סֵפֶר כְּרִיתוּת אִמְּכֶם אֲשֶׁר שִׁלַּחְתִּיהָ. וּכְתִיב, חִנָּם נִמְכַּרְתֶּם וְלֹא בְכֶסֶף תִּגָּאֵלוּ. וּמַאן דְּמָנַע אוֹרַיְיתָא מִנָּהּ, כְּמַאן דְּנָסַב מָארֵי דְּאִתְּתָא, וּמָנַע לֵיהּ מִנָּהּ, דָּא אִשְׁתְּאָרַת כְּאַרְמַלְתָּא, וְלָא אַרְמַלְתָּא. הה״ד, הָיְתָה כְּאַלְמָנָה, וְלָא אַלְמָנָה.

157. While they were sitting, Rabbi Shimon lowered his head and said, It is surely so. I have found this secret in the book of Rav Hamnuna Saba, who explained the following verse as referring to the Congregation of Yisrael, WHICH IS MALCHUT: "her food, her clothing, and her duty of marriage, shall he not diminish" (Shemot 21:10). NAMELY, BY STUDYING THE TORAH, THE UNION AND PLENTY ARE NOT DIMINISHED FROM MALCHUT. If it is withheld from her, it is written, "she shall go free without money" (Ibid. 11), as in, "Where is the bill of your mother's divorcement, with which I have put her away" (Yeshayah 50:1), and, "You were sold for naught; and you shall be redeemed without money" (Yeshayah 52:3). Whoever withholds Torah from MALCHUT is like one who takes away the husband from his wife and withholds her away from him, BECAUSE HE CAUSES THE DEPARTURE OF THE SUPERNAL TORAH, WHICH IS ZEIR ANPIN, HER HUSBAND, and she remains as a widow, though not AN ACTUAL widow. This is the meaning of, "how is she become like a widow" (Eichah 1:1), yet not a widow.

158. יָתְבוּ אִתְעַסְּקוּ בְּאוֹרַיְיתָא, עַד דְּנָהִיר יוֹמָא. בָּתַר דְּנָהִיר יוֹמָא, קָמוּ וְאָזְלוּ. עַד דַּהֲווֹ אָזְלוּ, חָמוּ חַד גְּבַר דַּהֲוָה אָזִיל בְּאָרְחָא, וְרֵישֵׁיהּ עָטִיף, קְרִיבוּ גַּבֵּיהּ, וַהֲוָה רָחִישׁ בְּשִׂפְוָותֵיהּ, וְלָא אָתִיב לוֹן מִדִּי. אָמַר רַבִּי אֶלְעָזָר, וַדַּאי הַאי אִמְלַךְ בְּמָארֵיהּ. יָתִיב רַבִּי אֶלְעָזָר וְרַבִּי אַחָא

וְצַלּוּ צְלוֹתָא, וְהַהוּא גְּבַר קָאִים בְּקִיּוּמֵיהּ בַּאֲתָר אַחֲרָא. בָּתַר דְּסַיְּימוּ צְלוֹתָא, אַזְלוּ בְּאָרְחָא, וְהַהוּא גַּבְרָא אִשְׁתְּמִיט מִנַּיְיהוּ. אָמַר רַבִּי אֶלְעָזָר, הַאי גַּבְרָא, אוֹ טִפְּשָׁא הוּא, אוֹ אָרְחוֹי לָא מִתְיַשְּׁרָן. אָמַר נִתְעֲסָק בְּאוֹרַיְיתָא, דְּהָא שַׁעֲתָא הִיא.

158. They sat and dealt with the Torah until daylight. With daylight they rose to go. While they were walking they saw a man walking on the way with his head covered. They approached him but he was muttering with his lips and did not respond at all to them. Rabbi Elazar said, Surely he takes counsel from his Master, NAMELY, HE RECITES THE WAYFARER’S PRAYER. Rabbi Elazar and Rabbi Acha sat down and prayed, while that man stood in another place. When they finished praying, they went on their way and that man slipped off from them. Rabbi Elazar said, This man is either a fool or his customs are improper. He said, Let us be occupied with the Torah, since it is time TO BE OCCUPIED WITH THE TORAH.

26. "The wise shall inherit honor"

A Synopsis

The rabbis examine the verse, "The wise shall inherit honor, but fools shall get shame," and they decide that Egypt is not among those nations that can be punished through lack of rain because they are watered by the Nile, but the Holy Land always drinks from heaven.

159. פָּתַח רַבִּי אֶלְעָזָר וְאָמַר, כָּבוֹד חֲכָמִים יִנְחָלוּ וּכְסִילִים מֵרִים קָלוֹן. כָּבוֹד חֲכָמִים יִנְחָלוּ, זַכָּאִין אִינּוּן דְּמִתְעַסְּקֵי בְּאוֹרַיְיתָא. עַד לָא פָּתַח מִלָּה, קָרִיב הַהוּא בַּר נָשׁ גַּבַּיְיהוּ. אָמַר ר׳ אֶלְעָזָר, לֵית לָן לְמִפְסַק מִלֵּי דְּאוֹרַיְיתָא, דְּכָל מַאן דְּאִשְׁתְּדַל בְּאוֹרַיְיתָא, זָכֵי לְמֵירַת יְרוּתָא דְּאַחֲסָנָא דִּלְעֵילָּא, בִּיקָרָא דְּמַלְכָּא עִלָּאָה קַדִּישָׁא, וְזָכֵי לְמֵירַת יְרוּתָא דְּאַחֲסָנָא בְּהַאי עָלְמָא, וּמַאי אִיהוּ. הַהוּא דְּאִקְרֵי כְּבוֹד יְיָ׳, דְּלָא פָּסַק מִנַּיְיהוּ לְעָלְמָא. הה״ד, כָּבוֹד חֲכָמִים יִנְחָלוּ, הַהוּא דְּאִקְרֵי כְּבוֹד יְיָ׳.

159. Rabbi Elazar said, "The wise shall inherit honor, but fools shall get shame" (Mishlei 3:35). "The wise shall inherit honor": happy are those who study Torah. Before he started talking, that man approached them. Rabbi Elazar said, We must not interrupt words of Torah, since whoever studies Torah, merits to receive the inheritance of possession from above of the glory of the King, ZEIR ANPIN, and merits to receive the inheritance of possession in this world. This is that which is called the glory of Hashem, NAMELY MALCHUT CALLED THIS WORLD, which never ceases from them. This is the meaning of, "The wise shall inherit honor," THAT IS, THEY SHALL INHERIT MALCHUT, which is called the glory of Hashem.

160. וּכְסִילִים מֵרִים קָלוֹן, מַאי הוּא. ת״ח, כַּד בַּר נָשׁ אָזַל בְּאֹרַח מֵישָׁר קַמֵּי קוּדְשָׁא ב״ה, וְאִשְׁתָּדַל בְּאוֹרַיְיתָא, הָא הַהוּא כְּבוֹד יְיָ׳ יָרִית לְגַרְמֵיהּ, וְכַמָּה אַפִּטְרוֹפְּסִין סַנֵּיגוֹרִין אִשְׁתַּכְּחוּ לְעֵילָּא עָלֵיהּ דְּב״נ, וְכֻלְּהוּ אוֹלְפִין עָלֵיהּ זְכוּ, קַמֵּי מַלְכָּא קַדִּישָׁא, וְאִי בַּר נָשׁ לָא אִשְׁתְּדַל בְּאוֹרַיְיתָא, וְלָא אָזַל בְּאָרְחָא דְּמָארֵיהּ, הוּא עָבֵיד קַטֵיגוֹרָא עָלֵיהּ. וְהַהוּא קַטֵיגוֹרָא שָׁאט בַּאֲוִירָא, וְלָא סָלִיק לְעֵילָּא, דִּלְמָא יְתוּב אָדָם מֵחוֹבוֹי. כֵּיוָן דְּחָמֵי דְּבַר נָשׁ לָא תָּב, וְלָא בָּעֵי לְאִשְׁתַּדְּלָא בְּאוֹרַיְיתָא,

כְּדֵין הוּא סָלִיק לְעֵילָּא, וְאוֹלִיף עָלֵיהּ חוֹבָא. הה״ד, וּכְסִילִים מֵרִים קָלוֹן, וְסָלִיק לְעֵילָּא וְעָבֵד קִטְרוּגָא.

160. HE ASKS what is meant by, "but fools shall get shame" AND ANSWERS, Come and see, when man walks the true way before the Holy One, blessed be He, and is occupied with the Torah, he inherits to himself that glory of Hashem. Many defenders and advocates are above over that man, who all speak in his favor before the Holy King. If that man does not study Torah and does not walk in his Master's way, he brings about prosecution over himself, but that prosecutor roams the air and does not yet rise up, THINKING that man might repent. After seeing that that man does not repent nor does he wish to study Torah, he then rises up and speaks ill of him. This is the meaning of, "but fools shall get (or: 'raise') shame," since he rises up and prosecutes.

161. פָּתַח וְאָמַר, וְאִם מִשְׁפַּחַת מִצְרַיִם לֹא תַעֲלֶה וְלֹא בָאָה וְלֹא עֲלֵיהֶם תִּהְיֶה הַמַּגֵּפָה וְגו׳. מַאי שְׁנָא מִצְרַיִם הָכָא, מִכָּל שְׁאַר עַמִּין, דְּהָא לְכֻלְּהוּ כְּתִיב וְלֹא עֲלֵיהֶם יְהִי הַגָּשֶׁם, וְהָכָא לָא. אֶלָּא הָא אוֹקְמוּהָ חַבְרַיָּיא, דְּהָא אַרְעָא דְּמִצְרַיִם לָא אִצְטְרִיךְ לְמִטְרָא, וְע״ד לָאו הִיא בִּכְלָלָא דְּאִינּוּן דְּבָעָן מִטְרָא, אֲבָל אִינּוּן דִּינָא אַחֲרָא אִסְתַּלָּק עָלַיְיהוּ, וְשַׁפִּיר קָאַמְרוּ.

161. He opened and said, "And if the family of Egypt does not go up, and does not come, then they shall have no overflow" (Zecharyah 14:18). HE ASKS, Why is Egypt different here than the rest of the nations? It is written of them all, "upon them shall be no rain" (Ibid. 17), yet here it is not WRITTEN SO. AND HE ANSWERS, The friends have explained that Egypt does not need rain, BECAUSE IT DRINKS THE WATERS OF THE NILE. Hence it is not among those in need of rain, but another punishment shall come to them. And it has been well said.

162. ת״ח, כְּתִיב כִּי הָאָרֶץ אֲשֶׁר אַתָּה בָא שָׁמָּה לְרִשְׁתָּהּ לֹא כְאֶרֶץ מִצְרַיִם הִיא אֲשֶׁר יְצָאתֶם מִשָּׁם וְגו׳. דְּהָא נַהֲרָא סָלִיק מִנֵּיהּ מִשְׁתַּקְיָיא אַרְעָא, אֲבָל הָכָא לִמְטַר הַשָּׁמַיִם תִּשְׁתֶּה מָּיִם, דְּהָא אַרְעָא קַדִּישָׁא מִן שְׁמַיָּא אִתְשַׁקְיָיא תָּדִיר. וְכַד יִשְׂרָאֵל הֲווֹ עַסְקִין בְּאוֹרַיְיתָא, הֲוָה

אִתְשַׁקְיָיא כַּדְקָא יָאוּת. וּמַאן דְּמָנַע אוֹרַיְיתָא מִנָּהּ, כְּאִילּוּ מָנַע טַב מִן כָּל עָלְמָא. עָאלוּ לְגוֹ מְעַרְתָּא חֲדָא דַּהֲוָה בְּאָרְחָא, עָאל הַהוּא גְּבַר עִמְּהוֹן, יָתְבוּ.

162. Come and see, it is written, "For the land, into which you go to possess it, is not as the land of Egypt, from whence you came out..." (Devarim 11:10), where the river rises and waters the land. But here, it "drinks water of the rain of heaven" (Ibid. 11), for the Holy Land always drinks from heaven. And when Yisrael were occupied with the Torah, it used to properly drink. And whoever withholds Torah from it, it is as if he withholds goodness from the whole world. They entered a cave on the way. The man entered with them and they sat down.

27. “Face to face”

A Synopsis

A stranger sits with the rabbis in a cave and speaks to them about Moses, saying that he was distinguished from all other prophets in the world. Moses was able to lift up his head and actually look at the supernal radiance, while still retaining a settled mind. As long as Joshua was with Moses he drew nourishment from Malchut and had no fear, but after he was on his own he could not even look directly at a messenger from God.

163. פָּתַח הַהוּא גַּבְרָא וְאָמַר, וְדִבֶּר יְיָ׳ אֶל מֹשֶׁה פָּנִים אֶל פָּנִים כַּאֲשֶׁר יְדַבֵּר וְגוֹ׳, הַאי קְרָא לָאו רֵישֵׁיהּ סֵיפֵיהּ וְלָאו סֵיפֵיהּ רֵישֵׁיהּ. וְלָא מִלָּה דָּא כְּמִלָּה דָּא, בְּקַדְמֵיתָא וְדִבֶּר ה׳ אֶל מֹשֶׁה פָּנִים אֶל פָּנִים שַׁפִּיר, לְבָתַר וְשָׁב אֶל הַמַּחֲנֶה, לְבָתַר וּמְשָׁרְתוֹ יְהוֹשֻׁעַ בִּן נוּן נַעַר, מַהוּ. א״ר אֶלְעָזָר וַדַּאי קוּדְשָׁא בְּרִיךְ הוּא אִתְרְעֵי בִּיקָרָא דִּילָן, דְּהַשְׁתָּא זִוּוּגָא דִּילָן בִּשְׁכִינְתָּא, וּשְׁכִינְתָּא לָא אִתְעֲדֵי מִנָּן. מַאן דְּפָתַח פִּתְחָא, לֵימָא מִלָּה.

163. The man began by saying, “And Hashem spoke to Moses face to face, as a man speaks…” (Shemot 33:11). In this verse the beginning does not fit the end nor does the end the beginning; a word does not fit with another. For at first it says, “And Hashem spoke to Moses face to face,” which is good. Then it says, “And he turned back to the camp” (Ibid.), WHICH IS NOT CONNECTED WITH, “AND HASHEM SPOKE…” Then, “but his servant Joshua, the son of Nun, a young man…” (Ibid.). What does that mean? IT HAS NO CONNECTION TO, “AND HE TURNED BACK TO THE CAMP.” Rabbi Elazar said, Surely the Holy One, blessed be He, wishes to honor us, for now we are connected with the Shechinah, who shall not leave us. Whoever opened this opening, let him speak.

164. פָּתַח וְאָמַר, וְדִבֶּר יְיָ׳ אֶל מֹשֶׁה פָּנִים אֶל פָּנִים, בְּכַמָּה דַּרְגִּין עִלָּאִין וְיַקִּירִין, אִתְפְּרַשׁ מֹשֶׁה נְבִיאָה מְהֵימָנָא, עַל כָּל שְׁאַר נְבִיאֵי דְּעָלְמָא. דְּהָא כֻּלְּהוּ לָקֳבְלֵיהּ, כְּקוֹף בִּפְנֵי בְּנֵי נָשָׁא. שְׁאַר נְבִיאֵי הֲווֹ מִסְתַּכְּלֵי בְּאַסְפַּקְלַרְיָא דְּלָא נָהִיר, וְעִם כָּל דָּא לָא הֲווֹ זַקְפָן אַנְפִּין

לְעֵילָּא לְאִסְתַּכְּלָא, אֶלָּא כְּמָה דִּכְתִּיב, וַאֲנִי הָיִיתִי נִרְדָּם עַל פָּנַי וּפָנַי אָרְצָה. וְלֹא עוֹד אֶלָּא דְּמִלִּין לָא הֲווֹ גַּבַּיְיהוּ בְּאִתְגַּלְיָיא.

164. He said, "And Hashem spoke to Moses face to face." With many supernal, precious grades Moses the faithful prophet was distinguished from all other prophets in the world, who were all before him as a monkey before man. The other prophets used to look at the non-shining mirror, yet they did not lift up their faces to behold, but, as written, "I was in a deep sleep on my face, and my face towards the ground" (Daniel 10:9). Moreover, these things were not in the open for them.

165. וּמֹשֶׁה נְבִיאָה מְהֵימְנָא לָאו הָכִי, דְּהוּא הֲוָה מִסְתָּכַּל בְּאַסְפַּקְלַרְיָא דְּנַהֲרָא, וְקָאִים בְּקִיּוּמֵיהּ. וְלֹא עוֹד, אֶלָּא דַּהֲוָה זָקִיף רֵישָׁא לְאִסְתַּכְּלָא, כְּמַאן דְּאָמַר לְחַבְרֵיהּ, זָקוֹף רֵישָׁךְ, וְיִסְתַּכְּלוּן אַנְפָּךְ בְּאַנְפִּי, בְּגִין דְּתִנְדַּע מִלַּי. כַּךְ מֹשֶׁה, פָּנִים אֶל פָּנִים זָקִיף רֵישָׁא, בְּלָא דְּחִילוּ, אַנְפּוֹי זַקְפָאן וּמִסְתַּכַּל בְּזִיו יְקָרָא עִלָּאָה, וְלָא אִשְׁתַּנֵּי דַּעְתּוֹי וְאַנְפּוֹי, כִּשְׁאַר נְבִיאִין, דְּכַד הֲווֹ נַבְאָן לְאִסְתַּכְּלָא, נַפְקָא מֵרְשׁוּתַיְיהוּ וּמִדַּעֲתַּיְיהוּ, וְאִשְׁתָּנֵי זִיו אַנְפַּיְיהוּ, וְלָא הֲווֹ יָדְעֵי מֵהַאי עָלְמָא כְּלוּם.

165. Moses the faithful prophet was not so, for he beheld the shining mirror and stood his ground. Furthermore, he used to lift up his head to look, as one saying to his neighbor, Lift up your head and let your face gaze at mine, so you shall know what I am saying. So did Moses do, who lifted up his head face to face without fear. His face was lifted UPWARDS and he was beholding the supernal, precious radiance. His mind and countenance did not change like other prophets, since OTHER PROPHETS, if they looked when prophesying, went out of their mind, their countenance changed, and they knew nothing of this world.

166. וּמֹשֶׁה לָאו הָכִי, דְּמֹשֶׁה בְּהַהוּא דַּרְגָּא עִלָּאָה מַמָּשׁ הֲוָה מִסְתָּכַּל, וְלָא נָפַק מֵרְשׁוּתֵיהּ וּמִן דַּעְתֵּיהּ, דְּהָא בְּשַׁעֲתָא דַּהֲוָה מִסְתָּכַּל בְּזִיו יְקָרָא עִלָּאָה, מִיַּד וְשָׁב אֶל הַמַּחֲנֶה, לְמַלְּלָא עִמְּהוֹן בְּכָל מַה דְּאִצְטְרִיכָאן, וְדַעְתּוֹי מִתְיַשְּׁבָא בֵּיהּ כְּקַדְמִיתָא, וְיַתִּיר. וְדָא הוּא וְשָׁב

אֶל הַמַּחֲנֶה. וּמְשָׁרְתוֹ יְהוֹשֻׁעַ בִּן נוּן נַעַר, וַדַּאי דַּהֲוָה יָנִיק מִתּוֹךְ הָאֹהֶל, אוֹלִיף לְאִסְתַּכְּלָא בְּרוּחַ קוּדְשָׁא, כד״א וְהַנַּעַר שְׁמוּאֵל מְשָׁרֵת אֶת יְיָ׳.

166. Moses was not so, since Moses used to behold that very highest grade, WHICH IS ZEIR ANPIN, and did not lose his mind, because when he beheld the precious supernal radiance, immediately, "he turned back to the camp" and talked with them about their needs. His mind was settled as before, and even more so. Hence, AFTER, "HASHEM SPOKE TO MOSES FACE TO FACE," it is said, "And he turned back to the camp." THEN IT IS SAID, "but his servant Joshua, the son of Nun, a young man..." Surely he received from the tent, for he was studying how to observe through the Holy Spirit, as written, "And the child Samuel ministered to Hashem" (I Shmuel 3:1).

167. ת״ח, כָּל זִמְנָא דַּהֲוָה יְהוֹשֻׁעַ לְגַבֵּי דְּמֹשֶׁה, הֲוָה אוֹלִיף וְאָנִיק מִתּוֹךְ הָאוֹהֶל, וְלָא דָּחִיל. בָּתַר דְּאִתְפְּרַשׁ מִמֹּשֶׁה, וַהֲוָה בִּלְחוֹדוֹי, מַה כְּתִיב, וַיִּפּוֹל יְהוֹשֻׁעַ אֶל פָּנָיו אַרְצָה וַיִּשְׁתָּחוּ, דְּלָא הֲוָה יָכִיל לְאִסְתַּכָּלָא, וְהַאי מֵחַד שְׁלִיחָא, כ״ש מֵאֲתָר אַחֲרָא.

167. Come and see, as long as Joshua was with Moses, he used to study and be nourished from within the tent, WHICH IS MALCHUT, and have no fear. After he separated from Moses and was on his own, it is written, "And Joshua fell on his face to the earth, and bowed down" (Joshua 5:14), because he could not look. This was before a messenger; all the more so from another place.

168. לְבַר נָשׁ, דְּאַפְקִיד מַלְכָּא גַּבֵּיהּ מָאנֵי דְּהַב וְאַבְנֵי יְקָר, כָּל זִמְנָא דְּמִשְׁתַּכַּח גַּבֵּיהּ, שַׁמָּשָׁא דְּבֵיתֵיהּ, אָחִיד בְּהוּ וְאִסְתַּכַּל בְּהוּ. כֵּיוָן דְּסָלִיק הַהוּא בַּר נָשׁ מֵעָלְמָא, לָא שָׁבִיק מַלְכָּא לְגַבֵּי שַׁמָּשָׁא כְּלוּם, וְאָחִיד פִּקְדּוֹנָא דִּילֵיהּ. אָמַר הַהוּא שַׁמָּשָׁא, וַוי דְּאָבַדִית. בְּיוֹמוֹי דְּמָארֵי, כָּל אִלֵּין הֲווֹ בִּידֵי.

168. THIS IS LIKENED to a man with whom the king deposited vessels of gold and precious stones. As long as it was with him, the servant of the house used to touch them and look at them. Once that man died, the king left nothing with the servant but came and took his keepsake. The servant said, Woe to me that I lost ALL THESE PRECIOUS THINGS. When my master was alive, they were all at my disposal.

169. כַּךְ יְהוֹשֻׁעַ, בְּיוֹמוֹי דְּמֹשֶׁה הֲוָה יָנִיק בְּכָל יוֹמָא מִתּוֹךְ הָאֹהֶל, וְלָא דָּחִיל. בָּתַר דְּשָׁכִיב, וַיִּפּוֹל יְהוֹשֻׁעַ אֶל פָּנָיו. וַאֲנָא בְּגִין דַּאֲנָא שְׁכִיחַ בְּגַוַּויְיכוּ, אֶסְתַּכַּל בְּמִלֵּי דְּאוֹרַיְיתָא, וְלָא אֱהֵא דָּחִיל. בָּתַר דְּאֶתְפְּרַשׁ מִנַּיְיכוּ, וְלָא אֵיכוּל לְאִסְתַּכְּלָא בִּלְחוֹדָאי.

169. Such was Joshua. When Moses was alive he used to be nourished daily from the tent, WHICH IS MALCHUT, and had no fear. After MOSES died, "Joshua fell on his face." And I, since I am among you, may look at words of Torah without fear. After withdrawing from you, I cannot look on my own.

28. "and you shall teach them diligently to your children"

A Synopsis

We read of a man's obligation to teach the Torah to his children and to be an example to them of how people should conduct themselves when they are guided by the Torah.

170. תּוּ פָּתַח וְאָמַר, וְשִׁנַּנְתָּם לְבָנֶיךָ וְדִבַּרְתָּ בָּם וְגוֹ'. כד"א חִצֶּיךָ שְׁנוּנִים. דְּבָעֵי ב"נ לְחַדְּדָא מִלֵּי דְּאוֹרַיְיתָא לִבְרֵיהּ, כְּחַרְבָּא דְּאִיהוּ שְׁנָנָא בִּתְרֵי סִטְרוֹי, בְּגִין דְּיֵיעוּל לֵיהּ חִדּוּדָא וְחֶדְוָה בְּאוֹרַיְיתָא, וְלָא יִשְׁתְּכַח לִבֵּיהּ בְּטִפְּשׁוּתָא. וְדִבַּרְתָּ בָּם, כָּל מִלִּין דְּאוֹרַיְיתָא, כָּל חַד וְחַד אוֹרְחָא לֵיהּ בִּלְחוֹדוֹי. וְדִבַּרְתָּ בָּם, וּתְדַבֵּר מִבָּעֵי לֵיהּ. אֶלָּא בָּעֵי ב"נ לְאַנְהָגָא גַּרְמֵיהּ בְּהוּ, וּלְאִתְנַהֲגָא גַּרְמֵיהּ, דְּלָא יִסְטֵי לִימִינָא וְלִשְׂמָאלָא.

170. He spoke further, "and you shall teach them diligently (Heb. *veshinantam*) to your children, and shall talk of them..." (Devarim 6:7). "VESHINANTAM" MEANS as in, "Your arrows are sharp (Heb. *shenunim*)" (Tehilim 45:6). For a man should teach his son words of Torah as a sword which is sharp on its two sides, so as to introduce into him sharpness and the joy of Torah, and his heart shall not be in folly. "and shall talk of them" means that all the things in the Torah, each THING has its own way. "and (shall) talk of them": HE ASKS, This verse should have been in the future tense, AND ANSWERS, The man himself should conduct himself by them and behave so as not to deviate right or left.

171. בְּשִׁבְתְּךָ בְּבֵיתֶךָ, לְאַנְהָגָא גַּרְמֵיהּ בְּבֵיתֵיהּ בְּאֹרַח מֵישָׁר וּבְאֹרַח תִּקּוּנָא, דְּיִלְפוּן מִנֵּיהּ בְּנֵי בֵּיתֵיהּ לְאַנְהָגָא גַּרְמֵיהּ עִמְּהוֹן בְּנַחַת וּבְחֵידוּ, וְלָא יָטִיל דְּחִילוּ בִּבְנֵי בֵּיתֵיהּ יַתִּיר, וְכָל עוֹבָדוֹי בְּבֵיתֵיהּ בְּאֹרַח תִּקּוּנָא. וּבְלֶכְתְּךָ בַדֶּרֶךְ, לְאַנְהָגָא בְּמִלֵּי דְּאוֹרַיְיתָא, וּלְתַקְּנָא גַּרְמֵיהּ בְּהוּ כְּמָה דְּאִצְטְרִיךְ, וּלְדַבְּרָא גַּרְמֵיהּ בְּאוֹרְחוֹי דְּאוֹרַיְיתָא. וּמַאי אִיהוּ. כְּמָה דְּיַעֲקֹב. לְדוֹרוֹן. לִקְרָבָא. לִצְלוֹתָא. וּצְלוֹתָא בָּעֵי לְצַלָּאָה לְמָארֵיהּ, וְעֵילָּא מִנְּהוֹן מִלֵּי דְּאוֹרַיְיתָא.

171. "when you sit in your house" (Devarim 6:7), namely conduct himself in his house in the right way, the correct way, so that his household will learn from him. He should deal with them composedly and joyfully, and not cause too much fear in his house. All his actions at home should be composed. "and when you walk by the way" means to be guided by words of Torah. And he should correct himself through them as proper to conduct himself by way of the Torah, which is like Jacob CONDUCTED HIMSELF ON THE WAY IN THREE THINGS, for a present, for prayer and for war. He should pray to his Master, BUT words of Torah are more valuable than prayer.

172. וּבְשָׁכְבְּךָ, לְדַבְּרָא גַּרְמֵיהּ בִּדְחִילוּ דְּמָארֵיהּ, בִּקְדוּשָּׁה, בַּעֲנָוָה דְּלָא יִשְׁתְּכַח חָצִיף לָקֳבְלֵיהּ דְּמָארֵיהּ. וּבְקוּמֶךָ, לְמֵיהַב תּוּשְׁבְּחָן לְמָארֵיהּ דְּאָתִיב נִשְׁמָתֵיהּ. דְּהָא בְּכַמָּה חִיּוּבִין אִשְׁתְּכַח קַמֵּי מָארֵיהּ, וְקוּדְשָׁא בְּרִיךְ הוּא עָבֵיד עִמֵּיהּ חֶסֶד, וְאָתִיב לָהּ לְגוּפֵיהּ. וּקְשַׁרְתָּם לְאוֹת עַל יָדְכָה. הָא אוּקְמוּהָ, עַל יַד כֵּהָה, וְדָא הוּא שְׂמָאלָא. וּבְסִפְרָא דְּאַגַּדְתָּא אָמַר, עַל יַד כֹּ"ה. כד"א כֹּ"ה יִהְיֶה זַרְעֶךָ.

172. "and when you lie down" (Ibid.) MEANS to conduct himself with fear of his Master, with holiness, with humility, not to be impudent before his Master. "and when you rise up" (Ibid.) means to give praise to his Master who returned his soul. For he is present before his Master with many sins, yet the Holy One, blessed be He, did kindness by him and returned his soul to his body. "And you shall bind them as frontlets between your eyes" (Ibid. 8), has been explained as referring to the dark hand, which is the left hand, WHICH IS DARKER AND WEAKER THAN THE RIGHT. In the book of Agadah it said, '*yadechah* (Eng. 'your hand')' means the hand (Heb. *yad*) of *koh*, WHICH IS MALCHUT CALLED *KOH*, as written, "Thus (Heb. *koh*) shall your seed be" (Beresheet 15:5).

29. The four compartments of the Tefilin

A Synopsis

We hear of how the friends who live in the south explained the four compartments of the Tefilin, but the rabbis say they do not agree with their interpretation because their inclusion of the supernal Keter as the first of the compartments is incorrect; this is because the supernal Keter includes everything. We learn about the four passages in the brain and the four passages in the heart; these are the four Mochin of Zeir Anpin and the four of Malchut. Rabbi Elazar talks about Judgment and Mercy, and says that one can always tell from which grade a prophet has drawn his prophecy.

173. וְחַבְרַיָּיא יַתְבֵי דָּרוֹמָא אוֹקְמוּהָ בְּרָזָא דִּלְהוֹן, אַרְבַּע בָּתֵּי דִּתְפִילִין כְּהַאי גַּוְונָא. קַדֶּשׁ לִי כָל בְּכוֹר סְתָם, לָקֳבֵל כִּתְרָא עִלָּאָה דִּכֹלָּא. וְהָיָה כִּי יְבִיאֲךָ, לָקֳבֵל חָכְמָה. שְׁמַע יִשְׂרָאֵל וְאָהַבְתָּ, לָקֳבֵל בִּינָה. וְהָיָה לָקֳבֵל חֶסֶד. לְבָתַר כְּלִילָן כֻּלְּהוּ בִּדְרוֹעָא שְׂמָאלָא, דְּאִקְרֵי עֹז. וּכְתִיב, וּבִזְרוֹעַ עֻזּוֹ. וְאֵין עֹז, אֶלָּא תּוֹרָה, וְאֵין עֹז, אֶלָּא תְּפִלִּין.

173. The friends who live in the south have explained, with their secrets, the four compartments of the Tefilin in the following manner. "Sanctify to Me (Heb. *kadesh li*) all the firstborn" (Shemot 13:2): FIRSTBORN unspecified corresponds to Keter, highest of all, WHICH IS CALLED FIRSTBORN. "And it shall be, when Hashem your Elohim shall bring you (Heb. *vehayah ki yeviacha*)" (Devarim 6:10) corresponds to Chochmah. "Hear, O Yisrael (Heb. *sh'ma Yisrael*)" together with "And you shall love Hashem your Elohim (Heb. *ve'ahavta*)" (Devarim 6:4-9) correspond to Binah. "And it shall come to pass, if you hearken (Heb. *vehayah im shamo'a*)" (Devarim 11:13-17) corresponds to Chesed. They are all then included in THE TEFILIN IN the left arm that is called might, as written, "and by the arm of His strength" (Yeshayah 62:8). Strength is nothing but Torah; strength is nothing but Tefilin.

174. וּמִלִּין לָא מִתְיַשְּׁבָן לְגַבָּן. מ"ט. בְּגִין דְּכִתְרָא עִלָּאָה הוּא כָּלִיל כֹּלָּא, דְּלָאו הוּא בְּחוּשְׁבְּנָא. וְעוֹד, וְהָיָה כִּי יְבִיאֲךָ בִּיצִיאַת מִצְרַיִם תַּלְיָיא, הַהוּא אֲתָר דְּאִשְׁתְּכַח בֵּיהּ חֵירוּ לְעַבְדִין, וְעַל דָּא לָא מִתְתַּקְּנָן בְּאָרְחַיְיהוּ. וַאֲנָן מֵחָכְמָה שַׁרְיָין, וְהָכִי הוּא וְקוּדְשָׁא בְּרִיךְ הוּא נָטִיל

לוֹן, אַרְבַּע לְעֵילָּא, אַרְבַּע לְתַתָּא, אַרְבַּע בַּאֲתַר דְּמוֹחָא. אַרְבַּע בַּאֲתַר דְּלִבָּא שַׁרְיָיא. בְּגִין דְּדָא בְּדָא אִתְקְשַׁר.

174. We do not agree with these words. The reason is that the supernal Keter includes everything, and is not part of the reckoning OF THE FOUR PASSAGES. Moreover, "And it shall be, when Hashem your Elohim shall bring you" derives from the exodus from Egypt, which is that place where freedom is bestowed on slaves, NAMELY BINAH. Hence the way OF OUR FRIENDS IN THE SOUTH is incorrect. But we start from Chochmah, THAT "SANCTIFY TO ME ALL THE FIRSTBORN" IS CHOCHMAH INSTEAD OF KETER, and it is so. And the Holy One, blessed be He, WHO IS ZEIR ANPIN, put on TEFILIN. There are four passages above and four below. HE EXPLAINS, there are four in the area of the brain, NAMELY, THEY ARE THE FOUR MOCHIN OF ZEIR ANPIN; there are four in the area where the heart dwells, WHICH IS MALCHUT, because the one is connected with the other; ZEIR ANPIN IS CONNECTED WITH MALCHUT.

175. וּבָעֵי ב"נ לְאִתְעַטְּרָא בְּהוּ, בְּגִין דְּאִיהוּ שְׁמָא קַדִּישָׁא עִלָּאָה. דִּכְתִּיב, וְרָאוּ כָּל עַמֵּי הָאָרֶץ כִּי שֵׁם יְיָ' וְגוֹ'. וְכָל מַאן דְּמִתְעַטַּר בְּעִטְרָא קַדִּישָׁא עִלָּאָה דָּא, אִקְרֵי מֶלֶךְ בְּאַרְעָא. וְקוּדְשָׁא בְּרִיךְ הוּא מֶלֶךְ בִּרְקִיעַ. הה"ד מֶלֶךְ אָסוּר בָּרְהָטִים. כְּמָה דְּקוּדְשָׁא בְּרִיךְ הוּא מֶלֶךְ לְעֵילָּא, הָכִי נָמֵי הוּא מֶלֶךְ לְתַתָּא. וּכְתַבְתָּם עַל מְזוּזוֹת בֵּיתֶךָ, בְּגִין דִּיהֱוֵי בַּר נָשׁ שְׁלִים בְּכֹלָּא, וְיִשְׁתְּכַּח שְׁלִים בְּפִקּוּדֵי דְּמָארֵיהּ, רָשִׁים לְעֵילָּא, רָשִׁים לְתַתָּא, זַכָּאָה חוּלָקֵהוֹן דְּיִשְׂרָאֵל.

175. Man should be crowned with them because they are the supernal Holy Name, NAMELY, YUD HEI VAV HEI, as written, "And all people of the earth shall see that you are called by the name of Hashem..." (Devarim 28:10). Whoever is adorned with this supernal holy crown is called a king on earth. And the Holy One, blessed be He, is a king in heaven. This is the meaning of, "a king caught in its tresses" (Shir Hashirim 7:6). Just as the Holy One, blessed be He, is king above, so is he a king below. "And you shall write them upon the doorposts of your house" (Devarim 6:9), so that the man shall be perfect in everything and perfect by his Master's commandments, marked above and marked below. Happy is the lot of Yisrael.

176. פָּתַח ר׳ אֶלְעָזָר וְאָמַר, תְּרֵי קְרָאֵי אַשְׁכַּחְנָא, דְּאע״ג דְּכֹלָּא בְּחַד דַּרְגָּא תַּלְיָין, לָאו אִינּוּן מִדַּרְגָּא חַד. חַד קְרָא כְּתִיב, כֹּה אָמַר יְיָ׳ צְבָאוֹת. וְחַד קְרָא כְּתִיב, כֹּה אָמַר יְיָ׳ אֱלֹהִים. מַה בֵּין הַאי לְהַאי. אֶלָּא בְּזִמְנָא דִּכְתִּיב כֹּה אָמַר יְיָ׳ צְבָאוֹת, כְּדֵין מִלָּה אַתְיָא בְּרַחֲמֵי. וּבְזִמְנָא דִּכְתִּיב כֹּה אָמַר יְיָ׳ אֱלֹהִים, כְּדֵין מִלָּה אַתְיָא בְּדִינָא.

176. Rabbi Elazar opened and said, I have found two verses, and though it comes from one grade, nevertheless they are not of the same grade. The one verse writes, "Thus says Hashem Tzva'ot (Eng. 'Lord of Hosts')" (Chagai 1:7), and another writes, "Thus says Hashem Elohim" (Yeshayah 7:7). What is the difference between them? HE ANSWERS, When it is written, "Thus says Hashem Tzva'ot" the matter comes with Mercy, and when it is written, "Thus says Adonai Elohim," it comes with Judgment.

177. כֹּה אָמַר יְיָ׳ צְבָאוֹת, בְּגִין דְּהַאי כֹּה, אִתְבָּרְכָא מִצַּדִּיק וּמִנֶּצַח וְהוֹד, דְּאִקְרֵי יְיָ׳ צְבָאוֹת. וּכְדֵין, מִלָּה בְּאִתְבַּסְּמוּתָא אַתְיָיא, דְּהָא מֵאֲתָר דָּא קָא אַתְיָא. כֹּה אָמַר יְיָ׳ אֱלֹהִים, כְּדֵין הַאי כֹּה יַנְקָא מִסִּטְרָא דְּדִינָא, מֵאֲתָר דִּגְבוּרָה עִלָּאָה, וְאוּלִיפְנָא מֵאַבָּא, דְּדִינָא הוּא בְּרַחֲמֵי, בְּגִין דִּכְתִּיב יְיָ׳ אֱלֹהִים.

177. HE EXPLAINS THE ISSUE: IN THE VERSE, "Thus (Heb. *koh*) says Hashem Tzva'ot," it is because '*koh*', WHICH IS MALCHUT, is blessed by the Righteous, WHO IS YESOD, and by Netzach and Hod that are called Hashem Tzva'ot. Then it comes out tempered because it issues from that place, YESOD. IN THE VERSE, "Thus says Adonai Elohim," this '*koh*', WHICH IS MALCHUT, is nourished from the aspect of Judgment and from the place of supernal Gvurah, THAT IS, GVURAH OF ZEIR ANPIN. I have learned from my father that Judgment is tempered with Mercy, since it is written, "Hashem Elohim," AND YUD HEI VAV HEI IS MERCY AND ELOHIM IS JUDGMENT.

178. דְּהָא אֱלֹהִים גְּבוּרָה הוּא בְּכָל אֲתָר, אֲדֹנָי, גְּבוּרָה תַּתָּאָה הִיא בְּכָל אֲתָר. וְעַל דָּא אִשְׁתְּמוֹדְעָן מִלֵּי מִפּוּמָא דִּנְבִיאָה, וְהוּא הֲוָה

מִתְכַּוֵּין לְמֵימַר מִלָּה מֵאַתְרֵיהּ. וּכְדֵין הֲווֹ יַדְעֵי אִלֵּין בְּנֵי מְהֵימְנוּתָא, מֵאָן אֲתָר תַּלְיָיא מִלְּתָא.

178. For Elohim is always Gvurah. Adonai is always lower Gvurah. Hence it is recognized from the mouth of the prophet, ACCORDING TO THE NAME HE MENTIONED, FROM WHICH GRADE HE PROPHESIZED as he directed his attention to say something from its own place. The faithful would then know whence the matter is from.

30. "Curse Meroz"

A Synopsis

The rabbis talk about the angel who will take revenge on the enemies of Yisrael in the future, and we also hear about "the stars in their courses fought against Sisera."

179. פָּתַח רַבִּי אַחָא וְאָמַר אוֹרוּ מֵרוֹז אָמַר מַלְאַךְ יְיָ׳ וְגוֹ׳. ת״ח, הַאי קְרָא רָזָא הוּא בְּרָזִין עִלָּאִין. בְּשַׁעֲתָא דְּמַלְכָּא קַדִּישָׁא מָסַר בֵּיתֵיהּ בִּידָא דְּמַטְרוֹנִיתָא כָּל זַיְינִין וְרוּמְחִין וּבַלִּיסְטְרָאוֹת דִּילֵיהּ אַפְקִיד בִּידָהָא, וְכָל אִינּוּן מַגִּיחֵי קְרָבָא דִּילֵיהּ אַפְקִיד עִמָּהּ. הה״ד, הִנֵּה מִטָּתוֹ שֶׁלִּשְׁלֹמֹה שִׁשִּׁים גִּבּוֹרִים סָבִיב לָהּ מִגִּבּוֹרֵי יִשְׂרָאֵל, וְהָא אוֹקְמוּהָ, וְכַד אֲגַח קוּדְשָׁא בְּרִיךְ הוּא קְרָבָא, בְּאִינּוּן גִּבּוֹרִין מַגִּיחֵי קְרָבָא דְּקָאָמַרָן אַגַח, וְאִינּוּן אִקְרוּן מְלוּמְדֵי מִלְחָמָה.

179. Rabbi Acha opened and said, "Curse Meroz, said the angel of Hashem" (Shoftim 5:23). Come and see, this verse is secret among supernal secrets. When the Holy King gave His house into the hands of the Queen, He put Her in charge over all weapons, lances and slings, and over all His soldiers. This is the meaning of, "Behold it is his litter, that of Solomon (THE SECRET OF MALCHUT)! Sixty valiant men are round about it, of the mighty men of Yisrael" (Shir Hashirim 3:7). It has already been explained THAT THEY ARE THE SECRET OF CHESED, GVURAH, TIFERET, NETZACH, HOD AND YESOD FROM THE SIDE OF GVURAH, EACH INCLUDING TEN. When the Holy One, blessed be He, wages war, He does so through these warring mighty men we spoke of. They are considered "expert in war" (Ibid. 8).

180. כְּתִיב מִן שָׁמַיִם נִלְחָמוּ הַכּוֹכָבִים מִמְּסִלּוֹתָם נִלְחֲמוּ עִם סִיסְרָא וְגוֹ׳. וּתְנַן, בְּהַאי שַׁעֲתָא דְּאִתְנְדִיבוּ יִשְׂרָאֵל לְגַלָּאָה רְשִׁימָא קַדִּישָׁא בִּבְשָׂרֵהוֹן, כְּדֵין הַאי חֶרֶב נוֹקֶמֶת נְקַם בְּרִית, כָּנַשׁ כָּל חֵילָא דִּילֵיהּ, וְכָל זַיְינִין, וְכָל אִינּוּן מַגִּיחֵי קְרָבָא, לְאַגָּחָא קְרָבָא עִמֵּיהּ דְּסִיסְרָא. וְכוֹכְבַיָּיא הֲווּ אוֹשְׁדִין נוּרָא מִלְּעֵילָא. וְאָמַר רַבִּי שִׁמְעוֹן, כָּל כּוֹכָב וְכוֹכָב אִית לֵיהּ שְׁמָא בִּלְחוֹדוֹי, וְכֻלְּהוּ בִּשְׁמָהָן אִקְרוּן.

180. It is written, "They fought from heaven; the stars in their courses fought against Sisera" (Shoftim 5:20). We have learned that when Yisrael were dedicated to exposing the holy imprint OF CIRCUMCISION in their flesh, the sword avenging the covenant, WHICH IS MALCHUT, gathered all its armies, all weapons and all soldiers to wage war with Sisera, and the stars were pouring fire from above. Rabbi Shimon said that every star has its own name, AS WRITTEN, "He calls them all by their names" (Tehilim 147:4).

181. אָמַר לוֹן קוּדְשָׁא בְּרִיךְ הוּא, אִתְעַתְּדוּ לְנַקְמָא נוּקְמָא דְּבָנַי. תְּרֵי נוּקְמֵי אֲנָא זַמִּין לְאִתְפָּרְעָא מִנַּיְיהוּ, חַד נוּקְמָא דְּשִׁית מְאָה רְתִיכִין דְּאוֹזִיף לֵיהּ לְרַבְרְבָא דְּמִצְרָאֵי, בְּגִין לְאַגָּחָא קְרָבָא בְּהוּ בְּיִשְׂרָאֵל, דִּכְתִּיב וַיִּקַּח שֵׁשׁ מֵאוֹת רֶכֶב בָּחוּר וְכֹל רֶכֶב מִצְרָיִם. וְחַד נוּקְמָא דְּבָנַי, דְּעָאקוּ לְהוּ עַד הַשְׁתָּא. וּבְגִין כַּךְ אִתְדָּנוּ בִּתְרֵין דִּינִין, חַד בְּמַיָּיא, וְחַד בְּאֶשָּׁא. בְּמַיָּיא, דִּכְתִּיב נַחַל קִישׁוֹן גְּרָפָם. בְּאֶשָּׁא, דִּכְתִּיב הַכּוֹכָבִים מִמְּסִלּוֹתָם.

181. The Holy One, blessed be He, said TO THE STARS, 'Prepare yourself to revenge ON SISERA the vengeance of My children. Two vengeances shall I take from them. The first vengeance is for the six hundred chosen chariots that he left to the ministers of Egypt so as to war against Yisrael, as written, "and he took six hundred chosen chariots, and all the chariots of Egypt" (Shemot 14:7). Another vengeance is for My children, for their distressing them until now'. For that reason they were sentenced to two punishments, one with water and one with fire; with water, as written, "The wadi of Kishon swept them away" (Shoftim 5:21), and by fire, as written, "the stars in their courses."

182. וּבְאִינּוּן כֹּכָבַיָּיא, אִית כֹּכָבָא חַד דְּלָא אָתָא לְהַהוּא נוּקְמָא, וְאִתְלַטְיָא לְעָלְמִין, דְּכַד שָׁארִי לְאַנְהֳרָא, אָתָאן שְׁאַר כֹּכָבַיָּיא וּבַלְעִין לֵיהּ, וּלְכָל סִיעָתָא דִּילֵיהּ, וְאִתְאֲבִידוּ כֻּלְּהוּ כַּחֲדָא. כד"א, אוֹרוּ מֵרוֹז אָמַר מַלְאַךְ יְיָ'. וְכִי רְשׁוּת אִית לְמַלְאָכָא בְּהַאי. אֶלָּא דָּא הוּא מַלְאָךְ, דִּכְתִּיב בֵּיהּ וַיִּסַּע מַלְאַךְ הָאֱלֹהִים הַהוֹלֵךְ לִפְנֵי מַחֲנֵה יִשְׂרָאֵל. וְדָא הוּא דְּכָל קְרָבִין דִּילֵיהּ אִינּוּן.

182. Among those stars there was one who did not come for that vengeance and was eternally cursed, so that when it starts to illuminate, the other stars come and swallow it with its whole camp and they perish together, as written, "Curse Meroz, said the angel of Hashem." HE ASKS, Does that angel have permission to do that, TO CURSE ANYONE? AND HE ANSWERS, This is the angel of whom it is written, "And the angel of Elohim, who went before the camp of Yisrael" (Shemot 14:19). It is he to whom these wars belong, NAMELY MALCHUT.

183. כִּי לֹא בָאוּ לְעֶזְרַת יְיָ׳, כַּד נַפְקוּ יִשְׂרָאֵל מִמִּצְרַיִם. לְעֶזְרַת יְיָ׳ בַּגִּבּוֹרִים, בְּאִינּוּן שִׁשִּׁים גִּבּוֹרִים כַּד אִזְדְּמָנוּ קְרָבָא עִם סִיסְרָא. וְדָא מַלְאָךְ, רָזָא דְּכָל דִּינִין וְכָל קְרָבִין דְּמַלְכָּא בִּרְשׁוּתֵיהּ. וְעַל דָּא אָמַר, מַלְאַךְ יְיָ׳. וְדָא הוּא דִּכְתִּיב, הַמַּלְאָךְ הַגּוֹאֵל אוֹתִי וְגוֹ׳, וְהָא אוּקְמוּהָ חַבְרַיָּיא. וְדָא זְמִינָא לְמֶהֱוֵי עִלָּאָה וְיַקִּירָא לְזִמְנָא דְּאָתֵי. וּבְדָא יִתְרַבֵּי שְׁמָא קַדִּישָׁא. וּבְדָא זַמִּין קוּדְשָׁא בְּרִיךְ הוּא לְאִתְפָּרְעָא מֵעַמִּין עכו״ם. וְעַל דָּא כְּתִיב, וְהִתְגַּדִּלְתִּי וְהִתְקַדִּשְׁתִּי וְגוֹ׳. אַזְלוּ, עַד דְּמָטוּ לְגַבֵּיהּ דְּר״ש, כֵּיוָן דְּחָמָא לוֹן, אָמַר ר״ש הָא שְׁכִינְתָּא הָכָא, וַדַּאי צְרִיכִין אֲנָן לְמֶחְזָק טִיבוּ לְאַנְפֵּי שְׁכִינְתָּא.

183. "because they did not come to the help of Hashem" (Shoftim 5:23), namely when Yisrael came out of Egypt, "to the help of Hashem against the mighty men" (Ibid.), namely the mighty men who came to fight together with Sisera, NAMELY, THE SIXTY MIGHTY MEN AROUND THE BED OF SOLOMON. The secret of this angel is that all punishment and all the King's wars are his responsibility. Hence it says, "the angel of Hashem." This is the meaning of, "the angel who redeemed me…" (Beresheet 48:16), NAMELY MALCHUT. The friends have already explained it. This ANGEL will be lofty and precious in the future to come. Thus the Holy Name will be magnified. By this ANGEL the Holy One, blessed be He, will take revenge on the heathen nations. Of this it is written, "Thus will I magnify Myself and sanctify Myself…" (Yechezkel 38:23). They walked until they reached Rabbi Shimon. When he saw them, Rabbi Shimon said, The Shechinah is here. Surely it behooves us to be grateful to the Shechinah.

31. "Lo, it is yet high day"

A Synopsis

Rabbi Shimon says that at the end of the exile Yisrael will return to the Holy Land through the merit of their study in the Torah, but this depends on their repentance. Another explanation of the title verse is that the day of exile was lengthened due to Yisrael's evil deeds. Yisrael cannot gather together until harsh Judgment is removed by the Holy Sfirot. We learn that "the end of days" refers to Malchut, who shall be returned to her place, and the great mating that will take place between Zeir Anpin and Malchut.

184. פָּתַח וְאָמַר הֵן עוֹד הַיּוֹם גָּדוֹל וְגוֹ׳. הַאי קְרָא אוּקְמוּהָ, דְּכַד יִשְׂרָאֵל יִתְעֲרוּן תְּשׁוּבָה לְקָמֵי קוּדְשָׁא בְּרִיךְ הוּא, בִּזְכוּ אוֹרַיְיתָא יְתוּבוּן לְאַרְעָא קַדִּישָׁא, וְיִתְכַּנְשׁוּן מִן גָּלוּתָא. דְּהָא וַדַּאי יוֹמָא חַד יְהֵא גָּלוּתָא לְיִשְׂרָאֵל, וְלָא יַתִּיר. הה״ד, נְתָנַנִי שׁוֹמֵמָה כָּל הַיּוֹם דָּוָה. וְאִי לָא יְתוּבוּן, קוּדְשָׁא בְּרִיךְ הוּא אָמַר, הֵן עוֹד הַיּוֹם גָּדוֹל לֹא עֵת הֵאָסֵף הַמִּקְנֶה בְּלָא זְכוּ וּבְלָא עוֹבָדִין דְּכַשְׁרָן. אֲבָל אַסְוָתָא חַד לְכוּ, הַשְׁקוּ הַצֹּאן, אִשְׁתַּדָּלוּ בְּאוֹרַיְיתָא, דְּאִתְשַׁקְיִיוּ מֵימֵי אוֹרַיְיתָא, וּלְכוּ רְעוּ, לַאֲתָר דְּנַיְיחָא לַאֲתָר טָבָא וְכִסּוּפָא דְּאַחֲסַנְתֵּיכוֹן.

184. He opened with the verse, "Lo, it is yet high day" (Beresheet 29:7). This verse has been explained that when Yisrael will rouse with repentance before the Holy One, blessed be He, they will return to the holy land and gather from exile by the merit of the Torah, since surely Yisrael will be in exile for but a day and no more, NAMELY, THE DAY OF THE HOLY ONE, BLESSED BE HE, WHICH IS A THOUSAND YEARS LONG, NAMELY THE FIFTH MILLENNIUM. This is the meaning of, "He has made me desolate and faint all the day" (Eichah 1:13). If they will not repent THEN, the Holy One, blessed be He, will say, "Lo, it is yet high day, neither is it time that the cattle should be gathered together" without merits and good deeds. But there is one remedy for you: "water the sheep" (Ibid.), delve into the Torah, so they will be watered by the waters of Torah, "and go and feed them," (Ibid.) AND GO to a resting place, a good place, the pleasantness of your possession.

185. ד״א הֵן עוֹד הַיּוֹם גָּדוֹל, דָּא הוּא יוֹם דְּאִקְרֵי יוֹם מְהוּמָה וּמְבוּסָה

וּמְבוּכָה, דִּי בְּהַהוּא יוֹם אִתְחֲרִיב בֵּי מַקְדְּשָׁא, וְנָפְלוּ יִשְׂרָאֵל בְּגָלוּתָא. וּבְגִין עוֹבָדִין בִּישִׁין, הַהוּא יוֹמָא אִתְמְשַׁךְ וְאִתְרְבֵּי, הה"ד הֵן עוֹד הַיּוֹם גָּדוֹל לֹא עֵת הֵאָסֵף הַמִּקְנֶה, בְּגִין דְּאִינּוּן מַשְׁכִין לֵיהּ לְהַהוּא יוֹמָא. הַשְׁקוּ הַצֹּאן, כְּמָה דְּאִתְּמַר בְּמִלֵּי דְּאוֹרַיְיתָא, דְּהָא בִּזְכוּתָא דְּאוֹרַיְיתָא יִפְּקוּן יִשְׂרָאֵל מִן גָּלוּתָא.

185. According to another explanation, "Lo, it is yet high day" is the day called, "a day of trouble, and of trampling, and of confusion" (Yeshayah 22:5), on which day the Temple was destroyed and Yisrael fell into exile. Because of the evil deeds YISRAEL DO, that day lengthens and increases. This is the meaning of, "Lo, it is yet high day, neither is it time that the cattle should be gathered together," because they lengthen that day OF EXILE. "water the sheep" is as we learned, namely with words of Torah, because through Torah Yisrael will come out of exile.

186. יִשְׂרָאֵל מַאי קָא אַמְרֵי. וַיֹּאמְרוּ לֹא נוּכַל עַד אֲשֶׁר יֵאָסְפוּ כָּל הָעֲדָרִים, עַד דְּיִתְכַּנְּשׁוּ כָּל שְׁאַר יוֹמִין עִלָּאִין, וְגָלְלוּ אֶת הָאֶבֶן, וְיִגַּנְדְּרוּן לְהַהוּא דִּינָא קַשְׁיָא דְּהַהוּא יוֹמָא דְּשַׁלְטָא עַל פִּי הַבְּאֵר, וְאִשְׁתְּכָחַת הַהִיא בא"ר בְּגָלוּתָא עִמָּנָא. וְכַד אִתְגַּלְיָיא הַאי בא"ר, וְהַהוּא אֶבֶן לָא שַׁלְטָא עָלָהּ, מִיַּד וְהִשְׁקִינוּ הַצֹּאן.

186. What do Yisrael say: "We cannot, until all the flocks are gathered together" (Beresheet 29:8), namely until all the rest of the supernal days, NAMELY THE HOLY SFIROT, will gather, "and till they roll the stone," roll the harsh Judgment that on that day rules over "the well's mouth" (Ibid.). FOR THIS REASON the well, WHICH IS MALCHUT, is with us in exile. As soon as that well will be exposed and that stone, WHICH IS HARSH JUDGMENT, will have no power over it, "we may water the sheep" (Ibid.).

187. וְזַמִּין קוּדְשָׁא בְּרִיךְ הוּא בְּסוֹף יוֹמַיָּא, לְאַהֲדְרָא לְיִשְׂרָאֵל לְאַרְעָא קַדִּישָׁא, וּלְאַכְנְשָׁא לוֹן מִגָּלוּתָא. וּמַאן אִינּוּן סוֹף יוֹמַיָּא הַהוּא דְּהִיא אַחֲרִית הַיָּמִים. בְּהַאי אַחֲרִית הַיָּמִים, יִשְׂרָאֵל סַבְלוּ גָּלוּתָא. הה"ד, בַּצַּר לְךָ וּמְצָאוּךָ כֹּל הַדְּבָרִים הָאֵלֶּה בְּאַחֲרִית הַיָּמִים, וּכְתִיב וְקָרָאת

אֶתְכֶם הָרָעָה בְּאַחֲרִית הַיָּמִים. בְּאַחֲרִית הַיָּמִים דַּיְיקָא, וְדָא הִיא כְּנֶסֶת יִשְׂרָאֵל בְּגָלוּתָא. וְעִם אַחֲרִית הַיָּמִים דָּא, קַבִּילוּ עוֹנְשָׁא בְּגָלוּתָא. וּבְדָא יַעְבִּיד קוּדְשָׁא בְּרִיךְ הוּא נוּקְמִין לְיִשְׂרָאֵל תְּדִירָא, הה״ד אֲשֶׁר יַעֲשֶׂה הָעָם הַזֶּה לְעַמְּךָ בְּאַחֲרִית הַיָּמִים. וּבְכָל אֲתָר דָּא הִיא, וְקוּדְשָׁא בְּרִיךְ הוּא זַמִּין לְאָתָבָא לָהּ לְאַתְרָהָא, הה״ד וְהָיָה בְּאַחֲרִית הַיָּמִים נָכוֹן יִהְיֶה הַר בֵּית יְיָ׳ וְגוֹ׳ וְדָא הוּא יוֹם.

187. The Holy One, blessed be He, at the end of days, will return Yisrael to the holy land and gather them from exile. The end of days is that which is the last of the days, NAMELY MALCHUT, WHICH IS THE LAST OF THE SFIROT, CALLED DAYS. During the end of days Yisrael suffer exile. This is what is meant by, "When you are in distress, and all these things are come upon you, in the latter days" (Devarim 4:30), and, "and evil will befall you in the latter days (lit. 'the end of days')" (Devarim 31:29). The "latter days" is precise, because it is the Congregation of Yisrael, WHICH IS MALCHUT, which is in exile. Together with this end of days they receive punishment in exile. With it the Holy One, blessed be He, will wreak vengeances for Yisrael constantly, as written, "what this people shall do to your people in the latter days" (Bemidbar 24:14). Wherever IT IS WRITTEN, 'THE END OF DAYS' it refers to her, MALCHUT. And the Holy One, blessed be He, will return her to her place. This is the meaning of, "And it shall come to pass in the last days, that the mountain of Hashem's house shall be established" (Yeshayah 2:2). This is that which is CALLED day, NAMELY THE LAST DAY, SINCE EACH SFIRAH IS CALLED DAY.

188. וּמִדְּשָׁארֵי צֵל לְמֶעְבַּד בְּשֵׁירוּתָא דְּיוֹמָא אָחֳרָא, כְּמָה בִּזְמְנָא דְּאִתְחֲרִיב מַקְדְּשָׁא הֲוָה, וְנָטָה צֵל לְמֵיעַל, הה״ד, אוֹי לָנוּ כִּי פָנָה הַיּוֹם כִּי יִנָּטוּ צִלְלֵי עָרֶב. יוֹם וְצֵל, הוּא סוֹף גָּלוּתָא. וְשִׁיעוּרָא דְּהַאי צֵל, שִׁית קְמָצִין וּפַלְגָּא. וּבְגוּדָל דְּמִשְׁחָא דְּבַר נָשׁ, גְּבַר בֵּין גּוּבְרִין. וְדוּכְרָנָא דְּהַאי רָזָא דְּבֵין חַבְרַיָּיא, דִּכְתִּיב כִּי תְמוֹל אֲנַחְנוּ וְלֹא נֵדָע כִּי צֵל יָמֵינוּ עֲלֵי אָרֶץ. כִּי תְמוֹל אֲנַחְנוּ בְּגָלוּתָא, וְלָא הֲוֵינָא יַדְעֵי כִּי צֵל יָמֵינוּ עֲלֵי אָרֶץ, לְאַשְׁרָאָה לוֹן קוּדְשָׁא בְּרִיךְ הוּא עֲלֵי אָרֶץ.

188. Once a shadow started to form at the beginning of the other day AFTER THE FIFTH MILLENNIUM, as during the time when the Temple was destroyed when the shadow was about to be gathered; THAT IS, JUST LIKE DURING THE DESTRUCTION OF THE TEMPLE WAS WHEN THE SHADOW BEGAN TO BE GATHERED, SO WILL REDEMPTION COME WHEN THE SHADOW WILL BEGIN TO EMERGE. WHEN THERE WILL BE day and shadow, it will be the end of exile. The measure of that shadow is six thumbs long for the height of a man among men, NAMELY, AN AVERAGE PERSON. This secret is remembered among the friends through the verse, "for we are but of yesterday, and know nothing, because our days upon earth are a shadow" (Iyov 8:9). "for we are but of yesterday," namely in exile; "and know nothing, because our days upon earth are a shadow," which means the Holy One, blessed be He, wants the shadow and day to rest upon the earth.

189. זַכָּאָה חוּלָקֵיהּ, מַאן דְּחָמֵי לֵיהּ, וְזַכָּאָה חוּלָקֵיהּ מַאן דְּלָא חָמֵי לֵיהּ. וַוי לְמַאן דְּיִזְדַּמַּן כַּד יִתְבַּע אַרְיָא רַבְרְבָא, לְאִתְחַבְּרָא לְנוּקְבֵיהּ. כָּל שֶׁכֵּן בְּשַׁעֲתָא דְּיִזְדַּוְּוגֵן כַּחֲדָא, עַל הַהִיא שַׁעֲתָא כְּתִיב, אַרְיֵה שָׁאָג מִי לֹא יִירָא וְגוֹ'.

189. Happy is the portion of he who sees him, MESSIAH, and happy is the portion of he who sees him not. Woe to him who shall be present when the great lion will demand to mate with his female, and more so when they will mate together, NAMELY ZEIR ANPIN WITH MALCHUT AT THE TIME OF REDEMPTION. Of that hour it is written, "The lion has roared, who will not fear..." (Amos 3:8).

190. ת"ח, בְּקַדְמֵיתָא כְּתִיב, שָׁאֹג יִשְׁאַג עַל נָוֵהוּ. וּבְהַהוּא זִמְנָא כַּד יִפּוּק לְקַבְּלָא לְבַת זוּגוֹ, כְּדֵין אַרְיֵה שָׁאָג מִי לֹא יִירָא יְיָ' אֱלֹהִים דִּבֶּר מִי לֹא יִנָּבֵא. בְּהַהִיא שַׁעֲתָא כְּתִיב, וְשָׁב יְיָ' אֱלֹהֶיךָ אֶת שְׁבוּתְךָ וְגוֹ', וְשָׁב מַאי הוּא. אֶלָּא קוּדְשָׁא בְּרִיךְ הוּא שָׁב כְּנֶסֶת יִשְׂרָאֵל מִגָּלוּתָא, וְשָׁב צַדִּיק לְאִזְדַּוְּוגָא בְּאַתְרֵיהּ. כְּדֵין כְּתִיב, אַךְ צַדִּיקִים יוֹדוּ לִשְׁמֶךָ יֵשְׁבוּ יְשָׁרִים אֶת פָּנֶיךָ.

190. Come and see, at first it is written, "He shall mightily roar because of His habitation" (Yirmeyah 25:30), WHICH IS DURING EXILE. When ZEIR

ANPIN will come out to receive his mate, MALCHUT, it is said, "The lion has roared, who will not fear"; "Adonai Elohim has spoken, who can but prophesy" (Amos 3:8). At that time it is written, "then Hashem your Elohim will turn your captivity" (Devarim 30:3). What is meant by "turn"? AND HE ANSWERS, The Holy One, blessed be He, returns the Congregation of Yisrael from exile, and the righteous returns to join its place. Then it is written, "Surely the righteous shall give thanks to Your name; the upright shall dwell in (or: 'return to') Your presence" (Tehilim 140:14).

32. From the top of Atzilut to the resurrection of the dead

A Synopsis

In this Mishnah we read an esoteric explanation of the story of Creation and the history of man that followed. To conclude Vaetchanan, we hear that at the time of the resurrection the vessels will be perfected and all sin will be removed from the world.

191. מַתְנִיתִין, לְכוֹן בְּנֵי נָשָׁא, מָארֵי דְּחָכְמְתָא, מָארֵי דְּסֻכַלְתָנוּ, קָלָא קָרֵי. מַאן מִנְּכוֹן דְּאִתְחַכָּם, וְיָדַע, בְּשַׁעֲתָא דְּרֵישָׁא חִיוָּורָא, אַתְקִין רֵישָׁא, רְשִׁימָא מֵעֵילָּא לְתַתָּא, וּמִתַּתָּא לְעֵילָּא. אַתְקִין סְטָר צָפוֹן, בְּעִטּוּרָא דְּקוּנָארִיתָא, בֵּיהּ רָשִׁים עוּמְקָא דִּתְהוֹמָא עִלָּאָה, דְּסָלִיק וְנָחִית בְּגַוֵּויהּ. נָחִית חַד דַּרְגָּא טְמִירָא, בַּאֲלַף וַחֲמֵשׁ מְאָה רְשִׁימִין, דַּאֲלַף וַחֲמֵשׁ מְאָה עָלְמִין.

191. Mishnah. To you, sons of men, men of wisdom, men of understanding, a voice is calling. Whoever of you attained wisdom and knows that when the white head, WHICH IS KETER, prepared a SECOND head, WHICH IS CHOCHMAH that is imprinted from above downwards and from below upwards, installed in the north direction, NAMELY THE LEFT COLUMN OF BINAH, an adornment of a pond of water, it imprinted in it the depth of the supernal abyss, NAMELY THE DEPTH OF BINAH CALLED THE SUPERNAL ABYSS that rises and falls inside it. A hidden grade descended with 1,500 imprints and 1,500 worlds.

192. תְּחוֹתֵיהּ תַּטְלֵל חַד חֵיוַת בָּרָא, וְקַרְנִין עֲשַׂר לָהּ. וַאֲרוּ עַיְינִין כְּעַיְינֵי אֱנָשָׁא לְחֵיוָתָא, וּפוּם מְמַלֵּל רַבְרְבָן. כַּד סַלְקָא, אַזְלַא בִּימָמָא, טְמִירָא בְּלֵילְיָא. כַּד נַחְתָּא, טְמִירָא בִּימָמָא, וְאַזְלָא בְּלֵילְיָא. כַּד נַטְלָא, מִזְדַּעְזְעָן אַרְבַּע מַגְרוּפֵי דַּאֲחִידָן בִּידָהָא. וְנַטְלִין עִמָּהּ שִׁתִּין פּוּלְסִין דְּנוּרָא, כָּל חַד חַרְבָּא שְׁנָנָא עַל יְרֵיכֵיהּ.

192. Underneath it, UNDER ZEIR ANPIN, a beast of the field strolls, NAMELY MALCHUT, which has ten horns, NAMELY TEN LIGHTS. That beast has eyes like human eyes and a mouth that speaks great things. When it rises, it walks by day and hides by night; when it journeys, the four shovels it holds in its hands tremble, and sixty blows of fire travel with it, each with a sharp edged sword on its hip.

193. סָלִיק בִּרְעוּתָא, לְאַפָּקָא בַּר נָשׁ שַׁלִּיטָא לְתַתָּא. אַתְקִין בְּהַאי חֵיוָתָא חַד, עַפְרָא דְּקִיקָא, כָּלִיל מִכֹּלָּא. נָשַׁב בֵּיהּ, אִתְפְּשַׁט בְּד׳ סִטְרֵי עָלְמָא. וְד׳ פּוּלְסִין אִתְגַּלְגָּלוּ, חַד לְעֵילָּא, חַד לְתַתָּא, חַד לַצָּפוֹן, חַד לַדָּרוֹם.

193. When He so desired to produce man to be ruler below, He implemented in that beast, WHICH IS MALCHUT, fine dust included of all SFIROT. He blew on it and it spread to the four directions of the world, THAT IS, IT SPREAD IN THE BODY TO THE FOUR DIRECTIONS OF THE WORLD. Four parts of the body rolled, one up, NETZACH, one down, HOD, WHICH ARE THE SECRET OF THE LEGS CALLED NETZACH AND HOD; one to the north, THE LEFT HAND, THE SECRET OF GVURAH, and one to the south, THE RIGHT HAND, THE SECRET OF CHESED.

194. אִילָנָא חַד רַבְרְבָא וְתַקִּיף, אִתְחַבָּר וְאִזְדְּוַג בָּהּ בְּחַד עַנְפָּא שַׁפִּירָא, דְּחֵזוּ חֶדְוָותָא דְּכֹלָּא. כד״א, יְפֵה נוֹף מְשׂוֹשׂ כָּל הָאָרֶץ. בֵּיהּ אִזְדְּוַג, אַפִּיקוּ חַד רוּחָא טְמִירָא, וּמַלְיָא לְהַהוּא גְּבִילוּ דְּעַפְרָא, וְקָאֵים עַל רַגְלוֹי, וְאַמְלְכֵיהּ עַל כָּל עָלְמָא, וְשַׁלְטֵיהּ עַל כֹּלָּא. הה״ד, תַּמְשִׁילֵהוּ בְּמַעֲשֵׂי יָדֶיךָ וְגוֹ׳. אִתְפְּקִיד עַל הַהוּא אִילָנָא, לָא נָטַר פִּקּוּדָא, אָתִיב מַלְכָּא רוּחֵיהּ לְגַבֵּיהּ, וְהַהוּא חֵיוָתָא נַטְלָא לֵיהּ.

194. A great and strong tree, THE TREE OF LIFE, NAMELY ZEIR ANPIN, was connected and joined to a comely bough, WHICH IS MALCHUT, the sight of which gladdens everybody, as written, "Beautiful for situation, the joy of the whole earth" (Tehilim 48:3). It united with it, and they produced a certain spirit that filled that dough of dust and MAN rose on his feet. He made him king over the whole world and ruler over everything. This is the meaning of, "You make him to have dominion over the works of Your hands…" (Tehilim 8:7). He was ordered regarding that tree, THE TREE OF KNOWLEDGE OF GOOD AND EVIL, NOT TO EAT FROM IT, but he did not observe that command. The King brought back the spirit OF MAN to Himself, and that beast, WHICH IS MALCHUT, took THAT SPIRIT FROM MAN.

195. כְּדֵין זְמִינִין מָנָא אַחֲרָא, וְקָאִים בֵּינַיְיהוּ. בְּקוּטְרָא דִּגְלִיפִין בֵּין מַלְאָכִין קַדִּישִׁין, בְּטִפְסָא דְּעִטּוּרִין אִתְאַחֲדָן.

195. ZEIR ANPIN AND MALCHUT prepared another vessel, NAMELY ANOTHER BODY, AND MAN rose between them with a connection OF NEFESH AND RUACH that are engraved among the holy angels that were united with the forming of the ANGELS' crowns.

196. דָּרִין בַּתְרָאִין, תְּפִיסִין בְּחוֹבַיְיהוּ. אִשְׁתְּלִיף רוּחֵיהוֹן מֵהַהוּא מָאנָא דִּלְבוּשָׁא, לְבָתַר אַגְנִיז בְּעַפְרָא, בֵּין רִגְבֵי נַחֲלָא. אִתְטְמָרוּ וְאִתְגְּנִיזוּ בְּחַד גַּרְמָא תַּקִּיף, דְּהַהוּא מָאנָא, יִתְבְּנוּן בְּקַדְמֵיתָא, וִיקוּמוּן חֵילִין חֵילִין תִּנְיָינוּת, בְּאַרְעָא קַדִּישָׁא מִתְעָרִין.

196. The following generations were punished for their sin OF THE TREE OF KNOWLEDGE OF GOOD AND EVIL, AND WERE SENTENCED TO DEATH, THAT EVENTUALLY their spirit is pulled out of THEIR vessel and garment, NAMELY THE BODY, AND THE BODY DIES. It is then buried in the dust among the clods of the valley, THAT IS, THE GRAVE, DERIVED FROM, "THE CLODS OF THE VALLEY SHALL BE SWEET TO HIM" (IYOV 21:33). AND ALL THE DEAD were hidden and concealed in one strong bone REMAINING from that vessel, NAMELY THE BONE OF LUZ THAT DOES NOT ROT IN THE GRAVE. From it they will be reconstructed again and rise in groups. And they will come again to the land of Yisrael, THAT IS, BY MEANS OF ROLLING IN TUNNELS, THEY WILL ALL COME TO THE LAND OF YISRAEL, WHERE THE COMPLETION OF THEIR RESURRECTION WILL BE ACHIEVED.

197. וְזַמִּין קוּדְשָׁא בְּרִיךְ הוּא, לְמִגְבַּל הַהוּא עַפְרָא קַדְמֵיתָא, דְּהַהוּא מָאנָא מַמָּשׁ. וּלְאַעֲלָא בֵּיהּ גְּבִילוּ דָּקִיק כְּהַאי חֲמִירָא דְּעִיסָה. וּמֵהַהוּא גְּבִילוּ דְּאִיהוּ צַחוּתָא דִּלְעֵילָּא, יִתְתָּקַּן וְיִתְיַשַּׁר מָאנָא דְּכַשְׁרָא. כְּגַוְונָא דְּאָמַר קְרָא, וּמַעְיָן מִבֵּית יְיָ' יֵצֵא וְהִשְׁקָה אֶת נַחַל הַשִּׁטִּים. בְּגִין דְּהַהוּא נַחַל אַסְגֵּי חֲבִיבוּתָא בְּעָלְמָא. וְכַד הַהוּא מַעְיָינָא קַדִּישָׁא, יִפּוּק וְיֵיעוּל לְגַבֵּיהּ, כְּדֵין יִתְתָּקַּן וְיִתְיְשַׁר, וְלָא יְהֵא בְּסוּרְחָנֵיהּ כְּקַדְמֵיתָא.

197. The Holy One, blessed be He, will knead that earlier dust of that actual vessel, NAMELY THE BODY THAT EXISTED PRIOR TO THE SIN OF THE TREE OF KNOWLEDGE OF GOOD AND EVIL, and introduce into it the finest dough, like leaven in the dough. From that dough, which is the highest clarity, the complete vessel will be constructed and straightened, like the verse says, "and a fountain shall issue from the house of Hashem, and shall water the valley of Shittim" (Yoel 4:18). For that fount increases love in the world. And when that holy fount will emerge and enter it, THE VALLEY OF SHITTIM, it will be constructed and made right and not be in its state of sinfulness.

198. וְאִינּוּן דְּלָא זָכָאן, יְקוּמוּן לְאִתְדְּנָא בְּדִינָא דְּמַלְכָּא עִלָּאָה. הה״ד וְרַבִּים מִיְּשֵׁנֵי אַדְמַת עָפָר יָקִיצוּ אֵלֶּה לְחַיֵּי עוֹלָם וְאֵלֶּה לַחֲרָפוֹת וּלְדִרְאוֹן עוֹלָם. וּכְדֵין כְּתִיב, כִּי כַאֲשֶׁר הַשָּׁמַיִם הַחֲדָשִׁים וְהָאָרֶץ הַחֲדָשָׁה אֲשֶׁר אֲנִי עוֹשֶׂה עוֹמְדִים לְפָנַי נְאֻם יְיָ׳ כֵּן יַעֲמוֹד זַרְעֲכֶם וְשִׁמְכֶם.

198. Those who have no merit will rise to be judged by the trial of the supernal King. This is the meaning of, "And many of those who sleep in the dust of the earth shall awake, some to everlasting life, and some to shame and everlasting contempt" (Daniel 12:2). Then, it is written, "For as the new heavens and the new earth, which I will make, shall remain before Me, says Hashem, so shall your seed and your name remain" (Yeshayah 66:22).

בָּרוּךְ יְיָ׳ לְעוֹלָם אָמֵן וְאָמֵן. יִמְלוֹךְ יְיָ׳ לְעוֹלָם אָמֵן וְאָמֵן

Blessed is the name of Hashem. Amen, amen. May Hashem rule forever Amen and Amen.

EKEV

Names of Articles

1. Meditation over a blessing

A Synopsis

We learn that it is a commandment to bless God, and that these blessings draw down the blessings from the supernal world – they draw life from the source of life. The blessing is like a gift to God that was sent by the person who prayed to Him. We learn about the secret meaning of Amen, that adorns the blessing, and about how the prayers and blessings ascend from below upwards through many levels. When the blessings descend all the patriarchs and the children are blessed. Baruch is the secret meaning of the highest source there is, and its flow is uninterrupted. We are also told of the secret meaning of the words "Atah" and "Melech" in the blessing. An explanation is given of the bowing and bending of the knee during the prayer service.

רעיא מהימנא

1. וְהָיָה עֵקֶב תִּשְׁמְעוּן אֵת הַמִּשְׁפָּטִים הָאֵלֶּה וְגוֹ׳, וְאָכַלְתָּ וְשָׂבָעְתָּ וּבֵרַכְתָּ אֶת יְיָ׳ אֱלֹהֶיךָ וְגוֹ׳. פִּקּוּדָא דָּא לְבָרְכָא לֵיהּ לְקוּדְשָׁא בְּרִיךְ הוּא, עַל כָּל מַה דְּאָכִיל וְשָׁתֵי, וְאִתְהֲנֵי בְּהַאי עָלְמָא. וְאִי לָא בָּרִיךְ, אִקְרֵי גַּזְלָן לְגַבֵּי קוּדְשָׁא בְּרִיךְ הוּא. דִּכְתִּיב גּוֹזֵל אָבִיו וְאִמּוֹ. וְהָא אוּקְמוּהָ חַבְרַיָּיא. בְּגִין דְּבִרְכָּאן דְּבָרִיךְ ב״נ לְקוּדְשָׁא בְּרִיךְ הוּא, אָתֵי לְאַמְשָׁכָא חַיִּין מִמְּקוֹרָא דְּחַיֵּי, לִשְׁמֵיהּ דְּקוּדְשָׁא בְּרִיךְ הוּא קַדִּישָׁא, וּלְאַרְקָא עָלֵיהּ מֵהַהוּא מִשְׁחָא עִלָּאָה, וְאָתֵי לְאִתְמַשְׁכָא מִתַּמָּן לְכָל עָלְמָא.

Ra'aya Meheimna (the Faithful Shepherd)

1. "Wherefore it shall come to pass, if you hearken to these judgments..." (Devarim 7:12). "When you have eaten, and are replete, then you shall bless Hashem your Elohim" (Devarim 8:10). We are commanded to bless the Holy One, blessed be He, for everything we eat and drink and enjoy in this world. He who does not bless is considered as stealing from the Holy One, blessed be He, as it is written: "he who robs his father or his mother" (Mishlei 28:24), and the friends explained THAT IT APPLIES TO THE HOLY

ONE, BLESSED BE HE. The blessings that a person gives the Holy One, blessed be He, are meant to draw life from the source of life, WHICH IS BINAH, to the Holy Name of the Holy One, blessed be He. And these blessings are to pour on top of Him from that supernal oil THAT IS THE ABUNDANCE OF CHOCHMAH. From there, it is then drawn upon the whole world.

2. וּכְתִיב וְאָכַלְתָּ וְשָׂבָעְתָּ וּבֵרַכְתָּ אֶת יְיָ׳ אֱלֹהֶיךָ וְאִינּוּן בִּרְכָאן, אָרִיק ב״נ בְּאִינּוּן מִלִּין מֵהַהוּא מְקוֹרָא עִלָּאָה, וְאִתְבָּרְכָאן כָּל אִינּוּן דַּרְגִּין וּמְקוֹרִין, וְאִתְמַלְיָין לְאַרְקָא עַל כָּל עָלְמִין. וְאִתְבָּרְכָאן כֻּלְּהוּ כַּחֲדָא.

2. It is also written: "when you have eaten, and are replete, then you shall bless Hashem your Elohim" (Ibid.). By these blessings, a person pours out through his words ABUNDANCE from the highest source, THAT IS BINAH. All the levels and sources OF ZEIR ANPIN AND MALCHUT are blessed and filled with abundance to pour upon all the worlds, and everything is blessed together.

3. וְע״ד אִצְטְרִיךְ ב״נ, לְשַׁוָּאָה רְעוּתֵיהּ בְּרָזָא דְּבִרְכָאן, בְּגִין דְּיִתְבָּרְכוּן אֲבָהָן וּבְנִין, כֹּלָּא כַּחֲדָא. וּמַאן דִּמְבָרֵךְ לְקוּדְשָׁא בְּרִיךְ הוּא, אִתְבְּרַךְ, וְנָטִיל חוּלָקֵיהּ מֵאִינּוּן בִּרְכָאן, בְּקַדְמֵיתָא דְּכָל עָלְמָא לְתַתָּא. כֵּיוָן דִּשְׁמָא דְּקוּדְשָׁא בְּרִיךְ הוּא מִתְבָּרֵךְ מִתַּמָּן, נָחִית וְשָׁרָא עַל רֵישֵׁיהּ חוּלָקָא קַדְמָאָה. וְהָא אוֹקִימְנָא דִּכְתִיב, בְּכָל הַמָּקוֹם אֲשֶׁר אַזְכִּיר אֶת שְׁמִי אָבֹא אֵלֶיךָ וּבֵרַכְתִּיךָ. כֵּיוָן דְּהַהִיא בְּרָכָה אַתְיָיא וְשַׁרְיָיא עַל רֵישֵׁיהּ, מִתַּמָּן אִתְפְּשַׁט בְּכָל עָלְמָא.

3. Therefore, a person needs to meditate on the secret of the blessings, so that the Patriarchs, WHO ARE CHESED, GVURAH AND TIFERET OF ZEIR ANPIN, and the children, WHO ARE NETZACH, HOD AND YESOD OF ZEIR ANPIN, shall all be blessed together. Whoever blesses the Holy One, blessed be He, is blessed and receives his part from these blessings before the rest of the lower world. As soon as the Name of the Holy One, blessed be He, is blessed from there, the initial portion of those blessings comes down and rests on the head OF THE ONE WHO SAID THE BLESSING. We have already provided an explanation for this, as it is written: "in all places where I cause

My Name to be pronounced, I will come to you, and I will bless you" (Shemot 20:21). After that particular blessing comes and rests on the head OF HE WHO BLESSED, it spreads from there to the rest of the world.

4. בְּשַׁעֲתָא דְּאִינּוּן בִּרְכָאן נַחְתִּין, מִתְעַטְּרָן גּוֹ חֲקַל תַּפּוּחִין קַדִּישִׁין, וּפַגְעֵי בְּהוּ כַּמָּה דַּרְגִּין דִּמְמַנָּן בְּעָלְמָא, וְנַחְתֵּי בְּהוּ, וְאַמְרֵי וּמַכְרִיזֵי דָּא אִיהוּ דּוֹרוֹנָא דְּשָׁדַר פְּלוֹנִי לְקוּדְשָׁא בְּרִיךְ הוּא. מַאן אֲתָר נַחְתֵּי, לְבָתַר דְּנַחְתֵּי מֵאֲתַר רֵישָׁא חֲדָא דְּצַדִּיק. תַּמָּן סַלְּקִין, מִתְעָרֵי לְנַחְתָּא אַחֲרָנִין מִלְּעֵילָּא, וְאִתְמַלְּיָיא מִלְּעֵילָּא וּמִתַּתָּא, הה״ד בְּרָכוֹת לְרֹאשׁ צַדִּיק. כֵּיוָן דְּהַאי דַּרְגָּא אִתְמַלְּיָיא, אָרִיק לְהַאי כַּלָּה, וּמִתַּמָּן נַגְדִּין וְאִתְמַשְּׁכָן לְתַתָּא.

4. When these blessings descend, they are adorned within the field of holy apple trees, THAT IS MALCHUT. Many levels of the those nominated over the world meet them there and come down together with them, announcing and proclaiming that it is the gift that this person sent to the Holy One, blessed be He. HE ASKS: From which place do the blessings descend? HE REPLIES: THE BLESSINGS descend afterward from the place of the head of the Righteous, THAT IS YESOD OF ZEIR ANPIN. THE BLESSINGS first go up and cause other BLESSINGS from above to go down, and it is filled from THOSE THAT DESCEND from above and from THOSE THAT ASCEND from below. This is the meaning of: "blessings are upon the head of the just" (Mishlei 10:6). Once that level is filled up, it pours upon the bride, WHICH IS MALCHUT, whence they flow and spread downward.

5. כַּד סַלְּקִין אִינּוּן בִּרְכָאן מִתַּתָּא, לֵית פִּתְחָא וּפִתְחָא לְעֵילָּא, וְלֵית מְמָנָא לְעֵילָּא, דְּלָא פָּתַח כָּל אִינּוּן פִּתְחִין. וּמַכְרְזֵי וְאַמְרֵי בְּכָל אִינּוּן רְקִיעִין, דָּא אִיהוּ דּוֹרוֹנָא דְּמַלְכָּא דְּשָׁדַר פְּלוֹנִי, דָּא הוּא דּוֹרוֹנָא בְּקִיּוּמָא כַּדְקָא יָאוּת. וּמַאן אִיהוּ. בְּרָכָה דְּאָתִיבוּ עָלֵיהּ אָמֵן. דְּכָל בְּרָכָה דְּאָתִיבוּ עָלֵיהּ אָמֵן, דָּא אִיהוּ בְּקִיּוּמָא כַּדְקָא יָאוּת.

5. When these blessings rise from below, there is no single opening above and there is no appointee from up high that does not open these openings, and declare throughout the firmaments: 'This is the gift to the King that so-and-so sent. That is a wholly proper gift.' What is A FULL blessing: IT IS A BLESSING to which Amen was said. For every blessing to which Amen was said is a properly full BLESSING.

6. וְכֵיוָן דְּהַאי בִּרְכָתָא סַלְקָא, כָּל דַּרְגִּין דִּלְעֵילָּא, כֻּלְּהוּ זְמִינִין לְגַבֵּי הַהוּא נְהוֹרָא דְּלָא נָהִיר, בְּגִין לְאַנְהָרָא לְגַבָּהּ. וְכָל שֶׁכֵּן אִי הִיא בִּרְכָתָא דְּסַגִּיאִין מְבָרְכָן לָהּ, וּמְעַטְּרִין לָהּ בְּעִטְרִין קַדִּישִׁין, בְּרָזָא דְּאָמֵן. אָמֵן הוּא רָזָא דְּקִשְׁרֵי, דְּכָל יִחוּדָא וּקְדוּשָּׁה בְּרָזָא דְּמָארֵיהּ. וּמְעַטֵּר לְהַהִיא בִּרְכָתָא בְּעִטְרִין עִלָּאִין כַּדְקָא יָאוּת.

6. When this blessing ascends, all the grades above summon the non-shining, NAMELY MALCHUT, to shine on it. Even more so, if it is a blessing said by many, it is adorned with holy crowns by means of SAYING Amen. Amen is the secret of the connections within each unification and sanctification in accordance with the secret of his Master. It properly adorns that blessing with sublime crowns.

7. וְקוּדְשָׁא בְּרִיךְ הוּא אִתְרְעֵי בְּהוּ, בְּאִינּוּן דִּמְבָרְכִין לֵיהּ, וְתִיאוּבְתֵּיהּ בְּבִרְכָתָא דִּלְתַּתָּא, דְּהַהִיא בִּרְכָתָא סַלְקָא, וְאַנְהִיר בּוּצִינָא דְּלָא נָהִיר, וְאַתְקִיף לָהּ בְּתוּקְפָּא תַּקִּיפָא, לְסַלְּקָא לְעֵילָּא. וְעַל רָזָא דָּא כְּתִיב, כִּי מְכַבְּדַי אֲכַבֵּד, אִלֵּין אִינּוּן דִּמְבָרְכִין לֵיהּ לְקוּדְשָׁא בְּרִיךְ הוּא. וּבוֹזַי יֵקָלּוּ, אִלֵּין אִינּוּן דְּלָא מְבָרְכִין לֵיהּ לְקוּדְשָׁא בְּרִיךְ הוּא, וּמַנְעִין בִּרְכָתָא מִפּוּמַיְיהוּ.

7. The Holy One, blessed be He, favors those that bless Him, and His passion is for the blessing that is below. That blessing rises and lights up the non-shining candle, WHICH IS MALCHUT, and strengthens it with a strong force to rise above, TO UNITE WITH ZEIR ANPIN. About this secret, it is written: "those who give Me honor, I will honor" (I Shmuel 1:30). This verse refers to those who give blessings to the Holy One, blessed be He. "..and they that despise Me shall be lightly esteemed" (Ibid.) refers to those who do not bless the Holy One, blessed be He, and withhold any blessings from their mouths.

8. רָזָא דְּרָזִין, לְאִינּוּן דְּיָדְעֵי חָכְמְתָא דְּמָארֵיהוֹן, לְמִנְדַּע רָזָא דְּבִרְכָּאן, בְּפִקּוּדֵי אוֹרַיְיתָא, וּבְכָל הֲנָאִין וְכִסּוּפִין דְּהַאי עָלְמָא, לְאַרְקָא בִּרְכָּאן מֵעֵילָּא לְתַתָּא.

8. The secret of secrets is for those who have knowledge in the Wisdom of their Master, to know the secret meanings of the blessings recited over the commandments of the Torah and over all the enjoyments and pleasures in this world, to pour out blessings from above downward.

9. בַּר בִּרְכָּאן דִּצְלוֹתָא, דְּאִינּוּן תִּקּוּנָא דְּמָארֵיהוֹן, מִתַּתָּא לְעֵילָּא וּמֵעֵילָּא לְתַתָּא. בִּרְכָּאן דְּלָאו אִינּוּן בִּצְלוֹתָא, סַלְּקִין מִתַּתָּא לְעֵילָּא, עַד דְּמָטוּ גּוֹ נְהוֹרָא דְּלָא נָהִיר, וּמִתְעָרֵי בְּתוּקְפָּא, לְהַהוּא נְהוֹרָא דְּלָא נָהִיר, בְּהַהִיא בְּרָכָה, וְסַלְּקָא אִתְּעֲרוּ לְעֵילָּא, עַד דְּמָטוּ לְכֻרְסְיָיא עִלָּאָה, מְקוֹרָא דְּכָל חַיִּין. כְּדֵין נָפְקוּ מֵהַהוּא מְקוֹרָא עִלָּאָה, בִּרְכָּאן אַחֲרָנִין, וְאִעֲרָעוּ אִלֵּין בְּאִלֵּין, וְנַשְּׁקֵי אִלֵּין לְאִלֵּין, וְאָתָאן וְשַׁרְיָין לְרֵישׁ צַדִּיק, לְאַרְקָא לְתַתָּא. וְכַד נַחְתִּין, אִתְבָּרְכָן אֲבָהָן וּבְנִין, וְכָל שְׁרָגִין דִּלְהוֹן.

9. HE EXPLAINS: The exception is the blessings in the prayer service, which are the correction of their Master. THEY BOTH RISE from below upwards and from above downwards, while the blessings that are not over the prayer rise from below upwards until they reach the non-shining light, WHICH IS MALCHUT, and awaken it with force by that blessing. This awakening rises high up until it reaches the highest Throne, WHICH IS BINAH, the source of all life, MEANING THAT ALL LIGHTS EMANATE FROM IT. Other blessings then flow out from that higher source and they meet and kiss one another. They approach and rest on the head of the Righteous THAT IS YESOD OF ZEIR ANPIN to pour down. When they descend, the Patriarchs, WHICH ARE CHESED, GVURAH AND TIFERET OF ZEIR ANPIN, and the children, WHICH ARE NETZACH, HOD AND YESOD OF ZEIR ANPIN, are blessed and all their candles, WHICH ARE THE SFIROT OF MALCHUT.

10. וְרָזָא דְּאִלֵּין בִּרְכָּאן לְאַתְעָרָא מֵעֵילָּא לְתַתָּא, בְּרָזָא דָּא, בָּרוּךְ: דָּא רָזָא דִּמְקוֹרָא עִלָּאָה מִכֹּלָּא, לְאַרְקָא וּלְאַמְשָׁכָא וּלְאַנְהָרָא כָּל בּוֹצִינִין.

וְאִיהוּ בָּרוּךְ תָּדִיר, דְּלָא פַּסְקִין מֵימוֹי. וּמִתַּמָּן שֵׁירוּתָא דְּאִקְרֵי עָלְמָא דְּאָתֵי, וְאִיהוּ קְצֵה הַשָּׁמַיִם, דְּהַהִיא קָצֶה קָצֶה עִלָּאָה אִיהוּ. בְּגִין דְּאִית קָצֶה כְּגַוְונָא דָּא לְתַתָּא, וְאִיהוּ עָלְמָא תַּתָּאָה. וְאִקְרֵי אוּף הָכִי בָּרוּךְ, לְקַבֵּל תַּתָּאֵי, לְאַרְקָא לְתַתָּא, וּלְאִתְעֲרָא מִתַּתָּא לְעֵילָּא בְּבִרְכָּאן דִּצְלוֹתָא. וּבָרוּךְ דָּא אִקְרֵי הָכָא, בְּרָזָא דְּחָכְמְתָא עִלָּאָה, דְּאַמְלֵי לְהַהוּא אֲתָר, בְּחַד שְׁבִיל דָּקִיק דְּאָעִיל בֵּיהּ.

10. The secret of these blessings that awaken from above to below pertains to this secret. 'Blessed' is the secret of the highest source, WHICH IS SUPERNAL ABA AND IMA, WHICH ARE CALLED CHOCHMAH. ONE NEEDS TO MEDITATE to pour, draw and kindle from there all the candles, MEANING THE LOWER GRADES. It is always blessed because its water never ceases flowing, MEANING THEY ARE IN A NEVER ENDING UNION AND THEIR ABUNDANCE TO THE LOWER BEINGS NEVER CEASES FLOWING. From there, the beginning that is called the World to Come, MEANING BINAH, RECEIVES. It is CALLED the end of heaven, because that end is the upper end OF ZEIR ANPIN CALLED HEAVEN. For there is a similar end below, which is the lower world, MALCHUT, which is also called 'blessed', in correspondence to the lower beings, MEANING to pour BLESSINGS downward and awaken from below upward by the blessing of the prayer. But here, REGARDING THE OTHER BLESSINGS, is called 'blessed', after the secret of Chochmah, DENOTING SUPERNAL ABA AND IMA, that which fills that place, BINAH CALLED THE WORLD TO COME, AS MENTIONED ABOVE, by means of a narrow path, MEANING YESOD OF CHOCHMAH, through which it enters it.

11. אַתָּה: לְבָתַר שָׁארִי לְאִתְגַּלְיָיא, דְּהָא הַאי בָּרוּךְ סָתִים אִיהוּ, וּבג"כ אִקְרֵי בְּאֹרַח סָתִים בָּרוּךְ, מְקוֹרָא עִלָּאָה דְּלָא אִתְגַּלְיָיא. אַתָּה, שֵׁירוּתָא לְאִתְגַּלְיָיא לְבַר, וּבג"כ אִקְרֵי אַתָּה. וּמַאן אִיהוּ. דָּא רָזָא דִּימִינָא, וְאִקְרֵי כֹּהֵן לְגַבֵּי הַהוּא אֲתָר. וְרָזָא דָּא אַתָּה כֹהֵן לְעוֹלָם, מַאן כֹּהֵן לְהַהוּא עוֹלָם, אַתָּה. וְדָא אִיהוּ יְמִינָא עִלָּאָה, דְּהָא אִשְׁתְּכַח לְאִתְגַּלְיָיא.

11. THE WORD 'you' IN THE BLESSING then begins to be revealed, because 'blessed' is hidden, WHICH ARE CHOCHMAH AND BINAH THAT ARE

INCOMPREHENSIBLE TO THE LOWER BEINGS. Therefore, it is called 'blessed' vaguely, IT BEING a higher unexposed source. HOWEVER, THE WORD 'you' is the start of the revelation outside. This is why it is called 'you', IN THE SECOND PERSON, WHO IS REVEALED. And who is it? It is the secret of the right, WHICH IS CHESED OF ZEIR ANPIN, called a priest to that place, BINAH. That is the meaning of: "you shall be a priest forever (lit. 'to a world')" (Tehilim 110:4), MEANING, who is "a priest" to that world, Binah, it is 'you'. This is the supernal right, CHESED OF ZEIR ANPIN, that is there to be revealed.

12. יְהֹוָה: דָּא רָזָא דְּאֶמְצָעִיתָא. רָזָא דִּמְהֵימְנוּתָא בְּכָל סִטְרִין. אֱלֹהֵינוּ: דָּא סִטְרָא דִּשְׂמָאלָא, דְּכָלִיל בִּימִינָא, וִימִינָא בֵּיהּ, וְאִתְכְּלִילוּ דָּא בְּדָא, לְמֶהֱוֵי חַד. וְעַד הָכָא, אִתְקְשָׁרוּ בִּרְכָאן, דְּכֵיוָן דְּאִלֵּין אִתְבָּרְכָאן, כֻּלְּהוֹן דִּלְתַתָּא אִתְבָּרְכָאן.

12. THE WORD 'Hashem' IN THE BLESSINGS is the secret of the Central Column IN ZEIR ANPIN, the secret meaning of the Faith in all directions. The WORD 'our Elohim' IN THE BLESSINGS is the left side OF ZEIR ANPIN. It is included in his right; the right is included in it, and one is included in the other into one. Up to this point, MEANING UP TO CHESED, GVURAH AND TIFERET OF ZEIR ANPIN, the blessings are connected TO ZEIR ANPIN. Once these CHESED, GVURAH AND TIFERET OF ZEIR ANPIN are blessed, everyone below is blessed.

13. לְבָתַר דְּאִינּוּן אִתְבָּרְכָאן, וְנַטְלֵי בִּרְכָאן לְגַרְמַיְיהוּ, אִתְהֲדָרוּ כְּלִילָן כְּחַד לְהַהוּא מְקוֹרָא, דְּאִינּוּן לָא יַכְלִין לְאִתְהַדְּרָא לְגַבֵּי הַהוּא אֲתָר, עַד דְּאִתְבָּרְכָן. כֵּיוָן דְּאִתְבָּרְכָן בְּקַדְמֵיתָא, אִתְהֲדָרוּ וְעָאלִין לְגַבֵּי הַהוּא אֲתָר, לְנַטְלָא בִּרְכָאן יַתִּירִין אַחֲרָנִין, לְאַרְקָא לְתַתָּא. וְעַד דְּאִינּוּן אִתְבָּרְכָאן, לָא עָאלִין וְלָא תָּאבִין לְגַבֵּיהּ. וְרָזָא דָּא וְלֹא יֵרָאוּ פָּנַי רֵיקָם.

13. After CHESED, GVURAH AND TIFERET OF ZEIR ANPIN are blessed and receive blessings for themselves, all return included into one to that source, WHICH IS BINAH, because they cannot return to that place before they are blessed. Once they are blessed first, they again enter that place THAT IS BINAH, to receive other additional blessings to bestow down. Before they are blessed, they do not enter or return TO BINAH. That is the secret meaning of the verse: "and none shall appear before Me empty" (Shemot 23:15).

14. וְכַד תָּבִין לְגַבֵּי הַהוּא אֲתָר, וְעָאלִין תַּמָּן, כְּדֵין אִקְרֵי הַהוּא אֲתָר מֶלֶךְ. וּמֶלֶךְ לָא אִתְקְרֵי, בַּר כַּד אִינּוּן מִתְקָרְבִין לְגַבֵּיהּ, וּמִתְבָּרְכָן. וּמַלְכָּא אֵימָתַי אִקְרֵי מֶלֶךְ. כַּד רַבְרְבָנוֹי אַתְיָין לְגַבֵּיהּ עֲתִירִין, מִסְתַּפְּקָן בְּכָל מַה דְּאִצְטְרִיכוּ, בְּלָא חֶסְרוֹנָא, כְּדֵין אִיהוּ מֶלֶךְ. מֶלֶךְ לְתַתָּא, כַּד אִלֵּין מְעַטְּרָן לֵיהּ בְּסִפּוּקָא, בְּעִטְרִין קַדִּישִׁין. וְהָכָא אִקְרֵי מֶלֶךְ. וּמַאן אִיהוּ. הָעוֹלָם אֲשֶׁר קִדְּשָׁנוּ וְצִוָּנוּ. וּבְגִין דְּאִיהוּ עָלְמָא דְּלָא אִתְגַּלְיָיא לְבַר, וְאִיהוּ סָתִים, קָרֵי לֵיהּ הָכִי בְּאֹרַח סָתִים. וְעַל דָּא לָא אִקְרֵי, אֶלָּא בְּאֹרַח סָתִים.

14. When they return to that place, BINAH, and enter there, that place is called 'king', WHICH IS THE SECRET OF THE WORD 'KING' IN THE BLESSING. BINAH is considered a king only when these – CHESED, GVURAH AND TIFERET OF ZEIR ANPIN, draw near it to be blessed. A king is considered a king when his chief ministers come to him when they are rich and have everything they need, without lacking anything. Then he is king. A king below, WHO IS MALCHUT, IS SO CONSIDERED when these, THE SFIROT OF ZEIR ANPIN, adorn her (Malchut) adequately with holy crowns. Here IN THE BLESSING, where a king is mentioned, who is THE KING? It is "The world, who has sanctified us and commanded us," WHICH IS BINAH. Since it is a world that is not revealed externally and is hidden, it is recited in a hidden manner, MEANING IN THE THIRD PERSON, 'WHO HAS SANCTIFIED US AND COMMANDED US', INSTEAD OF THE SECOND PERSON, NAMELY, "YOU WHO HAVE SANCTIFIED AND COMMANDED US." Therefore, it is recited in an undisclosed manner.

15. וּלְעוֹלָם יְמִינָא אַתָּה, כְּמָה דְּאִתְּמַר. וְעַל דָּא כֹּהֵן, כָּפִיף לְגַבֵּי הַהוּא אֲתָר, בְּרֵישָׁא וּבְסוֹפָא. וְעָלְמָא תַּתָּאָה, כַּד אִתְקָשַּׁר לִימִינָא, וְאִתְדַּבַּק בֵּיהּ, קָרֵי מִתַּתָּא לְעֵילָּא בָּרוּךְ, וְלָא אִקְרֵי בָּרוּךְ, בַּר בְּרָזָא

דִּמְקוֹרָא דְּאִתְדְּבַק בֵּיהּ, וְעָיֵיל בֵּיהּ, וְאַמְלֵי לֵיהּ. אַתָּה, רָזָא דְּהַהוּא כֹּהֵן, לְאִתְדַּבְּקָא בַּהֲדֵיהּ, וְע״ד, בִּצְלוֹתָא ב״נ כּוֹרֵעַ בְּבָרוּךְ, דְּאִיהוּ עָלְמָא כָּפוּף לְגַבֵּי עֵילָּא, וְדָא אִיהוּ שִׁנּוּי בֵּין בָּרוּךְ דִּצְלוֹתָא, וּבֵין בָּרוּךְ דִּשְׁאַר בִּרְכָאן. וְכֹלָּא בְּרָזָא עִלָּאָה אִיהוּ, לְאַרְקָא בִּרְכָאן לְכָל עָלְמִין.

15. As we learned, the right, WHICH IS CHESED, is always called 'you'. Therefore, the priest bows HIS HEAD towards that place, 'YOU', AT EACH AND EVERY BLESSING OF THE AMIDAH PRAYER, WHERE HE BOWS at the beginning OF THE BLESSING and at the end OF THE BLESSING. The lower world, THAT IS MALCHUT, when it is connected to the right, WHICH IS CHESED, and attached to it, is called from below upward 'blessed', and is not considered blessed except by means of the source to which it was attached, which entered it and filled it, WHICH IS CHESED. ONLY THEN IS MALCHUT CONSIDERED BLESSED. 'You' IN THE BLESSING is the secret of the priest, MEANING CHESED, to be attached to him. Therefore, in the prayer, one bends his knees at 'blessed', THAT IS MALCHUT, because it is a world bent at the top. That is the difference between 'blessed' in the prayer and 'blessed' in the other blessings; 'BLESSED' IN THE OTHER BLESSINGS IS IN CHOCHMAH AND BINAH, WHILE 'BLESSED' IN THE PRAYER IS IN MALCHUT. Everything follows a higher meaning to pour blessings to all the worlds.

16. בָּרוּךְ דִּצְלוֹתָא, ב״נ כּוֹרֵעַ בֵּיהּ בְּבִרְכּוֹי, וְגָחִין רֵישָׁא בְּאַתָּה, בְּגִין דְּאַתָּה אִקְרֵי רֹאשׁ. וְע״ד כֹּהֵן נָטִיל בָּרֹאשׁ, וְאִיהוּ רֹאשׁ תָּדִיר. וּבג״כ כְּרִיעָה בְּבָרוּךְ. וְגָחִינוּ דְּרֵישָׁא בְּאַתָּה. וְכֹהֵן בְּכָל אֲתָר דְּאִקְרֵי אַתָּה, גָּחִין בִּצְלוֹתָא. מֶלֶךְ בָּתַר דְּגָחִין, תּוּ לָא זָקִיף, מ״ט. קוּדְשָׁא בְּרִיךְ הוּא אָמַר לָהּ לְסִיהֲרָא, זִילִי אַזְעִירִי גַּרְמִיךְ, וְתוּ לָא זַקְפָא. וּבג״ד, בִּרְכָתָא דְּב״נ בָּרִיךְ לְקוּדְשָׁא בְּרִיךְ הוּא, אִתְעַר לְאַרְקָא בִּרְכָאן מִלְּעֵילָּא לְעָלְמִין כֻּלְּהוּ, כְּמָה דְּאִתְּמַר. זַכָּאִין אִינּוּן יִשְׂרָאֵל בְּעָלְמָא דֵּין, וּבְעָלְמָא דְּאָתֵי.

16. AT THE WORD 'blessed' in the AMIDAH prayer, one bends his knees, and bows his head at 'you', because 'you' is called 'head (or: 'first')'. Therefore, the priest receives his portion first and is always first in line.

That is why the knee bending is at 'blessed', and lowering of the head is at 'you'. Wherever the priest reads 'you', he bows down when praying. After a king lowers down his head AT THE BEGINNING OF THE AMIDAH PRAYER, he does not raise it again UNTIL HE FINISHES THE PRAYER. What is the reason? IT IS BECAUSE the Holy One, blessed be He, said to the moon: 'Go and diminish yourself', and THE MOON, WHICH IS MALCHUT, has not yet straightened herself FROM THIS DIMINISHING. A KING IS THE ASPECT OF MALCHUT; THEREFORE, HE LOWERS HIS HEAD AND DOES NOT RAISE IT UP. Hence, a blessing with which a person blesses the Holy One, blessed be He, is aroused to pour down blessings from above to all the worlds, as we have learned. Blessed are the children of Yisrael in this world and the World to Come.

17. כְּתִיב, כִּי אַתָּה אָבִינוּ כִּי אַבְרָהָם וְגוֹ'. תָּנֵינָן, לְזִמְנָא דְּאָתֵי אַמְרִין לֵיהּ לְיִצְחָק וְכוּ', בְּגִין דִּשְׂמָאלָא אִתְכְּלִיל בִּימִינָא, אֲבָל יְמִינָא מְנָלָן דְּאִקְרֵי אָב. דִּכְתִּיב וֶהְיֵה לִי לְאָב וּלְכֹהֵן, וְאע"ג דִּלְעֵילָּא אִקְרֵי אָב, וַאֲפִילּוּ לִנְהוֹרָא דְּלָא נָהִיר בְּשַׁעֲתָא דְּאִתְדְּבַק בִּימִינָא אִקְרֵי אַתָּה, כד"א אַתָּה יְיָ' אָבִינוּ גּוֹאֲלֵנוּ וְגוֹ'.

17. It is written: "You are our Father, though Abraham is ignorant of us..." (Yeshayah 63:16). We have learned that in the World to Come Isaac shall be told: 'YOU ARE OUR FATHER'. THUS ISAAC, WHO IS THE LEFT COLUMN, IS CALLED A FATHER. That is because the left is included in the right. HOWEVER, BEFORE IT WAS INCLUDED IN THE RIGHT IT WAS NOT CONSIDERED A FATHER, BECAUSE HARSH JUDGMENTS WERE FLOWING FROM HIM. But how do we know that the right too is considered a father? HE RESPONDS: It is written, "and be to me a father and a priest" (Shoftim 17:10). WE UNDERSTAND FROM THIS THAT THE PRIEST, WHO IS RIGHT AND CHESED, IS CONSIDERED A FATHER. Although above, even the non-shining light WHICH IS MALCHUT, is considered a father, when it is here attached to the right, it is called 'you', as it is written: "You, Hashem, are our Father, our Redeemer" (Yeshayah 63:16).

2. The owner of the house breaks the bread and the guest recites the blessing

A synopsis

The Faithful Shepherd explains the secret of the twelve letters of the blessings of the Kohen. The importance that the owner of the house making the blessing over the bread first.

18. אַדְּהָכִי, סָבָא אִזְדְּמַן לְגַבֵּיהּ, וְאָמַר, רַעְיָא מְהֵימָנָא, תַּקִּין פָּתוֹרָא לְמָארָךְ, לֵיהּ וּלְמַטְרוֹנִיתָא, מִכָּל מִינֵי עִדּוּנִין, לְקַיְּימָא בֵּיהּ זֶה הַשֻּׁלְחָן אֲשֶׁר לִפְנֵי יְיָ׳, וְהָא עַד כְּעַן כֻּלְּהוּ מִתְעַנְּגֵי מִפָּתוֹרָא דְּמַלְכָּא, הה״ד, לְכוּ לַחֲמוּ בְּלַחְמִי. וְדָא נַהֲמָא דְּאוֹרַיְיתָא דִּבְכְתָב, וְיֵינָא דְּאוֹרַיְיתָא דִּבְעַל פֶּה. וְתַמָּן כַּמָּה מַטְעַמִּים מִינֵי טַעֲמֵי תּוֹרָה, דִּמְתִיקִין, מִכָּל מַאֲכָלִין וְעִדּוּנִין דְּעָלְמָא, וּדְמַלְכָּא.

18. Meanwhile, an old person came to him and said: Faithful Shepherd, prepare a table for your Master, for Him and His Queen, with all kinds of delicacies, to fulfill in it: "this is the table that is before Hashem"' (Yechezkel 41:22). For until now, everyone was enjoying from the King's table, as it says: "Come, eat of my bread" (Mishlei 9:5). Bread is the Written Law, MEANING ZEIR ANPIN, and the wine of the Torah is the Oral Law, WHICH IS MALCHUT. IN MALCHUT, there are many dainties from the various sweet meanings of the Torah, and from all the victuals and delicacies in the world and of the King.

19. קָם רַעְיָא מְהֵימָנָא, פָּתַח וְאָמַר, אַהֲרֹן כַּהֲנָא קוּם מִשֵּׁינָתָךְ, לְמִדְבַּח תּוֹרִין וְעָאנִין וְאִמְּרִין וְעוֹפִין, וְכָל מִינִין דִּצְרִיכִין לִסְעוּדָתָא דְּמַלְכָּא. וְלֶחֶם הַפָּנִים, דְּאִינּוּן לָקֳבֵל תְּרֵין לוּחֵי דְּאוֹרַיְיתָא, דְּמִזֶּה וּמִזֶּה הֵם כְּתוּבִים. זֶה: תְּרֵיסָר אַנְפִּין. דְּאִינּוּן: יְבָרֶכְךָ יְיָ׳, יָאֵר יְיָ׳, יִשָּׂא יְיָ׳. זֶה תִּנְיָינָא, אֲדֹנָ״י אֲדֹנָ״י אֲדֹנָ״י. דְּאִינּוּן תְּרֵיסָר חֵיוָן, דְּאִתְּמַר בְּהוֹן, וּפְנֵי אַרְיֵה אֶל הַיָּמִין לְאַרְבַּעְתָּן, וּפְנֵי שׁוֹר מֵהַשְּׂמֹאל לְאַרְבַּעְתָּן, וּפְנֵי נֶשֶׁר לְאַרְבַּעְתָּן. וְאִתְּמַר עָלַיְיהוּ, אַרְבָּעָה פָּנִים לְאֶחָת. וְהַאי אִיהוּ,

וְקָרָא זֶה אֶל זֶה וְאָמַר, לָקֳבֵל עֶשְׂרִים וְאַרְבַּע סִפְרֵי תּוֹרָה. וְהַאי אִיהוּ זֶה הַשֻּׁלְחָן אֲשֶׁר לִפְנֵי יְיָ׳. מָאנִין דְּפָתוֹרָא דְּמַלְכָּא, אִינּוּן מָארֵי מַתְנִיתִין, מָארֵי צְלוֹתִין, דְּתָקִינוּ לוֹן לָקֳבֵל קָרְבְּנִין.

19. The Faithful Shepherd rose and began to speak: 'Aaron the priest, rise from your sleep to slaughter oxen and sheep and goats and lambs and fowl, and all the varieties needed for the King's feast. The shew-bread (lit. 'the bread of faces'), that is TWELVE, corresponding to the two tablets of Torah, "written on both their sides (lit. 'from this and this' (Heb. *zeh*))" (Shemot 32:15). *Zeh* IN NUMERICAL VALUE is the twelve faces, which are THE TWELVE LETTERS IN THREE TIMES YUD HEI VAV HEI IN THE VERSES: "Hashem bless you, and keep you; Hashem make His face shine upon you, and be gracious to you; Hashem lift up His countenance to you, and give you peace" (Bemidbar 6:24-25). The second *zeh* CORRESPONDS TO THE THREE TIMES ADONAI, WHICH CONTAIN IN THEM TWELVE LETTERS. They are the twelve living creatures about which it says, "and they four had the face of a lion, on the right side; and the four had the face of an ox on the left side; they four also had the face of an eagle" (Yechezkel 1:10). THESE ARE THREE LIVING CREATURES, LION, OX, AND EAGLE, and it says about them: "And every one had four faces" (Ibid. 6). THAT IS, IN EACH CREATURE OF THE THREE, THERE ARE FOUR FACES OF THE LION, OX, EAGLE, AND MAN, AND THREE TIMES FOUR AMOUNTS TO TWELVE LIVING CREATURES. That is the meaning of, "And one (Heb. *zeh*) cried to another (Heb. *zeh*), and said" (Yeshayah 6:3), THAT IS, THE TWELVE FACES OF YUD HEI VAV HEI TO THE TWELVE CREATURES OF ADONAI. They also correspond to the 24 books in the Torah, THAT IS, THE 24 BOOKS IN THE BIBLE. This is the meaning of: "this (Heb. *zeh*) is the table that is before Hashem" (Yechezkel 41:22), BECAUSE A TABLE IS MALCHUT. "*Zeh*" IS THE TWELVE CREATURES THAT ARE IN ADONAI, WHICH IS MALCHUT. "THAT IS BEFORE HASHEM" REFERS TO THE TWELVE FACES IN YUD HEI VAV HEI. The vessels on the King's table are the sages of Mishnah, versed in prayer, which THE SAGES composed to correspond to the sacrifices.

20. פָּתַח וְאָמַר, וְעָשִׂיתָ שֻׁלְחָן עֲצֵי שִׁטִּים וְגוֹ׳. תָּא חֲזֵי, מִנְהָגִין טָבִין וְשַׁפִּירָן הֲווֹ נַהֲגֵי מָארֵי דִּסְעוּדָתָא דְּמַלְכָּא, לְאַחֲזָאָה דְּאִינּוּן מִבְּנֵי פָתוֹרָה דְּמַלְכָּא. חַד רַבְרְבָא מִבְּנֵי סְעוּדָתָא, נָטִיל יְדוֹי בִּזְמְנָא דְּיֵיעֲלוּן

2. The owner of the house breaks the bread and the guest recites the blessing

לִסְעוּדָתָא לְהָסֵב, גָּדוֹל מֵסֵב בָּרֹאשׁ, תִּנְיָינָא תְּחוֹתֵיהּ, וּתְלִיתָאָה תְּחוֹת תִּנְיָינָא. וְאִלֵּין אִתְקְרִיאוּ ג' מִטּוֹת, לָקֳבֵל תְּלַת אֲבָהָן, וְלָקֳבֵל כֹּהֲנִים לְוִיִּם וְיִשְׂרְאֵלִים. מִכָּאן וְאֵילָךְ, לֵית לוֹן סֵדֶר, אֶלָּא כָּל הַקּוֹדֵם זָכָה.

20. He opened the discussion with the verse: "and you shall make a table of acacia wood" (Shemot 25:23). Come and behold: those present at the King's feast had goodly and comely customs to show they were members of the King's table. One was that the eldest would wash his hands FIRST. When they entered to sit for the meal, the oldest would sit at the head of the table. The second would be below him, and the third below the second. These are called the 'three beds', BECAUSE THEIR CUSTOM WAS EACH TO RECLINE ON A BED, to correspond to the three Patriarchs, and to the priests, the Levites and Yisrael THAT ARE CHESED, GVURAH AND TIFERET. From here on, they had no special order, rather whoever came first was seated.

21. תִּנְיָינָא, בַּעַל הַבַּיִת בּוֹצֵעַ, כְּדֵי שֶׁיִּבְצַע בְּעַיִן יָפָה. וּמַשְׁלִים בִּרְכָתָא, וּלְבָתַר בּוֹצֵעַ. וְאוֹקְמוּהָ רַבָּנָן דְּמַתְנִיתִין, דְּאֵין הַמְּסוּבִּין רַשָּׁאִין לִטְעוֹם, עַד שֶׁיִּטְעוֹם הַמְּבָרֵךְ. וְלֵית הַבּוֹצֵעַ רַשָּׁאי לִטְעוֹם, עַד שֶׁיִּכְלֶה אָמֵן מִפִּי הַמְּסוּבִּין. וְאִם רְעוּתֵיהּ לְחַלֵּק כָּבוֹד, הָרְשׁוּת בִּידֵיהּ. וְעוֹד אוֹקְמוּהָ, דְּאוֹרֵחַ מְבָרֵךְ, בְּגִין דִּיבָרֵךְ לְבַעַל הַבַּיִת.

21. The second CUSTOM is that the house owner breaks the bread so that he may apportion it generously. He first completes THE BLESSING OVER THE BREAD, and then breaks it. The sages of the Mishnah have set it so that none of those reclining at the feast table are permitted to taste until the giver of the blessing has tasted first. The one who apportions is not permitted to taste until all present have finished saying Amen. And if he wishes to delegate honor BY GIVING TO ANOTHER TO BREAK THE BREAD, he may do so. In addition, it had been stated that the guest blessed THE BLESSING AFTER THE MEAL so he will bless the landlord.

22. וְאֹרַח רָזָא, בַּעַל הַבַּיִת בּוֹצֵעַ, דָּא עַמּוּדָא דְּאֶמְצָעִיתָא, דְּאִיהוּ קַו הָאֶמְצָעִי. וּבְשַׁבָּת צָרִיךְ לִבְצוֹעַ מִשְּׁנֵי כִּכָּרוֹת, דְּאִינּוּן ה' ה'. בַּעַל

הַבַּיִת, דָּא ו׳ דְּאֶמְצָעִיתָא. וּבְגִין דְּלָא לְאִתְחֲזָאָה כְּרַעַבְתָּנוּתָא, יָכִיל לְמִבְצַע בָּהּ לְכָל חַד וְחַד כַּבֵּיצָה. מַאי כַּבֵּיצָה. י׳ וְי׳. אִינּוּן נְקוּדִין דִּשְׁמָא קַדִּישָׁא, אִתְקְרֵי פֵּרוּרֵי בִּכְזַיִת. וְאִלֵּין לָקֳבֵל טִפִּין דְּזֶרַע, וּמַאן דִּמְזַלְזֵל בְּהוֹן, וְזָרִיק לוֹן בַּאֲתַר דְּלָא אִצְטְרִיךְ, עֲנִיּוּתָא קָא רָדִיף אֲבַתְרֵיהּ, וְאָזִיל נָע וָנָד. הה״ד, נוֹדֵד הוּא לַלֶּחֶם אַיֵּה. וְלֵית לֶחֶם אֶלָּא תּוֹרָה, וְהוּא צוֹוֵחַ אַיֵּה מַאן דִּמְרַחֵם עֲלֵיהּ וְלָא יִשְׁכַּח.

22. In an esoteric interpretation, the landlord who breaks the bread is the central pillar, which is the Central Column, WHICH IS ZEIR ANPIN. On Shabbat, he needs to apportion from two loaves of challah bread, which are Hei-Hei OF YUD HEI VAV HEI. The house owner is Vav OF YUD HEI VAV HEI between THE TWO *HEI'S*. In order not appear a glutton, he may apportion to each one a piece the size of an egg. What is the size of an egg? It is Yud OF YUD HEI VAV HEI and Yud OF ADONAI, which are the dots of the Holy Name called crumbs the size of an olive, THAT IS, YUD OF YUD HEI VAV HEI IS THE SIZE OF AN EGG AND YUD OF ADONAI IS THE SIZE OF AN OLIVE. These CRUMBS correspond to drops of sperm. THEREFORE, poverty chases whoever belittles and disposes these crumbs in an inappropriate place, and he will constantly wander around. This is what is written: "he wanders abroad for bread, saying, where is it" (Iyov 15:23). Bread means Torah, and this verse implies that he cries out, looking for someone who will have mercy on him, but will find no one TO PITY HIM.

23. וּפֵרוּרִים בִּכְזַיִת, אִינּוּן בְּצַדִּיק, דְּאִיהוּ כָּתִישׁ כְּתִישׁוּ מֵאִינּוּן זֵיתִים. וְאוֹרֵחַ מְבָרֵךְ, וְאֹרַח צַדִּיקִים כְּאוֹר נֹגַהּ. בְּרָכוֹת לְרֹאשׁ צַדִּיק חַי עָלְמִין, וּבְגִ״ד אוֹרֵחַ מְבָרֵךְ.

23. Crumbs the size of an olive belong to the Righteous YESOD, who presses these olives, WHICH ARE THE SFIROT, EXTRACTING OIL FROM THEM, WHICH IS THE SECRET OF ABUNDANCE. The guest (Heb. *ore'ach*) blesses, NAMELY THE RIGHTEOUS, as is written: "but the path (Heb. *orach*) of just men is like the gleam of sunlight" (Mishlei 4:18), AND, "blessings are upon the head of the just" (Mishlei 10:6), the life of the world. Therefore, the guest, WHO IS THE RIGHTEOUS, NAMELY YESOD, makes the blessing.

2. The owner of the house breaks the bread and the guest recites the blessing

24. אַדְּהָכִי, הָא בּוּצִינָא קַדִּישָׁא אָתָא לְגַבֵּיהּ, וְאָמַר, רַעְיָא מְהֵימָנָא, יוֹמָא חַד אֲזִילְנָא אֲנָא וְחַבְרַיָּיא, לְאַכְסַנְיָא חֲדָא, וַהֲוָה תַּמָּן יַנּוּקָא חֲדָא, קָם וְתָקִין לָן מְנַרְתָּא וּפָתוֹרָא, אִיהוּ מִגַּרְמֵיהּ, כְּאִלּוּ הֲוָה מֵעֶשְׂרִין שְׁנִין, וְלָא הֲוָה אֶלָּא מִבֶּן חָמֵשׁ שְׁנִין, וְתָקִין פָּתוֹרָא מִכָּל מִינֵי מַאֲכָל וּמִשְׁתֶּה. אָמַר, הָא אוֹקְמוּהָ רַבָּנָן דְּבַעַל הַבַּיִת בּוֹצֵעַ וְאוֹרֵחַ מְבָרֵךְ, אֲבָל צָעִיר אֲנִי לְיָמִים וְאַתֶּם יְשִׁישִׁים עַל כֵּן זָחַלְתִּי וָאִירָא מֵחַוּוֹת דֵּעִי אֶתְכֶם. עַד דְּאֶטּוֹל רְשׁוּת מִכֶּם. א״ל, אֵימָא בְּרִי מַלְאֲכָא דַּיְיָ׳.

24. As he was speaking, the Holy Luminary came to him, TO THE FAITHFUL SHEPHERD and said: Faithful Shepherd, one day I went along with the friends to an inn. There was a child there who rose and by himself prepared for us a lamplight and a table, as if he were twenty years old. Yet he was approximately five years old. He set that table up with different dishes and drinks and said, The sages have decreed that the house owner breaks the bread and the guest makes the blessing. Yet, "I am young and you are very old; therefore, I was afraid and dared not declare my opinion to you" (Iyov 32:6), until I obtain permission from you. They said to him: Speak up my son, angel of Hashem.

25. אָמַר לָן, אַתּוּן בָּעֵיתוּן לֶחֶם תַּפְנוּקֵי בְּלָא קְרָבָא, אוֹ לֶחֶם בִּקְרָבָא. דְּהָכִי אוֹקְמוּהָ רַבָּנָן דְּמַתְנִיתִין, שְׁעַת אֲכִילָה שְׁעַת מִלְחָמָה. וְאִי בָּעִיתוּ לְמֶהֱוֵי קְרָבָא עָלֵיהּ, לֵית חַד אָכִיל, אֶלָּא מַאן דְּנָצַח קְרָבָא, אִיהוּ אָכִיל וּבוֹצֵעַ לְכֻלְּהוּ. א״ל חַבְרַיָּיא, בְּרִי אַנְתְּ זְעִיר, וַעֲדַיִין לָא יָדַעַת, אֵיךְ מְגִיחֵי גַּבְרִין רַבְרְבִין, בְּחַרְבָּא, בְּנִעְנוּעַ דְּחַרְבָּא. בְּרוֹמְחָא, בְּקַשְׁתָּא, בְּגִירִין דְּקַשְׁתָּא, בְּקִירְטָא, בְּאַבְנִין דְּקִירְטָא.

25. He said to us: 'Do you wish for delicacies without warring for them, or food by means of war?' That is how the sages of the Mishnah decreed that the mealtime is a time of war. If you desire to battle over it, let no one eat.

He who has won the battle shall eat first and apportion to the rest. The friends said to him: You are still small, my son, and you have yet to learn how mighty men wage war with a sword, with waving the sword, with a spear, with a bow and arrows, with a sling and stones.

26. א״ל, אַל יִתְהַלֵּל חוֹגֵר כִּמְפַתֵּחַ. דְּהָא וַדַּאי בְּק״ש אוֹקְמוּהָ, כָּל הַקּוֹרֵא ק״ש עַל מִטָּתוֹ, כְּאִילּוּ אוֹחֵז חֶרֶב פִּיפִיּוֹת, דִּכְתִּיב, רוֹמְמוֹת אֵל בִּגְרוֹנָם וְחֶרֶב פִּיפִיּוֹת בְּיָדָם. וְנִעְנוּעָא דְּחַרְבָּא, צָרִיךְ לְנַעְנְעָא לֵיהּ לְשִׁית סִטְרִין, כְּמָה דְּאוּקְמוּהָ, כְּדֵי שֶׁתַּמְלִיכוּהוּ עַל הַשָּׁמַיִם וְעַל הָאָרֶץ, וְעַל ד׳ רוּחוֹת הָעוֹלָם. וְדָא ו׳, גּוּף הַחֶרֶב. י׳ רֹאשׁ הַחֶרֶב. ה״ה, תְּרֵי פִּיּוֹת. נַרְתְּקָא דְּחַרְבָּא, אֲדֹנָי.

26. He said to us: "Let not him that girds on his harness boast himself as he that takes it off" (I Melachim 20:11). It has been explained, regarding the reading of the Sh'ma, that whoever recites the reading of Sh'ma by his bedside is as if he holds a double-edged sword, as it is written: "The high praises of Hashem are in their throats, and a two-edged sword in their hand" (Tehilim 149:6). The waving of the sword needs to be done to the six directions, WHICH ARE CHESED, GVURAH, TIFERET, NETZACH, HOD AND YESOD, as was explained, in order to make Him reign over the heavens, the earth, and the four corners of the world, WHICH ARE THE SIX DIRECTIONS. This Vav OF YUD HEI VAV HEI, THAT IS ZEIR ANPIN, is the body of the sword, and Yud OF YUD HEI VAV HEI IS the top of the sword. The two Hei's OF YUD HEI VAV HEI are the two edges OF THE SWORD. The sheath of the sword IS THE NAME Adonai, NAMELY MALCHUT.

27. רוּמְחָא רמ״ח בְּק״ש, עִם שִׁית תֵּיבִין דְּיִחוּדָא, הָא רוֹמַ״ח. מָגֵ״ן עִם חַרְבָּא, מִיכָאֵל גַּבְרִיאֵל נוּרִיאֵל שַׁמָּשִׁין דְּג׳ אֲבָהָן. קֶשֶׁת דְּזָרִיק חִצִּים, וְכָל זֶרַע דְּאֵינוֹ יוֹרֶה כַּחֵץ אֵינוֹ מוֹלִיד. קִירְטָא, דָּא ק״ש. ה׳ אַבְנִין דְּקִירְטָא, שְׁמַע יִשְׂרָאֵל יְיָ׳ אֱלֹהֵינוּ יְיָ׳. לְקַבְּלַיְיהוּ, וַיִּקַּח דָּוִד חֲמִשָּׁה חַלּוּקֵי אֲבָנִים מִן הַנַּחַל. וְכַד שַׁוֵּי לְהוֹן בְּקִירְטָא, דְּאִיהִי שָׂפָה, וְאִיהִי שְׁכִינְתָּא, אִתְעֲבֵידוּ חַד כֻּלְּהוּ ה׳, וְקָטִיל לְפְלִשְׁתָּאָה.

27. The spear (Heb. *romach*, Resh Vav Mem Chet) is the 248 (Resh Mem Chet) words in the reading of the Sh'ma, and together with the six words in the unification SH'MA YISRAEL, they total romach, THAT IS RAMACH PLUS VAV. The shield (Heb. *magen*) is with the sword, THAT IS, THE THREE ANGELS, Michael, Gabriel and Nuriel, WHOSE INTIALS FORM MAGEN. They serve the three Patriarchs, CHESED, GVURAH AND TIFERET, AS MICHAEL IS CHESED, GABRIEL GVURAH AND NURIEL TIFERET. The bow shoots arrows, and any sperm that does not shoot forth like an arrow does not beget offspring. THIS ALLUDES TO YESOD. The sling refers to the reading of the Sh'ma, and the five sling stones ARE THE FIVE WORDS: "Hear, O Yisrael, Hashem our Elohim, Hashem," WHICH ARE THE SECRET OF CHESED, GVURAH, TIFERET, NETZACH AND HOD, corresponding to the verse: "and chose him five smooth stones out of the brook" (I Shmuel 17:40). When he placed them into the sling, which is the mouth, BY READING THE SH'MA, which is the Shechinah, all five turned into one stone and killed the Philistine.

28. וְעַד כְּעַן זָרִיקְנָא הַאי אַבְנָא לְסָמָאֵל, דְּאִיהוּ אֶבֶן מָצוֹר, וְהָרַסְנָא מָצוֹר דִּילֵיהּ, וְאַשְׁפַּלְנָא לֵיהּ לְתַתָּא. וּבג״ד אֲמֵינָא לְכוֹן, אַל יִתְהַלֵּל חוֹגֵר כִּמְפַתֵּחַ. כְּעַן יִתְבָּרֵר לְכוֹן, דַּאֲנָא יְדַעְנָא אֵיךְ מַגִּיחִין גֻּבְרִין רַבְרְבִין בְּסַיְיפִין, בְּרוּמְחָא, בְּקַשְׁתָּא, בְּקִירְטָא. תַּוְּוהְנָא וְלָא יָכִילְנָא לְמַלְּלָא קַמֵּיהּ, א״ל רַבָּנָן, כְּעַן נֶחֱזֵי, מַאן יְהֵא מָרְוָוח נַהֲמָא, דְּאִיהוּ לֶחֶם הַמּוֹצִיא.

28. Up until now, I have been throwing the stone at Samael, a stone of siege. I have ruined his siege and lowered him down. Therefore, I said to you, "Let not him that girds on his harness boast himself as he that takes it off." Now it will become clear to you that I do know how mighty men wage war with swords, with spears, with bows and slings. We were astonished and could not speak to him. He said to us: Sages, let us now see who shall win bread, that is, the bread of the blessing over the bread.

29. פָּתַח וְאָמַר, וְהָיָה בַּאֲכָלְכֶם מִלֶּחֶם הָאָרֶץ תָּרִימוּ תְרוּמָה לַיְיָ׳. בְּמַאי אַתְרִימַת שְׁכִינְתָּא, דְּאִיהִי ה׳ דְּהַמּוֹצִיא, דְּאוּקִימוּ עָלָהּ מָארֵי מַתְנִיתִין, כָּל הַבּוֹצֵעַ, צָרִיךְ לְדַקְדֵּק בְּה׳. אֶלָּא וַדַּאי הָא אוּקְמוּהָ רַבָּנָן דְּמַתְנִיתִין, מוֹץ וְתֶבֶן פְּטוּרִין מִן הַמַּעֲשֵׂר. וְכַד הִיא בְּמוֹץ וְתֶבֶן, אִיהִי

בְּבֵית אֲסוּרִין, וְלֵית לָהּ רְשׁוּ לְאַרְמָא לְגַבֵּי מ׳, לְמֶעְבַּד עִמָּהּ מַ״ה. וְהַאי אִיהוּ תְּרוּמָה, תּוֹר״ה דְּאִיהִי ה׳ חוּמְשֵׁי תּוֹרָה, דְּבָהּ וַיְהִי מֹשֶׁה בָּהָר אַרְבָּעִים יוֹם וְגוֹ׳.

29. He opened the discussion saying: "When you eat of the bread of the land, you shall offer up (lit. 'raise') a gift (Heb. *trumah*) to Hashem" (Bemidbar 15:19). HE ASKS: How is the Shechinah raised, who is the Hei of *Hamotzi*, regarding which the sages of the Mishnah have decreed that 'Whoever breaks the bread of *Hamotzi* have to be precise in pronouncing the Hei'. HE RESPONDS: surely it has been decreed by the Mishnah sages that, 'chaff and straw do not require tithing'. When MALCHUT is in the chaff and straw, THAT IS, WHEN THE KLIPOT ARE SUSTAINED BY HER, she is in prison, and the Hei, THE SHECHINAH, does not have permission to rise to the Mem, WHICH IS ZEIR ANPIN, to become, with it, Mem Hei, MEANING YUD HEI VAV HEI FULLY SPELLED WITH ALEPH'S OF THE NUMERICAL VALUE OF MEM HEI (45). This is the meaning of Trumah, SPELLED AS TORAH AND MEM HEI, which is Hei (= 5) of the five books of the Torah, in which IS MEM, AS IS WRITTEN: "and Moses was in the mountain forty days..." (Shemot 24:18).

30. וּבְמוֹץ וְתֶבֶן דְּחִטָּה, עָלֵיהּ אוּקְמוּהָ רַבָּנָן, אִילָן שֶׁאָכַל אָדָם הָרִאשׁוֹן חִטָּה הֲוָה. קָרִיב ח״ט, דְּאִיהוּ מוֹץ וְתֶבֶן, לְאָת ה׳. וְאִסְתְּלִיק מִנֵּיהּ י׳, דְּאִיהוּ עִשּׂוּר דִּילָהּ. וּבג״ד כַּד אִיהוּ בְּמוֹץ וְתֶבֶן, דְּאִינּוּן לָקֳבֵל עָרְלָה וּפְרִיעָה, פָּטוּר מִן הַמַּעֲשֵׂר. וְלֵית רְשׁוּ לְאָת י׳, לְחַבְּרָא בְּאָת ה׳, דְּאִינּוּן אִישׁ וְאִשָּׁה. וּבְגִין דָּא, כָּל הַבּוֹצֵעַ צָרִיךְ לְדַקְדֵּק בָּהּ. וְצָרִיךְ לְמִבְצַע מֵאֲתָר דְּבִשּׁוּלוֹ יָפֶה, בְּגִין דְּבִשּׁוּל אִיהוּ גְּמַר פְּרִי, וְדָא ו׳.

30. Our sages referred to the chaff and straw of the wheat, when they said that the tree of which Adam ate was wheat. For by eating of the Tree of Knowledge of Good and Evil, he drew near Chet and Tet, WHICH ARE THE HUSKS (KLIPOT), chaff and straw, to the letter Hei, THAT IS MALCHUT. The Yud was gone from it, WHICH IS YESOD, its tithing. Therefore, when it is in straw and chaff – which correspond to the removal of the foreskin and the uncovering of the male organ, THAT IS, THEY CORRESPOND TO THE TWO LAYERS OF SKIN COVERING THE MALE ORGAN, ONE OF WHICH IS CUT OFF AND THE OTHER OF WHICH IS CUT OPEN, it does not require tithing. THAT IS YUD, for the letter Yud has no permission to join the letter Hei, which are a man and a woman, THAT IS, THE SECRET OF THE YUD IN THE SPELLING OF ISH (ENG. 'MAN') AND THE HEI IN THE SPELLING OF ISHAH (ENG. 'WOMAN'). Therefore, whoever breaks the bread must be precise pronouncing Hei and must break the bread where it is nicely baked, because the proper ripening is the completion of the fruit. That is the meaning of the Vav, WHICH IS ZEIR ANPIN THAT COMPLETES THE HEI, WHICH IS MALCHUT.

3. Ten things one must do for the meal

A Synopsis

The Faithful Shepherd begins to speak about the feast of the King – the display bread, the table, the utensils and vessels. He brings into the discussion the relevance of the Names of God and their numerical values, the four Holy Beasts and the 24 books in the Torah. Moses talks about the rituals that are performed before a King's table, and how beneficial and beautiful these are. We read about the distribution of the loaves of challah bread on Shabbat and about the blessings given by the guest. Next Rabbi Shimon appears and tells the Faithful Shepherd about a child of five years old who prepared the table all on his own as though he were twenty years old. The child knew the order of the blessings and lectured to the rabbis on the reading of the Sh'ma. We hear of the child's inner explanation of the wheat and the properly baked bread, and how he goes over the ten requirements that must be fulfilled for the Shabbat meal. The child talks about the Good Inclination and the Evil Inclination. We hear from the Faithful Shepherd the detailed explanation of the ten requirements mentioned by the child. In this explanation we hear about such things as the inner meaning of the ritual washing of the hands. Next Rabbi Shimon praises Moses, saying that he returns by reincarnation in every generation but that he did not reveal himself except in the generation when the Torah was received. At this point we learn that the souls of a generation who have just departed are reincarnated in the next generation immediately afterward. The Faithful Shepherd returns to his explication of the Shabbat meal, going over the injunction to break and hand out two loaves of bread, to eat three meals on the Shabbat, to have a lamp lit at the table, to have the cup of wine ready, to talk about matters of the Torah, to linger at the table for the sake of the poor and destitute, to do the final washing with water, to raise the cup of blessing with the proper ritual, and finally to perform the blessing after the meal.

31. וַעֲשָׂרָה דְּבָרִים צָרִיךְ אָדָם לְמֶעְבַּד בִּסְעוּדָתָא. חַד, נְטִילַת יָדַיִם. תִּנְיָינָא לְתַקְנָא שְׁתֵּי כִּכָּרוֹת לְשַׁבָּת. תְּלִיתָאָה, לְמֵיכַל תְּלַת סְעוּדָתִין, וּלְאוֹסָפָא מֵחוֹל עַל הַקֹּדֶשׁ. רְבִיעָאָה, לְאַנְהָרָא פָּתוֹרָא בִּשְׁרָגָא, כְּמָה דְּאוּקְמוּהָ, שֻׁלְחָן בַּצָּפוֹן, וּמְנוֹרָה בַּדָּרוֹם. וְצָרִיךְ הֲסֵבָּה, כְּמָה דְּאוֹקְמוּהָ הֵסֵבּוּ אֶחָד מְבָרֵךְ לְכֻלָּם.

3. Ten things one must do for the meal

31. There are ten things one must do for the meal: 1) the hand washing; 2) the preparation of the two Shabbat challah loaves; 3) to eat of three meals and add from weekdays to holiness; 4) to light a candle on the table, as was explained, that a table should be to the north side, and the candle on the south, and to recline, as was explained that if they recline together, one makes the blessing for everyone.

32. וּבְשַׁבָּת, בְּכָל מִלּוּי, צָרִיךְ לְאִתּוֹסְפָא מֵחוֹל עַל הַקֹּדֶשׁ, בֵּין בְּמַאֲכָלָיו, וּמִשְׁתָּיו, בֵּין בִּלְבוּשׁוֹי, בֵּין בַּהֲסֵבַתֵיהּ, דְּצָרִיךְ לְתַקְּנָא לֵיהּ מֵסִבָּה שַׁפִּירָא, בְּכַמָּה כָּרִים וּכְסָתוֹת מְרֻקָּמָן, מִכָּל דְּאִית בְּבֵיתֵיהּ, כְּמַאן דְּתַקִּין חוּפָּה לְכַלָּה. דְּשַׁבְּתָא אִיהִי מַלְכְּתָא, וְאִיהִי כַּלָּה. וּבְגִין דָּא הֲווֹ נַפְקֵי מָארֵי מַתְנִיתִין ע״ש, לְאַקְדְּמוּתָא לְאָרְחָא, וַהֲווֹ אַמְרֵי בֹּאִי כַלָּה בֹּאִי כַּלָּה. וּצְרִיכִין לְאַתְעָרָא שִׁירָה וְחֶדְוָה לְפָתוֹרָה לְגַבָּהּ.

32. On Shabbat, one should add from weekdays to holiness in everything he does, in his food and drink, his dress and his seating. He should prepare a comfortable reclining bed with many pillows and embroidered cushions from all that he has in his house, as when preparing the marriage canopy for the bride, because Shabbat is both a queen and a bride. Due to this, the sages of the Mishnah used to hasten to come out on Shabbat eve to welcome her on the way. And they used to say: 'Come bride, come bride.' There is a need to invoke on that table song and joy for her.

33. וְלֹא עוֹד, אֶלָּא דְּאִית רָזָא אָחֳרָא. כְּגַוְונָא דְּצָרִיךְ לְקַבְּלָא גְּבִירְתָּהּ, בְּכַמָּה נְהוֹרִין דִּשְׁרָגִין בְּשַׁבָּת, וּבְכַמָּה עִנּוּגִין, וּלְבוּשִׁין שַׁפִּירִין, וּבֵיתָא מְתֻקְּנָא, בְּכַמָּה מָאנֵי דְּתִקּוּנָא, בַּהֲסֵבָּה יָפָה לְכָל חַד וְחַד. וּבְהַאי חֶדְוָה וְתִקּוּנָא, גַּרְמִין דְּאִשְׁתְּאָרַת שִׁפְחָה בִּישָׁא בַּחֲשׁוֹכָא, בְּרַעֲבוֹן, בִּבְכִיָּה, בְּהֶסְפֵּד. בִּלְבוּשִׁין אוּכָמִין כְּאַרְמַלְתָּא. דְּאִי מְלֵאָה זוֹ, חֲרֵבָה זוֹ.

33. There is yet another secret meaning to it. ONE NEEDS TO WELCOME SHABBAT as it behooves one to welcome a lady by lighting many lamps for Shabbat, by many pleasures, beautiful clothes, a house set with many adorned vessels and nicely set up comfortable chairs for everyone. For joy and preparation cause the evil handmaid, THAT IS THE KLIPAH, to remain in the dark in hunger, in weeping, in mourning, and in black dress like a widow. When the one is filled, the other is destroyed, BECAUSE THE KLIPAH IS FILLED ONLY WITH THE DESTRUCTION OF HOLINESS. SIMILARLY, HOLINESS BECOMES FULL FROM THE DESTRUCTION OF THE KLIPAH.

34. יֵצֶר טוֹב, מַטְרוֹנִיתָא קַדִּישָׁא. מַלְכוּת הַקֹּדֶשׁ דְּנַחְתָּא בְּשַׁבָּת. כְּלִילָא מֵעֶשֶׂר סְפִירָן. מְעַטְּרָא בְּשֶׁבַע שְׁמָהָן, שֶׁאֵינָן נִמְחָקִין. בְּכַמָּה מַרְכְּבוֹת דְּחֵיוָון. וּבְכַמָּה חַיָּילִין וּמַשִׁרְיָין. וּמַלְכָּא נָפִיק לְקַבְּלָא בְּכַמָּה מַשִׁרְיָין. וְאִשְׁתָּאֲרַת יֵצֶר הָרָע שִׁפְחָה בִּישָׁא בַּחֲשׁוֹכָא, כְּאַרְמַלְתָּא בְּלֹא בַּעְלָהּ. בְּלָא מֶרְכָּבוֹת.

34. The Good Inclination is the Holy Queen, Malchut of holiness that descended on Shabbat that is comprised of ten Sfirot. She is decorated with seven names that are not erased, with the many Chariots of the living creatures, and with the many armies and camps OF ANGELS. The King goes out to her with many camps, and the Evil Inclination that is the wicked handmaid remains in the dark, like a widow without her husband, without any Chariots.

35. וְאִלֵּין דְּאִתְּמַר עֲלַיְיהוּ, לַמְזַבְּחִין וְלַמְקַטְּרִין לִמְלֶכֶת הַשָּׁמַיִם וְלַמַּזָּלוֹת אֲשֶׁר לֹא צִוִּיתִי, הוּא פּוּלְחָנָא דְּשִׁפְחָה בִּישָׁא, דְּשַׁלְטֵי בְּעַרְבֵי שַׁבָּתוֹת וְעַרְבֵי לֵילֵי רְבִיעִיּוֹת, מַה הֲווֹ אִלֵּין עַבְדִּין. הֲווֹ נַטְלִין לְבוּשִׁין אוּכָמִין, וְחַשְׁכָאן נְהוֹרִין, וְעַבְדִּין הֶסְפֵּדָא בְּלֵילֵי שַׁבָּתוֹת כְּדֵי לְאִשְׁתַּתְּפָא בַּהֲדָהּ כְּמָה דְּאִיהִי שַׁרְיָא, כִּי גַּם זֶה לְעוּמַּת זֶה עָשָׂה הָאֱלֹהִים.

35. It was said about them: "to those who sacrifice and burn incense to the queen of the heavens, and the constellation which I have not commanded" (Devarim 17:3), which is the worship WITH WHICH THEY SERVE the wicked handmaid that rules on Shabbat eve and on Wednesday eves. What do they do ON SHABBAT? HE RESPONDS: They wear black clothes, extinguish their lights, and lament on Shabbat eve to participate WITH THE WICKED HANDMAID, TO BE IN SADNESS, TROUBLE AND DARKNESS as she is, because "Elohim has made the one as well as the other" (Kohelet 7:14).

36. בָּתַר דְּחָאבוּ יִשְׂרָאֵל, וְאִתְחָרַב בֵּי מַקְדְּשָׁא, אִתְּמַר בִּשְׁכִינְתָּא אִימָּא קַדִּישָׁא, אֵיכָה יָשְׁבָה בָדָד הָעִיר רַבָּתִי עָם הָיְתָה כְּאַלְמָנָה, וּמְכַבִּין בְּלֵיל תִּשְׁעָה בְּאָב נְהוֹרִין וּשְׁרָגִין, וְעַבְדִּין הֶסְפֵּד, וְיַתְבִין כַּאֲבֵלִים לְאִשְׁתַּתְּפָא בְּדוֹחֲקָא דִּשְׁכִינְתָּא. בְּגִין דְּאִינּוּן גַּרְמוּ לָהּ כָּל הַהוּא תְּבִירוּ.

36. After Yisrael sinned and the Temple was destroyed, it is said regarding the Shechinah, holy Ima: "How does the city sit solitary, that was full of people! How is she become like a widow" (Eichah 1:1). THEREFORE, people extinguish lamps and candles on Tishah B'Av, and sit like mourners to participate in the sorrow of the Shechinah, because they caused Her all this calamity IN THEIR INIQUITIES.

37. חֲמִשָּׁאָה, כּוֹס דְּוַיְכֻלּוּ. שְׁתִיתָאָה, לְמֶהֱוֵי עַל פָּתוֹרָא מִלֵּי דְּאוֹרַיְיתָא. שְׁבִיעָאָה, לְאַרְכָּאָה עַל פָּתוֹרָא, בְּגִין דַּעֲנִיִּים יֵיתוּן עַל פָּתוֹרֵיהּ. תְּמִינָאָה, נְטִילַת יָדַיִם בְּמַיִם אַחֲרוֹנִים. תְּשִׁיעָאָה, בִּרְכַּת הַמָּזוֹן. עֲשִׂירָאָה, כּוֹס דִּבְרָכָה. וְצָרִיךְ לְאַחְזְרָא עֲלַיְיהוּ, וּלְתַקְּנָא לוֹן בְּרָזָא קַדִּישָׁא, דְּאִיהִי כְּלוּלָה מֵעֶשֶׂר סְפִירָאן, וְאִיהוּ פָּתוֹרָא דְּקוּדְשָׁא בְּרִיךְ הוּא, מִסִּטְרָא דִּגְבוּרָה. וּבְגִין כָּךְ אוֹקְמוּהָ רַבָּנָן, שֻׁלְחָן בַּצָּפוֹן.

37. The fifth THING IT BEHOOVES US TO PREPARE ON SHABBAT is the cup OF WINE for saying, "Thus the heavens and the earth were finished (Heb. *vaychulu*)..." (Beresheet 2:1) NAMELY, KIDDUSH. The sixth is to speak words of Torah at the table. The seventh is to extend the meal and allow the poor to come to the table. The eighth is washing the hands with fingerbowl water. The ninth is the blessing after the meal. The tenth is the cup for the blessing AFTER THE MEAL. It is necessary to repeat THESE TEN THINGS and to prepare them in accordance with the holy meaning, for she, MALCHUT, is comprised of ten Sfirot. MALCHUT IS CONSIDERED the table of the Holy One, blessed be He, from the side of Gvurah. Hence, the sages have explained that the table should face the north, WHICH IS FROM THE SIDE OF GVURAH.

38. חַד נְטִילַת יָדַיִם, דְּהָכִי אוֹקְמוּהָ רַבָּנָן דְּמַתְנִיתִין, יָדַיִם מְזוּהָמוֹת

פְּסוּלוֹת לַבְּרָכָה, בְּגִין דְּאִינּוּן שְׁנִיּוֹת לַטּוּמְאָה, דְּאִיהוּ אַב הַטּוּמְאָה, דְּאִיהוּ רִאשׁוֹן כַּד אִינּוּן מְסֻאָבוֹת, וְכַד אִינּוּן טְהוֹרוֹת אִינּוּן שְׁנִיּוֹת לַבְּרָכָה, דִּבְרָכָה לָא שַׁרְיָא אֶלָּא עַל טַהֲרָה. כַּהֲנָא דְּאִיהוּ אִישׁ טָהוֹר, אִישׁ חֶסֶד, שַׁרְיָא עָלֵיהּ בִּרְכָתָא. הה״ד, כַּשֶּׁמֶן הַטּוֹב עַל הָרֹאשׁ וְגוֹ׳. וּבְגִין דָּא, דַּבֵּר אֶל אַהֲרֹן וְאֶל בָּנָיו לֵאמֹר כֹּה תְבָרֲכוּ אֶת בְּנֵי יִשְׂרָאֵל וְגוֹ׳. וְאוּקְמוּהָ, כָּל כֹּהֵן הַמְּבָרֵךְ, מִתְבָּרֵךְ. וְשֶׁאֵינוֹ מְבָרֵךְ, אֵין מִתְבָּרֵךְ. וְאוּקְמוּהָ מָארֵי מַתְנִיתִין, כָּל בְּרָכָה שֶׁאֵין בָּהּ אַזְכָּרָה וּמַלְכוּת לָאו שְׁמֵיהּ בְּרָכָה. מַלְכוּת אֲדֹנָי.

38. NOW COME THE WORDS OF THE FAITHFUL SHEPHERD, WHO EXPLAINS THESE TEN THINGS IT BEHOOVES ONE TO DO AT SHABBAT MEAL. The first, the washing of hands, MEANS THAT the sages of the Mishnah explained that: ‘filthy hands are unfit for blessing, because they are twice removed from uncleanness’. When hands are unclean, they are considered a principle cause of defilement, which is once removed from uncleanness, and when the hands are clean, they are considered twice removed from uncleanness and are fit to bless, because blessing rests only on purity, because blessing rests on a priest, who is a pure man, a man of kindness. This is the meaning of: “It is like the precious ointment upon the head...” (Tehilim 133:2). Therefore, “speak to Aaron and to his sons, saying, ‘In this way you shall bless the children of Yisrael…’” (Bemidbar 6:23). It was explained that every priest who blesses is blessed, and if he does not bless he is not blessed. The sages of the Mishnah have further explained that any blessing that does not have a recitation of the Name OF YUD HEI VAV HEI and Malchut, THAT IS, ‘KING OF THE WORLD’, is not considered a blessing, as Malchut is the name of Adonai. THUS, EVERY BLESSING SHOULD CONTAIN A RECITATION OF THE NAME YUD HEI VAV HEI, AND MALCHUT, WHICH IS ADONAI.

39. וְעוֹד, נְטִילַת יָדַיִם צָרִיךְ לִיטּוֹל לוֹן עַד פִּרְקָא, דְּגָזְרוּ עָלֵיהּ י״ד פִּרְקִין, בְּהַהוּא שַׁעֲתָא שַׁרְיָא יַד יְיָ׳ עָלֵיהּ, וְאִיהִי יַד דִּבְרָכָה מִסִּטְרָא דְּחֶסֶד דְּבֵיהּ חָכְמָה בְּיַד יְמִינֵיהּ. וְאִיהִי יַד דִּקְדוּשָּׁה, מִסִּטְרָא דִּגְבוּרָה, וְשַׁרְיָיא בְּדִינָא. וְאִיהִי יַד דְּיִחוּדָא, מִסִּטְרָא דְּת״ת, דְּשַׁרְיָא בְּי״ד פִּרְקִין דְּגוּפָא, דְּאִינּוּן שְׁנֵים עָשָׂר פִּרְקִין בִּתְרֵין דְּרוֹעִין, וּתְרֵין שׁוֹקִין. וּתְרֵין

בְּגוּפָא וּבְרִית.

39. In addition, the hands need to be washed up to the joint THAT ATTACH THE FIVE FINGERS, because it was decreed TO WASH fourteen (Yud Dalet) joints IN THE FIVE FINGERS. EACH FINGER HAS THREE JOINTS AND THE THUMB TWO. At that time, the hand (Heb. *yad*, Yud Dalet) of Hashem rests on him. It is the hand of blessing from the aspect of Chesed, wherein Chochmah lies in the right hand, BECAUSE DURING THE GREATNESS OF ZEIR ANPIN CHESED ASCENDS TO BECOME CHOCHMAH. It is the hand of holiness from the aspect of Gvurah that prevails on Judgment. It is also the hand of unification from the aspect of Tiferet THAT UNIFIES RIGHT AND LEFT INTO ONE. This rests on the fourteen joints of the body, because there are twelve joints in the two arms, THREE JOINTS IN EACH ARM THERE, and in the two legs WITH THREE JOINTS IN EACH LEG, WHICH ADDS UP TO SIX, AND TOGETHER THEY ARE TWELVE. TOGETHER WITH the two in the body and genital organ, they total fourteen. AND IT WAS EXPLAINED THAT THREE TIMES FOURTEEN ALSO REFERS TO THE THREE SFIROT – CHESED, GVURAH AND TIFERET.

40. וּתְלַת זִמְנִין י״ד, אִיהוּ מ״ב, יו״י, מִן י״ד י״ד, י״ד, רָמוּז יְבָ״רֶכְךָ יָאֵ״ר יִשָּׂ״א, מִן הוי״ה הוי״ה הוי״ה. ד׳ ד׳ ד׳ מִי״ד י״ד י״ד, אִינּוּן רְמִיזִין בַּאֲדֹנָ״י אֲדֹנָ״י אֲדֹנָ״י. וְאָמַר הַנָּבִיא עָלַיְיהוּ, הֵיכַל יְיָ׳ הֵיכַל יְיָ׳ הֵיכַל יְיָ׳ הֵמָּה. וְהַאי נְטִילָא בְּיַד דְּאִתְּתְקָנַת.

40. Three times fourteen equals 42, and the three Yuds in three times hand (Yud Dalet) are indicated in "Hashem bless you (Heb. *yevarechecha*) ...Hashem make His face shine upon you (Heb. *ya'er*)...Hashem lift up His countenance to you (Heb. *yisa*)" (Bemidbar 6:24-25) of Yud Hei Vav Hei, Yud Hei Vav Hei, Yud Hei Vav Hei IN THE VERSES, MEANING THE THREE YUDS IN THE THREE times YUD HEI VAV HEI IN, "HASHEM BLESS YOU...HASHEM MAKE HIS FACE SHINE UPON YOU...HASHEM LIFT UP HIS COUNTENANCE TO YOU." The three Dalets in three hands (Yud Dalet) are implied in Adonai, Adonai, Adonai. The prophet said about them, THE THREE TIMES YUD HEI VAV HEI AND THREE TIMES ADONAI: "The temple of Hashem, the temple of Hashem, the temple of Hashem, are these" (Yirmeyah 7:4). THIS TEMPLE IS THE SECRET OF MALCHUT THAT IS CALLED ADONAI. THEREFORE, IT REPEATS THREE TIMES "THE TEMPLE

OF HASHEM," WHICH IS THE SECRET OF THREE TIMES ADONAI AND THREE TIMES YUD HEI VAV HEI, AS MENTIONED. Hence the decree of washing the hands, TO INDICATE THE SECRET OF THE FOURTEEN JOINTS AND THE THREE TIMES FOURTEEN IN CHESED, GVURAH AND TIFERET, WHICH IS THE SECRET MEANING OF THREE TIMES YUD HEI VAV HEI AND THREE ADONAI, AS MENTIONED.

41. וְכָל סְטָר מִג׳ אַנְפֵּי חֵיוָן, דְּאִינּוּן יְדָ׳ יְדָ׳ יְדָ׳. וּמִתְּלַת גַּדְפֵּי חֵיוָן, דְּאִינּוּן ד׳ ד׳ ד׳, כֻּלְּהוּ צָרִיךְ לְמֶהֱוֵי מִכֹּחַ אָדָם. וְאִיהוּ יוֹ״ד הֵ״א וָא״ו הֵ״א. כֹּחַ דִּילֵיהּ, יוֹ״ד וָא״ו דָּלֶ״ת, הֵ״א אָלֶ״ף, וָא״ו אָלֶ״ף וָא״ו, הֵ״א אָלֶ״ף. וּמַטְרוֹנִיתָא לָא שַׁרְיָא בְּכֹחַ דִּילֵיהּ, בְּפִרְקִין דְּאֶצְבְּעָן, עַד דְּאִתְעֲבָר מִנַּיְיהוּ זוּהֲמָא, שִׁפְחָה בִּישָׁא פְּסוּלָה, אִנְתּוּ דְּפָסוּל. וּבְגִין דָּא אוּקְמוּהָ מָארֵי מַתְנִיתִין, יָדַיִם מְזוּהָמוֹת פְּסוּלוֹת לַבְּרָכָה.

41. Every side OF THE THREE COLUMNS – CHESED, GVURAH AND TIFERET, WHICH ARE RIGHT, LEFT AND CENTRAL THAT ARE THREE TIMES FOURTEEN, is comprised of the three faces of the living creatures, THE LION, OX, AND EAGLE, which are Yud Hei Vav Hei, Yud Hei Vav Hei, Yud Hei Vav Hei, and the three wings in the living creatures are Dalet, Dalet, Dalet, THAT IS, THREE TIMES ADONAI, AS MENTIONED. They all need to derive from the power (Heb. *ko'ach*, = 28) of man (Adam), THAT IS, YUD HEI VAV HEI FULLY SPELLED WITH ALEPHS, that is, Yud Vav Dalet, Hei Aleph, Vav Aleph Vav, Hei Aleph, which has the same numerical value as Adam. His power, THE FULLY SPELLED YUD HEI VAV HEI, AGAIN FULLY SPELLED, is Yud Vav Dalet, Vav Aleph Vav, Dalet Lamed Tav; Hei Aleph, Aleph Lamed Pe; Vav Aleph Vav, Aleph Lamed Pe, Vav Aleph Vav; Hei Aleph, Aleph Lamed Pe. THESE ARE 28 LETTERS THAT CORRESPOND TO THE 28 JOINTS IN THE TEN FINGERS OF THE HAND. The Queen does not dwell in his power, in the 28 finger joints, until all the filth of the wicked, unfit handmaid, wife to the unfit, is removed. Therefore, the sages of the Mishnah explained that 'dirty hands are unfit to make a blessing', BECAUSE THE HANDMAID RESTS ON THEM.

42. וְאִינּוּן מַיִם לְדַכְּאָה יַד, דְּשַׁרְיָיא תַּמָּן יַד יְדָ׳. יַד יְדָ׳, דָּא מַיִם דְּאוֹרַיְיתָא. דְּעַמֵּי הָאָרֶץ אִינּוּן שֶׁרֶץ, מַה מוֹעִיל לוֹן טְבִילָה, וְהַשֶּׁרֶץ

שִׁפְחָה בִּישָׁא בִּידַיְהוֹן, בְּגָזֵל דְּבִידַיְהוֹן. בְּגֶזֶל דְּבִרְכָּאן דְּגַזְלִין לְקוּדְשָׁא בְּרִיךְ הוּא, דְּלָא יַדְעֵי לְבִרְכָא, וְלָא יַדְעֵי מַאי אִיהִי בְּרָכָה, וּמַאי אִיהִי זוּהֲמָא.

42. This water is for cleansing the hand upon which the hand of Yud Hei Vav Hei rests, AS MENTIONED NEARBY. The hand of Yud Hei Vav Hei is the water of the Torah. The ignorant people are considered like unclean reptiles, WITHOUT KNOWLEDGE OF THE TORAH TO TAKE AWAY THEIR IMPURITY. What good will immersing in water do them, holding in their hand that reptile, which is the wicked handmaid, stolen goods in their possession, the stolen blessings they stole from the Holy One, blessed be He. They do not know what a blessing is, or what filth is.

43. מִיַּד כְּשֶׁשָּׁמְעוּ מִלִּין אִלֵּין חַבְרַיָּיא וַאֲנָא עִמְּהוֹן, לָא יָכִילְנָא לְמִסְבַּל דְּיַשְׁלִים עֲשָׂרָה מִלִּין דִּבְרָכָה, וְאִשְׁתְּטַחְנָא לְגַבֵּיהּ. וּבְוַדַּאי לֵית בַּר נָשׁ דְּיֵימָא מִלִּין אִלֵּין, אֶלָּא אַנְתְּ. דְּאַנְתְּ הוּא כְּגַוְונָא דד׳ מְחִיצוֹת דְּג״ע. דְּב״נ עָאל בְּהוֹן בִּמְחִיצַת יַנּוּקִין, וְאִתְעֲבֵיד תִּינוֹק. וּבִמְחִיצַת נְעָרִים, וְאִתְעֲבֵיד נַעַר. וּבִמְחִיצַת בַּחוּרִים, וְאִתְעֲבֵיד בָּחוּר. וּבִמְחִיצַת זְקֵנִים, וְאִתְעֲבֵיד זָקֵן. וּבג״כ אִתְּמַר עָלָךְ, ׳מִמְּכוֹן ׳שִׁבְתּוֹ ׳הִשְׁגִּיחַ אֶל כָּל יוֹשְׁבֵי הָאָרֶץ. וְאַנְתְּ הוּא דְּאִתְּמַר עָלָךְ, בְּשַׁגַּם הוּא בָּשָׂר בְּדָרָא דְּדוֹר הַפְּלָגָה הֲוֵית. וּבְכָל דָּרָא וְדָרָא בְּגִלְגּוּלָא. כְּגַלְגַּל דְּמִתְהַפֵּךְ לְכַמָּה גַּוְונִין. וְלָא נִגְלֵית, אֶלָּא בְּדָרָא דְּאִתְיְיהִיב בֵּיהּ אוֹרַיְיתָא עַל יָדָךְ.

43. Immediately after the friends and myself heard these words, we could not stand to wait for him to finish all these ten items pertaining to blessings. We prostrated ourselves before him AND SAID TO HIM: Certainly, there is no one who could speak these things except for you, since you are comparable to the four sections in the Garden of Eden. If a person enters the children's section, he becomes a child; in the youths' section he becomes a youth; in the young men's section, he becomes a young man, and in the old people's section, he becomes an old man. Hence, it is written about you: "from the place of His habitation He looks upon all the inhabitants of the earth" (Tehilim 33:14), WHICH INITIALS IN HEBREW FORM MOSES. Also, it is about you that it says: "for that he also (Heb. *beshagam*) is flesh"

(Beresheet 6:3). THE WORD *BESHAGAM* CONTAINS THE LETTERS OF THE WORD MOSES, AS IT CONTAINS *MEM* AND *SHIN*, AND *BET AND GIMEL* BECOME *HEI*. You were present in the generation of the Tower of Babel, and in every generation YOU RETURN by incarnation like a wheel that turns around in many ways, yet you revealed yourself only at the generation when the Torah was given at your hands.

44. מִיַּד דְּאִתְכְּנִישַׁת מֵעָלְמָא, אַנְתְּ הוּא כְּשִׁמְשָׁא דְּנָהִיר בְּכָל דָּרָא וְדָרָא, דְּכַד אִתְכְּנַשׁ שִׁמְשָׁא בְּלֵילְיָא, נָהִיר בְּסִיהֲרָא, וּבְשִׁתִּין רִבּוֹא כֹּכְבַיָּא. הָכִי אַתְּ, דְּאַנְתְּ נָהִיר בְּשִׁתִּין רִבּוֹא בְּכָל דָּרָא וְדָרָא. וְהַאי אִיהוּ דְּקָא רָמַז קֹהֶלֶת, דּוֹר הוֹלֵךְ וְדוֹר בָּא. וְאוּקְמוּהָ רַבָּנָן, אֵין דּוֹר פָּחוּת מִשִּׁשִּׁים רִבּוֹא. וְעוֹד אוּקְמוּהָ, הַדּוֹר שֶׁהוֹלֵךְ הוּא שֶׁבָּא, לְקַיֵּים מַה שֶּׁהָיָה הוּא שֶׁיִּהְיֶה. מִכָּאן וְאֵילָךְ, אַשְׁלִים עַשְׂרָה דְּבָרִים דִּפְתוֹרָא בְּאִתְגַּלְיָיא. אָמַר רַעְיָא מְהֵימְנָא, בּוּצִינָא קַדִּישָׁא זַכָּאָה חוּלָקָךְ, דְּקוּדְשָׁא בְּרִיךְ הוּא גַּלֵּי לָךְ, מַה דְּלָא גַּלֵּי לְכָל נָבִיא וְחוֹזֶה, וְלָא לְמַאן וּלְמַאן.

44. As soon as you departed from the world, you became like a sun that shines in every generation. Even when the sun is gathered at night, it illuminates the moon and 600,000 stars. So are you who shine on the 600,000 people in each and every generation. That is what Kohelet indicated in the verse: "One generation passes away, and another generation comes" (Kohelet 1:4). The sages have explained that a generation does not consist of less than 600,000 people. They also explained THIS VERSE TO MEAN the generation that passes away is the one that comes. THAT IS, THE SOULS OF THE PREVIOUS GENERATION REINCARNATE AND COME IN THE FOLLOWING GENERATION. This fulfills THE VERSE: "That which has been, it is that which shall be" (Kohelet 1:9). From here on, complete the ten items about Shabbat table openly. The Faithful Shepherd said TO RABBI SHIMON: Holy Luminary, blessed is your lot that the Holy One, blessed be He, revealed to you what He has not revealed to any prophet or seer.

45. תְּנֵיָינָא, לְמִבְצַע עַל שְׁנֵי כִּכָּרוֹת בְּשַׁבָּת, דְּאִינּוּן רְמִיזִין בִּתְרֵי לוּחֵי אוֹרַיְיתָא, דְּאִתְיְיהִיבוּ בְּשַׁבָּת זוּגוֹת. דִּבְיוֹמָא תְּלִיתָאָה נַחְתּוּ, דְּבֵיהּ תְּרֵי

זִמְנֵי טוֹב, וּבְשַׁבָּת אִתְיְיהִיבַת, תְּרֵין נוּקְבִין לִתְרֵין טָבִין. וְאע״ג דְּאוּקְמוּהָ דְּשֵׁדִים מְמֻנָּן עַל זוּגוֹת, כְּמָה דְּאוּקְמוּהָ שְׁנֵי בֵּיצִים, שְׁנֵי אֱגוֹזִים. הֲלָכָה לְמֹשֶׁה מִסִּינַי שְׁלוּחֵי מִצְוָה אֵינָן נִזּוֹקִין.

45. The second SETTING REGARDING SHABBAT TABLE is to break bread over two loaves of bread on Shabbat, which are alluded to in the two tablets of the Torah that were given on Shabbat in pairs. On the third day, THAT IS TIFERET, they descended FROM HEAVEN, on which it was said twice 'good', SINCE IT COMPRISES RIGHT AND LEFT. On Shabbat, WHICH IS MALCHUT, the Torah was given, in which, IN MALCHUT, THERE ARE TWO FEMALES, ONE FROM THE CHEST OF ZEIR ANPIN AND UPWARD, AND ONE FROM THE CHEST OF ZEIR ANPIN DOWNWARD. THESE ARE two females, which correspond to twice 'good', SAID ON THE THIRD DAY, WHICH IS TIFERET. Though it was explained that demons are assigned TO HARM pairs – as has been explained THAT ONE MUST NOT EAT two eggs or two walnuts, YET IF THIS IS SO, WHY ARE TWO LOAVES OF BREAD USED ON SHABBAT, SEEING THEY ARE A PAIR? HE RESPONDS, it is a usage dating from Moses as delivered from Sinai that those sent on pious missions will meet no evil. THEREFORE, THERE IS NO NEED TO FEAR PERFORMING A PRECEPT DUE TO IT BEING IN PAIRS.

46. וְאִי תֵּימָא, וְהָא תָּנֵינָן, אֵין מַתְחִילִין בְּשֵׁנִי, וְאֵין מְסַיְּימִין בְּד׳, דְּהַיְינוּ בְּב׳ ד׳ עִם עֶרֶב רַב, דְּלָא הֲווֹ שְׁלוּחֵי מִצְוָה, דְּלָא אִתְגַּיְּירוּ לְשֵׁם שָׁמַיִם, וּלְבָתַר דְּאִתְעַבָּרוּ מֵעָלְמָא, מָנֵי קוּדְשָׁא בְּרִיךְ הוּא לְנַטְלָא שְׁנֵי לוּחוֹת אֲבָנִים כָּרִאשׁוֹנִים, וְאָמַר, וְכָתַבְתִּי עַל הַלּוּחוֹת אֶת הַדְּבָרִים אֲשֶׁר הָיוּ עַל הַלּוּחוֹת וְגוֹ׳.

46. You may wonder why we learned that one should not begin anything on the second day of the week or finish on Wednesday – MEANING ON THE SECOND AND ON THE FOURTH BECAUSE THEY ARE PAIRS, WHICH APPLIES TO MATTERS OF PRECEPTS AS WELL, EVEN THOUGH THOSE SENT ON PIOUS MISSIONS WILL MEET NO EVIL. HE ANSWERS, THIS IS when with the mixed multitude, THAT IS, WHEN THE CHILDREN OF YISRAEL ARE MINGLED WITH THE MIXED MULTITUDE, who are never sent on pious missions, because they have not converted for Heaven's sake. THEN, IT IS

FORBIDDEN TO BEGIN ON MONDAY OR WEDNESDAY. HOWEVER, THE RIGHTEOUS, WHO HAVE NO CONNECTION WITH THE MIXED MULTITUDE MAY START ON MONDAY AND WEDNESDAY FOR THE SAKE OF PERFORMING A PRECEPT, BECAUSE THOSE SENT ON A PIOUS MISSION SHALL COME TO NO HARM. THEREFORE, after they were gone from the world, AFTER THE SIN OF THE GOLDEN CALF, the Holy One, blessed be He, commanded to take "two tablets of stone like the first" (Shemot 34:1), saying:" "And I will write on the tablets the words that were on the first tablets..." (Ibid.). AND HE DID NOT MIND THE PAIRS.

47. וּתְרֵין כִּכָּרוֹת בְּשַׁבָּת, רְמִיזִין לִתְרֵין יוֹדִין יְאֲהדוֹנָהִי. דַּאֲדֹנָי אִיהִי יְחִידָה מִבַּעְלָהּ בְּשִׁית יוֹמִין דְּחוֹל, וּבְשַׁבָּת נָחִית לְגַבָּהּ. וּבְגִין דָּא בְּשַׁבָּת, כָּל נִשְׁמָתִין וְרוּחִין וְנַפְשִׁין נָפְקִין וְנַחְתִּין זוּגוֹת, וְאֵין שָׂטָן וְאֵין מַזִּיק שַׁלִּיט בְּיוֹמָא דְּשַׁבְּתָא. וַאֲפִילּוּ גֵּיהִנָּם לָא שַׁלִּיט, וְלָא אוֹקִיד בְּשַׁבָּת. וּבְגִין דָּא, לֹא תְבַעֲרוּ אֵשׁ בְּכֹל מוֹשְׁבוֹתֵיכֶם בְּיוֹם הַשַּׁבָּת. וְדָא אֵשׁ נוּכְרָאָה, אֶלָּא אֵשׁ דְּקָרְבְּנָא, אֵשׁ דִּקְדוּשָּׁה. וְלֵית לְאַרְכָּאָה בִּבְצִיעָא דִּלְהוֹן, דְּהָא אִתְּמַר לְעֵילָּא.

47. The two loaves of bread on Shabbat indicate the two Yuds IN THE COMBINATION OF YUD HEI VAV HEI AND ADONAI, WHICH IS Yud Aleph Hei Dalet Vav Nun Hei Yud. For Adonai, WHICH IS MALCHUT, is alone without her husband, WHICH IS YUD HEI VAV HEI, during the six weekdays, BECAUSE THEY ARE NOT THEN IN A COMPLETE UNION. On Shabbat, YUD HEI VAV HEI descends TO ADONAI AND THE COMBINATION IS FORMED OF YUD ALEPH HEI DALET VAV NUN HEI YUD. THEREFORE, TWO LOAVES OF BREAD ARE USED TO INDICATE THE TWO YUDS AT THE BEGINNING AND END OF THIS COMBINATION OF THE NAME YUD-ALEPH-HEI-DALET VAV-NUN-HEI-YUD. Hence, all Neshamot, Ruchot and Nefashot leave and come down in pairs on Shabbat, and no devil or demon has power on Shabbat day. Even Gehenom has no power and does not burn on Shabbat. Therefore, "you shall kindle no fire throughout your habitations on Shabbat day" (Shemot 35:3). That refers to strange fire, but the fire of sacrifice is a fire of holiness, WHICH IS PERMISSIBLE IN THE TEMPLE ON SHABBAT. THUS, WE NEED TO TAKE TWO LOAVES OF BREAD ON SHABBAT AND NOT TO BE AFRAID OF PAIRS. There is no need to speak at length on THE SUBJECT OF their apportioning, MEANING, ABOUT THE MEASURE OF AN

OLIVE'S SIZE OR AN EGG'S SIZE, as it was already explained above.

48. תְּלִיתָאָה לְמֵיכַל שְׁלֹשָׁה סְעוּדָתִין בְּשַׁבָּת, כְּמָה דְּאוּקְמוּהָ רַבָּנָן דְּמַתְנִיתִין, דְּאָמַר חַד מִינַיְיהוּ, יְהֵא חֶלְקִי עִם גּוֹמְרֵי שָׁלֹשׁ סְעוּדוֹת בְּשַׁבָּת, דְּאִינּוּן שְׁלִימוּ דְּשֶׁבַע בִּרְכָאן דִּצְלוֹתָא, לְאַשְׁלְמָא בְּהוֹן לַעֲשַׂר. וְרָזָא דְּעֹנֶג, וְנָהָר יוֹצֵא מֵעֵדֶן לְהַשְׁקוֹת אֶת הַגָּן. וּמַאן דְּלָא מְקַיֵּים לוֹן, וְאִית לֵיהּ רְשׁוּ לְקַיְּימָן, אִתְהַפָּךְ לֵיהּ לְנֶגַע צָרַעַת. וּבְגִין דְּלָא יֵיתֵי לְהַאי, אָמַר קוּדְשָׁא בְּרִיךְ הוּא, לְווּ עָלַי וַאֲנִי פּוֹרֵעַ, אָז תִּתְעַנַּג עַל יְיָ'.

48. The third SETTING REGARDING THE SHABBAT TABLE IS to eat three meals on Shabbat, as was explained by the sages of the Mishnah. One of them said: 'Let my lot be with those who eat on three meals on Shabbat', which complete the seven blessings in the Amidah prayer by bringing them to a total of ten. The secret of delight (Heb. *oneg*, Ayin Nun Gimel) is THE SECRET MEANING OF: "and a river went out of Eden to water that garden" (Beresheet 2:10). FOR EDEN MEANS DELIGHT, AND THE GARDEN IS MALCHUT, THE SECRET MEANING OF SHABBAT. ALSO, *ONEG* IS THE INITIALS OF EDEN, NAHAR (ENG. 'RIVER') AND GAN (ENG. 'GARDEN'). Whoever can but does not observe them, for him the *oneg* turns into a plague (Heb. *nega*) of leprosy, AS THEY ARE SPELLED WITH THE SAME LETTERS. In order that he should not come to this, the Holy One, blessed be He, says: 'Borrow on Me and I will pay', AND IT IS WRITTEN: "then shall you delight yourself in Hashem" (Yeshayah 58:14).

49. רְבִיעָאָה, לְאַנְהָרָא פָּתוֹרָא בִּמְנַרְתָּא. כְּמָה דְּאוּקְמוּהָ קַדְמָאִין, שֻׁלְחָן בַּצָּפוֹן, מְנוֹרָה בַּדָּרוֹם, דְּפָתוֹרָא דְּקוּדְשָׁא בְּרִיךְ הוּא הָכִי צְרִיכָא לְמֶהֱוֵי. חֲמִישָׁאָה כּוֹס דְּוַיְכֻלּוּ. כּוֹ"ס, בְּחֻשְׁבּוֹן אֱלֹהִים. וַיְכֻלּוּ ע"ב, דִּכְלִיל לוֹן כַּלָּה קַדִּישָׁא, דְּהַאי כּוֹס מָלֵא יֵינָא דְּאוֹרַיְיתָא, צָרִיךְ לְאַסְהֲדָא עַל עוֹבָדָא דִּבְרֵאשִׁית.

49. The fourth SETTING is to light the table with a lamp, as was decreed by ancient sages that a table should be at the north and the lamp at the south, for the table of the Holy One, blessed be He, MALCHUT, needs to be that way. The fifth SETTING is the wine cup of '*vaychulu*', MEANING THE

KIDDUSH CUP. The numerical value of 'kos (Eng. 'cup')' is that of Elohim, THAT IS, 86. '*Vaychulu*' is 72 IN NUMERICAL VALUE, which the holy Bride, MALCHUT, includes, NAMELY, THE NAME ELOHIM AND THE NAME OF AYIN BET (72). The cup, WHICH IS MALCHUT, filled with the wine, MEANING THE ABUNDNBCE OF THE ILLUMINATION OF CHOCHMAH, of the Torah, WHICH IS ZEIR ANPIN CALLED TORAH, needs to bear testimony to the act of Creation, WHICH IS THE SECRET OF BINAH, BECAUSE THE ABUNDANCE OF THE ILLUMINATION OF CHOCHMAH IS CONSIDERED A TESTIMONY (HEB. *EDUT*), BASED ON EDEN, AND BINAH IS THE SOURCE THAT POURS IT. THAT IS THE REASON WHY ONE SHOULD TESTIFY TO THE ACT OF CREATION.

50. שְׁתִיתָאָה, לְמֶהֱוֵי עַל פָּתוֹרָא דִּבְרֵי תּוֹרָה, דְּהָכִי אוֹקְמוּהָ מָארֵי מַתְנִיתִין, ג׳ שֶׁאָכְלוּ עַל שֻׁלְחָן אֶחָד וְלָא אָמְרוּ עָלָיו דִּבְרֵי תּוֹרָה וְכוּ׳. וְרָזָא דְּמִלָּה, בְּגִין דְּהָא אוֹקְמוּהָ שֻׁלְחָן בַּצָּפוֹן, וְאוֹרַיְיתָא אִתְיְיהִיבַת מִימִינָא. לְחַבְּרָא יְמִינָא דְּאִיהוּ רַחֲמֵי, בִּשְׂמָאלָא דְּאִיהוּ דִּינָא. דְּאוֹרַיְיתָא אִיהִי יְיָ׳ מִימִינָא, פָּתוֹרָא אֲדֹנָי מִשְּׂמָאלָא, וְצָרִיךְ לְחַבְּרָא לוֹן. דִּבְגִין דְּפָתוֹרָא מִשְּׂמָאלָא, אוֹקְמוּהָ רַבָּנָן דְּמַתְנִיתִין, קָשִׁין מְזוֹנוֹתָיו שֶׁל אָדָם כִּקְרִיעַת יַם סוּף. וּבְגִין כַּךְ, צָרִיךְ ת״ח לְזַמְּנָא עִמֵּיהּ, לְמַאן דְּיִשְׁתְּדַּל בְּפִתְגָּמֵי אוֹרַיְיתָא.

50. The sixth SETTING is to have words of Torah at one's table, because that is how the sages of the Mishnah decreed about 'three who ate on the same table yet have not spoken on it words of Torah...' The secret meaning is that they have decreed that the table should be to the north and that the Torah was given from the right. THEREFORE, IT BEHOOVES ONE TO SAY WORDS OF TORAH AT THE TABLE in order to join the right, which is Mercy, with the left, which is Judgment. The Torah is Yud Hei Vav Hei, ZEIR ANPIN, WHICH WAS GIVEN from the right, and the table is Adonai, MALCHUT, which is from the left, WHICH IS AT THE NORTH. THEREFORE, one needs to join them, BECAUSE THE LEFT WITHOUT THE RIGHT CONFERS HARSH JUDGMENTS. Since that table is at the left side, the sages of the Mishnah have explained that a person's sustenance is as difficult to obtain as the splitting of the Red Sea. Therefore, one needs to invite him a Torah scholar, who will study Torah.

51. שְׁבִיעָאָה, לְאַרְכָאָה עַל פָּתוֹרָא, בְּגִין עֲנִיִּים. וּבְגִין דָּא, כָּל הַמַּאֲרִיךְ עַל שֻׁלְחָנוֹ מַאֲרִיכִין לוֹ יָמָיו וּשְׁנוֹתָיו. וּבג״כ וּצְדָקָה תַּצִּיל מִמָּוֶת. דְּעָנִי חָשׁוּב כַּמֵּת, וְאִיהוּ מְחַיֶּה לֵיהּ, אוּף הָכִי קוּדְשָׁא בְּרִיךְ הוּא מְחַיֶּה לֵיהּ.

51. The seventh SETTING is to stay a long time at the table for the poor TO COME. Whoever stays long at the table will have his days and years extended. For that reason: "charity delivers from death" (Mishlei 10:2). Since a poor man is like a dead man, whom he revives WITH CHARITY, the Holy One, blessed be He, also revives him.

52. וְעוֹד בְּאוֹרַח רָזָא, דְּכֻלְּהוּ עֲנִיִּים מִסִּטְרָא דְּאָת ד׳, דְּאִתְּמַר בָּהּ דַּלּוֹתִי וְלִי יְהוֹשִׁיעַ. וְאוֹת ד׳ דְּאֶחָד, דְּצָרִיךְ לְאַרְכָאָה בָּהּ, הה״ד לְהַאֲרִיךְ יָמִים עַל מַמְלַכְתּוֹ, וּבג״ד, צָרִיךְ לְאַרְכָאָה עַל פָּתוֹרָא, דְּאִיהִי ד׳, כְּלִילָא מִד׳ רַגְלִין דְּפָתוֹרָא. בְּגִין יְקָרָא דְּאָת דָּלֶ״ת, צָרִיךְ לְאַרְכָאָה עַל פָּתוֹרָא, בְּגִין עֲנִיִּים.

52. Furthermore, an esoteric explanation is that all the poor people originate from the part of the letter Dalet, about which it is said: "I was brought low (Heb. *daloti*), and He saved me" (Tehilim 116:6). The pronunciation of the letter Dalet in 'Echad' (lit. 'one') should be prolonged. That is meant by the verse: "that he may prolong his days in his kingdom" (Devarim 17:20). Therefore, it behooves one to stay long at the table, which is Dalet (=four), because it has the four legs of the table. In honor of that letter Dalet, one should stay long at the table for the sake of the poor.

53. וּבְגִינֵהּ אוֹקְמוּהָ רַבָּנָן, דְּבִקֵּשׁ קוּדְשָׁא בְּרִיךְ הוּא מִדָּה יָפָה לְיִשְׂרָאֵל, וְלָא אַשְׁכַּח כְּמִדָּה דְּדַלּוּת. וְאַקְשׁוּ עֲלָהּ, בְּגִין דְּאוֹקְמוּהָ קַדְמָאֵי, כְּחוּשְׁבַן מִינֵי מִיתוֹת דְּאִינוּן כְּחוּשְׁבַן תּוֹצָאוֹת, וְחֶסְרוֹן כִּיס קָשֶׁה מִכּוּלָן, וְאֵיךְ אַמְרִין אִינוּן, דְּלָא אַשְׁכַּח לְיִשְׂרָאֵל מִדָּה יָפָה כַּעֲנִיּוּתָא.

53. In relation to it the sages explained that the Holy One, blessed be He, sought a comely virtue for Yisrael, and found only the virtue of poverty. A difficulty was raised here, since the ancient sages explained that the number of different deaths is equivalent to the numerical value of the word '*totzaot* (lit. 'modes')' (=903) (Tehilim 68:21), and that an empty pocket is the most difficult. How could it be said He found no better virtue for Yisrael than poverty?

54. אֶלָּא, בְּגִין דְּכָל עַמָּא וְלִישָּׁנָא, וְהָיָה כִּי יִרְעַב וְהִתְקַצַּף וְקִלֵּל בְּמַלְכּוֹ וּבֵאלֹהָיו וּפָנָה לְמָעְלָה. אֲבָל יִשְׂרָאֵל, אִינּוּן קַיָּימָא דְּקוּדְשָׁא בְּרִיךְ הוּא בְּהַאי מִדָּה, וְלָא אַכְחִישִׁין בֵּיהּ. וּבג״ד, בְּמִדָּה דָּא יִתְפָּרְקוּן. הה״ד, וְאֶת עַם עָנִי תּוֹשִׁיעַ. וְעָנִי לִישָּׁנָא דְּעִנּוּי, דַּאֲפִילּוּ אִית לֵיהּ לְב״נ עוּתְרָא, וְאִיהוּ בְּמַרְעִין וּבְמַכְתְּשִׁין, עָנִי אִתְקְרֵי, אוֹ דְּדַחֲקִין לֵיהּ בְּגִינֵיהּ, וְצַעְרִין לֵיהּ כָּל יוֹמָא. כָּל שֶׁכֵּן מַאן דְּאִיהוּ רָשׁ מִנֵּיהּ, וְאִיהוּ הוֹלֵךְ מֵאֲתָר לַאֲתָר.

54. He RESPONDS: It is only because about each nation and people, IT IS SAID: "and it shall come to pass, that when they shall be hungry, they shall fret themselves, and curse their king and their Elohim, and look upward" (Yeshayah 8:21). However, the children of Yisrael are in the Covenant with the Holy One, blessed be He, also with this virtue and do not deny His existence. Hence they shall be redeemed by this virtue. This is the meaning of: "and the afflicted people You shall save" (II Shmuel 22:28). 'Ani (Eng.. 'poor')' is derived from 'inui (Eng. 'suffering')', since even when one has wealth but suffers from illnesses and afflictions, he is considered poor. Or he is distressed FOR HIS WEALTH and is afflicted every day. This is surely true for one who is poorer than him, MEANING THAT HE LACKS EVEN ENOUGH TO FULFILL HIS NEEDS and must wander from place to place, WHO IS MOST CERTAINLY CONSIDERED POOR.

55. וְעוֹד אִית עָנִי, דְּאִסְתְּלָק מִנֵּיהּ דַּעְתֵּיהּ, כְּגוֹן אִיּוֹב, דְּאִתְּמַר בֵּיהּ, אִיּוֹב לֹא בְדַעַת יְדַבֵּר. אוּף הָכִי אִיהִי ד׳, דְּאִיהִי שְׁכִינְתָּא, כַּד אִסְתַּלָּק מִנָּהּ א״ח דְּאִיהוּ עַמּוּדָא דְּאֶמְצָעִיתָא, דְּאִקְרֵי דַּעַת. וְהַאי לֵית לָהּ חוּבִין בְּמִלָּה דְּיֵימָא. וְעוֹד, א״ח אִיהוּ תּוֹרָה, כָּלִיל תרי״ג פִּקּוּדִין הה״ד זֶה שְׁמִי לְעוֹלָם וְגוֹ׳. שְׁמִ״י עִם י״ה שס״ה. זִכְרִי עִם ו״ה רמ״ח.

וּבְגִין דָּא אוּקְמוּהָ, אֵין עָנִי אֶלָּא מִן הַתּוֹרָה וּמִן הַמִּצְוֹת דִּשְׁאַר עָנִי לָאו אִיהוּ אֶלָּא עִנּוּי. וְאָת ד׳ מִן אֲדֹנָי, אוּף הָכִי אִיהִי עָנִי בְּלָא יְהֹוָ״ה.

55. There is another kind of poor man, who lost his mind like Job, about whom, it is said: "Job has spoken without knowledge" (Iyov 34:35). So too is the Dalet, which is the Shechinah; when Aleph and Chet OF ECHAD were gone from it, which is the Central Pillar called Da'at (knowledge), IT IS POOR. And one, WHO IS WITHOUT KNOWLEDGE, does not incur iniquity by speaking IMPROPERLY. Furthermore, Aleph Chet is the Torah that is comprised of the 613 commandments. This is the meaning of: "this is My name (Heb. *shmi*) forever, and this is My memorial (Heb. *zichri*) to all generations" (Shemot 3:15). Shmi plus Yud-Hei IS NUMERICALLY 365, and zichri plus Vav-Hei is NUMERICALLY 248. Therefore it has been explained that one is poor only in Torah and commandments. This is because the other poor people suffer BUT ARE NOT POOR. The letter Dalet of Adonai, WHICH IS MALCHUT, is also poor without Yud Hei Vav Hei. SIMILARLY, THE DALET OF ECHAD, WHICH IS MALCHUT, IS POOR WITHOUT ALEPH AND CHET OF ECHAD THAT IS THE 613 COMMANDMENTS OF THE TORAH THAT ARE CHASSADIM.

56. תְּמִינָאָה, מַיִם אַחֲרוֹנִים דְּתַקִּינוּ לוֹן, בְּגִין מֶלַח סְדוֹמִית, הַמְסַמֵּא אֶת הָעֵינַיִם. אֲמַאי אִקְרוּן חוֹבָה. אֶלָּא בְּאֹרַח רָזָא, סַם הַמָּוֶת שַׁרְיָא, עַל יְדוֹי מְזוּהָמִין, דְּעַבְדֵּי בְּהוּ בְּרָכָה. וְעַל כּוֹס דִּמְבָרְכֵי עָלֵיהּ בְּלֹא טָהֳרָה, אִקְרֵי טָמֵא. וּמַה כּוֹס דְּשׁוֹתִין בּוֹ, טָמֵא לִבְרָכָה עַד דַּהֲווֹ מְטָהֲרֵי לֵיהּ בְּהַדָּחָה מִלְּגוֹ וּמִלְּבַר. כָּל שֶׁכֵּן יְדוֹי. וּבְגִין דָּא, מַיִם אַחֲרוֹנִים חוֹבָה. וְרָזָא דְּמִלָּה, וְהִתְקַדִּשְׁתֶּם: אֵלּוּ מַיִם רִאשׁוֹנִים. וִהְיִיתֶם קְדוֹשִׁים: אֵלּוּ מַיִם אַחֲרוֹנִים. כִּי קָדוֹשׁ: זֶה שֶׁמֶן עָרֵב. לָקֳבֵל, קק״ק יְיָ׳ צְבָאוֹת. וּבְגִין דָּא וְהִתְקַדִּשְׁתֶּם וְגוֹ׳, לְאִשְׁתְּמוֹדְעָא דְּאַתּוּן בְּנִין לְקוּדְשָׁא בְּרִיךְ הוּא, הה״ד בָּנִים אַתֶּם לַיְיָ׳ אֱלֹהֵיכֶם.

56. The eighth SETTING is the fingerbowl water that was instituted due to the salt of S'dom that is blinding to the eyes. Why is it considered obligatory? HE ANSWERS: According to the esoteric interpretation, deadly poison rests on dirty hands, with which one makes a blessing, and on a cup, over which one makes a blessing without cleanliness, and it is considered defiled. Just as a cup from which people drank is considered unclean for a blessing until it is cleansed by rinsing it inside and out, the hands all the more so. Hence fingerbowl water is obligatory. The secret of this is in the verse: "You shall therefore sanctify yourself" (Vayikra 26:2), which refers to the washing of hands before the meal. "And you shall be holy" (Ibid.) refers to fingerbowl water. "for I am holy" (Ibid.), refers to fragrant ointment, WHICH WAS USED TO ANOINT THE HANDS AFTER FINGERBOWL WATER. THESE THREE THINGS correspond to "Holy, holy, holy." "You shall therefore sanctify yourself" so that it shall be known that you are children of the Holy One, blessed be He. That is what is meant by: "You are the children of Hashem your Elohim" (Devarim 14:1).

57. תְּשִׁיעָאָה, כּוֹס דִּבְרָכָה. וְאוֹקְמוּהָ מָארֵי דְּמַתְנִיתִין, עֲשָׂרָה דְּבָרִים נֶאֶמְרוּ בְּכוֹס דִּבְרָכָה וְאִלֵּין אִינּוּן. עִטּוּ״ר. עִטּוּ״ף. הַדָּחָ״ה. שְׁטִיפָ״ה. חַ״י. מָלֵ״א. וּמְקַבְּלוֹ בִּשְׁתֵּי יָדָיו. וְנוֹתְנוֹ בַּיָּמִין. וּמְסַלְּקוֹ מִן הַקַּרְקַע טֶפַח. וְנוֹתֵן עֵינָיו בּוֹ. וּמְשַׁגְּרוֹ בְּמַתָּנָה לְאַנְשֵׁי בֵּיתוֹ. וְעַכְשָׁיו, אֵין לָנוּ אֶלָּא אַרְבָּעָה שֶׁהֵן הַדָּחָה. וּשְׁטִיפָה. חַי. מָלֵא. וְיֵשׁ אוֹמְרִים חַי מִן הֶחָבִית, וְיֵשׁ אוֹמְרִים חַי, הַכּוֹס שָׁלֵם. שֶׁשְּׁבִירָתוֹ זוֹ הִיא מִיתָתוֹ.

57. The ninth SETTING is the cup of blessing. As has been explained by the sages of the Mishnah, ten things were said about this cup of blessing, which are: decorating, wrapping, washing, rinsing, unmixed wine, full cup, receiving it with both hands and leaving it with the right, raising it from the surface a handbreadth, looking at it, and sending it as a gift to the members of his household. Now we have only four, which are washing, rinsing, unmixed wine, and a full cup. Some say the wine should be taken unmixed from the cask, BUT IN THE CUP, WATER MAY BE ADDED TO IT. Some say that unmixed (lit. living) wine means the cup should be whole, AND NOT THAT IT MAY NOT BE DILUTED, because its breaking is its death. THEREFORE, WHEN IT IS WHOLE, IT IS CONSIDERED LIVING. THE OTHER ITEMS ARE EXPLAINED BEFORE US.

58. כּוֹס עַל דֶּרֶךְ הַחָכְמָה, הוּא אֱלֹהִים. וְהוּא מָלֵא בְּיָ״הּ וְהֵם שָׁלֵם, כּ״ס בְּלָא ו׳ כְּמוֹ כֵּס שֶׁהוּא פָּגוּם וְחָסֵר בְּלָא אָלֶף, כֵּן הוּא חָסֵר בְּלָא וָי״ו, וְהוּא פָּגוּם. הַכִּסֵּ״א כֵּן עוֹלֶה בְּגִימַטְרִיָּא כּוֹס.

58. He EXPLAINS WHAT A WHOLE CUP IS. A cup, according to wisdom, is MALCHUT THAT IS CALLED Elohim (Aleph Lamed Hei Yud Mem), when it is full with Yud Hei. WHEN IT IS IN SMALLNESS, MALCHUT IS CONSIDERED MUTE (HEB. *ILEM*, ALEPH LAMED MEM) WITHOUT YUD HEI. And they are whole, MEANING THAT BOTH NAMES, THE CUP AND ELOHIM, ARE COMPLETE THIS WAY. HOWEVER, a cup (Heb. *kos*) without Vav is like *kes* (Caf Samech) instead of *kise* (Eng. 'throne', Caf Samech Aleph), which would be defective and lacking without Aleph. Therefore, KES INSTEAD OF KISE is lacking without Vav, and is defective. The Throne does amount numerically to *kos*, SINCE *HAKISE* (ENG. 'THE THRONE') IS ALSO A NAME OF MALCHUT, AS IS *KOS*.

59. כּוֹס הִיא הֵ״א, וְצָרִיךְ עֲשָׂרָה דְּבָרִים, כְּנֶגֶד י׳. וְהֵם: עִטּוּ״ר בְּסוֹד הָעֲטָרָה, עֲטֶרֶת תִּפְאֶרֶת. וְזֶהוּ סוֹד עִטּוּר, שֶׁאָז״ל מְעַטְּרוֹ בְּתַלְמִידִים, וְהִיא עֲטֶרֶת הַבְּרִית. עִטּוּ״ף, תְּפִלָּה לְעָנִי כִּי יַעֲטוֹף. שֶׁכָּל הַבְּרָכוֹת וְהַתְּפִלּוֹת מִתְעַטְּפִים, עַד שֶׁתַּעֲלֶה תְּפִלַּת הֶעָנִי.

59. The cup is MALCHUT, WHICH IS THE SECRET OF Hei (=five) OF YUD HEI VAV HEI. Ten items are needed that correspond to Yud (=ten) TO MULTIPLY TEN BY FIVE AND DRAW THE FIFTY GATES OF BINAH. They are: 1) crowning that indicates the secret of the corona, meaning the crown of Tiferet, WHICH IS MALCHUT OF YESOD. This is the secret of the crowning, of which the sages of blessed memory said that he used to crown it by placing scholars around it, that is, the corona of the member of the Covenant, IN ORDER TO JOIN WITH IT MALCHUT OF YESOD, WHICH INDICATES THE UNION OF YESOD AND MALCHUT, TO GIVE BIRTH TO SOULS, THE SECRET OF SCHOLARS. 2) Wrapping INDICATES the verse: "a prayer of the poor when he faints (or: 'wraps')" (Tehilim 102:1) because all these blessings and prayers are covered together, MEANING THEY ARE DELAYED IN BEING RECEIVED until the prayer of the poor rises. THE PRAYER OF THE POOR IS THE CORRECTION OF MALCHUT FROM THE SIDE OF DALET OF ECHAD, WHICH IS CALLED POOR. THE WRAPPING INDICATES THIS CORRECTION.

60. הַדָּחָ״ה וּשְׁטִיפָ״ה, כְּמוֹ וְטִהֲרוֹ וְקִדְּשׁוֹ. הַטָּהֳרָה מִיָּמִין הַחֶסֶד. וְהַקְּדוּשָּׁה מִשְּׂמֹאל דִּגְבוּרָה. כּוֹס דִּבְרָכָה מַלְכוּת מִצַּד בִּינָה הַנִּקְרֵאת

אֱלֹהִים. וְנִקְרָא עֲטָרָה מִצַּד הַכֶּתֶר. חַ״י, מִצַּד יְסוֹד, הַנִּקְרָא שָׁלוֹם, שֶׁנֶּאֱמַר וּבְרִית שְׁלוֹמִי לֹא תָמוּט אָמַר מְרַחֲמֵךְ יְיָ׳. מָלֵא, מִצַּד ת״ת. מְקַבְּלוֹ בִּשְׁתֵּי יָדָיו, ה׳ ה׳.

60. 3) and 4) are washing and rinsing, which are like: "and cleanse it, and hallow it" (Vayikra 16:19). Cleansing is from the right, WHICH IS Chesed, and the hallowing is from the left, WHICH IS Gvurah. The cup of blessing IS CALLED Malchut from the part of Binah that is called Elohim, and called a wreath from the part of Keter. 5) IT IS CALLED unmixed (living) from the aspect of Yesod that is also called peace, as is written: "'neither shall the covenant of My peace be removed', said Hashem that has mercy on you" (Yeshayah 54:10). RATHER, IT WILL BE ALIVE FOREVER. THEREFORE, MALCHUT IS CALLED LIVING FROM THIS ASPECT. 6) Full is from the aspect of Tiferet, MEANING WHEN IT RECEIVES FROM TIFERET THAT IS ABOVE THE CHEST, IT IS WHOLE AND FULL. 7) Accepting it with both hands, THAT INDICATE THE TWO HEIS OF YUD HEI VAV HEI, in WHICH THE UPPER HEI, WHICH IS BINAH, IS CHESED, AND THE LOWER HEI IS MALCHUT, IS GVURAH.

61. וְנוֹתְנוֹ בַּיָּמִין, כִּי ה׳ עֶלְיוֹנָה לָחֶסֶד, ה׳ שְׁנִיָּה לַגְּבוּרָה. וּמְסַלְּקוֹ מִן הַקַּרְקַע טֶפַח, בְּסוֹד יוֹ״ד כִּי סִלּוּק ה׳ הוּא יוֹ״ד. וְנוֹתֵן עֵינָיו בּוֹ, שֶׁהֵם בְּסוֹד יְאֲהדֹוָנָהִי. יְיָ׳ מֵאִיר בְּבַת עַיִן. יֶדֹו״ד בִּשְׁלֹשָׁה צִבְעֵי הָעַיִן. אֲדֹנָי מְאִירָה, בִּשְׁנֵי כְּרוּבֵי הָעַיִן, וְאִישׁוֹנֵי עַפְעַפֵּי הָעַיִן. וּמְשַׁגְ״רוֹ בְּמַתָּנָה לְאַנְשֵׁי בֵּיתוֹ. הִיא בִּינָה, שֶׁנֶּאֱמַר בָּהּ, יִשְׂמַח מֹשֶׁה בְּמַתְּנַת חֶלְקוֹ.

61. Leaving it with the right hand, because the upper Hei IS Chesed, and the second Hei IS Gvurah. THEREFORE, HE SHOULD GIVE IT WITH THE RIGHT HAND, WITH THE FIRST HEI. 8) Lifting it off the surface a handbreadth. THE HANDBREATH INDICATES the secret of the letter Yud, because Hei is raised by Yud, MEANING THAT ONE SHOULD RAISE THE FIVE SFIROT OF MALCHUT FROM HER PLACE, WHICH IS THE SECRET OF THE SURFACE, MULTIPLY HER BY YUD, AND MEDITATE ON HER RECEIVING THE FIFTY GATES OF BINAH. 9) Looking at it with the eyes, which are the secret OF THE UNIFICATION of Yud-Aleph-Hei-Dalet-Vav-Nun-Hei-Yud, NAMELY, THE COMBINATION OF YUD HEI VAV HEI AND ADONAI. ONE SHOULD

MEDITATE THAT Yud Hei Vav Hei, WHICH IS ZEIR ANPIN, shines in the pupil of the eye, WHICH IS ADONAI. Yud Hei Vav Hei SHINES IN THE THREE COLORS OF THE EYES, WHITE, RED AND GREEN, WHICH ARE CHESED, GVURAH AND TIFERET OF ZEIR ANPIN. Adonai shines in the two eyelids, as well as the two pupils OF THE EYE AND THE HAIR OF THE EYELASHES. 10) Sending it as a gift to the members of the household. ONE'S HOUSE is Binah, regarding which it is written: 'Let Moses rejoice in the gift of his portion'. This is BECAUSE MOSES MERITED BINAH AND ONE NEEDS TO ATTACH THE CUP, WHICH IS MALCHUT, TO THE LIGHTS OF BINAH.

62. עֲשִׂירָאָה, בִּרְכַּת מְזוֹנָא, הָא אוֹקְמוּהָ רַבָּנָן, בִּשְׁלֹשָׁה, צָרִיךְ כּוֹס. וְרָזָא דְּמִלָּה, בְּגִין דְּאִיהִי אַהֲבַת כְּלוּלוֹתָיִךְ, דְּאִינּוּן אֲבָהָן, בַּכֹּ״ל מִכֹּ״ל כֹּ״ל. וְלֵית לְאַרְכָּאָה יַתִּיר.

62. The tenth SETTING OF THE SHABBAT TABLE is the blessing after the meal. It was explained by the sages that three, WHO EAT TOGETHER, need a cup. The secret meaning of this is that THREE are THE ASPECT OF: "your love as a bride (Heb. *kelulotayich*)" (Yirmeyah 2:2), NAMELY, THE LOVE OF ALL THREE 'KOL', who are the patriarchs, regarding whom it is written: 'in all, of all, all (Heb. *bakol mikol kol*)', SINCE *KELULOTAYICH* IS DERIVED FROM *KOL*; IN RESPECT TO ABRAHAM, IT SAYS, "HASHEM BLESSED ABRAHAM IN ALL THINGS (HEB. *BAKOL*)" (BERESHEET 24:1); IN RESPECT TO ISAAC, IT SAYS, "AND I HAVE EATEN OF ALL (HEB. *MIKOL*)," AND IN RESPECT TO JACOB, IT SAYS, "I HAVE ENOUGH (ALL) (HEB. *KOL*)" (BERESHEET 33:11). We should not speak at length about it, BECAUSE IT IS A HIDDEN MYSTERY.

63. בִּרְכַּת הַמָּזוֹן מִן הַתּוֹרָה מִנַּיִן. שֶׁנֶּאֱמַר, וְאָכַלְתָּ וְשָׂבָעְתָּ וְגוֹ׳. וְשָׁנִינוּ בַּבְּרַיְיתָא, וּבֵרַכְתָּ זוּ הַזָּן. אֶת ה׳ אֱלֹהֶיךָ זוּ בִּרְכַּת הַמָּזוֹן. עַל הָאָרֶץ, זוּ בִּרְכַּת הָאָרֶץ. הַטּוֹבָה, זוּ בּוֹנֵה יְרוּשָׁלַיִם. וְכֵן הוּא אוֹמֵר, הָהָר הַטּוֹב הַזֶּה וְהַלְּבָנוֹן. אֵין לִי אֶלָּא לְאַחֲרָיו, לְפָנָיו מִנַּיִן. שֶׁנֶּאֱמַר אֲשֶׁר נָתַן לָךְ, מִשָּׁעָה שֶׁנָּתַן לְךָ, חַיָּיב אַתָּה לְבָרְכוֹ.

63. How do we know that the blessing after the meal is prescribed by the Torah? Because it is written: "When you have eaten, and are replete, then you shall bless Hashem your Elohim FOR THE GOOD LAND WHICH HE HAS GIVEN YOU" (Devarim 8:10). We have studied in the *Baraita* that "you shall bless" refers to the blessing 'Who sustains (Heb. *hazan*) EVERYTHING'. "Hashem your Elohim" REFERS TO THE BLESSING FOR THE LAND AND FOR SUSTENANCE (HEB. *AL HA'ARETZ VE'AL HAMAZON*), IN WHICH "HASHEM YOUR ELOHIM" refers to blessing for the food, and "for the land" refers to the blessing, 'Who builds Jerusalem (Heb. *boneh Yerushalaim*)'. It also says, "that goodly mountain region and the Lebanon" (Devarim 3:25). This explains only THE BLESSINGS after THE MEAL. YET where is THE BLESSING before THE MEAL indicated? It is indicated in the words: "which He has given you," WHICH MEANS THAT from the time He has given you, EVEN BEFORE EATING, you must bless Him.

64. וְדָרְשׁוּ חֲכָמִים ז״ל, מֹשֶׁה תִּיקֵן לָהֶם לְיִשְׂרָאֵל בִּרְכַּת הַזָּן, בְּשָׁעָה שֶׁיָּרַד לָהֶם הַמָּן. יְהוֹשֻׁעַ תִּיקֵן לָהֶם בִּרְכַּת הָאָרֶץ, בְּשָׁעָה שֶׁהֶכְנִיסָן לָאָרֶץ. דָּוִד וּשְׁלֹמֹה תִּקְנוּ בּוֹנֶה יְרוּשָׁלַיִם. עוֹד נִמְצָא בְּפָרָשַׁת הַמָּן, רֶמֶז לְבִרְכַּת מָזוֹן בַּמָּן עַצְמוֹ, שֶׁנֶּאֱמַר וּבַבֹּקֶר תִּשְׂבְּעוּ לֶחֶם וִידַעְתֶּם כִּי אֲנִי ה׳ אֱלֹהֵיכֶם.

64. The sages of blessed memory have interpreted that Moses instituted for the children of Yisrael the blessing 'Who sustains (Heb. *hazan*)' when manna descended on them. Joshua instituted for them the blessing over the land when he entered them into the Holy Land. David and Solomon instituted the blessing for the building of Jerusalem. In addition, there is an indication of the blessing after the meal in the passage relating to the manna, as it is written: "in the morning you shall be filled with bread; and you shall know that I am Hashem your Elohim" (Shemot 16:12).

65. אָר״ש, רָזָא דְּאִינּוּן שֶׁבַע זַיְינִין דִּרְשִׁימִין בִּתְפִילִין, דְּהוּא ז׳ שְׁבַשִּׁינִין, דִּרְמִיזִין לְז׳ אוּנֵי דְּרֵיאָה דְּב״נ, דִּבְהוֹן שָׁאִיב רוּחָא, וּמִנֵּיהּ מַפִּיק צוּצִיתָא דְּנוּר, דְּדָלִיק מִפּוּמֵיהּ. וְעוֹד דְּאִינּוּן רֶמֶז, לְשִׁבְעָה יוֹמֵי, וּשְׁבוּעֵי דְּמִפֶּסַח לַעֲצֶרֶת. וְעוֹד דְּאִינּוּן רְמִיזִין לְשִׁבְעָה קְנֵי מְנֹרָתָא, דְּאִית עֲלַיְיהוּ שֶׁבַע בּוּצִינֵי קַדִּישִׁין. וְעוֹד דְּאִינּוּן רְמִיזִין, לְשִׁבְעָה כֹּכְבֵי לֶכֶת, דְּאִינּוּן מְנַהֲרֵי בִּרְקִיעָא. וְעוֹד דְּאִינּוּן רְמִיזִין לְשִׁבְעָה מַדְרֵגִין,

דְעָלְמָא עֲלַיְיהוּ קַיְימָא. וְאִינוּן יְסוֹדָא וְשָׁרְשָׁא וְעִיקָרָא דְּכֹלָּא. וַעֲלֵיהוֹן אֲמָרֵי חַבְרַיָיא, כָּל מַאן דְּבָעֵי לְאַנְחָא תְּפִלִּין דְּרֵישָׁא, מִבָּעֵי לֵיהּ לְאִסְתַּכְּלָא בְּאִינוּן תְּרֵי שִׁינִין, דְּאִינוּן רְמִיזִין לְאִינוּן ז׳ זַיְינִין, דְּאִית בְּהוֹן רֶמֶז רָזִין סְתִימִין, עֲמִיקִין רְמִיזִין.

65. Rabbi Shimon said: The secret of these seven Zayins – THE THREE ZAYINS IN THE THREE HEADED SHIN AND THE FOUR ZAYINS IN THE FOUR HEADED SHIN – that are inscribed on the Tefilin, is that the Zayins in the Shins INSCRIBED ON BOTH SIDES OF THE TEFILIN allude to the seven lobes in man's lung, by which he draws air and exhales with it a fiery spark from his mouth – BECAUSE AIR IS COMPOSED OF FIRE, WATER AND AIR. They also allude to the seven days OF THE WEEK and the SEVEN weeks from Pesach to Shavuot. Also, they indicate the seven branches of the candelabra, on which there are seven holy lamps. They also indicate the seven planets that shine in the firmament and they indicate the seven grades – CHESED, GVURAH, TIFERET, NETZACH, HOD, YESOD AND MALCHUT – by which the world is maintained, which are the foundation, root and essence of everything. The friends said about these SEVEN ZAYINS that whoever wishes to put on the head Tefilin has to examine these two Shins hinted in the seven Zayins, for there are an allusion in them to hidden mysteries and deep allusions.

4. "As for the likeness of their faces, they had the face of a man"

A Synopsis

Rabbi Shimon draws a correspondence between the seven letters inscribed on the Tefilin, the seven lobes of the lungs, the seven days of the week, the seven weeks from Pesach to Shavuot, the seven candles of the candelabra, the seven planets, and the seven levels or Sfirot upon which the universe endures. He talks about the four countenances of the Holy Beasts. He emphasizes that Adam is male and female. We learn that there is a correspondence between the four countenances and the four enshrined Names of God as read in 'the Great, Mighty, and Awesome El'. The human face observes all the creatures, and all ascend and observe him. Rabbi Shimon talks about the secret of the throne, ascending and descending, and how the four countenances of the creatures are depicted – engraved, illuminating, shining, sparkling and glowing – and how they sow seeds upon the world.

66. כִּי יי׳ אֱלֹהֵיכֶם הוּא אֱלֹהֵי הָאֱלֹהִים וַאֲדֹנֵי הָאֲדֹנִים הָאֵל הַגָּדוֹל וגו׳. תַּנְיָא, וּדְמוּת פְּנֵיהֶם פְּנֵי אָדָם. אִלֵּין לָאו אִינּוּן כְּאִינּוּן כְּרוּבִים, אִינּוּן אַנְפֵּי רַבְרְבִין, כְּרוּבִים אַנְפֵּי זוּטְרֵי, כְּרַבְיָא. פְּנֵי אָדָם, כָּל דְּיוּקְנָא כְּלִילָן בְּהוֹ, בְּגִין דְּאִינּוּן אַנְפֵּי רַבְרְבִין, וּמִתְצַיְּירִין בְּהוֹ צִיּוּרִין גְּלִיפִין, בְּגִלּוּפֵי שְׁמָא דִּמְפָרַשׁ, בְּד׳ סִטְרִין, מִזְרָ״ח מַעֲרָ״ב צָפוֹ״ן דָּרוֹ״ם.

66. "Hashem, your Elohim, is the Elohim of Elohim, Lord of lords, a great El..." (Devarim 10:17). We have learned that "As for the likeness of their faces, they had the face of a man" (Yechezkel 1:10). These are unlike the Cherubs. These are large faces, while Cherubs are small faces like those of children. All images are comprised in "the face of a man," because they are large faces. Engraved shapes are formed in them by the engraving of the Name explicitly pronounced to the four directions of the world – east, west, north and south.

67. מִיכָאֵ״ל רָשִׁים בִּרְשִׁימוּ לִסְטַר דָּרוֹם, וְכָל אַנְפִּין מִסְתַּכְּלִין לְגַבֵּי פְּנֵי אָדָ״ם, פְּנֵי אַרְיֵ״ה פְּנֵי נֶשֶׁ״ר פְּנֵי שׁוֹ״ר. אָדָם אִיהוּ דְּכַר וְנוּקְבָא, וְלֹא אִתְקְרֵי אָדָם בַּר הָכִי. וּמִנֵּיה אִתְצַיְּירִין צִיּוּרִין, דְּרֶכֶב אֱלֹהִים רִבּוֹתַיִם אַלְפֵי שִׁנְאָן.

67. Michael made a mark to the south side and all three faces – the face of a lion, the face of an ox, and the face of an eagle – look toward the face of a man. A man is male and female, and is not called a man without them. From it, FROM THE FACE OF A MAN, all shapes were formed IN THE SECRET OF THE VERSE: "The chariots of Elohim are twice ten thousand, thousands upon thousands (Heb. *shin'an*)" (Tehilim 68:18).

68. שִׁנְאָן, כְּלָלָא דְּכֻלְהוּ צִיוּרֵי, שׁוֹ"ר, נֶשֶׁ"ר, אַרְיֵ"ה, ן' דָא אִיהוּ אָדָם. פְּשִׁיטוּ דְּאִתְכְּלִיל כַּחֲדָא, בְּרָזָא דְכַר וְנוּקְבָא. וְכֻלְהוּ אַלְפִין וְרִבְבָן, כֻּלְהוּ נָפְקִין מֵהַנֵּי רָזָא שִׁנְאָן. מֵהַנֵּי דְיוּקְנִין מִתְפַּרְשָׁן כָּל חַד וְחַד בִּסְטְרַיְיהוּ, כְּמָה דְּאִתְחַזֵּי לוֹן.

68. Shin'an IN THE VERSE contains all the shapes, BECAUSE IT IS THE INITIALS of *shor* (Eng. 'ox), *aryeh* (Eng. 'lion'), *nesher* (Eng. 'eagle'), and final Nun is *Adam* (Eng. 'man'), which is the expansion of the meaning of male and female that are included together. All the thousands and tens of thousands come out of these LIVING CREATURES that are in the secret of *shin'an*, and from these shapes, each parts to its aspect as befits it.

69. אֵלִין אִינוּן דְּקָא מְשַׁלְבָן חַד בְּחַד, וְכָלִיל חַד בְּחַד, לְמֶהֱוֵי כֹּל חַד כָּלִיל בְּחַבְרֵיה, שׁוֹ"ר נֶשֶׁ"ר אַרְיֵ"ה אָדָ"ם, אִתְנַהֲגָן בְּרָזָא דְּאַרְבַּע שְׁמָהָן גְּלִיפָן סַלְקִין לְאִתְנַהֲגָא וּלְאִסְתַּכְּלָא.

69. All these are integrated into each other and are comprised of each other, so that one should be included in the other. THESE, the ox, eagle, lion, and man are maintained by the secret of the four engraved names, WHICH ARE 'THE GREAT AND MIGHTY AND AWFUL EL', which rise to maintain and observe.

70. סַלִּיק לְאִתְנַהֲגָא וּלְאִסְתַּכְּלָא שׁוֹר לְאַנְפֵּי אָדָם, סָלִיק שְׁמָא אַחֲרָא, מִתְעַטְּרָא מְחָקְקָא בְּרָזָא דִּתְרֵין גְּוָונִין, וְאִיהוּ אֵל. כְּדֵין אִתְהֲדַר לַאֲחוֹרָא, כֻּרְסְיָיא חָקִיק וְגָלִיף לֵיהּ, וְאִתְרְשִׁים לְאִתְנַהֲגָא בְּרָזָא דִּשְׁמָא דָא.

70. The ox rose to be maintained by and observe the face of a man. Another name is adorned and inscribed by two colors. It is the name 'El'. It then goes back, and the Throne engraves and carves it, and it is marked BY IT to be maintained by the secret of this name.

71. וְסַלִּיק לְאִתְנַהֲגָא וּלְאִסְתַּכְּלָא נֶשֶׁר לְאַנְפֵּי אָדָם, סָלִיק שְׁמָא חָדָא, מִתְעַטְּרָא מִתְנַהֲגָא בְּרָזָא דִּתְרֵין אַנְפִּין וּגְוָונִין, לְאִתְנַהֲגָא לְאִסְתַּלְּקָא בִּסְלִיקוּ ג בְּעִטּוּרָא, וְאִיהוּ גָּדוֹל, כְּדֵין אִתְהֲדַר לְאַחוֹרָא, וְכֻרְסְיָיא חָקִיק וְגָלִיף לֵיהּ, וְאִתְרְשִׁים לְאִתְנַהֲגָא בְּרָזָא דִּשְׁמָא דָא.

71. The eagle rose to be maintained by and observe the face of a man. A name rises, and is adorned and inscribed by two faces and colors, to observe in rising the wreath, which is THE NAME 'Great'. It then goes back, and the Throne engraves and carves it, and it is marked so as to be maintained by the secret of this name.

72. סַלִּיק לְאִתְנַהֲגָא וּלְאִסְתַּכְּלָא אַרְיֵה לְאַנְפֵּי אָדָם, סַלִּיק שְׁמָא חָדָא מִתְעַטְּרָא מְחָקְקָא בְּרָזָא דִּתְרֵין אַנְפִּין וּגְוָונִין, לְאִתְתַּקְּפָא וּלְאִתְקַשְּׁרָא בְּתוּקְפֵיהּ, וְאִיהוּ גִּבּוֹר. כְּדֵין אִתְהֲדַר לְאֲחוֹרָא, וְכֻרְסְיָיא חָקִיק וְגָלִיף לֵיהּ, וְאִתְרְשִׁים לְאִתְנַהֲגָא בְּרָזָא דִּשְׁמָא דָא.

72. The lion rose to be maintained by and observe the face of a man. A name rises, and is adorned and inscribed by two faces and colors, to be strengthened and connected to Gvurah (might); it is the name 'Mighty'. It then goes back, and the Throne engraves and carves it, and it is marked so as to be maintained by the secret of this name.

73. אָדָם אִסְתַּכֵּל בְּכֻלְּהוּ, וְכֻלְּהוּ סַלְקִין וּמִסְתַּכְּלִין בֵּיהּ, כְּדֵין כֻּלְּהוּ אִצְטַיְּירָן בִּגְלוּפַיְיהוּ בְּצִיּוּרָא דָא, בְּרָזָא דִּשְׁמָא חַד, דְּאִקְרֵי נוֹרָא. וּכְדֵין כְּתִיב עֲלַיְיהוּ, וּדְמוּת פְּנֵיהֶם פְּנֵי אָדָם. כֻּלְּהוּ כְּלִילָן בְּהַאי דְּיוֹקְנָא, וְהַאי דְּיוֹקְנָא כָּלִיל לוֹן.

73. The FACE OF a man observes all the living creatures, and all rise and observe it. They all take form, by their engravings, in this form in the secret by means of a name called ‘Awful’. It is then written about them that: “As for the likeness of their faces, they had the face of a man.” They are all included in this form, and this form encompasses them.

74. וְעַל רָזָא דָא, אִתְקְרֵי קב״ה, הָאֵל הַגָּדוֹל הַגִּבּוֹר וְהַנּוֹרָא. דְּהָא שְׁמָהָן אִלֵּין גְּלִיפִין אִינּוּן לְעֵילָא, בְּרָזָא דִּרְתִּיכָא עִלָּאָה, כְּלִילָא בְּאַרְבַּע אַתְוָון ידוד, דְּאִיהוּ שְׁמָא דְּכָלִיל כָּל דְּיוּקְנִין, אִלֵּין מְחָקְקָן גְּלִיפִין בְּכֻרְסַיָּיא, וְכֻרְסַיָּיא גְּלִיפָא מְרַקְמָא בְּהוּ. חַד לִימִינָא, וְחַד לִשְׂמָאלָא, וְחַד לְקַמָּא, וְחַד לְאַחוֹרָא. רְשִׁימָא בְּד׳ סִטְרִין דְּעַלְמָא.

74. Because of this secret meaning, the Holy One, blessed be He, is called ‘the great, mighty and awful El’, because these names are high corrections by the supernal Chariot, and it is included in the four letters of Yud Hei Vav Hei, which is the Name encompassing all forms. These forms are engraved and carved into the Throne and the Throne is engraved and embroidered with them, one to the right and one to the left and one to the front and one to the rear, assigned to the four directions of the world.

75. כֻּרְסְיָיא כַּד סַלְקָא, רְשִׁימָא בְּאַרְבַּע דְּיוּקְנִין אִלֵּין. אִלֵּין אַרְבַּע שְׁמָהָן עִלָּאִין, נָטְלִין לְהַאי כֻּרְסְיָיא. וְכֻרְסְיָיא אִתְכְּלֵל בְּהוּ, עַד דְּנָקְטָא וְלָקְטָא אִינּוּן עִנּוּגִין וְכִסּוּפִין, נָחֲתָא מַלְיָיא כְּאִילָנָא דְּמַלֵּי עַנְפִין לְכָל סְטַר, וּמַלְיָיא אִיבִּין. כֵּיוָן דְּנָחֲתָא, נָפְקוּ אִלֵּין ד׳ דְּיוּקְנִין, מְצוּיָּרִין בְּצִיּוּרַיְיהוּ, גְּלִיפִין מְנַהֲרָן, נְצִיצָן מְלַהֲטָן, וְאִינּוּן זַרְעִין זַרְעָא עַל עָלְמָא.

75. When the Throne ascends, it is marked in these four shapes. These four lofty names bear this Throne, and the Throne is composed of them until the Throne receives and collects these pleasures and delights. AFTERWARDS THE THRONE descends fully laden, like a tree full with branches in every direction and loaded with fruits. After THE THRONE descends, the four forms OF THE LIVING CREATURES come out formed, engraved, illuminating, glittering and glowing, and they sow seeds over the world.

SHOFTIM

Names of Articles

1. "He puts one up, and sets up another"

A Synopsis

The Zohar talks here about the precepts regarding the appointment of the judiciary and law enforcement officers.

רעיא מהימנא

1. שׁוֹפְטִים וְשׁוֹטְרִים תִּתֶּן לְךָ בְּכָל שְׁעָרֶיךָ אֲשֶׁר יְיָ׳ אֱלֹהֶיךָ נוֹתֵן לְךָ וְגוֹ׳. בְּפִקּוּדָא דָּא, מָנֵי שׁוֹפְטִים וְשׁוֹטְרִים. וְעוֹד כִּי אֱלֹהִים שׁוֹפֵט, כִּי: מ׳, מִנֵּיהּ יוּ״ד דְּחוּשְׁבָּנֵיהּ כ׳, בָּתַר הָכָא, אֱלֹהִים שׁוֹפֵט, זֶה יַשְׁפִּיל ה״ה, וְזֶה יָרִים דָּא וָ״ו.

Ra'aya Meheimna (the Faithful Shepherd)

1. "Judges and officers shall you make you in all your gates, which Hashem your Elohim, gives you, throughout your tribes" (Devarim 16:18). In this precept, He commanded regarding judges and officers. Moreover, "but (Heb. *ki*, Caf Yud) Elohim is the Judge" (Tehilim 75:8). The numerical value of 'ki' is forty if you take into account that *Yud* in its full spelling equals twenty and *Caf* is twenty for a total of forty. After that, "Elohim is the Judge: He puts one up," *Hei* OF YUD HEI VAV HEI does "and sets up another" (Ibid.), THAT IS, *Vav* OF YUD HEI VAV HEI.

2. The four deaths of Samael

A Synopsis

We learn about the recommended sentencing for various crimes. The secret meaning of "justice, justice you shall pursue" is shown to be found in the construction of the name Yud Hei Vav Hei, that corresponds to the top, body and sides of the sword. We read about the Judgment from the court on high and the judgment from the court here in the world. The scabbard of the sword of justice is said to be the name Adonai, and we see the relevance to the eighteen graces of the prayer that is recited while standing. We read that Samael must be sentenced by the sword, as he is the chief minister of Edom above, and the text talks about the strangulation and stoning of Samael and the serpent as well. The name Yud Hei Vav Hei is said to be the death of Samael and the Snake, and life to the children of Yisrael. Here we read about the burning of Samael, and we are brought to see how our bodies are the trees that are combustible, and how the light inside us enables us to incinerate Samael through higher Wisdom; when the fire of exaltation comes down to the firewood of the sacrificial offering, any foreigner who approaches will be burned in the fire.

2. פִּקּוּדָא בָּתַר דָּא, לָדוּן בְּסַיִיף. לָדוּן בְּחֶנֶק. לָדוּן בְּדִין סְקִילָה. לָדוּן בְּדִין שְׂרֵיפָה. לָדוּן בְּסַיִיף לְמַאן. לְסָמָאֵל. הה"ד, כִּי רִוְּתָה בַשָּׁמַיִם חַרְבִּי הִנֵּה עַל אֱדוֹם תֵּרֵד.

2. The following precept is to punish by sword, by strangulation, by stoning, and by fire. Whom do you punish by the sword? HE RESPONDS: Samael, as it is written, "for My sword sated in heaven, behold, it shall come down upon Edom" (Yeshayah 34:5), MEANING OVER SAMAEL, WHO IS THE MINISTER OF EDOM.

3. חֶרֶב דְּקוּדְשָׁא בְּרִיךְ הוּא, י' רֵישָׁא דְּחַרְבָּא. ו' גּוּפָא דְּחַרְבָּא. הֵ"א הֵ"א, תְּרֵין פִּיפִיּוֹת דִּילָהּ. צֶדֶק צֶדֶק תִּרְדּוֹף, חַתְכִין תְּרֵין דִּינִין, דִּינָא מִפִּי ב"ד דִּלְעֵילָּא, וְדִינָא מִפִּי ב"ד דִּלְתַתָּא. וּמֵהָכָא אִשְׁתְּמוֹדַע, אֵין אָדָם נוֹקֵף אֶצְבָּעוֹ מִלְּמַטָּה עַד שֶׁנִּתַּן לוֹ רְשׁוּת מִלְּמַעְלָה.

3. The sword of the Holy One, blessed be He, *Yud* OF YUD HEI VAV HEI, is the top of the sword. The *Vav* OF YUD HEI VAV HEI IS the body of the sword, while the two *Hei's* OF YUD HEI VAV HEI are the two edges of the sword, WHICH ARE THE SECRET MEANING OF: "justice, only justice, shall you pursue" (Devarim 16:20). Two verdicts are decided (lit. 'cut'), one from the celestial court and one from the terrestrial court. From this we understand that a person cannot do the least thing down here unless permission is given from up high.

4. נַרְתְּקָא דְּחַרְבָּא אֲדֹנָי. תַּמָּן אִשְׁתְּכַח דִּינָא. בְּק״ש יֱדֹוִד. חַרְבָּא דְּקוּדְשָׁא בְּרִיךְ הוּא, עָלָהּ אִתְּמַר רוֹמְמוֹת אֵל בִּגְרוֹנָם וְחֶרֶב פִּיפִיּוֹת בְּיָדָם. בְּצַדִּיק חַי עָלְמִין, כָּלִיל חַ״י בִּרְכָאן, דְּבֵיהּ אֲדֹנָי שְׂפָתַי תִּפְתָּח, וּפִי בֵּיהּ עָאל חַרְבָּא בְּנַרְתִּיקָהּ, וַחֲמַת הַמֶּלֶךְ שָׁכָכָה, וּמִתְחַבְּרִין תְּרֵין שְׁמָהָן יְאֲהדֹוָנָהִי.

4. The sheath of the sword, THE CONTAINER WHERE THE SWORD IS HIDDEN, is the name Adonai. There IN ADONAI, the letters of Judgments are found, SINCE IN ADONAI ARE THE LETTER *ALEPH* AND *DIN* (ENG. 'JUDGMENT'). In the reading of Sh'ma is the secret meaning of Yud Hei Vav Hei, that is the sword of the Holy One, blessed be He, AS MENTIONED ABOVE. About it, it is written: "The high praises of Elohim in their throat, and a two edged sword in their hand" (Tehilim 149:6), AS WAS EXPLAINED ABOVE. In the righteous, the life of the world, are included all the eighteen blessings, MEANING THAT THROUGH THE RIGHTEOUS, YESOD OF ZEIR ANPIN, IS ACCOMPLISHED THE UNION OF ZEIR ANPIN AND MALCHUT OF GREATNESS, WHICH IS THE SECRET OF THE EIGHTEEN BLESSINGS IN THE AMIDAH PRAYER. In it, "Adonai my lips open, and my mouth" (Tehilim 51:17) "My mouth," MEANS THAT YESOD OPENS MALCHUT, WHICH IS CALLED 'ADONAI'. In it, IN YESOD, the sword enters into its sheath. THAT IS THE MEANING OF THE UNION OF YUD HEI VAV HEI WITH ADONAI THAT IS ACCOMPLISHED THROUGH YESOD. "Then the king's wrath was pacified" (Ester 7:10), BECAUSE THE KLIPOT WERE CONSUMED BY THE UNIFICATION OF THE READING OF SH'MA. NOW BY THE AMIDAH PRAYER, THEY NO LONGER HAVE A HOLD AND THE ANGER SUBSIDES. The two names are joined, Yud-Aleph-Hei-Dalet-Vav-Nun-Hei-Yud, WHICH IS THE INTEGRATION OF THE TWO NAMES YUD HEI VAV HEI AND ADONAI.

5. לָדוּן בְּחֶנֶק. זַרְקָא, תַּמָּן קַו, י׳ כְּרִיכָא בֵּיהּ, וְקַו, ו׳ דְּאִתְפַּשְּׁטָא מִנֵּיהּ. בֵּיהּ תָּפִיס לְסָמָאֵל, וַיִּשָּׂאוּהוּ בַמּוֹט בִּשְׁנָיִם. מַאי מוֹט דְּהַהוּא רָשָׁע.

אָדָם דְּאִיהוּ יוֹ"ד הֵ"א וָא"ו הֵ"א, מַ"ה, וְד' אַתְוָון יְדֹוִ"ד, הֲרֵי תִּשְׁעָה וְאַרְבָּעִים, כְּחוּשְׁבַּן תִּשְׁעָה וְאַרְבָּעִים אַתְוָון, דְּאִינּוּן בְּשִׁית תֵּיבִין דְּיִחוּדָא עִלָּאָה, וּבְשִׁית תֵּיבִין דְּיִחוּדָא תַּתָּאָה, דְּאִינּוּן ו' ו', וְהַאי וַיִּשָּׂאוּהוּ בַמּוֹט בִּשְׁנָיִם, בִּפְרוּדָא מִנַּיְיהוּ, בְּלָא א' בְּאֶמְצַע וָ"ו, דְּלֵית יִחוּדָא לְסִטְרָא אַחֲרָא, אֶלָּא וַיִּשָּׂאוּהוּ בַמּוֹט בִּשְׁנָיִם, סָמָאֵל וּבַת זוּגֵיהּ, עוֹלָם הַנִּפְרָדִים.

5. THE PRECEPT to punish by strangulation. IN THE CANTILLATION MARK *Zarka* there is a line with a *Yud* entwined around it; the line is the *Vav* that extended from the *Yud*. With THAT *VAV*, Samael is caught. THIS ACCORDS WITH THE MEANING OF: "and they carried it between two on a pole" (Bemidbar 13:23). What is the pole of that wicked SAMAEL? HE RESPONDS: It is man, who is Yud-Vav-Dalet-Hei-Aleph-Vav-Aleph-Vav-Hei-Aleph, which is 45 IN NUMERICAL VALUE. Together with the four letters Yud Hei Vav Hei the total is 49, like the number of the 49 letters in the six words of the supernal unification, WHICH IS SH'MA YISRAEL and in the six words of the lower unification, WHICH IS 'BLESSED IS THE NAME OF HIS KINGDOM…', which are *Vav* (= 6), *Vav*. That is the meaning of: "and they carried it between two on a pole," separated from them, without the *Aleph* between the two *Vavs*, because there is no uniting the Other Side. Instead, "they carried it between two on a pole," Samael and his mate, the world of the separated.

6. בְּחֶבֶל דְּיִחָנֵק בָּהּ, אֲחִידָן הֵ"א הֵ"א, בְּה' אֶצְבְּעָאן דְּיַד יְמִינָא, וּבְה' דְּיַד שְׂמָאלָא. ו' חֶבֶל. י' חֲנִיקָא דִּלְהוֹן. שְׁמָא דַּיְדֹוָ"ד, מִיתָה לְסָמָאֵ"ל וְנָחָשׁ, וְחַיִּים לְיִשְׂרָאֵל. וּבְגִ"ד רְאוּ עַתָּה כִּי אֲנִ"י אֲנִי הוּא וְאֵין אֱלֹהִים עִמָּדִי אֲנִי אָמִית לֵאלֹהִים אֲחֵרִים בִּשְׁמִי, וּלְכָל דְּלָא הֵימְנוּ בִּי. וַאֲחַיֶּה לְאִינּוּן דְּהֵימְנִין וְנַטְרִין פִּקּוּדִין דִּילִי.

6. To the rope with which SAMAEL will be strangled are attached *Hei-Hei* (=five), meaning the five fingers of the right hand and the five fingers of the left hand. The *Vav* is the rope. The *Yud* is the strangulation OF SAMAEL AND THE SERPENT. The Name Yud Hei Vav Hei is death to Samael and the serpent and life to Yisrael. Therefore, it is written: "See now that I, even I, am He, and there is no Elohim with Me. I kill" (Devarim 32:39) other

Elohim with My Name and all those who do not believe in Me, "and I make alive" (Ibid.) those who believe in Me and observe My commandments.

7. לְדוּן בִּסְקִילָה לְסָמָאֵל, בְּאֶבֶן דְּאִיהִי יו"ד, זָרִיק לָהּ לְגַבֵּיהּ, בְּחָמֵשׁ אֶצְבְּעָן דְּאִינּוּן ה', וּבַקָּנֶה דִּדְרוֹעָא דְּאִיהוּ ו', וּבַכָּתֵף דְּתַמָּן ה'. וְזָרִיק לָהּ לְגַבֵּיהּ מַחֲשָׁבָה, דְּאִיהוּ שְׁמָא מְפֹרָשׁ יו"ד הֵ"א וָא"ו הֵ"א.

7. To punish Samael with stoning, THAT IS with a stone, which is the *Yud*. It is thrown at him with five fingers, that are the *Hei*, and with the outstretched arm, that is the *Vav*, and with the shoulder, where the *Hei* lies. And the thought throws THAT STONE at him, which is the explicitly pronounced Name Yud Hei Vav Hei.

8. לְדוּן בִּשְׂרֵפָה לְסָמָאֵל. עֵצִים לְאַדְלְקָא בְּהוֹן נוּרָא. זַכָּאָה אִיהוּ גּוּפָא דְּאִיהוּ עֵץ, וְאֵבָרִים דִּילֵיהּ עֵצִים, לְאוֹקְדָא בְּהוֹן אֶשָּׁא, דְּאִיהוּ נֵר מִצְוָה, בְּכָל אֵבֶר, לְאוֹקְדָא לְסָמָאֵל, בִּשְׁכִינְתָּא עִלָּאָה, בְּעֵץ דְּאִיהוּ תִּפְאֶרֶת, וּבְכָל עֵצִים דַּאֲחִידָן בֵּיהּ, דִּבְזִמְנָא דְּאֵשׁ עַל גָּבוֹהַּ נָחִית. הֲוָה, עַל גַּבֵּי עֵצִים דְּקָרְבְּנָא, וְהַזָּר הַקָּרֵב יוּמָת, דְּאִתּוֹקַד בֵּיהּ, הה"ד וְהָאֵשׁ עַל הַמִּזְבֵּחַ תּוּקַד בּוֹ. זַכָּאָה אִיהוּ מַאן דְּאָחִיד בְּאִילָנָא דְּחַיֵּי, בְּגוּפֵיהּ, בְּאֵבָרִים דִּילֵיהּ, נֵר כָּל עַנְפָּא וְעַנְפָּא נֵר מִצְוָה ברמ"ח פִּקּוּדִין דִּילֵיהּ.

8. To punish Samael with burning, THROUGH wood (or: 'tree') with which to kindle fire. Blessed is that body that is wood. Its members are pieces of wood in which a fire will burn, which is the fire of the commandment, in each member, to burn Samael BY the supernal Shechinah, THAT IS BINAH, with a tree that is Tiferet, and with all the trees, MEANING SFIROT, that are attached TO TIFERET. When the fire of the higher descends over the wood of the sacrifice, "the stranger that comes near shall be put to death" (Bemidbar 1:51), because he will be burned IN THE FIRE. That is the meaning of: "And the fire on the altar shall be kept burning in it" (Vayikra 6:5). Blessed is he who is attached to the Tree of Life, WHICH IS ZEIR ANPIN, with his body and limbs, for he is a candle. Each branch is a candle of a commandment with his 248 positive commandments THAT CORRESPOND TO THE 248 BODY PARTS, THAT IS, A COMMANDMENT'S CANDLE FOR EACH BODY PART.

9. כַּד אֲחִידָן בֵּיהּ תַּרְוַויְהוּ, יִתְקַיָּים וַיַּרְא וְהִנֵּה הַסְּנֶה בּוֹעֵר בָּאֵשׁ וְהַסְּנֶה אֵינֶנּוּ אוּכָּל. וְסָמָאֵל וְנָחָשׁ וְכָל מְמָנָן דִּילֵיהּ, דְּאִינּוּן קוֹצִין, אִתּוֹקָדוּ. וַעֲנְפִין דִּסְנֶה, וְאִיבָּא דִּילֵיהּ, וְעָלִין דִּילֵיהּ, לָא אִתּוֹקָדוּ. דָּא אַחֲזֵי לֵיהּ קוּדְשָׁא בְּרִיךְ הוּא.

9. When both THE TREE OF LIFE AND THE COMMANDMENT'S CANDLE, WHICH ARE ZEIR ANPIN AND MALCHUT, are attached TO THAT MAN, this verse will be applied: "the bush burned with fire, but the bush was not consumed" (Shemot 3:2), NAMELY, MAN. Samael and the serpent and all his ministers, ATTACHED TO THE MAN'S BODY, which are thorns, will be combusted but the branches of the bush and its fruits and leaves will not be combusted. The Holy One, blessed be He, pointed this out to Moses.

3. "At the mouth of two witnesses...shall the matter be established"

A Synopsis

Rabbi Shimon tells the Faithful Shepherd that the children of Yisrael are dry wood, being connected to secular fire, and that they do not deserve to have miracles performed for them. But as soon as Moses descends on them with the Torah the Tree of Life descends on them as well, and so does the mitzvah that is the candlelight of God – all for Moses' sake. Through that candlelight the heathen nations of the world will be burned. Rabbi Shimon talks about the two witnesses necessary in any trial, and says that even the walls of one's house will bear witness; the walls of one's house are said to be the inner walls of the heart, and the members of one's household are the 248 organs and limbs. Rabbi Shimon says that a wicked person's sins are even engraved on his bones. We learn that the reason sins are engraved on the bones is because the bones are white and the black script is easily recognizable. This is like the Torah with the white parchment and the black ink, black and white being darkness and light. In addition to this reason for the sins being carved into the bones, the body is destined to be reinstated with its bones, so all its merits and demerits are engraved there. If it is not worthy it will not be resurrected from the dead. Returning to the issue of the two testimonials, Rabbi Shimon calls them the seeing eye and the hearing ear. He says that even the sun and moon testify about a person, and he speaks a good deal about those who give testimony.

10. אָמַר בּוּצִינָא קַדִּישָׁא, וַדַּאי יִשְׂרָאֵל אִינּוּן עֵצִים יְבֵשִׁים בְּאוֹרַיְיתָא, בְּגִין דַּאֲחִידוּ בְּאֵשׁ דְּהֶדְיוֹט, לָאו אִינּוּן כַּדְּקָא חֲזֵי, לְמֶעְבַּד בְּהוֹן נִיסָא, מִיַּד דְּאַנְתְּ נְחִיתַת עָלַיְיהוּ בְּאוֹרַיְיתָא, בְּגִינָךְ נָחַת עָלַיְיהוּ אִילָנָא דְּחַיֵּי, וּמִצְוָה דְּאִיהוּ נֵר יְיָ׳ וַאֲחִידַת בְּהוֹן וְיֵהוֹן חַיִּין. וְאוּמִין עכו״ם דְּעָלְמָא, אִתּוֹקְדָן בְּהַהוּא נֵר, וְהַאי אִיהוּ דְּאָמַר נָבִיא, וְאַתָּה אַל תִּירָא עַבְדִּי יַעֲקֹב וְאַל תֵּחַת יִשְׂרָאֵל כִּי אִתְּךָ אָנִי וְגוֹ׳.

10. The Holy Luminary, THAT IS RABBI SHIMON, said TO THE FAITHFUL SHEPHERD: Surely Yisrael are dry wood in the Torah, because they are connected to a fire of a layperson. They do not deserve to have a miracle performed for them. As soon as you descend on them with Torah, for your sake the Tree of Life descends on them, WHICH IS ZEIR ANPIN, and the commandment, WHICH IS MALCHUT, the candle of Hashem, which holds on to them and so they live. But the heathen nations will be burned by that candle. This is what the prophet said: “Therefore fear you not, O My servant Jacob…neither be dismayed, Yisrael…for I am with you” (Yirmeyah 30:10-11).

11. לֹא יָקוּם עֵד אֶחָד בְּאִישׁ לְכָל עָוֹן וְגוֹ׳. עַל פִּי שְׁנֵי עֵדִים אוֹ עַל פִּי שְׁלֹשָׁה עֵדִים יָקוּם דָּבָר. פִּקּוּדָא דָּא, לְהָעִיד עֵדוּת בב״ד, דְּלָא יַפְסִיד חַבְרֵיהּ מָמוֹנָא בְּגִינֵיהּ, אִי אִית לֵיהּ עֵדוּת בַּהֲדֵיהּ. וְלֵית סַהֲדוּתָא פָּחוּת מִתְּרֵין, הה״ד עַל פִּי שְׁנַיִם עֵדִים וְגוֹ׳ יָקוּם דָּבָר, לֹא יָקוּם עַל פִּי עֵד אֶחָד. וּבג״ד אוּקְמוּהָ מָארֵי מָתְנִיתִין, מִי מֵעִיד עַל הָאָדָם, קִירוֹת בֵּיתוֹ. וְלֹא עוֹד אֶלָּא אַנְשֵׁי בֵּיתוֹ מְעִידִין עָלָיו. מַאי קִירוֹת בֵּיתוֹ. אִינּוּן קִירוֹת לִבּוֹ. וַיַּסֵּב חִזְקִיָּהוּ פָּנָיו אֶל הַקִּיר, וְאוּקְמוּהָ רַבָּנָן, מְלַמֵּד שֶׁהִתְפַּלֵּל חִזְקִיָּהוּ מִקִּירוֹת לִבּוֹ.

11. “One witness shall not rise up against a man for any iniquity…at the mouth of two witnesses or at the mouth of three witnesses shall the matter be established” (Devarim 19:15). It is a precept to testify at court so his neighbor shall not lose money, because HE DOES NOT TESTIFY if he knows of a testimony in his favor. A testimony requires no less than two witnesses. That is the meaning of: “at the mouth of two witnesses or at the mouth of three witnesses shall the matter be established,” but not at the mouth of one witness. That is why the sages of Mishnah have explained, who bears testimony on a person - the walls of his house do. Moreover, the members of his household testify about him. What are the walls of his house? They are the walls of his heart, AS WRITTEN: “Then Hezekiah turned his face towards the wall” (Yeshayah 38:2). The sages of the Mishnah have explained this to teach us that Hezekiah was praying from the walls of his heart.

12. אַנְשֵׁי בֵּיתוֹ, אִינּוּן רמ״ח אֵבָרִים דִּילֵיהּ. דְּהָכִי אוּקְמוּהָ מָארֵי מָתְנִיתִין, רָשָׁע עֲוֹנוֹתָיו חֲקוּקִים עַל עַצְמוֹתָיו. וְהָכִי צַדִּיק, זָכִיּוֹתָיו חֲקוּקִים לוֹ עַל עַצְמוֹתָיו. וּבג״כ אָמַר דָּוִד כָּל עַצְמוֹתַי תֹּאמַרְנָה. וּבְגִינֵהּ אִתְּמַר, וּמִי מְעִידִין עַל הָאָדָם קוֹרוֹת בֵּיתוֹ. גַּרְמִין בְּנוּיִין עַל

מוֹחָא דְּאִיהוּ מַיָּא. וְעַלַיְיהוּ קָא רָמִיז, הַמְקָרֶה בַמַּיִם עֲלִיּוֹתָיו, הַמְקָרֶה לָשׁוֹן קוֹרוֹת.

12. The members of his household are his 248 body parts, SINCE THE BODY IS CALLED HOUSE. This is how the sages of the Mishnah have explained that a wicked person's sins are engraved on his bones. Similarly, the merits of a righteous man are engraved on his bones. Therefore, David said: "all my bones shall say" (Tehilim 35:10). That is why we were taught: who testifies on a person – the beams of his house... THE BEAMS OF HIS HOUSE are the bones OF THE SKULL that are constructed over the brain that is water. About this, it is written: "Who lays the beams of His chambers in the waters" (Tehilim 104:3).

13. וַאֲמַאי בְּגַרְמִין יַתִּיר מִבִּשְׂרָא וְגִידִין וּמַשְׁכָא. בְּגִין דְּגַרְמִין אִינּוּן חִוָּורִין, וּכְתִיבָא אוּכָמָא, לָא אִשְׁתְּמוֹדְעָא אֶלָּא מִגּוֹ חִוָּורוּ. כְּגַוְונָא דְּאוֹרַיְיתָא, דְּאִיהִי חִוָּורוּ מִלְּגָאו, אוּכָם מִלְּבַר. אוּכָם וְחִוָּור, חֹשֶׁךְ וְאוֹר וְאִית חֹשֶׁךְ תְּכֵלֶת, וְאִתְּמַר בֵּיהּ גַּם חֹשֶׁךְ לֹא יַחְשִׁיךְ מִמֶּךָּ. וּתְכֵלֶת אוּכָם, אִיהוּ נוּקְבָא לְגַבֵּי חִוָּורוּ. וְלֹא עוֹד, אֶלָּא דְּגוּפָא עַל גַּרְמִין עָתִיד לְמֵיקַם. וּבְגִ"ד זַכְווֹי וְחוֹבוֹי חֲקוּקִין עַל גַּרְמִין דִּילֵיהּ, וְאִם יִזְכֶּה יְקוּם גּוּפָא עַל גַּרְמִין דִּילֵיהּ. וְאִי לָאו, לָא יְקוּם, וְלָא יְהֵא לֵיהּ תְּחִיַּית הַמֵּתִים.

13. Why are THE INIQUITIES ENGRAVED in the bones rather than in the flesh, the tendons and the skin? That is because the bones are white, and a black script is not recognizable except over white. This is similar to the Torah, which is white on the inside, THAT IS, THE PARCHMENT, and black on the outside, MEANING THE INK. Black and white are darkness and light. There is darkness that is blue, WHICH IS MALCHUT, about which it is written: "even the darkness is not dark for You" (Tehilim 139:12). Blue is black and is a female to the white, THAT IS ZEIR ANPIN, SINCE MALCHUT HAS NO LIGHT OF HER OWN EXCEPT WHAT SHE RECEIVES FROM ZEIR ANPIN. Furthermore, the body will be reinstated with its bones. Therefore, the merits and demerits are engraved on its bones and, if it is deserving, the body will be reinstated with its bones. If it is not DESERVING, it will not be reinstated and will not have a resurrection from the dead.

14. וְלָא עוֹד, אֶלָּא תְּרֵין סָהֲדִין אִינּוּן עַל ב"נ, עַיִן רוֹאָה וְאוֹזֶן שׁוֹמַעַת, וּב"ד סוֹפֵר, וְדָן חוֹבוֹי. וְלֹא עוֹד, אֶלָּא שִׁמְשָׁא וְסִיהֲרָא סָהֲדִין עַל ב"נ, כְּמָה דְּאוֹקְמוּהָ תִּקְעוּ בַחֹדֶשׁ שׁוֹפָר בַּכֶּסֶה לְיוֹם חַגֵּנוּ. מַאי בַּכֶּסֶה. בְּיוֹמָא דְסִיהֲרָא מִתְכַּסְּיָא. וַאֲמַאי מִתְכַּסֵּית. בְּגִין דְּכַד מָטֵי רֹאשׁ הַשָּׁנָה, יֵיתֵי סָמָאֵל לְמִתְבַּע דִּינָא לִבְנוֹי קָמֵי קוּדְשָׁא בְּרִיךְ הוּא, וְהוּא יֵימָא לֵיהּ דְּיֵיתֵי סָהֲדִין. וְהוּא יֵיתֵי לְשִׁמְשָׁא עִמֵּיהּ. אָזֵל לְמַיְיתֵי סִיהֲרָא, וְהִיא מִתְכַּסְּיָא. בְּאָן אֲתָר מִתְכַּסֵּית. אֶלָּא סְלִיקַת, לְהַהוּא אֲתָר, דְּאִתְּמַר בֵּיהּ בַּמְכוּסֶּה מִמְּךָ אַל תַּחְקוֹר, לְפַיְּיסָא לֵיהּ עַל בְּנָהָא.

14. Furthermore, there are two witnesses regarding the person: a seeing eye and a hearing ear. The court counts and judges his iniquities. Furthermore, even the sun and moon testify about the person, as we explained: "Blow a Shofar at the new moon, at the full moon (lit. 'on the covering') on our feast day" (Tehilim 81:4). What is the meaning of "covering"? That is the day when the moon, WHICH IS MALCHUT, is covered. Why is it covered? That is because when Rosh Hashanah (the Jewish New Year) arrives, Samael will approach to demand punishment against her children, MEANING YISRAEL, WHO ARE THE CHILDREN OF MALCHUT, before the Holy One, blessed be He. And He will tell him to bring forth the witnesses, so he will bring with him the sun. As he is about to bring the moon, she is covered. At which place is she covered? HE RESPONDS: She goes up to that place regarding which it is said: 'Do not investigate into what is hidden from you', in order to reconcile the Holy One, blessed be He, with her children.

15. וְהַאי הוּא דְּאָמַר קְרָא, תִּקְעוּ בַחֹדֶשׁ שׁוֹפָר בַּכֶּסֶה לְיוֹם חַגֵּנוּ. לַאֲתָר דְּבֵיהּ סְלִיקַת שְׁכִינְתָּא, דְּאִתְּמַר בֵּיהּ וּבַמְכוּסֶּה מִמְּךָ אַל תַּחְקוֹר. וְחוֹבִין בְּאִתְכַּסְיָיא, תַּמָּן צָרִיךְ לְמֵידָן בֵּינוֹ לְבֵין קוֹנוֹ. וְחוֹבִין דְּאִתְגַּלְיָיא דְּעָבֵד לוֹן, אִתְּמַר מְכַסֶּה פְּשָׁעָיו לֹא יַצְלִיחַ. דִּשְׁכִינְתָּא מִסִּטְרָא דְּכֶתֶר אִיהִי עָלְמָא דְּאִתְכַּסְיָא, וְאוֹקְמוּהָ מָארֵי מַתְנִיתִין, דְּצָרִיךְ ב"נ לְחַבְּרָא לָהּ לְהַהוּא אַתְרָא, בְּהַהוּא זִמְנָא מָטֵי זִמְנָא דְּרַחֲמֵי, וְאַעְבַּר דִּינָא. וּבג"ד לְחַבְרֵיהּ אָמַר לְזַכָּאָה לֵיהּ בְּעֵדוּתֵיהּ. אֲבָל לְרָשָׁע אֵין מְזַכִּין לוֹ.

15. That is what the scripture says, "Blow a Shofar at the new moon, at the covering on our feast day" (Ibid.), meaning the area to which the Shechinah ascended. Regarding this, it is said, 'Do not investigate into what is hidden from you'. The iniquities that are in concealment need to be judged there between himself and his Creator. About the iniquities he committed in public, it is written: "He that covers up his sins shall not prosper" (Mishlei 28:13). The Shechinah from the side of Keter is the hidden world and the sages of the Mishnah have explained that a person needs to connect HIS INIQUITIES to that place, WHICH IS KETER. At that time, a period of Mercy arrives and Judgment passes away. Therefore, he recommends to connect ONE'S INIQUITIES TO KETER, to free him from the testimony OF MALCHUT. However, the wicked is not acquitted.

16. וְעוֹד, קוּדְשָׁא בְּרִיךְ הוּא וּשְׁכִינְתֵּיהּ סָהֲדִין עַל ב"נ, הה"ד הַעִדוֹתִי בָכֶם הַיּוֹם אֶת הַשָּׁמַיִם וְאֶת הָאָרֶץ. אֶת הַשָּׁמַיִם, הַהוּא דְּאִתְּמַר בֵּיהּ וְאַתָּה תִּשְׁמַע הַשָּׁמַיִם. וְאֶת הָאָרֶץ, הַהוּא דְּאִתְּמַר בָּהּ וְהָאָרֶץ הֲדוֹם רַגְלָי. וְעוֹד, תְּרֵין סָהֲדִין: עַמּוּדָא דְּאֶמְצָעִיתָא, וְצַדִּיק. וְאִינּוּן ע"ד, מִן שְׁמַ"ע אֶחָד. עֵד, מִן בָּרוּךְ שֵׁם כְּבוֹד מַלְכוּתוֹ לְעוֹלָם וָעֶד.

16. Furthermore, the Holy One, blessed be He, and His Shechinah give CONSTANT testimony about the person AND NOT ONLY ON ROSH HASHANAH, AS MENTIONED. This is what is written: "I call heaven and earth to witnesses against you this day" (Devarim 4:26). Heaven is the one about which is written: "hear You (in) heaven" (I Melachim 8:32), THAT IS ZEIR ANPIN. Earth is the one about which is written, "and the earth is My footstool" (Yeshayah 66:1), THAT IS MALCHUT. In addition, the two witnesses are the Central Column, THAT IS ZEIR ANPIN, and the Righteous IS YESOD. They are *Ayin* and *Dalet* of Sh'ma and Echad (lit. 'one'), NAMELY *AYIN* FROM THE SPELLING OF SH'MA, AND *DALET* FROM ECHAD. THIS IS THE WITNESS (HEB. *ED*, *AYIN-DALET*) FROM THE ASPECT OF ZEIR ANPIN; there is another witness from, 'blessed is the Name of the glory of His Kingdom forever and ever (Heb. *va'ed*)', NAMELY *ED* FROM THE WORD '*VA'ED*', WHICH IS A WITNESS FROM THE ASPECT OF YESOD IN ZEIR ANPIN, WHICH IS INCLUDED IN MALCHUT.

17. עַל פִּי שְׁנַיִם עֵדִים אוֹ שְׁלֹשָׁה עֵדִים יוּמַת הַמֵּת, דָּא סָמָאֵל, מֵת מֵעִקָּרוֹ וַיִּשָּׂאוּהוּ בַמּוֹט בִּשְׁנָיִם. לֹא יוּמַת עַל פִּי עֵד אֶחָד, דְּלָא יְהֵא לֵיהּ חוּלָקָא בְּאֵל אֶחָד.

17. "At the mouth of two witnesses, or three witnesses, shall he that is worthy of death be put to death" (Devarim 17:6). That is Samael, who is essentially dead: "they carried it between two on a pole" (Bemidbar 13:23). "But at the mouth of one witness he shall not be put to death" (Devarim 17:6), meaning he shall have no portion in the one El.

18. כִּי יָקוּם עֵד חָמָס בְּאִישׁ וְגוֹ׳ וְדָרְשׁוּ הַשּׁוֹפְטִים הֵיטֵב וְגוֹ׳, וַעֲשִׂיתֶם לוֹ כַּאֲשֶׁר זָמַם וְגוֹ׳. פִּקּוּדָא דָּא לִדְרוֹשׁ וְלַחֲקוֹר הָעֵדִים בְּז׳ חֲקִירוֹת, קוֹדֶם דְּיָדִין לֵיהּ בְּעוֹנְשָׁא דְּמוֹתָא, בְּשֶׁבַע חֲקִירוֹת, שְׁבַע לָקֳבֵל שִׁבְעָה אֵלֶּה עֵינֵי יְיָ׳ הֵמָּה מְשׁוֹטְטִים בְּכָל הָאָרֶץ. בְּהוֹן וְיִסַּרְתִּי אֶתְכֶם אַף אָנִי שֶׁבַע.

18. "If a false witness rise up against any man...and the judges shall make diligent inquiry...then shall you do to him as he had thought to have done to his brother" (Devarim 19:16-19). This precept is to examine the witnesses seven times before sentencing one to death. The seven examinations are seven that correspond to: "those seven...the eyes of Hashem, they rove to and fro through the whole earth" (Zecharyah 4:10). THEY ARE THE SECRET OF CHESED, GVURAH, TIFERET, NETZACH, HOD, YESOD AND MALCHUT. Regarding them, it is said: "and will chastise you seven times for your sins" (Vayikra 26:28).

4. "then shall you do to him as he had thought to have done"

A Synopsis

Rabbi Shimon talks about the fate of a corrupt witness, and we learn that such corrupt witnesses include Samael and the Serpent.

19. פִּקּוּדָא בָּתַר דָּא, לַעֲשׂוֹת לְעֵד זוֹמֵם כַּאֲשֶׁר זָמַם לַעֲשׂוֹת לְאָחִיו. תְּרֵין סַהֲדֵי שִׁקְרָא דְּאִינּוּן סָמָאֵל וְנַחָשׁ, אִי יֵיתוּן לְאַסְהֲדָא סָהֲדוּתָא דְּשֶׁקֶר עַל יִשְׂרָאֵל, דְּטָעוּ בֵּין ו׳ לְז׳ דְּאִינּוּן אַתְוָון זוּ. וְהַאי אִיהוּ עַם זוּ יָצַרְתִּי לִי תְּהִלָּתִי יְסַפֵּרוּ.

19. The following precept is to do to a witness convicted of false testimony as he thought to do to his brother. If the two false witnesses, Samael and the serpent, come to give false testimony against Yisrael that they confused between *Vav* and *Zayin*, NAMELY BETWEEN ZEIR ANPIN THAT IS CHESED, GVURAH, TIFERET, NETZACH, HOD, YESOD AND MALCHUT, THAT IS *ZAYIN*. THAT IS, THAT THEY HAVE SINNED AND DISTANCED BY THEIR SIN THE *VAV*, WHICH IS ZEIR ANPIN, FROM THE *ZAYIN*, WHICH IS MALCHUT, which are the letters of '*zu* (Zayin Vav)'. This is the meaning of, "This people which (Heb. *zu*) I have formed for Myself; they shall relate My praise" (Yeshayah 43:21), NAMELY, THIS ALLUDES TO THE PEOPLE THAT UNITES THE *ZAYIN* WITH THE *VAV*.

20. וְלָא יִתְיַיחֵד ו׳ עִם ז׳, אֶלָּא בִּשְׂרֵפַת חָמֵץ, דְּבֵין ו׳ לְז׳. וְאע״ג דְּמִדְּאוֹרַיְיתָא אִיהוּ עַד סוֹף שִׁית, גָּזְרוּ רַבָּנָן, אוֹכְלִין כָּל אַרְבַּע, וְתוֹלִין כָּל חָמֵשׁ, וְשׂוֹרְפִין בִּתְחִלַּת שֵׁשׁ. וְאוֹלְפִי מָארֵי מַתְנִיתִין מִסַּהֲדוּתָא דְּשַׁעְתֵּי דְּחָמֵץ, לְסַהֲדוּתָא דִּבְדִיקוֹת דְּסָהֲדֵי, דְּהַהוּא דְּהָרַג אֶת הַנֶּפֶשׁ. וְכֹלָּא מְפֹרָשׁ בְּמַתְנִיתִין. וִיקַיָּים בְּהוֹן, אֲרֵי בְּפִתְגָּמָא דְּחָשִׁיבוּ מִצְרָאֵי לְמֵידָן וְכוּ׳. וְהַאי אִיהוּ וַעֲשִׂיתֶם לוֹ כַּאֲשֶׁר זָמַם.

20. The *Vav* will be united with the *Zayin* only by burning leavened bread, MEANING TO BURN THE KLIPOT THAT TAKE HOLD between the *Vav* and the *Zayin* – THAT IS, BETWEEN ZEIR ANPIN AND MALCHUT. Even though according to the laws of the Torah IT IS PERMISSIBLE TO EAT to the end of the sixth hour of the day, the sages have decreed that you may eat to the end of the fourth hour, hold it in suspense during the fifth hour, and burn it at the beginning of the sixth. The sages of the Mishnah deduced from the testimony regarding the hours of the disposition of leaven THAT ACCORDING TO THE LAWS OF THE TORAH THE TIME TO BURN IS PAST THE SIXTH HOUR – AT THE SEVENTH HOUR, to the testimonial regarding the examination of witnesses about one who has killed someone, WHICH ALSO REQUIRE SEVEN EXAMINATIONS, AS MENTIONED ABOVE, and everything is explained in the Mishnah. It shall be fulfilled REGARDING SAMAEL AND THE SERPENT, “in the thing wherein they dealt proudly” (Shemot 18:11), WHICH MEANS, IN THE SAME THING THE EGYPTIANS PLANNED TO PUNISH YISRAEL, THEY WERE PUNISHED. That is the meaning of: “then shall you do to him, as he had thought” (Devarim 19:19).

5. The Small Sanhedrin and the Great Sanhedrin

A Synopsis

Speaking about the higher court, Rabbi Shimon next tells the Faithful Shepherd that he was Gadol, the highest above the seventy greater Sanhedrin. He says that Moses is the friend of God and the friend of Malchut. He also talks about the lower court, and about the greater and smaller lamp lights. The greater lamp light is the light of God and the smaller is the song of the Levites.

21. פִּקּוּדָא בָּתַר דָּא, לְקַבֵּל בֵּית דִּין הַגָּדוֹל עֲלַיְיהוּ, בִּינָה, מִסִּטְרָא דִּגְדוּלָּה אִקְרֵי אֱלֹהִים, בֵּית דִּין הַגָּדוֹל, רַב בְּדִינוֹי, וְרַב בְּזַכְווֹי, כְּגַוְונָא דְּאִתְּמַר שׂוֹם תָּשִׂים עָלֶיךָ מֶלֶךְ בְּפִקּוּדָא, שׂוֹם לְעֵילָּא, תָּשִׂים לְתַתָּא. הָכִי לְקַבֵּל עָלֵיהּ ב״ד רַבְרְבָא, אע״ג דְּקַבִּיל עָלֵיהּ ב״ד זְעֵירָא. בֵּית דִּין זְעֵירָא, בֵּית דִּין שֶׁל שְׁלֹשָׁה, מִסִּטְרָא דִּשְׁכִינְתָּא תַּתָּאָה. ב״ד רַבְרְבָא, מֵאִלֵּין סַנְהֶדְרֵי גְּדוֹלָה.

21. The following precept is to accept the ruling of the Great Sanhedrin on them, which is Binah, which, from the aspect of Chesed, is called Elohim, WHICH IS BINAH, the great Sanhedrin, SINCE GREAT IS CHESED. It is great in judgment, WHICH IS THE LEFT, and great in finding merit, WHICH IS THE RIGHT. THIS MEANS THAT WHEN THE LEFT SIDE OF BINAH IS INCLUDED WITHIN THE RIGHT, WHICH IS CHESED, BOTH ARE CONSIDERED GREAT, as we learned in relation to the precept, "you may appoint (lit. 'appoint you shall appoint') a king over you" (Devarim 17:15), in which "appoint" is above IN BINAH, and "you shall appoint" is below, IN MALCHUT. In the same way one must accept upon himself the Great Sanhedrin FROM THE ASPECT OF BINAH, although he accepted upon himself the Small Sanhedrin FROM THE ASPECT OF MALCHUT. The small court consists of three from the aspect of the lower Shechinah – WHICH IS MALCHUT. The great court consists of those in the Great Sanhedrin OF 72 MEMBERS, SEVENTY SANHEDRIN JUDGES AND TWO SCRIBES.

22. אָמַר בּוּצִינָא קַדִּישָׁא, שִׁבְעִים סַנְהֶדְרֵי גְּדוֹלָה הֲווֹ, וְאַנְתְּ רַבְרְבָא עַל כֻּלְּהוּ, וְהָיָה כָּל הַדָּבָר הַגָּדוֹל יָבִיאוּ אֵלֶיךָ וְכָל הַדָּבָר הַקָּטֹן יִשְׁפְּטוּ

הֵם. אֵלּוּ. הֵם סַנְהֶדְרֵי גְּדוֹלָה, סַנְהֶדְרֵי קְטַנָּה. סַנְהֶדְרֵי גְּדוֹלָה מִסִּטְרָא דִשְׁכִינְתָּא עִלָּאָה, סַנְהֶדְרֵי קְטַנָּה מִסִּטְרָא דִשְׁכִינְתָּא תַּתָּאָה.

22. The Holy Luminary, RABBI SHIMON, said TO THE FAITHFUL SHEPHERD: The Great Sanhedrin consisted of seventy members, and you are the greatest of them all, as is written: "every great matter they shall bring to you, but every small matter they shall judge" (Shemot 18:22), which relates to the Great Sanhedrin and the Small Sanhedrin, ABOUT WHICH IT IS SAID, "GREAT MATTER" AND "SMALL MATTER." The Great Sanhedrin are from the aspect of the supernal Shechinah, WHICH IS BINAH, and the Small Sanhedrin are from the aspect of the lower Shechinah, WHICH IS MALCHUT.

23. מֹשֶׁה שׁוּשְׁבִינָא דְּמַלְכָּא, אַהֲרֹן שׁוּשְׁבִינָא דְּמַטְרוֹנִיתָא. וְעִמְּהוֹן שַׁבְעִין וּתְרֵין סַנְהֶדְרִין, כְּמִנְיַן חֶסֶד, וּמֵהָכָא סַנְהֶדְרֵי גְּדוֹלָה. סַנְהֶדְרֵי קְטַנָּה, מִסִּטְרָא דִשְׂמָאלָא, אֶת הַמָּאוֹר הַקָּטֹן לְמֶמְשֶׁלֶת הַלַּיְלָה.

23. Moses is the best man of the King, ZEIR ANPIN; Aaron is the best man of the Queen. Together with them there are 72 members to the Sanhedrin, MEANING WITH THE SEVENTY SANHEDRIN JUDGES OVER WHOM MOSES AND AARON PRESIDE, which have the same number as Chesed, WHICH HAS THE NUMERICAL VALUE OF 72. Hence, THEY ARE CONSIDERED the Great Sanhedrin, SINCE CHESED IS CALLED GREAT, AS MENTIONED ABOVE. The Small Sanhedrin are from the aspect of the left, THAT IS MALCHUT, WHICH IS ERECTED FROM THE LEFT, ABOUT WHICH IT IS WRITTEN: "and the lesser light to rule the night" (Beresheet 1:16).

24. וּבְגִ"ד, תִּפְאֶרֶת אֶת הַמָּאוֹר הַגָּדוֹל לְמֶמְשֶׁלֶת הַיּוֹם, דְּאִתְּמַר בֵּיהּ יוֹמָם יְצַוֶּה יְיָ' חַסְדּוֹ. אֶת הַמָּאוֹר הַקָּטֹן לְמֶמְשֶׁלֶת הַלַּיְלָה, וּבַלַּיְלָה שִׁירֹה עִמִּי. שִׁיר דִּלְוִיִּם, וְדָא יְסוֹד. בֶּן יִשַׁי חַי עַל הָאֲדָמָה. דְּתָקִין עֶשֶׂר מִינֵי תְּהִלִּים, בְּשִׁירָה. וְאִיהוּ צַדִּיק לִשְׂמָאלָא, אֶת הַמָּאוֹר הַקָּטֹן, וְדָא שְׁכִינְתָּא, דְּאִתְנְטִילַת מִשְּׂמָאלָא.

24. Due to this, Tiferet IS CONSIDERED "the greater light to rule the day" (Ibid.), BECAUSE it says about it, "Hashem will command His steadfast love

(Heb. *Chesed*) in the daytime" (Tehilim 42:9). SINCE IT IS CHESED, IT IS CALLED THE GREATER LIGHT. "And the lesser light to rule the night" means: "and in the night His song shall be with me" (Ibid.), that is, the song of the Levites, which is Yesod IN MALCHUT, ACCORDING TO THE MEANING OF THE WORDS: "the son of Jesse lives on the ground" (I Shmuel 20:31), IN WHICH 'LIVES' REFERS TO YESOD, AND THE GROUND IS MALCHUT. He has composed ten types of songs in Tehilim, MEANING 'BLESSED', 'A SONG', 'A POEM', ETC. The Righteous is to the left, MEANING YESOD IN MALCHUT, AND THE LEFT, "the lesser light" is the Shechinah that was taken from the left.

Ki Tetze

Names of Articles

1. He who brings out an evil name

A Synopsis

The Faithful Shepherd begins Ki Tetze by talking about people who defame someone's character, and how they must be punished. He refers in this context to a person who defames a virgin of Yisrael, to the spies who went out and gave false reports about the land they saw, and to Esther, who was worthy of the Holy Spirit. He says that those who know only the surface or revealed interpretation of the Torah know nothing of its mysteries; they are poor in knowledge and are referred to as riding upon an donkey. They are from the aspect of the Tree of Knowledge of Good and Evil. Moses talks about the mystery of Esther and her relationship with the Shechinah who gives a person many special attributes. Esther was protected from Ahasuerus just like Sarai was protected from the Pharaoh. The Faithful Shepherd returns to the issue of defamation, and says that those who speak ill of the Shechinah will be stricken in their souls. He talks about the righteous man with whom things do not go well, and the evil man with whom they do. We learn that when the Torah was given, the first tablets that were broken were comparable to virginity in that they testified to the whole Torah; the Torah's groom, Moses, broke her virginity. Next Elijah and all the heads of the Yeshivah bless the Faithful Shepherd. Elijah speaks to Moses about his role and the role of Abraham in relationship to Malchut; he says that Moses spoke out against Yisrael when they made the golden calf and thus he defamed Malchut.

רעיא מהימנא

1. וְעָנְשׁוּ אוֹתוֹ מֵאָה כֶסֶף וְגוֹ׳. פִּקּוּדָא דָא, לָדוּן בְּדִין, מוֹצִיא שֵׁם רָע. הה״ד, וְעָנְשׁוּ אוֹתוֹ מֵאָה כֶסֶף וְנָתְנוּ לַאֲבִי הַנַּעֲרָה כִּי הוֹצִיא שֵׁם רָע עַל בְּתוּלַת יִשְׂרָאֵל. רַבָּנָן, וְהַאי אִיהוּ בָּתַר נִשּׂוּאִין, דְּאָמַר לָא מָצָאתִי לְבִתְּךָ בְּתוּלִים, וְלָאו כָּל שֵׁם רָע שָׁקוּל, דִּמְרַגְּלִים דְּאַפִּיקוּ שׁוּם בִּישׁ עַל אַרְעָא, אִתְעֲנָשׁוּ בְּגִינָהּ, וּמִיתוּ וְלָא זָכוּ לָהּ. וְאִתְּתָא קַרְקַע אִיהִי בְּאַרְעָא, כְּמָה דְּאוּקְמוּהָ, אֶסְתֵּר קַרְקַע עוֹלָם הָיְתָה.

Ra'aya Meheimna (the Faithful Shepherd)

1. He who brings out an evil name

1. "and they shall fine him a hundred shekels of silver..." (Devarim 22:19). We are commanded to punish whoever defames someone's character. This is the meaning of, "and they shall fine him a hundred shekels of silver, and give them to the father of the girl, because he has brought out an evil name upon a virgin of Yisrael." THE FAITHFUL SHEPHERD SAID, Sages, this applies to after the wedding, since he says, "I found not your daughter a virgin" (Ibid. 17). Not all evil names are alike, since the spies who spread an evil name on the land were punished for it by dying and not meriting it. A woman is like ground, WHICH IS WHY THE SPIES WERE CONSIDERED AS ONE DEFAMING THE CHARACTER OF A WOMAN. It is like the explanation that Esther was the ground.

2. וְאִי תֵּימְרוּן שׁוּם בִּישׁ עָלָהּ, דְּאִסְתְּאָבַת בַּאֲחַשְׁוֵרוֹשׁ, וְזָכְתָה לְאִתְלַבְּשָׁא בָּהּ רוּחָא דְּקֻדְשָׁא הה״ד וַתִּלְבַּשׁ אֶסְתֵּר מַלְכוּת. הָא אָמַר קוּדְשָׁא בְּרִיךְ הוּא, אֲנִי יְיָ׳ הוּא שְׁמִי וּכְבוֹדִי לְאַחֵר לֹא אֶתֵּן וּתְהִלָּתִי לַפְּסִילִים. וְרוּחָא דְּקֻדְשָׁא שְׁכִינְתָּא הֲוַת, דְּאִיהִי שֵׁם דְּאִתְלַבְּשַׁת בְּאֶסְתֵּר.

2. You may say that Esther has a bad reputation BY SAYING that she was defiled with Ahasuerus, YET she was worthy that the Holy Spirit, WHICH IS MALCHUT, would be clothed in her as written, "Esther put on her royal apparel" (Ester 5:1). IN THAT CASE, YOU ARE BRINGING OUT AN EVIL NAME ON MALCHUT. Yet the Holy One, blessed be He, said, "I am Hashem, that is My name, and My glory will I not give to another, neither My praise to carved idols" (Yeshayah 42:8), WHICH IS THE SHECHINAH CALLED 'NAME', 'GLORY' AND 'PRAISE'. The Holy Spirit is the Shechinah and is a name that was clothed with Esther. HOW CAN YOU SAY SHE WAS DEFILED WITH AHASUERUS?

3. אֲבָל רַבָּנָן, וַוי לְאִינּוּן דְּאַכְלִין תֶּבֶן תֶּבֶל דְּאוֹרַיְיתָא וְלָא יָדַע בְּסִתְרֵי דְּאוֹרַיְיתָא, אֶלָּא קַלִּין וַחֲמוּרִין דְּאוֹרַיְיתָא, קַלִּין תֶּבֶן דְּאוֹרַיְיתָא, חוּמְרָא דְּאוֹרַיְיתָא, חִטָּה, חֵט ה׳, אִילָנָא דְּטוֹב וָרָע.

3. Yet sages, woe to those who eat the chaff and ears of corn of the Torah, THAT IS, WHOSE TORAH IS MIXED OF GOOD AND EVIL LIKE CHAFF AND

EARS OF CORN THAT ARE A MIXTURE OF FOOD AND KLIPOT. Such a man knows nothing of the mysteries of the Torah, but only light and weighty precepts; the light is the chaff of the Torah, NAMELY THE REFUSE, and the weighty precepts of the Torah are wheat, WHICH CONTAINS BOTH FOOD AND REFUSE. CHET AND TET OF WHEAT (HEB. *CHITAH*) ARE THE REFUSE AND HEI IS GOOD. THIS IS THE SECRET OF the Tree of Knowledge of Good and Evil, AS THE SAGES SAID THAT THE TREE OF KNOWLEDGE OF GOOD AND EVIL WAS WHEAT.

4. לֵית דַּרְכָּא דְּמַלְכָּא וּמַטְרוֹנִיתָא, לְמִרְכַּב עַל חֲמָרָא, אֶלָּא עַל סוּסְוָון. הה"ד כִּי תִרְכַּב עַל סוּסֶיךָ מַרְכְּבוֹתֶיךָ יְשׁוּעָה. דְּאֵין מְזַלְזְלִין בְּמַלְכוּתָא, לְמִרְכַּב מַטְרוֹנִיתָא עַל חֲמָרָא. כ"ש מַלְכָּא, לֵית דֵּין אֲתָר הֶדְיוֹט עֶבֶד, דְּאָרְחֵיהּ לְמִרְכַּב עַל חֲמָרָא. וּבג"ד כְּתִיב בֵּיהּ בְּמָשִׁיחַ, עָנִי וְרוֹכֵב עַל חֲמוֹר. עָנִי אִיהוּ תַּמָּן בְּסִימָן, עֵרוּבִין נִדָּה יְבָמוֹת, וּשְׁאַר מַתְנִיתִין בִּכְלָל. וְלָא אִתְקְרֵי תַּמָּן מֶלֶךְ, עַד דְּרָכִיב בְּסוּסְיָא דִּילֵיהּ כְּנֶסֶת יִשְׂרָאֵל.

4. It is not the custom of the King and the Matron to ride a donkey (Heb. *chamor*), NAMELY THE LITERAL UNDERSTANDING (HEB. *CHOMER*) OF THE TORAH, WHICH IS WHEAT AND THE TREE OF KNOWLEDGE OF GOOD AND EVIL AS MENTIONED. Instead they ride on horses, THE SECRET OF THE MYSTERIES OF THE TORAH. This is the meaning of, "you ride upon your horses, your chariots of salvation" (Chavakuk 3:8). For Malchut is not treated lightly so as to have the Queen ride on a donkey, and even more so the King, for it is no place for commoners and servants, THAT IS METATRON THAT IS CALLED A COMMONER AND A SERVANT, whose way is to ride a donkey. This is why it says of Messiah, WHEN YISRAEL WILL HAVE NO MERIT, "humble (Heb. *ani*), and riding upon an donkey" (Zecharyah 9:9). Ani stands for the Mishnah orders of Eruvin, Nidah and Yevamot, THE INITIALS OF WHICH FORM '*ANI* (ENG. 'POOR')'. The rest of the orders of the Mishnah are comprised in these, WHICH INDICATES THAT AS LONG AS ONE DOES NOT KNOW THE MYSTERIES OF THE TORAH BUT ONLY THE REVEALED TORAH, ONE IS POOR IN KNOWLEDGE AND RIDING UPON AN DONKEY, WHICH IS THE ASPECT OF THE TREE OF KNOWLEDGE OF GOOD AND EVIL. THE HOLY ONE, BLESSED BE HE, is not considered a King until He rides on His horse, which is the Congregation of Yisrael,

NAMELY MALCHUT, ACCORDING TO THE SECRET OF, "I COMPARE YOU, O MY LOVE, TO A MARE OF THE CHARIOTS OF PHARAOH" (SHIR HASHIRIM 1:9), WHICH IS WHOLLY GOOD WITHOUT ANY EVIL.

5. קוּדְשָׁא בְּרִיךְ הוּא כַּד אִיהוּ לְבַר מֵאַתְרֵיהּ, לָאו אִיהוּ מֶלֶךְ. וְכַד אִתְהַדָּר לְאַתְרֵיהּ, וְהָיָה יְיָ׳ לְמֶלֶךְ. וְהָכִי יִשְׂרָאֵל, אִתְּמַר בְּהוֹן, כָּל יִשְׂרָאֵל בְּנֵי מְלָכִים. כְּגַוְונָא דְּאַבָּא, אִינּוּן בְּנוֹי. לָאו אִינּוּן בְּנֵי מְלָכִים, עַד דִּיהַדְרוּן לְאַרְעָא דְּיִשְׂרָאֵל. וְאִי תֵּימָא דְּהֶדְיוֹט דָּא, אַף ע״ג דְּאִיהוּ הֶדְיוֹט לְגַבֵּי מָארֵיהּ, עָלֵיהּ אִתְּמַר, אַל תְּהִי בִּרְכַּת הֶדְיוֹט קַלָּה בְּעֵינֶיךָ. וְהֶדְיוֹט דָּא לְגַבֵּי מַלְכָּא עֶבֶד מְטַטְרוֹן. וְאָדָם קַדְמָאָה דְּלָא נָטַר יְקָר דְּיָהֲבוּ לֵיהּ, נַחְתּוּ לֵיהּ לְמֵיכַל עִם חֲמָרֵיהּ, וְאָמַר אֲנִי וַחֲמוֹרִי נֹאכַל בְּאֵבוּס אֶחָד. וְיִשָּׂשכָר בְּהַאי חֲמָרָא, זָכָה לְאִתְקְרֵי יִשָּׂשכָר חֲמוֹר גָּרֶם.

5. The Holy One, blessed be He, outside His place is not a King. When He returns to His place, "Hashem shall be King" (Zecharyah 14:9). It is said of Yisrael as well that all Yisrael are princes. Like the father the children are not princes until they return to the land of Yisrael. You may say that he WHO RIDES A DONKEY is a commoner, AND HE ANSWERS, though he is a commoner in relation to his Master, do not treat lightly a blessing from a commoner, for this commoner is the servant Metatron, AND IT IS HE WHO RIDES THIS DONKEY. The first man, who did not keep the glory he was given BY EATING OF THE TREE OF KNOWLEDGE OF GOOD AND EVIL, was brought down to eat together with his donkey, WHICH IS THE ASPECT OF THE TREE OF KNOWLEDGE OF GOOD AND EVIL and he said TO THE HOLY ONE, BLESSED BE HE, I and my donkey shall eat from the same trough. Issachar merited this donkey by being called, "Issachar is a strong donkey" (Beresheet 49:14), BECAUSE HE SUBDUED THIS DONKEY CALLED A STRONG (HEB. *GEREM*) DONKEY BY BRINGING HIM DOWN THE STAIRCASE (HEB. *GEREM*).

6. וְרַבָּנָן מָארֵי מָתְנִיתִין, מַטְרוֹנִיתָא אִתְּמַר בָּהּ וּמַלְכוּתוֹ בַּכֹּל מָשָׁלָה, בָּתַר דְּאִתְלַבְּשָׁא בֵּיהּ אֶסְתֵּר, שְׁלִיטַת אֶסְתֵּר עַל אֲחַשְׁוֵרוֹשׁ וְאוּמָּתֵיהּ. וְאִתְּמַר בְּהוּ וְהָרוֹג בְּשׂוֹנְאֵיהֶם. וְאִי תֵּימָא דְּאִתְיָיחַד עִמָּהּ. אַף עַל גַּב

דַּהֲווֹ בְּבֵיתָא חֲדָא, ח״ו. אֶלָּא, כְּגַוְונָא דְּיוֹסֵף, דְּאִתְּמַר בֵּיהּ, וַתַּנַּח בִּגְדוֹ אֶצְלָהּ, וְלָא לְבוּשׁוֹ, אֶלָּא בִּגְדוֹ, לִישָּׁנָא דְּבוֹגְדִים בָּגָדוּ.

6. The sages who wrote the Mishnah SAID THAT it is said of the Matron, WHO IS MALCHUT, "and His kingdom rules over all" (Tehilim 103:19), SINCE SHE RULES OVER THE KLIPOT AS WELL. THEREFORE, after Esther put on THE ROYAL APPAREL, IN ACCORDANCE WITH THE SECRET OF THE VERSE, "ESTHER PUT ON HER ROYAL APPAREL (HEB. *MALCHUT*)," Esther ruled over Ahasuerus and his people, and it is said of them, "and slew of their foes" (Ester 9:16). If you say that AHASUERUS mated with her, heaven forbid. Though they were in the same house, SHE DID NOT MATE WITH HIM, but was like Joseph of whom it says, "And she laid up his garment (Heb. *bigdo*) by her" (Beresheet 39:16). The word 'bigdo' is employed, which is derived from, "traitors have dealt treacherously (Heb. *bagdu*)" (Yeshayah 24:16). THIS IS HIS MOST OUTER ASPECT, WHICH THE KLIPOT CAN BE ATTACHED TO.

7. וְהָכָא סִתְרָא רַבְרְבָא. וּבְגִין דָּא, אֶסְתֵּר: לִישָּׁנָא דְּסִתְרָאָה, אַתָּה סֵתֶר לִי, שְׁכִינְתָּא אַסְתִּירַת לָהּ מֵאֲחַשְׁוֵרוֹשׁ, וְיָהִיב לֵיהּ שֵׁידָה בְּאַתְרָהּ, וְאִתְהַדְּרַת אִיהִי בִּדְרוֹעֵיהּ דְּמָרְדְּכַי. וּמָרְדְּכַי דַּהֲוָה יָדַע שְׁמָא מְפָרַשׁ, וְשַׁבְעִין לָשׁוֹן, עֲבַד כָּל דָּא בְּחָכְמְתָא. וּבְגִין דָּא אוּקְמוּהָ מָארֵי מַתְנִיתִין, דַּאֲפִילּוּ בְּלָא דָּא, אִית לֵיהּ לְב״נ קוֹדֶם דְּיִתְיָחֵד עִם אִתְּתֵיהּ, לְמַלְּלָא עִמָּהּ, בְּגִין דְּשֶׁמָּא שֵׁידָה אִתְחַלְּפָא בְּאִתְּתֵיהּ.

7. There is a great mystery here, which is why 'Esther' is derived from mystery (Heb. *seter*), as written, "You are my hiding place (Heb. *seter*)" (Tehilim 32:7), since the Shechinah hid her from Ahasuerus and gave him a female demon instead while she returned to Mordechai's arm. And Mordechai, who knew the explicit Name and the seventy tongues, did all this with wisdom. This is why the sages of the Mishnah stated that even regardless of this, a man must speak with his wife before he mates with her, because she might have been exchanged with a female demon.

8. וְדָא בְּאִתְּתָא מֵאִילָנָא דְּטוֹב וָרָע, אֲבָל אִם הִיא מִשְּׁכִינְתָּא, לֵית לָהּ

שִׁנּוּי, הה"ד אֲנִי יְיָ' לֹא שָׁנִיתִי. אֲנִי: דָּא שְׁכִינְתָּא. וְלֵית לָהּ דְּחִילוּ מִכָּל סִטְרִין אַחֲרָנִין. הה"ד, כָּל הַגּוֹיִם כְּאַיִן נֶגְדּוֹ.

8. This is true for a woman who comes from the aspect of the Tree of Knowledge of Good and Evil, AND AN EXCHANGE WITH A FEMALE DEMON APPLIES TO HER, but if she is from the Shechinah she remains unchanged. This is the meaning of, "For I am Hashem, I do not change" (Malachi 3:6). "I" is the Shechinah, who has no fear from the other sides, NAMELY THE KLIPOT. This is the meaning of, "All nations before Him are as nothing" (Yeshayah 40:17).

9. וּבְאַתְרָא דִּשְׁכִינְתָּא תַּמָּן, כַּמָּה סְגוּלוֹת תַּמָּן. וּבְגִין דְּאֶסְתֵּר אִתְלַבְּשַׁת שְׁכִינְתָּא בָּהּ, חַזְיָא הֲוַת לְמֶעְבַּד עִמָּהּ כַּמָּה סְגוּלוֹת. כְּגַוְונָא דְּשָׂרָה, קוּדְשָׁא בְּרִיךְ הוּא נָטִיר לָהּ, בְּגִין שְׁכִינְתָּא דַּהֲוַת עִמָּהּ, נָטִיר לָהּ מִפַּרְעֹה, וַאֲפִילּוּ לְבוּשָׁהּ וְתַכְשִׁיטֶיהָ בְּכֻלְּהוּ שַׁוֵּי קוּדְשָׁא בְּרִיךְ הוּא סְגוּלוֹת, בְּגִין שְׁכִינְתָּא. וּבְגִין דָּא, אָתָא פַּרְעֹה לְסַנְדָּלָא, מָחָא לֵיהּ עִמֵּיהּ. וְהָכִי נָמֵי בְּכָל תַּכְשִׁיטִין דִּילָהּ. בְּכָל תַּכְשִׁיט וְתַכְשִׁיט דַּהֲוָה נָגַע בֵּיהּ, מָחֵי לֵיהּ, עַד דְּאִתְפְּרַשׁ מִנָּהּ הַהוּא טָמֵא, וְאַחְזַר לָהּ לְבַעְלָהּ.

9. Wherever the Shechinah is, there are many special attributes. Hence, since the Shechinah was clothed in her, Esther was worthy of having special things done to her like Sarah, whom the Holy One, blessed be He, kept, and since the Shechinah was with her He kept her from Pharaoh. The Holy One, blessed be He even made her clothes and jewels have special qualities due to the Shechinah that was with her. For that reason, when Pharaoh came to TOUCH her sandal, THE ANGEL struck him with it, and the same happened with all her jewelry. Each jewel he would touch struck him until that defiled one left her and brought her back to her husband.

10. וְאִי בְּתַכְשִׁיטִין דִּילָהּ כַּךְ, כ"ש מַאן דְּנָגַע בְּגוּפָא. וַאֲפִילּוּ בְּאֶצְבַּע דִּילָהּ, לְסִטְרָא דְּיִחוּדָא, וְהַזָּר הַקָּרֵב יוּמָת. דְּקוּדְשָׁא בְּרִיךְ הוּא לָא יְהִיב לֵיהּ רְשׁוּ לְמִקְרַב גַּבָּהּ, הה"ד אֲנִי יְיָ' הוּא שְׁמִי וּכְבוֹדִי לְאַחֵר לֹא אֶתֵּן.

10. If this is true for her jewels, it is much more so that whoever touched her body, even her finger, for the purpose of mating, THEN, "and the stranger that comes near shall be put to death" (Bemidbar 1:51), since the Holy One, blessed be He, did not give him permission to come near her. This is the meaning of, "I am Hashem, that is My name, and My glory will I not give to another" (Yeshayah 42:8).

11. וּבְגִין דָּא, לָא כָּל ש״ר שָׁקוּל. מְרַגְּלִים דְּאַפִּיקוּ שׁוּם בִּישׁ עַל אַרְעָא דְּיִשְׂרָאֵל מִיתוּ. מַאן דְּאַפִּיק שׁוּם בִּישׁ עַל שְׁכִינְתָּא, כָּל שֶׁכֵּן דִּלְקְיָין בְּנִשְׁמָתְהוֹן. דְּאִלֵּין דְּאַפִּיקוּ שׁוּם בִּישׁ עַל אַרְעָא, לָקוּ בְּגוּפַיְיהוּ, וּמִיתַת גַּרְמַיְיהוּ מִיתוּ. אֲבָל מַאן דְּאַפִּיק שׁוּם בִּישׁ עַל שְׁכִינְתָּא, נִשְׁמְתָא דִּלְהוֹן לָקְאָה. וְהַאי לְמַאן דְּיָדַע רָזָא דָּא, וְעֵינוֹי פַּתְחִין. אֲבָל מַאן דְּעֵינוֹי סְתִימִין, לֵית לֵיהּ עוֹנְשָׁא כָּל כַּךְ.

11. For that reason not every SPREADING OF an evil name is the same. The spies who defamed the land of Yisrael died. Those who speak ill of the Shechinah are most certainly struck in their souls, for those who spoke ill about the land were struck bodily and committed suicide. But whoever defames the Shechinah, his soul is stricken. This applies to whoever knows this secret OF BRINGING OUT AN EVIL NAME ON THE SHECHINAH, and whose eyes are open. But a person whose eyes are shut is not punished as severely.

12. וּמַה דְּרַבָּנָן דְּמַתְנִיתִין שַׁוְיָין קַמַּיְיהוּ, דְּאִתְּתָא אֲנוּסָה מוּתֶּרֶת לְבַעְלָהּ. וַדַּאי אִיסּוּר וְהֶיתֵּר דְּמַתְנִיתִין לָא מְמַלֵּל אֶלָּא בְּמִילֵּיהּ דְּב״נ, וְאִתְּתָא דְּאִיהִי מֵאִילָנָא דְּעֵץ הַדַּעַת טוֹב וָרָע. אֲבָל אִתְּתָא דְּאִיהִי מֵאִילָנָא דְּחַיֵּי, לָאו לָהּ דִּינָא כְּאִלֵּין, דְּהַהוּא דְּאִילָנָא דְּחַיֵּי, צַדִּיק וְטוֹב לוֹ. וּבְגִינֵיהּ אִתְּמַר, לֹא יְאוּנֶּה לַצַּדִּיק כָּל אָוֶן, וְלָא לְבַת זוּגוֹ צַדֶּקֶת. וְאוֹלִיפְנָא מִשָּׂרָה בְּבֵיתָא דְּפַרְעֹה, דְּלָא הֲוָה לֵיהּ רְשׁוּ לְמִקְרַב בַּהֲדָהּ.

12. As for what the sages of the Mishnah said to them that a raped wife is permitted to remain with her husband, permission and prohibition in the Mishnah speak only of human matters and a woman who is from the Tree of

Knowledge of Good and Evil. But the case of a woman who is from the Tree of Life is not as that of those FROM THE TREE OF KNOWLEDGE OF GOOD AND EVIL, since whoever is from the Tree of Life is a righteous person with whom things are well. Of him it is said, "No evil shall happen to the just" (Mishlei 12:21), nor to his just wife. We learned that from Sarah in the house of Pharaoh – that he had no permission to come near her.

13. וּמַאן דְּאִיהוּ צַדִּיק וְרָע לוֹ, הַאי דְּאִיהוּ מֵאִילָנָא דְּטוֹב וָרָע, דְּכֵיוָן דְּרָע עִמֵּיהּ, אֵין צַדִּיק אֲשֶׁר לֹא יֶחֱטָא בְּהַהוּא רָע, בָּתַר דְּאִיהוּ עִמֵּיהּ. רָשָׁע וְטוֹב לוֹ, דְּאִתְגַּבָּר יֵצֶר הָרָע עַל יֵצֶר טוֹב, אִתְּמַר וְטוֹב לוֹ, טוֹב אִיהוּ תְּחוֹת רְשׁוּתֵיהּ, וּבְגִין דְּרָע שַׁלִּיט עַל טוֹב, רָשָׁע אִיהוּ, דְּהַהוּא דְּאִתְגַּבָּר נָטִיל שְׁמָא. רָשָׁע וְרָע לוֹ, אֵל אַחֵר סָמָאֵל, וְרָע לוֹ, סַם הַמָּוֶת דִּילֵיהּ עכו"ם, תְּמוֹתֵת רָשָׁע רָעָה. וּבג"ד, אֲנוּסָה לָאו אִיהִי, אֶלָּא אִי אִית בָּהּ תַּעֲרוֹבֶת בְּהַהִיא נִשְׁמְתָא, דְּטוֹב וָרָע.

13. Whoever is righteous but for whom things go badly, namely, he who is from the Tree of Knowledge of Good and Evil, since there is evil PRESENT with him, "For there is not a just man upon earth who...never sins" (Kohelet 7:20). As for an evil man for whom things go well, it is that the Evil Inclination overpowered his Good Inclination. HENCE they said that it is well with him, because the good is under the power OF THE EVIL MAN. And since the evil dominates the good, he is an evil man, since whoever is stronger receives the name. IF THE GOOD OVERCOMES THE EVIL, HE IS CALLED A RIGHTEOUS MAN THAT IT IS EVIL WITH HIM, SINCE EVIL IS UNDER HIS POWER. IF EVIL OVERCOMES GOOD HE IS CALLED AN EVIL MAN THAT IT IS WELL WITH HIM, SINCE GOOD IS UNDER HIS POWER. An evil man with whom things are evil is another El, who is Samael. It is evil with him, namely the poison of death, which is idol worshiping, OF WHICH IT IS WRITTEN, "Evil shall slay the wicked" (Tehilim 34:22). For that reason a raped WOMAN is considered so only if that soul has a mixture of good and evil.

14. וְאוֹרַיְיתָא דְּאִתְיְיהִיבַת, אִתְּבָּרוּ לוּחִין דִּילָהּ, דְּאִינּוּן מְשׁוּלִים לַבְּתוּלִים. וְקוּדְשָׁא בְּרִיךְ הוּא הֲדַר יָהִיב לוֹן לְיִשְׂרָאֵל, לְנַטְרָא לָהּ, אוֹרַיְיתָא דבע"פ אִתְקְרִיאַת הֲלָכָה לְמֹשֶׁה מִסִּינַי. וְחָתָן דִּידָהּ, תָּבַר

בְּתוּלִים דִּילָהּ. וּמַאן דְּאַפִּיק שׁוּם בִּישׁ עָלָהּ, דְּיֵימָא דְּהָא הַהִיא אוֹרַיְיתָא לָאו אִיהִי דָּא, דְּהָא לוּחִין דִּילָהּ אִתְּבָרוּ. קוּדְשָׁא בְּרִיךְ הוּא יֵימָא לֵיהּ, דְּאִיהוּ אֲבִי הַנַּעֲרָה, בַּת, דְּאִיהוּ בְּתֵיבַת בְּרֵאשִׁית, אִיהִי בְּרַתָּא דְּמַלְכָּא, קוּדְשָׁא בְּרִיךְ הוּא אָמַר וּפָרְשׂוּ הַשִּׂמְלָה, וְאִתְפַּתְחַת יְרִיעָה מס״ת, וְיֶחֱזוּן דְּאִתְמַר בֵּיהּ, פְּסָל לְךָ שְׁנֵי לוּחוֹת אֲבָנִים כָּרִאשׁוֹנִים וְכָתַבְתִּי עַל הַלּוּחוֹת אֶת הַדְּבָרִים אֲשֶׁר הָיוּ עַל הַלּוּחוֹת הָרִאשׁוֹנִים אֲשֶׁר שִׁבַּרְתָּ.

14. When the Torah was given, her tablets that were likened to virginity were broken. JUST AS VIRGINITY IS A TESTIMONY TO THE VIRGIN'S HONESTY, SO THE TABLETS THAT WERE GIVEN BEFORE THE EYES OF ALL YISRAEL WERE A TESTIMONY TO THE WHOLE TORAH. And the Holy One, blessed be He, again gave her to Yisrael to keep her. And the oral Torah is called Halachah given to Moses on Sinai. MOSES WAS THEREFORE CALLED THE BRIDE'S GROOM OF THE TORAH. And the groom of the Torah broke her virginity, WHICH IS THE FIRST SET OF TABLETS. Whoever speaks ill of her and says that Torah is not LIKE THE FIRST ONE, since her tablets were broken, the Holy One, blessed be He, will speak to him, who is the girl's father, NAMELY OF that daughter who is IMPLIED in the word Beresheet (In the beginning), SINCE BERESHEET IS SPELLED WITH THE LETTERS OF '*BAT ROSHI* (ENG. 'THE DAUGHTER OF MY HEAD')', TO INDICATE THAT THE TORAH IS the King's daughter. THEN the Holy One, blessed be He, spoke: "And they shall spread the cloth" (Devarim 22:17), and the parchment of the Torah scroll unfolds, and they shall see that it is written in it, "Hew for yourself two tablets of stone like the first, and I will write upon these tablets the words that were on the first tablets, which you did break" (Shemot 34:1).

15. מִיַּד קָם אֵלִיָּהוּ, וְכָל מָארֵי מְתִיבְתָּא, וּבָרִיכוּ לֵיהּ, וְאָמְרוּ סִינַי סִינַי, הָכִי אִתְחַזְיָיא לְמִשְׁמַע מִלִּין דִּילָךְ וְלִשְׁתּוּק, אֲבָל בִּרְשׁוּתָא דְּקוּדְשָׁא בְּרִיךְ הוּא וּשְׁכִינְתֵּיהּ, אֲנָא בָּעֵי לְמַלְּלָא מִלָּה לְגַבָּךְ, לִיקָרָא דִּילָךְ. א״ל אֵימָא.

15. Immediately Elijah rose with all the heads of the Yeshivah and they blessed him. And ELIJAH said TO THE FAITHFUL SHEPHERD, Sinai, Sinai, it would have been worthy for us to listen to your words and be silent, yet with permission from the Holy One, blessed be He, and His Shechinah, I wish to say something to you, in your honor. He said to him, speak.

16. פָּתַח וְאָמַר, רַעְיָא מְהֵימְנָא, הַאי כַּלָּה דִּילָךְ, קוּדְשָׁא בְּרִיךְ הוּא יָהַב לָהּ לְאַבְרָהָם לְגַדְּלָא לָהּ לְגַבָּךְ, וּבְגִין דְּאִיהוּ נָטִיר לָהּ, אִתְקְרִיאַת בְּרָתֵיהּ. הה״ד, בַּת הָיְתָה לוֹ לְאַבְרָהָם וּבַכֹּל שְׁמָהּ. וּבָהּ קִיֵּים כָּל אוֹרַיְיתָא כֻּלָּהּ, וַאֲפִילוּ עֵירוּבֵי תַּבְשִׁילִין. הה״ד, וַיִּשְׁמוֹר מִשְׁמַרְתִּי וְגוֹ׳. וְאִיהוּ הֲוָה לְגַבָּהּ אוֹמֵן, כְּגוֹן וַיְהִי אוֹמֵן אֶת הֲדַסָּה. וְקוּדְשָׁא בְּרִיךְ הוּא בָּרִיךְ לֵיהּ בְּגִינָהּ, הה״ד וַיְיָ׳ בֵּרַךְ אֶת אַבְרָהָם בַּכֹּל. וְגַדִּיל לָהּ מִכָּל מִדּוֹת טָבִין, וְגָמִיל לָהּ חֶסֶד, וְסָלִיק לָהּ בִּגְדוּלָה בְּמִדַּת חֶסֶד דְּאַבְרָהָם, וַהֲוָה בֵּיתֵיהּ בְּגִינָהּ פָּתוּחַ לָרְוָוחָה, לְמִגְמַל חֶסֶד עִם כָּל בָּאֵי עוֹלָם.

16. ELIJAH opened and said, Faithful Shepherd, the Holy One, blessed be He gave this bride of yours, NAMELY MALCHUT to Abraham to bring up for you. And since he kept her she is called his daughter. This is what is meant by the saying that Abraham had a daughter whose name was 'Bakol (Eng. 'in all')'. By her he observed the whole Torah even to the Eruv Tavshilin (an action allowing one to cook on holiday for Shabbat). This is the meaning of, "and kept My charge" (Beresheet 26:5). And he brought her up, as written, "And he brought up Hadassa" (Ester 2:7). And the Holy One, blessed be He, blessed him for her sake, as written, "and Hashem had blessed Abraham in all things (Heb. *bakol*)" (Beresheet 24:1). He brought her up with every good virtue and was charitable to her. He raised her to greatness, with the quality of kindness (Chesed) of Abraham. His house was, for her sake, wide open to do kindness to all the people of the world.

17. וּבְגִין דְּאִיהוּ גָּמִיל חֶסֶד עִמָּהּ, כַּד בְּנוֹי דְּאַבְרָהָם הֲווֹ מְמוּשְׁכָּנִין בְּכַמָּה חוֹבִין בְּמִצְרַיִם, אָמַר קוּדְשָׁא בְּרִיךְ הוּא לָךְ רַעְיָא מְהֵימָנָא, זִיל וְגָמִיל טִיבוּ, לְמַאן דְּגָמִיל לֵיהּ עִמָּךְ, דְּדָא כַּלָּה דִּילָךְ, יְהִיבַת לָהּ לֵיהּ, לְגַדְּלָא לָהּ בְּמִדּוֹת טָבִין, וְאִיהוּ גָּדִיל לָהּ בִּתְלֵיסָר מְכִילָן דְּרַחֲמֵי, דִּרְמִיזִין בִּתְלַת תֵּיבִין וָה״ו אֲנִ״י וָה״ו, דְּאִינּוּן וָא״ו. דְּכָלִיל בְּהוֹן ע״ב

שְׁמָהָן, כְּמִנְיַן חֶסֶד. דִּבְהוֹן הֲוָה אִתְגַּבַּר אַבְרָהָם עַל ע״ב אוּמִין וּבְכַלָּה דִּילָךְ, הֲוָה לֵיהּ סְגוּלָּה בְּע״ב שְׁמָהָן, וַהֲוָה נָצַח לְכָל אוּמָּה וְלִישָּׁן.

17. Since he was kind to her, when Abraham's children were exiled because of their many iniquities in Egypt, the Holy One, blessed be He, said, 'Faithful Shepherd, go and be kind to him who did kindness by you, since I gave him your bride, WHO IS MALCHUT, to raise with good qualities'. And he raised her BY DRAWING HER thirteen attributes of mercy implied in the three words, Vav Hei Vav, Aleph Nun Yud, Vav Hei Vav, which are THE INITIALS OF Vav, since the 72 names are comprehended in them AS THE FIRST OF THE 72 NAMES IS VAV HEI VAV, THE MIDDLE ONE IS ALEPH NUN YUD AND TOWARDS THE END IS THE SECOND VAV HEI VAV. 72 IS the numerical value of Chesed, with which Abraham overcame the 72 nations, WHICH ARE THE SEVENTY NATIONS, ESAU AND ISHMAEL. Through your bride, NAMELY MALCHUT, he had a special property through the 72 names AFTER MALCHUT RECEIVED THEM, and he overcame every nation and tongue.

18. וּבְגִין דָּא, מוֹלִיךְ לִימִין מֹשֶׁה זְרוֹעַ תִּפְאַרְתּוֹ. וּבוֹקֵעַ מַיִם, דְּיַמָּא קַרְעַת לֵיהּ קֳדָם בְּנוֹי, בִּתְרֵיסַר קְרָעִין, בְּחוּשְׁבָּן וָ״ו, וּבִזְכוּת א׳ עַבְדַת יַמָּא יַבֶּשְׁתָּא. וּבָהּ טוּבְעוּ מִצְרַיִם, דְּלָא מְהֵימְנִין בְּוָא״ו דְּאִיהוּ אֶחָד. וּלְזִמְנָא דְּאָתֵי, כִּימֵי צֵאתְךָ מֵאֶרֶץ מִצְרָיִם אַרְאֶנּוּ נִפְלָאוֹת, יִתְקַיֵּים בְּיִשְׂרָאֵל זַרְעָא דְּאַבְרָהָם. וּבָךְ יִתְקַיֵּים, מוֹלִיךְ לִימִין מֹשֶׁה זְרוֹעַ תִּפְאַרְתּוֹ וּבוֹקֵעַ מַיִם דְּאוֹרַיְיתָא קֳדָמֵהוֹן, לְמֶהֱוֵי לָךְ שֵׁם עוֹלָם. וְתַמָּן תַּרְוִיחַ כַּלָּה דִּילָךְ.

18. For that reason IT IS WRITTEN, "That caused His glorious arm to go at the right hand of Moses" (Yeshayah 63:12), WHICH IS MALCHUT, and "dividing the water" (Ibid.) by tearing the water into twelve pieces, the numerical value of Vav Vav. And by merit of Aleph IN THE FULLY SPELLED VAV (VAV ALEPH VAV) THAT INDICATES THE ILLUMINATION OF BINAH, You turned the sea into dry land. In it the Egyptians drowned, who did not believe in the Vav, WHICH IS ZEIR ANPIN, which is THE NUMERICAL VALUE OF one. In the future to come it will be fulfilled in Yisrael, the seed of Abraham, "As in the days of your coming out of the land of Egypt I will show him marvelous things" (Michah 7:15). In you it shall be fulfilled, "That caused His glorious arm to go at the right hand of Moses, dividing the water" of the Torah, to make yourself, "an everlasting name" (Yeshayah 63:12). There you shall attain your bride.

19. וּבְגִין דְּבַת דָּא, אִתְיְיהִיבַת לְיִשְׂרָאֵל, דְּאִיהִי הֲלָכָה דִּילָךְ, מִסִּטְרָא דִּשְׂמָאלָא, הֲלָכָה לְמֹשֶׁה מִסִּינַי. דְּהָא מִסִּטְרָא דִּימִינָא, ה' הֲלָכָה דִּילָךְ, מִסִּטְרָא דִּשְׁמָא דְּאַבְרָהָם. י' דְּיִצְחָק. וְכֹלָּא ה"י מִן אֱלֹהִים. וְאַנְתְּ וָא"ו, מָלֵא דִּילָהּ, שְׁלֵימוּת דִּילָהּ, כּוֹס מָלֵא. בְּקַדְמֵיתָא כֵּ"ס יָ"הּ, וּלְבַסּוֹף כּוֹס מָלֵא בִּרְכַּת יְיָ'.

19. Since this daughter, NAMELY MALCHUT, was given to Yisrael, it is your Halachah from the left side, Halachah attributed to Moses from Sinai, SINCE HALACHAH IS SPELLED WITH THE SAME LETTERS AS 'THE BRIDE (HEB. *HAKALAH*)'. For on the right side, your Halachah is the letter Hei, NAMELY HEI from the side of the name Abraham, AND IT IS Yud from THE SIDE OF THE NAME Isaac. And everything is Hei Yud of THE NAME Elohim. And you are Vav, SINCE MOSES IS THE ASPECT OF ZEIR ANPIN, WHICH IS VAV, which is the full spelling of MALCHUT and her perfection. AND SHE IS CALLED a full cup. For at first she was the throne of Yud Hei, IN WHICH 'THRONE' (HEB. *KES*, *CAF SAMECH*) HAS NO VAV AND THE NAME YUD HEI IS WITHOUT VAV HEI. At the end it is a cup (Heb. *kos*, *Caf Vav Samech*) full of the blessing of Yud Hei Vav Hei, SINCE THE CUP IS FULL AND THE NAME IS COMPLETE.

20. וּבְגִין דְּאִתְיְיהִיבַת לְיִשְׂרָאֵל עַל יְדָךְ, דְּאִינּוּן מִסִּטְרָא דְּעַמּוּדָא דְּאֶמְצָעִיתָא, אִית לְגַלָּאָה אֲמַאי אִתְיְיהִיבַת לוֹן דְּהָא וַדַּאי אַבְרָהָם הָא אִתְּמַר אֲמַאי אִתְיְיהִיבַת לֵיהּ. וְאַנְתְּ גְּמִילַת חֶסֶד עִם בְּנוֹי, כְּגַוְונָא דְּגָמִיל הוּא עִמָּךְ. לְיִצְחָק יָהַב לֵיהּ קוּדְשָׁא בְּרִיךְ הוּא לֵיהּ וּלְזַרְעֵיהּ, לְנַטְרָא לָהּ מֵאִילָנָא דְּטוֹב וָרָע. וְעַבְדוּ לָהּ כַּמָּה גְּדָרִין, וַחֲתִיכוּ לָהּ כַּמָּה לְבוּשִׁין, דְּאִינּוּן לְבוּשֵׁי דַּהֲבָא, בְּכַמָּה פְּסָקוֹת. וַהֲווֹ חוֹלְקִין וּמַקְשִׁין עֲלַיְיהוּ עַל אִלֵּין פְּסָקוֹת, לְתַקְּנָא לָהּ בְּכַמָּה פֵּרוּקִין, לְקַשֵּׁט לָהּ בְּכַמָּה מִינֵי קִשּׁוּטִין, לְשַׁבָּתוֹת וְי"ט, לְמֶהֱוֵי מְקֻשְּׁטָא לְגַבָּךְ בְּזִמְנָא

דְתֵיתֵי לְגַבָּהּ בְּפוּרְקָנָא בַּתְרַיְיתָא, דְּאִתְּמַר בָּהּ מַ"ה שֶׁ"הָיָה ה"וּא.

20. And since MALCHUT was given through you to Yisrael, who are the Central Pillar THAT INCLUDES RIGHT AND LEFT it behooves us to reveal why it was given them. For surely we learned why she was given to Abraham, BECAUSE HE DREW ON HER THE ATTRIBUTE OF CHESED, and you were kind (bestowing Chesed) to his children just as he was kind to you. And the Holy One, blessed be He, gave her to Isaac, to him and his descendants to keep her from the Tree of Knowledge of Good and Evil. And they made her some boundaries and cut for her some garments, golden garments with some laws. And they used to disagree and ask questions regarding these laws, to supply them with explanations, to decorate her with many decorations for Shabbat and holidays, to redeem her at the last redemption, as it says of her, "That (Heb. *mah*) which has been (Heb. *shehayah*), it is (Heb. *hu*)" (Kohelet 1:9) (making the initials of Moses). (THE CONTINUATION IS MISSING)

21. וּבְגִין דְּאִינּוּן גָּרְמוּ לָךְ, וַעֲבִידוּ עִמָּךְ טָבִין, אַנְתְּ סְבִילַת בְּגִינַיְיהוּ כַּמָּה מַכְתְּשִׁין, בְּגִין דְּלָא יִתְקְטִיל מָשִׁיחַ בֶּן יוֹסֵף, דְּאִתְּמַר בֵּיהּ וּפְנֵי שׁוֹר מֵהַשְּׂמֹאל, מִזַּרְעָא דְּיוֹסֵף, דְּאִתְּמַר בֵּיהּ בְּכוֹר שׁוֹרוֹ הָדָר לוֹ. וּבְגִין דְּלָא יִתְחַלֵּל הוּא וְזַרְעֵיהּ בֵּין עכו"ם, בְּחוֹבֵיהּ דְּיָרָבְעָם דַּעֲבַד ע"ז, הֲוָה הוּא לְאִתְחַלְּלָא בעכו"ם הוּא וְזַרְעֵיהּ, בְּגִין דְּיָרָבְעָם בֶּן נְבָט מִזַּרְעֵיהּ אִיהוּ, בְּגִינֵיהּ אִתְּמַר בָּךְ, וְהוּא מְחוֹלָל מִפְּשָׁעֵינוּ וְגוֹ', וּבַחֲבוּרָתוֹ נִרְפָּא לָנוּ.

21. Since they brought it on you and did good things for you, you have suffered for their sakes many troubles so that Messiah the son of Joseph shall not be killed, of whom it says, "the face of an ox on the left side" (Yechezkel 1:10), who is a descendant of Joseph, of whom it says, "The firstling of his herd, grandeur is his" (Devarim 33:17). That is because he and his descendants shall not be violated among the heathen nations because of the sin of Jeroboam who worshipped idols, for which he and his seed were to be violated among the idol worshiping nations. For Jeroboam the son of Nebat is a descendant of Joseph and it is because of him that it says of you, "But he was wounded because of our transgressions…and by his injury we are healed" (Yeshayah 53:5).

22. וְיִשְׂרָאֵל בְּגִין דְּאִינּוּן כְּלִילָן יְמִינָא וּשְׂמָאלָא, תַּמָּן הֵ״י דִּילָךְ בִּשְׁלִימוּ הֲוָה, אִית לָךְ לְאִתְיַחֲדָא עִמָּהּ בֵּינַיְיהוּ. וּבְגִין דְּאִתְּמַר בָּךְ, כִּי הוֹצִיא שֵׁם רָע עַל בְּתוּלַת יִשְׂרָאֵל, אִתְּמַר בָּךְ וְלוֹ תִהְיֶה לְאִשָּׁה, לֹא יוּכַל לְשַׁלְּחָהּ כָּל יָמָיו, בְּגָלוּתָא לָא יָכִיל לְמִפְרַשׁ לֵיהּ מִנָּהּ כָּל יוֹמוֹי.

22. And since Yisrael are included of right and left, BEING OF THE CENTRAL COLUMN, where your Hei and Yud are in a state of completion, it behooves you to unite with her, WITH MALCHUT, between them. And since it says of you, "because he has brought out an evil name upon a virgin of Yisrael," it says of you, "and she shall be his wife; he may not put her away all his days" (Devarim 22:19), NAMELY WHEN SHE IS in exile he may not be away from her all his days.

23. וְאֵיךְ הוּא שֵׁם רָע דְּאַפִּיקַת עָלָהּ. אֶלָּא בָּתַר דְּאִתְיְיהִיבַת אִיהִי לְיִשְׂרָאֵל, כָּל מַאן דְּאַפִּיק שׁוּם בִּישׁ עַל יִשְׂרָאֵל, כְּאִילּוּ אַפִּיק עָלָהּ. וְשׁוּם בִּישׁ הֲוָה, דְּאַמָרְתְּ לְקוּדְשָׁא בְּרִיךְ הוּא, לָמָּה יְיָ׳ יֶחֱרֶה אַפְּךָ בְּעַמֶּךָ. וְקוּדְשָׁא בְּרִיךְ הוּא אָמַר, וְכִי אַנְתְּ אַפִּיק שׁוּם בִּישׁ עַל יִשְׂרָאֵל דְּעַבְדוּ יַת עֶגֶל, לֵךְ רֵד כִּי שִׁחֵת עַמְּךָ. עֶרֶב רַב וַדַּאי, דְּאַנְתְּ גַּיְירַת לוֹן עַבְדוּ יַת עֶגְלָא. וּבְגִין דָּא כִּי הוֹצִיא שֵׁם רָע עַל בְּתוּלַת יִשְׂרָאֵל וְלוֹ תִהְיֶה לְאִשָּׁה.

23. Where is the evil name you brought upon her? After MALCHUT was given to Yisrael, whoever brings out an evil name on Yisrael is as one who brings out an evil name on MALCHUT. And the evil name was in what you said to the Holy One, blessed be He, "Hashem, why does Your wrath burn against Your people" (Shemot 32:11), NAMELY YISRAEL, and the Holy One, blessed be He, said, 'because you spoke ill on Yisrael when they made the golden calf'. "Go, get you down; for your people…have become corrupt" (Ibid. 7), NAMELY YOUR PEOPLE, who are the mixed multitudes whom you converted and who made the golden calf. And therefore, "because he has brought out an evil name upon a virgin of Yisrael," THEN, "she shall be his wife" AS WE SAID.

24. קָם רַעְיָא מְהֵימְנָא, נָשִׁיק לֵיהּ בְּאַנְפּוֹי, וְעַל עֵינוֹי וּבָרִיךְ לֵיהּ, וְאָמַר

לֵיהּ, תְּהֵא מְבֹרַךְ מִפּוּמָא דְקוּדְשָׁא בְּרִיךְ הוּא וּשְׁכִינְתֵּיהּ, בְּכָל מִדָּה וּמִדָּה דִּילֵיהּ, וּבַעֲשַׂר סְפִירָן דִּילֵיהּ, וּבְכָל שְׁמָהָן דִּילֵיהּ, וּבְכָל מָארֵי מְתִיבְתָּאן, וּבְכָל מַלְאָכִין. וְעָנוּ כֻּלְּהוּ וְאָמְרוּ אָמֵן. וְקוּדְשָׁא בְּרִיךְ הוּא וּשְׁכִינְתֵּיהּ הוֹדוּ בְּבִרְכָתֵיהּ. אֵלִיָּהוּ, קוּם אַפְתַּח פּוּמָךְ בְּפִקּוּדִין עִמִּי, דְּאַנְתְּ הוּא עוֹזֵר דִּילִי, מִכָּל סִטְרָא, דְּהָא עֲלָךְ אִתְּמַר בְּקַדְמֵיתָא, פִּנְחָס בֶּן אֶלְעָזָר בֶּן אַהֲרֹן הַכֹּהֵן, בֶּן אַהֲרֹן וַדַּאי, בֶּן אָח דִּילִי הוּא, וְאָח לְצָרָה יִוָּלֵד.

24. The Faithful Shepherd rose and kissed him, ELIJAH, on his face and his eyes and blessed him. And he said to him, may you be blessed by the mouth of the Holy One, blessed be He, and His Shechinah, by each of His attributes and His ten Sfirot and all His names and all the heads of Yeshivah and all the angels. And they all answered and said Amen. And the Holy One, blessed be He, and His Shechinah acknowledged his blessing. Elijah, rise, open your mouth regarding the precepts with me, because you are my assistant in every aspect, for it first says of you, "Pinchas, the son of Elazar, the son of Aaron the priest" (Bemidbar 25:11), BECAUSE PINCHAS IS ELIJAH. Surely he is the son of Aaron, my nephew, as written, "and a brother is born for adversity" (Mishlei 17:17).

2. “If a man find a girl that is a virgin”

A Synopsis

We read two esoteric explanations of the title verse, from which we learn that one must lay hold of one’s higher aspect through the agency of the Tefilin and the Tzitzit and the prayers and meditations that are prescribed. People must always study the Torah even if not for its own sake in order that some day they may come to study it for its own sake. We are also shown that God has seduced Yisrael and opened for them the fifty gates of mercy and freedom. Even though the Shechinah is in exile, God will never forsake Her.

25. כִּי יִמְצָא אִישׁ נַעֲרָה בְתוּלָה אֲשֶׁר לֹא אוֹרָשָׂה וְגוֹ׳. פִּקּוּדָא דָּא, לָדוּן בִּמְפַתֶּה חֲמִשִּׁים כֶּסֶף. הה״ד, כִּי יִמְצָא אִישׁ נַעֲרָה בְתוּלָה אֲשֶׁר לֹא אוֹרָשָׂה. אִלֵּין יִשְׂרָאֵל, מִסִּטְרָא דִּשְׁכִינְתָּא אִתְקְרִיאוּ בַּת. וּתְפָשָׂהּ וְשָׁכַב עִמָּהּ וְנִמְצָאוּ וְנָתַן לַאֲבִי הַנַּעֲרָה חֲמִשִּׁים כֶּסֶף וְלוֹ תִהְיֶה לְאִשָּׁה לֹא יוּכַל לְשַׁלְּחָהּ כָּל יָמָיו. רַבָּנָן וְכָל מָארֵי מְתִיבְתָּא, אִישׁ: אִלֵּין יִשְׂרָאֵל, מִסִּטְרָא דְּקוּדְשָׁא בְּרִיךְ הוּא. וּתְפָשָׂהּ, בְּקִשּׁוּרָא דִּתְפִלִּין. וּתְפָשָׂהּ, בְּכַנְפֵי מִצְוָה. אֲשֶׁר לֹא אוֹרָשָׂה, בַּת יְחִידָה, דָּא נְשָׁמָה. וְשָׁכַב עִמָּהּ, בִּצְלוֹתָא דִּשְׁכִיבָא, בְּהַשְׁכִּיבֵנוּ. וְנָתַן לַאֲבִי הַנַּעֲרָה חֲמִשִּׁים כָּסֶף, כ״ה כ״ה אַתְוָון דְּיִחוּדָא.

25. “If a man find a girl that is a virgin, who is not betrothed…” (Devarim 22:28). This precept is to punish the seducer with fifty shekels of silver. This is the meaning of, “If a man find a girl that is a virgin, who is not betrothed”: these are Yisrael, who, from the aspect of the Shechinah are called daughter. “and lay hold of her, and lie with her, and they be found; then the man that lay with her shall give to the girl’s father fifty shekels of silver, and she shall be his wife; because he has humbled her, he may not put her away all his days” (Ibid. 28-29). The sages and all the members of the Yeshivah SAID, “a man” refers to Yisrael from the aspect of the Holy One, blessed be He, WHO IS CALLED A MAN; “and lay hold of her” with the knot of Tefilin, “and lay hold of her” with the Tzitzit. “who is not betrothed,” namely an only daughter, who is the soul FOR BY THE KNOT OF TEFILIN AND TZITZIT YISRAEL LAY HOLD OF THEIR SOUL. “and lie with her," namely with the prayer of lying down, that is, '*Hashkivenu* (Eng. 'cause us to lie down')'. "shall give to the girl's father fifty shekels of silver," namely 25 LETTERS OF THE MEDITATION OF SH'MA and 25 letters of the meditation OF 'BLESSED BE THE NAME…'.

26. קוּם רַעְיָא מְהֵימָנָא, דְּוַדַּאי מַאן דְּאִשְׁתְּדַל בַּהֲלָכָה שֶׁלֹּא לִשְׁמָהּ, וְרָוַוח הֲלָכָה, וַדַּאי בִּתְפִישָׂה אִיהִי לְגַבֵּיהּ. וְעִם כָּל דָּא אוֹקְמוּהָ, לְעוֹלָם יַעֲסוֹק אָדָם בַּתּוֹרָה אֲפִילּוּ שֶׁלֹּא לִשְׁמָהּ, שֶׁמִּתּוֹךְ שֶׁלֹּא לִשְׁמָהּ בָּא לִשְׁמָהּ. וְהַאי הֲלָכָה מִסִּטְרָא דְּנַעַר טוֹב, דְּאִתְפְּרַשׁ מֵאִילָנָא דְּטוֹב וָרָע, דְּאִיהוּ אִיסּוּר וְהֶיתֵּר, טוּמְאָה וְטָהֳרָה, כָּשֵׁר וּפָסוּל. וְעַל שֵׁם נַעַר, אִתְקְרִיאַת אִיהִי נַעֲרָה. דְּעָתִיד לְקַיֵּים בָּהּ, וְיִנָּעֲרוּ רְשָׁעִים מִמֶּנָּה, דְּאִינּוּן אִיסּוּר טָמֵא וּפָסוּל, סָמָאֵל וּמַשִׁרְיָיתֵיהּ.

26. Rise, Faithful Shepherd, for surely whoever studies Halachah, WHICH IS MALCHUT, not for its own sake, and understands the Halachah, surely it is seized by him, THAT IS, UNWILLINGLY. Yet it has been explained that man should always study Torah even if not for its own sake, so that from studying not for its own sake it shall become for its own sake. And this Halachah is from the aspect of the good lad, WHO IS METATRON, who separated from the Tree of Knowledge of Good and Evil, which comprises the forbidden and the permissible, the unclean and the clean, the fit and the unfit. After the lad METATRON, MALCHUT is called a girl, by whom it will be fulfilled, "that the wicked might be shaken out of it" (Iyov 38:13), who are the forbidden, the unclean and unfit, Samael and his legions.

27. ד"א כִּי יִמְצָא אִישׁ נַעֲרָה בְתוּלָה, אִלֵּין יִשְׂרָאֵל, דִּכְתִּיב כִּי נַעַר יִשְׂרָאֵל וָאוֹהֲבֵהוּ, נַעַר מִסְּטָר דִּמְטַטְרוֹ"ן. וְאֵין אִישׁ אֶלָּא קוּדְשָׁא בְּרִיךְ הוּא, שֶׁנֶּאֱמַר יְיָ' אִישׁ מִלְחָמָה. כִּי יִמְצָא אִישׁ נַעֲרָה בְתוּלָה, בְּתוּלַת יִשְׂרָאֵל, דְּאִתְּמַר בָּהּ נָפְלָה לֹא תוֹסִיף קוּם בְּתוּלַת יִשְׂרָאֵל. הִנֵּה אָנֹכִי מְפַתֶּיהָ וְהוֹלַכְתִּיהָ הַמִּדְבָּר, וּלְבָתַר אַפְתַּח לוֹן חַמְשִׁין תַּרְעִין דְּחֵירוּ, דְּאִינּוּן חַמְשִׁין תַּרְעִין דְּרַחֲמֵי, מִסִּטְרָא דְּאַבְרָהָם אֲבוּהוֹן. וְהַאי אִיהוּ וְנָתַן לַאֲבִי הַנַּעֲרָה חֲמִשִּׁים כָּסֶף, וְכֶסֶף מִדַּרְגָּא דְּחֶסֶד, דַּרְגָּא דְּאַבְרָהָם.

27. According to another explanation, “If a man find a girl that is a virgin” refers to Yisrael, as written, “When Yisrael was a child, then I loved him” (Hoshea 11:1), AND THEY ARE CALLED lad from the aspect of Metatron, NAMELY, THEIR SOULS ARE FROM BRIYAH WHERE METATRON IS. The man is none other than the Holy One, blessed be He, as written, “Hashem is a man of war” (Shemot 15:3). “If a man find a girl that is a virgin,” namely the virgin of Yisrael, of whom it says, “The virgin of Yisrael is fallen; she shall no more rise” (Amos 5:2). THE MAN IS THE HOLY ONE, BLESSED BE HE, WHO SEDUCED HER, AS WRITTEN, “behold, I will allure her, and bring her into the wilderness” (Hoshea 2:16). Then He opened for them fifty gates of freedom, which are the fifty gates of mercy of the side of their father Abraham, WHO IS CHESED. This is what is meant by, “shall give to the girl’s father fifty shekels of silver,” silver being of the grade of Chesed, the grade of Abraham.

28. דִּבְמִפְקָנוּ דְּמִצְרַיִם, חַמְשִׁין תַּרְעִין דְּחֵירוּ אַפְתַּח לוֹן, מִסִּטְרָא דְּדִינָא דִּשְׂמָאלָא, דְּאִיהוּ אֲדֹנָי, דְּתַמָּן דָּן אָנֹכִי. קָדֶם דִּינָא דָּן אָנֹכִי, וּלְבָתַר נַפְקוּ. אֲבָל בְּפוּרְקָנָא בַּתְרַיְיתָא, וּבְרַחֲמִים גְּדוֹלִים, מִסִּטְרָא דְּאַבְרָהָם, וּגְדוּלָּה דַּרְגָּא דְּאַבְרָהָם, דְּבִינָה, תַּמָּן אִיהִי יַד הַגְּדוֹלָה, תַּמָּן אִיהִי נ׳ כֶּסֶף. וּלְבָתַר לֹא יוּכַל שַׁלְּחָהּ בְּגָלוּתָא כָּל יָמָיו, בְּגִין דְּלוֹ תִהְיֶה לְאִשָּׁה, כְּמָה דְּאִתְּמַר וְאֵרַשְׂתִּיךְ לִי לְעוֹלָם. וּקְרָא אַחֲרִינָא, כִּי בוֹעֲלַיִךְ עוֹשַׂיִךְ יְיָ׳ צְבָאוֹת שְׁמוֹ. לֹא יֵאָמֵר לָךְ עוֹד עֲזוּבָה. דְּאע״ג דִּשְׁכִינְתָּא אִיהִי בְּגָלוּתָא, קוּדְשָׁא בְּרִיךְ הוּא לָא זָז מִנָּהּ.

28. For at the exodus from Egypt the fifty gates of freedom were opened to them from the side of Judgment, which is left, which is Adonai, NAMELY MALCHUT FROM THE LEFT SIDE, where, “will I judge” (Beresheet 15:14), SINCE ADONAI CONTAINS THE LETTERS OF JUDGMENT (HEB. *DIN*), for first I judge and then they shall come out. But at the last redemption IT IS SAID, “with great mercies WILL I GATHER YOU” (Yeshayah 54:7), which is the grade of Abraham. And Greatness, WHICH IS CHESED, is the grade of Abraham, since Binah there is CALLED the great hand, and there are fifty shekels of silver there, NAMELY THE FIFTY GATES OF BINAH. Later, “he may not put her away” into exile, “all his days” because “she shall be his wife.” This is like the words, “And I will betroth you to Me forever”

(Hoshea 2:21), and another verse, "For your Maker is your husband. Hashem Tzva'ot is His name" (Yeshayah 54:5). "You shall no more be termed forsaken" (Yeshayah 62:4). For even though the Shechinah is in exile, the Holy One, blessed be He, does not move from her.

3. “and she shall be his wife”

A Synopsis

We read about the precept for one to marry the woman he violated. An allegory is used to show how the soul reincarnates with its evil inclination from a previous life, and how that evil inclination or demon can be turned back into an angel through repentance and worship. Some students of the Torah are like the ministering angels in that they know about the past and the future; many other people are like beasts who hate the Torah students and sages of the Mishnah.

29. פִּקּוּדָא בָּתַר דָּא, לִישָּׂא אֲנוּסָתוֹ. דְּוַדַּאי אֲנוּסָה אִית מִתְּרֵין סִטְרִין, אֲנוּסָה בִּרְחִימוּ דִּילֵיהּ לְגַבָּהּ, וְאִיהִי לָא רְחִימַת לֵיהּ. וְאִית אֲנוּסָה דִּרְחִימַת אִיהִי לֵיהּ, וּדְחִילַת לְאִזְדַּוְּוגָא עִמֵּיהּ בְּלָא קִדּוּשִׁין וּבְרָכָה, וְאִיהִי לָא בָּעָאת אִם הִיא הֶדְיוֹטָא לְגַבֵּיהּ, וְלוֹ תִּהְיֶה לְאִשָּׁה.

29. The following precept is for one to marry the woman he violated. For surely there are two kinds of violated women, SINCE THERE IS one who is violated because he loves her but she doesn’t love him. Another is violated because she loves him but fears to mate with him without marriage and being blessed, or she doesn’t want him if he is a commoner. Of him it says, “and she shall be his wife” (Devarim 22:19).

30. בְּסִתְרֵי תּוֹרָה, אִית לָן לְהַמְשִׁיל מָשָׁל, נִשְׁמְתָא אִית דְּאִיהִי מַטְרוֹנִיתָא. וְנִשְׁמְתָא אִית, דְּאִיהִי אָמָה. כְּגוֹן וְכִי יִמְכּוֹר אִישׁ אֶת בִּתּוֹ לְאָמָה. וְנִשְׁמְתָא אִית, דְּאִיהִי שִׁפְחָה הֶדְיוֹטָא, דְּב״נ, אוּף הָכִי. אִית דְּאִיהוּ עֶבֶד שִׁפְחָה לְגַבֵּי נִשְׁמְתָא. וּלְזִמְנִין נִשְׁמְתָא אַזְלָא בְּרָזָא דְּגִלְגּוּלָא, הה״ד, וְלֹא מָצְאָה הַיּוֹנָה מָנוֹחַ לְכַף רַגְלָהּ, וְיֵצֶר הָרָע רָדִיף אֲבַתְרָהָא, לְאַעֲלָא בְּגוּפָא, דְּאִיהוּ שִׁפְחָה לְגַבֵּי יֵצֶר הָרָע. אִיהוּ שֵׁד יְהוּדִי. וְנִשְׁמְתָא י׳, אָמָה הָעִבְרִיָּה. וּבָהּ הַהוּא שֵׁד, אִתְהַדָּר שַׁדַּי, דְּנָטִיר לָהּ לְהַהִיא נִשְׁמְתָא, וְתָב בָּהּ בְּתִיּוּבְתָּא, וּמְבָרֵךְ בָּהּ לְקוּדְשָׁא בְּרִיךְ הוּא בְּכָל יוֹמָא בְּבָרוּךְ. וּמְקַדֵּשׁ בָּהּ לְקוּדְשָׁא בְּרִיךְ הוּא, בקק״ק. וּמְיַחֵד עִמָּהּ לְקוּדְשָׁא בְּרִיךְ הוּא, בְּק״ש.

30. In relation to mysteries of the Torah we have to employ an allegory. There is a soul that is the Matron, NAMELY, DRAWN FROM MALCHUT OF ATZILUT, and there is a soul that is a handmaid, THAT IS, DRAWN FROM THE WORLD OF BRIYAH, such as in, "And if a man sell his daughter to be a maidservant" (Shemot 21:7). And there is a soul that is a common maid, THAT IS, FROM THE WORLD OF ASIYAH. And so is man. There is a man who is a servant to the soul. Sometimes the soul goes by means of incarnation, SINCE THE MAN SINNED WITH IT IN A PREVIOUS INCARNATION. THEN, "the dove found no rest for the sole of her foot" (Beresheet 8:9), SINCE THE SOUL FINDS NO REST IN HIM, BECAUSE OF THE INIQUITIES IN THE PREVIOUS INCARNATION. And the Evil Incarnation chases it to enter that body, which is a maid to the Evil Inclination. THAT IS, THE FORCE OF INIQUITIES FROM THE FORMER INCARNATION THAT LIES IN THIS BODY IS CONSIDERED A MAID TO THE EVIL INCARNATION. It is a Jewish demon SUBSERVIENT TO THE EVIL INCLINATION and the soul is Yud CALLED a Hebrew maidservant, BEING OF THE WORLD OF BRIYAH, in which this demon (Heb. *shed*) becomes Shadai, because it kept the soul and repented through it, and with it blessed the Holy One, blessed be He, daily with 'Blessed... (Heb. *baruch*)', and with it sanctifies the Holy One, blessed be He, with 'Holy, holy, holy', and with it declares the unity of the Holy One, blessed be He, by Kriat Sh'ma.

31. מַה דַּהֲוָה אִיהוּ שֵׁד, אִתְהַדָּר מַלְאָךְ דִּידֵיהּ מְטַטְרוֹן, וְאִתְהַדָּר שַׁדַּי דְּהָכִי סָלִיק בִּמְטַטְרוֹן, בְּחוּשְׁבַּן שַׁדַּי. וּמִיַּד יִתְקְיָים בֵּיהּ, וְלוֹ תִהְיֶה לְאִשָּׁה לֹא יוּכַל לְשַׁלְּחָהּ כָּל יָמָיו. וְאִי לָא חָזַר בְּתִיוּבְתָּא, אִיהִי לְגַבֵּיהּ מִשְׁתַּעְבְּדָא בְּחוֹבִין דְּעַבְדַּת, וְיִתְקְיָים בֵּיהּ הָאִשָּׁה וִילָדֶיהָ תִּהְיֶה לַאדוֹנֶיהָ. וְאִתְּמַר בְּהַהוּא שֵׁד בַּעַל חוֹבֵיהּ, וְהוּא יֵצֵא בְּגַפּוֹ. וְהַאי שֵׁד, אִיהוּ כְּמַטֶּה דְּמֹשֶׁה, דְּאִתְהַפָּךְ מִמַּטֶּה לְנָחָשׁ, וּמִנָּחָשׁ לְמַטֶּה, הָכִי הַאי שֵׁד, אִתְהַפָּךְ מִשֵּׁד לְמַלְאָךְ, וּמִמַּלְאָךְ לְשֵׁד, כְּפוּם עוֹבָדוֹי דְּבַר נָשׁ.

31. AFTER DOING ALL THIS, what used to be a demon, WHICH BRINGS HARM, NAMELY THE FORCE OF INIQUITIES IN THE BODY, turns around to be its angel OF THE ASPECT OF Metatron and turned TO BE Shadai, because the numerical value of Metatron is that of Shadai. Immediately there is fulfilled in it REGARDING THE SOUL, "and she shall be his wife; he may not put her away all his days" (Devarim 22:19). But if he does not repent, THE

SOUL is enslaved in him through the iniquities he committed and it shall be fulfilled in him, "the wife and her children shall be her master's" (Shemot 21:4), THAT IS, THE SOUL WILL LEAVE HIM TO ITS ROOT, and it says of the demon which is its debtor, NAMELY THE FORCE OF INIQUITIES IN THE BODY FROM THE PREVIOUS INCARNATION, "and he shall go out by himself" (Ibid.), THAT IS, IT SHALL LEAVE WITHOUT REMEDY. That demon is like Moses' staff that turns from a staff into a snake and from a snake into a staff. So does this demon turn from a demon into an angel and from an angel into a demon, according to man's deeds.

32. וְע"ש שֵׁדִים דְּאָתוּ מֵהַאי, אוֹקְמוּהָ מָארֵי מַתְנִיתִין, דְּאִית מִנְּהוֹן כְּמַלְאָכֵי הַשָּׁרֵת, וְאִינּוּן תַּלְמִידֵי חֲכָמִים דְּיַדְעִין מַאי דַּהֲוָה, וּמַה דְּעָתִיד לְמֶהֱוֵי. וְאִינּוּן בְּדִיוּקְנַיְיהוּ בְּאַרְעָא, אִינּוּן מָארֵי פִּילוֹסוֹפְיָא, אִצְטַגְנִינֵי יִשְׂרָאֵל, דְּיַדְעִין מַאי דַּהֲוָה, וּמַאי דְּעָתִיד לְמֶהֱוֵי, מֵאוֹתוֹת דְּחַמָּה וְסִיהֲרָא, לָקוּתָא דִּלְהוֹן, וְכָל כֹּכָב וּמַזָּל, וּמָה אַחְזֵי בְּעָלְמָא.

32. Of the demons that come from this, NAMELY THE DEMON THAT TURNS INTO AN ANGEL, the sages of the Mishnah explained that some are like the ministering angels. They are the students of the Torah that know what was and what will be. They have their form DOWN on earth, being philosophers, astrologers of Yisrael, who know what was and what will be ACCORDING TO the signs on the sun and moon and their eclipses and each star and constellation; in this way they know what is seen in the world.

33. וְאִית מִנְּהוֹן כַּבְּהֵמָה, פָּרִין וְרָבִין כַּבְּהֵמָה, דִּיוּקְנָא דִּלְהוֹן לְתַתָּא אִינּוּן עַמֵּי הָאָרֶץ, וְאוֹקְמוּהָ מָארֵי מַתְנִיתִין, דְּאִינּוּן שֶׁקֶץ, וּבְנוֹתֵיהוֹן שֶׁרֶץ. וְעַל בְּנוֹתֵיהֶן נֶאֱמַר, אָרוּר שׁוֹכֵב עִם כָּל בְּהֵמָה. וְאִינּוּן שׂוֹנְאִים לְת"ח מָארֵי מִשְׁנָה, דְּאִינּוּן מַלְאֲכֵי הַשָּׁרֵת מַמָּשׁ. וּבְגִין דָּא אוֹקְמוּהָ מָארֵי מַתְנִיתִין, עַל ב"נ אִי יְהֵא כְּמַלְאַךְ יְיָ', צְבָאוֹת תּוֹרָה יְבַקְשׁוּ מִפִּיהוּ, וְאִי לָאו לֹא יְבַקְשׁוּ תּוֹרָה מִפִּיהוּ.

33. Some of them, OF THE DEMONS, are like beasts that increase and multiply like animals, and their form below ON EARTH is ignorant people, who, as the sages of the Mishnah explained, are vermin and whose daughters are abominable. Of their daughters it says, "Cursed be he that lies with any manner of beast" (Devarim 27:21). They hate Torah students, sages of the Mishnah, who are veritable ministering angels. For that reason the sages of the Mishnah explained about man that if he is as "a messenger of Hashem Tzva'ot" (Malachi 2:7), one should seek Torah out of his mouth. Otherwise, one must not seek Torah out of his mouth.

4. Ten, not nine

A Synopsis

We read about those people who have knowledge of the mysteries of the Torah and who receive their souls from the aspect of the holy Malchut of Atzilut, including all ten Sfirot. They keep the Torah and the precepts with love and awe of God, not for the sake of receiving any reward. There is also a Malchut of Briyah; this is Malchut to the angels in Briyah, and she is a maid to Malchut of Atzilut, having her form comprised of ten Sfirot. However, this Malchut may be desecrated because of the sins of Yisrael. The Faithful Shepherd says that not all demons are alike and not all the servants of the Shechinah are alike; she even has some foreign servants of the Other Side who serve her.

34. וְאִית אַחֲרָנִין מָארֵי סִתְרֵי תּוֹרָה, מָארֵי מִדּוֹת, דְּאִינּוּן יָרְתִין נִשְׁמָתִין מִסִּטְרָא דְּמַלְכוּתָא קַדִּישָׁא, דְּאִיהוּ כְּלִילָא מֵעֲשַׂר סְפִירָן. דְּמַאן דְּיָרִית לָהּ, וְזָכֵי לָהּ, זָכֵי לַעֲשַׂר סְפִירָן בְּלָא פְּרוּדָא, עֲשַׂר וְלָא תְּשַׁע, דְּאִי הֲווֹ יָרְתִין לְמַלְכוּתָא יְחִידָאָה, הֲווֹ תְּשַׁע בְּפֵרוּדָא מִנָּהּ, בְּגִין דְּלֵית תַּמָּן פְּרוּדָא, אָמַר בַּעַל סֵפֶר יְצִירָה עֶשֶׂר וְלֹא תֵּשַׁע.

34. There are others who have knowledge of the mysteries of the Torah, men of qualities, who receive souls from the aspect of the holy Malchut OF ATZILUT, which includes ten Sfirot. Whoever receives her and attains her, merits ten indivisible Sfirot, ten, not nine, since had they inherited Malchut alone the nine Sfirot would have been separated from her. But since there is no division there, IN ATZILUT, the author of the Book of Formation said 'ten, not nine', WHICH MEANS THAT THE NINE UPPER SFIROT ARE NEVER APART FROM HER.

35. וְאִי תֵּימָא דִּסְלִיקַת לְעֵילָּא מֵעֲשַׂר. שְׁמָא מְפֹרָשׁ יוֹ״ד הֵ״א וָא״ו הֵ״א, הָא עֲשַׂר, יוֹ״ד דְּמִתְיַיחֵד בָּהּ, וְלָא סְלִיק לְעֵילָּא מֵעֲשַׂר. וּבְגִין דָּא י׳, וְלָא י״א. אֲבָל מַאן דִּמְחַבֵּר יוֹ״ד, דְּאִיהִי אוֹת בְּרִית, בְּשִׁפְחָה. וּמַטְרוֹנִיתָא כְּלִילָא מִי׳, בְּשֵׁד דע״ז סָמָאֵ״ל אִתְּדָן בַּגֵּיהִנָּם.

35. You may say that MALCHUT rises above the ten, AND IS THERE ALONE. HE ANSWERS, the explicit Name Yud Vav Dalet, Hei Aleph, Vav Aleph

Vav, Hei Aleph, WHICH COMPRISES TEN LETTERS, is the ten Sfirot OF ZEIR ANPIN, and the ten SFIROT, WHICH ARE ZEIR ANPIN, unite with her, WITH MALCHUT, and she does not rise above the ten OF ZEIR ANPIN, BUT NEVER SEPARATES FROM HIM. Hence THE AUTHOR OF THE BOOK OF FORMATION SAYS, 'ten, not eleven'. But whoever joins Yud (= 10), which is the sign of the covenant, WHICH IS YESOD, with the maidservant, or JOINS the Matron that includes the Yud with the demon of idol worship that is Samael is punished in Gehenom.

36. דְּמַאן דְּיָרִית בְּרַתָּא דְּמַלְכָּא מַלְכוּת, לָא זָכֵי לָהּ, אֶלָּא בְּרָא דְּמַלְכָּא, דְּאִתְקְרֵי בְּנִי בְכוֹרִי יִשְׂרָאֵל, דְּמִסְטְרָא דָּא אִתְקְרִיאוּ יִשְׂרָאֵל בְּנִין לְקוּדְשָׁא בְּרִיךְ הוּא, הה"ד בָּנִים אַתֶּם לַיְיָ' אֱלֹהֵיכֶם, וּמַלְכוּת דָּא דַּאֲצִילוּת.

36. Whoever inherits the King's daughter, who is Malchut, merits her only if he is the King's son called, "Yisrael is my son, my firstborn" (Shemot 4:22). For from that aspect Yisrael are called children of the Holy One, blessed be He, as meant by, "You are the children of Hashem your Elohim" (Devarim 14:1). This is Malchut of Atzilut.

37. וְאִית לְקַבְלָהּ מַלְכוּת דִּבְרִיאָה, וְאִיהִי מַלְכוּת לְמַלְאָכִים דִּבְרִיאָה. וְאִיהִי נַעֲרָה דְּמַטְרוֹנִיתָא, מְשַׁמְשָׁא דִּילָהּ, וְאִיהִי דְּיוּקְנָא דִּגְבִירְתָּא דִּילָהּ, כְּלוּלָה מִי'. הַאי בְּחוּבִין דְּיִשְׂרָאֵל, יָכִילַת לְאִתְחַלְלָא בֵּין אוּמִין דְּעָלְמָא. אֲבָל מַלְכוּת דַּאֲצִילוּת דְּקוּדְשָׁא בְּרִיךְ הוּא, עָלָהּ אִתְּמַר אֲנִי יְיָ' הוּא שְׁמִי וּכְבוֹדִי לְאַחֵר לֹא אֶתֵּן וּתְהִלָּתִי לַפְּסִילִים, לָא יָהִיב לָהּ לְמַאן דִּמְחַלֵּל שַׁבָּתוֹת וְיָמִים טוֹבִים, אֶלָּא לְמַאן דְּאִיהוּ בְּרָא דְּמַלְכָּא, וְנָטִיר אוֹרַיְיתָא וּפִקּוּדִין, בִּדְחִילוּ וּרְחִימוּ דְּמָארֵיהּ, וְלָא עַל מְנָת לְקַבֵּל פְּרָס, אֶלָּא כְּבֵן דְּאִיהוּ מְחוּיָּב לְמֶעְבַּד צִוּוּיֵיהּ דַּאֲבוֹי, דְּעָלֵיהּ אִתְּמַר כַּבֵּד אֶת אָבִיךָ וְאֶת אִמֶּךָ. אֶת אָבִיךָ: דָּא קוּדְשָׁא בְּרִיךְ הוּא. וְאֶת אִמֶּךָ: דָּא שְׁכִינְתָּא. וְעִם כָּל דָּא, מַאן דִּמְחַלֵּל נַעֲרָה דְּמַלְכָּא, אִתְחֲשִׁיב לֵיהּ כְּאִלּוּ מְחַלֵּל מַטְרוֹנִיתָא דִּילֵיהּ.

37. There is a corresponding Malchut of Briyah, which is Malchut to the angels in Briyah. She is a maid to Malchut OF ATZILUT and her attendant. She has the form of her mistress OF ATZILUT, comprised of ten SFIROT. THIS MALCHUT OF BRIYAH, because of the iniquities of Yisrael, might be desecrated among the nations of the world. But of Malchut of Atzilut of the Holy One, blessed be He, it says, "I am Hashem, that is My name, and My glory will I not give to another, neither My praise to carved idols" (Yeshayah 42:8). For He gives her not to him who desecrates Shabbat and holidays but to him who is the King's son and keeps the Torah and the precepts with love and awe of his Master, not for the sake of receiving a reward but as a child who is obligated to do his father's bidding, of which it says, "Honor your father and your mother" (Shemot 20:12). Your father is the Holy One, blessed be He, and your mother is the Shechinah. Nevertheless, whoever desecrates the King's maid, WHO IS MALCHUT OF BRIYAH, is considered as if he violated His Queen.

38. וְרַבָּנָן, כָּל שֵׁדִין לָאו אִינּוּן שְׁקוּלִין, וְלָא כָּל עַבְדִין דִּשְׁכִינְתָּא, דִּכְתִּיב בָּהּ, וּמַלְכוּתוֹ בַּכֹּל מָשָׁלָה. אִית לָהּ כַּמָּה נַעֲרוֹת עִבְרִיּוֹת, וּשְׁפָחוֹת עִבְרִיּוֹת. וְאִית לָהּ עֲבָדִים וּשְׁפָחוֹת נָכְרִיּוֹת, בְּגִין דְּלָא יִשְׁתְּכַּח מַלְכוּתָא אָחֳרָא בְּעָלְמָא, בְּזִמְנָא דְּאִיהִי שַׁלְטָא.

38. HEAR, sages, not all demons are alike, and not all the servants of the Shechinah ARE ALIKE, since it is written of her, OF THE SHECHINAH, "and His kingdom rules over all" (Tehilim 103:19). She has some Hebrew maids, WHO ARE MALCHUYOT OF BRIYAH, and Hebrew maidservants, WHO ARE MALCHUYOT OF ASIYAH. She has foreign servants and maidservants OF THE OTHER SIDE, WHO SERVE HER, so there shall be no other Malchut in the world when she rules. THEREFORE EVEN THE OTHER SIDE IS SUBSERVIENT TO HER THEN AND DOES HER BIDDING.

5. "I will cause...the unclean spirit to pass out of the land"

A Synopsis

Moses talks about the foreign maidservants that correspond to the Shechinah and that are from the aspect of the poison of death. He says they are the female aspect of Samael, and we learn that Samael and his female used to be servants of God until they made themselves into deities. They became deities because the people on earth worshipped them, and they are materialized in this world among the mixed multitudes. We learn that God will destroy them in the future.

39. וְאִלֵּין שְׁפָחוֹת נָכְרִיּוֹת, מִסִּטְרָא דְּסַם הַמָּוֶת, נוּקְבָּא דְּסָמָאֵל. דְּשִׁפְחָה הֲוַת לְמַטְרוֹנִיתָא. נוּקְבָּא וְסָמָאֵל אֵל אַחֵר, עֶבֶד הֲוָה לֵיהּ לְקוּדְשָׁא בְּרִיךְ הוּא, לְבָתַר דַּעֲבִידוּ גַּרְמַיְיהוּ אֱלוֹהוּת, וְקוּדְשָׁא בְּרִיךְ הוּא עָתִיד לְאַעְבָּר לוֹן מֵעָלְמָא, וּלְמִמְחֵי לוֹן.

39. These foreign maidservants THAT CORRESPOND TO THE SHECHINAH are from the aspect of the poison of death. They are the female aspect of Samael, where the maidservant became the Matron, NAMELY A MAIDSERVANT WHO TAKES THE PLACE OF HER MATRON. Samael and his female, who is another El, were servants to the Holy One, blessed be He, but later made themselves into deities. And the Holy One, blessed be He, will remove them out of the world and wipe them away.

40. וְאִי תֵּימְרוּן, אִי בְּנֵי נָשָׁא עַבְדִּין לוֹן אֱלָהוּת, וְלָא בִּרְעוּתָא דִּלְהוֹן, אֲמַאי אִתְעֲנָשׁוּ. אֶלָּא כַּד הֲווֹ דּוֹר הַמַּבּוּל וְדוֹר הַפְּלָגָה יַדְעֵי בְּהוֹן, וַהֲווֹ מְקַטְּרִין לוֹן, וְסַגְדִּין לוֹן, וּבְהַהוּא חֵילָא דַּהֲווֹ מְקַטְּרִין לוֹן, וְסַגְדִּין לוֹן, הֲווֹ נַחְתֵּי לְגַבַּיְיהוּ, וְעַבְדֵי רְעוּתַיְיהוּ, וּמְמַלְּלָן בְּהוֹן בְּאִינּוּן צוּלְמִין, הָא אִתְעֲבֵידוּ אֱלוֹהוּת וַעֲבוֹדַת כו״ם. בְּגִין דָּא, קוּדְשָׁא בְּרִיךְ הוּא עָתִיד לְאַעְבְּרָא לוֹן, וְיִמְחֵי לוֹן מֵעָלְמָא, צוּלְמִין דִּלְהוֹן דַּהֲווֹ פַּלְחִין בְּהוֹן, וְאִשְׁתַּאֲבוּ מִנְּהוֹן רוּחִין וְצוּלְמִין.

40. If you argue that people made them into deities and it was not their own desire, why then were they punished BY BEING DESTROYED FROM THE

WORLD? AND HE ANSWERS, when the generation of the Flood and the generation of the Tower of Babel knew of them they burned sacrifices to them and bowed before them. By the power of burning offerings to them and bowing to them, they would descend upon them and do their bidding and speak through the forms THEY MADE. Thus they became deities and idol worship. For that reason the Holy One, blessed be He, intended to wipe them away from the world, NAMELY their images that they worshipped from which they received spirits and images.

41. וְכַד אִית בְּעָלְמָא עֵרֶב רַב, נַחְתִּין לְאִתְגַּשְּׁמָא בְּהוֹן, וְקוּדְשָׁא בְּרִיךְ הוּא יַעֲבַר לוֹן מִן עָלְמָא, הה״ד וְאֶת רוּחַ הַטּוּמְאָה אַעֲבִיר מִן הָאָרֶץ. וְאִי תֵּימְרוּן, בִּזְמְנָא דְּגָלוּתָא בַּתְרָאָה, לֵית עכו״ם, בְּגִין דְּלָא יַדְעִין בְּנֵי עָלְמָא בְּהוֹן. וְאִינּוּן דְּיַדְעִין בְּעֵרֶב רַב תַּמָּן, אִשְׁתְּכַח לוֹן דְּמַכְעִיסִין לְקוּדְשָׁא בְּרִיךְ הוּא וּשְׁכִינְתֵּיהּ, וְיִשְׂרָאֵל בֵּינַיְיהוּ, וְעֵרֶב רַב מַצְלִיחִין בְּהוֹן, לְקַיֵּים מַאי דִּכְתִּיב וּמְשַׁלֵּם לְשׂוֹנְאָיו אֶל פָּנָיו לְהַאֲבִידוֹ.

41. When mixed multitudes live in the world, SAMAEL AND HIS FEMALE descend INTO THOSE IMAGES to be materialized in them. THEREFORE the Holy One, blessed be He, will remove them from the world. This is the meaning of the words, "and also I will cause…the unclean spirit to pass out of the land" (Zecharyah 13:2). If you say that during the last exile there is no idol worship because people don't know about them, HE ANSWERS, those among the mixed multitudes who do know anger the Holy One, blessed be He, and His Shechinah and Yisrael that are among them. And they have success against the mixed multitudes to fulfill the words, "and repays them that hate Him to their face, to destroy them" (Devarim 7:10).

42. קָמוּ כֻּלְּהוּ תַּנָּאִין וַאֲמוֹרָאִין וּבָרִיכוּ לְרַעְיָא מְהֵימְנָא, וְאָמְרוּ לֵיהּ סִינַי סִינַי, מַאן יָכִיל לְמַלְּלָא קֳדָמָךְ, דְּאַנְתְּ בִּדְיוּקְנָא דְּמָארָךְ, דִּבִזְמְנָא דְּמַלִּיל בְּטוּרָא דְּסִינַי, כָּל חֵיוָן דְּמַלְאָכִין, וְחֵיוָן דְּכֻרְסְיָיא, וְעִלָּאִין וְתַתָּאִין, שַׁתְקוּ, וְלָא אִשְׁתְּכַח דִּבּוּר אָחֳרָא אֶלָּא דִּילֵיהּ. וּבְגִין דְּאַתְּ בְּרֵיהּ בִּדְיוּקְנָא דִּילֵיהּ, צָרִיךְ לְמִשְׁמַע כֻּלְּהוּ מָארֵי מְתִיבְתָּא מִלִּין מִפּוּמָךְ, אַל תִּתֵּן שְׁתִיקָה לְמִלּוּלָךְ.

42. All the Tannaim and Amoraim rose and blessed the Faithful Shepherd, and said to him, Sinai, Sinai, who could speak before you, for you have your Master's form. When He spoke on Mount Sinai, all the living creatures among the angels and all the living creatures of the throne, the higher and lower were silent. And there was no other speech but his. Since you are his son of his form, all the heads of the Yeshivah need to hear things from you. Do not silence your words.

6. "and shall cheer his wife whom he has taken"

A Synopsis

We learn of the precept for a man to rejoice in his new bride for a whole year, during which he needn't go to war or pay taxes. Here everything pertains to the mystery of the year, that is said to be Malchut, and the number twelve is the linkage between the twelve months, the twelve oxen that supported the molten sea, the four Sfirot in each of three columns, and the twelve stones that Jacob took.

43. כִּי יִקַּח אִישׁ אִשָּׁה חֲדָשָׁה לֹא יֵצֵא בַּצָּבָא וְגוֹ'. וְשִׂמַּח אֶת אִשְׁתּוֹ אֲשֶׁר לָקָח. פִּקּוּדָא דָּא, חָתָן לְמֶחְדֵּי בְּאִתְּתֵיהּ שַׁתָּא חַד, דִּכְתִּיב נָקִי יִהְיֶה לְבֵיתוֹ שָׁנָה אֶחָת. וְאִינּוּן י"ב יַרְחִין אִינּוּן מִדִּילָהּ. דְּהָא שָׁנָה אִיהִי כַּלָּה, וְלֵית כַּלָּה בַּר בִּי"ב יַרְחִין, דִּכְתִּיב עוֹמֵד עַל שְׁנֵים עָשָׂר בָּקָר. וְהוֹאִיל וְלֵית תִּקּוּנָא דְּכַלָּה, בַּר בִּי"ב, אִצְטְרִיךְ חָתָן לְמֶחְדֵּי לָהּ, וּלְבֵיתָהּ, לָהּ וּלְתִקּוּנָהָא, כְּגַוְונָא דִּלְעֵילָּא. וְע"ד יַעֲקֹב כְּתִיב בֵּיהּ, וַיִּקַּח מֵאַבְנֵי הַמָּקוֹם. אַבְנֵי הַמָּקוֹם י"ב הֲווֹ, וּמַאן דְּחַדֵּי לְכַלָּה, חַדֵּי לְעוֹלֵימְתָהָא, וְעוּלֵימָתָן י"ב הֲווֹ. וְכֹלָּא אִיהוּ רָזָא דְּשָׁנָה. בְּגִין כַּךְ אִצְטְרִיךְ לְחָתָן לְמֶחְדֵּי בְּאִתְּתֵיהּ שָׁנָה אֶחָת.

43. "When a man has taken a new wife, he shall not go out to war…and shall cheer his wife whom he has taken" (Devarim 24:5). This precept is for the groom to rejoice in his wife for one year, as written, "but he shall be free at home one year" (Ibid.), since these twelve months are hers. For the year is a bride, NAMELY MALCHUT THAT IS CALLED A YEAR, and the bride is present only with twelve months, as written, "AND HE MADE A MOLTEN SEA… It stood upon twelve oxen" (I Melachim 7:23-25). FOR THE SEA IS MALCHUT; TWELVE OXEN ARE THE SECRET OF FOUR SFIROT, CHOCHMAH, BINAH, TIFERET AND MALCHUT, EACH OF THREE COLUMNS, WHICH ARE ALWAYS TWELVE. And since the bride is perfected only with twelve, the groom needs to cheer her and her household, her and her equipment, as it is above. Hence it is written of Jacob, "and he took of the stones of that place" (Beresheet 28:11), THE PLACE BEING MALCHUT. There are twelve stones to that place, and whoever cheers the bride cheers her maids, HER SFIROT IN BRIYAH. There are twelve maids FOR THE SAME

REASON. Everything pertains to the mystery of the year. For that reason the groom has to rejoice in his bride for one year.

44. וְהָא אוֹקִימְנָא, דְּחֶדְוָה דָּא, לָאו דִּילֵיהּ הִיא, אֶלָּא דִּילָהּ. דִּכְתִּיב וְשִׂמַּח אֶת אִשְׁתּוֹ. וְיִשְׂמַח אֶת אִשְׁתּוֹ לָא כְּתִיב, אֶלָּא וְשִׂמַּח, יַחְדֵּי לְכַלָּה. כְּגַוְונָא דָּא, לָאו חֵדוּ לְכַלָּה, בַּר בְּגוּפָא וְתִקּוּנָהָא. וּמַאן חַדֵּי לוֹן. צַדִּיק. וְעַל דָּא נָקִי יִהְיֶה לְבֵיתוֹ. נָקִי, דְּלָא יַעֲמוֹל בְּמִלֵּי דְּעָלְמָא, דִּיהֵא בֵּיהּ רַעֲוָא לְמֶחְדֵּי לָהּ. נָקִי מִכֹּלָּא. נָקִי לְמַסִּין וּלְאַרְנוֹנִין וְגוּלְגַּלְתִּין. נָקִי דְּלָא יִפּוּק לְחֵילָא לְאַגָּחָא קְרָבָא. לְאִשְׁתַּכְּחָא חֶדְוָה עֵילָּא וְתַתָּא, וּלְאַתְעֲרָא חֶדְוָה לְעֵילָּא. זַכָּאִין עַמָּא קַדִּישָׁא, דְּמָארֵיהוֹן חַדֵּי בְּהוֹן, זַכָּאִין אִינּוּן בְּהַאי עָלְמָא, וְזַכָּאִין אִינּוּן בְּעָלְמָא דְּאָתֵי.

44. Yet we have explained that this joy is not his but hers, as written, "and shall rejoice with his wife." It does not say that he shall rejoice in his wife but "shall rejoice with," which means that he shall rejoice with the bride. Similarly, the bride has no joy save in the body and her jewels. Who rejoices with them? The righteous does. For that reason, "he shall be free at home," free from toiling in worldly matters, so that he shall have the desire to rejoice with her. He shall be free of all, free of taxes, crop taxes and poll tax. He shall be free from going to the army to war, so there shall be joy above and below and to evoke joy above. Blessed is the holy nation, whose Master rejoices in them. Blessed are they in this world and blessed they are in the World to Come.

7. "At his day you shall give him his hire"

A Synopsis

The Faithful Shepherd says that one must pay his hired servant on time, and tells us about Metatron who is the messenger from the eighteen worlds and who receives the eighteen blessings of the Amidah prayer three times every day. We hear about the Shacharit service, the Minchah service, and the Arvit service, and there is emphasis on charity to the poor. Moses talks about the stranger, who is anyone outside his own place, and in this sense every person on earth is a stranger because his soul has come naked from the other world. Whoever repents and returns his soul to its place is as if he returned God and His Shechinah to God's place. Next the Mishnah sages tell Moses that the two Messiahs cannot redeem Yisrael without him. Moses says that when reciting the benedictions of the Amidah prayer a man should at first be as a servant arranging praises before his master, and then as a servant receiving wages from his master, and then as a servant who received his wages and is now going on his way. We hear that God tells Metatron that he will recognize the presence of the Shechinah in a prayer by looking at the purpose of the prayer, and seeing if the prayer was said to give pleasure to God.

45. בְּיוֹמוֹ תִתֵּן שְׂכָרוֹ וְגוֹ׳. פָּתַח רַעְיָא מְהֵימְנָא וְאָמַר, פִּקּוּדָא בָּתַר דָּא לָתֵת שְׂכַר שָׂכִיר בִּזְמַנּוֹ. הֲדָא הוּא דִכְתִיב, בְּיוֹמוֹ תִתֵּן שְׂכָרוֹ וְלֹא תָבֹא עָלָיו הַשֶּׁמֶשׁ. מָארֵי מְתִיבְתָּאן עִלָּאֵי וְתַתָּאֵי, שְׁמָעוּ. מְטַטְרוֹן אִיהוּ שְׂכַר שָׂכִיר, מֵחַ״י עָלְמִין, שְׁלִיחַ דִּילֵיהּ, לְקַבְּלָא חַ״י בִּרְכָאן דִּצְלוֹתָא, בְּכָל יוֹמָא, תְּלַת זִמְנִין. וּבְגִין דָּא, בְּיוֹמוֹ תִתֵּן שְׂכָרוֹ, דָּא צְלוֹתָא דְּשַׁחֲרִית. וְלֹא תָבֹא עָלָיו הַשֶּׁמֶשׁ, דָּא צְלוֹתָא דְּמִנְחָה, דְּאִי עָבַר יוֹמוֹ, בָּטֵל קָרְבָּנוֹ. כִּי עָנִי הוּא וַדַּאי, עָנִי הוּא בְּגָלוּתָא, לֵית לֵיהּ מִדִּילֵיהּ, אֶלָּא מַאי דְּיַהֲבֵינָן לֵיהּ בִּצְלוֹתָא, בְּגִין דָּא צְלוֹתָא תְּפִלָּה דִּילֵיהּ, תְּפִלָּה לְעָנִי כִּי יַעֲטוֹף, בַּעֲטִיפַת צִיצִית, תְּפִלָּה דְּיָד אִיהִי.

45. "At his day you shall give him his hire..." (Devarim 24:15). The Faithful Shepherd opened and said, the following precept is to give a hired servant his hire in time. This is the meaning of, "At his day you shall give him his hire, neither shall the sun go down upon it." Listen, heads of

Yeshivot high and low. Metatron is the hire of the hired servant, a messenger from the eighteen worlds, BEING YESOD OF ATZILUT CALLED EIGHTEEN, to receive the eighteen blessings of the Amidah prayer FOR MALCHUT every day, three times a day. For that reason, "At his day you shall give him his hire" refers to the Shacharit service; "neither shall the sun go down upon it" refers to the Minchah service, for if the day is past, the offering is no longer valid. "for he is poor" (Ibid.). Surely he is poor in exile and has nothing but what he is given in prayer. For that reason his prayer is, "A prayer (Heb. *tfilah*) of the poor, when he faints (or: 'wraps')" (Tehilim 102:1), namely the wrap of the Tzitzit and the hand Tefilin. THAT IS, THE PRAYER OF THE POOR IS THE HAND TEFILIN (OR TFILAH), WHICH IS MALCHUT.

46. וְאֵלָיו הוּא נוֹשֵׂא אֶת נַפְשׁוֹ, דָּא תְּפִלַּת עַרְבִית, דְּאִיהִי אֵמוּרִים וּפְדָרִים, שִׁיּוּרִין דְּקָרְבְּנִין דְּיוֹמָא. וְאִינּוּן כְּגוֹן פֶּרֶט הַכֶּרֶם, וּפְאַת שָׂדְךָ, דְּעָלַיְיהוּ אִתְּמַר, שִׁיְּרֵי מִצְוָה מְעַכְּבִין אֶת הַפּוּרְעָנוּת. לֶעָנִי וְלַגֵּר תַּעֲזוֹב אוֹתָם, דְּעַמּוּדָא דְּאֶמְצָעִיתָא בַּר מֵאַתְרֵיהּ, גֵּר אִתְקְרֵי. וּבְגִין דָּא, אֲנָא דְּדַרְגָּא דִּילִי עַמּוּדָא דְּאֶמְצָעִיתָא, קָרֵינָא גַּרְמָאי גֵּר בְּגָלוּתָא קַדְמָאֵי. הה"ד, גֵּר הָיִיתִי בְּאֶרֶץ נָכְרִיָּה, דְּאִיהוּ בְּגָלוּתָא רְבִיעָא בְּגִינַיְיהוּ.

46. "and sets his heart upon it" (Devarim 24:15) refers to the Arvit service, which CORRESPONDS TO the parts of the sacrifice and the fatty parts that are left from the offerings of the day. They are like single grapes of the vineyard and "the corners of your field" (Vayikra 19:9) of which we learned that leaving things over in the form of charity hinders divine punishment. "you shall leave them for the poor and stranger" (Ibid. 10), THAT IS, TO THE CENTRAL PILLAR THAT IS ZEIR ANPIN. For the Central Pillar, when it is outside its place, NAMELY IN EXILE, is called a stranger. For that reason, THE FAITHFUL SHEPHERD SAID, I, my grade being of the Central Pillar, termed myself a stranger in the first exile. This is the meaning of, "I have been a stranger in a strange land" (Shemot 2:22), for he, ZEIR ANPIN, lies in exile for the sake OF YISRAEL.

47. שָׁאִילוּ לֵיהּ מָארֵי מַתְנִיתִין, רַעְיָא מְהֵימָנָא, הָא פִּקּוּדָא דָּא הֲווֹ מְקַיְּימִין יִשְׂרָאֵל בְּאַרְעָא דְּיִשְׂרָאֵל. אָמַר לוֹן, בְּגִין לְאִתְעָרָא רַחֲמֵי, עַל

אִלֵּין דְּמִתָרְכֵי מֵאַתְרַיְיהוּ. דְּבַר נָשׁ כַּד אִיהוּ לְבַר מֵאַתְרֵיהּ, גִּיּוֹרָא אִתְקְרֵי, כ"ש עַל נִשְׁמָתִין דְּאַזְלִין עַרְטִילָאִין מֵהַהוּא עָלְמָא, וְאַתְיָין לְעָלְמָא דֵּין. בְּגִינַיְיהוּ, הַאי אִיהוּ דְּאָמַר קְרָא, כְּצִפּוֹר נוֹדֶדֶת מִן קִנָּהּ, דָּא נִשְׁמְתָא, דִּשְׁכִינְתָּא לָא זָזָה מִנָּהּ. כֵּן אִישׁ, דְּאִתְּמַר בֵּיהּ יְיָ' אִישׁ מִלְחָמָה, נוֹדֵד מִמְּקוֹמוֹ, דְּאִיהוּ נָע וָנָד מֵאַתְרֵיהּ, דְּאִיהוּ עָלְמָא דְּאָתֵי, בִּינָה. וָנָד אֲבַתְרָהּ בְּעָלְמָא דֵּין, עַד דְּתַשְׁלִים יוֹמִין דְּאִתְחַיְּיבַת לְמֵיזַל לְבַר מֵאַתְרָהָא. וְאִיהוּ נָטִיר לָהּ, עַד דְּיַחֲזִיר לָהּ לְאַתְרָהָא. וְאוֹמֵי דְּלָא יַחֲזוֹר אִיהוּ לְאַתְרֵיהּ, עַד דְּיַחֲזִיר לָהּ לְאַתְרָהָא. וּמַאן דְּחָזַר בְּתִיּוּבְתָּא, כְּמַאן דְּאַחְזָר לְקוּדְשָׁא בְּרִיךְ הוּא וּשְׁכִינְתָּא לְאַתְרָהָא. וְדָא רָזָא דְּפוּרְקָנָא, דְּאָמַר הַיּוֹם אִם בְּקוֹלוֹ תִשְׁמָעוּ.

47. The sages of the Mishnah asked him, Faithful Shepherd, yet Yisrael performed this precept REGARDING THE CORNERS OF THE FIELD AND THE GLEANING OF THE HARVEST in the land of Yisrael, WHEN THE HOLY ONE, BLESSED BE HE, WAS IN HIS PLACE AND NOT A STRANGER. WHY IS IT WRITTEN, "FOR THE POOR AND STRANGER"? He said to them, this is in order to invoke mercy on those SOULS driven away from their place. For a man outside his own place is called a stranger, and all the more so the souls that walk naked from that world and come into this world. Of them the verse says, "As a bird that wanders from her nest," which is the soul from which the Shechinah does not move, "so is a man" (Mishlei 27:8), THE HOLY ONE, BLESSED BE HE, of whom it says, "Hashem is a man of war" (Shemot 15:3), "wanders from His place" (Mishlei 27:8), roaming and roving from His place, which is the World to Come, namely Binah, and wanders after her, AFTER THE SHECHINAH THAT IS THE SOUL in this world, until the days that the soul needs to go outside its place are completed. He guards it until He returns it to its place and swears He shall not return to His place before He returns it to its own. THEREFORE, whoever repents AND RETURNS HIS SOUL TO ITS PLACE is as if he returned the Holy One, blessed be He, and His Shechinah to His place. This is the secret of redemption as it said, "today even, if you will only hearken to His voice" (Tehilim 95:7).

48. אָמְרוּ מָארֵי מַתְנִיתִין דִּמְתִיבְתָּא עִלָּאָה וְתַתָּאָה, רַעְיָא מְהֵימָנָא,

אֲנָן שְׁלִיחָן דְּמָארֵי עָלְמָא לְגַבָּךְ, זַכָּאָה חוּלָקָךְ, דְּאַנְתְּ בַּעַל תְּשׁוּבָה, שָׁקוּל לְשִׁתִּין רִבְוָון דְּיִשְׂרָאֵל, וְאַנְתְּ הַדְרַת לְקוּדְשָׁא בְּרִיךְ הוּא וּשְׁכִינְתֵּיהּ לְאַתְרֵיהּ, עֵילָּא וְתַתָּא. וּבְגִינָךְ יִתְפָּרְקוּן יִשְׂרָאֵל וְיַחְזְרוּן לְאַתְרַיְיהוּ. וְלֵית חֵילָא לַמְּשִׁיחִין. לְמִפְרַק לְיִשְׂרָאֵל, בַּר מִינָּךְ. וּבְגִינָךְ אִינּוּן מִתְעַכְּבִין. אַשְׁלִים מִלִּין יְקָרִין אִלֵּין, דְּעָלַיְיהוּ אִתְּמַר, הַנֶּחֱמָדִים מִזָּהָב וּמִפָּז רָב וּמְתוּקִים מִדְּבַשׁ וְנוֹפֶת צוּפִים.

48. The Mishnah sages of the lofty Yeshivah OF THE HOLY ONE, BLESSED BE HE, and of the lower Yeshivah OF METATRON said, Faithful Shepherd, we are messengers of the Master of the universe to you. Blessed is your portion that you are penitent and equal to the 600,000 of Yisrael and that you returned the Holy One, blessed be He, and His Shechinah to their place above and below. Due to you, Yisrael will be redeemed and return to their place. The TWO Messiahs, MESSIAH THE SON OF JOSEPH AND MESSIAH THE SON OF DAVID, have no power to redeem Yisrael except with you. It is because of you that they are held back FROM REDEEMING YISRAEL. Finish saying these precious things of which it says, "More to be desired are they than gold, even much fine gold; sweeter also than honey and the honeycomb" (Tehilim 19:11).

49. אָמַר לוֹן, מָארֵי מְתִיבְתָּאן, בְּגִין הַאי שָׂכִיר, דְּאִיהוּ עֶבֶד, דְּאָתֵי לְקַבְּלָא תְּלַת צְלוֹתִין, תַּקִּינוּ מָארֵי מַתְנִיתִין דִּלְכוֹן, לְמֶהֱוֵי בַּר נָשׁ, בִּתְלַת בִּרְכָאן קַדְמָאִין, כְּעֶבֶד דִּמְסַדֵּר שְׁבָחִין קַמֵּי מָארֵיהּ. וּבְאֶמְצָעִיּוֹת, כְּעֶבֶד דִּמְקַבֵּל פְּרָס מִמָּארֵיהּ. וּבְבַתְרָאֵי, כְּעֶבֶד דְּנָטַל פְּרָס מִמָּארֵיהּ, וְאָזִיל לֵיהּ.

49. He said to them, Yeshivah heads, for that hired servant, who is the servant METATRON, who comes to receive three prayers, your masters of the Mishnah decreed that man should be when reciting the first three benedictions OF THE AMIDAH PRAYER as a servant arranging praises before his master, and during the middle benedictions as a servant receiving wages from his master, and during the last benedictions as a servant who received his wages from his master and walked his way.

50. וּבְגִין דָּא, עֶבֶד אַבְרָהָם, וְרִבְקָה, אִיהוּ אַמְתְּלָא לְהַאי, כַּד קוּדְשָׁא בְּרִיךְ הוּא, יִשְׁלַח לְמְטַטְרוֹן דְּאִיהוּ עַבְדָּא דִּילֵיהּ, בְּגִין צְלוֹתָא אִיהוּ יֵימַר לְגַבֵּיהּ, אוּלַי לֹא תֹאבֶה הָאִשָּׁה לָלֶכֶת אַחֲרַי. כְּלוֹמַר, אוּלַי צְלוֹתָא לָא בָּעֵי לְמֵיזַל אֲבַתְרָאִי. אָמַר לֵיהּ קוּדְשָׁא ב״ה, וְנִקִּיתָ מִשְּׁבוּעָתִי זֹאת. דְּחָכְמָה אִיהוּ אַבָּא, דְּנָחִית בְּצַדִּיק, לְנַטְרָא שְׁכִינְתָּא בְּגָלוּתָא, וּמִתַּמָּן שָׁלַח בְּגִינָהּ.

50. For that reason the servant of Abraham and Rebecca was likened to this that when the Holy One, blessed be He, will send Metatron His servant to receive the prayer, THE SECRET OF MALCHUT, he shall say to Him, "Perhaps the woman will not be willing to follow me" (Beresheet 24:5), that is, perhaps the prayer will not want to follow me. The Holy One, blessed be He, answered him, "then you shall be clear from this my oath" (Ibid. 8). AND HE EXPLAINS that Chochmah is Aba, THAT IS, ABRAHAM WHO IS CALLED A FATHER, WHO IS CHESED, RISES AND BECOMES CHOCHMAH IN THE STATE OF GREATNESS, and he descends to the Righteous, YESOD, to keep the Shechinah in exile. And from there, FROM YESOD, the servant, WHO IS METATRON OF THE NUMERICAL VALUE OF SHADAI, SINCE IT CORRESPONDS TO YESOD, sent after her, AFTER THE PRAYER, WHERE THE SHECHINAH LIES.

51. אָמַר לֵיהּ הַהוּא שָׁלִיחַ, הַב לִי סִימָנִין, לְאִשְׁתְּמוֹדְעָא בִּצְלוֹתָא, דְּתַמָּן בְּרַתָּא, אָמַר קוּדְשָׁא בְּרִיךְ הוּא, וְהָיָה הַנַּעֲרָה אֲשֶׁר אוֹמַר אֵלֶיהָ הַטִּי נָא כַדֵּךְ וְאֶשְׁתֶּה וְאָמְרָה שְׁתֵה. וְאִם לָאו, אֶלָּא דְּאַשְׁכַּח כָּל אֵבָרִין דְּגוּפָא מַלְיָין חוֹבִין, וְלָא אַשְׁכָּחַת בֵּיהּ אֵבֶר לְשַׁרְיָיא בֵּיהּ תּוֹרָה, דְּאִיהוּ בְּדִיוּקְנָא דְּעַמּוּדָא דְּאֶמְצָעִיתָא. וְלָא מִצְוָה, דְּאִיהוּ דִּיוּקְנָא דְּרִבְקָה, דַּהֲוָה שׁוֹשַׁנָּה בֵּין הַחוֹחִים, דְּאִינּוּן רְשָׁעִים גְּמוּרִים. מָנֵי לְעַבְדֵיהּ מְטַטְרוֹן, הִשָּׁמֶר לְךָ פֶּן תָּשִׁיב אֶת בְּנִי שָׁמָּה, דְּאִיהוּ רוּחָא דְּקוּדְשָׁא, דְּהָא מִצְוָה אִיהוּ נַפְשָׁא, רוּחָא אִיהוּ תּוֹרָה.

51. The messenger, METATRON, said to Him, Give me a token with which to recognize the prayer where the daughter is, NAMELY THE SHECHINAH. The Holy One, blessed be He said, "and let it come to pass, that the girl to whom I shall say, Let down your pitcher, I pray you, that I may drink; and she shall say, Drink" (Ibid. 14). THAT IS, IF THE PURPOSE OF THE PRAYER WILL BE TO GIVE ME DRINK, TO PLEASE ME, THEN YOU SHALL KNOW THE SHECHINAH IS THERE. If it does not, but he finds all the body parts full of iniquities, AND ALL ITS INTENTIONS DURING PRAYER ARE ONLY FOR ITSELF ALONE, AND NOT TO GIVE ME PLEASURE, and there is no WHOLE body part where Torah dwells, WHICH IS THE LIGHT OF RUACH, which has the form of the Central Pillar, and no precept, WHICH IS THE LIGHT OF NEFESH of the form of Rivkah, NAMELY THE SHECHINAH, who was a lily among the thorns, who are completely evil people, He ordered His servant Metatron, "Beware lest you bring my son back there" (Ibid. 6), who is the spirit of holiness, since a precept is Nefesh and the Ruach is Torah, MEANING THAT RUACH IS DRAWN FROM ZEIR ANPIN CALLED TORAH. AND HE DOES NOT MERIT THE RUACH AND NEFESH OF HOLINESS.

8. One's fear of sin precedes one's wisdom

A Synopsis

The sages of the Mishnah have explained that action is more valuable than speech. They also said that a person acquires wisdom if he fears sin first and that the Torah will rest on him if he first does all the precepts. If he reverses these then he comes from the aspect of Judgment. Suffering and Judgment must also precede mercy: 'as the suffering so the reward'. We hear what Moses' role will be during the last exile.

52. וּבג״ד אוּקְמוּהָ מָארֵי מַתְנִיתִין, לֹא הַמִּדְרָשׁ הוּא הָעִיקָּר אֶלָּא הַמַּעֲשֶׂה. וּבַאֲתָר אַחֲרָא אָמְרוּ, כָּל שֶׁיִּרְאַת חֶטְאוֹ קוֹדֶמֶת לְחָכְמָתוֹ, חָכְמָתוֹ מִתְקַיֶּימֶת וְכוּ׳. יִרְאַת חֶטְאוֹ, אִימָּא עִלָּאָה, תְּשׁוּבָה. חָכְמָה, אַבָּא עִלָּאָה. כַּד אַקְדִּים ה׳ זְעֵירָא, דְּאִיהִי מִצְוָה, שַׁרְיָא עָלֵיהּ תּוֹרָה, דְּאִיהוּ ו׳. וְכַד אַקְדִּים יִרְאָה לַחָכְמָה, דְּאִיהִי ה׳ עִלָּאָה, שַׁרְיָיא עָלֵיהּ חָכְמָה, דְּאִיהִי י׳. וְאִקְרֵי בֵּן. וּמִכָּאן, בָּנִים אַתֶּם לַיְיָ׳ אֱלֹהֵיכֶם.

52. For that reason the sages of the Mishnah explained that action, not talk, is more valuable. In another place they said that one whose fear of sin precedes his wisdom, his wisdom prevails… One's fear of sin is supernal Ima, BINAH THAT IS CALLED repentance. Chochmah is supernal Aba. And when one precedes small Hei, NAMELY MALCHUT, which is the precepts, the Torah, WHICH IS ZEIR ANPIN that is Vav, rests on him. And when he places fear, which is upper Hei, before Chochmah, Chochmah rests on him, which is Yud, and he is called a son, NAMELY THE SON OF YUD HEI. Hence, "You are the children of Hashem your Elohim" (Devarim 14:1).

53. וְהַאי אִיהוּ זֶה שְׁמִי י״ה לְעוֹלָם, וְזֶה זִכְרִי ו״ה. שְׁמִי עִם י״ה, שס״ה. זִכְרִי עִם ו״ה, רמ״ח. וְכֻלְּהוּ תרי״ג. דְּהַיְינוּ תרי״ג פִּקּוּדִין, דְּאִתְיְיהִיבוּ לִבְנִין קַדִּישִׁין, לְמֶהֱוֵי לוֹן חוּלָקָא בִּשְׁמֵיהּ, הה״ד כִּי חֵלֶק יְיָ׳ עַמּוֹ.

53. This is, "this is My name (Heb. *shmi*)," Yud Hei, "forever, and this is My memorial (Heb. *zichri*)" (Shemot 3:15), Vav Hei. 'Shmi' plus Yud Hei

IS IN NUMERICAL VALUE 365, and 'zichri' plus Vav Hei IS IN NUMERICAL VALUE 248. All together HAVE THE NUMERICAL VALUE OF 613, namely the 613 commandments given to the holy children so they will have a portion in His name. This is the meaning of, "For Hashem's portion is His people" (Devarim 32:9).

54. וְכַד אַקְדִּים תּוֹרָה לְמִצְוָה, אוֹ חָכְמָה לְיִרְאָה. אִתְהַפָּךְ שְׁמֵיהּ עָלֵיהּ לְנוּקְבָּא, מִדַּת הַדִּין, כְּגַוְונָא דָּא הוה״י. דְּאִתְהַפָּךְ לֵיהּ כֹּלָּא לְדִינָא, וְקָשִׁין מְזוֹנוֹתָיו בְּאוֹרַיְיתָא, כִּקְרִיעַת יַם סוּף. וּכְגַוְונָא דָּא פּוּרְקָנָא, אִם זָכוּ יִפְּקוּן בְּרַחֲמֵי, הה״ד, בְּטֶרֶם יָבֹא חֵבֶל לָהּ וְהִמְלִיטָה זָכָר, וְיִפְּקוּן בְּרַחֲמֵי. וְאִי לָאו אַקְדִּים רַחֲמֵי, וְיִפְּקוּן בְּצַעֲרָא. וְשַׁפִּיר דְּאַקְדִּים צַעֲרָא וְדִינָא לְרַחֲמֵי. וּבג״ד אוֹקְמוּהָ רז״ל, מָארֵי מַתְנִיתִין לְפוּם צַעֲרָא אַגְרָא.

54. When one puts the Torah before the precepts or wisdom before fear, the Name turns for him into the female aspect, into the attribute of Judgment thus: Hei Vav Hei Yud. FOR WHEN THE NAME IS WRITTEN STRAIGHT IT INDICATES THE QUALITY OF MERCY AND WHEN IT IS BACKWARD IT INDICATES THE QUALITY OF JUDGMENT. Everything turns into Judgment for such a man and his Torah sustenance is as difficult to acquire as the splitting of the red sea. Redemption WILL BE similar. If they have merit, they will come out with mercy, as written, "before her pain came, she was delivered of a man child" (Yeshayah 66:7), and they shall come out with mercy. It is good if suffering and Judgment precede SO AS TO DRAW mercy, which is why the sages of the Mishnah said, 'as the suffering so the reward'.

55. וּמִפִּקְנוּ דְּנַפְשָׁא, מִקּוֹדֶם דְּנַפְקַת אִית לָהּ צַעֲרָא, לְבָתַר דִּנְפִיקַת בְּרַחֲמֵי. וְרָזָא דְּמִלָּה בִּבְכִי יָבֹאוּ, לְבָתַר וּבְתַחֲנוּנִים אוֹבִילֵם, וּבג״ד, וְעֵת צָרָה הִיא לְיַעֲקֹב וּמִמֶּנָּה יִוָּשֵׁעַ, וְיִפְּקוּן בְּרַחֲמֵי. וּכְגַוְונָא דְּשָׁלַח קוּדְשָׁא בְּרִיךְ הוּא לְיוֹנָה, וְלָא אַשְׁכַּח אֲתַר לְשַׁרְיָא. הָכִי שָׁלַח לָךְ רַעְיָא מְהֵימָנָא בְּקַדְמֵיתָא.

55. When the Nefesh comes out, WHEN IT IS BORN INTO THE WORLD, it is in pain before it comes out, NAMELY LABOR PAIN, but after it has come out it is in a state of mercy. This is the meaning of, "They shall come with weeping" and then, "and with supplications will I lead them" (Yirmeyah 31:8). For that reason, "it is a time of trouble to Jacob; but he shall be saved out of it" (Yirmeyah 30:7), and they shall come out with mercy. Just like the Holy One, blessed be He, sent out the dove, AS NOAH IS OF THE ASPECT OF YESOD, but she did not find a place to rest, AS WRITTEN, "BUT THE DOVE FOUND NO REST" (BERESHEET 8:9), so did he send for you, Faithful Shepherd first. HE SENT FOR HIM, BECAUSE HE DID NOT FIND A PLACE TO BE HIDDEN FROM HIM, WHICH IS WHY HE WAS REVEALED TO HIM.

56. וּמַה כְּתִיב בְּהוֹן. וַיִּפֶן כֹּה וָכֹה וַיַּרְא כִּי אֵין אִישׁ. דְּכֻלְּהוֹן חַיָּיבִין, וְלָא אַשְׁכָּחַת בְּהוֹן אִישׁ זוֹכֶה לְאַפָּקָא מִן גָּלוּתָא. וּבג״ד סָרְבַת לְמֵיזַל תַּמָּן, וַאֲמַרְתְּ, שְׁלַח נָא בְּיַד תִּשְׁלָח. וְהָא אַנְתְּ כְּגוֹן בְּהַהוּא זִמְנָא, בָּךְ יִתְקַיֵּים עִם יִשְׂרָאֵל, כִּימֵי צֵאתְךָ מֵאֶרֶץ מִצְרָיִם אַרְאֶנּוּ נִפְלָאוֹת. וּבְגָלוּתָא בַּתְרָאָה, תְּרֵין מְשִׁיחִין יִשְׁלַח עִמָּךְ, לָקֳבֵל תְּרֵין גַּדְפִּין דְּיוֹנָה. דְּאַנְתְּ כְּגוּפָא בְּגָלוּתָא רְבִיעָאָה, לֵית לָךְ גַּדְפִּין. וְלֹא עוֹד, אֶלָּא בְּקַדְמֵיתָא הֲווֹ יִשְׂרָאֵל כְּגוּפָא, וְאַנְתְּ וְאַהֲרֹן, כִּתְרֵין גַּדְפִּין דְּיוֹנָה, וּבְהוֹן פָּרְחוּ יִשְׂרָאֵל.

56. It is written of them, "And he looked this way and that, and when he saw that there was no man" (Shemot 2:12), WHICH MEANS HE SAW they were all guilty and there was no man among them who had the merit to get out of exile. For that reason you refused to go there but said, "send, I pray You, by the hand of him whom You will send" (Shemot 4:13). Yet NOW you are like at that time OF THE EXODUS FROM EGYPT. In you it shall be fulfilled together with Yisrael, "As in the days of your coming out of the land of Egypt I will show him marvelous things" (Michah 7:15). During the last exile He will send with you two Messiahs, MESSIAH SON OF JOSEPH AND MESSIAH SON OF DAVID, who correspond to the two wings of the dove, WHO IS THE SHECHINAH, because you are in the fourth exile like a body without wings. Moreover, at first Yisrael were like a body, and you and Aaron like the two wings of the dove, with which Yisrael flew OUT OF EXILE.

9. Each precept includes the ten Sfirot

A Synopsis

Moses says that every precept has ten Sfirot in it. He speaks about the three stories of the ark, and the priests, Levites and Yisrael; he says that the ark as a whole, that is the Shechinah, is with them. We learn that the Name Yud Hei Vav Hei has dominion over the image of man and over every one of his limbs.

57. לֵית פִּקּוּדָא, דְּלָא אִתְכְּלִילוּ תַּמָּן עֶשֶׂר סְפִירוֹת. בַּתֵּיבָה תַּחְתִּיִּים שְׁנִיִּים וּשְׁלִישִׁים תַּעֲשֶׂיהָ. לְאַכְלְלָא בָּהּ, כֹּהֲנִים לְוִיִּם וְיִשְׂרְאֵלִים. תֵּיבָה שְׁכִינָה עִמְּהוֹן, תּוֹרַת יְיָ׳, אִיהִי רְבִיעִית הַהִין, ה׳ רְבִיעָאָה. וּמְשׁוּלֶּשֶׁת בְּיה״ו, לְאַשְׁלְמָא בֵּיהּ יֶדוֹ״ד. וַעֲשָׂרָה דַּרְגִּין דְּאִתְכְּלִילוּ בֵּיהּ, דְּאִינּוּן יו״ד הֵ״א וָא״ו הֵ״א. לְאִתְקַיְּימָא בְּהוּ בְּיִשְׂרָאֵל, וְאַתֶּם הַדְּבֵקִים בַּיְיָ׳ אֱלֹהֵיכֶם וְגוֹ׳, בָּנִים אַתֶּם לַיְיָ׳ אֱלֹהֵיכֶם. הַאי שְׁמָא שֻׁלְטָנוּתֵיהּ בְּצוּלְמָא דְּבַר נָשׁ, וְעַל כָּל אֵבֶר וְאֵבֶר דִּילֵיהּ.

57. There is no precept but that has ten Sfirot included in it. Of the ark IT IS WRITTEN, "with lower, second, and third stories shall you make it" (Beresheet 6:16), to include in it the priests, Levites and Yisrael, WHO ARE CHESED, GVURAH AND TIFERET. The ark AS A WHOLE, WHICH IS the Shechinah, is with them. The Torah of Hashem, WHICH IS THE SHECHINAH, is the fourth part of a hin, NAMELY, FOURTH TO CHESED, GVURAH AND TIFERET, a fourth letter IN THE NAME YUD HEI VAV HEI. It is trebled by RECEIVING THE THREE LETTERS Yud Hei Vav, to complete it into A NAME OF FOUR LETTERS, Yud Hei Vav Hei. Ten grades are included in it, NAMELY, IT RECEIVES THEM FOR THE SAKE OF YISRAEL, which are Yud Vav Dalet, Hei Aleph, Vav Aleph Vav, Hei Aleph, TEN LETTERS THROUGH WHICH it shall be fulfilled in Yisrael, "But you that did cleave of Hashem your Elohim..." (Devarim 4:4), and, "You are the children of Hashem your Elohim" (Devarim 14:1). For this name, YUD HEI VAV HEI, FULLY SPELLED WITH ALEPHS, has dominion over the image of man and over each and every limb of his.

10. Fish and locusts do not require slaughtering

A Synopsis

The Faithful Shepherd says that fish and locusts are permitted to be eaten because they can be gathered without slaughtering. He says this is like the sages of the Mishnah, that do not need to be killed by the Angel of Death, but are gathered up. And just as the fish live in the sea and die if they are taken out, the students of the Torah die if they are separated from the sea of the Torah. We learn that the Kabbalah sages are above all, and that they have dominion over the fish of the sea and the birds of the air. Moses says that if a younger student who is not yet fit to teach goes out and teaches, he must die. He also speaks about the sages of Mishnah as being crocodiles and talks about what happens when they disagree.

58. פִּקּוּדָא בָּתַר דָּא, לָדוּן בְּדִינֵי חֲגָבִים, דְּאִתְּמַר דָּגִים וַחֲגָבִים אֵינָן טְעוּנִין שְׁחִיטָה, אֶלָּא אֲסִיפָתָם הִיא הַמַּתֶּרֶת אוֹתָם. הָכִי מָארֵי מַתְנִיתִין, אֵינָן צְרִיכִין שְׁחִיטָה, אֶלָּא דְּאִתְּמַר בְּהוֹן וַיִּגְוַע וַיֵּאָסֶף עַל עַמָּיו. מַה נוּנֵי יַמָּא, חִיּוּתָן בְּיַמָּא, אוּף תַּלְמִידֵי חֲכָמִים, מָארֵי מַתְנִיתִין, חִיּוּתַיְיהוּ בְּאוֹרַיְיתָא, וְאִי אִתְפָּרְשָׁן מִנָּהּ מִיָּד מֵתִים. תַּנִּינָא דְּמַתְנִיתִין, דְּבָהּ אִתְרָבּוּ תַּנִּינֵי יַמָּא. וְאִי אִינּוּן דְּבְיַבֶּשְׁתָּא יִפְּלוּן לְמַיָּא, וְלָא יַדְעִין לְשַׁטְטָא, אִינּוּן מַיְיתִין. אֲבָל אָדָם דְּאִינּוּן מָארֵי קַבָּלָה, אִינּוּן לְעֵילָּא מִכֻּלְּהוּ, בְּהוּ אִתְּמַר וְיִרְדּוּ בִדְגַת הַיָּם וּבְעוֹף הַשָּׁמַיִם, דְּאִינּוּן מָארֵי מַתְנִיתִין, תַּנִּינַיָּא. הַתַּנִּין הַגָּדוֹל, נָחָשׁ בָּרִיחַ, לְקָבֵל וְהַבְּרִיחַ הַתִּיכוֹן בְּתוֹךְ הַקְּרָשִׁים.

58. The following precept is to discuss the laws concerning locusts. We learned that fish and locusts do not require slaughter, but it is their gathering that makes it permissible to eat them. Such are the sages of the Mishnah. They do not need slaughtering BY THE ANGEL OF DEATH but it says of them, "and expired, and was gathered to his people" (Beresheet 49:33). Just as the fish of the sea live in the sea, so do the Torah students and the sages of the Mishnah live in the sea, and if they are separated from the Torah they immediately die. THEY ARE the crocodiles of the Mishnah wherein grow the sea crocodiles. And if those who live on dry land, NAMELY THOSE WHO HAVE NO TORAH IN THEM, fall into the water, NAMELY INTO THE TORAH, but cannot swim, NAMELY A STUDENT WHO DID NOT BECOME A TEACHER YET TEACHES, they die. But 'Man', who are the Kabbalah sages are above all. Of them it says, "and have dominion over the fish of the sea, and over the birds of the air" (Beresheet 1:28), who are the Mishnah sages the crocodiles. The great crocodile is "the flying (Heb. *bariach*) serpent" (Yeshayah 27:1) that corresponds to "the middle bar (Heb. *bariach*) in the midst of the boards" (Shemot 26:28), WHICH IS THE CENTRAL COLUMN, TIFERET.

59. בְּזִמְנָא דְּתַנִּינִין מָארֵי מִשְׁנָה, אִית בְּהוֹן מַחֲלוֹקֶת, וּמַקְשִׁין דָּא לְדָא, בָּלַע לְחַבְרֵיהּ. וְהַאי אִיהוּ תַּלְמִיד זְעֵיר, שֶׁלֹּא הִגִּיעַ לְהוֹרָאָה, וּמוֹרֶה, חַיָּיב מִיתָה. וְאִי אִינּוּן שָׁוִין דָּא לְדָא, וְאִית בְּהוֹן מַחֲלוֹקֶת וְקוּשְׁיָא, אִתְּמַר בְּהוֹן לְסוֹף, וְאֶת וָהֵב בְּסוּפָה, וְאוֹקְמוּהָ אַהֲבָה בְּסוֹפָהּ.

59. When the crocodiles – the Mishnah sages – have a disagreement among them and ask each other difficult questions, ONE THEN swallows his colleague LIKE THE FISH OF THE SEA, WHERE THE BIGGER SWALLOWS THE SMALLER. This concerns a younger student who has not reached the position of teaching yet teaches, which is punishable by death. But if they are on equal footing, BOTH BEING LARGE, and have a disagreement and difficult question, it says of them at the end, "Vahev in Sufah" (Bemidbar 21:14), which has been explained TO MEAN love at its end (Heb. *sofah*), SINCE VAHEV MEANS LOVE (HEB. *AHAVAH*).

11. “and you put your nest in a rock”

A Synopsis

Rav Hamnuna Saba, who is here referred to as a great fish, speaks to the Faithful Shepherd about the title verse, and he says that the Mishnah sages must be strong and have a sharp tongue to bore through to reach the great abyss. He tells Moses that he will descend to the great abyss to find the time of the redemption because of his righteousness. Other sages tried to go there into the depth of the Halachah but did not come back up again, as they were not strong enough. Rav Hamnuna Saba says that whoever pierces the rock without permission will be bitten by a serpent.

60. אַדְּהָכִי, הָא נוּנָא רַבָּא אִזְדְּמַן לְגַבֵּיהּ, וְאָמַר רַעְיָא מְהֵימָנָא, אֵיתָן מוֹשָׁבֶךָ וְשִׂים בַּסֶּלַע קִנֶּךָ. תַּנְיָא דִּמְסַיֵּיעַ לָךְ. דְּהָא נוּנִין בַּסֶּלַע קִנָּא דִּלְהוֹן, אֵיתָן בְּהִפּוּכָא, תַּנְיָא. אֵיתָנִים בְּהִפּוּךְ אַתְוָון, תַּנָּאִים. אִסְתְּמַר מִנַּיְיהוּ, דְּהָא אַנְתְּ כְּבַד פֶּה וּכְבַד לָשׁוֹן, וּמַאן דְּבָעֵי לְאַתְקְפָא בַּסֶּלַע דְּנוּנֵי יַמָּא, דְּמָארֵי מַתְנִיתִין, דְּאִינּוּן תַּנָּאִים, בָּעֵי לְמֶהֱוֵי תַּקִּיף, לִישָּׁנָא חֲדִידָא חֲרִיפָא, לִינְקוּב עַד דְּמָטֵי לִתְהוֹמָא רַבָּא דְּתַמָּן.

60. In the meantime a great fish came to him, RAV HAMNUNA SABA, and said, Faithful Shepherd, “Strong (Heb. *eitan*) is your dwelling place, and you put your nest in a rock” (Bemidbar 24:21). Tania, THAT IS, THE TANNAIM, helps you IN EXILE TO RAISE THE SHECHINAH, because the fish, THE TANNAIM, have their nest in the rock, WHICH IS MALCHUT. Eitan is Tania written backwards; Eitanim (plural) is Tannaim spelled in a different order. Beware of them, because you are slow of speech and of a slow tongue. And whoever wishes to attack the sea fish in the rock, who are the Mishnah sages, the Tannaim, needs to be strong and of a sharp and polished tongue that bores and reaches the great abyss that lies there.

61. כִּי עוֹד חָזוֹן לַמּוֹעֵד וְיָפֵחַ לַקֵּץ וְלֹא יְכַזֵּב, וְאוֹקְמוּהָ דְּהַאי קְרָא נוֹקֵב וְיוֹרֵד, עַד תְּהוֹמָא רַבָּא. מַאן הוּא דְּנָחִית לִתְהוֹם רַבָּא, לְאַשְׁכְּחָא זִמְנָא דָּא, אֶלָּא אַנְתְּ, דְּאִתְּמַר בָּךְ צִדְקָתְךָ כְּהַרְרֵי אֵל מִשְׁפָּטֶיךָ תְּהוֹם רַבָּה. כַּמָּה מָארֵי מַתְנִיתִין, דְּבָעוּ לְנַחְתָּא לְעוּמְקָא דַּהֲלָכָה, לְאַשְׁכְּחָא

תַּמָּן קֵץ דְּפֻרְקָנָא, וְנַחְתּוּ תַּמָּן, וְלָא סָלִיקוּ. וְאע״ג דְּלִישָׁנְהוֹן הֲוַת כְּפַטִּישׁ יְפוֹצֵץ סֶלַע, חֲלִישׁ פַּטִּישׁ דִּלְהוֹן, לְנַקְבָא בְּהַהוּא סֶלַע. וּמַאן דִּנְקִיבוּ דִּילֵיהּ בְּהַהוּא סֶלַע בְּלָא רְשׁוּ, אָתָא חִוְיָא לְנַשְׁכָא לֵיהּ. וְאִית אַחֲרָנִין דִּנְקִיבוּ לָהּ, עַד דְּמָטוּ לִתְהוֹמָא רַבָּא, וְלָא סָלִיקוּ מִתַּמָּן.

61. "For there is still a vision for the appointed time; and it speaks concerning the end, and does not lie. THOUGH IT TARRY, WAIT FOR IT; BECAUSE IT WILL SURELY COME, IT WILL NOT DELAY" (Chavakuk 2:3). It has been explained that this verse pierces and descends to the great abyss. Who is it that shall descend to the great abyss to find that time OF THE END but you, of whom it says, "Your righteousness is like the great mountain; your judgments are a great deep" (Tehilim 36:7). Many Mishnah sages wanted to reach down to the depth of the Halachah, WHICH IS MALCHUT CALLED HALACHAH, to find there THAT TIME, NAMELY the time of the coming of the redemption, and went down there but did not come up. Though their tongue was "like a hammer that breaks the rock in pieces" (Yirmeyah 23:29), their hammer was too weak and could not pierce that rock, NAMELY PIERCE IT TO KNOW ABOUT THE END. Whoever pierces that rock without permission, a serpent will come to bite him; others bore it until they reach the great abyss but do not come up from there.

12. Fallen

A Synopsis

We hear about two Messiahs who fell into the gulf together with the Shechinah. Rav Hamnuna Saba tells Moses that he is the one who will repair the pit. He talks about four exiles and four Klipot, the fourth of which is called a pit. We hear that the fourth exile is a generation of evil people, and that it is empty without the Torah; this is how it will be at the end of the exile. We hear that death is poverty of knowledge, and that for Moses' sake all the Tannaim and Amoraim above will descend into the deep to help him.

62. וּבְזִמְנָא דְנוּקְבָּא פְּתִיחָא, כָּל מַאן דַּהֲוָה נָפִיל תַּמָּן, לָא הֲוָה סָלִיק. וּמָשִׁיחַ בֶּן דָּוִד נָפַל תַּמָּן עִם מָשִׁיחַ בֶּן יוֹסֵף. דְּחָד אִיהוּ עָנִי וְרוֹכֵב עַל חֲמוֹר. וְחַד אִיהוּ, בְּכוֹר שׁוֹרוֹ, דָּא מָשִׁיחַ בֶּן יוֹסֵף. וְהַאי אִיהוּ כִּי יִכְרֶה אִישׁ בּוֹר וְלֹא יְכַסֶּנּוּ וְנָפַל שָׁמָּה שׁוֹר אוֹ חֲמוֹר. וּבג"ד אִקְרֵי מָשִׁיחַ בַּר נַפְלֵי. וְאִיהִי נַפְלַת בַּתְרַיְיהוּ, וְאִתְּמַר עָלָהּ, נָפְלָה לֹא תוֹסִיף קוּם בְּתוּלַת יִשְׂרָאֵל. וְאַנְתְּ הוּא בַּעַל הַבּוֹר יְשַׁלֵּם כֶּסֶף יָשִׁיב לִבְעָלָיו. וְהַמֵּת יִהְיֶה לוֹ, דָּא מָשִׁיחַ בֶּן יוֹסֵף, דְּעָתִיד לְאִתְקַטְלָא.

62. And when the gulf is open, whoever falls there does not come up. And Messiah the son of David fell there together with Messiah the son of Joseph, of whom one is, "humble, and riding upon an donkey" (Zecharyah 9:9) and the other is, "The firstling of his herd" (Devarim 33:17), who is Messiah the son of Joseph. This is the meaning of, "if a man shall dig a pit, and not cover it, and an ox or an donkey fall into it" (Shemot 21:33). For that reason Messiah is called 'the one who fell', and She, NAMELY THE SHECHINAH, fell with them, and of Her it says, "The virgin of Yisrael is fallen; she shall no more rise" (Amos 5:2). And you, FAITHFUL SHEPHERD, are "the owner of the pit shall make it good, and give money to the owner of them; and the dead (beast) shall be his" (Shemot 21:34). The dead refers to Messiah the son of Joseph that will be killed.

63. נָחַת בְּגִינֵיהּ. דְּוַדַּאי אַרְבַּע גָּלְיוֹת הֲווֹ, תְּלַת, לָקֳבֵל תְּלַת קְלִיפִּין דֶּאֱגוֹזָא, דְּאִינּוּן תֹּהוּ, קַו יָרוֹק, קְלִיפָּה יְרוֹקָא דֶּאֱגוֹזָא. תִּנְיָינָא בֹּהוּ,

אֲבָנִין מְפוּלָמִין, דְּאִינוּן סְלָעִים תַּקִּיפִין, דְּמ״מ פַּסְקוּ מִינַּיְיהוּ כַּמָּה פְּסָקוֹת, וְנָקִיט לוֹן, לְאַפָּקָא מַיָּא דְּאוֹרַיְיתָא. וּבג״ד אִתְקְרִיאוּ אֲבָנִים מְפוּלָמוֹת, דְּמִנַּיְיהוּ מַיִין נָפְקִין. קְלִיפָּה תְּלִיתָאָה, דְּקִיקָא, גָּלוּתָא תְּלִיתָאָה, דַּהֲוָה זְעֵיר, וְהַאי אִיהוּ וְחֹשֶׁךְ. גָּלוּתָא רְבִיעָאָה, תְּהוֹם רַבָּה, חָלָל דֶּאֱגוֹזָא. וְהַאי אִיהוּ, וְחֹשֶׁךְ עַל פְּנֵי תְהוֹם.

63. (THE BEGINNING IS MISSING) descended for his sake. For surely there were four exiles, three corresponding to the three nutshells. The first is without form (Heb. *tohu*), which is a green line, namely the green shell of the nut. The second is void (Heb. *bohu*), which is viscous stones, which are strong boulders, from which the Mishnah sages legislated some decrees, and they hold on to them since water will come out of them. The third Klipah is the thick shell OF THE NUT, which is the third exile that was short. This is darkness. The fourth exile is a great abyss, which is the space inside the nut. This is "darkness was on the face of the deep" (Beresheet 1:2).

64. וְאִתְקְרֵי בּוֹר, דְּנָפַל שָׁמָּה שׁוֹר, דָּא דִּכְתִיב בְּיוֹסֵף, בְּכוֹר שׁוֹרוֹ הָדָר לוֹ. דְּאִתְּמַר בֵּיהּ, וַיַּשְׁלִיכוּ אוֹתוֹ הַבּוֹרָה. נוּקְבָא בִּישָׁא. וְהַבּוֹר רֵק, דְּכוּרָא, רֵק בְּלָא תּוֹרָה, אֲבָל נְחָשִׁים וְעַקְרַבִּים יֵשׁ בּוֹ. וְדָא גָּלוּתָא רְבִיעָאָה, דּוֹר דִּרְשָׁעִים מָלֵא נְחָשִׁים וְעַקְרַבִּים, רַמָּאִים כִּנְחָשִׁים וְעַקְרַבִּים, דְּעָקְרִין מִלֵּי דְּרַבָּנָן, וְדַיְינִין לְשִׁקְרָא, עֲלַיְיהוּ אִתְּמַר, הָיוּ צָרֶיהָ לְרֹאשׁ.

64. THE FOURTH KLIPAH, THE DEEP, is called a pit where an ox has fallen. This is why it is written of Joseph, "The firstling of his herd, grandeur is his" (Devarim 33:17), of whom it says, "And they…cast him into a pit" (Beresheet 37:24), which is the evil female OF THE KLIPAH; "and the pit was empty" (Ibid.) is the male OF THE KLIPAH, which is empty, without Torah THAT IS CALLED WATER. But there are snakes and scorpions in it. This is the fourth exile, WHICH IS EMPTY WITHOUT TORAH, which is a generation of evil people, filled with snakes and scorpions that are scoundrels like snakes and who are scorpions (Heb. *akrabim*) since they uprooted (Heb. *akru*) the words of the sages and give false sentence. Of them it says, "Her adversaries have become the chief" (Eichah 1:5).

65. וַיִּפֶן כֹּה וָכֹה וַיַּרְא כִּי אֵין אִישׁ דְּיִשְׂרָאֵל, בְּאִלֵּין רַשִׁיעַיָּא עֵרֶב רַב, וְדָא בְּסוֹף גָּלוּתָא. וּבְגִין דָּא קֵץ דְּפוּרְקָנָא נוֹקֵב עַד הַתְּהוֹם רַבָּה. וְרַעְיָא מְהֵימְנָא, תְּהוֹם הוּא הַמָּוֶת בְּהִיפּוּךְ אַתְוָון, וְלֵית מָוֶת אֶלָּא עֲנִיּוּתָא, אַנְתְּ נְחִיתַת תַּמָּן. וְהָא קָא אִתְבְּרִיר לְעֵילָּא, קַמֵּי תַּנָּאִים וַאֲמוֹרָאִים, וְכֻלְּהוּ נַחְתִּין בְּגִינָךְ בִּתְהוֹמָא לְסַיְּיעָא לָךְ.

65. "And he looked this way and that, and when he saw that there was no man" (Shemot 2:12) of Yisrael among the wicked OF THAT GENERATION, BUT THAT THEY ARE the mixed multitude. This will be at the end of exile. And because of that the end, the coming of the exile, bores all the way to the great abyss, WHICH IS THE FOURTH EXILE CALLED A GREAT ABYSS. Faithful Shepherd, you came down there. *Tehom* (Eng. 'abyss') is *Hamavet* (Eng. 'the death') spelled backwards, and death is no other than poverty, THAT IS, POVERTY IN KNOWLEDGE. It has been clarified up high, before the Tannaim and Amoraim, that they will all descend for your sake into the deep, IN THE FOURTH EXILE, to help you.

13. The Leviathan

A Synopsis

Rav Hamnuna Saba tells Moses that he is the Leviathan of the sea of the Torah, the master of all fishes. The sages of the Mishnah have stated that the Torah is maintained only by those who are willing to die for it, and part of the meaning here is that death is poverty. In response to Moses' query about the Leviathan, Rabbi Shimon answers that is it he whose grade is the Central Pillar, a righteous man who grows in the sea of supernal Ima where God is unified through the Sh'ma and the prayer 'Blessed be...' Moses says that the world is supported by that Leviathan.

66. וְאַנְתְּ תַּנְיָא דִּמְסַיֵּיעַ לָךְ יַתִּיר מִכֻּלְּהוּ, בְּגִין דְּאַנְתְּ לִוְיָתָן דְּיַמָּא דְּאוֹרַיְיתָא, מָארֵיהּ דְּכָל נוּנִין לִוְיָתָן אִתְקְרֵי, עַל שֵׁם אוֹרַיְיתָא, דְּאִתְּמַר בֵּיהּ כִּי לִוְיַת חֵן הֵם לְרֹאשֶׁךָ. וּבָךְ אָדָם וּבְהֵמָה תּוֹשִׁיעַ יְיָ'. אָדָם דְּאִתְּמַר בֵּיהּ אָדָם כִּי יָמוּת בְּאֹהֶל, וְאוֹקְמוּהָ מָארֵי מַתְנִיתִין, אֵין הַתּוֹרָה מִתְקַיֶּימֶת אֶלָּא בְּמִי שֶׁמֵּמִית עַצְמוֹ עָלֶיהָ, וְלֵית מִיתָה אֶלָּא עֲנִיּוּתָא. וּבְהֵמָה, אִלֵּין עַמֵּי הָאָרֶץ, דְּאִינּוּן מִתְכַּפְּיָין כַּסּוּס כַּפֶּרֶד תְּחוֹת מָארֵי מַתְנִיתִין.

66. And you support yourself by your sage's statement more than all of them, since you are the Leviathan of the sea of the Torah. For the master of all fishes is called Leviathan, named after the Torah of which it says, "for they are a graceful garland (Heb. *liviat*) for your head" (Mishlei 1:9). By you, "Hashem, You preserve man and beast" (Tehilim 36:7). Of man, NAMELY TIFERET, it has been said, "when a man dies in a tent" (Bemidbar 19:14), and the sages of the Mishnah have stated that the Torah is maintained only by whoever is willing to die for it, death being no other than poverty. 'Beast' refers to the ignorant, who are submissive like horses and mules to the sages of the Mishnah.

67. אַדְּהָכִי הָא בּוּצִינָא קַדִּישָׁא אָתָא, פָּתַח רַעְיָא מְהֵימָנָא וְאָמַר, מָארֵי מַתְנִיתִין מַאן אִיהוּ לִוְיָתָן. אָמַר לֵיהּ בּוּצִינָא קַדִּישָׁא, הַאי אִיהוּ דְּדַרְגֵּיהּ עַמּוּדָא דְּאֶמְצָעִיתָא, וְצַדִּיק, דְּאִתְּמַר בֵּיהּ, גּוּף וּבְרִית חֲשִׁיבֵינָן

חַד. וְאִתְרַבֵּי בְּיַמָּא דָא, דְּאִיהִי אִימָּא עִלָּאָה, יָם, דְּבָהּ מְיַיחֲדִין לְקוּדְשָׁא בְּרִיךְ הוּא כ״ה כ״ה אַתְוָון, דְּאִינּוּן יָם בְּחוּשְׁבָּן, וְאִיהוּ בָּהּ. אָמַר ר״מ, וַדָּאי לִוְיָתָן דְּקָאֵים עַל שְׂפַת הַיָּם, וְעָלְמָא קָאֵי עַל סְנַפִּירוֹי, דָּא צַדִּיק יְסוֹד עוֹלָם, דְּכָל עָלְמָא קָאֵים עֲלוֹי. אָמַר בּוּצִינָא קַדִּישָׁא, זַכָּאָה חוּלָקָךְ ר״מ.

67. In the meantime the Holy Luminary, RABBI SHIMON, came. The Faithful Shepherd opened and said, Mishnah sages, who is the Leviathan? The Holy Luminary answered him, it is he whose grade is the Central Pillar and a righteous man of whom it says that we consider his body, TIFERET, and member of the covenant, YESOD, as one. And he grows in that sea, which is supernal Ima, NAMELY BINAH, which is a sea where the Holy One, blessed be He, is unified in 25 and 25 letters IN SH'MA YISRAEL AND IN 'BLESSED BE...', the numerical value of which is that of '*yam* (Eng. 'sea')', THAT IS, FIFTY, and who is in it, BEING IN THAT SEA THAT IS BINAH. The Faithful Shepherd said, surely this Leviathan stands on the beach and the world is poised on his fins, AS THIS LEVIATHAN is, "the righteous is an everlasting foundation" (Mishlei 10:25). The Holy Luminary said, blessed is your portion, Faithful Shepherd.

14. "and the betrothed maiden cried out, but there was none to save her"

A Synopsis

As the beginning of this section is missing, the meaning is not entirely clear, but it begins by talking about the daughter of sound, Malchut, who is in temporary exile until Moses will come for her. The title verse means that the Shechinah cries out for her children, Yisrael, but there is no one to save them until the savior comes. We learn that when the tablets were broken the Shechinah fell, and we are also told that the mixed multitudes cannot separate from Yisrael until the final redemption. Moses is said to be God's son, the Central Pillar. We hear about the joy that will be known at the time of redemption, and about the Destroyer, Anger and Wrath that are in the world now.

68. בַּת קוֹל בְּגָלוּתָא, עַד דְּתֵיתֵי אַנְתְּ לְגַבָּהּ, דְּאַנְתְּ קוֹל דִּילָהּ, דְּכָל אִשָּׁה בַּת בַּעְלָהּ, כְּמָה דְּאַתְּ אָמֵר וַתְּהִי לוֹ לְבַת. מְאוֹרָשָׂה אִיהִי לָךְ, עֲדַיִין לָא עָאלַת עִמָּהּ לַחוּפָּה.

68. (THE BEGINNING IS MISSING) echo (lit. 'daughter of sound'), WHICH IS MALCHUT, is in exile until you come for her, since you are her sound SINCE MALCHUT IS THE SECRET OF SPEECH; MOSES, ZEIR ANPIN, IS THE SOUND IN SPEECH, AND SPEECH IS THE DAUGHTER OF SOUND. IT IS CALLED DAUGHTER since every wife is a daughter to her husband, as written, "took her for his own daughter" (Ester 2:7). SHE IS THEREFORE CALLED DAUGHTER OF SOUND. She is betrothed to you since you have not come under the *Chupah*, WHICH IS REDEMPTION, with her.

69. אִתְּמַר, צָעֲקָה הַנַּעֲרָה הַמְאוֹרָשָׂה וְאֵין מוֹשִׁיעַ לָהּ. הָכִי שְׁכִינְתָּא, אִימָּא עִלָּאָה, צוֹעֶקֶת עַל בְּנָהּ, וְאֵין מוֹשִׁיעַ לָהּ, עַד דְּיֵיתֵי עַמּוּדָא דְּאֶמְצָעִיתָא בְּגִינָהּ, דְּאִיהוּ מוֹשִׁיעַ. דִּבְגִינָהּ אִתְּמַר, הִנֵּה מַלְכֵּךְ יָבֹא לָךְ צַדִּיק וְנוֹשָׁע. הוּא מוֹשִׁיעַ לְעֵילָּא, וְאַנְתְּ לְתַתָּא. וּבְגִין דְּאַנְתְּ בְּדִיּוּקְנֵיהּ, אִתְּמַר בָּךְ, וְאַתָּה פֹּה עֲמוֹד עִמָּדִי. דְּכֻלְּהוּ יִשְׂרָאֵל אַהַדְרוּ לַאֲהָלֵיהוֹן, וְאַנְתְּ לָאו, עַד פּוּרְקָנָא בַּתְרַיְיתָא. וּמַאן גָּרַם דָּא, עֵרֶב רַב. דִּבְגִינַיְיהוּ, וַיַּשְׁלֵךְ מִיָּדָו אֶת הַלּוּחוֹת. וּמֵהַהִיא שַׁעֲתָא נָפְלָה, וְלָא אִתְפָּרְקַת מֵעֶרֶב

רַב, דְּאִתְּמַר בְּהוֹן וְגַם עֵרֶב רַב עָלָה אִתָּם. בְּכָל דָּא לָא אִתְפָּרְשָׁן מִיִּשְׂרָאֵל. וְשִׁפְחָה מִגְּבִרְתָּהּ, עַד פּוּרְקָנָא בַּתְרַיְיתָא.

69. It is said, "and the betrothed maiden cried out, but there was none to save her" (Devarim 22:27). So does the Shechinah, the highest mother, cry for Her children, WHO ARE YISRAEL, but there is none to save them AND TAKE THEM OUT TO REDEEM THEM, until the Central Pillar, ZEIR ANPIN, will come for Her, who is the savior. For Her it is said, "behold, our king comes to you. He is just, and victorious" (Zecharyah 9:9). He is savior above and you below. And since you have His form OF ZEIR ANPIN it is said of you, "But as for you, stand here by Me" (Devarim 5:28). All Yisrael returned to their tents but you do not, until the final redemption. Who caused that? The mixed multitude, because of whom, "he threw the tablets out of his hands" (Shemot 32:20). From that time THE SHECHINAH FELL and was not redeemed from the mixed multitude of whom it says, "And a mixed multitude went up also with them" (Shemot 12:38). Nevertheless, they do not separate from Yisrael and the maidservant DOES NOT SEPARATE from her mistress until the final redemption.

70. אַנְתְּ בְּרָא דְּמַלְכָּא, כְּגַוְונָא דִּילָךְ אִתְּמַר בְּעַמּוּדָא דְּאֶמְצָעִיתָא בְּכֹלָּא, חֶדְוָה דִּילָךְ, כְּחֶדְוָה דִּילֵיהּ יְהֵא, כַּד יֵיתֵי לְמִפְרַק לְכַלָּתֵיהּ, וְהוּא כֶּחָתָן יוֹצֵא מֵחוּפָּתוֹ וְגוֹ'. דְּהָא לְבוּשִׁין דִּילָהּ בְּגָלוּתָא חֲשׁוֹכִין, וּבִזְמְנָא דְּאִיהִי מִתְלַבְּשַׁת בְּהוֹן, אִיהִי אָמְרָה אַל תִּרְאוּנִי שֶׁאֲנִי שְׁחַרְחוֹרֶת. וְאִלֵּין קְלִיפִּין אִינּוּן, מַשְׁחִית אַף וְחֵמָה, נוּקְבָּא בִּישָׁא, שִׁפְחָה בִּישָׁא, שַׁבְתַּאי, וְשִׁפְחָה כִּי תִירַשׁ גְּבִירְתָּהּ, דְּאִיהִי שַׁבָּת מַלְכְּתָא. מַשְׁחִית אַף וְחֵמָה, סָחֲרִין לִתְלָתָא אֲבָהָן.

70. You are the King's son; according to your example we deduced about the Central Pillar in all THINGS. Your joy shall be like its joy when it will come to redeem the Shechinah, "which is like a bridegroom coming out of his chamber…" (Tehilim 19:6). For Her garments in exile are dark, and when she wears them she says, "Do not gaze upon me, because I am black" (Shir Hashirim 1:6). They are the Klipot, Destroyer, Anger and Wrath, WHICH ARE CHESED, GVURAH AND TIFERET OF THE KLIPOT, NAMELY

THE MALE OF THE KLIPAH THAT INCLUDES THEM. His evil female is an evil maidservant. She is Shabtai (Eng. 'Saturn') OF WHOM IT SAYS, "and a handmaid that is heir to her mistress" (Mishlei 30:23), who is Queen Shabbat. Destroyer, Anger and Wrath, WHICH ARE CHESED, GVURAH AND TIFERET OF THE KLIPAH, surround the three patriarchs, WHO ARE CHESED, GVURAH AND TIFERET OF HOLINESS.

15. A crown on his head and a beautiful tree before him

A Synopsis

We learn that the Shechinah used to be the crown, the Yud, on top of Hei Vav Hei, until she reverted to be below it.

71. וְלֹא עוֹד, אֶלָּא מַה דַּהֲוַת בְּרַתָּא דְמַלְכָּא, י׳ עַל הו״ה, דִּכְלִילָן בַּאֲבָהָן, ה׳ קַדְמָאָה בְּאַבְרָהָם. ה׳ תִּנְיָינָא בְּיִצְחָק. ו׳ בְּיַעֲקֹב. וַהֲוַת י׳ רֵישָׁא עֲלַיְיהוּ. אִתְּמַר, נָפְלָה עֲטֶרֶת רֹאשֵׁנוּ. וְאַמְתִּילוּ רַבָּנָן מְתָלָא, לְמַלְכָּא דַּהֲוָה לֵיהּ עֲטָרָה עַל רֵישֵׁיהּ, וְאִילָן יָאֶה קֳדָמֵיהּ, אַתְיָא לֵיהּ שְׁמוּעָה בִּישָׁא, אַרְמֵי עֲטָרָה מֵעַל רֵישֵׁיהּ. וּמַה דַּהֲוַת י׳ עַל הו״ה. י׳ לְעֵילָּא, אִתְהַדַּר הוה״י, י׳ לְתַתָּא. וּבְגִין דָּא אָמַר דָּוִד, אֶבֶן מָאֲסוּ הַבּוֹנִים הָיְתָה לְרֹאשׁ פִּנָּה מֵאֵת יְיָ׳ הָיְתָה זֹּאת.

71. Moreover, the King's daughter, THE SHECHINAH, used to be Yud on top of Hei Vav Hei that are included in the patriarchs, first Hei in Abraham, WHO IS CHESED, and second Hei in Isaac, WHO IS GVURAH; Vav WAS INCLUDED in Jacob, WHO IS TIFERET. Yud was on top of them. It then said, "The crown is fallen from our head" (Eichah 4:16). The sages used a simile of a king who had a crown on his head and a beautiful tree before him. When he heard bad news he flung the crown from off his head. What was, THE SHECHINAH, Yud on top of Yud Hei Vav Hei, WHEN Yud was on top, reverted to THE PERMUTATION Hei Vav Hei Yud, WHERE Yud is below. For that reason David said, "The stone which the builders rejected has become the head stone of the corner. This is Hashem's doing" (Tehilim 118:22-23).

16. "and speak to the rock"

A Synopsis

The Faithful Shepherd is invited to take the stone in his hand in order to break the Klipot. While other leaders tried to do this they were effective only in removing the outer shell, but they could not bring water from the stone as Moses could; these drops of water are wisdom and the wisdom of the Kabbalah. The Faithful Shepherd talks about the stone of the Name of Yud Hei Vav Hei, the stone which is Moses' rock, and the rock called Mishnah. He says that his rock is the King's daughter, Malchut of Atzilut, and that since he hit that rock he was sentenced never to enter the land of Yisrael, and was buried in a strange land.

72. קוּם ר"מ, טוֹל אַבְנָא דָּא בִּידָךְ, דְּאִתְּמַר בָּהּ, עַל אֶבֶן אַחַת שִׁבְעָה עֵינָיִם. לְתַבְרָא קְלִיפִּין דֶּאֱגוֹזָא, דְּהָא כַּמָּה רוֹעִים פַּרְנָסֵי דָּרָא, אִתְכְּנָשׁוּ עַל הַאי אַבְנָא, דְּאִיהִי סֶלַע דִּילָךְ, לְאַפָּקָא מַיָּא מִתַּמָּן, דְּכַלָּה דִּילָךְ מַעְיַן הַחָכְמָה. בְּהַאי סֶלַע, דְּנְבִיעָא דִּילָהּ בְּאוֹרַיְיתָא, בְּרָזִין סְתִימִין לֵית סוֹף. וְעָלָהּ אִתְּמַר, וְהַחָכְמָה מֵאַיִן תִּמָּצֵא.

72. Rise, Faithful Shepherd, take this stone, WHICH IS MALCHUT, in your hand, of which it says, "upon one stone are seven facets" (Zecharyah 2:9), in order to break the shells (Klipot) of the nut. For many shepherds, leaders of the generation were gathered by that stone, which is your rock, to bring water out of it, since your bride, MALCHUT, is the fount of Chochmah in this river that is flowing with Torah in infinite hidden secrets. It says of it, "But where shall wisdom be found" (Iyov 28:12).

73. וְכָל תּוּקְפָּא דִּלְהוֹן לְאַעְבְּרָא קְלִיפָּה דִּלְעֵילָּא, וְכַד מָטָן לַקְּלִיפָּה תִּנְיָינָא, דְּאִיהִי תַּקִּיפָא, אִיהִי קַשְׁיָא לוֹן, וּמָחָאן בָּהּ כָּל יוֹמֵיהוֹן כֻּלְּהוּ, בְּלִישָׁנֵהוֹן דְּאִינּוּן תַּקִּיפִין כְּפַטִּישִׁין, וְלֵית לוֹן רְשׁוּ לְאַפָּקָא מִינָהּ מַיָּא. אֶלָּא אִלֵּין טִפִּין דְּנָפְקִין עַל יְדָךְ, בְּזִמְנָא דְּאִתְּמַר בָּהּ, וַיַּךְ אֶת הַסֶּלַע בְּמַטֵּהוּ פַּעֲמָיִם. וּבִמְחָאָה תִּנְיָינָא נַפְקֵי אִלֵּין טִפִּין. וְאִלֵּין אִינּוּן רְמִיזִין דְּחָכְמָה, רְמִיזִין דְּקַבָּלָה, דְּאִינּוּן בַּחֲגִיגָה, וּשְׁאַר מַתְנִיתִין. וְהַאי אֶבֶן לֵית מַאן דְּאַפִּיק מִינָהּ חָכְמָה, דְּאִיהִי מִלְּגָאו, דְּלֵית לָהּ סוֹף, בַּר אַנְתְּ,

דְּאִתְּמַר בָּךְ הֲלָכָה לְמֹשֶׁה מִסִּינַי.

73. Their whole power is effective in removing the outer shell. When they reach the second shell, which is strong, they find it difficult and strike it all their lives with their tongues that are as strong as hammers, but they have no permission to bring water out of it, except for those drops that came out through you, when it said of it, "and with his rod he smote the rock twice" (Bemidbar 20:11). At the second smiting these drops came out. They are the allusions of wisdom and the allusions OF THE WISDOM of Kabbalah, which are in TRACTATE Chagigah and other Mishnayot. No one can bring forth from this stone wisdom that is inside it, which is infinite, except you, of whom it says, 'Halachah given to Moses on Sinai'.

74. פָּתַח רַעְיָא מְהֵימָנָא וְאָמַר, סָבָא סָבָא, אִית סֶלַע, וְאִית סֶלַע, אִית אֶבֶן, וְאִית אֶבֶן. אִית אֶבֶן דִּשְׁמָא דִּיְהֹוָ"ה, עָלָהּ אִתְּמַר וְאַבְנָא דִּי מְחָת לְצַלְמָא הֲוַת לְטוּר רַב. וְאִית אֶבֶן דְּאִיהִי אֶבֶן מַשְׂכִּית, דְּלֵית תַּמָּן נְבִיעוּ דְּמַיָּא דְּחָכְמְתָא, וְלָא דִּבּוּר.

74. The Faithful Shepherd opened and said, Old man, there is a rock and there is a rock; there is a stone and there is a stone. There is a stone of the Name of Yud Hei Vav Hei, WHICH RISES TO YUD OF YUD HEI VAV HEI AND BECOMES A CROWN OVER HEI VAV HEI OF YUD HEI VAV HEI. It says of it, "and the stone that smote the image became a great mountain" (Daniel 2:35), SINCE YUD OF YUD HEI VAV HEI IS THE SECRET OF A GREAT MOUNTAIN. And there is a stone that is "a figured stone" (Vayikra 26:1), OF WHICH IT SAYS, "NOR SHALL YOU INSTALL A FIGURED STONE IN YOUR LAND, TO BOW DOWN UPON IT" (IBID.) where there is neither flow of the waters of Chochmah nor speech.

75. אֶלָּא אֶבֶן דְּאִיהִי סֶלַע, דְּמֹשֶׁה, עָלָהּ אִתְּמַר וְדִבַּרְתֶּם אֶל הַסֶּלַע לְעֵינֵיהֶם וְנָתַן מֵימָיו. דְּאִיהִי בַּת קוֹל וְלָא תַּלְיָא בָּהּ אֶלָּא דִּבּוּר וּפִיוּסָא. אֲבָל שִׁפְחָה, סֶלַע אַחֲרָא, דְּאִתְקְרִיאַת מִשְׁנָה. נוּקְבָא דְּעֶבֶד נַעַר. עָלָהּ אִתְּמַר, בִּדְבָרִים לֹא יִוָּסֶר עָבֶד, אֶלָּא דְּמָחָאן וּמְתַבָּרִין מִינָּהּ כַּמָּה פְּסָקוֹת, וְלַקְטִין לוֹן, וְאִתְקְרוּן לְקוּטוֹת. וְעַל דִּמְלַקְּטֵי לוֹן,

אִתְקְרִיאוּ לְקוּטוֹת, בְּלָא נְבִיעוּ דְּחָכְמָה וְקַבָּלָה.

75. But of the stone which is Moses' rock it says, "and speak to the rock before their eyes; and it shall give forth its water" (Bemidbar 20:8). FOR THIS ROCK is a divine echo, NAMELY MALCHUT OF ATZILUT, and only speech and reconciliation applies to it. But of the handmaid OF MALCHUT OF ATZILUT that is another rock called Mishnah, which is the female of the serving lad METATRON it says, "A servant will not be corrected by words" (Mishlei 29:19), but it is smitten and several decrees are broken of it, NAMELY EXPLANATIONS, and are gathered, which are called compilations. They are called compilations because they are gathered without a fount of wisdom or Kabbalah.

.76 אֲבָל סֶלַע דִּילִי, אִיהִי בְּרַתָּא דְּמַלְכָּא, בְּגִינָהּ אִתְּמַר, וְדִבַּרְתֶּם אֶל הַסֶּלַע לְעֵינֵיהֶם וְנָתַן מֵימָיו, בְּדִבּוּר וּפִיּוּס, כִּבְרַתָּא דְּמַלְכָּא. וּבְגִין דְּמָחֵינָא בָּהּ, לָקֵינָא עָלָהּ, וְאִתְגְּזַר עֲלָנָא מוֹתָא. דְּמַאן דְּמְסָרֵב לְמַטְרוֹנִיתָא, חַיָּיב מִיתָה. כָּל שֶׁכֵּן מַאן דְּמָחָא לִבְרַתֵּיהּ דְּמַלְכָּא. וּבְגִין דָּא אִתְגְּזַר עָלַי, דְּלָא אֵיעוּל לְאַרְעָא דְּיִשְׂרָאֵל, וַאֲנָא קָבוּר בְּאַרְעָא נוּכְרָאָה, וְאִתְעַבְּרַת מִינִי. וְאִתְּמַר, וַיֵּרֶד אֵלָיו בַּשָּׁבֶט. וְהַאי שֵׁבֶט, אִיהוּ חַד מִשִּׁבְטַיָּא דִּילִי, דַּאֲנָא עָתִיד לְנַחְתָּא תַּמָּן לְמֶהֱוֵי עִם יִשְׂרָאֵל בְּגָלוּתָא. וְכֹלָּא אִתְרְמִיז, וּבַאֲתַר אוֹחֲרָא אוֹקְמוּהָ מָארֵי מַתְנִיתִין.

76. But my rock is the King's daughter, NAMELY MALCHUT OF ATZILUT, about which it says, "and speak to the rock before their eyes; and it shall give forth its water," namely with words and reconciliation as befitting a King's daughter. But since I smote her I was smitten because of her and we were sentenced to death. For whoever refuses the queen is punishable by death, and all the more so whoever smites the King's daughter. Because of that I was punished not to enter the land of Yisrael, AS THE LAND OF YISRAEL CORRESPONDS TO THE KING'S DAUGHTER, but instead I am buried in a strange land, MALCHUT BEING THE LAND OF YISRAEL, and she is angry with me. And it says, "he went down to him with a staff (also: 'tribe')" (II Shmuel 23:21). This is one of my tribes, because I will descend there to be with Yisrael in exile. Everything is alluded to and explained in another place by the sages of the Mishnah.

17. The Faithful Shepherd, the son of the King

A Synopsis

We are told that Moses is man in the likeness of Adam above. The speaker appears to be the first man, and Rabbi Shimon addresses him and the Faithful Shepherd, telling Moses that his gathering into the world above is spoken of in Bemidbar, and the inference is drawn that Moses did not die as other people do. We are told that Moses shines on the sages of Halachah and Kabbalah like the sun, and also that they are watered in secret from him as though he were a spring.

77. דְּבֵי מַקְדְּשָׁא, וּשְׁמָא דְּמָשִׁיחַ, אִתְקְרִיאוּ בְּשֵׁם יְדוָ"ד. וְדָא אַרְבַּע אַנְפֵּי אָדָם, וְאִינּוּן דְּשִׁבְטָא דְּלֵוִי, אִינּוּן נַפְקָן מֵחֵיוָן דְּאִינּוּן שְׁאַר שְׁבָטִין, וְעָאלוּ בְּחוּלָקָא דְּאָדָם, דְּאִינּוּן אַרְבַּע אַנְפִּין דִּילֵיהּ. וּמֹשֶׁה אִיהוּ אָדָם בְּדִיּוּקְנָא דְּהַהוּא אָדָם קַדְמָאָה דִּלְעֵילָּא. מַה שְּׁמוֹ וּמַה שֵּׁם בְּנוֹ. וּבְגִין דָּא, כַּהֲנַיָּיא וְלֵיוָאֵי, מְזוֹנֵיהוֹן עַל יְדָא דְּמַלְכָּא אָכִיל בְּפָתוֹרֵיהּ, וּשְׁאַר חַיָּילִין דְּמַלְכָּא, כָּל חַד יָהֲבִין לֵיהּ לְמֵיכַל בְּבֵית מוֹשָׁב דִּילֵיהּ. וְרַעְיָא מְהֵימָנָא אִיהוּ כִּבְרָא דְּמַלְכָּא, קָרִיב לְמַלְכָּא יַתִּיר מֵאִלֵּין דְּאַכְלִין לְפָתוֹרֵיהּ, דְּלֵית מַאן דְּקָרִיב לְמַלְכָּא מִכָּל בְּנֵי מַלְכוּתָא , כִּבְרֵיהּ.

77. (THE BEGINNING OF THE ARTICLE IS MISSING. THE FOLLOWING ARE NOT THE WORDS OF THE FAITHFUL SHEPHERD) since the Temple and Messiah's name are named after the Name Yud Hei Vav Hei, AND THESE FOUR LETTERS YUD HEI VAV HEI ARE the four faces of man and belong to the tribe of Levi, since they came out of the living creatures of the rest of the tribes, WHICH ARE THE FACE OF A LION, THE FACE OF AN OX AND THE FACE OF AN EAGLE and entered the portion of man's face, being his four faces, AS THE FACE OF MAN INCLUDES ALL FOUR FACES. And Moses is man of the likeness of Adam above. "what is his name" IS THE FIRST MAN "and what is his son's name" (Mishlei 30:4) REFERS TO MOSES. Because of that, the priests and Levites are fed by the King and eat at His table, and the rest of the King's armies each give them food in their abode. The Faithful Shepherd is like the King's son, who is closer to the King than

those who eat at His table, for none is closer to the King among all His people than His son.

78. קָם בּוּצִינָא קַדִּישָׁא וְאָמַר, סָבָא סָבָא, בְּמִלִּין דִּילָךְ אִשְׁתְּמוֹדַע מַאן אַנְתְּ. אַנְתְּ הוּא אָדָם קַדְמָאָה. מַה שְּׁמוֹ, אִתְּמַר עָלָךְ. מַה שֵּׁם בְּנוֹ, אִתְּמַר עַל רַעְיָא מְהֵימְנָא. וּבְגִין דְּאִיהוּ חִדֵּשׁ כַּמָּה חִדּוּשִׁין בְּאוֹרַיְיתָא, חֶדְוָה זְמִינָא לְגַבָּךְ, דְּבֵן חָכָם יְשַׂמַּח אָב.

78. The Holy Luminary, RABBI SHIMON, rose and said TO THE SPEAKER, Old, old man, through your words your identity is recognized. You are the first man; "what is his name" was spoken of you, "and what is his son's name" relates to the Faithful Shepherd. And because THE FAITHFUL SHEPHERD made new expositions in the Torah, you rejoice since, "A wise son makes a glad father" (Mishlei 10:1).

79. רַעְיָא מְהֵימְנָא, בְּפַרְשְׁתָּא דָּא, הֲוָה אַדְכַּר כְּנִישׁוּ דִּילָךְ לְהַהוּא עָלְמָא, דִּכְתִּיב עֲלֵה אֶל הַר הָעֲבָרִים הַזֶּה הַר נְבוֹ וְגוֹ', וְרָאִיתָ אוֹתָהּ וְנֶאֱסַפְתָּ אֶל עַמֶּךָ וְגוֹ', כַּאֲשֶׁר נֶאֱסַף אַהֲרֹן אָחִיךָ וְגוֹ'. וּבְהַאי פַּרְשְׁתָּא, אִית לָךְ לְאַהְדְּרָא לְעָלְמָא, וּלְהַחֲיוֹת, וּלְאַעֲלָא לְאַרְעָא דְּיִשְׂרָאֵל, וּלְאִתְחַבְּרָא בְּפַרְשְׁתָּא דָּא בְּכַלָּה דִּילָךְ, דִּכְתִּיב בָּהּ, הִנְנִי נוֹתֵן לוֹ אֶת בְּרִיתִי שָׁלוֹם. וּבג"ד לָא אָמַר לָךְ קוּדְשָׁא בְּרִיךְ הוּא הָכָא רֵד, אֶלָּא עֲלֵה. דְּמִנֵּיהּ, אַנְתְּ תְּהֵא עָאל לְאַרְעָא דְּיִשְׂרָאֵל.

79. Faithful Shepherd, in this portion your gathering into that world is mentioned, as written, "Go into this mount Avarim," mount Nebo, "And when you have seen it, you shall be gathered to your people, as Aaron your brother was gathered" (Bemidbar 27:12-13). And in this portion it behooves you to return to the world and live and enter the land of Yisrael and join in this portion your bride, WHO IS THE LAND OF YISRAEL, NAMELY MALCHUT, of whom it says, "Behold, I give to him My covenant of peace" (Bemidbar 25:12), WHICH WAS HIS, AND WHICH HE GAVE TO PINCHAS YET HE HIMSELF REMAINED NOT IN WANT. This is why the Holy One, blessed be He, did not say to him 'descend' but rather, "Go (lit. 'ascend') INTO MOUNT AVARIM," because from THIS MOUNTAIN you shall enter the land of Yisrael.

80. וּמַה דְּאָמַר בָּךְ, וְלֹא יָדַע אִישׁ אֶת קְבוּרָתוֹ עַד הַיּוֹם הַזֶּה. וַי לְאִינּוּן אֲטִימִין לִבָּא, סְתִימִין עַיְינִין, דְּלָא יַדְעֵי קְבוּרָה דִּילָךְ, דַּהֲוֵית אַנְתְּ בָּעֵי רַחֲמֵי מִקּוּדְשָׁא בְּרִיךְ הוּא, דְּלָא יֵיעוּל לָךְ בְּהַהוּא קְבוּרָה, דְּבָהּ אַנְתְּ מִתְקְרֵי מֵת. הה״ד, מֹשֶׁה עַבְדִּי מֵת. וְאִינּוּן טִפְּשָׁאֵי אַמְרִין, וְכִי מֹשֶׁה הֲוָה מְפַחֵד מִמִּיתָה, לְנָפְקָא מֵהַאי עָלְמָא, לְעָלְמָא דְּאָתֵי, כִּשְׁאַר בִּרְיָין. וְאִינּוּן לָא יַדְעִין דִּקְבוּרָה דִּילָךְ, וּמוֹתָא דִּילָךְ אֵיךְ הִיא.

80. And as for what has been said of you, "but no man knows his grave to this day..." (Devarim 34:6), woe to those of a closed heart and shut eyes who do not know your burial that you sought mercy before the Holy One, blessed be He, not to be taken into a burial in which you are considered dead. This is the meaning of, "Moses My servant is dead" (Yehoshua 1:2). And these fools used to say that Moses was afraid of death like other people, of leaving this world into the next. They do not know how your burial and death took place.

81. דְּהָכִי אוֹקְמוּהָ מָארֵי מַתְנִיתִין, דְּמֵתֵי חוּצָה לָאָרֶץ אֵינָם חַיִּים. לָא אַמְרֵי דְּאֵינָם עֲתִידִים לְהַחֲיוֹת, דְּאִלְמָלֵי כַּךְ הֲווֹ כַּפְרִין בִּתְחִיַּית הַמֵּתִים. אֶלָּא הָכָא רָזָא רַבְרְבָא, קְבוּרָה דִּילֵיהּ בְּצוּלְמָא דְּלָאו הֲגוּנָה לֵיהּ, דְּאִיהִי אֶרֶץ צִיָּה וְעָיֵף בְּלִי מָיִם, וְלֵית מַיִם אֶלָּא תּוֹרָה, וּבָהּ לֹא תֹאַר לוֹ וְלֹא הָדָר. וּמַאן דְּחָזֵי לֵיהּ בְּהַהוּא צוּלְמָא, וְנִרְאֵהוּ וְלֹא מַרְאֶה וְנֶחְמְדֵהוּ. וּבג״ד, נְבוּאַת יְשַׁעְיָה הִנֵּה יַשְׂכִּיל עַבְדִּי, קָא רָמִיז עָלֵיהּ.

81. For so did the sages of the Mishnah explain that those who die outside the land of Yisrael are not living. They do not say that they shall not live, for had they said that they would have denied the resurrection of the dead. But there is a great secret here, for his, MOSES', burial was in a form not befitting him, which is, "in a dry and thirsty land, where no water is" (Tehilim 63:2), NAMELY IN THE WILDERNESS; and water is none other than Torah, WHICH MEANS THE WILDERNESS IS A PLACE OF KLIPOT, where, "he had no form nor comeliness" (Yeshayah 53:2). And whoever saw him in that form, IT IS SAID, "that we should look at him, and no countenance, that we should desire him" (Ibid.). This is why the prophecy of Isaiah THAT

BEGINS WITH, "Behold, My servant shall prosper" (Yeshayah 52:13) alludes to him.

82. וּבְגִין הַהוּא קְבוּרָה, הֲוָה בָּעֵי רַחֲמֵי דְּלָא יְמוּת תַּמָּן בח"ל, לְפוּם דַּהֲוָה בְּאֶרֶץ צִיָּה רָעֵב וְעָיֵף וְצָמֵא בְּלִי מַיִם, דְּאִיהִי אוֹרַיְיתָא. וּבג"ד אִתְּמַר עָלֵיהּ, עֲלֵה אֶל הַר הָעֲבָרִים הַזֶּה. מִשִּׁפְלוּתָא דִּילֵיהּ, אַחְזֵי לֵיהּ מַעֲלָתֵיהּ, אע"ג דְּאַנְתְּ קָבוּר בַּאֲתָר דְּלָאו הָגוּן לָךְ, עָרוּם בְּלָא לְבוּשִׁין דִּילָךְ, דְּאִינּוּן עוֹר וּבָשָׂר, נָע וָנָד מֵאֲתָר דִּילָךְ, וּמְטַלְטֵל וְגָלֵי. הָא פִּנְחָס דְּעַבְדַּת טִיבוּ עִמֵּיהּ, דְּאִתְּמַר עָלָךְ, הִנְנִי נוֹתֵן לוֹ אֶת בְּרִיתִי שָׁלוֹם, הָא אִיהוּ יַעְבִּיד טִיבוּ עִמָּךְ, וּבֵיהּ תִּסְתְּלַק בְּפַרְשְׁתָּא דִּילֵיהּ. דְּבָהּ כַּלָּה דִּילָךְ, תַּמָּן תִּתְיַיחֵד עִמָּהּ, כֶּחָתָן עִם כַּלָּתֵיהּ.

82. Because of this burial, he sought mercy not to die there outside the land of Yisrael because it was, "in a dry and thirsty land, where no water is," which is the Torah. Thus it says of him, "Go into this mount Avarim"; from his lowliness He showed him his loftiness, namely though you are buried in a place not befitting you, without your garments, which are skin and flesh, moving and roving from your place, wandering and exiled, yet Pinchas, with whom you did kindness, as it says of you, "Behold, I give to him My covenant of peace," will be kind to you and in his portion you shall rise, THAT IS, IN THE PASSAGE "BEHOLD, I GIVE TO HIM MY COVENANT OF PEACE." FOR PINCHAS IS ELIJAH, THE ANGEL OF THE COVENANT, WHO WILL HELP MOSES CONNECT WITH THE TWO MESSIAHS TO BRING YISRAEL OUT OF EXILE. In it is your bride, MALCHUT, and there you shall join her like a groom joins his bride.

83. דְּהָא אַנְתְּ, אִי לָא הֲוֵית קָבוּר לְבַר מֵאַרְעָא קַדִּישָׁא, לְבַר מִכַּלָּה דִּילָךְ, לָא הֲווֹ יִשְׂרָאֵל נָפְקִין מִגָּלוּתָא. וּבְגִינָךְ אִתְּמַר, וְהוּא מְחוֹלָל מִפְּשָׁעֵינוּ. אִתְעֲבִידַת חוֹל בְּגִין חוֹבָה וָפֶשַׁע דְּיִשְׂרָאֵל בִּקְבוּרָה דִּילָךְ, דְּאִתְּמַר בָּךְ וַיִּקְבּוֹר אוֹתוֹ בַגַּיְא. וּמַה כְּתִיב בִּקְבוּרָה דִּילָךְ. כָּל גֶּיא יִנָּשֵׂא, כָּל שָׁפֵל וְנָמוּךְ יִנָּשֵׂא בְּגִינָךְ, דְּאִינּוּן יִשְׂרָאֵל, דְּאִינּוּן שְׁפָלִים מִכָּל אוּמָּה וְלִישָּׁן. וְכָל הַר וְגִבְעָה יִשְׁפָּלוּ, דְּאִינּוּן רַשִׁיעַיָּיא, וְגַסֵּי הָרוּחַ.

83. For had you not been buried outside the Holy Land, outside your bride, Yisrael would not have come out of exile. Of you it says, “But he was wounded (Heb. *mecholal*) because of our transgressions” (Yeshayah 53:5), becoming not sacred (Heb. *chol*) due to the iniquity and transgression of Yisrael, as it says of you, “And He buried him in the valley” (Devarim 34:6). It says of your burial, “Every valley shall be exalted” (Yeshayah 40:4), namely, all that is lowly shall be exalted for your sake, which is Yisrael who are humbler and lower than any nation and tongue. “and every mountain and hill shall be made low” (Ibid.) are the wicked and the impudent.

84. וְהַאי אִיהוּ, וּבַחֲבוּרָתוֹ נִרְפָּא לָנוּ, בְּחִבּוּרָה דְּאִתְחַבָּר עִמָּנָא בְּגָלוּתָא, נִרְפָּא לָנוּ. דְּאַנְתְּ הוּא כְּשִׁמְשָׁא דְּנָהִיר, דְּאע״ג דְּאִתְכְּנַשׁ בְּלֵילְיָא, נָהִיר הוּא בְּסִיהֲרָא, וּבְכָל כֹּכְבַיָּא וּמַזָּלֵי. הָכִי אַנְתְּ נָהִיר, בְּכָל מָארֵי הֲלָכוֹת וְקַבָּלוֹת. וְלָךְ אִשְׁתַּקְיָין בִּגְנִיזוּ, כְּמַבּוּעָא דְּאַשְׁקֵי לְאִילָנִין תְּחוֹת שָׁרְשֵׁיהוֹן בִּגְנִיזוּ, עַד דְּאִתְבְּקַע מֵימוֹי בְּאִתְגַּלְיָיא. הה״ד, יָפוּצוּ מַעְיְנוֹתֶיךָ חוּצָה.

84. This is the meaning of, “and by his injuries (Heb. *chavurato*) we are healed” (Yeshayah 53:5), namely, with the connection (Heb. *chibur*) he made with us in exile “we are healed.” For you are like the shining sun, since though the sun sets at night it shines on the moon and all the stars and constellations. So do you shine upon all the sages of all kinds of Halachah and Kabbalah who are watered in secret from you like a spring that waters the trees under their root unbeknownst until its water breaks into the open. This is what is meant by, “So will your spring be dispersed abroad” (Mishlei 5:16).

85. דְּאַנְתְּ הוּא אוֹף הָכִי, כְּשִׁמְשָׁא דְּאָזִיל בִּימֵי הַחוֹרֶף תְּחוֹת מַבּוּעִין, וְכַד מָטֵי פּוּרְקָנָא, תְּהֵא כְּשִׁמְשָׁא דְּאָזִיל בַּקַּיִץ לְעֵילָּא מִמַּבּוּעִין, וְיֶהוֹן צוֹנְנִין בְּרַחֲמֵי. דְּכַד אַנְתְּ תְּחוֹתַיְיהוּ, אִינּוּן חַמִּין בְּדִינָא. אָתָא רַעְיָא מְהֵימָנָא, וּבָרִיךְ לְבוּצִינָא קַדִּישָׁא, וְאָמַר וַדַּאי אַנְתְּ הוּא דְּנָהִיר לִי, בִּזְמְנָא דְּאִתְּמַר עָלַי, כִּי בָא הַשֶּׁמֶשׁ, כָּבָה הַשֶּׁמֶשׁ, דְּאַחֲשִׁיךְ נְהוֹרֵיהּ. יְהֵא רַעֲוָא, דידו״ד יַנְהִיר שְׁמֵיהּ עֲלָךְ.

85. For you are also like the sun that travels during winter underneath the streams SECRETLY AND WARMS THEM. With the time of redemption, you shall be like the sun that travels during summer above the springs and they shall be cool WITHOUT JUDGMENT but with Mercy. For when you are underneath them they are warm with Judgment. The Faithful Shepherd approached and blessed the Holy Lamp, saying, surely you shine upon me when it says of me, "because the sun was set (Heb. *ki va*)" (Beresheet 28:11), WHICH IS SPELLED LIKE 'the sun was extinguished (Heb. *kavah*)' when its light is darkened. May it be that the Name Yud Hei Vav Hei will shine its Name upon you.

18. Visions by vision, simile and dream

A Synopsis

Rabbi Shimon says how the five lights of Binah used to shine on Moses, which was why his face was like the face of the sun. He talks about the five times light was mentioned in the first day of creation and the five fingers of the right hand and the five Sfirot that are the secret of the five times that firmament was mentioned. The Faithful Shepherd talks about visions, saying that they are from the right, and Rabbi Shimon replies with his interpretation of Moses' vision of the burning bush, and of why the bush did not burn. The two of them talk about visions and prophetic apparitions and dreams. We learn that visions are known through the eye of the mind of the heart.

86. וְעוֹד אָמַר בּוּצִינָא קַדִּישָׁא, וַדַּאי אַנְתְּ הוּא כֹּלָּא, דְּאָמַר, אִם יִהְיֶה נְבִיאֲכֶם וְגוֹ'. ובג"ד, כַּד אִתְגַּלְיָיא אִימָּא עִלָּאָה לָךְ, אֲמַרְתְּ אָסוּרָה נָּא וְאֶרְאֶה אֶת הַמַּרְאֶה הַגָּדוֹל הַזֶּה מַדּוּעַ לֹא יִבְעַר הַסְּנֶה. בְּגִין דְּאִיהִי רַחֲמֵי, אִתְּמַר בָּהּ לֹא יִבְעַר הַסְּנֶה.

86. The Holy Luminary said further, surely you are all that, as said, "If there be a prophet among you" (Bemidbar 12:6). For that reason, when supernal Ima, WHO IS BINAH, was revealed to you, you said, "I will now turn aside, and see this great sight (or: 'vision'), why the bush is not burnt" (Shemot 3:3). For since BINAH is Mercy, it says of it, "the bush is not burnt," THAT IS, THAT WHICH IS CALLED BUSH WILL NOT BURN.

87. וְחָמֵשׁ נְהוֹרִין אִית לָהּ, דְּאִתְקְרִיאוּ קַרְנֵי הַחַמָּה, עַד הוֹד, וּמִתַּמָּן עַד הוֹד, הֲווֹ נְהִרִין בָּךְ ר"מ, וְהַאי אִיהוּ וְנָתַן הוֹד לְמֹשֶׁה, לְאִשְׁתְּמוֹדְעָא דְּכֻלְּהוּ לָךְ אִתְיְיהִיבוּ, אֲפִילּוּ עַד הוֹד. וּבג"ד, פְּנֵי מֹשֶׁה כִּפְנֵי חַמָּה. וְאִלֵּין חָמֵשׁ, סַלְּקִין לְחַמְשִׁין תַּרְעִין דְּבִינָה.

87. There are five lights TO BINAH called sunrays, SINCE BINAH IS CALLED SUN, FROM CHESED to Hod. And from there, FROM BINAH, to Hod they used to shine on you, Faithful Shepherd. This gave Hod to Moses, to let it be known that all FIVE SFIROT, CHESED, GVURAH, TIFERET, NETZACH

AND HOD gave to you since even Hod WAS GIVEN TO YOU. This is why the face of Moses is like the face of the sun, THAT IS, LIKE BINAH CALLED SUN. And these five SFIROT amount to the fifty gates of Binah SINCE EVERY SFIRAH COMPREHENDS TEN SFIROT.

88. וּבְאִלֵּין חָמֵשׁ דְּאִתְּמַר, דְּאִינּוּן חָמֵשׁ אוֹר דְּיוֹמָא קַדְמָאָה, דְּאִינּוּן לָקֳבֵל חָמֵשׁ אֶצְבְּעָן דִּימִינָא אִתְחֲזְיָא לָךְ בַּסְּנֶה. בְּגִין דְּעָתִיד אַנְתְּ, לְאַפָּקָא זַרְעָא דְּאַבְרָהָם מִן גָּלוּתָא, דְּאִיהוּ דַּרְגָּא יְמִינָא. וּמִתַּמָּן בִּינָה אִיהוּ רַחֲמִים גְּמוּרִים, יַד הַגְּדוֹלָה. אֲבָל מִסְּטְרָא דִּגְבוּרָה, יַד הַחֲזָקָה, חָמֵשׁ רָקִיעַ, בְּיוֹם שֵׁנִי, לָקֳבֵל חָמֵשׁ אֶצְבְּעָן דִּשְׂמָאלָא. אֲבָל מִסְּטְרָא דְּדַרְגָּא דִּילָךְ, וּבְנֵי יִשְׂרָאֵל יוֹצְאִים בְּיָד רָמָה. דְּגוּף וּתְרֵין דְּרוֹעִין וּתְרֵין שׁוֹקִין, לָקֳבֵל חָמֵשׁ אֶצְבְּעָן, ה' ה' ה'. ה' אֶצְבְּעָן דְּיַד יָמִין, וה' דְּיַד שְׂמָאל, וּתְרֵין דְּרוֹעִין וּתְרֵין שׁוֹקִין וְגוּף, דְּאִינּוּן חָמֵשׁ דְּסַלְּקִין יָ"הּ. א"ל רַעְיָא מְהֵימְנָא, בְּרִיךְ אַנְתְּ לְאִמָּא עִלָּאָה. אֲבָל הַאי י"ה שַׁוְיָא לִי ה', בְּגִין מַטֵּה הָאֱלֹהִים, דְּאִיהוּ ו'. וְאָמַר וַדַּאי הָכִי הוּא.

88. And these five we mentioned, which are the five TIMES 'light' mentioned in the first day OF CREATION, WHICH IS CHESED, which correspond to the five fingers of the right hand, WHICH IS CHESED, appeared to you at the bush, since you are destined to bring out Abraham's descendants from exile, who is the grade of right, WHICH IS CHESED. From there Binah is complete Mercy, IN ACCORDANCE WITH THE SECRET OF the great hand, WHICH IS CHESED. But from the aspect of Gvurah, CALLED the strong hand, ITS FIVE SFIROT ARE THE SECRET OF five times 'firmament' MENTIONED in the second day OF THE WORKS OF CREATION that correspond to the five fingers of the left hand. But from your grade, WHICH IS THE CENTRAL COLUMN, IT SAYS, "and the children of Yisrael went out with a high hand" (Shemot 14:8) THAT CORRESPONDS TO THE BODY, WHICH IS THE CENTRAL COLUMN, INCLUDING the body, the two arms and two legs, which are FIVE ASPECTS corresponding to the five fingers IN THE HAND. THIS THE THREE HANDS ARE five, five, five, NAMELY five fingers of the right hand, five fingers of the left hand and the two arms, two legs and the body, which are five. TOGETHER they amount to Yud Hei (= 15). The Faithful Shepherd said to him, blessed are you to supernal Ima, BINAH. Yet these Yud Hei, THE THREE HANDS, CHESED, GVURAH AND TIFERET, form for me the last Hei for the rod of Elohim, which is Vav, NAMELY ZEIR ANPIN. NAMELY, YUD HEI, WHICH ARE CHESED, GVURAH AND TIFERET, BUILD MALCHUT FOR ZEIR ANPIN. He said, surely it is so.

89. אָמַר לֵיהּ רַעְיָא מְהֵימְנָא, בּוֹצִינָא קַדִּישָׁא, לְאִתַּתְקְפָא מִלִּין דִּילָךְ, דְּמַרְאֶה אִיהִי לִימִינָא, חָשׁוּב בַּמַּרְאָה דְּאִתְּמַר בֵּיהּ בַּמַּרְאָה אֵלָיו אֶתְוַדָּע, וַתִּשְׁכַּח רמ״ח, דְּסָלִיק בְּחֻשְׁבַּן אַבְרָהָם. אָמַר בּוֹצִינָא קַדִּישָׁא, בְּקַדְמֵיתָא אִתְחֲזֵי לָךְ הַאי חֵיזוּ, דְּאִתְּמַר בֵּיהּ בַּמַּרְאָה אֵלָיו אֶתְוַדָּע. וּלְבָתַר דְּאַמְרַת, אָסוּרָה נָּא וְאֶרְאֶה אֶת הַמַּרְאֶה הַגָּדוֹל הַזֶּה. דְּאַדְכִּיר בֵּיהּ ה׳ זִמְנִין הַסְּנֶה. כְּעַן אִתְגַּלְיָיא לָךְ חֵיזוּ דָּא, ברמ״ח פִּקּוּדִין אִלֵּין, דְּאִינּוּן בַּחֲמִשָּׁה חוּמְשֵׁי תּוֹרָה. קָם ר״מ, וְנָשִׁיק לֵיהּ, וּבָרִיךְ לֵיהּ.

89. THE FAITHFUL SHEPHERD said to the Holy Luminary, I come to support your words as YOU SAID THAT VISION IS BINAH, YET a vision is to the right, since if you calculate THE NUMERICAL VALUE OF 'in a vision', of which it says, "make Myself known to him in a vision (Heb. *bemar'eh*)" (Bemidbar 12:6), you shall find it is IN NUMERICAL VALUE 248 that is the same numerical value as Abraham, WHICH IS CHESED. THIS SEEING IN A VISION IS CHESED OF ZEIR ANPIN RATHER THAN FROM BINAH. The Holy Luminary said TO HIM, at first the vision appeared to you of which it says, "make Myself known to him in a vision," WHICH IS BINAH. Then you said, "I will now turn aside, and see this great sight (or: 'vision'), why the bush is not burnt," NAMELY BINAH, wherein the bush is mentioned five times. THEY CORRESPOND TO THE FIVE LIGHTS OF THE RIGHT IN BINAH THAT ILLUMINATE THE BUSH FIVE TIMES, WHICH ARE ITS FIVE JUDGMENTS THAT TURN INTO MERCY LIKE BINAH. THIS IS WHY THE BUSH DID NOT BURN. Now this vision is revealed to you again with the 248 positive precepts in the five books of the Torah, NAMELY THE FIVE LIGHTS OF CHESED OF ZEIR ANPIN CALLED TORAH. The Faithful Shepherd rose, kissed him and blessed him. WE SHOULD KNOW THERE ARE TWO MIRRORS (OR VISIONS), THE SHINING MIRROR THAT IS ZEIR ANPIN AND ALSO BINAH, AS HE SAYS HERE, AND THE NON-SHINING MIRROR THAT IS MALCHUT.

90. אָמַר לֵיהּ בּוֹצִינָא קַדִּישָׁא, הַאי מַרְאֶה, לְזִמְנִין אִיהוּ בְּאוֹת ה׳

הַמַּרְאֶה הַגָּדוֹל. וּלְזִמְנִין אִיהוּ בְּאוֹת ב׳, בַּמַּרְאָה אֵלָיו אֶתְוַדָּע. וּלְזִמְנִין בְּמ״ם, מִמַּרְאֶה מָתְנָיו וּלְמַטָּה. וּלְזִמְנִין בְּכ׳ כְּמַרְאֵה אָדָם עָלָיו. וּלְזִמְנִין בְּו׳, וּמַרְאֶה כְּבוֹד יְיָ׳. וּלְזִמְנִין לְמַרְאֵה. לָא הו״ל לְמֶהֱוֵי תּוֹסֶפֶת אָת כְּלַל, בַּר ב׳ מִן בַּמַּרְאָה. אֶלָּא וַדַּאי, הַאי מַרְאֶה כְּלִילָא אִיהִי מֵעֶשֶׂר סְפִירָן, וְכָל אָת אַחְזֵי סְפִירָה דִּילָהּ, כְּגוֹן כְּמַרְאֵה בְּאָת כ׳, אַחְזֵי עַל כֶּתֶר, וְהָכִי שְׁאַר אַתְוָון, כָּל חַד אַחְזֵי עַל סְפִירָה דִּילָהּ. וְלָא צָרִיךְ לְאַרְכָא הָכָא, וּלְחַכִּימָא בִּרְמִיזָא.

90. THE FAITHFUL SHEPHERD said to him, Holy Luminary, this vision is at times preceded by the letter Hei, "the great vision (Heb. *hamar'eh*)," and at times by the letter Bet, "make Myself known to him in a vision (Heb. *bemar'eh*)"; at times by Mem, "from what appeared (Heb. *mimar'eh*) to be his loins downward" (Yechezkel 1:27), at times with Caf, "the appearance (Heb. *kemar'eh*) of a man above" (Ibid. 26); sometimes by Vav, "And the sight (Heb. *umar'eh*) of the glory of Hashem" (Shemot 24:17), and, "after the sight (Heb. *lemar'eh*). Yet it did not need an additional letter at all except Bet of '*bemar'eh*.' But surely this mirror comprehends ten Sfirot, and each letter indicates its Sfirah, namely '*kemar'eh*' with Caf indicates Keter, and so on; the rest of the letters shows each its own Sfirah. And there is no need to speak here at length; a hint would be sufficient to the wise.

91. וְכַמָּה חֶזְיוֹנוֹת אִית לָהּ, וְדִמְיוֹנוֹת וּמַרְאוֹת אִית לָהּ, וְכֹלָּא אִשְׁתְּמוֹדַע בְּעֵין הַשֵּׂכֶל דְּלִבָּא, דְּאִתְּמַר בָּהּ הַלֵּב יוֹדֵעַ הַלֵּב מֵבִין. וּמַה דְּאָמַר, וּבְיַד הַנְּבִיאִים אֲדַמֶּה. דִּמְיוֹן לָאו אִיהוּ, אֶלָּא בְּשֵׂכֶל דְּלִבָּא, וְלָאו כְּדִמְיוֹן דְּעֵינָא. הֲדָא הוּא דִּכְתִּיב, וְאֶל מִי תְּדַמְּיוּנִי וְאֶשְׁוֶה. וְאֶל מִי תְּדַמְּיוּן אֵל. וְאִית חֶזְיוֹנוֹת כְּגוֹן הַחוֹזִים בַּכּוֹכָבִים, אֲבָל חֶזְיוֹן דִּנְבוּאָה אִיהוּ כְּחֶזְיוֹן לַיְלָה.

91. How many apparitions it has, how many similes and visions, all known through the eye of the mind of the heart, WHICH IS MALCHUT, of which it says, 'a knowing heart', and, 'an understanding heart', and the words OF THE VERSE, "and used similes by means of the prophets" (Hoshea 12:11). Simile is only by means of the mind of the heart, WHICH IS MALCHUT, and is unlike the imaging of the eye. This is what is meant by, "To whom then will you liken Me, that I should be his equal" (Yeshayah 40:25), and, "To whom then will you liken El" (Ibid. 18). There are sights like those of the stargazers, WHICH ARE FROM THE OTHER SIDE. But a prophetic apparition is like a nightly apparition, WHICH IS MALCHUT CALLED NIGHT, BUT NOT OF SFIROT HIGHER THAN HER.

92. דִּמְיוֹנוֹת וְחֶזְיוֹנוֹת, כְּגוֹן הַמֵּבִין דָּבָר מִתּוֹךְ דָּבָר, וְהַמְדַמֶּה דָּבָר לְדָבָר. אֲבָל מַרְאֶה דְּאִיהִי בְּעֵין הַשֵּׂכֶל, אִיהִי כְּאוֹר דְּנָהִיר בְּבַת עֵינָא. דְּבַת עֵינָא אִיהִי אוּכָּמָא. שְׁחוֹרָה אֲנִי וְנָאוָה, אוֹר דְּנָהִיר בָּהּ הַהוּא חִוָּורוּ דִּלְגוֹ. וְהַאי בַּת עֵינָא, אִיהִי נֵר מִצְוָה. נְהוֹרָא דְּנָהִיר בָּהּ מִלְּגוֹ, וְתוֹרָה אוֹר.

92. Similes and apparitions are like deducing one thing from another; likening one thing to another, but a vision that is in the mind's eye is like a light that shines on the pupil of the eye, WHICH IS MALCHUT, since the pupil is black, as written, "I am black" (Shir Hashirim 1:5), NAMELY THE PUPIL OF THE EYE, "but comely" (Ibid.) with the white light in the eye that shines ON THE PUPIL OF THE EYE. This pupil of the eyes is called "the commandment is a lamp" (Mishlei 6:23), and the light that shines within it from inside NAMELY THE WHITE, is, "and Torah is light" (Ibid.), THAT IS, ZEIR ANPIN THAT IS CALLED TORAH.

93. אָמַר בּוּצִינָא קַדִּישָׁא הַיְינוּ מַאי דַּאֲמֵינָא דִּכְעָן בְּאוֹרַיְיתָא אִתְגַּלְיָא לָךְ קוּדְשָׁא בְּרִיךְ הוּא וּשְׁכִינְתֵּיהּ, וְהַאי אִיהוּ יְהֹוָ"ה, בַּמַּרְאָה אֵלָיו אֶתְוַדָּע. בַּמַּרְאָה: אִימָּא עִלָּאָה. אִתְיְדַע, לָךְ בְּדַעַת. בֵּן יָ"ה. בַּחֲלוֹם אֲדַבֶּר בּוֹ, הֵ"א בַּתְרָאָה.

93. The Holy Luminary said, That is what I said, that now through the Torah the Holy One, blessed be He, and His Shechinah were revealed to you. That is WHAT IS MEANT BY, "make Myself known to him in a vision" (Bemidbar 12:6). The vision is supernal Ima. "Make Myself known" MEANS IT IS KNOWN to you through knowledge (Da'at), WHICH IS the son of Yud Hei, NAMELY ZEIR ANPIN THAT IS VAV OF YUD HEI VAV HEI. "and speak to him in a dream" (Bemidbar 12:6) refers to last Hei, WHICH IS THE SHECHINAH.

94. חֶלְמָא, בִּסְתִימוּ דְּעַיְינִין. וּבְג״ד אִתְקְרִיאַת אַסְפַּקְלַרְיָאה שְׁאֵינָהּ מְאִירָה. נְבוּאָה אִיהִי מַרְאֶה בִּפְתִיחוּ דְּעַיְינִין. וּשְׁלֹשָׁה גַּוְונִין בְּעֵינָא, לָקֳבֵל תְּלַת אֲבָהָן. דִּבְהוֹן נְהִירָא בַּת יְחִידָאָה, תְּרֵין כַּנְפֵי עֵינָא, נֶצַח וְהוֹד. מַרְאֶה לָא אִתְחַזְיָא אֶלָּא בְּהוֹן, כַּד אִינּוּן פְּתִחִין, אִיהִי מַרְאֶה בְּהָקִיץ. וְכַד אִינּוּן סְגִירִין, אִיהוּ מַרְאֶה בַּחֲלוֹם.

94. The dream is with the eyes shut, NAMELY MALCHUT, for which reason it is called the non-shining mirror. Prophecy is a vision with open eyes, since the three colors of the eye correspond to the three patriarchs CHESED, GVURAH AND TIFERET in which the only daughter, WHICH IS MALCHUT, NAMELY THE PUPIL OF THE EYE, shines. The two sides of the eyes are Netzach and Hod, and the vision OF PROPHECY is seen only through them, NETZACH AND HOD. When they are open it is a waking vision and when they are shut it is a vision in a dream.

95. א״ל רַעְיָא מְהֵימְנָא, בְּרִיךְ אַנְתְּ לְקוּדְשָׁא בְּרִיךְ הוּא, קוּם אַשְׁלִים פִּקּוּדִין, לְאַנְהֲרָא מַרְאֶה עִלָּאָה בְּהוֹן, לְקוּדְשָׁא בְּרִיךְ הוּא. אָמַר לֵיהּ בּוּצִינָא קַדִּישָׁא, י׳, אִיהִי בַּת עֵינָא, כִּי נֵר מִצְוָה וְתוֹרָה אוֹר ה״ו מַנְהִיר בָּהּ ה׳, ג׳ גַּוְונִין דְּעֵינָא, וּתְרֵין כַּנְפֵי עֵינָא. חָמֵשׁ אוֹר נְהִרִין בָּהּ מִלְּגָאו, ה׳ עִלָּאָה דְּאִיהִי אוֹר הַמַּרְאֶה.

95. The Faithful Shepherd said to him, blessed are you to the Holy One, blessed be He. Rise and complete the precepts so the supernal vision, WHICH IS BINAH, shall shine with them, WITH THE PRECEPTS towards the Holy One, blessed be He. The Holy Luminary said to him, Yud is the pupil of the eye, NAMELY MALCHUT, OF WHICH IT SAYS, "For the commandment is a lamp; and Torah is light," SINCE THE COMMANDMENT IS A LAMP REFERS TO MALCHUT AND THE TORAH IS LIGHT REFERS TO ZEIR ANPIN. SHE IS Hei Vav AS VAV shines on her, ON THE PUPIL OF THE EYE, five SFIROT, WHICH ARE the three colors in the eye, CHESED, GVURAH AND TIFERET, and the two sides of the eye, NETZACH AND HOD. And five TIMES 'light' shine on THE PUPIL OF THE EYE from within, SINCE THEY ARE FROM supernal Hei, WHICH IS BINAH, which is the light of the (Hei) vision.

19. Forty minus one

A Synopsis

We are told that God will strike Samael fifty times for turning himself into a deity, and that Adam and Eve and the serpent and the land were given a total of 39 stripes because they all sinned against the letter Hei.

96. אַרְבָּעִים יַכֶּנּוּ לֹא יוֹסִיף וְגוֹ', פִּקּוּדָא דָּא לְהַלְקוֹת לְרָשָׁע, דְּאִיהוּ סָמָאֵל, דְּעָתִיד קוּדְשָׁא בְּרִיךְ הוּא לְמַחֲאָה לֵיהּ חַמְשִׁין מָחָאן. בְּגִין דְּעָבֵד גַּרְמֵיהּ אֱלוֹהַּ. יֵיתֵי יִחוּדָא, דִּמְיַיחֲדָן בֵּיהּ יִשְׂרָאֵל בְּכָל יוֹמָא, בְּכ"ה אַתְוָון, וְיִמְחֵי בְּהוֹן, לְמַאן דְּשַׁוֵּי גַּרְמֵיהּ אֱלוֹהַּ, וְלָאו אִיהוּ אֶלָּא עֶבֶד מְטוּנָּף. וְאִלֵּין דְּסָרְחוּ בה' תַּקִּין לוֹן קוּדְשָׁא בְּרִיךְ הוּא, לְמָחָאָה בְּיוֹ"ד הֵ"א וָא"ו, דְּאִינּוּן אַרְבָּעִים חָסֵר חַד. וּבְהַאי שְׁמָא, מָחָא קוּדְשָׁא בְּרִיךְ הוּא עַשְׂרָה מַכְתְּשִׁין לְאָדָם. וְעַשְׂרָה לְחַוָּה. וְעַשְׂרָה לְנָחָשׁ. וְתִשְׁעָה לְאַרְעָא. בְּגִין דְּכֻלְּהוּ סָרְחוּ בְּאָת ה'. וּבג"ד, כִּי עָשִׂיתָ זֹּאת.

96. "Forty stripes he may give him, and not exceed" (Devarim 25:3). This precept is to strike the wicked, who is Samael, who the Holy One, blessed be He, will give fifty stripes for turning himself into a deity. Let the unification OF KRIAT SH'MA AND 'BLESSED BE…' that Yisrael meditate on twice a day in the 25 plus 25 letters in them, come and strike with them whoever turns himself into a deity, and who is nothing but a filthy servant. And as for those who sinned against LAST Hei, WHICH IS MALCHUT, the Holy One, blessed be He, decreed to strike them with Yud Vav Dalet, Hei Aleph, Vav Aleph Vav, which are of the numerical value of forty minus one. With this name the Holy One, blessed be He, gave ten stripes to Adam, ten to Eve, ten to the serpent and ten to the land, WHICH AMOUNT TO 39 STRIPES, since they all sinned against the letter Hei, WHICH IS MALCHUT. Hence IT IS WRITTEN, "Because you have done this" (Beresheet 2:14), 'THIS' BEING A NAME OF MALCHUT.

20. Levirate marriage and Chalitzah

A Synopsis

This section talks about the precept for a man to marry the widow of his childless brother. The man must concentrate on unification and not on his own pleasure, otherwise he creates a separation and brings Samael in between. We are told that spilling seed in vain withholds many blessings from a man, and it brings separation instead of union.

97. כִּי יֵשְׁבוּ אַחִים יַחְדָּו וּמֵת אַחַד מֵהֶם וּבֵן אֵין לוֹ וְגוֹ׳, יְבָמָהּ יָבֹא עָלֶיהָ וּלְקָחָהּ לוֹ לְאִשָּׁה וְיִבְּמָהּ. פִּקּוּדָא דָא, לְיַבֵּם אֵשֶׁת אָח דְּאֵשֶׁת אָח אִיהִי ד׳, וְעִם א״ח אִיהִי אֶחָד. וְאִם ח״ו לִבֵּיהּ לָאו אִיהוּ, לְמַיְיתֵי אָח עַל ד׳, דְּאִיהִי אִתְּתֵיהּ בַּת זוּגֵיהּ דא״ח, עָבֵיד פִּרוּדָא, וְעָאל סָמָאֵל אֵל אַחֵר בְּאֶמְצָעִיתָא, וְאִתְּמַר בֵּיהּ, וְשִׁחֵת אַרְצָה לְבִלְתִּי וְגוֹ׳, דְּאִסְתַּלָּק קוֹצָא דְּאָת ד׳ מִן אֶחָד. וּבְגִין דָּא, וְהָיָה אִם בָּא אֶל אֵשֶׁת אָחִיו וְשִׁחֵת אַרְצָה לְבִלְתִּי נְתָן זֶרַע לְאָחִיו. וְהַשְׁחָתַת זַרְעָא, מָנַע מִנֵּיהּ כַּמָּה בִּרְכָאן, וּפִרוּדָא דְּיִיחוּדָא. וּבג״ד וַיְהִי עֵר בְּכוֹר יְהוּדָה רַע בְּעֵינֵי ה׳ וַיְמִיתֵהוּ ה׳.

97. "If brothers dwell together, and one of them die, and have no child…her husband's brother shall go in to her, and take her to him to wife" (Devarim 25:5). This precept is to marry one's brother's widow, since a brother's widow is Dalet OF ONE (HEB. *ECHAD, ALEPH CHET DALET*), and together with Aleph Chet OF ECHAD it is one. THAT IS, THE BROTHER (HEB. *ACH, ALEPH CHET*) SHOULD MEDITATE ON THIS UNIFYING. And if, heaven forbid, THE BROTHER does not with a WHOLE heart wish to bring Aleph Chet to Dalet, THE DALET being the wife and mate of the brother, BUT CONCENTRATE ON HIS OWN PLEASURE, he creates a separation and brings Samael, another El, in between. It says of him "that he spilled it on the ground…" (Beresheet 38:9). THEN the tip is gone from the letter Dalet of *Echad* AND IT TURNS INTO RESH; AND THE WORD *ECHAD* BECOMES *ACHER* (ENG. 'OTHER'). This is why, "and it came to pass, when he went in to his brother's wife, that he spilled it on the ground, lest he should give seed to his brother" (Ibid.). Spilling seed in vain withholds many blessings from one, and IT BRINGS separation to union. This is why, "And Er, Judah's firstborn, was wicked in the sight of Hashem; and Hashem slew him" (Ibid. 7).

98. וְיִיחוּדָא דְּאָח עִם ד׳ בְּצַדִּיק. וּבֹעַז בְּגִין דְּאִתְתְּקַף עַל יִצְרֵיהּ, אִקְרֵי צַדִּיק. וְהַאי אִיהוּ בּוֹעַ״ז, בּ״וֹ עֹ״ז, תַּקִּיף בְּיִצְרֵיהּ. הֵן כָּל אֵלֶּה יִפְעַל אֵל פַּעֲמַיִם שָׁלֹשׁ עִם גָּבֶר, וְדָא יה״ו דִּכְלִילָן תְּלַת אַתְוָון בְּצַדִּיק, לְיַבֵּם ה׳.

98. Uniting Aleph Chet with Dalet is done by means of the righteous, and Boaz, since he overcame his impulse SO AS TO PERFORM LEVIRATE MARRIAGE FOR THE SAKE OF PERFORMING A PRECEPT is considered righteous. This is why he is CALLED Boaz, WHICH IS SPELLED LIKE *Bo Az* (Eng. 'strength in him'), namely, he has a strong impulse. "Lo, El does all these things twice or three times with a man" (Iyov 33:29). This is Yud Hei Vav that include three letters of the Righteous, WHO IS YESOD CALLED MAN, in order to levirate the LAST Hei, WHICH IS MALCHUT.

21. "to confirm all manner of transactions; a man pulled off his shoe"

A Synopsis

We read about the custom in old times concerning redeeming and exchanging where a man pulled off his shoe and gave it to his neighbor; this alludes to a change of name, a change of place and a change of action. We are given the inner meaning of this custom. The Shechinah does not change when she is with God, nor does He change when with her. The meaning of the ritual of the shoe is linked to the meaning of levirate marriage as well.

99. וּבִינָה בֶּן יָ״הּ, בְּגִינָהּ אִתְּמַר, וְזֹאת לְפָנִים בְּיִשְׂרָאֵל עַל הַגְּאוּלָּה וְעַל הַתְּמוּרָה לְקַיֵּים כָּל דָּבָר. הָכָא קָא רָמִיז שִׁנּוּי הַשֵּׁם, וְדָא מצפ״ץ הָכָא, וְזֹאת לְפָנִים בְּיִשְׂרָאֵל. וְדָא שִׁנּוּי מָקוֹם, אֶהְיֶ״ה, אַיֵּה מְקוֹם כְּבוֹדוֹ לְהַעֲרִיצוֹ. יה״ו, אִיהוּ אֶהְיֶ״ה, וְדָא שִׁנּוּי מָקוֹם. שִׁנּוּי מַעֲשֶׂה, אֲדֹנָ״י, א׳ אֶדְיֶ״ד, י׳ יֶדוֹ״ד, תַּרְוַויְיהוּ מִשְׁתַּנִּים בַּאֲדֹנָ״י.

99. Of Binah, the son of Yud Hei, it says, "Now this was the custom in former times in Yisrael concerning redeeming and concerning exchanging, to confirm all manner of transactions; a man pulled off his shoe, and gave it to his neighbor" (Rut 4:7). This alludes to changing name, which is Mem Tzadi Pe Tzadi here. Eheyeh - 'where (Heb. *ayeh*)' is the place of His glory to adore Him – Yud Hei Vav is Eheyeh, which is a change of place. A change in action: in Adonai Aleph OF ADONAI is Eheyeh, Yud OF ADONAI is Yud Hei Vav Hei, and both change in Adonai.

100. וְזֹאת הַתְּעוּדָה בְּיִשְׂרָאֵל, הַתְּעוּדָה, אִימָּא עִלָּאָה, צוֹר תְּעוּדָה חֲתוֹם תּוֹרָה בְּלִמּוּדָי. אִיהוּ חוֹתָם דְּעָלְמָא, חוֹתָם דִּשְׁמַיָּא וְאַרְעָא. עַל הַתְּמוּרָה, שְׁכִינְתָּא תַּתָּאָה. בְּאָן אֲתָר אִתְטַמְּרַת. בְּעוּלֵימָא דִּילָהּ, מְטַטְרוֹ״ן, וְיִשְׁנֶה תַּמָּן, אִיהִי מְשַׁנָּה. וְאָדָם דְּאִתְּמַר בֵּיהּ כְּתִפְאֶרֶת אָדָם לָשֶׁבֶת בָּיִת, מְשַׁנֶּה פָּנָיו וַתְּשַׁלְּחֵהוּ.

100. "and this was the manner of attesting in Yisrael" (Rut 4:7). The attestation is supernal Ima, WHO IS BINAH, AS WRITTEN, "Bind up the testimony, seal the Torah among My disciples" (Yeshayah 8:16). BINDING

IS BINAH, AND SINCE IT IS WRITTEN, "BIND UP THE TESTIMONY" WE DERIVE THAT TESTIMONY OR ATTESTATION IS BINAH, which is the seal of the world, namely the seal of heaven and earth, WHICH ARE ZEIR ANPIN AND MALCHUT. Exchanging refers to the lower Shechinah, NAMELY MALCHUT. Where did MALCHUT hide HERSELF? In her lad, THE ANGEL Metatron, and he changed her. There MALCHUT is CALLED Mishnah. And of man, of whom it says, "according to the beauty of a man; that it (he) may remain in the house" (Yeshayah 44:13), IT SAYS, "You change (Heb. *meshaneh*) his countenance, and send him away" (Iyov 14:20).

101. וּבגִ"ד אוּקְמוּהָ מָארֵי מַתְנִיתִין, לֹא כְּשֶׁאֲנִי נִכְתָּב אֲנִי נִקְרָא בָּעוֹלָם הַזֶּה, נִכְתָּב יֱדֹו"ד, וְנִקְרָא אֲדֹנָ"י. וְהָא כְּתִיב אֲנִי יְיָ' לֹא שָׁנִיתִי. בִּכְתִיבָה לֹא אִשְׁתַּנֵּי, אֲבָל בִּקְרִיאָה אִשְׁתַּנֵּי. דִּכְתִיבָה דְּאִיהוּ אַתְרֵיהּ, לָא אִשְׁתַּנֵּי. בִּקְרִיאָה דְּאִיהִי לְבַר מֵאַתְרֵיהּ, אִשְׁתַּנֵּי. הִשָּׁמֶר מִפָּנָיו וּשְׁמַע בְּקוֹלוֹ אַל תַּמֵּר בּוֹ. בְּגִין דְּשִׁפְחָה דִּילֵיהּ אֲדֹנָ"י, שְׁמָהּ כְּשֵׁם מַטְרוֹנִיתָא. וְקוּדְשָׁא בְּרִיךְ הוּא בֵּיהּ אִשְׁתַּנֵּי, בְּגִין דְּאִיהוּ נַעַר. בֵּיהּ רָזָא יָשׁוּב לִימֵי עֲלוּמָיו.

101. This is why the sages of the Mishnah have explained that 'the way I am spelled is not the way I am pronounced in this world; but spelled Yud Hei Vav Hei and pronounced Adonai'. HE ASKS, yet it is written, "I am Hashem, I do not change" (Malachi 3:6), AND ANSWERS, it is not changed in spelling but is changed in pronunciation since writing INDICATES it does not change in its place, but in reading, WHICH IS THE GRADE OF MALCHUT CALLED SPEECH, when it is outside its place, it does change AND IS PRONOUNCED ADONAI. "Take heed of him, and obey his voice, provoke him not…for My name is in him" (Shemot 23:21), since His handmaid's name is Adonai like the Queen's name. And the Holy One, blessed be He, is changed in him, IN METATRON, because he is a lad. In him is the mystery of, "he shall return to the days of his youth" (Iyov 33:25).

102. אֲבָל שְׁכִינְתָּא אֵצֶל קוּדְשָׁא בְּרִיךְ הוּא לָא מִשְׁתַּנֵּית, וְקוּדְשָׁא בְּרִיךְ הוּא לְגַבָּהּ לָא אִשְׁתַּנֵּי, הה"ד, אֲנִי יְיָ' לֹא שָׁנִיתִי, אֲנִי: שְׁכִינְתָּא. יְיָ': עַמּוּדָא דְּאֶמְצָעִיתָא. שָׁלַף אִישׁ נַעֲלוֹ: דָּא סַנְדַּלְפוֹן, סַנְדָּל אִיהוּ

לְגַבֵּי קוּדְשָׁא בְּרִיךְ הוּא, וְנַעַל לְגַבֵּי שְׁכִינְתָּא. אֲבָל תִּפְאֶרֶת, דִּכְלִיל שִׁית סְפִירָן, אִיהוּ גּוּפָא לַיְדֹוָ"ד. וּמַלְכוּת, גּוּפָא לִשְׁכִינְתָּא, דְּאִיהוּ אֲדֹנָי.

102. But the Shechinah, when with the Holy One, blessed be He, does not change, nor does the Holy One, blessed be He, change when with Her. This is the meaning of, "I am Hashem, I do not change." "I" is the Shechinah; Yud Hei Vav Hei is the Central Pillar, NAMELY ZEIR ANPIN; "a man pulled off his shoe" refers to Sandalphon, who is a sandal by the Holy One, blessed be He, and a shoe by the Shechinah. But Tiferet that includes six Sfirot is a body to the Name Yud Hei Vav Hei, and Malchut is a body to the Shechinah that is Adonai.

103. וְנִגְּשָׁה יְבִמְתּוֹ אֵלָיו לְעֵינֵי הַזְּקֵנִים וְחָלְצָה נַעֲלוֹ מֵעַל רַגְלוֹ וְגוֹ'. פִּקּוּדָא דָא, לַחֲלוֹץ. וְהַאי אִיהוּ חֲלִיצַת רוּחָא מֵהַהוּא גּוּפָא, דְּבָעֵי לְאַנְהָגָא עִמֵּיהּ כְּאָח, וְהַהוּא קְשִׁירָא דְּאַחְוָה דְּעִם אָחוּהָ מַתִּיר מִנֵּיהּ, וְהַהוּא רוּחָא אָזִיל נָע וָנָד, עַד דְּאַשְׁכַּח פָּרוֹקָא. הה"ד, אוֹ דוֹדוֹ אוֹ בֶן דּוֹדוֹ יִגְאָלֶנּוּ אוֹ מִשְּׁאֵר בְּשָׂרוֹ וְגוֹ'. וְאִי לָא אַשְׁכַּח, וְהִשִּׂיגָה יָדוֹ וְנִגְאָל. כְּאוֹרֵחַ דְּאָזִיל מֵאֲתָר לַאֲתָר, אוֹ כְּעֶבֶד דְּאָזִיל בְּשַׁלְשֶׁלֶת עַל צַוְּארֵיהּ, עַד דְּאַשְׁכַּח פִּדְיוֹן מֵאָדוֹן דִּילֵיהּ עַל חוֹבֵיהּ. וַוי לְמַאן דְּלָא אֲנָח בֵּן לְמִפְרַק יָתֵיהּ.

103. "then shall his brother's wife approach him in the presence of the elders, and loose his shoe from off his foot, and spit in his face…" (Devarim 25:9). It is a precept to perform Chalitzah. It is the loosening (Heb. *Chalitzah*) of the spirit from that body to which he needs to connect as a brother AND MARRY HIS WIFE; he releases him from the brother's tie, AND THE WIDOW NEEDS HIM NO LONGER. That spirit OF THE DEAD THAT IS SEPARATED FROM HIS BROTHER THROUGH THE CHALITZAH goes away and wanders until it is redeemed. This is what is meant by, "either his uncle, or his uncle's son, may redeem him, or any that is near of kin to him…" (Vayikra 25:49). But if he finds not, "his means suffice, he may redeem himself" (Ibid.), AND HE NEEDS TO WAIT UNTIL HE ACQUIRES ENOUGH FOR HIS OWN REDEMPTION. AND THE SPIRIT OF THE DEAD is like a guest going from place to place or like a servant walking with a chain around his neck until he achieves redemption from his Master from his iniquities, NAMELY BY MEANS OF REINCARNATION. Woe to him who did not leave a son who will redeem him.

22. One who acts with piety to his Master

A Synopsis

We are told that a prisoner cannot release himself from prison, and the Faithful Shepherd says that God regards one who prays and does charity and occupies himself with Torah to have redeemed Him and His children from among the heathen nations. Stress is placed on the necessity to meditate only on redeeming the Shechinah from exile. Elijah and the heads of the Yeshivot tells Moses that he is the son of the King and Queen, and that his worship is done with the love of a son who will risk his life for his parents' sakes. The Faithful Shepherd prostrates himself before God and says that even though he has nothing to offer Him, still God desires the heart of man to be willing to do anything for Him. Next God comes to bless and kiss the Faithful Shepherd, and says that he is indeed His son.

104. וְאֵלִיָּהוּ וְרַבָּנָן וּמָארֵי מְתִיבְתָּאן, הָכָא רָמִיז, אֵין חָבוּשׁ מַתִּיר עַצְמוֹ מִבֵּית הָאֲסוּרִין. דְּאִיהוּ קָשׁוּר בְּקִשּׁוּרָא דִּתְפִלִּין דְּיָד, וְאָסוּר בִּתְפִלִּין דְּרֵישָׁא, כַּד לֵית לֵיהּ בֵּן לְמִפְרַק לֵיהּ, מִסִּטְרָא דְּבֶן יָ״הּ. בְּהַהוּא קִשִּׁירוּ אִיהוּ אָח חָבוּשׁ וְאָסוּר, דְּלֵית לֵיהּ רְשׁוּ לְמִפְרַק יַת גַּרְמֵיהּ, דְּאִיהוּ ד׳ עַצְמוֹ דְּאָח, עֶצֶם מֵעֲצָמַי קָרָא לָהּ לְגַבֵּיהּ, בְּקַרְקַפְתָּא דִּתְפִלִּין דְּרֵישָׁא. וּבָשָׂר מִבְּשָׂרִי קָרָא לָהּ מִסִּטְרָא דְּלִבָּא.

104. Elijah and heads of the Yeshivot, LISTEN. It is indicated here that a prisoner cannot release himself from prison. For he, ZEIR ANPIN, is tied by the knot of the hand Tefilin and bound by the head Tefilin, when he has no son, NAMELY A MAN WHO WILL WORSHIP THE HOLY ONE, BLESSED BE HE, NOT FOR THE SAKE OF RECEIVING A REWARD, WHO IS CALLED A SON TO THE HOLY ONE, BLESSED BE HE, who will redeem him through the aspect of the son of Yud Hei. THAT IS, IF HE WHO PUTS ON TEFILIN IS NOT A CHARIOT TO THE SON OF YUD HEI, WHO IS ZEIR ANPIN, NAMELY, IF HE DOES NOT MEDITATE ON PLEASING HIS MAKER LIKE A SON WHO WORKS FOR HIS FATHER NOT TO RECEIVE A REWARD, THEN by that knot OF TEFILIN the Holy One, blessed be He, is a tied and bound brother, who has no permission to redeem himself, he being Dalet OF ECHAD, which is itself (or: is the bone) of Aleph and Chet OF ECHAD, WHICH IS ZEIR ANPIN. ZEIR ANPIN called it "bone of my bones" (Beresheet 2:23) in the skull where the head Tefilin is put, and called it "flesh of my flesh" (Ibid.) from the aspect of the heart.

105. וְלָא לְמַגָּנָא אָמַר קוּדְשָׁא בְּרִיךְ הוּא, כָּל הָעוֹסֵק בַּתּוֹרָה וּבִגְמִילוּת חֲסָדִים וּמִתְפַּלֵּל עִם הַצִּבּוּר, מַעֲלֶה אֲנִי עָלָיו כְּאִלּוּ פְּדָאַנִי לִי וּלְבָנַי מִבֵּין העכו"ם. וְכַמָּה בְּנֵי נָשָׁא דְּקָא מִשְׁתַּדְּלֵי בְּאוֹרַיְיתָא, וְעַבְדֵּי גְּמִילוּת חֲסָדִים, וּמְצַלִּין, וְלָא אִתְפְּרַק קוּדְשָׁא בְּרִיךְ הוּא וּשְׁכִינְתֵּיהּ וְיִשְׂרָאֵל. אֶלָּא דְּיִשְׁתַּדַּל בְּאוֹרַיְיתָא, לְחַבֵּר יָתָהּ בְּקוּדְשָׁא בְּרִיךְ הוּא. וּגְמִילוּת חֶסֶד, הָא אוֹקְמוּהָ, דְּהָא אֵין חָסִיד אֶלָּא הַמִּתְחַסֵּד עִם קוֹנוֹ, דְּכָל פִּקּוּדִין דְּעָבֵיד, לְמִפְרַק בְּהוּ שְׁכִינְתֵּיהּ, וּבְהָא עָבֵיד חֶסֶד עִם קוּדְשָׁא בְּרִיךְ הוּא.

105. Not in vain did the Holy One, blessed be He, say that 'whoever is occupied with the Torah and charity and prays with the congregation, I regard him as if he redeemed Me and My children from among the heathen'. HE ASKS, YET many people are occupied in the Torah and charity and pray with the congregation, yet the Holy One, blessed be He, and His Shechinah are not redeemed. AND HE ANSWERS that THE MEANING IS he should study Torah in order to unite the Shechinah with the Holy One, blessed be He, AND NOT FOR ANY OTHER PURPOSE. As for charity, we have explained that a Chasid (Eng. 'pious man') is a man who acts with kindness (Chesed) with his Maker, WHICH MEANS THAT all the commandments he performs are done in order to redeem THROUGH THEIR MERIT the Shechinah FROM EXILE, AND NOT FOR ANY OTHER PURPOSE. By that he acts with piety with the Holy One, blessed be He, AND IS CALLED PIOUS.

106. מַאן דְּגָמִיל חֶסֶד בִּשְׁכִינְתֵּיהּ, עִם קוּדְשָׁא בְּרִיךְ הוּא גָּמִיל. בְּגִין דְּכַד חָבוּ יִשְׂרָאֵל, וְקוּדְשָׁא בְּרִיךְ הוּא הֲוָה בָּעֵי לְיַסְּרָא לוֹן, אִימָּא הֲוַת רְבִיעָא עֲלַיְיהוּ, עַד דְּנַפְקוּ לְתַרְבּוּת רָעָה. קוּדְשָׁא בְּרִיךְ הוּא מַה עָבֵיד. תָּרִיךְ בְּנֵי מַלְכָּא וּמַטְרוֹנִיתָא. וְאִיהוּ אוֹמֵי, דְּלָא יְהַדַּר לְאַתְרֵיהּ, עַד דְּמַטְרוֹנִיתָא אִתְהַדְּרַת לְאַתְרָהָא. וּמַאן דְּהָדַר בִּתְשׁוּבָה, וְגָמִיל חֶסֶד בִּשְׁכִינְתָּא, וּבְכָל אוֹרַיְיתָא וּבְפִקּוּדִין דִּילָהּ, וְלָאו אִיהִי אֶלָּא לְמִפְרַק

שְׁכִינְתָּא, דָּא עָבֵיד חֶסֶד עִם קוֹנוֹ, וּכְאִילוּ פָּרִיק לֵיהּ וּלִשְׁכִינְתֵּיהּ וְלִבְנוֹי.

106. Whoever is charitable with the Shechinah, TO BRING HER OUT OF EXILE, is charitable with the Holy One, blessed be He, since when Yisrael sinned and the Holy One, blessed be He, wanted to afflict them, Ima, NAMELY THE SHECHINAH, brooded over them AND STOPPED THE HOLY ONE, BLESSED BE HE FROM AFFLICTING THEM. This was so until they fell into bad ways. The Holy One, blessed be He then exiled the King's children, NAMELY YISRAEL, together with the Queen, WHO IS THE SHECHINAH, and swore He shall not return to His place until the Queen returns to Hers. THUS a man who is charitable with the Shechinah and repents, and in all Her Torah and precepts MEDITATES only on redeeming the Shechinah FROM EXILE, acts with piety towards his Maker and it is as if he redeemed Him and His Shechinah and His children FROM EXILE.

107. אָמַר אֵלִיָּהוּ וְכָל רָאשֵׁי מְתִיבְתָּאן, רַעְיָא מְהֵימְנָא, אַנְתְּ הוּא הַאי ב"נ, אַנְתְּ הוּא בַּר מִן מַלְכָּא וּמַטְרוֹנִיתָא, דְּאִשְׁתַּדְּלוּתָא דִּילָךְ לְגַבֵּי קוּדְשָׁא בְּרִיךְ הוּא, לָאו כְּמַאן דְּעָבֵיד חֶסֶד עִם קוֹנוֹ, אֶלָּא כִּבְרָא דִּמְחוּיָּיב לְשַׁוּוֵיהּ גַּרְמֵיהּ וְתוּקְפֵּיהּ לְמִפְרַק אַבָּא וְאִימָּא, וּמָסַר גַּרְמֵיהּ לְמִיתָה עֲלַיְיהוּ. דְּמַאן דְּלָאו אִיהוּ בְּרָא דְּמַלְכָּא, וְעָבֵד טִיבוּ עִם מַלְכָּא וְעִם מַטְרוֹנִיתָא, וַדַּאי הַאי אִתְחֲשִׁיב דְּעָבֵיד חֶסֶד עִם קוֹנוֹ.

107. Elijah and all the heads of the Yeshivot said, Faithful Shepherd, you are that man, you are the son of the King and the Queen, whose worship to the Holy One, blessed be He is not EVEN that of one who is pious with his Maker, but that of a son who is obliged to gird himself and his strength to redeem his father and mother and risk his life for their sakes. For whoever is not the son of the King yet acts with kindness by the King and Queen, surely is regarded thus that he acts with kindness with his Maker. BUT YOU WHO ARE THE SON OF THE KING, FOR YOU IT IS A DUTY RATHER THAN KINDNESS.

108. קָם רַעְיָא מְהֵימְנָא, וְאִשְׁתְּטַח קַמֵּי קוּדְשָׁא בְּרִיךְ הוּא וּבָכָה, וְאָמַר כֵּן יְהֵא רַעֲוָא דִּילֵיהּ, דְּיִתְחֲשִׁיב לִי כְּבַר, דְּעוֹבָדִין דִּילִי לְגַבֵּי קוּדְשָׁא

בְּרִיךְ הוּא וּשְׁכִינְתֵּיהּ יְהוֹן לְגַבֵּיהּ כִּבְרָא דְּאִשְׁתְּדַּל בְּהוֹן בָּתַר אֲבוֹי וְאִמֵּיהּ, דְּרָחִים לוֹן יַתִּיר מִגַּרְמֵיהּ וְנַפְשֵׁיהּ רוּחֵיהּ וְנִשְׁמָתֵיהּ, וְכָל מַה דַּהֲוָה לֵיהּ הֲוָה חָשִׁיב לוֹן לְאַיִן, לְמֶעְבַּד בְּהוֹן רְעוּתֵיהּ דְּאַבָּא וְאִמָּא, וּלְמִפְרַק לוֹן בְּהוֹן. וְאע״ג דְּיָדַעְנָא דְּכֹלָּא בִּרְשׁוּתֵיהּ, רַחֲמָנָא לִבָּא בָּעֵי. בְּהַהוּא זִמְנָא אָתָא קוּדְשָׁא בְּרִיךְ הוּא וְנָשִׁיק לֵיהּ, וְאָמַר, רַעְיָא מְהֵימְנָא, וַדַּאי אַנְתְּ הוּא בְּרָא דִּילִי, וְדִשְׁכִינְתָּא. רַבָּנָן וּמַלְאָכִין נַשְּׁקוּ בַר קָמוּ כֻּלְּהוּ וְנַשְּׁקוּ לֵיהּ, וְקַבִּילוּ לֵיהּ לְרַב וּמַלְכָּא עֲלַיְיהוּ.

108. The Faithful Shepherd rose and prostrated himself before the Holy One, blessed be He. He wept and said, may it please Him to regard me as a son, that my doings towards the Holy One, blessed be He and His Shechinah will be considered by them as those of a son who strives to do them for his father and mother, whom he loves more than he loves himself, his own Nefesh, Ruach and Neshamah. Whatever he has he regards as naught, so as to do with them his father's and mother's wishes and redeem them through them. And though I know everything is His domain AND I HAVE NOTHING TO OFFER HIM, yet the Merciful desires the heart OF MAN TO BE WILLING TO DO ANYTHING. At that time the Holy One, blessed be He came to him, kissed him, and He said, Faithful Shepherd, you are indeed My son and the son of the Shechinah. Sages and angels, kiss the son. They all rose and kissed him and accepted him as a Rabbi and king over them.

23. Cutting off the seed of Amalek

A Synopsis

The Faithful Shepherd talks about Amalek and how the names of Bilaam and Balak are marked in it. He tells us of the four facets of Yisrael – Jacob and Rachel, and Israel and Leah – and says that these correspond to the four faces of the eagle. Similarly there are four facets to Amalek – divination, enchantment, iniquity and perverseness. Amalek above is Samael, whose facets tempt people to sin against God.

109. וְהָיָה בְּהָנִיחַ יְיָ׳ אֱלֹהֶיךָ וְגוֹ׳, תִּמְחֶה אֶת זֵכֶר עֲמָלֵק וְגוֹ׳. פִּקּוּדָא דָא, לְהַכְרִית זַרְעוֹ שֶׁל עֲמָלֵק. דְּהָא קוּדְשָׁא בְּרִיךְ הוּא אוֹמֵי, דְּלָא יַחֲזוֹר עַל כֻּרְסְיֵהּ, עַד דְּיִטּוֹל נוּקְמָא מִנֵּיהּ. פָּתַח רַעְיָא מְהֵימְנָא וְאָמַר. וַדַּאי, בְּגִ״ד הֲווֹ אַזְלֵי בְּמַדְבְּרָא וְעַל יַמָּא, וְלָא יֵיעֲלוּן בְּאַרְעָא דְּיִשְׂרָאֵל, עַד דְּיִטּוֹל נוּקְמָא מִנֵּיהּ דַּעֲמָלֵק.

109. "Therefore it shall be, when Hashem your Elohim has given you rest…you shall blot out the remembrance of Amalek…" (Devarim 25:19). For the Holy One, blessed be He has sworn not to return to His throne before He takes revenge from it. The Faithful Shepherd opened and said, surely this is why they were traveling in the wilderness and by the sea, and did not enter the land of Yisrael until He would take revenge on Amalek.

110. עֲמָלֵק מַאן הוּא לְעֵילָּא, דְּהָא חֲזֵינָן דְּבִלְעָם וּבָלָק מִתַּמָּן הֲווֹ נִשְׁמָתִין דִּלְהוֹן, וּבְגִין דָּא הֲווֹ שַׂנְאִין לְיִשְׂרָאֵל יַתִּיר מִכָּל אוּמָּה וְלִישָּׁן, וּבְגִ״ד עֲמָלֵק רָשִׁים בִּשְׁמֵהוֹן, ע״ם מִן בִּלְעָם, ל״ק מִן בָּלָק, וּדְכַר וְנוּקְבָּא אִינּוּן עֲמָלֵקִים. וְעָלַיְיהוּ אִתְּמַר, לֹא הִבִּיט אָוֶן בְּיַעֲקֹב וְלֹא רָאָה עָמָל בְּיִשְׂרָאֵל.

110. HE ASKS, who is THE ROOT OF Amalek above IN THE SPIRITUAL SENSE? We see that the souls of Bilaam and Balak came from there, FROM CELESTIAL AMALEK, and this is why they had more enmity towards Yisrael than any nation or tongue. This is why AMALEK is marked in their names, NAMELY Am of Bilaam and Lek of Balak. The Amalekites are male and female and of them it says, "He has not beheld iniquity in Jacob nor has he seen perverseness in Israel" (Bemidbar 23:21), WHERE INIQUITY IS THE MALE SIDE OF AMALEK AND PERVERSENESS IS ITS FEMALE.

111. כְּגַוְונָא דְּאִית בְּיִשְׂרָאֵל אַרְבַּע אַנְפִּין, יַעֲקֹב, יִשְׂרָאֵל, רָחֵל, לֵאָה. יִשְׂרָאֵל עִם לֵאָה, יַעֲקֹב עִם רָחֵל, לָקֳבֵל, וּפְנֵי נֶשֶׁר לְאַרְבַּעְתָּם. הָכִי אִית אַרְבַּע אַנְפִּין לַעֲמָלֵק, קֶסֶם, וְנַחַשׁ, עָמָל, וָאָוֶן. עָמָל רָשִׁים בַּעֲמָלֵק. וְהָמָן דַּהֲוָה מִסִּטְרָא דַּעֲמָלֵק, יָשׁוּב עֲמָלוֹ בְּרֹאשׁוֹ. וְכָל אַלּוּפֵי עֵשָׂו מֵעֲמָלֵק הֲווֹ. וּלְעֵילָּא עֲמָלֵק, סָמָאֵל. עָמָל, נַחַשׁ, אָוֶן, וּמִרְמָה. דְּמְפַתֵּי לֵיהּ לְב״נ לְמֶחֱטֵי לְקוּדְשָׁא בְּרִיךְ הוּא. קֶסֶ״ם, ק׳ מִן עֲמָלֵק ס״ם מִן סָמָאֵ״ל. נַחַ״שׁ, אֵ״ל מִסָּמָאֵל

111. Yisrael has four facets, Jacob, Israel, Rachel and Leah, IN WHICH Israel and Leah ARE MALE AND FEMALE and Jacob with Rachel ARE MALE AND FEMALE. THESE FOUR correspond to, "they four also had the face of an eagle" (Yechezkel 1:10), THAT IS, WHICH CORRESPOND TO THE FOUR FACES OF THE EAGLE, SINCE JACOB AND ISRAEL ARE THE ASPECT OF AN EAGLE THAT IS THE CENTRAL COLUMN. Similarly there are four facets to Amalek, which are divination, enchantment, iniquity and perverseness. The letters of iniquity (Heb. *amal*) are present in Amalek, and OF Haman, who descended from Amalek IT SAYS, "His mischief (Heb. *amal*) shall return upon his own head" (Tehilim 7:17). And all the chiefs of Esau came from Amalek. Amalek above is Samael WHO HAS FOUR OF THEIR FACETS, WHICH ARE iniquity, enchantment, perverseness and deceit. They tempt man to sin against the Holy One, blessed be He. Divination (Heb. *kesem*) is Kof of Amalek, poison (Heb. *sam*) from Samael, enchantment is El of Samael (THE END IS MISSING).

24. One must not start anything on Monday or Wednesday

A Synopsis

We learn of the astrological reasons for not starting anything on a Monday or a Wednesday. Both the children of Yisrael and the children of Ishmael calculate according to the moon, but Yisrael are attached to its good part and the children of Ishmael to its evil part. We are told that the dominion of both Saturn and Shabbat is on the seventh day, the day of rest. People should not start things on Mondays or Wednesdays because Gehenom was created on the second day and the eclipse of the luminaries on the fourth day.

112. עָלֵיהּ אִתְּמַר לְאַבְרָהָם, לֶךְ לְךָ מֵאַרְצְךָ וּמִמּוֹלַדְתְּךָ וּמִבֵּית אָבִיךָ, בֵּית מוֹלָד דִּילָךְ, מֵאִלֵּין בָּתֵּי סִיהֲרָא, אוֹ בָּתֵּי שַׁבְּתַאי, אוֹ בָּתֵּי מַאֲדִים. דְּבָתֵּי מַאֲדִים וּבָתֵּי שַׁבְּתַאי וּלְבָנָה, עָלַיְיהוּ אִתְּמַר, אֵין מַתְחִילִין בב"ד. דְּמַאֲדִים סוּמָקוּ דְּחַמָּה, גֵּיהִנָּם, אִימָּא דְּעֵשָׂו, דְּאִתְיְילִידַת בְּיוֹמָא תִּנְיָינָא. וְסִיהֲרָא, אִיהוּ טוֹב וָרָע, טוֹב בְּמִילוּאָהּ. וְרַע בְּחֶסְרוֹנָהּ.

112. Regarding it Abraham was told, "Get you out of your country, and from your kindred, and from your father's house" (Beresheet 12:1), namely, from your nativity, WHICH IS THE ASTROLOGY OF STARS AND CONSTELLATIONS, from those houses of the moon, of Saturn, or Mars – since it says of Mars, Saturn and the moon that one must not start things on Monday and Wednesday, because Mars has in itself the redness of the sun, WHICH INDICATES Gehenom, Esau's mother, who was born on the second day OF THE WORKS OF CREATION, WHICH IS WHY WE DO NOT START ON MONDAY. The moon is both good and evil, good when it shines FULLY and evil when it is in ITS DAYS OF wane.

113. וּבְגִין דְּאִיהִי כְּלִילָא מִטּוֹב וָרָע, מוֹנִין בָּהּ יִשְׂרָאֵל וּמוֹנִין בָּהּ בְּנֵי יִשְׁמָעֵאל. וְכַד לָקַת בְּמִלּוּאָה, סִימָנָא לָא טַב לְיִשְׂרָאֵל. וְכַד לָקַת בְּחֶסְרוֹנָהּ, סִימַן רָע לַיִשְׁמְעֵאלִים. וּבְהַאי וְאָבְדָה חָכְמַת חֲכָמָיו, חָכְמָה דְּיִשְׁמְעֵאלִים, וּבִינַת נְבוֹנִים תִּסְתַּתָּר, דְּאִינּוּן לָא יַדְעִין בִּבְרִיאָתָן, אֶלָּא בְּשִׁמּוּשָׁא דִּילְהוֹן, כְּפִי שִׁנּוּי עָלְמָא בַּהֲלִיכָתָן וְשִׁימּוּשָׁן. וְסִיהֲרָא אִתְבְּרִיאַת בְּיוֹמָא רְבִיעָאָה, וּבְחֶסְרוֹנָהּ דִּילָהּ עֲנִיּוּת, אִתְבְּרִיאַת לִילִית,

שַׁבְּתַאי, דְּאִיהוּ רָעָב וְצִמָּאוֹן וְלָקוּתָא דִּנְהוֹרִין. עָלָהּ אִתְּמַר, יְהִי מְאֹרֹת חָסֵר. מְאֵרַת יְיָ׳ בְּבֵית רָשָׁע. וְחוֹטֵא יִלָּכֶד בָּהּ, בְּבֵית הַסֹּהַר דִּילָהּ, וְצַדִּיק יִמָּלֵט מִמֶּנָּה.

113. Since THE MOON comprehends good and evil, Yisrael calculate according to it and the children of Ishmael calculate according to it. YISRAEL ARE ATTACHED TO ITS GOOD PART AND THE CHILDREN OF ISHMAEL TO ITS EVIL PART. When it is eclipsed during its fullness, WHICH IS ITS GOOD PART, it is a bad sign for Yisrael, and when it is eclipsed during its waning it is a bad sign for the Ishmaelites. Of it, IT IS WRITTEN, "for the wisdom of their wise men shall perish" (Yeshayah 29:14), namely the wisdom of the Ishmaelites, "and the understanding of their prudent men shall be hid" (Ibid.), because they do not know about the creation OF THE STARS but of their customs, according to changes in the world and their calculation. The moon was created on the fourth day OF THE WORKS OF CREATION and when it is waning, when there is poverty, Lilit was created, who is Saturn, which is hunger and thirst and the eclipse of the luminaries. It says of her, "Let there be lights (Heb. *me'orot*)" (Beresheet 1:14) spelled without Vav, WHICH MEANS A CURSE, AS WRITTEN, "The curse (Heb. *me'erat*) of Hashem is in the house of the wicked" (Mishlei 3:33), AND ALSO, "but the sinner shall be caught by her" (Kohelet 7:26) and the righteous, "shall escape from her" (Ibid.). THIS IS WHY WE DO NOT START THINGS ON WEDNESDAY.

114. וְאִית כֹּכָבָא אַחֲרָא, נְקוּדָה זְעֵירָא, נָקוּד עַל סִיהֲרָא דְּאִיהוּ מְאֹרֹת, וְדָא חוֹלָם, בַּת מֶלֶךְ, שַׁבָּת מַלְכְּתָא. דְּשֻׁלְטָנוּתָא דְּתַרְוַויְיהוּ בְּיוֹם שְׁבִיעִי, דְּאִתְּמַר בֵּיהּ, לְמַעַן יָנוּחַ עַבְדְּךָ וַאֲמָתְךָ. דְּסֵדֶר בְּרִיאָתָן לָאו כְּסֵדֶר שִׁמּוּשָׁן. וּבג״ד חַמָּ״ה וּמַ״אֲדִים סוּמָקֵי דְּגֵיהִנָּם, אִתְבְּרִיאוּ בְּיוֹמָא תִּנְיָינָא. לְבָנָה שַׁבְּתַאי, אִתְבְּרִיאוּ בְּיוֹמָא רְבִיעָאָה, כַּפְנָא וַחֲשׁוֹכָא. וּבג״ד אֵין מַתְחִילִין בב״ד, בְּגִין דְּגֵיהִנָּם אִתְבְּרֵי בְּיוֹמָא תִּנְיָינָא, וְלָקוּתָא דִּנְהוֹרִין בְּיוֹמָא רְבִיעָאָה.

114. There is another star, which is a small dot over the moon, which is a luminary. This is the dot Cholam CALLED a King's daughter, Queen

Shabbat. And the dominion of both SATURN (HEB. *SHABTAI*) AND SHABBAT is on the seventh day, of which it says, "that your manservant and your maidservant may rest" (Devarim 5:14). For the order of their creation is not like the order of calculation. This is why the sun and Mars, which are red and OF THE ASPECT OF Gehenom, were created on the second day OF THE WORKS OF CREATION, and the moon and Saturn were created on the fourth day OF THE WORKS OF CREATION, SINCE SATURN INDICATES hunger and darkness. This is why we do not start on Monday or Wednesday, since Gehenom was created on the second day and the eclipse of the luminaries on the fourth day.

25. "and a handmaid that is heir to her mistress"

A Synopsis

We are told that the sages of Mishnah disagree regarding the giving of the Torah, one thinking that it was given on the third day and another thinking that it was given on the seventh day. Mention of the stars and the moon and the sun and the planets are brought in to clarify the argument. We learn that there are twelve constellations from the good side and twelve from the evil side. Lastly we are told that the wicked are the forefathers of impurity and that an evil man is considered to be dead.

115. כֹּכָ"ב, עָלֵיהּ אִתְּמַר, דָּרַךְ כֹּכָב מִיַּעֲקֹב. דְּדַרְגֵּיהּ בְּיוֹמָא תְּלִיתָאָה. וּבֵיהּ וַיְהִי בַּיּוֹם הַשְּׁלִישִׁי בִּהְיוֹת הַבֹּקֶר, דְּבֵיהּ נָחִית קוּדְשָׁא בְּרִיךְ הוּא לְמֵיהַב אוֹרַיְיתָא לְיִשְׂרָאֵל, בַּת יְחִידָה, לְמֶהֱוֵי עִמֵּיהּ שַׁבָּת מַלְכְּתָא. דְּאִיהוּ יוֹם שְׁלִישִׁי, כָּלִיל תְּלַת עַנְפֵי אֲבָהָן, ש', בַּת יְחִידָאָה, דְּשֻׁלְטָנוּתָא דִילָהּ בְּלֵיל שַׁבָּת, בֵּיהּ אִתְעָבֵידַת שַׁבָּת.

115. Of the star it says, "there shall come a star out of Jacob" (Bemidbar 24:17), WHICH IS THE CENTRAL COLUMN. Its grade is in the third day OF THE WORKS OF CREATION and it says of it, "And it came to pass on the third day in the morning" (Shemot 19:16), in which the Holy One, blessed be He, descended to give the Torah to Yisrael, THE TORAH BEING an only daughter, NAMELY MALCHUT, to be with it, WITH THE THIRD DAY, WHICH IS TIFERET, as Queen Shabbat. For the third day includes the three branches of the patriarchs, NAMELY THE THREE BRANCHES OF SHIN, WHICH ARE CHESED, GVURAH AND TIFERET, and the only daughter, WHICH IS MALCHUT, whose dominion is on Shabbat eve, becomes Shabbat in it, IN THE THIRD DAY, BECAUSE SHABBAT IS COMPOSED OF THE LETTER SHIN PLUS *BAT* (ENG. 'DAUGHTER'), IN WHICH SHIN ALLUDES TO THE THREE SFIROT CHESED, GVURAH AND TIFERET, WHICH ARE ATTACHED TO THE DAUGHTER, MALCHUT.

116. וּבג"ד חוּלְקִין מָארֵי מַתְנִיתִין עַל מַתַּן תּוֹרָה, בַּת יְחִידָה. דָּא אָמַר, בַּשְּׁלִישִׁי נִתְּנָה תּוֹרָה. וְדָא אָמַר, בַּשְּׁבִיעִי נִתְּנָה תּוֹרָה. וְאִיהִי בַּת יְחִידָה, דַּאֲחִידַת בְּעַמּוּדָא דְּאֶמְצָעִיתָא, תְּלִיתָאָה לַאֲבָהָן. וּבְצַדִּיק,

שְׁבִיעִית לֵיהּ בַּת יְחִידָאָה. וְכַד אִיהִי עֲטָרָה עַל רֵישֵׁיהּ, אִתְקְרֵי בֵּיהּ שְׁבִיעִי, דְּהוּא שְׁשִׁי הֲוָה, דְּכֹכָב דִּילֵיהּ צֶדֶק, וּבַת יְחִידָה שַׁבָּת מַלְכְּתָא אִתְקְרֵי צֶדֶק. וּבְגִין דָּא, תּוֹרָה אֲחִידָא בֵּין יוֹם ג׳ וְז׳.

116. This is why the Mishnah sages disagree regarding the giving of the Torah, which is an only daughter. One said the Torah was given on the third day and another said it was given on the seventh day, since she is an only daughter attached to the Central Pillar, which is the third of the patriarchs, NAMELY TIFERET, ACCORDING TO WHICH THE TORAH WAS GIVEN ON THE THIRD DAY. AND MALCHUT is attached to the Righteous, WHO IS YESOD, NAMELY THE SIXTH DAY, and the only daughter, WHO IS MALCHUT, is seventh to him. And when she is a crown over his head, she is considered seventh with regard to him, as he, YESOD is sixth, and his planet is Jupiter (Heb. *tzedek*). And the only daughter, Queen Shabbat, is called righteousness (Heb. *tzedek*) and hence the Torah, MALCHUT, is attached between the third DAY and the seventh DAY. SOME THEREFORE SAY THAT THE TORAH WAS GIVEN ON THE THIRD DAY AND SOME SAY THE TORAH WAS GIVEN ON THE SEVENTH.

117. וְאִיהוּ כ״ב מִן כּוֹכָ״ב, כ״ו כִּי שֶׁמֶשׁ וּמָגֵן יְדֹוָ״ד צְבָאוֹת, שְׁכִינְתָּא מַלְכוּת הַקֹּדֶשׁ, בְּךָ יְבָרֵךְ יִשְׂרָאֵל, כ״ב אַתְוָון דְּאוֹרַיְיתָא. כּוֹכָב, כְּלִילָא מִתְּלַת דַּרְגִּין, כ׳, כֶּתֶר. ב׳ בִּינָה. יְדֹוָ״ד כָּלִיל תַּרְוַויְיהוּ, חָכְמָה. וְכֹלָּא כָּלִיל כּוֹכָ״ב, דַּרְגָּא דְּעַמּוּדָא דְּאֶמְצָעִיתָא, וּשְׁכִינְתָּא.

117. And she, MALCHUT, is Caf Bet of the star (Heb. *kochav*, *Caf Bet Caf Vav*). Caf Vav OF THE STAR IS THE NUMERICAL VALUE OF YUD HEI VAV HEI, ACCORDING TO THE SECRET OF, "For Hashem Elohim is a sun and shield" (Tehilim 84:12). The Shechinah is Malchut of holiness, OF WHOM IT SAYS, "By you (Heb. *becha*, *Bet Caf*) shall Yisrael bless" (Beresheet 48:20), BEING CAF BET OF THE STAR. And She is the secret of the Caf Bet (22) letters of the Torah. A star includes three grades. Caf OF KOCHAV is Keter, Bet is Binah, CAF VAV OF KOCHAV, WHICH IS Yud Hei Vav Hei, includes both, and is Chochmah. The star includes everything, INCLUDING ALSO the grade of the Central Pillar, WHICH IS CAF VAV OF MERCURY THAT HAS THE SAME NUMERICAL VALUE AS YUD HEI VAV HEI. IT INCORPORATES the Shechinah, WHO IS CAF BET OF KOCHAV, AS SAID BEFORE.

118. אִיהִי לְבָנָה, לִבּוּן הַהֲלָכָה, רַחֲמֵי, בְּסִטְרָא דְּחֶסֶד. וְאִתְקְרִיאַת חַמָּה, בָּרָה כַּחַמָּה, מִסִּטְרָא דִּגְבוּרָה, פְּנֵי מֹשֶׁה כִּפְנֵי חַמָּה. סִיהֲרָא אֲפֵילָה, מִעוּט דְּסִיהֲרָא, שִׁפְחָה דִּילָהּ גֵּיהִנָּם, חַמָּה בִּישָׁא. שִׁפְחָה דִּילֵיהּ שַׁבְּתַאי, לָקוּתָא דִּנְהוֹרִין, חִילּוּל שַׁבָּת. שִׁפְחָה, דְּאָהַדְרַת עוֹרֶף לִגְבִירְתָּהּ בְּכָל יוֹמָא וְיוֹמָא וְאִתְגַּבְּרַת עָלָהּ בְּחוֹבִין דְּיִשְׂרָאֵל בְּנָהָא. הה״ד, וְשִׁפְחָה כִּי תִירַשׁ גְּבִירְתָּהּ. דְּשׁוּלְטָנוּתָא דְּשִׁפְחָה, לָא הֲוֵי אֶלָּא בְּיוֹמָא תִּנְיָינָא, בַּגֵּיהִנָּם. וּבָרְבִיעִי, בְּלָקוּתָא דִּנְהוֹרִין. וְאִתְהַדְּרַת לְשַׁלְטָאָה בְּכָל יוֹמָא וְיוֹמָא.

118. She, THE SHECHINAH, is CALLED the moon (Heb. *levanah*), namely clarification (Heb. *libun*) of the Halachah, which is Mercy from the aspect of Chesed. She is also called the sun, clear as the sun, from the aspect of Gvurah, the face of Moses being as the face of the sun. A waning moon is a dark moon, her handmaid OF MALCHUT that is Gehenom and an evil sun. ALSO her handmaid is Saturn, which is the eclipse of the luminaries and the desecration of Shabbat. She is a handmaid that turns her back on her mistress, MALCHUT, every day and overcomes her because of the iniquities of Yisrael her children. This is the meaning of, “and a handmaid that is heir to her mistress” (Mishlei 30:23). The handmaid rules mainly on the second day, in which Gehenom WAS CREATED, and on the fourth day where the luminaries became defective. From them she came to rule every day.

119. וּבַת מֶלֶךְ, אֲסִירָא בְּסִרְכוֹת, בְּבֵית הַסֹּהַר, בְּגָלוּתָא דִּילָהּ. וְאִיהִי קִינָא דְּסָמָאֵל בֵּין כֹּכְבַיָּא. וְקוּדְשָׁא בְּרִיךְ הוּא אוֹמֵי, אִם תַּגְבִּיהַּ כַּנֶּשֶׁר וְאִם בֵּין כֹּכָבִים שִׂים קִנֶּךָ מִשָּׁם אוֹרִידְךָ נְאֻם יְיָ׳. וּשְׁכִינְתָּא נֹגַהּ, וְנֹגַהּ לָאֵשׁ, וּמֵהָכָא קָרוּ לְבֵי כְּנִשְׁתָּא אֵשׁ נוֹגַהּ.

119. The King’s daughter, WHO IS MALCHUT, is bound by ropes. THAT IS, JUST AS THE ADHESIONS OF THE LUNG STOP THE AIR FROM THE LUNG, SO DO THE INIQUITIES OF YISRAEL STOP THE LIGHT FROM MALCHUT in prison in her exile. She is a nest to Samael among the stars, THAT IS, SAMAEL IS ATTACHED TO HER, and the Holy One, blessed be He, swears, “Though you do soar aloft like the eagle, and though you do set your nest among the stars, from there I will bring you, says Hashem" (Ovadyah 1:4). And the Shechinah is CALLED Venus (Heb. *nogah*), AS WRITTEN, "the fire was bright (Heb. *nogah*)" (Yechezkel 1:13). Hence the synagogue is called 'a bright fire' IN A FOREIGN TONGUE.

120. **אֵשׁ מַאֲדִים לִישָׁנָא דְּאוֹדֶם, טוּר אוֹדֶם פִּטְדָה. נוֹגַהּ אֶשָּׁא חִיוָּרָא. וְתַרְוַויְיהוּ פְּנֵי חַמָּה וּפְנֵי סִיהֲרָא, נֶצַח וְהוֹד, אִינּוּן דְּנָטְלוּ חִוָּורוּ מֵחֶסֶד, וְסוּמָקוּ מִגְּבוּרָה. אַהֲרֹן וְדָוִד מִתַּמָּן הֲווֹ, חַד נָטִיל רַחֲמֵי, וְחַד נָטִיל דִּינָא, דָּוִד מִסִּטְרָא דִּשְׂמָאלָא, וְהוּא אַדְמוֹנִי. אַהֲרֹן אִישׁ חֶסֶד, וְתַרְוַויְיהוּ נְבִיאֵי קְשׁוֹט מִתַּמָּן. פְּנֵי מֹשֶׁה הֲווֹ נְהִירִין בִּנְבוּאָה דְּבִינָה, אִיהוּ חַמָּה עִלָּאָה מִתַּמָּן נְבוּאָה דִּילֵיהּ.**

120. The fire of Mars (Heb. *ma'adim*) IS RED SINCE MA'ADIM derives from redness (Heb. *odem*), ACCORDING TO THE SECRET OF, "the first row shall be a ruby (Heb. *odem*), a chrysolite, and a beryl" (Shemot 28:17). Venus is a white fire, and both are the face of the sun, the face of the moon. Netzach and Hod receive the whiteness from Chesed and the redness from Gvurah; Aaron and David came from there; one received Mercy and the other received Judgment. David came from the left side, AS WRITTEN, "Now he was ruddy" (I Shmuel 16:12). Aaron is a man of Chesed, and the two true prophets, NAMELY NETZACH AND HOD, are from them. The face of Moses used to shine with prophecy from Binah, which is the supernal sun, whence his prophecy came.

121. **בְּהוֹן עֵשָׂו חַיָּיבָא עֶבֶד אֱדוֹם, וְנוּקְבָא דִּילֵיהּ מַאֲדִים, אִיהִי שְׁפִיכוּת דָּמִים דְּיִשְׂרָאֵל, וְגַרְמָה דְּמַטְרוֹנִיתָא אִתְקַיָּים בָּהּ, נְתָנַנִי יְיָ' בִּידֵי לֹא אוּכַל קוּם, נְתָנַנִי שׁוֹמֵמָה כָּל הַיּוֹם דָּוָה. הוֹד דָּוָה אִתְהַדָּר. דְּנֶצַח וְהוֹד לָקֳבְלַיְיהוּ. יָכִין וּבוֹעַז. שְׁתֵּיהֶן אֲשֶׁר הַבַּיִת נִשְׁעַן עֲלֵיהֶם. דְּבֵי כְּנִשְׁתָּא אִתְקְרִיאַת עַל שְׁמַיְיהוּ אֵשׁ נוֹגַהּ כַּדְּקָא אֲמֵינָא.**

121. In them, Esau the wicked, the servant IS CALLED Edom, and his female IS CALLED Mars, which is bloodshed in Yisrael. She caused it to be fulfilled in the Queen, "he has made me desolate and faint (Heb. *davah*) all the day" (Eichah 1:13). Hod turned into Davah, since they correspond to Netzach and Hod. "I AM NOT ABLE TO RISE UP" (IBID. 14) CORRESPONDS TO

NETZACH AND "FAINT ALL THE DAY" CORRESPONDS TO HOD. THEY ARE Jachin and Boaz, NETZACH BEING JACHIN AND BOAZ HOD, on both of which the house is supported, since a synagogue, WHICH CORRESPONDS TO MALCHUT, is named after them 'a bright fire', as we said.

122. וְשִׁפְחָה רָעָה אִיהִי קְבוּרָה, וּבָהּ אֲסִירָא לִגְבִירְתָּא. וְאִיהִי שַׁבְּתַאי, קָרָה וִיבֵשָׁה, בִּקְבוּרְתָא דְעַפְרָא, וְאִיהִי מָוֶת דַּעֲנִיּוּתָא דְאוֹרַיְיתָא, וְאִיהִי קְבוּרַת עָנִי, מְכוּסֶּה בַּת בְּשֶׁבַע מִינֵי מְדוֹרוֹת, דְּאִיהִי כְּלִילָא מִשֶּׁבַע כֹּכָבַיָּא, כְּמָה דְשַׁבָּת מַלְכְּתָא כְּלִילָא מִשֶּׁבַע. וְאִינּוּן שֶׁבַע כֹּכָבַיָּא מִסִּטְרָא דִגְבִירְתָּא שֶׁבַע שְׁנֵי הַשָּׂבָע, מִסִּטְרָא דְשִׁפְחָה שֶׁבַע שְׁנֵי הָרָעָב. דְּעָלַיְיהוּ אָמַר נָבִיא לֹא רָעָב לַלֶּחֶם וְלֹא צָמָא לַמַּיִם כִּי אִם לִשְׁמוֹעַ אֶת דִּבְרֵי יְיָ'.

122. And an evil handmaid is THE ASPECT OF burial, and in it her mistress is imprisoned. THE EVIL HANDMAID is Saturn, which is cold and dry, buried in the dust, and is the death of poverty in the Torah, OF WHICH IT WAS SAID THAT A POOR MAN IS CONSIDERED AS DEAD. She is the grave of the poor man, who is covered within it with seven kinds of stories. For she includes seven planets, like HER MISTRESS Queen Shabbat includes seven SFIROT. And the seven planets from the aspect of the mistress are the seven years of plenty and those of the aspect of the handmaid are the seven years of famine, of which the prophet said, "not a famine for bread, nor a thirst for water, but for hearing the words of Hashem" (Amos 8:11).

123. גְּבִירְתָּהּ גַּן. שִׁפְחָה אַשְׁפָּה מְטוּנֶּפֶת, מִסִּטְרָא דְעֵרֶב רַב אַשְׁפָּה מְעוּרֶבֶת בַּגַּן, לְגַדְּלָא זְרָעִים, מִסִּטְרָא דְעֵץ הַדַּעַת טוֹב וָרָע. מִסִּטְרָא דַּע"ז, אִתְקְרִיאַת שַׁבְּתַאי, לִילִית, אַשְׁפָּה מְטוּנֶּפֶת, בְּגִין דְּצוֹאָה מְעוּרֶבֶת מִכָּל מִינֵי טִנּוּף וְשֶׁרֶץ, דְּזָרְקִין בָּהּ כְּלָבִים מֵתִים וַחֲמוֹרִים מֵתִים. בְּנֵי עֵשָׂו וְיִשְׁמָעֵאל קְבוּרִים בָּהּ. עכו"ם דְּאִינּוּן כְּלָבִים מֵתִים, קְבוּרִים בָּהּ. וְאִיהִי קֶבֶר דַּע"ז, דְּקָבְרִין בָּהּ עֲרֵלִים, דְּאִינּוּן כְּלָבִים מֵתִים, שֶׁקֶץ וְרֵיחַ רָע, מְטוּנָּף, מְסוֹרָח, מִשִּׁפְחָה בִּישָׁא אִיהִי סִרְכָא, דַּאֲחִידָא בְּעֵרֶב רַב, מְעוֹרָבִים בְּיִשְׂרָאֵל. וַאֲחִידַת בְּעֶצֶם וּבָשָׂר, דְּאִינּוּן

בְּנֵי עֵשָׂו וְיִשְׁמָעֵאל, עֶצֶם מֵת, וּבָשָׂר טָמֵא, בָּשָׂר בַּשָּׂדֶה טְרֵפָה, דְּעָלָהּ אִתְּמַר, לַכֶּלֶב תַּשְׁלִיכוּן אוֹתוֹ.

123. Her mistress is a garden. The handmaid is filthy refuse from the aspect of the mixed multitude. The refuse is mixed in the garden in order to grow seeds of the aspect of the Tree of Knowledge of Good and Evil. From the aspect of idolatry THE HANDMAID is called Saturn, Lilit, filthy refuse, because she is excrement mixed with different types of filth and vermin, into which dead dogs are thrown. The children of Esau and Ishmael are buried in it. She is a grave for idolatry, where the uncircumcised are buried, who are dead dogs, vermin, a bad smell and filthy, and who became foul through her, who is the adhesion attached to the mixed multitude that are mixed in Yisrael, and who is attached to the bones and flesh that are the children of Esau and Ishmael, who are a dead bone and unclean meat, meat that is torn by beasts in the field, of which it says, "you shall cast it to the dogs" (Shemot 22:30).

124. וּכְגַוְונָא דְּאִית תְּרֵיסָר מַזָּלוֹת, מִסִּטְרָא דְּטוֹב. הָכִי אִית תְּרֵיסַר מַזָּלוֹת, מִסִּטְרָא דְּרָע. הֲדָא הוּא דִּכְתִּיב, שְׁנֵים עָשָׂר נְשִׂיאִים לְאֻמֹּתָם. דְּזֶה לְעֻמַּת זֶה עָשָׂה הָאֱלֹהִים, וְרַשִׁיעַיָּיא אִינּוּן אֲבִי אֲבוֹת הַטּוּמְאָה, דְּאִינּוּן טְמֵא מֵת וְשֶׁרֶץ, דִּמְטַמֵּא לְב״נ מֵאֲוִירוֹ וּמִתּוֹכוֹ וּמִגַּבּוֹ. וַאֲפִילוּ תּוֹךְ תּוֹכוֹ דְּכַהֲנָא מִסְתְּאַב בְּהוֹן. וּבְגִין דָּא עַל כָּל נַפְשׁוֹת מֵת לֹא יָבֹא. דְּרָשָׁע קָרוּי מֵת. וּבוֹצִינָא קַדִּישָׁא, לְאָבִיו וּלְאִמּוֹ לֹא יִטַּמָּא.

124. Just as there are twelve constellations from the good side so there are twelve constellations from the Evil Side. This is what is meant by, "twelve princes according to their nations" (Beresheet 25:16), since, "the Elohim has made the one as well as the other" (Kohelet 7:14). And the wicked are the forefathers of impurity, being made impure by the dead and by vermin, who causes one to be unclean by their space, their inside, their back, and even their innermost parts, by which the priest becomes unclean. This is why, "neither shall he go in to any dead body" (Vayikra 21:11), since the evil man is considered dead. And the Holy Luminary EVEN "not defile himself for his father, or for his mother" (Ibid.).

26. Elijah, do not tarry in coming down

A Synopsis

Elijah is implored to come down quickly because God and His Shechinah are in exile and the Faithful Shepherd is buried among the wicked awaiting release. He begs Elijah to come with the celestial angels, and he speaks about the vessels of the Shechinah that are holy angels above and Yisrael below. If there are people of good qualities Malchut spreads over them with her ten Sfirot and the Cause of Causes descends upon her. Next Rabbi Shimon beseeches God to take note of the Faithful Shepherd who is worth 600,000 people of Yisrael and who embodies all ten attributes; he reminds God that He promised He would not destroy the world for the sake of ten righteous people. Finally Rabbi Shimon asks Elijah to swear an oath to reveal Moses to all the leaders of the Mishnah sages so they will recognize him and he will no longer have to bear the burden of the sins of Yisrael. He says that God will thank Elijah for doing this.

125. הָכָא אַשְׁכַּחְנָא אַסְוָותָא, לְגַבֵּי דְּאִתְּמַר בִּי וַיִּתֵּן אֶת רְשָׁעִים קִבְרוֹ. בָּתַר דִּקְבוּרָה דָּא בְּגִין אַבָּא וְאִימָּא, דְּאִינּוּן בְּגָלוּתָא עִם יִשְׂרָאֵל אִתְקַיָּים בִּי קְרָא וְלֹא יִטַּמָּא. אֵלִיָּהוּ, לָא תִּתְעַכֵּב מִלְּנַחְתָּא, דְּאע״ג דְּאַנְתְּ כַּהֲנָא, לְאָבִיו וּלְאִמּוֹ יִטַּמָּא, דְּהָא קוּדְשָׁא בְּרִיךְ הוּא וּשְׁכִינְתֵּיהּ בְּגָלוּתָא, דְּאִיהִי קְבוּרָה לוֹן, וַאֲנָא קָבוּר בֵּינַיְיהוּ. בְּאוֹמָאָה עֲלָךְ, בְּשֵׁם יְיָ' חַי וְקַיָּים, לָא תִּתְעַכֵּב מִלְּנַחְתָּא. מַלְאֲכִין קַדִּישִׁין, מָארֵי דְּגַדְפִּין, בְּאוֹמָאָה עֲלַיְיכוּ, טוּלוּ אוֹמָאָה דָּא, וּסְלִיקוּ לָהּ עַל גַּדְפַּיְיכוּ, שְׁבוּעַת יְיָ' בְּחַ״י צַדִּיק וְקַיָּים עַמּוּדָא דְּאֶמְצָעִיתָא, טוּלוּ אוֹמָאָה דָּא, וּסְלִיקוּ לָהּ עַל גַּדְפַּיְיכוּ. בְּמַטְרוֹנִיתָא בִּיקָרָא דִּילָהּ, לְגַבֵּי קוּדְשָׁא בְּרִיךְ הוּא.

125. I have found remedy here to that of which it says, "For they made his grave among the wicked" (Yeshayah 53:9). Since this is the burial site for Aba and Ima, WHO ARE ZEIR ANPIN AND MALCHUT, who are in exile with Yisrael, the verse was fulfilled in me, "not defile himself" (Vayikra 21:11). Elijah, do not tarry in coming down, for though you are a priest, PINCHAS BEING ELIJAH, such may be defiled for his father, or for his mother. For the Holy One, blessed be He, and His Shechinah are in exile, THEY BEING ABA

AND IMA TO WHOM EXILE is a grave, and I am buried among them. An oath upon you, by the name of the living, enduring Hashem, do not tarry in coming down. Holy, winged angels, an oath upon you, take this oath, WHICH IS THE SECRET OF MALCHUT THAT IS CALLED AN OATH, and raise her, the Queen, upon your wings with her glory to the Holy One, blessed be He.

126. מַלְאֲכִין עִלָּאִין, שְׁלִיחָן דְּקוּדְשָׁא בְּרִיךְ הוּא מִימִינָא. וּמַלְאָכִין שְׁלִיחָן דִּילֵיהּ, מִשְּׂמָאלָא. וּמַלְאָכִים דְּאַבָּא וְאִמָּא. יֵהוֹן סתרין לָהּ עֵילָּא וְתַתָּא, וּמְכַסִּין לָהּ בְּאָת ו׳, בְּשִׁית גַּדְפִּין דִּילֵיהּ, דְּאִתְּמַר בֵּיהּ שְׂרָפִים עוֹמְדִים מִמַּעַל לוֹ שֵׁשׁ כְּנָפַיִם וְגוֹ׳ בִּשְׁתַּיִם יְכַסֶּה פָּנָיו דִּשְׁבוּעָה דִּילֵיהּ, דְּאִיהִי ה׳, רְבִיעָאָה. וּבִשְׁתַּיִם יְכַסֶּה רַגְלָיו דִּילָהּ, וּבִשְׁתַּיִם מְעוֹפְפִים לָהּ.

126. Celestial angels, sent by the Holy One, blessed be He, from the right side, His angels messengers from the left, and angels of Aba and Ima, WHO ARE ZEIR ANPIN AND MALCHUT, WHICH ARE THE CENTRAL COLUMN, shall hide her, MALCHUT, above and below, and cover her with the letter Vav, WHICH IS ZEIR ANPIN, with his six wings, of whom it says, "Seraphs stood above him. Each one had six wings; WITH TWO HE COVERED HIS FACE" (Yeshayah 6:2) of his oath, which is Hei, the fourth LETTER OF YUD HEI VAV HEI, NAMELY MALCHUT, "and with two he covered his feet" (Ibid.) OF MALCHUT, and with two they cause her to fly TO ZEIR ANPIN.

127. וְאַנְתְּ אֵלִיָּהוּ, דִּסְלִיקַת לְעֵילָּא, לְעִילַּת הָעִילּוֹת, וְהוּא טָעִין לָךְ מִכָּל טוּב, נָחִית לְגַבָּהּ, וְתֶהֱוֵי כְּרוּב תְּחוֹתָא, לְנַחְתָּא לָהּ מְלֵאָה כָּל טוּב. וּמַלְאָכִין, דְּאַבָּא וְאִימָּא, דְּאִינּוּן יָ״ה, אַסְתֲּרוּ לָהּ, בִּנְחִיתוּ דִּילָהּ. וּמַלְאָכִין דְּבַעְלָהּ, בְּרָא דְּאַבָּא וְאִמָּא, ו׳, כַּסִּיאוּ לָהּ, וּמְעַפְפִין לָהּ, מִשִּׁית גַּדְפִּין אב״ג ית״ץ, ובל״ו דְּתַלְיָין מִנַּיְיהוּ כְּחֶשְׁבּוֹן ל״ו. וַדָּאי אִיהוּ שְׂרָפִים עוֹמְדִים מִמַּעַל לוֹ. וּנְחִיתַת ה׳ דִּילֵיהּ, טְמִירָא מְכוּסָּה בְּהוֹן. וּמַלְאָכִין דְּאִינּוּן דְּצַדִּיק חַ״י עָלְמִין, אַסְמִיכוּ לָהּ עֲלַיְיכוּ כְּחֵיוָן דְּסַמְכֵי לְכֻרְסְיָיא.

127. And you, Elijah, who have risen to the Cause of causes, who loaded you with every goodness, go down to her, TO MALCHUT, and be a cherub under her, to bring her down filled with goodness. And the angels of Aba and Ima, who are Yud Hei, shall cover her during your descent and make her fly with six wings OF THE SIX LETTERS Aleph Bet Gimel, Yud Tav Tzadi and the 36 LETTERS IN THE SIX NAMES derived FROM ALEPH BET GIMEL, YUD TAV TZADI, WHICH ARE KOF RESH AYIN, SIN TET NUN; NUN GIMEL DALET, YUD CAF SHIN; BET TET RESH, TZADI TAV GIMEL; CHET KOF BET, TET NUN AYIN; YUD GIMEL LAMED, PE ZAYIN KOF; SHIN KOF VAV, TZADI YUD TAV, THE numerical value OF WHICH is 36. Surely, "Seraphs stood above him (Heb. *lo*, *Lamed Vav*)," NAMELY WITH THE ABOVE-MENTIONED LAMED VAV (36) LETTERS. And his Hei descends, NAMELY MALCHUT, hidden and covered by them. And angels coming from the Righteous, the life of the worlds, support her over you like the living creatures that support the throne.

128. דְּאע״ג דְּהֵ״א דַּאֲצִילוּת, דִּשְׁמָא דְּיִדוָ״ד, אִיהִי סְמִיכַת לְכֻלְּהוּ, לֵית לְכוֹן לְפָרְחָא לְעֵילָּא, וּלְנַחְתָּא לְתַתָּא, בַּר מִינָהּ. כְּאֵבָרִין דְּגוּפָא, דְּלֵית לְהוֹן תְּנוּעָה בַּר מִנִּשְׁמָתָא, דְּאֵבָרִין דְּאִית לָהּ, אִתְפְּשָׁטוּ עֲלַיְיכוּ, לְסַמְכָא לְכוֹן בְּהוֹן. דְּהָכִי אִיהִי ה׳, כְּיַמָּא, אִי אִית לָהּ מָאנִין, מִתְמַלְיָין מִנָּהּ, וּמִתְפַּשְׁטִין בְּהוֹן, כַּנְחָלִים דְּמִתְפַּשְׁטִן מִן יַמָּא עַל אַרְעָא. וְאִי לָאו, אִיהִי ה׳ בִּגַרְמָא יְחִידָאָה, בְּלָא אִתְפַּשְׁטוּתָא דְּנַחֲלִין.

128. For though Hei of Atzilut, of the Name Yud Hei Vav Hei, WHICH IS MALCHUT, supports everything, you must not fly up and down, except with her, WITH MALCHUT. Just like the body parts cannot move except with the soul, so do her parts, NAMELY HER SFIROT, expand over you to support you with them. For such is Hei, like the sea. If it has vessels TO FILL, they are filled from it and it spreads within them like streams that spread from the sea onto the earth. If it does not have vessels, it is Hei only, alone without the expansion of streams.

129. הָכִי מָאנִין דִּשְׁכִינְתָּא, אִינּוּן מַלְאֲכִין קַדִּישִׁין לְעֵילָּא, וְיִשְׂרָאֵל לְתַתָּא, אִי אִית בְּהוֹן מָארֵי מִדּוֹת, מָארֵי חֶסֶד חֲסִידִים, גִּבּוֹרִים מָארֵי תּוֹרָה, נְבִיאִים וּכְתוּבִים, צַדִּיקִים, אַנְשֵׁי מַלְכוּת, דְּאִתְּמַר בְּהוּ, וַאֲשֶׁר

כֹּחַ בָּהֶם לַעֲמוֹד בְּהֵיכַל הַמֶּלֶךְ, בַּעֲמִידָה דִּצְלוֹתָא, בְּהֵיכָלָא דְּמַלְכָּא אֲדֹנָ"י, מַלְכָּא דִּילָהּ יְדֹוָ"ד. וְהֵם חֲכָמִים וּנְבוֹנִים רָאשֵׁי יִשְׂרָאֵל. וְלָא רָאשֵׁי עֵרֶב רַב, דְּאִתְּמַר בְּהוֹן, הָיוּ צָרֶיהָ לְרֹאשׁ. אִיהִי אִתְפַּשְׁטַת עֲלַיְיהוּ בַּעֲשַׂר סְפִירָן דִּילָהּ. בְּהַהוּא זִמְנָא, נָחִית עִלַּת הָעִלּוֹת, בְּיוֹ"ד הֵ"א וָא"ו הֵ"א, לְנַחְתָּא עֲלַיְיהוּ, לְאָקָמָא שְׁכִינְתָּא עֲלַיְיהוּ.

129. Such are the vessels of the Shechinah, which above are holy angels and below are Yisrael. If there are people of good qualities among them, kind, pious and mighty, learned in the Torah, the Prophets and the Writings, righteous, people of Malchut, of whom it says, "and such as had ability in them to stand in the king's palace" (Daniel 1:4), namely during the Amidah (lit. 'standing') prayer in the King's palace, which is Adonai, whose King is Yud Hei Vav Hei. If they are wise and intelligent, leaders of Yisrael, not leaders of the mixed multitude, of whom it says, "Her adversaries have become the chief" (Eichah 1:5), then she, MALCHUT, spreads over them with her ten Sfirot. At that time the Cause of causes descends upon her with Yud Vav Dalet, Hei Aleph, Vav Aleph Vav, Hei Aleph, to establish the Shechinah on them.

130. וּבְזִמְנָא דְּוַיִּפֶן כֹּה וָכֹה וַיַּרְא כִּי אֵין אִישׁ, אִיהִי אָמְרַת, שַׁלָּמָה אֶהְיֶה כְּעוֹטְיָה, מְעוּטֶּפֶת בְּגַרְמָא דְּלָא אִתְפַּשְׁטַת עֲלַיְיהוּ, וְקוּדְשָׁא בְּרִיךְ הוּא צָוַוח עָלֵהּ וְאָמַר, אֵיכָה יָשְׁבָה בָדָד.

130. When, "he looked this way and that, and when he saw that there was no man" (Shemot 2:12), she says, "for why should I be like one who cloaks himself" (Shir Hashirim 1:7), namely wrapping herself and not expanding over them. And the Holy One, blessed be He, cries aloud for her, saying, "How does the city sit solitary" (Eichah 1:1).

131. אַדְּהָכִי, קָם בּוּצִינָא קַדִּישָׁא, וְאָמַר רִבּוֹן עָלְמָא, הָא הָכָא רַעְיָא מְהֵימָנָא, דְּאִתְּמַר בֵּיהּ וְהָאִישׁ מֹשֶׁה עָנָו מְאֹד, עַד כְּעַן וַיַּרְא כִּי אֵין אִישׁ. הָא הָכָא וְהָאִישׁ מֹשֶׁה, דְּשָׁקִיל לְשִׁתִּין רִבּוֹא דְּיִשְׂרָאֵל. וּבֵיהּ מִמְּכוֹן שִׁבְתּוֹ הִשְׁגִּיחַ. דְּבֵיהּ אִתְּמַר לְגַבֵּי דָּרָא דְּגָלוּתָא בַּתְרָאָה, וַיִּי'

הִפְגִּיעַ בּוֹ אֵת עֲוֹן כֻּלָּנוּ. וְאִיהוּ כָּלִיל בַּעֲשַׂר מִדּוֹת, דִּבְגִינַיְיהוּ אַמָרְתְּ לֹא אַשְׁחִית בַּעֲבוּר הָעֲשָׂרָה. נְחִית עָלֵיהּ, לְאַשְׁגְּחָא עַל עָלְמָא, וְקַיֵּים מִילָּךְ, דְּאַנְתְּ קְשׁוֹט, וְכָל מִילָּךְ קְשׁוֹט.

131. As he was speaking, the Holy Luminary, RABBI SHIMON, rose and said, Master of the universe, here is the Faithful Shepherd, of whom it says, "Now the man Moses was very meek" (Bemidbar 12:3). Until this moment, "he saw that there was no man." But here the man Moses is equivalent to 600,000 of Yisrael, and in him, "From the place of His habitation He looks" (Tehilim 33:14), THE INITIALS OF WHICH FORM THE WORD MOSES, of whom it says in relation to the last exile, "and Hashem has caused the iniquity of us all to fall upon him" (Yeshayah 53:6). He comprehends the ten attributes for which You said, "I will not destroy it for the sake of the ten" (Beresheet 18:32). Go down over him to oversee the world and fulfill Your words that You are true and that all Your words are true.

132. דְּאִיהוּ גָּמַל חֶסֶד עִם שְׁכִינְתָּא, וְקָטִיר שִׁפְחָה דִּילָהּ בִּגְבוּרָה, לְמֶהֱוֵי שִׁפְחָה אֲסִירָא תְּחוֹת גְּבִירְתָּהּ, בְּקִשּׁוּרָא דִּתְפִלִּין. וְאִשְׁתְּדַל בְּגִינָהּ, בְּתוֹרַת אֱמֶת, תּוֹרַת אֱמֶת הָיְתָה בְּפִיהוּ. וְאִשְׁתְּדַל בָּהּ, בַּנְּבִיאִים וּכְתוּבִים. בִּנְבִיאֵי, בְּכַמָּה נֶחָמוֹת. בַּכְּתוּבִים, בַּעֲשָׂרָה מִינֵי תְּהִלִּים. בְּצַדִּיק, בְּי״ח בִּרְכָאן דִּצְלוֹתָא.

132. For he acted kindly by the Shechinah and tied her handmaid to Gvurah, so the handmaid shall be bound under her mistress with the knot of Tefilin. And he endeavored for Her sake with the Torah of truth, AS WRITTEN, "The Torah of truth was in his mouth" (Malachi 2:6). And he strove in it in the Prophets and the Writings: in the Prophets in different kinds of comforts and in the Writings, WHICH ARE MALCHUT, in ten kinds of Psalms, WHICH ARE HER TEN SFIROT; in the Righteous WHICH IS YESOD in the eighteen blessings in the AMIDAH prayer.

133. וּמָארֵי מַתְנִיתִין, לָא אִשְׁתְּמוֹדְעָן לֵיהּ לְרַעְיָא מְהֵימְנָא. אֵלִיָּהוּ, בְּאוּמָאָה עֲלָךְ בִּשְׁמָא דִּידֹוָ״ד, וּבִשְׁמֵיהּ מְפֹרָשׁ, גַּלֵּי לֵיהּ לְכָל רֵישֵׁי מָארֵי מַתְנִיתִין, דְּיִשְׁתְּמוֹדְעוּן לֵיהּ, וְלָא יִתְחַלֵּל יַתִּיר, דְּאִתְּמַר בֵּיהּ,

וְהוּא מְחוֹלָל מִפְּשָׁעֵינוּ, לֵית לָךְ צוֹרֶךְ לְמֵיטַל רְשׁוּ דְּהָא אֲנָא שְׁלִיחָא דְּמָארֵי עָלְמָא, וְיָדַעְנָא דְּאִי אַנְתְּ עָבֵיד דָּא, דְּיוֹדֵי לָךְ קוּדְשָׁא בְּרִיךְ הוּא עָלֵיהּ, וְיִסְתַּלְּקוּן בְּנָךְ בְּגִינֵיהּ, עֵילָּא וְתַתָּא. וְלָא תִּתְעַכָּב לְמֶעְבַּד, לָא שָׁבוּעַ, וְלָא חֹדֶשׁ, וְלָא שָׁנָה, אֶלָּא מִיַּד.

133. But the sages of the Mishnah do not know the Faithful Shepherd. Elijah, an oath upon you in the Name Yud Hei Vav Hei and in the explicit Name, reveal him to all the leaders of the Mishnah sages so they will recognize him and he shall no more be violated, "But he was wounded (or: 'violated') because of our transgressions" (Yeshayah 53:5). You do not have to receive permission FROM THE HOLY ONE, BLESSED BE HE, because I am a messenger from the Master of the universe and I know that if you do that, the Holy One, blessed be He, will thank you for it and your descendants shall be exalted for it above and below. Do not tarry in doing it, neither a week nor a month, nor a year, but do it immediately.

27. Pesach, Chametz and Matzah

A Synopsis

We read of the importance of keeping the precepts about food and drink, including most importantly the restriction on leaven during Pesach. The conclusion is that any misdeed below causes damage above.

134. רַעְיָא מְהֵימָנָא, מָאנֵי דִּפְסְחָא, בִּזְמְנָא דְּשָׁלִיט עָלַיְיהוּ לֵיל שִׁמּוּרִים, כֻּלְּהוּ צְרִיכִים לְמֶהֱוֵי שִׁמּוּרִים, וּנְטוּרִים מֵחָמֵץ וּשְׂאוֹר בְּכָל שֶׁהוּא, וְכָל מַאֲכָלִים וּמַשְׁקִים כֻּלְּהוּ נְטוּרִין. וּמַאן דְּנָטִיר לוֹן מֵחָמֵץ וּשְׂאוֹר, גּוּפֵיהּ, אִיהוּ נָטִיר מיצה״ר לְתַתָּא, וְנִשְׁמָתֵא לְעֵילָּא. וְאִתְּמַר בֵּיהּ, לֹא יְגוּרְךָ רָע. בְּגִין דְּהָא אִתְעָבֵיד גּוּפֵיהּ קֹדֶשׁ, וְנִשְׁמָתֵיהּ קֹדֶשׁ קֳדָשִׁים. וְאִתְּמַר בְּיֵצֶר הָרָע וְכָל זָר לֹא יֹאכַל קֹדֶשׁ, וְהַזָּר הַקָּרֵב יוּמָת.

134. Faithful Shepherd, when the night of watchfulness, WHICH IS THE SHECHINAH, has power over the vessels of Pesach, everybody should be guarded, kept from Chametz and any kind of leaven. Every food and drink SHOULD BE watched, and whoever keeps them from Chametz and leaven, his body is kept from the Evil Inclination below, and his soul IS KEPT from above, and it says of it, "nor shall evil dwell with you" (Tehilim 5:5), for his body becomes holy and his soul the holy of holies. And it says of the Evil Inclination, "No stranger shall eat of the holy thing" (Vayikra 22:10), "and the stranger that comes near shall be put to death" (Bemidbar 1:51).

135. פֶּסַח, דְּרוֹעָא יְמִינָא דְּאַבְרָהָם, כֶּסֶף מְזוּקָּק, מַאן דְּעָרַב בֵּיהּ עוֹפֶרֶת, מְשַׁקֵּר לֵיהּ. הָכִי מַאן דְּעָרַב חָמֵץ אוֹ שְׂאוֹר כָּל שֶׁהוּא בְּמַצָּה, כְּאִלּוּ מְשַׁקֵּר בְּמוֹנִיטָה דְּמַלְכָּא. וְהָכִי מַאן דְּעָרַב בְּטִפָּה דִּילֵיהּ שׁוּם תַּעֲרוֹבֶת, כְּאִילוּ מְשַׁקֵּר חוֹתָמָא דְּמַלְכָּא, דָּא בְּדָא תַּלְיָיא.

135. Pesach is the right arm, which is Abraham, NAMELY CHESED, refined silver. Whoever mixes lead in it is false to it. Similarly, for anyone who mixes Chametz or leaven at all in the Matzah it is as if he is false to the King's coin, WHICH IS MALCHUT CALLED MATZAH. So is whoever mingles any admixture into his drop of semen BY FORBIDDEN INTERCOURSE OR BY THINKING OF SOMEONE ELSE, as if he is false to the King's seal, WHICH IS YESOD. For they are interdependent – THE DEED BELOW CAUSES DAMAGE ABOVE.

28. Head and hand Tefilin

A Synopsis

We are told about Rosh Hashanah and the meaning of the knot of the hand Tefilin. Rabbi Shimon addresses Metatron calling him a servant to his Master and yet a king over all other peoples and over the angels. He says that the sound of prayer and the sound of the Shofar are like spears stabbing and killing the Evil Inclination.

136. רֹאשׁ הַשָּׁנָה, דְּרוֹעָא שְׂמָאלָא דְּיִצְחָק, תַּמָּן דִּינֵי נְפָשׁוֹת, וַעֲקֵדָה דְּיִצְחָק תַּמָּן הֲוָה. דְּעָקִיד לֵיהּ אַבְרָהָם. קְשׁוּרָא דִּתְפִלָּה דְּיָד, דּוּמְיָא דַּעֲקֵדָה דְּיִצְחָק. זַכָּאָה אִיהוּ בְּרָא דְּאִתְעֲקַד בַּאֲבוֹי, וְאִתְקְשַׁר בֵּיהּ, לְמֶעְבַּד עוֹבָדוֹהִי, בְּאוֹרַיְיתָא וּבְמִצְוָה. וְזַכָּאָה עֶבֶד דְּאִתְקְשַׁר תְּחוֹת רַבֵּיהּ, לְמֶעְבַּד רְעוּתֵיהּ, אִיהוּ בַּאֲתָר דִּבְרָא דְּמַלְכָּא.

136. Rosh Hashanah (the Jewish New Year) is the left arm, which is Isaac, where criminal laws are SENTENCED, JUDGING WHO SHALL LIVE AND WHO SHALL DIE. The sacrifice of Isaac was there, whom Abraham bound. The knot of the hand Tefilin resembles the binding of Isaac. BOTH RELATE TO THE BINDING OF GVUROT WITH CHASSADIM. Blessed is the son who is bound to his father, connected to him to do as he does with the Torah and the precepts, and blessed is the servant bound under his master to do his bidding, who is in the place of a king's son.

137. מְטַטְרוֹ"ן, זַכָּאָה אַנְתְּ, וְזַכָּאִין בְּנָךְ, דְּאִינּוּן קְשִׁירִין וַעֲקִידִין בִּתְפִלִּין תְּחוֹת רְשׁוּתָא דְּמָארָךְ. וּבְג"ד, אע"ג דְּאַנְתְּ עֶבֶד לְמָארָךְ, מַלְכָּא אַנְתְּ עַל כָּל מְמָנָן דִּשְׁאַר עַמִּין. מַלְכָּא עַל כָּל מַלְאָכִין. מַלְכָּא, דְּשֵׁדִים וְכָל מַשִּׁרְיָיתֵיהּ, דַּחֲלִין מִנָּךְ. מַאן גָּרִים דָּא, בְּגִין דְּאַנְתְּ שְׁרַכְרָךְ לְמָארָךְ, וְאַנְתְּ מְשַׁמֵּשׁ לְמָארָךְ. שַׁדַּי דִּמְזוּזָה לְבַר, שׁוֹמֵר הַפֶּתַח. יְדֹוָ"ד דְּאִיהוּ מָארָךְ, מִלְּגָאו.

137. Metatron, blessed are you and blessed are your children, NAMELY, THOSE DERIVED FROM METATRON, WHO HAVE NOT YET MERITED TO BE CHILDREN TO MALE AND FEMALE OF ATZILUT, who are bound and tied by the Tefilin under your Master's authority. For that reason, though you are a servant to your Master, you are a king over all the ministers of the other peoples, king over all the angels, a king of whom all demons and their legions are afraid. Who brought that about? Your being a stool for your Master's feet. You serve your Master as Shadai of the Mezuzah from outside, guarding the entrance. Yud Hei Vav Hei, who is your Master, is inside, AND SHADAI, WHO IS THE ASPECT OF METATRON, IS OUTSIDE.

138. וְהָכִי אִיהוּ כַּד קוּדְשָׁא בְּרִיךְ הוּא נָחִית לְשַׁלְטָאָה עַל עֵץ הַדַּעַת טוֹב וָרָע, דְּאִיהוּ טוֹב מְטַטְרוֹ"ן. רָע סָמָאֵל, שֵׁד, מַלְכָּא דְּשֵׁדִים. מְטַטְרוֹן מַלְאָךְ, מַלְכָּא דְּמַלְאָכִים. אֲבָל מִסִּטְרָא דְּאִילָנָא דְּחַיֵּי, שַׁדַּי אִיהוּ יְסוֹד. וּבג"ד לְמַטָּה, שְׁנַיִם, עֶבֶד וְרַבּוֹ, דְּלָאו אִינּוּן יִחוּדָא חֲדָא, וּלְמַעְלָה, אֶחָד. תִּפְאֶרֶת יְסוֹד, דְּגוּף וּבְרִית חַשְׁבִינָן חַד, דְּאִיהִי עַמּוּדָא דְּאֶמְצָעִיתָא וְצַדִּיק.

138. It is so THAT METATRON IS SHADAI when the Holy One, blessed be He, descends TO BRIYAH to rule over the Tree of Knowledge of Good and Evil, good being Metatron and evil Samael, who is a devil, the king of demons. Metatron is an angel, the king of angels, but from the aspect of the Tree of Life the name Shadai is Yesod OF ATZILUT. This is why below IN BRIYAH THERE ARE two, a servant and his Master. THE SERVANT IS SHADAI OUTSIDE AND HIS MASTER IS YUD HEI VAV HEI INSIDE, and they are not unified into one. And above IN ATZILUT Tiferet and Yesod are one, since we consider the body and the member of the covenant as one, the Central Column and the Righteous, NAMELY TIFERET AND YESOD.

139. כְּגַוְונָא דִּתְפִלִּין דְּרֹאשׁ, דְּאִיהוּ בִּינָה עַל תִּפְאֶרֶת, מִסִּטְרָא דְּאִילָנָא דְּחַיֵּי דַּאֲצִילוּת, וּמַלְכוּת תְּפִלָּה דְּיָד. הָכִי לְתַתָּא בְּאִילָנָא דְּחַיֵּי דִּבְרִיאָה, מִסִּטְרָא דְּכֻרְסְיָיא עִלָּאָה, תְּפִלִּין דְּרֹאשׁ מְטַטְרוֹן. תְּפִלִּין דְּיַד דִּילֵיהּ, כִּסֵּא תַּחְתּוֹן. וְהַאי אִיהוּ דְּאָמַר נָבִיא עָלֵיהּ, כִּסֵּא כָבוֹד מָרוֹם מֵרִאשׁוֹן.

139. Just like the head Tefilin are MOCHIN OF Binah above Tiferet that is the Tree of Life in Atzilut, and Malchut is the hand Tefilin, so it is below in the Tree of Life in Briyah. From the aspect of the supernal throne, BINAH OF BRIYAH, there is the head Tefilin of Metatron, and his hand Tefilin are the lower throne, NAMELY MALCHUT OF BRIYAH. Of this the prophet says, "A glorious throne exalted from the beginning" (Yirmeyah 17:12).

140. אֲבָל מִסִּטְרָא דְּעֵץ הַדַּעַת טוֹב וָרָע, בְּקִשּׁוּרָא דִּתְפִלִּין, אִתְקְשַׁר יצה״ר תְּחוֹת יֵצֶר הַטּוֹב, כְּעַבְדָּא תְּחוֹת מָארֵיהּ, בְּקָלָא דְּאוֹרַיְיתָא, בְּקָלָא דִּצְלוֹתָא, בְּקוֹל דְּשׁוֹפָר. קָלָא אִיהוּ רוֹמַ״ח לְגַבֵּיהּ. וְדָא קוֹל הַשּׁוֹפָר, קוֹל דְּעַמּוּדָא דְּאֶמְצָעִיתָא, דְּאִיהוּ כָּלִיל אֶשָּׁא מַיָּא וְרוּחָא. דְּאִינּוּן תְּלַת אֲבָהָן, דִּבְהוֹן הי״ו, ה׳ בְּאַבְרָהָם, י׳ בְּיִצְחָק, בְּכָל אֲתָר ה׳ דְּשָׁלִיט עַל י׳ דִּינָא הוּא, וְהַאי אִיהוּ ה״י מִן אֱלֹהִים. וּבג״ד עָלָה אֱלֹהִים בִּתְרוּעָה. ו׳ מִן וֵאלֹהֵי יַעֲקֹב, וְדָא רוּחַ הַשּׁוֹפָר, שְׁכִינְתָּא מָנָא דִּכְלְהוּ תְּלַת, וְאִיהוּ ה׳ מִן הַשּׁוֹפָר.

140. But from the aspect of the Tree of Knowledge of Good and Evil, the Evil Inclination is bound under the Good Inclination by the knot of Tefilin like a servant under his master by the sound of Torah, the sound of prayer and the sound of the Shofar, since a sound UTTERED FOR PERFORMING A PRECEPT is like a spear in relation to it, STABBING AND KILLING THE EVIL INCLINATION. Such is the sound of the Shofar, which is the sound of the Central Pillar, NAMELY ZEIR ANPIN, which includes fire, water and air, which are the three patriarchs GVURAH, CHESED AND TIFERET that have Hei Yud Vav in them, Hei in Abraham and Yud in Isaac. NAMELY, HEI IN THE NAME ABRAHAM ALLUDES TO JUDGMENT AND YUD IN THE NAME ISAAC ALLUDES TO CHESED IN JUDGMENT. Wherever Hei rules over Yud, NAMELY WRITTEN BEFORE YUD, it is Judgment. This is Hei Yud of Elohim, NAMELY THE MOCHIN OF THE NAME ELOHIM. THESE HEI YUD ARE THE SECRET OF THE FIRE AND WATER IN THE SHOFAR, and this is why, "Elohim is gone up with a shout" (Tehilim 47:6). Vav of, 'and (Heb. *Vav*) the Elohim of Jacob' is the wind of the Shofar, NAMELY TIFERET. The Shechinah is the vessel THAT RECEIVES all three, FIRE, WATER AND AIR OF THE SHOFAR, and is the Hei of the word HaShofar.

29. Ten sounds of the Shofar

A Synopsis

This section begins by reiterating the statement that blowing the Shofar has an effect on evil like spears and swords, but the part following this paragraph is missing. After that we read about the effect of Yisrael reciting the Sh'ma and how this links them to the Shechinah.

141. דְּאִינּוּן י׳ שׁוֹפָרוֹת, דְּאִינּוּן קשר״ק קש״ק קר״ק, מִתְלַבְּשִׁין בְּהוֹן הֵ״א יוֹ״ד וָא״ו הֵ״א, דְּכָל אַתְוָון אִלֵּין אִינּוּן לְסִטְרִין אַחֲרָנִין וּלְחַיָּיבַיָּא כְּשַׁלְשְׁלָאִין וְרוּמְחִין וְסַיְיפִין. תְּרוּעָה שַׁלְשֶׁלֶת אִיהִי. וּתְרֵי תְּרוּעוֹת אִית בְּעַשְׂרָה שׁוֹפָרוֹת. וְאִינּוּן חַד.

141. There are ten sounds of the Shofar, which are T'kiah Sh'varim T'ruah T'kiah, T'kiah Sh'varim T'kiah, T'kiah T'ruah T'kiah, in which Hei Aleph, Yud Vav Dalet, Vav Aleph Vav, Hei Aleph are clothed. All these letters, towards the other aspects and towards the evil are like chains and spears and swords. One blow is a chain and the two blows are accomplished by ten sounds of the Shofar, and are one. (THE CONTINUATION IS MISSING)

142. דְּאִתְּמַר בָּהּ וְהָאֵם רוֹבֶצֶת עַל הָאֶפְרוֹחִים. יִשְׂרָאֵל מְצַפְצְפִן לָהּ בְּכַמָּה צִפְצוּפִין דִּצְלוֹתִין, וְאִיהִי לָא בָּעְיָא לְנַחְתָּא לְגַבַּיְיהוּ. יִשְׂרָאֵל מַה עָבְדִין. נָטְלִין אִימָּא דְּאִיהִי שְׁכִינְתָּא בַּהֲדַיְיהוּ, וְקַשְׁרִין לָהּ בְּקִשּׁוּרָא דִּתְפִלִּין, כַּד מָטָאן לק״ש, קָרָאן בְּנִין דִּילָהּ בְּשִׁית תֵּיבִין דְּיִיחוּדָא, דְּאִינּוּן שְׁמַע יִשְׂרָאֵל יְיָ׳ אֱלֹהֵינוּ יְיָ׳ אֶחָד, הָא קָא נַחְתִּין לְגַבֵּי אִמְּהוֹן, קַשְׁרִין לוֹן עִמָּהּ. וְהַאי אִיהִי אֲשֶׁר תִּקְרְאוּ אוֹתָם, דְּאִיהוּ עוֹנָתָהּ, כְּמוֹ מוֹעֲדֵי.

142. It says of it, "and the mother bird sitting upon the young" (Devarim 22:6). Yisrael chirp to her with many chirps of prayers, but she does not want to descend to them. Yisrael then take the mother with them, who is the Shechinah, and tie her by the knot of Tefilin. And when they reach Kriat Sh'ma, Her children call the six words of the declaration of unity, which are, "Hear, O Yisrael. Hashem our Elohim; Hashem is one" (Devarim 6:4). They then go down to their mother, THE SHECHINAH, and tie themselves to her BY MEANS OF THE MEDITATION OF 'BLESSED BE THE NAME...'. This is the meaning of, "which you shall proclaim" (Vayikra 23:2). This is her duty of matrimony, NAMELY HER TIME OF MATING, as WRITTEN, "WHICH YOU SHALL PROCLAIM TO BE HOLY gatherings (or: 'appointed times')," MEANING, DURING MY TIME OF MATING.

30. Rosh Hashanah, Pesach, Shavuot and Sukkot

A Synopsis

Rabbi Shimon tells us how each festival uses its own kind of item (like the Matzah and the Lulav, for example) to draw the Mochin of Zeir Anpin to Malchut. By these rituals Malchut is raised up to Thought, that is the explicit Name Yud Hei Vav Hei fully spelled with Alephs.

143. הָכִי בְּגַוְונָא דָּא מַצָּה, בָּהּ מְזַמְּנִין לְשִׁבְעָה יוֹמִין דְּפֶסַח. מְזַמְּנִין לְשִׁבְעָה יוֹמִין דְּסֻכּוֹת, בְּשִׁבְעָה מִינֵי, דְּאִינּוּן לוּלָב, וְאֶתְרוֹג, וְג׳ הֲדַסִּים, וּב׳ בַּדֵּי עֲרָבָה. שְׁבוּעוֹת, קָרָאן לוֹן בְּאוֹרַיְיתָא. ר״ה יוֹמָא דְּדִינָא, כָּל חַד בְּמִינֵיהּ.

143. In the same manner we call UPON THE MOCHIN FROM ZEIR ANPIN TO SHINE DURING THEIR TIME OF MATING ON THE SHECHINAH in the Matzah, which is summoned for the seven days of Pesach. Thus we summon for the seven days of Sukkot the seven kinds, which are the Lulav, the Etrog, the three branches of myrtle and two branches of willow. On Shavuot we call THE MOCHIN OF ZEIR ANPIN by the Torah. Rosh Hashanah is the day of Judgment. Each uses its own kind.

144. כָּל מַאן דְּקָרָא, כָּל דַּרְגָּא בְּמִינֵיהּ, יִתְקַיֵּים בֵּיהּ, אָז תִּקְרָא וַיְיָ׳ יַעֲנֶה. אָ״ז, ז׳ יוֹמִין דְּסֻכּוֹת, וְחַג שְׁמִינִי עֲצֶרֶת. אָ״ז, מַצָּה, וְז׳ יוֹמִין דְּפֶסַח. אָ״ז, סוּכָּה, וְז׳ מִינִין דְּלוּלָב, דְּאִינּוּן שָׁלֹשׁ הֲדַסִּים, וּשְׁנֵי עֲרָבוֹת, לוּלָב, וְאֶתְרוֹג, וּכְלִילָן בְּד׳, הָא חַד סָרֵי, כְּחוּשְׁבַּן ה״ו. וְצָרִיךְ לוֹמַר הַלֵּל עֲלַיְיהוּ, הַלְלוּיָהּ, לְאַשְׁלְמָא שֵׁם יְדֹוָד.

144. Whoever called, NAMELY DREW MOCHIN FROM ZEIR ANPIN TO MALCHUT, each grade with its own kind, the words shall be fulfilled in him, "Then (Heb. *az* = eight) shall you call, and Hashem shall answer" (Yeshayah 58:9). Az is the seven days of Sukkot together with ONE DAY OF Shmini Atzeret; Az is the Matzah and the seven days of Pesach; Az IS one Sukkah together with the seven kinds of the Lulav, which are three branches of myrtle, two branches of willow, Lulav and Etrog. When included in the four kinds, NAMELY MYRTLE, WILLOW, LULAV AND ETROG, they are TOGETHER WITH THE SEVEN PARTICULARS eleven, which is the numerical value of Hei Vav. Halel should be recited over them with Haleluyah in it, namely Yah (Yud Hei) to complete the Name Yud Hei Vav Hei.

145. וְצָרִיךְ לְסַלְּקָא לָהּ בְּמַחֲשָׁבָה, בְּאַרְבַּע מִינִין, הה״ד אָמַרְתִּי אֶעֱלֶה בְתָמָר. אֶעֱלֶ״ה סִימַן: אֶתְרוֹ״ג, עֲרָבָ״ה, לוּלָ״ב, הֲדָ״ס. וּמַחֲשָׁבָה שְׁמָא מְפֹרָשׁ, אִשְׁתְּלִים בָּהּ י״ד, כְּגַוְונָא דְּי״ד פִּרְקִין דִּיְדָא דִּימִינָא, דְּבֵיהּ צָרִיךְ לְנַטְלָא לוּלָב. הֲרֵי מַתַּן תּוֹרָה, שָׁבֻעוֹת, שִׁבְעָה בְּשִׁבְעָה י״ד. בְּר״ה, י״ד בְּקוֹל הַשּׁוֹפָר, וּבְעֶשֶׂר שׁוֹפָרוֹת, כִּדְאוּקִימְנָא לְעֵילָּא.

145. MALCHUT is raised by the four kinds up to Thought, WHICH IS CHOCHMAH. This is the meaning of, "I will go up (Heb. *e'eleh*) into the palm tree" (Shir Hashirim 7:10). E'eleh is a mark, NAMELY THE INITIAL OF Etrog, Aravah (Eng. 'willow'), Lulav and Hadas (Eng. 'myrtle'), and Thought is the explicit Name, NAMELY YUD HEI VAV HEI FULLY SPELLED WITH ALEPHS, WHICH IS CHOCHMAH OF ZEIR ANPIN, WHICH HAS TEN LETTERS, YUD VAV DALET, HEI ALEPH, VAV ALEPH VAV, HEI ALEPH, WHICH, TOGETHER WITH THE FOUR KINDS, reaches the number fourteen like the fourteen joints in the right hand OF ZEIR ANPIN, WHICH IS CHESED, with which one should take the Lulav. The giving of the Torah, NAMELY SHAVUOT, is seven within seven, NAMELY SEVEN DAYS IN SEVEN WEEKS, which amount to the number of fourteen, WHICH IS THE HIGH HAND (HEB. *YAD* = FOURTEEN), THE SECRET OF THE CENTRAL COLUMN, AS SHALL BE EXPLAINED. On Rosh Hashanah THERE ARE ALSO fourteen: the sound of the Shofar TOGETHER WITH ITS THREE PARTICULARS, WHICH ARE FIRE, AIR AND WATER, ARE FOUR, and with the ten sounds of the Shofar, as we explained before, ARE FOURTEEN.

146. בַּפֶּסַח, אִיהִי שְׁכִינְתָּא יָ״ד הַגְּדוֹלָה, מִסִּטְרָא דְּחֶסֶד. בְּרֹאשׁ הַשָּׁנָה, אִיהִי יָ״ד הַחֲזָקָה, מִסִּטְרָא דִּגְבוּרָה. בְּמַתַּן תּוֹרָה, יָ״ד רָמָה, מִסִּטְרָא דְּעַמּוּדָא דְּאֶמְצָעִיתָא. וּתְלַת זִמְנִין י״ד, מ״ב. וּתְלַת אֲבָהָן דְּתַלְיָין מִנַּיְיהוּ, סַלְּקִין חֲמִשָּׁה וְאַרְבָּעִים, כְּחוּשְׁבַּן יוֹ״ד הֵ״א וָא״ו הֵ״א.

146. On Pesach, the Shechinah is the great hand from the aspect of Chesed. On Rosh Hashanah She is the mighty hand from the aspect of Gvurah. At the giving of the Torah She is a high hand from the aspect of the Central Column, WHICH IS TIFERET. Three times fourteen equal 42, and together with the three patriarchs, CHESED, GVURAH AND TIFERET, from whom they derive, they equal 45, the number of Yud Vav Dalet, Hei Aleph, Vav Aleph Vav, Hei Aleph.

בָּרוּךְ יְיָ׳ לְעוֹלָם אָמֵן וְאָמֵן יִמְלוֹךְ יְיָ׳ לְעוֹלָם אָמֵן וְאָמֵן.

Blessed is Hashem forever Amen and Amen; May Hashem reign forever Amen and Amen.

Vayelech

Name of Articles

1. וַיֵּלֶךְ מֹשֶׁה וַיְדַבֵּר אֶת הַדְּבָרִים הָאֵלֶּה אֶל כָּל יִשְׂרָאֵל. ר' חִזְקִיָּה פָּתַח, מוֹלִיךְ לִימִין מֹשֶׁה זְרוֹעַ תִּפְאַרְתּוֹ בּוֹקֵעַ מַיִם מִפְּנֵיהֶם וְגוֹ', זַכָּאִין אִינּוּן יִשְׂרָאֵל, דְּקוּדְשָׁא בְּרִיךְ הוּא אִתְרְעֵי בְּהוּ, וּבְגִין דְּאִתְרְעֵי בְּהוּ, קָרָא לוֹן בְּנִין בּוּכְרִין קַדִּישִׁין, אַחִין כִּבְיָכוֹל, נָחַת לְדַיְירָא עִמְּהוֹן. הה"ד, וְעָשׂוּ לִי מִקְדָּשׁ וְשָׁכַנְתִּי בְּתוֹכָם. וּבָעָא לְאַתְקְנָא לְהוּ כְּגַוְונָא דִּלְעֵילָּא, וְשָׁארִי עָלַיְיהוּ שִׁבְעָה עֲנָנֵי יְקָר, שְׁכִינְתֵּיהּ אַזְלָא קַמַּיְיהוּ, הה"ד וַיְיָ' הוֹלֵךְ לִפְנֵיהֶם יוֹמָם.

1. "And Moses went and spoke these words to all Yisrael" (Devarim 31:1). Rabbi Chizkiyah opened with the verse, "That caused His glorious arm to go at the right hand of Moses, dividing the water before them…" (Yeshayah 63:12). Blessed are Yisrael that the Holy One, blessed be He, favored them. Since He favored them, He called them holy firstborn sons, and brethren. He, so to speak, went down to dwell with them. This is the meaning of, "And let them make Me a sanctuary, that I may dwell among them" (Shemot 25:8). And He wished to establish them in the likeness of above, and He caused the seven clouds of glory to rest over them, and His Shechinah goes before them, as it is written: "and Hashem went before them by day" (Shemot 13:21).

1. Moses, Aaron and Miriam

A Synopsis

Rabbi Chizkiyah talks about God's desire for Yisrael and His special treatment of them. We learn that Moses, Aaron and Miriam had higher gifts, and that Aaron was the right arm of Moses. During Moses' lifetime Yisrael ate manna or heavenly bread, but as soon as Joshua took over, the manna ceased to fall and the people reverted to eating the bread of the land.

2. תְּלַת אַחִין קַדִּישִׁין אַזְלִין בֵּינַיְיהוּ, וּמַאן אִינּוּן. מֹשֶׁה, אַהֲרֹן, וּמִרְיָם. וּבִזְכוּתֵהוֹן, יָהַב לוֹן קוּדְשָׁא בְּרִיךְ הוּא, מַתְנָן עִלָּאִין. כָּל יוֹמוֹי דְּאַהֲרֹן, לָא אַעְדוּ עֲנָנֵי יְקָר מִיִשְׂרָאֵל. וְהָא אוֹקְמוּהָ, דְּאַהֲרֹן דְּרוֹעָא יְמִינָא דְּיִשְׂרָאֵל הֲוָה. וְהַיְינוּ דִּכְתִיב, וַיִּשְׁמַע הַכְּנַעֲנִי מֶלֶךְ עֲרָד וְגוֹ', כִּי בָּא יִשְׂרָאֵל דֶּרֶךְ הָאֲתָרִים וְגוֹ'. כְּבַ"נ דְּאָזִיל בְּלָא דְּרוֹעָא, וְסָמִיךְ גַּרְמֵיהּ לְכָל אֲתָר, וּכְדֵין וַיִּלָּחֶם בְּיִשְׂרָאֵל וַיִּשְׁבְּ מִמֶּנּוּ שֶׁבִי, בְּגִין דַּהֲווֹ בְּלָא דְּרוֹעָא יְמִינָא. ת"ח, אַהֲרֹן דְּרוֹעָא יְמִינָא דְּגוּפָא הֲוָה. וְעַל דָּא כְּתִיב, מוֹלִיךְ לִימִין מֹשֶׁה זְרוֹעַ תִּפְאַרְתּוֹ. וּמַאן אִיהוּ. אַהֲרֹן.

2. Three holy siblings went among them. They are Moses, Aaron and Miriam. It is for their merit that the Holy One, blessed be He, gave them supernal gifts. Throughout Aaron's days the clouds of glory did not move away from Yisrael. We have established that Aaron is the right arm of Yisrael, as written, "the Canaanite, the king of Arad…heard tell that Yisrael came by the way of Atarim…" (Bemidbar 21:1). THE WAY OF ATARIM MEANS THAT YISRAEL WERE like a man walking without an arm, supporting himself in each AND EVERY place, AS ATARIM MEANS PLACES. Then, "he fought against Yisrael, and took some of them prisoners" (Ibid.). THIS HAPPENED because they were without the right arm. Come and see, Aaron was the right arm of the body, WHICH IS TIFERET. Hence it is written, "That caused His glorious arm to go at the right hand of Moses." Which is that? It is Aaron, THE RIGHT ARM OF TIFERET.

3. וַיֵּלֶךְ מֹשֶׁה, מַאי וַיֵּלֶךְ, לְאָן הָלַךְ. אֶלָּא וַיֵּלֶךְ, כְּגוּפָא בְּלָא דְּרוֹעָא. כד"א, וַיֵּלְכוּ בְּלֹא כֹחַ לִפְנֵי רוֹדֵף. דְּהָא מִית אַהֲרֹן דְּרוֹעָא יְמִינָא,

וּבָעָא לְאִסְתַּלְּקָא גּוּפָא.

3. HE ASKS, What is meant by "went" in "And Moses went"? Whither did he go? AND HE ANSWERS, "went" MEANS HE WENT like an armless body, as in, "and they are gone without strength before the pursuer" (Eichah 1:6), because Aaron, the right arm, died, and the body, WHICH IS MOSES, wanted to go away BECAUSE OF IT.

4. כָּל יוֹמוֹי דְּמֹשֶׁה, אַכְלוּ יִשְׂרָאֵל לֶחֶם מִן הַשָּׁמַיִם. כֵּיוָן דְּאָתָא יְהוֹשֻׁעַ, מַה כְּתִיב וַיִּשְׁבּוֹת הַמָּן מִמָּחֳרָת וְגוֹ'. וַיֹּאכְלוּ מֵעֲבוּר הָאָרֶץ מִמָּחֳרַת הַפֶּסַח. מַה בֵּין הַאי לְהַאי. אֶלָּא דָּא מִלְעֵילָּא. וְדָא לְתַתָּא. כָּל זִמְנָא דְּמֹשֶׁה, אִשְׁתְּכַח גּוּפָא דְּשִׁמְשָׁא שַׁלִּיט, וְנָהִיר לְעָלְמָא. כֵּיוָן דְּאִסְתְּלַּק מֹשֶׁה, אִתְכְּנַשׁ גּוּפָא דְּשִׁמְשָׁא, וְנָפִיק גּוּפָא דְּסִיהֲרָא.

4. Throughout Moses' life Yisrael ate bread from heaven. When Joshua came, it is written, "and the manna ceased on the morrow…" (Yehoshua 5:12), "And they did eat of the corn of the land on the morrow after the Passover" (Ibid. 11). What is the difference between them, THE MANNA AND THE CORN OF THE LAND? It is that the manna is from above, HEAVEN, WHICH IS ZEIR ANPIN, while that, THE BREAD OF THE LAND, is from below, FROM MALCHUT CALLED LAND. As long as Moses was alive, the body of the sun, WHICH IS ZEIR ANPIN, ruled and shone on the world. Once Moses departed, the body of the sun was gone, and the body of the moon came out, WHICH IS MALCHUT, THE ASPECT OF JOSHUA. THUS THE BREAD FROM HEAVEN STOPPED AND THEY ATE OF THE CORN OF THE LAND, WHICH IS MALCHUT.

2. Moses is the rule of the sun, Joshua of the moon

A Synopsis

Rabbi Chizkiyah tells us how the people were led by the sun itself, Zeir Anpin, during Moses' lifetime, but after his death they were led by the moon, Malchut, as the moon was the aspect of Joshua. Next the topic turns to the difficulty of matching people with those who are the other half of their spirits, since sometimes they are not incarnated at the same time. If a husband who is not a woman's true counterpart has behaved immorally, he is gathered up so that the counterpart can come and marry her. Rabbi Eleazar wonders why the man has to die, and why they cannot just separate. The answer is that the death saves the man from seeing his wife belong to another. This is compared to Saul's kingship which happened because David's time for kingship had not yet come. When David was ready, Saul was gathered up for his iniquities so that he would not have to see his servant ruling over him. This is also why Moses died when the rule of the moon, Joshua, arrived; the moon could not rule as long as the sun was around. The question is asked why, when Moses was about to die, many instructions were given by God to him rather than to Joshua. We learn that even after Moses' departure he would still exist to illuminate God's messages for Joshua, just as the sun in hiding illuminates the moon.

5. כְּתִיב אִם אֵין פָּנֶיךָ הוֹלְכִים אַל תַּעֲלֵנוּ מִזֶּה וּבַמֶּה יִוָּדַע אֵפוֹא וְגוֹ', הָכִי אוֹלִיפְנָא, כֵּיוָן דְּאָמַר קוּדְשָׁא בְּרִיךְ הוּא לְמֹשֶׁה הִנֵּה מַלְאָכִי יֵלֵךְ לְפָנֶיךָ, אָמַר מֹשֶׁה, וּמַה קַסְטִיפָא דְּשִׁמְשָׁא דְּיִתְכְּנִישׁ, וְיַדְבַּר סִיהֲרָא, גּוּפָא דְּסִיהֲרָא לָא בָּעֵינָא. אִם אֵין פָּנֶיךָ הוֹלְכִים, גּוּפָא דְּשִׁמְשָׁא בָּעֵינָא, וְלָאו דְּסִיהֲרָא. כְּדֵין גּוּפָא דְּשִׁמְשָׁא אִתְנְהִיר, וְאִתְעֲבֵיד מֹשֶׁה, כְּגַוְונָא דְּגוּפָא דְּשִׁמְשָׁא קַמַּיְיהוּ דְּיִשְׂרָאֵל. כֵּיוָן דְּאִתְכְּנִישׁ מֹשֶׁה, אִתְכְּנִישׁ שִׁמְשָׁא, וְאִתְנְהִיר סִיהֲרָא, וַהֲוָה יְהוֹשֻׁעַ מִשְׁתַּמֵּשׁ לִנְהוֹרָא דְּסִיהֲרָא. וַוי לְהַהוּא כְּסוּפָא.

5. It is written, "If Your presence go not with me, carry us not up from here. For in what shall it be known..." (Shemot 33:15-16). We have learned that when the Holy One, blessed be He, said to Moses, 'Behold My angel to walk before you', Moses said, And why is it that the guidance of the sun shall be gathered, WHICH IS THE GUIDANCE OF ZEIR ANPIN, and the moon shall guide. I do not want the body of the moon, THE GUIDANCE OF

MALCHUT CALLED AN ANGEL. AND HE SAID TO ZEIR ANPIN, "If Your presence go not with me, CARRY US NOT UP FROM HERE." I want neither the body of the sun, WHICH IS ZEIR ANPIN, nor the moon, WHICH IS MALCHUT. Then the body of the sun shone, and Moses became as the body of the sun before Yisrael. When Moses was gathered, the sun was gathered and the moon shone, which is Joshua ministering to the light of the moon. Woe to that shame.

6. וַיֹּאמֶר אֲלֵיהֶם בֶּן מֵאָה וְעֶשְׂרִים שָׁנָה וְגוֹ'. הַיְינוּ דא"ר אֶלְעָזָר, אַרְבְּעִין שְׁנִין נָהִיר שִׁמְשָׁא לוֹן לְיִשְׂרָאֵל, וְאִתְכְּנִישׁ לְסוֹף אַרְבְּעִין שְׁנִין, וְנָהִיר סִיהֲרָא. אר"ש וַדַּאי הָכִי הוּא, הַיְינוּ דִּכְתִּיב וְיֵשׁ נִסְפֶּה בְּלֹא מִשְׁפָּט וְהָא אַתְעֲרוּ חַבְרַיָּיא. וַאֲנָן נוֹקִים לֵיהּ לַקְּרָא, אֲבָל עַל מַה דְּאַתְעֲרוּ חַבְרַיָּיא כֹּלָּא הוּא אִצְטְרִיךְ לְעָלְמָא, לְתוֹעַלְתָּא דב"נ, דְּיִתְכְּנַשׁ עַד לָא מָטוֹן יוֹמוֹי.

6. "And he said to them, I am a hundred and twenty years old…" (Devarim 31:2). It is as Rabbi Elazar said that the sun shone on Yisrael for forty years and was gathered at the end of forty years and then the moon shone. HE THEREFORE SAID, "I CAN NO MORE GO OUT AND COME IN" (IBID.), BECAUSE THE TIME HAS COME FOR THE MOON TO RULE, WHICH IS THE ASPECT OF JOSHUA. Rabbi Shimon said, surely it is thus, as written, "but sometimes ruin comes for want of judgment" (Mishlei 13:23), which the friends have already explained, and we shall expound on this verse. But in relation to what the friends have said, everything is needed in the world for the good of man, who will be gone before his time, THAT IS, THAT HE IS RUINED WITHOUT JUDGMENT, AS SHALL BE EXPLAINED.

7. ת"ח, וְהָא אִתְּמַר, דְּכָל רוּחִין דְּנָפְקִין מִלְעֵילָּא, דְּכַר וְנוּקְבָּא נַפְקֵי, וּמִתְפָּרְשָׁן. וּלְזִמְנִין תִּפּוּק נִשְׁמְתָא דְּנוּקְבָא, עַד לָא נַפְקַת דְּכַר, דְּהוּא בַּר זוּגָהּ. וְכָל זִמְנִין דִּדְכוּרָא לָא מָטָא זִמְנֵיהּ לְאִזְדַּוְּוגָא בַּהֲדֵי נוּקְבֵיהּ, וְאָתֵי אַחֲרָא וְאִתְנְסִיב בַּהֲדָהּ, כֵּיוָן דְּמָטָא זִמְנָא דְּהַאי לְאִזְדַּוְּוגָא, כַּד אִתְּעַר צֶדֶק בְּעָלְמָא, לְמִפְקַד עַל חוֹבֵי עָלְמָא, כָּנִישׁ לֵיהּ לְהַאי אַחֲרָא, דַּהֲוָה נָסִיב בַּהֲדָהּ, וְאָתֵי אַחֲרָא וְנָטִיל לָהּ. וְעַל דָּא קָשִׁין זִוּוּגִין קַמֵּי קוּדְשָׁא בְּרִיךְ הוּא.

7. Come and see, we learned that all spirits that emerge from above come out male and female, and separate WHEN THEY COME INTO THE WORLD TO BE CLOTHED IN BODIES. At times the female soul will emerge into the world before THE SOUL OF the male has come out, who is her mate. Whenever it is not the time of the man to join his woman and another came, WHO IS NOT HER MATE, and married her, then when his, HER SOULMATE'S, time comes to unite with her, righteousness, WHICH IS THE ATTRIBUTE OF JUDGMENT, is awakened in the world to punish for the iniquities of the world. It gathers that man who married her, THAT IS, IT TAKES HIS SOUL SO HE DIES, and the other comes, WHO IS HER MATE, and marries her. This is why matching couples is difficult for the Holy One, blessed be He, LIKE THE SPLITTING OF THE RED SEA.

8. וְכָל דָּא בְּגִין דְּסָרַח דְּכוּרָא עוֹבָדוֹי, ואע״ג דְּלָא סָרַח כ״כ עוֹבָדוֹי בַּחֲטָאֵיהּ, אִתְכְּנִישׁ בְּהַהוּא זִמְנָא, עַד לָא מָטוֹן יוֹמוֹי, דְּלָא עָבֵיד הָכִי בְּמִשְׁפָּט וְעָלֵיהּ כְּתִיב, וְיֵשׁ נִסְפֶּה בְּלֹא מִשְׁפָּט. וְאָעְרַע בֵּיהּ דִּינָא דְּצֶדֶק בְּחוֹבוֹי. בְּגִין דְּמָטָא זִמְנֵיהּ דְּאַחֲרָא, וְנָסִיב לָהּ, דְּהָא דִּידֵיהּ הִיא.

8. This is true if the man, WHO IS NOT HER MATE, sinned in his actions, THAT HE IS TAKEN OUT OF THE WORLD WHEN THE TIME HAS COME FOR HER MATE TO MARRY HER. Even if he did not sin much TO BE SENTENCED TO DEATH, NEVERTHELESS he dies then before his time comes TO DIE and it is not done so ACCORDING TO judgment. Of him it is written, "but sometimes ruin comes for want of judgment." The Judgments of righteousness, WHICH IS MALCHUT OF THE ATTRIBUTE OF JUDGMENT, contact him because of his sins, because the time of the other, HER MATE, has come to marry her, because she is his, EVEN THOUGH ACCORDING TO JUDGMENT HE DOES NOT DESERVE DEATH.

9. א״ל ר״א, וַאֲמַאי, יַפְרִישׁ לוֹן קוּדְשָׁא בְּרִיךְ הוּא, וְיֵיתֵי אַחֲרָא וְיָהִיב לֵיהּ. אֲמַר לֵיהּ דָּא הוּא תּוֹעַלְתָּא דְּבַר נָשׁ, וְטִיבוּ דְּעָבֵיד עִמֵּיהּ, דְּלָא יֶחֱמֵי אִתְּתֵיהּ בִּידָא אַחֲרָא. ות״ח, אִי הַאי לָא כַּשְׁרָן עוֹבָדוֹי, אע״ג דְּדִילֵיהּ הִיא הַהִיא אִתְּתָא, לָא אִתְדְּחֵי הַאי אַחֲרָא מִקַּמֵּיהּ.

9. Rabbi Elazar said to him, and why DOES HE DIE? Let the Holy One, blessed be He, separate them from each other and let him WHO IS HER

MATE come and marry her. He said to him, it is for the good of man, and He does kindly by him, so he will not see his wife under someone else's authority. Come and see, if he, HER MATE, is not of fitting deeds, then even if the woman is his, NEVERTHELESS the other is not rejected, WHO IS NOT HER MATE, from before him.

10. ת״ח, שָׁאוּל מַלְכָּא נָטַל מַלְכוּ. בְּגִין דְּעַד לָא מָטָא זִמְנֵיהּ דְּדָוִד לְהַאי. דְּהָא מַלְכוּ הֲוָה וַדַּאי דְּדָוִד, וְאָתָא שָׁאוּל וְנָטִיל לֵיהּ. כֵּיוָן דְּמָטָא זִמְנֵיהּ דְּדָוִד לְמֵירַת דִּילֵיהּ, כְּדֵין אִתְּעַר צֶדֶק וְכָנִישׁ לֵיהּ לְשָׁאוּל בְּחוֹבוֹי, וְאִתְדְּחֵי מִקַּמֵּי דָּוִד, וְאָתָא דָּוִד וְנָטַל דִּילֵיהּ.

10. Come and see, King Saul took the kingship because although the kingship was David's the time of David had not yet come for it. THEREFORE when David's time had come to inherit his own, righteousness awoke and gathered Saul in his sins, and he was pushed aside before David. And David came and took what was his.

11. וַאֲמַאי לָא אַעְדֵּי קוּדְשָׁא בְּרִיךְ הוּא לְשָׁאוּל מִמַּלְכוּ, וְלָא יְמוּת. אֶלָּא טִיבוּ עָבֵד קוּדְשָׁא בְּרִיךְ הוּא עִמֵּיהּ, דְּכָנִישׁ לֵיהּ בְּמַלְכוּתָא, וְלָא יֶחֱמֵי עַבְדֵּיהּ שַׁלִּיט עָלֵיהּ, וְנָטִיל מַה דַּהֲוָה דִּילֵיהּ בְּקַדְמֵיתָא. כַּךְ הַאי. בג״כ, בָּעֵי ב״נ לְמִבְעֵי רַחֲמֵי קָמֵי קוּדְשָׁא בְּרִיךְ הוּא, כַּד אִזְדַּוּוג, דְּלָא יִתְדְּחֵי מִקַּמֵּי אַחֲרָא.

11. Why did the Holy One, blessed be He, not take away the kingship from Saul TO GIVE IT TO DAVID, so he would not HAVE TO die? AND HE ANSWERS, the Holy One, blessed be He, did kindness with him by gathering his soul while he was still reigning, so he would not see his servant ruling over him and taking what had been his. It is so THAT HE MARRIED HIS NEIGHBOR'S MATE, AND THE TIME HAS COME FOR HIS NEIGHBOR TO MARRY HER, HE GATHERS HIS SOUL AND THEN MARRIES THE WOMAN TO HER MATE, SO HE WILL NOT SEE HIS WIFE IN ANOTHER AUTHORITY. This is why man has to beg for mercy from the Holy One, blessed be He, when he marries, that he will not be pushed aside before another.

12. כְּתִיב, וַיֹּאמֶר יְיָ׳ אֵלַי רַב לָךְ אַל תּוֹסֶף דַּבֵּר אֵלַי וְגוֹ׳ וְהָא

אוֹקִימְנָא, אָמַר לֵיהּ קוּדְשָׁא בְּרִיךְ הוּא לְמֹשֶׁה מֹשֶׁה, תִּבְעֵי לְאַחְדְּשָׁא עָלְמָא, חָמֵית מִן יוֹמָךְ שִׁמְשָׁא פָּלַח לְסִיהֲרָא. חָמֵית מִן יוֹמָךְ דְּיִשְׁלוֹט סִיהֲרָא בְּעוֹד דְּשִׁמְשָׁא קַיְּימָא. אֶלָּא הֵן קָרְבוּ יָמֶיךָ לָמוּת קְרָא אֶת יְהוֹשֻׁעַ, יִתְכְּנִישׁ שִׁמְשָׁא, וְיִשְׁלוֹט סִיהֲרָא. וְלֹא עוֹד, אֶלָּא אִי אַנְתְּ תֵּיעוּל לְאַרְעָא, יִתְכְּנִישׁ סִיהֲרָא מִקַּמָּךְ, וְלָא יִשְׁלוֹט. וַדַּאי שׁוּלְטָנוּתָא דְּסִיהֲרָא מָטָא, וְלָא תִּשְׁלוֹט בְּעוֹד דְּאַנְתְּ קַיְּימָא בְּעָלְמָא.

12. It is written, “and Hashem said to me, Let it suffice you; speak no more to Me of this matter…” (Devarim 3:26). We explained that the Holy One, blessed be He, said to Moses, ‘Moses, you want the world to change. Have you ever seen in your days that the sun will serve the moon? Have you ever seen in your days that the moon will rule while the sun is present? But, “Behold, your days approach that you must die. Call Joshua” (Devarim 31:14). Let the sun be gathered and the moon reign. Moreover, if you enter the land, the moon shall be gathered for you and will not be able to rule. Surely the dominion of the moon is come, WHICH IS JOSHUA, but it cannot rule as long as you are in the world.’

13. קְרָא אֶת יְהוֹשֻׁעַ וְגוֹ'. וּמַאי קָאָמַר הִנְּךָ שׁוֹכֵב עִם אֲבוֹתֶיךָ וְקָם הָעָם הַזֶּה וְגוֹ'. וְלָא אַשְׁכַּחְנָא, דְּפָקִיד קוּדְשָׁא בְּרִיךְ הוּא לִיהוֹשֻׁעַ, אֶלָּא לְמֹשֶׁה, דא"ל לְמֹשֶׁה כָּל הַאי, דִּכְתִּיב וַעֲזָבַנִי וְהֵפֵר אֶת בְּרִיתִי, וְחָרָה אַפִּי בוֹ בַיּוֹם הַהוּא. וְעַתָּה כִּתְבוּ לָכֶם אֶת הַשִּׁירָה הַזֹּאת וְלַמְּדָהּ אֶת בְּנֵי יִשְׂרָאֵל שִׂימָהּ בְּפִיהֶם, אִי הָכִי מַהוּ וַאֲצַוֶּנּוּ.

13. “Call Joshua, AND PRESENT YOURSELVES IN THE TENT OF MEETING, THAT I MAY GIVE HIM A CHARGE…” (Ibid.). What about His words, “Behold, you shall sleep with your fathers; and this people will rise up…” (Ibid. 16). We never found the Holy One, blessed be He, giving charge to Joshua but to Moses, as He said all that to Moses, as written, “and will forsake Me, and break My covenant…Then My anger will burn against them on that day” (Ibid. 16-17), “Now therefore write this poem for yourselves, and teach it to the children of Yisrael. Put it in their mouths” (Ibid. 19). ALL THIS WAS SAID TO MOSES. In that case what is meant by, “that I may give him a charge,” SEEING THAT HE CHARGED HIM WITH NOTHING?

14. אֶלָּא קְרָא אָמַר, הִנְּךָ שׁוֹכֵב עִם אֲבוֹתֶיךָ, אָמַר לֵיהּ קוּדְשָׁא בְּרִיךְ הוּא לְמֹשֶׁה, אע״ג דְּאַנְתְּ תִּשְׁכּוֹב עִם אֲבָהֳתָךְ, הָא אַנְתְּ קַיְּימָא תָּדִיר לְאַנְהֲרָא לְסִיהֲרָא. כְּמָה דְּשִׁמְשָׁא, דאע״ג דְּאִתְכְּנִישׁ, לָא אִתְכְּנִישׁ אֶלָּא לְאַנְהֲרָא לְסִיהֲרָא. וּכְדֵין אַנְהִיר לְסִיהֲרָא, כַּד אִתְכְּנִישׁ. וְעַל דָּא, הִנְּךָ שׁוֹכֵב לְאַנְהֲרָא, וְדָא הוּא וַאֲצַוֶּנּוּ. וּכְדֵין אִתְבְּשַׂר יְהוֹשֻׁעַ לְאִתְנַהֲרָא, וְעַל דָּא כְּתִיב, הִנְּךָ שׁוֹכֵב עִם אֲבוֹתֶיךָ, לְאַנְהֲרָא לִיהוֹשֻׁעַ, וְדָא הוּא וְצַו אֶת יְהוֹשֻׁעַ וְחַזְּקֵהוּ. וְצַו אֶת יְהוֹשֻׁעַ כֻּלְּהוּ לְאַנְהֲרָא.

14. AND HE ANSWERS, the verse says, "Behold, you shall sleep with your fathers." The Holy One, blessed be He, said to Moses, 'Though you shall sleep with your fathers, yet you will always shine on the moon, NAMELY JOSHUA, WHO IS THE ASPECT OF THE MOON, MALCHUT, like the sun that, although it set, set only to shine on the moon. For then, after it set, it shines on the moon. Hence, "you shall sleep" to shine.' This is what is meant by, "that I may give him a charge." FOR WITH THE DEPARTURE OF MOSES, HE SHINES WITH WORDS OF HASHEM TO JOSHUA, LIKE THE SUN SHINES ON THE MOON AFTER IT SETS. THUS then Joshua was instructed to shine. Hence the verse, "you shall sleep with your fathers," that is, to shine on Joshua. And that is, "But charge Joshua" (Devarim 3:28); the purpose of everything is to illuminate HIM.

15. כִּי אַתָּה תָּבֹא, וּלְבָתַר תָּבִיא מַה בֵּין הַאי לְהַאי. אֶלָּא חַד תָּבֹא, לְבַשְּׂרָא לֵיהּ דְּיֵיעוּל לְאַרְעָא, וְיִתְקַיֵּים בָּהּ. וְחַד תָּבִיא, לְבַשְּׂרָא לֵיהּ שֻׁלְטָנוּתָא עַל יִשְׂרָאֵל, וְאִתְבְּשַׂר עַל קִיּוּמָא דְּגַרְמֵיהּ, וְאִתְבְּשַׂר עַל שֻׁלְטָנוּ דְּיִשְׂרָאֵל.

15. "For you must go (Heb. *tavo*)" (Devarim 31:7). Afterwards IT IS WRITTEN, "for you shall bring (Heb. *tavi*)" (Ibid. 23). What is the difference between them? AND HE ANSWERS, one 'tavo' is to announce to him that he shall enter the land and dwell in it; and one 'tavi' is to announce to him about the dominion over Yisrael. HE THUS WAS TOLD TWO THINGS: he was told about his own dwelling in the Land of Yisrael and about the dominion over Yisrael.

3. "From the uttermost part of the earth have we heard songs"

A Synopsis

Rabbi Shimon talks about those people who pay no attention to the glory of God and who have no interest in becoming holy. He says that Malchut is ready and available to praise God after midnight every night. Prior to that the wicked prosecutors go about in the world to harm people, but from midnight onward their power is removed. We hear that if people are sanctified in their own union they also inspire a spiritual sanctity above, assisting in the union of God and His Shechinah. If they do not, there are flaws both above and below and the children born of the union are deceitful. Rabbi Shimon tells us about the time that Yisrael entered the Holy Land with the Ark of the Covenant traveling before them, and the songs of praise and joy that were sung. He says how unfortunate it is that Yisrael were destined later to treacherously betray God and become uprooted from their land; they would have to be cleansed of their iniquities in a foreign land.

16. ר׳ שִׁמְעוֹן פָּתַח, מִכְּנַף הָאָרֶץ זְמִירוֹת שָׁמַעְנוּ צְבִי לַצַּדִּיק וְגוֹ׳, וַוי לוֹן לִבְנֵי נָשָׁא, לְאִינּוּן דְּלָא מַשְׁגְּחִין וְלָא מִשְׁתַּדְּלִין בִּיקָרָא דְּמָארֵיהוֹן, וְלָא מִסְתַּכְּלִין בִּקְדוּשָּׁא עִלָּאָה, לְאִתְקַדְּשָׁא בְּהַאי עָלְמָא, לְמֶהֱוֵי קַדִּישִׁין בְּעָלְמָא דְּאָתֵי. מִכְּנַף הָאָרֶץ, דָּא כְּסוּתָא עִלָּאָה קַדִּישָׁא. זְמִירוֹת שָׁמַעְנוּ, כד״א נוֹתֵן זְמִירוֹת בַּלָּיְלָה, זְמִירוֹת תּוּשְׁבְּחָן דִּכְנֶסֶת יִשְׂרָאֵל, קַמֵּי קוּדְשָׁא בְּרִיךְ הוּא בַּלָּיְלָה. בַּלָּיְלָה: בִּזְמְנָא דְּאִיהִי אִזְדַּמְּנָא וּשְׁכִיחָא לְשַׁבְּחָא לֵיהּ לְקוּדְשָׁא בְּרִיךְ הוּא וּמִשְׁתַּעֲשָׁע עִם צַדִּיקַיָּיא בְּגִנְתָּא דְּעֵדֶן.

16. Rabbi Shimon opened with, "From the uttermost part of the earth have we heard songs, glory to the righteous. BUT I SAID, MY LEANNESS, MY LEANNESS, WOE TO ME! TRAITORS HAVE DEALT TREACHEROUSLY..." (Yeshayah 24:16). Woe to people, that they do not care and are not occupied with the glory of their Master, nor do they behold the supernal holiness, to be sanctified in this world so as to be holy in the World to Come. "The uttermost part of the earth" refers to the supernal covering, NAMELY MALCHUT. "We heard songs," as in, "who gives songs in the night" (Iyov 35:10), that is, the songs and praises of the Congregation of Yisrael, MALCHUT, before the Holy One, blessed be He, WHO IS ZEIR

ANPIN, at night. "In the night" MEANS when she is ready and present to praise the Holy One, blessed be He, and takes pleasure in the righteous in the Garden of Eden.

17. וְאֵימָתַי. מִפַּלְגּוּת לֵילְיָא וְאֵילָךְ. וּכְדֵין זְמִירוֹת שָׁמַעְנוּ, תּוּשְׁבְּחָן. וּזְמִירוֹת: כד״א לֹא תִזְמוֹר. וּכְתִיב זְמִיר עָרִיצִים יַעֲנֶה, אַעְקְרוּתָא מֵאַתְרַיְיהוּ כָּל אִינּוּן תַּקִּיפִין, דְּהָא כַּד עָיֵיל לֵילְיָא, כַּמָּה עֲרִיצִים גַּרְדִּינֵי נִימוּסִין שְׁכִיחִין בְּעָלְמָא, אָזְלִין וְשַׁיְיטָן בְּעָלְמָא לְקַטְרְגָא. מִפַּלְגּוּת לֵילְיָא וְאֵילָךְ, אִתְּעַר רוּחָא חֲדָא וְאַעְקַר לְכֻלְּהוּ מֵאַתְרַיְיהוּ, וְאַעְבַּר לוֹן דְּלָא יִשְׁלְטוּן. זְמִירוֹת שָׁמַעְנוּ, תּוּשְׁבְּחָן דִּכְנֶסֶת יִשְׂרָאֵל בְּלֵילְיָא, וְכָל דָּא לָמָּה. צְבִי לַצַּדִּיק, לְאִזְדַּוְּוגָא בְּזִוּוּגָא חֲדָא דְּקוּדְשָׁא בְּרִיךְ הוּא, וּלְאִתְקַדְּשָׁא בִּקְדוּשָּׁה חֲדָא.

17. When IS SHE READY TO PRAISE THE HOLY ONE, BLESSED BE HE? It is from midnight onward. Then, "we heard songs," namely praises. "Songs (Heb. *zemirot*)" MEANS as in, "nor prune (Heb. *tizmor*)" (Vayikra 25:4), and ALSO, "so the song of the tyrant shall be brought low" (Yeshayah 25:5), which refers to pulling out all the tyrants from their places. For when the night comes, many tyrannical litigants are present in the world, walking and roaming the world to bring accusations. From midnight onward, a spirit is roused, which pulls them all from their places and removes them so they shall not have power. "We heard songs" refers to the praises of the Congregation of Yisrael TO THE HOLY ONE, BLESSED BE HE, at night. What is the reason for all that? It is "glory to the righteous," WHICH MEANS MALCHUT WISHES to unite in a single union with the Holy One, blessed be He, and be sanctified with him in the same holiness. "Glory" is derived from desire, while the righteous is Yesod.

18. וָאוֹמַר רָזִי לִי רָזִי לִי, דָּא הוּא רָזָא עִלָּאָה. דָּא הוּא רוּחַ קַדִּישָׁא, אֲבָל אוֹי לִי עַל דָּרָא, וְעַל עָלְמָא, בּוֹגְדִים בָּגָדוּ, דְּכֻלְּהוּ מְשַׁקְּרָן בֵּיהּ, מְשַׁקְּרָן בְּהוּ בְּגַרְמַיְיהוּ, וְלָא דַּי דִּמְשַׁקְּרָן בְּגַרְמַיְיהוּ, אֶלָּא אִינּוּן בְּבִנְין דְּאוֹלִידוּ מִתְשַׁקְּרָן בְּהַהוּא שִׁקְרָא דִּלְהוֹן, וְאִשְׁתְּכָחוּ פְּגִימִין לְעֵילָּא וְתַתָּא.

18. "But I said, My leanness, my leanness, woe to me." "MY LEANNESS (HEB. *RAZI*)" is a supernal mystery, BECAUSE 'RAZ' MEANS A SECRET. THE SECOND SECRET is TO DRAW a Holy Spirit. THAT IS, THE UNION OF THE HOLY ONE, BLESSED BE HE, WITH HIS SHECHINAH AT MIDNIGHT IS A SUPERNAL MYSTERY. IF PEOPLE BELOW ARE THEN SANCTIFIED IN THEIR MATING, AND MEDITATE ON IT, THEY DRAW A HOLY SPIRIT. But "woe to me" for the generation and for the world; "traitors have dealt treacherously," for they are all false to Him, THAT IS, THEY DENY THE SUPERNAL PROVIDENCE; they are false to themselves BY NOT SANCTIFYING THEMSELVES DURING MATING. Not only are they false to themselves, but the children they beget would be false because of their falsity DURING MATING, WHICH WAS WITHOUT SUPERNAL HOLINESS, and they are blemished above and below.

19. כֵּיוָן דְּאִסְתָּכַּל יְשַׁעְיָהוּ בְּהַאי, כָּנִישׁ לְאִינּוּן דַּחֲלִין חַטָּאָה, וְאוֹלִיף לוֹן אֹרַח קַדִּישָׁא לְאִתְקַדְּשָׁא בִּקְדוּשָּׁה דְּמַלְכָּא, וּלְאִשְׁתַּכְּחָא בְּנַיְיהוּ קַדִּישִׁין. כֵּיוָן דְּאִתְקְדָּשׁוּ אִלֵּין, אִינּוּן בְּנִין דְּאוֹלִידוּ אִקְרוּן עַל שְׁמֵיהּ. הה"ד הִנֵּה אָנֹכִי וְהַיְלָדִים אֲשֶׁר נָתַן לִי יְיָ' לְאוֹתוֹת וּלְמוֹפְתִים בְּיִשְׂרָאֵל, דִּפְרִישָׁן מִשְּׁאַר עַמִּין.

19. When Isaiah saw this, he gathered all those who fear sin and taught them the holy way of being sanctified with the holiness of the King DURING MATING so their children would be holy. Once they were sanctified, the children they begot were named after Him. This is the meaning of, "Behold, I and the children whom Hashem has given me are for signs and for portents in Yisrael" (Yeshayah 8:18), which means they are separated from the other nations.

20. ד"א מִכְּנַף הָאָרֶץ זְמִירוֹת שָׁמַעְנוּ, בְּשַׁעֲתָא דְּעָאלוּ יִשְׂרָאֵל לְאַרְעָא, וַאֲרוֹן קַיְימָא קַדִּישָׁא קַמַּיְיהוּ, שָׁמְעוּ יִשְׂרָאֵל דְּמִסְטְרָא חַד דְּאַרְעָא, תּוּשְׁבְּחָן וְחֵדוּ וְקַל מְזַמְּרֵי עִלָּאֵי, דִּמְזַמְּרֵי בְּאַרְעָא, כְּדֵין צְבִי לַצַּדִּיק, תּוּשְׁבְּחָא דְּמֹשֶׁה הֲוָה בְּהַהִיא שַׁעֲתָא, דִּבְכָל אֲתָר דְּאָרוֹן, הֲוָה שָׁארִי בְּאַרְעָא, הֲווֹ שַׁמְעֵי קָלָא דְּאַמְרֵי, וְזֹאת הַתּוֹרָה אֲשֶׁר שָׂם מֹשֶׁה לִפְנֵי בְּנֵי יִשְׂרָאֵל. אֲבָל אוֹי לִי דְּבוֹגְדִים בָּגָדוּ, דִּזְמִינִין יִשְׂרָאֵל לְשַׁקְּרָא

בְּקוּדְשָׁא בְּרִיךְ הוּא, וּלְאִתְעַקְּרָא מֵאַרְעָא זִמְנָא חֲדָא. וּבְגִין דְּאִתְאֲחָדוּ בֵּינַיְיהוּ שִׁקְרָא דִּלְהוֹן, יִתְעַקְּרוּן זִמְנָא תִּנְיָינָא, עַד דְּיִשְׁתְּלִים חוֹבַיְיהוּ בְּאַרְעָא אַחֲרָא.

20. Another explanation for, "From the uttermost part of the earth have we heard songs" is that when Yisrael entered the land with the holy ark of the covenant before them, Yisrael heard from one side in the land praises and joy and the voice of lofty singers that sing in the land. Then, "glory to the righteous," as the praises at that time were directed to Moses, SINCE GLORY IS A WORD OF PRAISE AND GLORIFICATION, AND THE RIGHTEOUS IS MOSES. Wherever the ark dwelt in the land, they would hear a voice saying, "And this is the Torah which Moses set before the children of Yisrael" (Devarim 4:44). But, "woe to me, traitors have dealt treacherously," since Yisrael will betray the Holy One, blessed be He, and be pulled out of the land once. Since falsehood has taken hold in their midst they shall be torn out a second time FROM THE LAND until their iniquities shall be made good in another land.

4. There are three who testify

A Synopsis

Rabbi Aba and Rabbi Yitzchak discuss the witnesses that bear testimony about Yisrael, and we learn that they are the well of Isaac, the lottery, the stone that Joshua placed and the song of praise that God taught Moses just before his death.

21. לָקוֹחַ אֵת סֵפֶר הַתּוֹרָה הַזֶּה וְגוֹ'. הָא אוּקִימְנָא מִלֵּי. אֱלֹהֵיכֶם. אֱלֹהֶיךָ. אֵל. אֱלֹהֵינוּ.

21. "Take this book of the Torah, and put it in the side of the Ark of the Covenant of Hashem your Elohim..." (Devarim 31:26). HE WAS ASKED WHY HE SAID, "HASHEM YOUR ELOHIM," RATHER THAN 'HASHEM OUR ELOHIM'. AND HE ANSWERS, we have explained this IN SEVERAL PLACES, THE REASON FOR THE NAMES 'your (plur.) Elohim', 'your (sing.) Elohim', 'El', 'our Elohim'.

22. דְּאָמַר ר' אַבָּא אָמַר ר' יְהוּדָה, מַאי דִּכְתִּיב כִּי הַמָּקוֹם אֲשֶׁר אַתָּה עוֹמֵד עָלָיו אַדְמַת קֹדֶשׁ הוּא. אַדְמַת קֹדֶשׁ וַדַּאי, דְּהַיְינוּ אֶרֶץ הַחַיִּים. אֲשֶׁר אַתָּה עוֹמֵד עָלָיו, עָלָיו וַדַּאי, הַיְינוּ בְּקַדְמֵיתָא, וכ"ש לְבָתַר. תָּאנָא, אָמַר ר' יוֹסֵי, כְּתִיב וְהָיָה שָׁם בְּךָ לְעֵד, לְעֵד וַדַּאי דְּיַסְהִיד סַהֲדוּתָא.

22. As Rabbi Aba said in the name of Rabbi Yehuda, what is the meaning of, "for the place on which you do stand is holy ground" (Shemot 3:5)? It is surely holy ground, namely the land of the living, WHICH IS MALCHUT. "On which you do stand": surely it is on it, that is in the beginning and all the more so later. We learned that Rabbi Yosi said, it is written, "that it may be there for a witness against you" (Devarim 31:26), a witness surely to give testimony.

23. תְּלָתָא אִינּוּן דְּקַיְימוּ בְּסַהֲדוּתָא לְאַסְהֲדָא, וְאִלֵּין אִינּוּן: בְּאֵר דְּיִצְחָק, גּוֹרָל, וְאַבְנָא דְּשַׁוֵּי יְהוֹשֻׁעַ. וְדָא שִׁירָתָא, סַהֲדוּתָא יַתִּיר

מִכֹּלָּא. אָמַר ר׳ יִצְחָק אִי הָכִי אַרְבַּע אִינּוּן. אָמַר לֵיהּ וַדַּאי, אֲבָל גּוֹרָל לָא כְּתִיב בֵּיהּ סַהֲדוּתָא.

23. There are three who testify. They are Isaac's well, the lot and the stone, which Joshua placed. And this poem more than all, AS IT SAYS, "THAT THIS POEM MAY BE A WITNESS FOR ME..." (IBID. 19). Rabbi Yitzchak said, in that case there are four. He said to him, surely THIS IS SO, but no testifying is mentioned in relation to the lot.

24. בְּאֵר דְּיִצְחָק מְנָלָן. דִּכְתִּיב בַּעֲבוּר תִּהְיֶה לִּי לְעֵדָה וְגוֹ׳. גּוֹרָל, דִּכְתִּיב עַל פִּי הַגּוֹרָל תֵּחָלֵק נַחֲלָתוֹ, דַּהֲוָה אָמַר דָּא לִיהוּדָה, וְדָא לְבִנְיָמִין, וְכֵן לְכֻלְּהוּ. אַבְנָא דִּיהוֹשֻׁעַ, דִּכְתִּיב הִנֵּה הָאֶבֶן הַזֹּאת תִּהְיֶה בָּנוּ לְעֵדָה. וְהָכָא, וְהָיָה שָּׁם בְּךָ לְעֵד. וּכְתִיב, וְעָנְתָה הַשִּׁירָה הַזֹּאת לְפָנָיו לְעֵד, הִיא וַדַּאי אַסְהִידַת בְּהוּ בְּיִשְׂרָאֵל.

24. Whence do we know about Isaac's well? From the verse, "that they (it) may be a witness to me" (Beresheet 21:30); about the lot, from the words, "According to the lot shall their inheritance be divided" (Bemidbar 26:56), which used to say, 'this is to Judah', and 'this is to Benjamin', and so on. HENCE IT SAID, "ACCORDING TO (LIT. 'BY THE MOUTH OF') THE LOT," WHICH MEANS THE LOT SPOKE. As for Joshua's stone, it is written, "Behold, this stone shall be a witness to us" (Yehoshua 24:27). And here IT IS WRITTEN, "that it may be there for a witness against you," and, "that this poem shall testify against them as a witness" (Devarim 31:21). Surely it testified against Yisrael.

5. Song and poem

A Synopsis

The matter of Moses' song is examined in great detail, and we are reminded that the song was meant to testify against Yisrael later when they transgressed the laws of God. Rabbi Shimon clarifies which is the most valuable and important song ever written, since the discussion has also included the Song of Songs and the song that David sang towards the end of his life. The purpose of the song is to connect everyone to God and to unify His Name.

25. תָּאנָא, א״ר אֶלְעָזָר, מַאי דִּכְתִּיב וַיְדַבֵּר מֹשֶׁה וְגוֹ׳, אֶת דִּבְרֵי הַשִּׁירָה הַזֹּאת עַד תּוּמָּם. הָכָא אִית לְאִסְתַּכְּלָא, מַהוּ אֶת דִּבְרֵי, אֶת הַשִּׁירָה הַזֹּאת מִבָּעֵי לֵיהּ. וּמַהוּ עַד תּוּמָּם. אֶלָּא הָכִי תָּאנָא בְּרָזָא דְּמַתְנִיתִין, כָּל אִינּוּן מִלֵּי דְּאָמַר מֹשֶׁה, כֻּלְּהוּ מִתְגַּלְּפֵי בִּשְׁמָא דְקוּדְשָׁא בְּרִיךְ הוּא, וְכָל אִינּוּן מִלִּין הֲווֹ אַתְיָין, וְסַלְקִין וְנַחְתִּין, וּמִתְגַּלְּפִין תַּמָּן. וְכָל מִלָּה וּמִלָּה הֲוָה אַתְיָיא קַמֵּי מֹשֶׁה לְאִתְגַּלְּפָא עַל יְדוֹי וְקַיְּימָא קַמֵּיהּ. וְהַיְינוּ דִּכְתִּיב עַד תּוּמָּם.

25. We learned that Rabbi Elazar said, regarding the verse, "And Moses spoke...the words of this poem, until they were ended" (Devarim 31:30), we have to observe here the meaning of, "the words of." It should have said, 'the poem'. And what is, "until they were ended"? AND HE ANSWERS, we have so learned according to the secret of the Mishnah. All the words Moses spoke were engraved with the name of the Holy One, blessed be He, and all these words were coming, going up and down engraved there WITH THE NAME OF THE HOLY ONE, BLESSED BE HE. Each word would come before Moses to be engraved by him, and stood before him. THAT IS, IT IS WRITTEN, "THE WORDS OF THIS POEM" BECAUSE EACH WORD WOULD COME BEFORE HIM TO BE ENGRAVED. This is the meaning of, "until they were ended," THAT IS, UNTIL THEY FINISHED BEING ENGRAVED WITH THE NAME OF HASHEM.

26. ר׳ אַבָּא אָמַר, אֶת דִּבְרֵי הַשִּׁירָה הַזֹּאת, שִׁירָה הַזֹּאת מִבָּעֵי לֵיהּ: מַאי קָא רְמִיזָא. אֶלָּא שִׁירָתָא דְקוּדְשָׁא בְּרִיךְ הוּא אָמַר, כד״א שִׁיר הַשִּׁירִים אֲשֶׁר לִשְׁלֹמֹה, מַלְכָּא דִּשְׁלָמָא כֹּלָּא דִילֵיהּ, וְהָא אוּקִימְנָא

מִלֵּי. מִזְמוֹר שִׁיר לְיוֹם הַשַּׁבָּת, לְיוֹם הַשַּׁבָּת מַמָּשׁ. שִׁיר דְקוּדְשָׁא בְּרִיךְ הוּא אָמַר.

26. Rabbi Aba said, "the words of this poem." HE ASKS, it should have said, 'a poem', AND NOT "THE POEM." What does THE DEFINITE ARTICLE (HEI) allude to? AND HE ANSWERS, it is the poem the Holy One, blessed be He, recited, as in, "The song of songs, which is Solomon's (Heb. *Shlomo*)" (Shir Hashirim 1:1), who is the King that the peace (Heb. *shalom*) is His, WHO IS THE HOLY ONE, BLESSED BE HE. We have already explained this matter. "A Psalm, a song for the Shabbat day" (Tehilim 92:1), precisely for the Shabbat day, WHICH IS MALCHUT, a song the Holy One, blessed be He, recited FOR THE SHABBAT DAY, WHICH IS MALCHUT.

27. אֶלָּא הָכָא אִית לְאִסְתַּכְּלָא, הָתָם שִׁיר, וְהָכָא שִׁירָה. דָּא דְּכַר, וְדָא נוּקְבָּא. וְהָא תָּנֵינָן, כָּל נְבִיאֵי כֻּלְּהוּ לְגַבֵּי מֹשֶׁה, כְּקוֹף בְּעֵינַיְיהוּ דִּבְנֵי נָשָׁא, וְאִינּוּן אָמְרוּ שִׁיר, וּמֹשֶׁה אָמַר שִׁירָה. מֹשֶׁה הֲוָה לֵיהּ לְמֵימַר שִׁיר, וְאִינּוּן שִׁירָה. אֶלָּא דָּא הִיא רָזָא דְּמִלָּה, מֹשֶׁה לְגַרְמֵיהּ לָא קָאָמַר דָּא, אֶלָּא לְיִשְׂרָאֵל.

27. Yet we should examine this. There it says "a song (Heb. *shir*)," while there, "a poem (Heb. *shirah*). Shir is masculine, ZEIR ANPIN, and shirah is feminine, MALCHUT. We learned that all the prophets, in relation to Moses, are like a monkey in the sight of men. They said 'shir', THAT IS, "THE SONG OF SONGS," "A SONG FOR THE SHABBAT DAY," while Moses recited 'shirah', and they are shirah. The esoteric meaning is that Moses did not say it for himself but for the sake of Yisrael.

28. א"ל ר"ש, לָאו הָכִי, אֶלָּא, מֹשֶׁה וַדַּאי מֵהָכָא אִשְׁתְּמוֹדַע, דְּאִיהוּ בְּדַרְגָּא עִלָּאָה יַתִּיר מִכֹּלָּא. מֹשֶׁה סָלִיק מִתַּתָּא לְעֵילָּא, וְאִינּוּן נַחְתֵּי מֵעֵילָּא לְתַתָּא. הוּא סָלִיק מִתַּתָּא לְעֵילָּא, כְּמָה דְּתָנֵינָן מַעֲלִין בַּקֹּדֶשׁ וְאֵין מוֹרִידִין. מֹשֶׁה סָלִיק מִתַּתָּא לְעֵילָּא, דְּאָמַר שִׁירָה תּוּשְׁבַּחְתָּא דְּמַטְרוֹנִיתָא, דְּאִיהִי מְשַׁבַּחַת לְמַלְכָּא. וּמֹשֶׁה בְּמַלְכָּא אִתְאֲחַד. וְאִינּוּן נַחְתֵּי מֵעֵילָּא לְתַתָּא, דְּאַמְרוּ שִׁיר, דְּהוּא שְׁבָחָא דִּמְשַׁבְּחָא מַלְכָּא

לְמַטְרוֹנִיתָא, וְאִינּוּן בְּמַטְרוֹנִיתָא אִתְאֲחָדוּ. וְעַל דָּא, בְּהַאי אִשְׁתְּמוֹדַע שְׁבָחָא דְּמֹשֶׁה, יַתִּיר מִכֻּלְּהוּ. וְהַיְינוּ דִּכְתִּיב, אָז יָשִׁיר מֹשֶׁה וּבְנֵי יִשְׂרָאֵל אֶת הַשִּׁירָה הַזֹּאת לַיְיָ', שִׁירָתָא דְּמַטְרוֹנִיתָא לְמַאן. לַיְיָ'. ובג"כ, וַיִּכְתּוֹב מֹשֶׁה אֶת דִּבְרֵי הַשִּׁירָה הַזֹּאת, וְעָנְתָה הַשִּׁירָה הַזֹּאת.

28. Rabbi Shimon said to him, this is not so. But it is known from here that Moses was of a much higher grade than all of them. Moses rose from below upward and they descended from above downward. He, MOSES, rose from below upwards, as we learned that we increase in holiness, not decrease. Moses rose from below upwards by reciting a shirah, which is the praise of the Queen, with which she praises the King. HE STARTED WITH MALCHUT. And Moses himself joined the King, SO HIS SHIRAH ROSE FROM BELOW UPWARDS. But they descended from above downward, as they recited a shir, WHICH IS THE ASPECT OF THE MALE, which is the praise with which the King praises the Queen. They joined the Queen, SO THEIR SHIR WAS FROM ABOVE DOWNWARDS, FROM ZEIR ANPIN TO MALCHUT. This praise of Moses was made known which is above them all. This is the meaning of, "Then sang Moses and the children of Yisrael this song (Heb. *shirah*) to Hashem" (Shemot 15:1), that is, the shirah of the Queen. To whom? To Hashem. Hence it is written, "Moses therefore wrote this poem the same day" (Devarim 31:22), AND ALSO "that this poem shall testify" (Ibid. 21).

29. וְעָנְתָה הַשִּׁירָה הַזֹּאת, וְעָנוּ הַדְּבָרִים הָאֵלֶּה מִבָּעֵי לֵיהּ. אֶלָּא רָזָא דְּמִלָּה כְּמָה דְּאוֹקִימְנָא, דִּכְתִּיב וְאֶרֶץ מִתְקוֹמָמָה לוֹ, וּמֹשֶׁה בְּכֹלָּא אִסְתָּכַּל, וְעַל דָּא אָמַר שִׁירָה, בְּגִין לְאִתְאַחֲדָא מִלִּין בַּאֲתָר דָּא, לְמֶהֱוֵי עֲלַיְיהוּ דִּינָא, דִּכְתִּיב וְעָנְתָה הַשִּׁירָה הַזֹּאת לְפָנָיו. וְלָמָּה. דִּכְתִּיב כִּי אֲנִי יָדַעְתִּי אֶת יִצְרוֹ, וּכְתִיב כִּי יָדַעְתִּי אַחֲרֵי מוֹתִי וְגוֹ'. וְכַד תַּעְבְּדוּ דָּא, מִיַּד וְעָנְתָה הַשִּׁירָה הַזֹּאת לְפָנָיו לְעֵד.

29. "That this poem shall testify." HE ASKS, it should have said, 'these words shall testify'. AND HE ANSWERS that the secret meaning of this is as we explained that it is written, "and the earth shall rise up against him" (Iyov 20:27), WHICH MEANS THAT THE EARTH, WHICH IS MALCHUT, RISES UP TO EXECUTE JUDGMENT AGAINST MAN. And Moses observed everything, and so he said a shirah, WHICH IS AN ASPECT OF MALCHUT, in order to give the words a hold in that place, MALCHUT FROM WHICH they will be judged, as written, "that shall testify against them as a witness." Why is that? Because, it is written, "for I know their inclination" (Devarim 31:21), and, "For I know that after my death..." (Ibid. 29). When you shall do that, forthwith, "this poem shall testify against them as a witness," WHICH MEANS THAT MALCHUT SHALL PUNISH YOU.

30. ת"ח, כְּתִיב יְגַלּוּ שָׁמַיִם עֲוֹנוֹ וְלָא יַתִּיר, אֲבָל וְאֶרֶץ מִתְקוֹמְמָה לוֹ. בְּהַאי, דִּינָא אִתְעֲבֵיד לְמַאן דְּאִתְעֲבֵיד.

30. Come and see, it is written, "The heaven shall reveal his iniquity" (Iyov 20:27), WHICH IS ZEIR ANPIN THAT IS CALLED HEAVEN, and no more, REVEALING THE INIQUITY ALONE. But, "the earth shall rise up against him." By this, THE EARTH, WHICH IS MALCHUT, judgment is executed on whomever it is executed.

31. כְּתִיב, וַיְדַבֵּר דָּוִד לַיְיָ' אֶת דִּבְרֵי הַשִּׁירָה הַזֹּאת. הַשְׁתָּא תּוּשְׁבַּחְתָּא דְּדָוִד הוּא, בְּגִין דְּאָמַר שִׁירָה מִתַּתָּא לְעֵילָּא, וְזָכָה לְהַאי דַּרְגָּא, וְלָא אָמַר הַאי שִׁירָה, אֶלָּא בְּסוֹף יוֹמוֹי, דַּהֲוָה בִּשְׁלִימוּ יַתִּיר, מֵהַאי שִׁירָה. כְּמָה דִּתְנֵינָן, אַל תַּאֲמֵן בְּעַצְמְךָ עַד יוֹם מוֹתְךָ. וְהָכָא, אַמַּאי זָכָה דָּוִד לְמֵימַר שִׁירָתָא מִתַּתָּא לְעֵילָּא, בְּסוֹף יוֹמוֹי. דַּהֲוָה בְּנַיְיחָא מִכָּל סִטְרוֹי, דִּכְתִּיב בְּיוֹם הִצִּיל יְיָ' אוֹתוֹ מִכַּף כָּל אוֹיְבָיו.

31. It is written, "And David spoke to Hashem the words of this song (Heb. *shirah*)" (II Shmuel 22:1). It is to David's praise because he recited the shirah from below upward, FROM MALCHUT TO ZEIR ANPIN LIKE MOSES, and attained that grade OF RECITING SHIRAH FROM BELOW UPWARD. He said this shirah only at the end of his days when he was exceedingly perfected by this shirah, as we learned, 'Do not believe in yourself until the day you die'. And here, why did David merit to say a shirah from below upward at the end of his days? It is because he was then at rest in every respect, as written, "in the day that Hashem delivered him out of the hand of all his enemies" (Ibid.).

32. אר"ש, שִׁירָתָא מְעַלְיָא מִכֹּלָּא מַאי הִיא. כְּמָה דְּתָנֵינָן בְּרָזָא דְּמַתְנִיתִין, בְּמִלִּין וּבְעוֹבָדָא הָכִי נָמֵי מִתַּתָּא לְעֵילָּא, וּמֵעֵילָּא לְתַתָּא. וּלְבָתַר לְכַוְּונָא בְּלִבָּא, וּלְקַשְּׁרָא כֹּלָּא בְּחַד קִשְׁרָא.

32. Rabbi Shimon said, shirah is the most valuable. What is it? AND HE ANSWERS, it is according to what we learned in the secret of the Mishnah THAT SERVICE SHOULD BE in speech and action, IN THE TWO DECLARATIONS OF UNITY FROM BELOW UPWARD AND FROM ABOVE DOWNWARD. Here also it is from below upward and from above downward. Then one is to meditate in the heart and bind everything into one bond.

6. "Because I will call on the name of Hashem; ascribe greatness to our Elohim"

A Synopsis

Rabbi Shimon tells us that people have to arrange their praise to God in a certain way so that the glory can be raised upward and the blessings can be drawn downward; then they need to create the bond of Faith in order to unify the Holy Name.

33. מְנָלָן מִמֹּשֶׁה, בְּקַדְמֵיתָא, מִתַּתָּא לְעֵילָּא, כִּי שֵׁם יְיָ׳ אֶקְרָא. מַאי אֶקְרָא. כְּמָה דִּכְתִּיב, וַיִּקְרָא אֶל מֹשֶׁה, דָּא שְׁכִינְתָּא. לְבָתַר, הָבוּ גֹּדֶל לֵאלֹהֵינוּ, דָּא מַלְכָּא עִלָּאָה. לְבָתַר נָחִית בְּדַרְגּוֹי מֵעֵילָּא לְתַתָּא, דִּכְתִּיב צַדִּיק וְיָשָׁר. לְבָתַר קָשִׁיר קִשְׁרָא דִּמְהֵימְנוּתָא וְאָמַר, הוּא, וְדָא הוּא קִשְׁרָא לְכֹלָּא.

33. Whence do we know that? From Moses. At first HE SPOKE from below upward, SAYING, "Because I will call on the name of Hashem" (Devarim 32:3). What is "call"? It is as in, "called to Moses" (Vayikra 1:1), which is the Shechinah. Then he said, "ascribe greatness to our Elohim," which is the supernal King, NAMELY ZEIR ANPIN. Then he descended the grades from above downward, FROM ZEIR ANPIN TO MALCHUT, as written, "just and right is He" (Devarim 32:4), WHICH ARE YESOD THAT IS CALLED 'RIGHTEOUS', AND 'JUST' THAT IS MALCHUT. Then he bound the bond of Faith and said, "is He," NAMELY "JUST AND RIGHT is He," which binds everything, BECAUSE "HE" IS THE THIRD, HIDDEN PERSON THAT ALLUDES TO THE BLESSED INFINITY THAT BINDS EVERYTHING.

34. בג״כ, בָּעֵי בַּר נָשׁ לְסַדְּרָא שְׁבָחָא דְּמָארֵיהּ כְּהַאי גַּוְונָא, בְּקַדְמֵיתָא מִתַּתָּא לְעֵילָּא, לְסַלְּקָא יְקָרָא דְּמָארֵיהּ, לַאֲתַר דְּשַׁקְיוּ דַּעֲמִיקָא דְּבֵירָא נָגִיד וְנָפִיק. לְבָתַר לְאַמְשָׁכָא מֵעֵילָּא לְתַתָּא, מֵהַהוּא שַׁקְיוּ דְּנַחֲלָא, לְכָל דַּרְגָּא וְדַרְגָּא, עַד דַּרְגָּא בַּתְרָאָה, לְאַמְשָׁכָא בִּרְכָאן לְכֹלָּא, מִלְּעֵילָּא לְתַתָּא. לְבָתַר בָּעֵי לְקַשְּׁרָא קִשְׁרָא בְּכֹלָּא, קִשְׁרָא דִּמְהֵימְנוּתָא. וְדָא הוּא ב״נ דְּאוֹקִיר לִשְׁמָא דְּמָארֵיהּ, לְיַחֲדָא שְׁמָא קַדִּישָׁא. וְעַל דָּא

כְּתִיב, כִּי מְכַבְּדַי אֲכַבֵּד, כִּי מְכַבְּדַי לְעָלְמָא דָּא, אֲכַבֵּד בְּעָלְמָא דְּאָתֵי.

34. For that reason man needs to arrange his Master's praise in the same way, at first from below upward, to raise the glory of his Master, WHICH IS MALCHUT, to the place where the water of the depth of the well flows and emerges, THAT IS, TO THE PLACE OF BINAH. Then to draw from above downward to each and every grade OF THE SEVEN LOWER SFIROT down to the last grade, WHICH IS MALCHUT, in order to draw blessings to everything from above downward. Then we need to bind the bond on everything, the bond of Faith, THAT IS, TO BIND EVERYTHING TO BLESSED INFINITY AS MENTIONED. Such a man glorifies his Master, to unify the Holy Name. Hence it is written, "for them that honor Me I will honor" (I Shmuel 2:30), for those who honor Me in this world shall I honor in the World to Come.

35. וּבוֹזַי יֵקָלּוּ, מַאי וּבוֹזַי יֵקָלּוּ. דָּא הוּא מַאן דְּלָא יָדַע לְיַחֲדָא שְׁמָא קַדִּישָׁא, וּלְקַשְּׁרָא קִשְׁרָא דִּמְהֵימְנוּתָא, וּלְאַמְשָׁכָא בִּרְכָאן לַאֲתָר דְּאִצְטְרִיךְ, וּלְאוֹקִיר שְׁמָא דְּמָארֵיהּ. וְכָל מַאן דְּלָא יָדַע לְאוֹקִיר שְׁמָא דְּמָארֵיהּ, טַב לֵיהּ דְּלָא אִבְרֵי.

35. "And they that despise Me shall be lightly esteemed" (Ibid.). HE ASKS, what is meant by, "And they that despise Me shall be lightly esteemed," AND ANSWERS, this is one who does not know how to unify the Holy Name and bind the bond of Faith and draw blessings where they should be and glorify the name of his Master. Whoever does not know how to glorify the name of his Master, it would have been better for him had he not been created.

7. Answering Amen

A Synopsis

Rabbi Yehuda says that the person who says the 'Amen' is even greater than the person who makes the blessing because the 'Amen' draws blessings from the fountain of Binah. There follows a long discussion of the importance of the 'Amen'.

36. א״ר יְהוּדָה, וּבוֹזַי יֵקָלּוּ, מַאן דְּלָא יָדַע לְאוֹקִיר לְמָארֵיהּ, וְלָא אִתְכַּוָּון בְּאָמֵן, דְּתָנֵינָן גָּדוֹל הָעוֹנֶה אָמֵן יוֹתֵר מִן הַמְּבָרֵךְ. וְהָא אוֹקִימְנָא קַמֵּיהּ דר״ש, דְּאָמֵן, מָשִׁיךְ בִּרְכָאן מִמַּבּוּעָא לְמַלְכָּא, וּמִמַּלְכָּא לְמַטְרוֹנִיתָא. וּבְאַתְוָון גְּלִיפִין דְּרִבִּי אֶלְעָזָר, מֵאָלֶ״ף לְמֵ״ם, וּמִמֵּ״ם לְנוּ״ן. כֵּיוָן דְּמָטוּ בִּרְכָאן לְנוּן, מִתַּמָּן נַגְדִּין וְנָפְקִין בִּרְכָאן לְעִלָּאֵי וְתַתָּאֵי, וּמִתְפַּשְּׁטֵי בְּכֹלָּא. וְקָלָא נָפִיק אִתְשַׁקְיוּ מִשַּׁקְיוּתָא דְּבִרְכָן, דְּאַפִּיק פְּלַנְיָא עַבְדָּא דְּמַלְכָּא קַדִּישָׁא.

36. Rabbi Yehuda said, "And they that despise Me shall be lightly esteemed" (I Shmuel 2:30), refers to he who does not know how to glorify his Master and does not concentrate when saying Amen. For we learned that he who answers Amen is more valuable than he who makes the blessings. We have presented it before Rabbi Shimon WHO SAID THAT HE WHO ANSWERS Amen draws blessings from the spring, WHO IS BINAH, to the King, ZEIR ANPIN, and from the King to the Queen. In the Engraved Letters by Rabbi Elazar HE SAID 'FROM Aleph OF AMEN, WHICH IS BINAH, to Mem OF AMEN, WHICH IS ZEIR ANPIN, and from Mem of Amen to final Nun, WHICH IS MALCHUT.' When the blessings reach final Nun, WHICH IS MALCHUT, blessings come out from there to the upper and lower beings and expand through everything. When the sound comes out, they drink of the blessings so-and-so has brought forth, a servant of the Holy King. finite

37. וְכַד יִשְׂרָאֵל לְתַתָּא, מְשַׁמְּרִין לְאָתָבָא אָמֵן, לְכַוְּונָא לִבַּיְיהוּ כְּמָה דְּאִצְטְרִיךְ, כַּמָּה פִּתְחִין דְּבִרְכָּאן פְּתִיחָן לֵיהּ לְעֵילָּא, כַּמָּה טָבָאן מִשְׁתַּכְּחִין בְּכֻלְּהוּ עָלְמִין, כַּמָּה חֵדוּ בְּכֹלָּא. מַאי אֲגָר לְהוּ לְיִשְׂרָאֵל דְּגַרְמִין הַאי. אֲגָר לְהוּ בְּעָלְמָא דֵּין, וּבְעָלְמָא דְּאָתֵי. בְּעָלְמָא דֵּין בְּשַׁעֲתָא דְּעָאקִין לְהוּ, וּמְצַלָּן צְלוֹתָא קַמֵּי מָארֵיהוֹן, קָלָא מַכְרְזָא

בְּכֻלְּהוּ עָלְמִין, פִּתְחוּ שְׁעָרִים וְיָבוֹא גּוֹי צַדִּיק שׁוֹמֵר אֱמוּנִים אַל תִּקְרֵי אֱמוּנִים, אֶלָּא אָמֵנִים. פִּתְחוּ שְׁעָרִים, כְּמָה דְּיִשְׂרָאֵל פַּתְחִין לְהוּ תַּרְעִין דְּבִרְכָּאן, כַּךְ הַשְׁתָּא פִּתְחוּ שְׁעָרִים, וְתִתְקַבֵּל צְלוֹתְהוֹן מֵאִינּוּן דְּעָאקִין לְהוּ.

37. When Yisrael below guard themselves to answer Amen and meditate in their heart as needs be, how many openings of blessings are open above, how much goodness is present throughout the worlds, how much joy abounds in everything! What is the reward of Yisrael to have brought this about? Their reward is in this world and in the World to Come. In this world, when they are beset by enemies and they say their prayer before their Master, the sound proclaims throughout the worlds, "Open the gates, that the righteous nation that keeps faithfulness (Heb. *emunim*) may enter in" (Yeshayah 26:2). Do not pronounce it 'emunim' but 'Amenim (Amen plural)', WHICH MEANS THAT THEY ARE CAREFUL TO ANSWER AMEN. "Open the gates," as Yisrael opened to them the gates of blessings, so now "open the gates" and let their prayer be accepted which is about those who distress them.

38. הַאי בְּעָלְמָא דֵּין, בְּעָלְמָא דְּאָתֵי מַאי אַגְרַיְיהוּ. דְּכַד יִפּוּק ב״נ מֵהַאי עָלְמָא, דַּהֲוָה שׁוֹמֵר לְאָתָבָא אָמֵן. מַאי שׁוֹמֵר. כְּלוֹמַר, נָטִיר, הַהִיא בְּרָכָה דְּאָמַר הַהוּא דִּמְבָרֵךְ, וּמְחַכֶּה לֵיהּ לְאָתָבָא אָמֵן, כְּמָה דְּאִצְטְרִיךְ. נִשְׁמָתֵיהּ סַלְקָא וּמַכְרְזֵי קַמֵּיהּ, פִּתְחוּ שְׁעָרִים קַמֵּיהּ, כְּמָה דְּאִיהוּ הֲוָה פָּתַח תַּרְעִין כָּל יוֹמָא, כַּד הֲוָה שׁוֹמֵר אֱמוּנִים.

38. This is THEIR REWARD in this world. What is their reward in the World to Come? AND HE ANSWERS, it is when a man leaves this world, where he observed answering Amen. By "observed" is meant that he observes the blessing that is said and awaits the man who says it so as to answer Amen AFTER IT, as needs be. Then his soul rises and proclaims before him, "open the gates" before him, as he used to open gates every day, when he observed emunim, THAT IS AMENIM.

39. א״ר יוֹסֵי א״ר יְהוּדָה, מַאי אָמֵן. א״ר אַבָּא, הָא אוּקְמוּהָ כֹּלָּא,

אָמֵן אִקְרֵי מַבּוּעָא דְּהַהוּא נַחֲלָא דְּנָגִיד, אָמֵן אִקְרֵי, דִּכְתִּיב וָאֶהְיֶה אֶצְלוֹ אָמוֹן, אַל תִּקְרֵי אָמוֹן, אֶלָּא אָמֵן. קִיּוּמָא דְּכֻלְּהוּ הַהוּא נַחֲלָא דְּנָגִיד וְנָפִיק, אָמֵן אִקְרֵי, דְּתַנְיָא מִן הָעוֹלָם וְעַד הָעוֹלָם, עוֹלָם דִּלְעֵילָּא, עוֹלָם דִּלְתַתָּא. אוֹף הָכָא אָמֵן וְאָמֵן, אָמֵן דִּלְעֵילָּא, אָמֵן דִּלְתַתָּא. אָמֵן קִיּוּמָא דְּכֻלְּהוּ, וְהָא אוֹקִימְנָא אָמֵן בְּאִינּוּן אַתְוָון.

39. Rabbi Yosi said, what is Amen? Rabbi Aba said, everything has been explained. Amen is called the spring of the flowing river, WHICH IS BINAH, and is called Amen, because it is written, "then I was by him, as a nursling (Heb. *amon*)" (Mishlei 8:30). Do not pronounce it amon but Amen. The sustenance of all THE GRADES, NAMELY that river that emerges and flows, WHICH IS BINAH, is called Amen. As we have learned, "from everlasting to everlasting (lit. 'world to world')" (Tehilim 106:48), means from the world above, WHICH IS BINAH, to the world below, WHICH IS MALCHUT. Here too, "Amen, and Amen" is Amen of above, WHICH IS BINAH, Amen of below, WHICH IS MALCHUT. Amen MEANS sustenance for everyone. We have already explained Amen according to its letters.

40. ר"ש אָמַר, אָלֶף עֲמִיקָא דְּבֵירָא דְּכָל בִּרְכָאן מִתַּמָּן נַבְעִין וְנָפְקִין, וּמִשְׁתַּכְחִין. מֵ"ם פְּתוּחָה, נַהֲרָא דְּנָגִיד וְנָפִיק, וְאִקְרֵי מֵ"ם. וְהוּא רָזָא דְּתָנֵינָן, מֵ"ם פְּתוּחָה, מֵ"ם סְתוּמָה. כְּמָה דְּאוֹקִימְנָא, לְמַרְבֵּה הַמִּשְׂרָה.

40. Rabbi Shimon said, Aleph OF AMEN is the depth of the well, whence all the blessings flow and come out and exist. Open Mem is the river that emerges and flows, WHICH IS YESOD, and is called Mem. This is the meaning of what we learned that open Mem IS YESOD, closed final Mem IS BINAH, as we established BY THE VERSE, "for the increase (Heb. *lemarbeh*, spelled with final Mem) of the realm" (Yeshayah 9:6).

41. נוּן פְּשׁוּטָה, כְּלָלָא דִּתְרֵין נוּנִין, נוּן פְּשׁוּטָה, נוּן כְּפוּפָה. נוּן פְּשׁוּטָה כְּלָלָא דְּאָת וָא"ו, בג"כ כֹּלָּא אִקְרֵי נוּן וָאו נוּן. וּבְרָזָא דְּמַתְנִיתָא הָכִי תָּאנָא, ו' דְּכַר, ן' פְּשׁוּטָה כְּלָלָא דִּדְכַר וְנוּקְבָא, נוּן כְּפוּפָה, בִּכְלָלָא דִּפְשׁוּטָה הִיא. וּבְסִפְרָא דְּרַב הַמְנוּנָא סָבָא, מֵם דְּהָכָא,

הִיא נוֹטָרִיקוֹן מֶלֶ״ךְ, וְהַיְינוּ אָמֵן, אָמֵ״ן נוֹטָרִיקוֹן, אֵ״ל מֶ״לֶךְ נֶ״אֱמָן. כְּלָלָא דְּכֹלָּא, וְשַׁפִּיר הוּא, וְהָא אִתְּמַר.

41. Extended final Nun comprises both Nun's, extended Nun and bent Nun, WHICH MEANS IT INCLUDES IN ITSELF THE NUKVA OF ZEIR ANPIN AS WELL CALLED BENT NUN. Extended final Nun comprises the letter Vav, BECAUSE IT INCLUDES WITHIN IT THE MALE AS WELL, WHICH IS THE LETTER VAV, WHICH IS ZEIR ANPIN. FOR EXTENDED FINAL NUN IS EXPANDED, INCLUDING BOTH MALE AND FEMALE, WHICH ARE ZEIR ANPIN THAT IS VAV AND MALCHUT THAT IS NUN. For that reason everything TOGETHER is called Nun Vav final Nun. We have learned it according to the secret of the Mishnah: Vav is masculine, extended final Nun is both masculine and feminine, bent Nun is comprised in extended final Nun. In the book of Rav Hamnuna Saba, the Mem here IN AMEN is the initial of *Melech* (Eng. 'king'), namely Amen. Amen is the initials of *El Melech Ne'aman* (Eng. 'El a faithful King'), which comprises everything. It is good and we have already learned that.

42. תָּאנָא, כָּל מַאן דְּשָׁמַע בְּרָכָה מֵהַהוּא דִּמְבָרֵךְ, וְלָא אִתְכְּוָון בְּאָמֵן, עָלֵיהּ נֶאֱמַר וּבוֹזַי יֵקָלּוּ. כד״א, לָכֶם הַכֹּהֲנִים בּוֹזֵי שְׁמִי מַאי עוֹנְשֵׁיהּ. כְּמָה דְּלָא פָּתַח בִּרְכָאן לְעֵילָּא, כַּךְ לָא פַּתְחִין לֵיהּ. וְלֹא עוֹד אֶלָּא כַּד נָפִיק מֵהַאי עָלְמָא, מַכְרִיזֵי קַמֵּיהּ, וְאַמְרֵי, טְרוּקוּ גַּלֵּי קַמֵּיהּ דִּפְלַנְיָיא, וְלָא לֵיעוּל, וְלָא תְּקַבְּלוּן לֵיהּ, וַוי לֵיהּ וַוי לְנִשְׁמָתֵיהּ.

42. We learned that whoever heard a blessing someone made but did not meditate IN HIS HEART on the Amen, of him it says, "And they that despise Me shall be lightly esteemed," as in, "to you, O priests, who despise My name" (Malachi 1:6). What is his punishment? Just as he did not make an opening for blessings above, no blessings are opened for him. Moreover, when he comes out of this world, a proclamation resounds before him, saying, close the gates before so-and-so, so he may not enter. Do not accept him. Woe to him, woe to his soul.

8. The openings of the Garden of Eden and the openings of Gehenom

A Synopsis

We learn about the fate of those who do not say 'Amen' with their whole heart. It is said that there is a corresponding opening for each gate in the Garden of Eden to a gate in Gehenom. The lowest chamber of Gehenom is described as Hell and Destruction, and those who enter there never rise again, but are lost from all the worlds; to this place it is said that those who are contemptuous of the 'Amen' are sent.

43. תָּאנָא, חַיָּיבֵי דְּגֵיהִנָּם, כֻּלְּהוּ סַלְקֵי בִּמְדוֹרִין יְדִיעָן, וְכַמָּה פִּתְחִין אִית לֵיהּ לַגֵּיהִנָּם, וְכֻלְּהוּ פִּתְחִין לָקֳבֵל פִּתְחִין דְּגַן עֵדֶן. וּבְשַׁעֲתָא דְּאַפְקֵי לְאִינּוּן חַיָּיבַיָּא דְּקַבִּילוּ עוֹנְשַׁיְיהוּ, אִינּוּן פַּתְחֵי פְּתִיחִין, וְשַׁוְיָין לוֹן לְבַר. וְכֻלְּהוּ פִּתְחִין בִּשְׁמָהָן אִקְרוּן, לָקֳבְלֵיהוֹן דְּפִתְחִין דְּגַן עֵדֶן, וְכָל פִּתְחָא וּפִתְחָא, אִקְרֵי שְׁמָא, לָקֳבְלֵי הַהוּא פִּתְחָא דְּגֵיהִנָּם, וְאִשְׁתְּמוֹדְעָן פִּתְחִין לָקֳבְלֵיהוֹן פִּתְחִין, אִינּוּן פִּתְחִין דג"ע.

43. We learned that the wicked in Gehenom all go up through certain compartments and that there are many openings to Gehenom. All the openings correspond to the openings in the Garden of Eden. When the wicked are taken out after receiving their punishments, they open the gates and put them outside. All the gates bear names corresponding to those in the Garden of Eden, and each and every gate IN THE GARDEN OF EDEN is called by a name corresponding to the RESPECTIVE gate in Gehenom. The gates in the Garden of Eden are known, gate for gate, WHICH MEANS, UPON SEEING THE KIND OF GATE IN GEHENOM, ONE IS ABLE TO KNOW THROUGH IT THE OPPOSING GATE IN THE GARDEN OF EDEN, WHAT KIND OF GATE IT IS.

44. בַּגֵּיהִנָּם אִית מָדוֹרָא בַּתְרָאָה תַּתָּאָה דְּכֻלְּהוּ, וְהַהוּא מָדוֹרָא הֲוֵי מָדוֹרָא עַל מָדוֹרָא, וְאִקְרֵי אֶרֶץ עֵיפָתָה. מַהוּ עֵיפָתָה. כד"א רָבוּעַ יִהְיֶה כָּפוּל, וּמְתַרְגְּמִינָן מְרוּבַּע יְהֶיֶה עִיף, אוּף הָכָא עֵיפָתָה, כְּלוֹמַר כְּפוּלָה. וְהַהוּא אִקְרֵי שְׁאוֹל תַּחְתִּית, שְׁאוֹל הוּא מָדוֹרָא חַד. תַּחְתִּית, הוּא מָדוֹרָא תַּתָּאָה. ובג"כ אִקְרֵי אֶרֶץ עֵיפָתָה תַּחְתִּית, וְאִקְרֵי אֲבַדּוֹן.

וע״ד כְּתִיב, שְׁאוֹל וַאֲבַדּוֹן. וְכֻלְּהוּ מָדוֹרִין לָא אַכְפָּלוּ, וְכֻלְּהוּ לָא עֲיִיפִין בַּר מֵהַאי.

44. The last compartment in Gehenom is the lowest. That compartment is DOUBLE, a compartment over a compartment, and is called, "A land of gloom (Heb. *efatah*)" (Iyov 10:22). What is gloom? It is as in, "Foursquare it shall be" (Shemot 28:16), which is '*if*' in Aramaic. Here too, efatah means double. That COMPARTMENT is called the bottom of Sheol. Sheol is one UPPER compartment and the bottom is the lower compartment. Therefore it is called the lower land of gloom, and ALSO called Avadon. Hence it is written, "Sheol and Avadon" (Mishlei 27:20), WHICH ARE THE DOUBLE COMPARTMENTS, ONE ON TOP OF THE OTHER. Not all compartments are double, and not all are gloomy, THAT IS, THEY ARE NOT CALLED "A LAND OF GLOOM," except for this one.

45. וְתָאנָא, מַאן דְּנָחִית לַאֲבַדּוֹן דְּאִקְרֵי תַּחְתִּית, לָא סָלִיק לְעָלְמִין. וְהַהוּא אִקְרֵי גֶּבֶר דְּאִשְׁתְּצֵי וְאִתְאֲבִיד מִכֻּלְּהוּ עָלְמִין. וְתָאנָא, לְהַהוּא אֲתָר נַחְתִּין לְהַנְהוּ גַּבְרֵי דִּמְבַזֵּי לְאָתָבָא אָמֵן, וְעַל אָמֵן סַגִּיאִין דְּאִתְאֲבִידוּ מִנֵּיהּ, דְּלָא חָשִׁיב לְהוּ, דַּיְינִין לֵיהּ בַּגֵּיהִנָּם, וְנַחְתִּין לֵיהּ בְּהַהוּא מָדוֹרָא תַּתָּאָה, דְּלֵית בָּהּ פִּתְחָא, וְאִתְאֲבִיד וְלָא סָלִיק מִנֵּיהּ לְעָלְמִין. וע״ד כְּתִיב, כָּלָה עָנָן וַיֵּלַךְ כֵּן יוֹרֵד שְׁאוֹל לֹא יַעֲלֶה. וְלָא, וְהָא כְּתִיב מִבֶּטֶן שְׁאוֹל שִׁוַּעְתִּי שָׁמַעְתָּ וְגוֹ׳. וּכְתִיב מוֹרִיד שְׁאוֹל וַיָּעַל. אֶלָּא הָכָא שְׁאוֹל, הָתָם תַּחְתִּית. וְאוֹקִימְנָא הָא דְּאַהְדַּר בֵּיהּ, הָא דְּלָא אַהְדַּר בֵּיהּ.

45. And we learned that whoever descends to Avadon, that is called bottom, never rises. That MAN is called a man who was destroyed and lost to all worlds. And we learned that to that place are lowered those men who despised saying Amen. Such a man is punished in Gehenom for the many Amen's that were lost to him, that he did not consider, and he is lowered to the lowest compartment, which has no opening, and he is lost and never rises from there. Hence it is written, "As the cloud is consumed and vanishes away, so he who goes down to Sheol shall come up no more" (Iyov 7:9). HE ASKS, but no; it is written, "out of the belly of Sheol I cried and

You did hear..." (Yonah 2:3), AND HE ROSE FROM THERE. It is also written, "He brings down to Sheol and brings up" (I Shmuel 2:6). AND HE ANSWERS, but this is Sheol FROM WHICH ONE ASCENDS, and there is the bottom FROM WHERE ONE DOES NOT RISE. We explained that this refers to one who repented BY DOING PENANCE, and there to one who did not.

46. א"ר יוֹסֵי, מַאי דִּכְתִּיב כִּי שְׁתַּיִם רָעוֹת עָשָׂה עַמִּי אוֹתִי עָזְבוּ מְקוֹר מַיִם חַיִּים לַחְצוֹב לָהֶם בֹּארוֹת וְגוֹ'. אוֹתִי עָזְבוּ מְקוֹר מַיִם חַיִּים, דָּא הוּא דְּלָא בָּעֵי לְקַדְּשָׁא שְׁמָא דְקוּדְשָׁא בְּרִיךְ הוּא, בְּאָמֵן. מַאי עוֹנְשֵׁיהּ. כְּתִיב לַחְצוֹב לָהֶם בֹּארוֹת בֹּארוֹת נִשְׁבָּרִים, דְּנַחְתִּין לַגֵּיהִנָּם דַּרְגָּא בָּתַר דַּרְגָּא, עַד דְּנַחְתִּין לַאֲבַדּוֹן דְּאִקְרֵי תַּחְתִּית. וְאִי אִיהוּ קַדִּישׁ שְׁמָא דְקוּדְשָׁא בְּרִיךְ הוּא, לְכַוָּונָה בְּאָמֵן כַּדְקָא יָאוּת, סָלִיק דַּרְגָּא בָּתַר דַּרְגָּא, לְאִתְעַדְּנָא מֵהַהוּא עָלְמָא דְּאָתֵי, דְּנָגִיד תָּדִיר לָא פָּסִיק, הה"ד אֱמוּנִים נוֹצֵר יְיָ' וּמְשַׁלֵּם עַל יֶתֶר עוֹשֵׂה גַאֲוָה.

46. Rabbi Yosi said, as for the words, "For My people have committed two evils; they have forsaken Me the fountain of living waters, and have hewn them out cisterns..." (Yirmeyah 2:13), "they have forsaken Me the fountain of living waters" is by not wanting to sanctify the Name of the Holy One, blessed be He, with Amen. What is his punishment? It is as is written, "and have hewn them out cisterns, broken cisterns," by going to Gehenom one level after another until they reach Avadon that is called bottom. If he sanctifies the Name of the Holy One, blessed be He, by meditating properly on Amen, he rises, level after level, to have delight in the World to Come, that ever flows and does not cease. This is the meaning of, "for Hashem preserves the faithful, and plentifully repays him who acts haughtily" (Tehilim 31:24).

9. The song of the well

A Synopsis

We learn that song draws blessings from above downward until they are available in all the worlds, and that the children of Yisrael are destined to proclaim the song both from below upward and from above downward. In this way they will connect a bond of Faith and Trust. And at the time of redemption they will say the entire perfect song that is composed of and includes all other songs, and God will be proclaimed the only God.

47. תָּאנָא, שִׁירָה מָשִׁיךְ בִּרְכָאן מֵעֵילָּא לְתַתָּא, עַד דְּיִשְׁתַּכְּחוּן בִּרְכָאן בְּכֻלְּהוּ עָלְמִין. א״ר אֶלְעָזָר, זְמִינִין אִינּוּן יִשְׂרָאֵל לְמֵימַר שִׁירָתָא, מִתַּתָּא לְעֵילָּא, וּמֵעֵילָּא לְתַתָּא. וּלְקַשְּׁרָא קִשְׁרָא דִּמְהֵימְנוּתָא. דִּכְתִּיב, אָז יָשִׁיר יִשְׂרָאֵל אֶת הַשִּׁירָה הַזֹּאת. אָז שָׁר לֹא נֶאֱמַר, אֶלָּא אָז יָשִׁיר. וְכֵן כֻּלְּהוּ כְּהַאי גַּוְונָא. אֶת הַשִּׁירָה הַזֹּאת, מִתַּתָּא לְעֵילָּא. עֲלִי בְאֵר עֱנוּ לָהּ, עֲלִי בְאֵר, כְּלוֹמַר סַק לְאַתְרִיךְ, לְאִתְאַחֲדָא בְּבַעְלִיךְ, דָּא הוּא מִתַּתָּא לְעֵילָּא.

47. We learned that shirah (Eng. 'poem') draws blessings from above downward, until there are blessings throughout the worlds. Rabbi Elazar said, Yisrael will recite a poem from below upward and from above downward, and to bind the bond of Faith, as written, "Then Yisrael sang (lit. 'will sing') this song (Heb. *shirah*)" (Bemidbar 21:17). It speaks in the future tense rather than in the past. And so is everything the same way, IN THE FUTURE TENSE. "This shirah" is from below upward, BECAUSE SHIRAH IS IN MALCHUT THAT SINGS UPWARDS TO ZEIR ANPIN, "Spring up, O well, sing to it" (Ibid.). "Spring up, O well," namely, THEY SPOKE TO MALCHUT CALLED A WELL, rise to your place to join your husband ZEIR ANPIN. This is from below upward, RAISING MALCHUT TO ZEIR ANPIN.

48. וּלְבָתַר מֵעֵילָּא לְתַתָּא, בְּאֵר חֲפָרוּהָ שָׂרִים, דְּאוֹלִידוּ לָהּ אַבָּא וְאִימָּא, כָּרוּהָ נְדִיבֵי הָעָם, אִלֵּין אֲבָהָן, דְּאִקְרוּן נְדִיבֵי עַמִּים. כָּרוּהָ, אֲתָר לְאִזְדַּוְּוגָא בָּהּ מַלְכָּא, בְּבִרְכָּן. וּבְמָה, הוּא זִווּגָא. בִּמְחוֹקֵק: דָּא יְסוֹד. בְּמִשְׁעֲנוֹתָם: דָּא נֶצַח וְהוֹד, מֵעֵילָּא לְתַתָּא. וּמִמִּדְבָּר מַתָּנָה,

וּמִמַּתָּנָה נַחֲלִיאֵל, וּמִנַּחֲלִיאֵל בָּמוֹת. הָא קִשּׁוּרָא שְׁלֵימָא, קִשּׁוּרָא דִּמְהֵימְנוּתָא, קִשּׁוּרָא קַיְּימָא דְּכֹלָּא בֵּיהּ.

48. Afterwards THEY DRAW from above downward, "the well that the princes dug out" (Ibid. 18). THE WELL IS MALCHUT; "the princes dug out," as Aba and Ima begot her, BECAUSE ABA AND IMA FORMED MALCHUT ACCORDING TO THE SECRET OF, "THE SIDE, WHICH HASHEM ELOHIM HAD TAKEN" (BERESHEET 2:22); "the nobles of the people delved" (Bemidbar 21:18) are the patriarchs, NAMELY CHESED, GVURAH AND TIFERET OF ZEIR ANPIN called the nobles of the people. They delved it, NAMELY THEY DELVED A PLACE for the King to unite with her with blessings. With what? Through union. "with the scepter" (Ibid.) refers to Yesod, "with their staves" (Ibid.) refers to Netzach and Hod. UP TO HERE is from above downward. "From the wilderness" (Ibid. 19), WHICH IS MALCHUT CALLED SPEECH, "to Matanah" (Ibid.) IT RISES TO YESOD CALLED MATANAH. "And from Matanah it rises to Nahaliel," WHICH IS TIFERET, "and from Nahaliel to Bamot" (Ibid.), WHICH IS ABA AND IMA. This is the complete bond, the bond of Faith, the bond that incorporates sustenance for everything.

49. א"ר יוֹסֵי, זְמִינִין יִשְׂרָאֵל לְמֵימַר שִׁירָתָא שְׁלֵימָתָא. שִׁירָתָא דְּכָלִיל כָּל שְׁאַר שִׁירִין. הה"ד, וַאֲמַרְתֶּם בַּיּוֹם הַהוּא הוֹדוּ לַה' קִרְאוּ בִשְׁמוֹ הוֹדִיעוּ בָעַמִּים עֲלִילוֹתָיו. בְּהַהוּא זִמְנָא כְּתִיב, וְהָיָה יְיָ' לְמֶלֶךְ עַל כָּל הָאָרֶץ בַּיּוֹם הַהוּא יִהְיֶה יְיָ' אֶחָד וּשְׁמוֹ אֶחָד. וּכְתִיב אָז יִמָּלֵא שְׂחוֹק פִּינוּ וּלְשׁוֹנֵנוּ רִנָּה, אָז יֹאמְרוּ בַגּוֹיִם הִגְדִּיל יְיָ' לַעֲשׂוֹת עִם אֵלֶּה.

49. Rabbi Yosi said, Yisrael will recite a complete poem, a poem including all other songs. This is the meaning of, "O give thanks to Hashem; call upon His name. Make known His deeds among the people" (Tehilim 105:1). Of that time it is written, "on that day Hashem shall be one, and His Name One" (Zacharia 14:9), and, "Then was our mouth filled with laughter, and our tongue with singing. Then they said among the nations, Hashem has done great things for them" (Tehilim 126:2).

בָּרוּךְ יְיָ' לְעוֹלָם אָמֵן וְאָמֵן

Blessed be Hashem forever, Amen and Amen.

יִמְלוֹךְ יְיָ' לְעוֹלָם אָמֵן וְאָמֵן.

May Hashem reign forever, Amen and Amen.

HA'AZINU

Names of Articles

Continuation of Ha'azinu

1. “Give ear, O heavens”

A Synopsis

Rabbi Yehuda speaks of the many times that Moses reproved Yisrael, but tells us that Moses said all these things with love, always reminding the people how much God loved them. Rabbi Yitzchak says that Moses had always refused to be guided by anyone other than God Himself; he would not be guided by any angel or messenger. Moses never trembled before the voice of God or any messenger, and yet after he died Joshua was afraid of God’s messengers. God was no longer as available to Yisrael as He had been during Moses’ lifetime.

1. הַאֲזִינוּ הַשָּׁמַיִם וַאֲדַבֵּרָה וְתִשְׁמַע הָאָרֶץ אִמְרֵי פִּי, רִבִּי יְהוּדָה פָּתַח, פָּתַחְתִּי אֲנִי לְדוֹדִי וְדוֹדִי חָמַק עָבָר וְגוֹ׳, בִּקַּשְׁתִּיהוּ וְלֹא מְצָאתִיהוּ קְרָאתִיו וְלָא עָנָנִי. מַה כְּתִיב לְעֵילָּא. אֲנִי יְשֵׁנָה וְלִבִּי עֵר וְגוֹ׳. אֲנִי יְשֵׁנָה, אָמְרָה כְּנֶסֶת יִשְׂרָאֵל. אֲנִי יְשֵׁנָה, מִפִּקּוּדֵי אוֹרַיְיתָא, בִּזְמְנָא דַּאֲזִילְנָא בְּמַדְבְּרָא. וְלִבִּי עֵר, לְאַעֲלָא לְאַרְעָא, לְמֶעְבַּד לְהוּ נִימוּסִין דְּהָא כָּל פִּקּוּדֵי אוֹרַיְיתָא בְּאַרְעָא מִשְׁתַּכְּחִין. קוֹל דּוֹדִי דוֹפֵק, דָּא מֹשֶׁה. דְּאוֹכַח לְהוּ לְיִשְׂרָאֵל בְּכַמָּה וִיכּוּחִין, בְּכַמָּה קְטָטִין. דִּכְתִּיב, אֵלֶּה הַדְּבָרִים וְגוֹ׳, מַמְרִים הֱיִיתֶם וְגוֹ׳. וּבְחוֹרֵב הִקְצַפְתֶּם וְגוֹ׳. הה״ד דוֹפֵק.

1. “Give ear, O heavens, and I will speak; and hear, O earth, the words of my mouth” (Devarim 32:1). Rabbi Yehuda opened with, “I opened to my beloved; but my beloved had turned away, and was gone…I sought him, but I could not find him; I called him, but he gave me no answer” (Shir Hashirim 5:6). Before that it is written, “I sleep, but my heart wakes…” (Ibid. 2). “I sleep,” says the Congregation of Yisrael, “I sleep” away from the commandments of the Torah when I traveled the wilderness; “but my heart wakes” to bring them to the land of Yisrael to legislate laws for them. For all the commandments of the Torah are present in the land of Yisrael. “hark, my beloved is knocking” (Ibid.) refers to Moses, who reproved Yisrael with many arguments and quarrels, as written, “These are the words…” (Devarim 1:1), “You have been rebellious” (Devarim 9:24), and, “Also in Horeb you provoked…” (Ibid. 8). This is the meaning of, “knocking.”

2. ועכ״ד דְּמֹשֶׁה אוֹכַח לְהוֹ לְיִשְׂרָאֵל, בִּרְחִימוּתָא הֲווֹ כָּל מִלּוֹי, דִּכְתִּיב כִּי עַם קָדוֹשׁ אַתָּה לַיְיָ׳ אֱלֹהֶיךָ. וּבְךָ בָּחַר יְיָ׳ אֱלֹהֶיךָ לִהְיוֹת לוֹ לְעָם וְגוֹ׳ בָּנִים אַתֶּם לַיְיָ׳ אֱלֹהֵיכֶם וְאַתֶּם הַדְּבֵקִים בַּיְיָ׳. וְעַל דָּא וְשָׁמַעְתָּ בְּקוֹל יְיָ׳ אֱלֹהֶיךָ. כִּי מֵאַהֲבַת יְיָ׳ אֶתְכֶם. הה״ד פִּתְחִי לִי אֲחוֹתִי רַעְיָתִי.

2. Though Moses reproved Yisrael, all his words were with love, as written, "For you are a holy people to Hashem your Elohim. Hashem your Elohim has chosen you to be a special people to Himself..." (Devarim 7:6), "You are the children of Hashem your Elohim" (Devarim 14:1), "But you that did cleave" (Devarim 4:4). Therefore, "obey the voice of Hashem your Elohim" (Devarim 27:10), "because Hashem loved you" (Devarim 7:8). This is the meaning of, "Open to me, my sister, my love" (Shir Hashirim 5:2), SPOKEN AFFECTIONATELY.

3. מַה כְּתִיב. קַמְתִּי אֲנִי לִפְתּוֹחַ לְדוֹדִי, אָמְרוּ יִשְׂרָאֵל בְּעוֹד דַּהֲוֵינָן זְמִינִין לְמֵיעַל לְאַרְעָא, וּלְקַבְּלָא אִינּוּן פִּקּוּדֵי אוֹרַיְיתָא, עַל יְדוֹי דְּמֹשֶׁה, מַה כְּתִיב. וְדוֹדִי חָמַק עָבָר, דִּכְתִּיב, וַיָּמָת שָׁם מֹשֶׁה עֶבֶד יְיָ׳. בִּקַּשְׁתִּיהוּ וְלֹא מְצָאתִיהוּ, דִּכְתִּיב וְלֹא קָם נָבִיא עוֹד בְּיִשְׂרָאֵל כְּמֹשֶׁה. קְרָאתִיו וְלֹא עָנָנִי, דְּלָא הֲוָה דָּרָא כְּדָרָא דְּמֹשֶׁה, דְקוּדְשָׁא בְּרִיךְ הוּא שָׁמַע לְקַלֵיהוֹן, וְעָבֵד לְהוּ נִסִּין וְנִימוּסִין, כְּמָה דְעָבֵד עַל יְדוֹי.

3. It is written, "I rose up to open to my beloved" (Ibid. 4). Yisrael said, while we were ready to enter the land of Yisrael and accept the commandments of the Torah through Moses, it is written, "but my beloved had turned away, and was gone," as written, "So Moses the servant of Hashem died there" (Devarim 34:5). "I sought him, but I could not find him," as written, "And there arose not a prophet since in Yisrael like Moses" (Ibid. 10). "I called him, but he gave me no answer," since there was no generation like the generation of Moses that the Holy One, blessed be He, obeyed their voices and performed miracles and made laws for them, as He did through him.

4. ר׳ יִצְחָק אָמַר, קַמְתִּי אֲנִי לִפְתּוֹחַ לְדוֹדִי, דָּא קוּדְשָׁא בְּרִיךְ הוּא

בְּיוֹמוֹי דְּמֹשֶׁה, דְּכָל יוֹמוֹי לָא בָּעָא דְּמַלְאָכָא וּשְׁלִיחָא לְדַבְּרָא עִמֵּיהּ, דִּכְתִּיב אִם אֵין פָּנֶיךָ הוֹלְכִים וְגוֹ׳. זַכָּאָה חוּלָקֵיהּ דְּמֹשֶׁה, דְּקוּדְשָׁא בְּרִיךְ הוּא אִסְתְּכַם לִרְעוּתֵיהּ. וְדוֹדִי חָמַק עָבָר, בְּיוֹמוֹי דִּיהוֹשֻׁעַ, דִּכְתִּיב, לֹא כִּי אֲנִי שַׂר צְבָא יְיָ׳.

4. Rabbi Yitzchak said, “I rose up to open to my beloved” refers to the Holy One, blessed be He, during the life of Moses, who refused all his days to be guided by an angel or messenger, as written, “If Your presence go not with me…” (Shemot 33:15). Blessed is the portion of Moses that the Holy One, blessed be He, approved of his desire. “but my beloved had turned away, and was gone,” during the life of Joshua, as written, “No, but I am captain of the host of Hashem” (Yehoshua 5:14).

5. ת״ח, מֹשֶׁה הֲוָה שָׁמַע קָלָא קַדִּישָׁא דְּמַלְכָּא עִלָּאָה, וְלָא אִזְדַּעְזָע, וכ״ש מַלְאָכָא, דְּלָא בָּעָא. בָּתַר דְּשָׁכִיב מַה כְּתִיב. וַיֹּאמֶר לֹא כִּי אֲנִי שַׂר צְבָא יְיָ׳. וּכְתִיב וַיִּפּוֹל יְהוֹשֻׁעַ אֶל פָּנָיו אַרְצָה. עַתָּה בָאתִי, בְּיוֹמוֹי דְּמֹשֶׁה רַבָּךְ אֲתֵינָא, וְלָא קַבְּלָנִי. בֵּיהּ שַׁעֲתָא, יָדְעוּ יִשְׂרָאֵל שְׁבָחָא דְּמֹשֶׁה. בְּהַהוּא זִמְנָא בָּעוּ יִשְׂרָאֵל לְקוּדְשָׁא בְּרִיךְ הוּא, וְלָא אִזְדְּמַן לְהוּ הָכִי כְּיוֹמוֹי דְּמֹשֶׁה, הה״ד בִּקַּשְׁתִּיהוּ וְלֹא מְצָאתִיהוּ וְגוֹ׳.

5. Come and see, Moses used to hear the holy sound of the supernal King yet did not tremble, nor did he tremble before an angel, whom he did not wish TO ACCEPT. After he died, it is written, “And he said, No, but I am captain of the host of Hashem…And Joshua fell on his face to the earth.” “I am now come” (Ibid.), during the days of Moses your master, yet I was not accepted. At that time, Yisrael recognized the value of Moses. At that time Yisrael sought the Holy One, blessed be He, but He was not as available as during Moses’ lifetime. This is the meaning of, “I sought him, but I could not find him…”

2. "Give ear, O heavens - hear heavens"

A Synopsis

Rabbi Chiya tells us about the time that Isaiah said, "Hear, heavens, and give ear, earth"; when Isaiah was then challenged by a voice he answered that it was not he himself who was speaking. And yet when Moses spoke it was indeed his own voice. Rabbi Yosi's interpretation is that Moses was addressing the supernal heaven and earth while Isaiah was addressing the lower heavens and earth.

6. הַאֲזִינוּ הַשָּׁמַיִם וַאֲדַבֵּרָה, רִבִּי חִיָּיא אָמַר, זַכָּאָה חוּלָקֵיהּ דְּמֹשֶׁה, יַתִּיר מִכָּל נְבִיאֵי עָלְמָא. ת״ח, כְּתִיב שִׁמְעוּ שָׁמַיִם וְהַאֲזִינִי אֶרֶץ כִּי יְיָ׳ דִּבֵּר. שִׁמְעוּ שָׁמַיִם, יְשַׁעְיָה דַּהֲוָה יַתִּיר רְחִיקָא מִמַּלְכָּא, כְּתִיב שִׁמְעוּ שָׁמַיִם. מֹשֶׁה דַּהֲוָה יַתִּיר קָרִיב לְמַלְכָּא, כְּתִיב הַאֲזִינוּ הַשָּׁמַיִם.

6. "Give ear, O heavens, and I will speak." Rabbi Chiya said, Moses' portion is blessed above that of any prophet in the world. Come and see, it is written, "Hear, heavens, and give ear, earth, for Hashem has spoken" (Yeshayah 1:2). "Hear, heavens": it is written in Isaiah, who was further away from the King, "Hear, heavens." As for Moses, who was nearer to the King, it is written, "Give ear, O heavens."

7. תָּאנָא, בְּהַהוּא זִמְנָא דְּאָמַר יְשַׁעְיָהוּ שִׁמְעוּ שָׁמַיִם וְהַאֲזִינִי אֶרֶץ. כַּמָּה גַּרְדִּינֵי טְהִירִין אִזְדְּמָנוּ לְתַבְרָא רֵישֵׁיהּ, נָפְקָא קָלָא וְאָמַר, מַאן הוּא דֵּין דְּבָעֵי לְאַרְעֲשָׁא עָלְמִין, עַד דְּפָתַח וְאָמַר, לָאו אֲנָא, וְלָאו דִּידִי, אֶלָּא כִּי יְיָ׳ דִּבֵּר, וְלָא אֲנָא. בְּמֹשֶׁה מַה כְּתִיב. הַאֲזִינוּ הַשָּׁמַיִם וַאֲדַבֵּרָה, אֲנָא וְלָא אַחֲרָא. וַאֲדַבֵּרָה בְּלָא דְּחִילוּ. וְתִשְׁמַע הָאָרֶץ אִמְרֵי פִי, וְלָא מֵאַחֲרָא. זַכָּאָה חוּלָקֵיהּ. א״ר אַבָּא, בְּאַתְוָון גְּלִיפָן דר׳ אֶלְעָזָר, הַאֲזִינוּ הַשָּׁמַיִם וַאֲדַבֵּרָה וְתִשְׁמַע הָאָרֶץ, הָכָא אִתְרְמִיז שְׁמָא קַדִּישָׁא עִלָּאָה.

7. We learned that when Isaiah said, "Hear, heavens, and give ear, earth," many prosecutors came to break his head. A voice resounded, saying, Who is that who wishes to shake worlds! Then he opened with the words, It is not I nor is it mine, but, "Hashem has spoken" and not I. Of Moses it is written, "Give ear, O (lit. 'the') heavens, and I will speak," I and no other. "I will speak" without fear, "and hear O (lit. 'the'), earth, the words of my mouth" and not anybody else's. Blessed is his portion. Rabbi Aba said, In the engraved letters of Rabbi Elazar HE SAID, in "Give (spelled with Vav) ear, the (Heb. *Hei*) heavens, and (Heb. *Vav*) I will speak; and hear, the (Heb. *Hei*) earth" the holy, supernal Name is alluded to, NAMELY YUD HEI VAV HEI.

8. ר׳ יוֹסֵי אָמַר, תּוּ מַה בֵּין מֹשֶׁה לִישַׁעְיָהוּ. מֹשֶׁה אָמַר הַאֲזִינוּ הַשָּׁמַיִם, הַשָּׁמַיִם, שָׁמַיִם עִלָּאִין, אִינּוּן דְּאִשְׁתְּמוֹדְעָן, דְּאִקְרוּן שְׁמָא דְקוּדְשָׁא בְּרִיךְ הוּא. וְתִשְׁמַע הָאָרֶץ, אֶרֶץ עִלָּאָה, הַהִיא דְּאִשְׁתְּמוֹדְעָא, וְאִיהִי אֶרֶץ הַחַיִּים. בִּישַׁעְיָה כְּתִיב, שִׁמְעוּ שָׁמַיִם וְלָא הַשָּׁמַיִם. הַאֲזִינִי אֶרֶץ, וְלָא הָאָרֶץ. וְאִינּוּן שָׁמַיִם וָאָרֶץ תַּתָּאִין. וְעִם כָּל דָּא, בָּעוּ לְאַעַנְשָׁא לֵיהּ, עַד דְּאָמַר כִּי יְיָ׳ דִּבֵּר, וְלֹא אֲנָא. וּמֹשֶׁה אָמַר כּוּלֵּי הַאי, דִּכְתִּיב הַאֲזִינוּ הַשָּׁמַיִם וַאֲדַבֵּרָה וְתִשְׁמַע הָאָרֶץ אִמְרֵי פִּי.

8. Rabbi Yosi said, Another difference between Moses and Isaiah is that Moses said, "Hear, the heavens" WITH THE DEFINITE ARTICLE, "the heavens," namely the supernal heavens, those known to be called the Name of the Holy One, blessed be He. "and hear, the earth" is the supernal earth, the one known to be the land of the living, NAMELY MALCHUT. In Isaiah it is written, "Hear, heavens," instead of "the heavens," because these are the lower heavens and earth. Nevertheless, they wanted to punish him until he said, "for Hashem has spoken" and not I. Moses spoke much more, as written, "Give ear, the heavens, and I will speak; and hear, the earth, the words of my mouth," WHO ARE ZEIR ANPIN AND MALCHUT. HE DID NOT FEAR, AND NONE WANTED TO PUNISH HIM.

3. The apple tree and the lily

A Synopsis

Rabbi Yitzchak says how blessed Yisrael is to be under the direct care of God rather than to have been assigned to one of His appointed ministers. He says that God is like an apple that has three colors and the Congregation of Yisrael, Malchut, is like a lily that has two colors. The three colors of the apple allude to Chesed, Gvurah and Tiferet, while the two colors of the lily allude to Judgment and Chesed. The Patriarchs are also the three colors joined in the apple.

9. רִבִּי יִצְחָק פָּתַח, כְּתַפּוּחַ בַּעֲצֵי הַיַּעַר וְגוֹ'. זַכָּאָה חוּלָקֵהוֹן דְּיִשְׂרָאֵל מִכָּל עַמִּין עכו"ם, דְּהָא כָּל שְׁאַר עַמִּין אִתְיְהִיבוּ לְרַבְרְבָן מְמַנָּן, בְּשֻׁלְטָנוּתָא עֲלַיְיהוּ. וְיִשְׂרָאֵל קַדִּישִׁין, זַכָּאָה חוּלָקֵהוֹן בְּעָלְמָא דֵּין וּבְעָלְמָא דְּאָתֵי, דְּלָא יָהַב לוֹן קוּדְשָׁא בְּרִיךְ הוּא לָא לְמַלְאָכָא, וְלָא לְשָׁלִיטָא אַחֲרָא, אֶלָּא הוּא אָחִיד לוֹן לְחוּלָקֵיהּ, הה"ד כִּי חֵלֶק יְיָ' עַמּוֹ. וּכְתִיב, כִּי יַעֲקֹב בָּחַר לוֹ יָהּ. כְּתַפּוּחַ בַּעֲצֵי הַיַּעַר, מַה תַּפּוּחַ מִתְפָּרְשָׁא בִּגְוָונוֹי, עַל כָּל שְׁאַר אִילָנֵי חַקְלָא, כַּךְ קוּדְשָׁא בְּרִיךְ הוּא מִתְפָּרַשׁ וְאִתְרְשִׁים עַל כָּל חֵילִין עִלָּאִין וְתַתָּאִין, בג"כ יְיָ' צְבָאוֹת שְׁמוֹ, אוֹת הוּא בְּכָל חֵילָא דִּלְעֵילָּא.

9. Rabbi Yitzchak opened with, "Like the apple tree…" (Shir Hashirim 2:3). Happy is the portion of Yisrael more than all the idolatrous nations, because all the other nations were handed to appointed ministers to control them. As for holy Yisrael, happy is their portion in this world and in the World to Come that the Holy One, blessed be He, gave them neither to an angel nor to another ruler, but took them for His own portion. This is the meaning of, "For Hashem's portion is His people" (Devarim 32:9), and, "For Hashem has chosen Jacob to Himself" (Tehilim 135:4). "Like the apple tree among the trees of the wood": just as the apple tree is different in color from all the other trees in the field, so is the Holy One, blessed be He, separated and marked above all higher and lower legions. Hence His name is Hashem Tzva'ot, WHICH MEANS He is a sign (Heb. *ot*) throughout the celestial army (Heb. *tzava*).

10. ת״ח, קוּדְשָׁא בְּרִיךְ הוּא כְּתַפּוּחַ, דְּאִית בֵּיהּ תְּלַת גַּוְונִין. כ״י כְּשׁוֹשַׁנָּה מַאן שׁוֹשַׁנָּה. א״ר אַבָּא, שׁוֹשַׁנָּה סְתָם, שׁוֹשַׁנָּה דְּאִתְכְּלִילַת בְּשִׁית טַרְפֵּי, שׁוֹשַׁנָּה דָּא גְּוָונֵיהּ חִוָּור וְסוּמָק. וְכֹלָּא הוּא תְּרֵין גְּוָונֵי, סוּמָק וְחִוָּור, הָכִי כ״י.

10. Come and see, the Holy One, blessed be He is like an apple that has in it three colors, WHITE, RED AND GREEN THAT INDICATE CHESED, GVURAH AND TIFERET. The Congregation of Yisrael, WHO IS MALCHUT, is like a lily. What is a lily? Rabbi Aba said, It is a generic lily, a lily of six petals. The colors of such a lily are white and red, and it is all of two colors, red and white THAT INDICATE JUDGMENT AND CHESED. Such is the Congregation of Yisrael, WHO IS MALCHUT.

11. קוּדְשָׁא בְּרִיךְ הוּא כְּתַפּוּחַ, כ״י כְּשׁוֹשַׁנָּה. דְּהָכִי אָמְרָה כ״י, תַּחַת הַתַּפּוּחַ עוֹרַרְתִּיךָ. תַּחַת הַתַּפּוּחַ בְּאָן אֲתָר הִיא. אֶלָּא אִלֵּין אֲבָהָתִין דְּאָמָרָן. ר׳ יוֹסֵי אָמַר, דָּא יוֹבְלָא. ר׳ אַבָּא אָמַר, כֹּלָּא שַׁפִּיר, אֶלָּא אִלֵּין אֲבָהָן דְּקָאמְרָן, אִלֵּין אִינּוּן ג׳ גְּוָונֵי, דְּמִתְחַבְּרָן בְּתַפּוּחַ.

11. The Holy One, blessed be He, is like an apple tree; the Congregation of Yisrael is like a lily. For thus spoke the Congregation of Yisrael, "I roused you under the apple tree" (Shir Hashirim 8:5). HE ASKS, Where is this, under the apple tree, AND ANSWERS, These are the Patriarchs we mentioned, CHESED, GVURAH AND TIFERET THAT ARE CALLED PATRIARCHS. Rabbi Yosi said, It is Jubilee, NAMELY BINAH CALLED APPLE TREE. Rabbi Aba said, Everything is correct, because the Patriarchs we mentioned are the three colors joined in the apple.

12. ר׳ יִצְחָק אָמַר, בְּאָן אֲתָר אִתְכְּלִילַת כ״י בְּשׁוֹשַׁנָּה. בְּאִינּוּן נְשִׁיקִין דִּרְחִימוּתָא, דְּאִתְדַּבְּקַת בְּמַלְכָּא עִלָּאָה, נַטְלָה תְּרֵי שׁוֹשַׁנִּים, כד״א שִׂפְתוֹתָיו שׁוֹשַׁנִּים. ובג״כ אָמְרָה כ״י, יִשָּׁקֵנִי מִנְּשִׁיקוֹת פִּיהוּ. בְּגִין דְּאִתְכְּלִילַת בְּשׁוֹשַׁנִּים, בִּתְרֵי שִׂפְוָון דִּילֵיהּ.

12. Rabbi Yitzchak said, How did the Congregation of Yisrael become a part of the lily? By loving kisses with which MALCHUT cleaved to the supernal King ZEIR ANPIN. Then she took FROM HIS TWO LIPS two roses, as written, "his lips like lilies" (Shir Hashirim 5:13). This is why the Congregation of Yisrael said, "Let him kiss me with the kisses of his mouth" (Shir Hashirim 1:2), since then she is included in the lilies in his two lips THAT ARE CALLED LILIES.

4. Seven firmaments and seven planets

A Synopsis

Rabbi Yehuda says that God is called heaven, and thus all the firmaments are also included in this name; when the firmaments are joined together they are called heaven and therefore they are also called the Name of God. Rabbi Yehuda goes on to list these seven firmaments. Rabbi Yitzchak recalls that Rabbi Shimon compared all the seventy Sfirot of the King to seven firmaments and seven planets, and that although the planets are called by physical names they actually conceal all the firmaments. We are told the names of the seven planets and given their relationship to the seven supernal Sfirot. Rabbi Yosi says that the rabbis find these matters easy to understand even though they are concealed by certain terms. Rabbi Shimon admonishes the other rabbis to forget about the Baraithas because they know the greater wisdom of the Kabbalah and have revealed what was never revealed to ancient sages.

13. ר׳ יְהוּדָה אָמַר, קוּדְשָׁא בְּרִיךְ הוּא שָׁמַיִם אִקְרֵי. וּבְגִין דְּאִקְרֵי שָׁמַיִם, כָּל אִינּוּן רְקִיעִין דְּאִתְכְּלִילָן בִּשְׁמָא דָּא, כַּד מִתְחַבְּרָן כַּחֲדָא, אִקְרוּ שָׁמַיִם, וְאִקְרוּ שְׁמָא דְקוּדְשָׁא בְּרִיךְ הוּא. מַאן אִינּוּן רְקִיעִין. שִׁבְעָה אִינּוּן. כְּמָה דְּתָנֵינָן, וִילוֹן, רָקִיעַ, שְׁחָקִים, זְבוּל, מָעוֹן, מָכוֹן, עֲרָבוֹת. וּבְאַגַּדְתָּא דְּבֵי רַב הַמְנוּנָא סָבָא, הָכִי תָּנֵינָן. ר׳ יִצְחָק אָמַר, הָנֵי בָּרַיְיתֵי דְּבֵי רַב הַמְנוּנָא סָבָא הָכִי, וְסַגִּיאִין אִינּוּן בְּכָל הָנֵי גְּוָונֵי.

13. Rabbi Yehuda said, The Holy One, blessed be He, WHO IS ZEIR ANPIN, is called heaven, and since He is called heaven, all the firmaments that are included in this name, when they are joined together are called heaven and called the Name of the Holy One, blessed be He. What are these firmaments COMPREHENDED IN HEAVEN? AND HE ANSWERS, There are seven as we learned: Vilon (Eng. 'curtain'), Raki'a (Eng. 'firmament'), Shechakim (Eng. 'skies'), Zvul (Eng. 'dwelling'), Ma'on (Eng. 'temple'), Machon (Eng. 'sanctuary'), and Aravot (Eng. 'heaven'). In the Agadah of Rav Hamnuna Saba we learned it thus IN THESE WORDS. Rabbi Yitzchak said, The B'raitot of Rav Hamnuna Saba are thus, SPEAKING ABOUT LOWER THINGS BUT ALLUDING TO LOFTY ONES, THAT IS, JUST LIKE HERE THE SEVEN FIRMAMENTS ARE DISCUSSED THAT REFER TO ZEIR ANPIN THAT HAS

SEVEN SFIROT. There are many B'RAITOT THAT SPEAK in all these manners.

14. כְּמָה דְּתָנֵינָן, אר"ש, תָּנֵינָן בְּאִינּוּן בָּרַיְיתֵי, דִּלְגַבֵּי דְּכָל הָנֵי שַׁבְעִין כִּתְרִין דְּמַלְכָּא. לָקֳבְלֵיהוֹן שַׁוְויָן ז' רְקִיעִין, וְז' כֹּכְבַיָּא דְּרַהֲטִין וְאַזְלִין, וְקָרֵי לוֹן שְׁמָהָן בִּשְׁמָהָן. ואע"ג דְּשַׁוְוייִן כֻּלְּהוּ כִּסְאֵי דִּרְקִיעִין, דְּשִׁבְעָה כֹּכְבַיָּא, שַׁבְּתַאי, צֶדֶק, מַאֲדִים, חַמָּה, נוֹגַהּ, כּוֹכָב, לְבָנָה. וְשָׁוִין אִלֵּין לָקֳבֵיל אִלֵּין, בִּכְסוּיָא דְּמִלִּין. לְגַבֵּי אִינּוּן דִּכְתִּיב, יַעַמְדוּ נָא וְיוֹשִׁיעוּךָ הוֹבְרֵי שָׁמַיִם הַחוֹזִים בַּכֹּכָבִים. כֻּלְּהוּ מִלִּין מִתְכַּסְיָין, ואע"ג דְּלָאו אוֹרְחֵי דְּאוֹרַיְיתָא. וַאֲנָן בָּתַר אוֹרְחִין דְּאוֹרַיְיתָא קָא אַזְלֵינָן, כְּמָה דִּכְתִּיב וַיִּקְרָא לָהֶן שֵׁמוֹת כַּשֵּׁמוֹת אֲשֶׁר קָרָא לָהֶן אָבִיו, כְּמָה דְּמַלִּיל קוּדְשָׁא בְּרִיךְ הוּא, אָזְלִינָן, וּבַהֲדֵיהּ אָזְלֵינָן, כְּמָה דִּכְתִּיב וְהָלַכְתָּ בִּדְרָכָיו.

14. As we learned, Rabbi Shimon said, We learned in all these B'raitot that all these seventy Sfirot of the King are compared to seven firmaments and seven planets that run to and fro, and they are called by PHYSICAL names. But though they conceal all the firmaments, THAT IS, THEY ARE CALLED BY NAMES THAT ALLUDE TO THEIR INNER, SECRET ASPECT, as for the seven planets, Shabtai (Saturn), Tzedek (Jupiter), Ma'adim (Mars), Chamah (Sun), Nogah (Venus), Cochav (Mercury), Levanah (Moon) they relate these SEVEN SUPERNAL SFIROT to those NAMES OF THE PLANETS, WISHING to conceal matters, NAMELY, regarding those OF WHOM it is written, "Let now the astrologers, the stargazers, the monthly prognosticators, stand up, and save you" (Yeshayah 47:13). They conceal matters UNDER THESE NAMES, even though they are not the ways of the Torah BUT ASTROLOGICAL LANGUAGE. But we follow the ways of the Torah, NAMELY, ALLUDE TO EVERYTHING AND CONCEAL IT WITH WORDS OF TORAH, as written, "and he called their names after the names by which his father had called them" (Beresheet 26:18), namely, we follow the words of the Holy One, blessed be He, NAMELY THE LANGUAGE OF THE TORAH, and walk with Him, as written, "and walk in His ways" (Devarim 28:9).

15. אָמַר רִבִּי יוֹסֵי, פְּשִׁיטִין מִלִּין אִלֵּין לְגַבֵּי חַבְרַיָּיא, וְאִשְׁתְּמוֹדְעָן מִלֵּי

בְּהוּ, וְאע״ג דְּאִתְכַּסְיָין. א״ל וְהָכִי תְּנָן, כְּמָה דא״ר יְהוּדָה א״ר חִיָּיא לְקַמָּן. וְהָכִי אוֹלִיפְנָא מֵאִינּוּן בָּרַיְיתֵי, דִּתְנָא בְּיוֹמוֹי דִּשְׁלֹמֹה מַלְכָּא, קַיְּימָא סִיהֲרָא בְּאַשְׁלְמוּתָא, וּבְאַתְרִין סַגִּיאִין אִשְׁתְּמוֹדְעָן מִלֵּי דְּאִינּוּן בָּרַיְיתֵי.

15. Rabbi Yosi said, These words, NAMELY, OUTER NAMES MENTIONED ABOVE, are easy to the friends, and the words are understood, though they are concealed BY FOREIGN TERMS. He said to him, And so have we learned like Rabbi Yehuda said that Rabbi Chiya said before us. And so have we learned from these B'raitot, that during Solomon's days the moon stood full, THAT IS, MALCHUT WAS FULL AND FACE TO FACE WITH ZEIR ANPIN, WHICH IS WHY WISDOM WAS SO PREVALENT THEN. Many people understood the words of these B'raitot.

16. אר״ש, אֲרִימִית יְדַי בִּצְלוֹ לְקַדִּישָׁא עִלָּאָה, דְּמִלִּין אִלֵּין אִתְגַּלְיָאוּ עַל יְדִי, בְּהַהוּא עָלְמָא, כְּמָה דְּאִתְכַּסִּיאוּ בְּלִבָּאִי. וְלֵית אֲנָן בְּאִינּוּן אָרְחִין דְּאִינּוּן בָּרַיְיתֵי, אוֹרְחֵי דְּאוֹרַיְיתָא נַקְטִינָן.

16. Rabbi Shimon said, I have raised my hands in prayer to the holy supernal One that these subjects, THE WISDOM OF KABBALAH, were uncovered by me in that world the way they were covered in my heart. And we do not USE these ways of the B'raitot but apply the ways of the Torah TO INTERPRET THIS DISCIPLINE.

17. תָּאנָא א״ר יְהוּדָה, מַאן לָךְ רַב בְּחָכְמְתָא כְּדָוִד מַלְכָּא, וּשְׁלֹמֹה מַלְכָּא בְּרֵיהּ, בְּהַאי כִּתְרָא דְּאִשְׁתְּמוֹדַע בְּבָרַיְיתֵי אִלֵּין. וְסִיהֲרָא קַרְיֵיהּ דָּוִד מַלְכָּא צֶדֶק, דְּהָא דִּילֵיהּ הוּא, דִּכְתִּיב פִּתְחוּ לִי שַׁעֲרֵי צֶדֶק אָבֹא בָם אוֹדֶה יָהּ. שְׁלֹמֹה מַלְכָּא הָכִי נָמֵי, וְאִיהוּ אִתְקְרֵי צֶדֶק, וְשִׁמְשָׁא דְּאִתְקְרֵי בְּבָרַיְיתֵי בְּרִית, אִיהוּ אִקְרֵי מִשְׁפָּט. וְאִינּוּן כֻּרְסֵי יְקָרָא דְּמַלְכָּא, דִּכְתִּיב צֶדֶק וּמִשְׁפָּט מְכוֹן כִּסְאֶךָ. צַדִּיק וְצֶדֶק הָכִי נָמֵי בְּחַד דַּרְגָּא הֲווֹ. תָּאנָא, ז׳ כִּתְרִין אוֹקְמוּהָ, תִּשְׁעָה אִקְרוּן. וַאֲפִילּוּ בְּאִינּוּן בָּרַיְיתֵי, שִׁבְעָה רְקִיעִין אִינּוּן תִּשְׁעָה הֲווֹ.

17. We learned that Rabbi Yehuda said, Who is great in wisdom like King David and his son King Solomon in ATTAINING that Sfirah known by these B'raitot, THAT IS THE SFIRAH OF MALCHUT. King David called the moon, WHICH IS MALCHUT, righteousness because it is his, HE BEING A CHARIOT TO MALCHUT, as written, "Open to me the gates of righteousness. I will go in to them, and I will praise Yah" (Tehilim 118:19). King Solomon also CALLED IT RIGHTEOUSNESS, and it is called righteousness. The sun that is called in the B'raitot a covenant, NAMELY YESOD, is called justice. And both are the Throne of Glory of the King, ZEIR ANPIN, as written, "Righteousness and justice are the foundation of Your throne" (Tehilim 89:15), because the Righteous and Righteousness, YESOD AND MALCHUT, are also in the same grade, WHICH IS WHY THEY ARE MENTIONED TOGETHER IN THE WORDS, "RIGHTEOUSNESS AND JUSTICE ARE THE FOUNDATION OF YOUR THRONE." We learned that the seven Sfirot, CHESED, GVURAH, TIFERET, NETZACH, HOD, YESOD AND MALCHUT, ARE NINE, THAT IS, TOGETHER WITH CHOCHMAH AND BINAH. And even in these B'raitot, seven firmaments are nine.

18. אר"ש, עַד אֵימָתַי יִקְרוּן חַבְרַיָּיא בְּהָנֵי מִלִּין. הָא אֲנָן בָּתַר קוּדְשָׁא בְּרִיךְ הוּא אַזְלֵינָן, וַאֲנָן יַדְעֵי מִלִּין, וְהָא אִתְגְּלֵי עַל יְדָן מִלָּה דָּא, מַה דְּלָא אִתְגְּלֵי לְקַדְמָאֵי. מִכָּאן וּלְהָלְאָה, כָּל אִינּוּן מִלִּין, וְכָל אִינּוּן בָּרַיְיתֵי, סְלִיקוּ לְהוּ לְאִינּוּן דְּלָא עָאלוּ וְנַפְקוּ, וּבְנֵיהוֹן אַתְיָין לְשָׁאֲלָא. וְכַד יִשְׁאֲלוּן, יֵימְרוּן חַבְרַיָּיא, וַוי לְדָרָא דר"ש בֶּן יוֹחָאי אִסְתְּלִיק מִנֵּיהּ. אֲבָל ת"ח מִכָּאן וּלְהָלְאָה, לָא יְהֵא דָּרָא כְּדָרָא דָּא, וְלָא אוֹרַיְיתָא אִתְגְּלֵי עַל חַבְרַיָּיא.

18. Rabbi Shimon said, How long will the friends read these things, NAMELY THE B'RAITOT! We follow the Holy One, blessed be He, and we know the subjects OF THE WISDOM OF KABBALAH. We have revealed what was not revealed to ancient sages. From now on, leave all these things and all the B'raitot to those who did not go in and out, NAMELY THOSE WHO ENTERED THE WISDOM BUT DID NOT LEAVE IT BECAUSE THEY DID NOT UNDERSTAND IT. Let their children come and inquire about this wisdom, and when they will, the friends will say TO THEM, Woe to the generation from which Rabbi Shimon bar Yochai has departed. Yet come and see, from now on there shall be no generation like this one, and Torah will not be disclosed by the friends.

5. Moses revealed on the day he passed away

A Synopsis

Rabbi Shimon says that the last generation that left Egypt knew everything, because Moses revealed it all to them during the forty years that they wandered in the wilderness. Rabbi Yitzchak had taught that even Moses only revealed secrets on the last day before he died, once he was given permission to reveal them. The poem that Moses delivered to the people was drawn from the Holy Spirit downwards, and he called on the name of God when he spoke.

19. ת״ח, דָּרָא בַּתְרָאָה דְּנַפְקוּ מִמִּצְרַיִם, יָדְעוּ כֹּלָּא, דְּהָא מֹשֶׁה גַּלֵּי לוֹן כָּל אִינּוּן מ׳ שְׁנִין דַּהֲווֹ בְּמַדְבְּרָא, כְּמָה דַּאֲמֵינָא. תָּאנָא א״ר יִצְחָק, וְאַף מֹשֶׁה לָא גַּלֵּי דָּא, אֶלָּא בְּהַהוּא יוֹמָא דַּהֲוָה סָלִיק מִן עָלְמָא, דִּכְתִּיב בֶּן מֵאָה וְעֶשְׂרִים שָׁנָה אָנֹכִי הַיּוֹם, בְּהַהוּא יוֹמָא מַמָּשׁ, ועכ״ד לָא אָמַר, עַד דְּיָהֲבוּ לֵיהּ רְשׁוּתָא. דִּכְתִּיב, וְעַתָּה כִּתְבוּ לָכֶם אֶת הַשִּׁירָה הַזֹּאת. וְכַד גַּלֵּי, לָא אָמַר הַאֲזִינוּ יִשְׂרָאֵל, אֶלָּא הַאֲזִינוּ הַשָּׁמַיִם.

19. Come and see, the last generation that left Egypt knew everything because Moses revealed it to them all the forty years they were in the wilderness, as I said. We learned that Rabbi Yitzchak said, Even Moses revealed it only on the day he departed from the world, as written, "I am a hundred and twenty years old this day" (Devarim 31:2), on the very day HE PASSED AWAY. Hence he did not speak until he was given permission as written, "Now therefore write this poem for yourselves" (Ibid. 19). When he did reveal, he did not say 'Give ear, Yisrael', but, "Give ear, O heavens" (Devarim 32:1).

20. א״ר יוֹסֵי, כְּתִיב אֶת הַשִּׁירָה, וְכִי שִׁירָה אִקְרֵי. א״ר יִצְחָק שִׁירָה וַדַּאי, מַה שִׁירָה אִתְמַשְׁכָא בְּרוּחַ הַקֹּדֶשׁ מֵעֵילָּא לְתַתָּא, אוֹף הָכִי מִלִּין אִלֵּין אִתְמַשְׁכָן בְּרוּחַ הַקֹּדֶשׁ מֵעֵילָּא לְתַתָּא, ובג״כ אָמַר מֹשֶׁה שִׁירָה.

20. Rabbi Yosi said, It is written, "this poem," THAT IS, "NOW THEREFORE WRITE THIS POEM FOR YOURSELVES." Could it be called a poem? IT

SHOULD HAVE SAID 'THIS TORAH'. Rabbi Yitzchak said, It is surely a poem. As a poem is drawn through the Holy Spirit from above downwards, SO these words also were drawn through the Holy Spirit from above downwards. This is why Moses spoke of a poem.

21. ת״ח, כּוּלֵי הַאי אָמַר מֹשֶׁה, וְקָרָא לְעִלָּאִין, עַד לָא יֵימָא מִלָּה, דִּכְתִּיב הַאֲזִינוּ הַשָּׁמַיִם. יַעֲרוֹף כַּמָּטָר וְגוֹ׳. וְכָל כַּךְ לָמָּה. מִשּׁוּם כִּי שֵׁם יְיָ׳ אֶקְרָא. עַד דְּיֵימָא מִלָּה, אַרְעִישׁ כֻּלְּהוּ עָלְמִין.

21. Come and see all that Moses has spoken and called to the high ones before he uttered a word, as written, "Give ear, O heavens." "My doctrine shall drop as the rain..." (Ibid. 2). Why all that? Because "I will call on the name of Hashem" (Ibid. 3). Before he said that, he caused all the worlds to tremble.

22. תָּאנָא בְּהַהִיא שַׁעֲתָא דְּאָמַר מֹשֶׁה הַאֲזִינוּ הַשָּׁמַיִם וַאֲדַבֵּרָה, אִתְרְגִּישׁוּ עָלְמִין. נָפַק קָלָא וְאָמַר, מֹשֶׁה מֹשֶׁה, אֲמַאי אַתְּ מַרְעִישׁ עָלְמָא כֹּלָּא. אַתְּ בְּרֵיהּ דְּבַר נָשׁ, וּבְגִינָךְ אִתְרְגִּישׁ עָלְמָא. פָּתַח וְאָמַר כִּי שֵׁם יְיָ׳ אֶקְרָא. בְּהַהִיא שַׁעֲתָא אִשְׁתְּתָקוּ, וַאֲצִיתוּ מִלּוֹי.

22. We learned that when Moses said, "Give ear, O heavens, and I will speak," the worlds shook. A voice resounded saying, Moses, Moses, why are you shaking the whole world? You are human, shall the world shake because of you? He opened and said, "I will call on the name of Hashem." At that moment they became silent and listened to his words.

האדרא זוטא קדישא

The holy Idra Zuta (the smaller assembly)

6. The day when Rabbi Shimon wanted to depart from the world

A Synopsis

This section begins to tell about the events surrounding Rabbi Shimon's voluntary departure from the world. Many of the friends are with him, although they come and go as Rabbi Shimon requests them to. A fire encircles the whole house as he prepares to reveal things that he has never before had permission to reveal, and Rabbi Aba is charged with writing down his revelations. Rabbi Shimon begins by saying that the living are the righteous, and anyone who is wicked is considered to be dead. He says that God delights in the honor of the righteous even more than His own honor. Next Rabbi Shimon tells the other rabbis that he can see two rabbis who died some time earlier together with seventy righteous people all shining with the radiance of the most hidden Atika Kadisha; at this statement the other rabbis tremble. Rabbi Shimon says that during his whole life he was attached to God, and now at the end God and all His holy followers have come joyfully to listen to hidden secrets and to the praise of Atika Kadisha.

23. תָּאנָא בְּהַהוּא יוֹמָא דר״ש בָּעָא לְאִסְתַּלְּקָא מִן עָלְמָא, וַהֲוָה מְסַדֵּר מִלּוֹי, אִתְכְּנָשׁוּ חַבְרַיָּיא לְבֵי ר״ש, וַהֲווֹ קַמֵּיהּ ר׳ אֶלְעָזָר בְּרֵיהּ, וְר׳ אַבָּא, וּשְׁאָר חַבְרַיָּיא, וַהֲוָה מַלְיָא בֵּיתָא. זָקִיף עֵינוֹי ר״ש, וְחָמָא דְּאִתְמְלֵי בֵּיתָא. בָּכָה ר״ש וְאָמַר, בְּזִמְנָא אַחֲרָא כַּד הֲוֵינָא בְּבֵי מַרְעִי, הֲוָה רִבִּי פִּנְחָס בֶּן יָאִיר קַמָּאִי, וְעַד דְּבָרִירְנָא דּוּכְתָּאִי אוֹרִיכוּ לִי עַד הַשְׁתָּא. וְכַד תַּבְנָא, אַסְחַר אֶשָּׁא מִקַּמָּאִי, וּמֵעָלְמִין לָא אִתְפְּסָק, וְלָא הֲוָה עָאל בַּר נָשׁ, אֶלָּא בִּרְשׁוּתָא. וְהַשְׁתָּא חֲמֵינָא דְּאִתְפְּסַק, וְהָא אִתְמְלֵי בֵּיתָא.

23. We learned that on the day Rabbi Shimon wanted to depart from the world and was putting his affairs in order, the friends gathered in the house of Rabbi Shimon. Before him were Rabbi Elazar his son and Rabbi Aba and other friends, and the house was full. Rabbi Shimon lifted up his eyes and saw that the house became full. Rabbi Shimon wept and said, Another time when I was ill Rabbi Pinchas ben Yair was before me, and they waited for me until I inquired about my place IN THE GARDEN OF EDEN. When I returned, a fire circled me, which never stopped. No one entered MY HOUSE except by permission. Now I see THE FIRE stopped, and behold the house is full.

24. עַד דַּהֲווֹ יַתְבֵי, פָּתַח עֵינוֹי ר״ש, וְחָמָא מַה דְּחָמָא, וְאַסְחַר אֶשָּׁא בְּבֵיתָא, נַפְקוּ כּוּלְּהוּ, וְאִשְׁתָּאֲרוּ רִבִּי אֶלְעָזָר בְּרֵיהּ, וְרִבִּי אַבָּא. וּשְׁאַר חַבְרַיָּיא יָתְבוּ אַבְּרָאי. אר״ש לְרִבִּי אֶלְעָזָר בְּרֵיהּ, פּוּק חֲזֵי, אִי הָכָא רִבִּי יִצְחָק, דַּאֲנָא מְעָרְבְנָא לֵיהּ, אֵימָא לֵיהּ דִּיסַדֵּר מִלּוֹי, וְיֵתִיב לְגַבָּאי, זַכָּאָה חוּלָקֵיהּ.

24. While they were sitting, Rabbi Shimon opened his eyes and saw what he saw, and fire encircled the house. Everybody left, and only Rabbi Elazar his son and Rabbi Aba remained, while the rest of the friends stayed outside. Rabbi Shimon said to Rabbi Elazar his son, Go out and see if Rabbi Yitzchak is here, because I was a guarantor for him. Tell him to settle his affairs and sit by me. Happy is his portion.

25. קָם ר״ש, וְיָתִיב, וְחַיִיךְ, וְחַדֵּי. אָמַר, אָן אִינּוּן חַבְרַיָּיא. קָם רִבִּי אֶלְעָזָר, וְאָעִיל לוֹן. יָתְבוּ קַמֵּיהּ. זָקִיף יְדוֹי ר״ש, וּמְצַלֵּי צְלוֹתָא, וַהֲוֵי חַדֵּי, וְאָמַר, אִינּוּן חַבְרַיָּיא דְּאִשְׁתְּכָחוּ בְּבֵי אִדָּרָא, יִזְדַּמְנוּן הָכָא. נַפְקוּ כֻּלְּהוּ, וְאִשְׁתָּאֲרוּ רִבִּי אֶלְעָזָר בְּרֵיהּ, וְרִבִּי אַבָּא, וְרִבִּי יְהוּדָה, וְרִבִּי יוֹסֵי, וְרִבִּי חִיָּיא. אַדְּהָכִי, עָאל רִבִּי יִצְחָק, א״ל ר״ש, כַּמָּה יָאוּת חוּלָקָךְ, כַּמָּה חֵידוּ בָּעֵי לְאִתּוֹסְפָא לָךְ בְּהַאי יוֹמָא, יָתִיב רִבִּי אַבָּא בָּתַר כַּתְפּוֹי, וְרִבִּי אֶלְעָזָר קַמֵּיהּ.

25. Rabbi Shimon rose and sat down, laughed and rejoiced. He said, Where are the friends? Rabbi Elazar rose and let them in, and they sat before him. Rabbi Shimon raised his hands, recited a prayer and was glad. He said, Let the friends that were present at the assembly, NAMELY THE IDRA RABA, come here. They all left, and Rabbi Elazar his son, Rabbi Aba, Rabbi Yehuda, Rabbi Yosi and Rabbi Chiya stayed. In the meanwhile Rabbi Yitzchak entered. Rabbi Shimon said to him, How deserved is your portion.

How much joy should be added to you on this day. Rabbi Aba sat behind him and Rabbi Elazar before him.

26. אר"ש, הָא הַשְׁתָּא שַׁעֲתָא דִּרְעוּתָא הוּא, וַאֲנָא בָּעֵינָא לְמֵיעַל בְּלֹא כִּסּוּפָא לְעָלְמָא דְּאָתֵי. וְהָא מִלִּין קַדִּישִׁין דְּלָא גָּלִיאָן עַד הַשְׁתָּא, בָּעֵינָא לְגַלָּאָה קַמֵּי שְׁכִינְתָּא, דְּלָא יֵימְרוּן דְּהָא בִּגְרִיעוּתָא אִסְתַּלַּקְנָא מֵעָלְמָא. וְעַד כְּעַן טְמִירִן הֲווּ בְּלִבָּאִי, לְמֵיעַל בְּהוּ לְעָלְמָא דְּאָתֵי.

26. Rabbi Shimon said, Now it is time of goodwill, and I want to come without shame into the World to Come. Here are holy matters that I have not revealed until now. I wish to reveal them before the Shechinah so it shall not be said that I have gone from this world in want – until now they have been hidden in my heart, so I can enter through them into the World to Come.

27. וְכַךְ אַסְדַּרְנָא לְכוּ, רִבִּי אַבָּא יִכְתּוֹב, וְרִבִּי אֶלְעָזָר בְּרִי יִלְעֵי, וּשְׁאַר חַבְרַיָּיא יִרַחֲשׁוּן בְּלִבַּיְיהוּ. קָם רִבִּי אַבָּא מִבָּתַר כַּתְפּוֹי. וְיָתִיב רִבִּי אֶלְעָזָר בְּרֵיהּ קַמֵּיהּ, א"ל קוּם בְּרִי, דְּהָא אַחֲרָא יְתִיב בְּהַהוּא אֲתָר, קָם רִבִּי אֶלְעָזָר.

27. This is how I am going to arrange you: Rabbi Aba shall write, Rabbi Elazar my son shall recite orally, and the other friends shall speak in their hearts. Rabbi Aba rose from behind his back. Rabbi Elazar was sitting in front of him. RABBI SHIMON said to him, Rise my son, for another shall sit in this place. Rabbi Elazar rose.

28. אִתְעֲטַף ר"ש, וְיָתִיב. פָּתַח וְאָמַר, לֹא הַמֵּתִים יְהַלְלוּ יָהּ וְלֹא כָּל יוֹרְדֵי דוּמָה. לֹא הַמֵּתִים יְהַלְלוּ יָהּ, הָכִי הוּא וַדַּאי, אִינּוּן דְּאִקְרוּן מֵתִים, דְּהָא קוּדְשָׁא בְּרִיךְ הוּא חַי אִקְרֵי, וְהוּא שָׁארִי בֵּין אִינּוּן דְּאִקְרוּן חַיִּים, וְלָא עִם אִינּוּן דְּאִקְרוּן מֵתִים. וְסוֹפֵיהּ דִּקְרָא כְּתִיב, וְלֹא כָּל יוֹרְדֵי דוּמָה, וְכָל אִינּוּן דְּנַחְתִּין לְדוּמָה, בַּגֵּיהִנָּם יִשְׁתַּאֲרוּן. שֶׁאֲנִי אִינּוּן דְּאִקְרוּן חַיִּים, דְּהָא קוּדְשָׁא בְּרִיךְ הוּא בָּעֵי בִּיקָרֵיהוֹן.

28. Rabbi Shimon wrapped himself IN HIS GARMENT, and sat down. He started by saying, "The dead cannot praise Yah, nor can any who go down into silence (Heb. *dumah*)" (Tehilim 115:17). Surely "The dead cannot praise Yah," those who are considered dead, because the Holy One, blessed be He, is called living and dwells among those who are called living, NAMELY THE RIGHTEOUS, and not with those that are considered dead, NAMELY THE WICKED. The end of the verse PROVES IT, as written, "nor can any who go down into Dumah," namely all those who go down to THE ANGEL Dumah, and remain in Gehenom. But it is not so with those who are called living, THE RIGHTEOUS, that the Holy One, blessed be He, delights to honor.

29. אר״ש, כַּמָּה שַׁנְיָא שַׁעֲתָא דָּא מֵאִדְּרָא. דִּבְאִדְּרָא אִזְדַּמַּן קוּדְשָׁא בְּרִיךְ הוּא וּרְתִיכוֹי. וְהַשְׁתָּא, הָא קוּדְשָׁא בְּרִיךְ הוּא הָכָא, וְאָתֵי עִם אִינּוּן צַדִּיקַיָּיא דִּבְגִנְתָּא דְּעֵדֶן, מַה דְּלָא אִעֲרָעוּ בְּאִדְּרָא. וְקוּדְשָׁא בְּרִיךְ הוּא בָּעֵי בִּיקָרֵיהוֹן דְּצַדִּיקַיָּיא יַתִּיר מִיקָרָא דִּילֵיהּ, כְּמָה דִּכְתִּיב בִּירָבְעָם, דַּהֲוָה מְקַטֵּר וּמַפְלַח לע״ז, וְקוּדְשָׁא בְּרִיךְ הוּא אוֹרִיךְ לֵיהּ. וְכֵיוָן דְּאוֹשִׁיט יְדֵיהּ לָקֳבְלֵי דְּעִדּוֹ נְבִיאָה, אִתְיְיבַשׁ יְדֵיהּ, דִּכְתִּיב וַתִּיבַשׁ יָדוֹ וְגוֹ׳. וְעַל דְּפָלַח לע״ז לָא כְּתִיב, אֶלָּא עַל דְּאוֹשִׁיט יְדֵיהּ לְעִדּוֹ נְבִיאָה. וְהַשְׁתָּא קוּדְשָׁא בְּרִיךְ הוּא בָּעֵי בִּיקָרָא דִּילָן, וְכֻלְּהוּ אָתָאן עִמֵּיהּ.

29. Rabbi Shimon said, How different is this time from the Idra RABA IN THE PORTION OF NASO, since in the Idra the Holy One, blessed be He, came with His Chariots. Now the Holy One, blessed be He, is here, coming with the righteous that are in the Garden of Eden, which has not happened at the Idra. And the Holy One, blessed be He, delights in the honor of the righteous more than His own honor, as written about Jeroboam that he used to make offerings and worship idols, yet the Holy One, blessed be He, waited for him AND DID NOT PUNISH HIM. But once he stretched his hands against Ido the prophet, his hand dried up, as written, "And his hand…dried up" (I Melachim 13:4). It is not mentioned because he worshipped idols, but because he put out his hand against Ido the prophet. Now the Holy One, blessed be He, delights in our honor as all THE RIGHTEOUS IN THE GARDEN OF EDEN came with Him.

30. אָמַר, הָא רַב הַמְנוּנָא סָבָא הָכָא, וְסַחֲרָנֵיהּ ע׳ צַדִּיקֵי גְּלִיפָן בְּעִיטְרִין, מְנַהֲרִין כָּל חַד וְחַד מִזִּיהֲרָא דְּזִיוָא דְּעַתִּיקָא קַדִּישָׁא, סְתִימָא דְּכָל סְתִימִין. וְהוּא אָתֵי לְמִשְׁמַע בְּחֶדְוָותָא, אִלֵּין מִלִּין דַּאֲנָא אֵימָא. עַד דַּהֲוָה יָתִיב, אָמַר, הָא רִבִּי פִּנְחָס בֶּן יָאִיר הָכָא, אַתְקִינוּ דּוּכְתֵּיהּ, אִזְדַּעְזָעוּ חַבְרַיָּיא דַּהֲווּ תַּמָּן, וְקָמוּ וְיָתְבוּ בְּשִׁיפּוּלֵי בֵּיתָא. וְרִבִּי אֶלְעָזָר וְרִבִּי אַבָּא, אִשְׁתָּאֲרוּ קַמֵּיהּ דר״ש. אר״ש, בְּאִדְּרָא אִשְׁתְּכַחְנָא דְּכָל חַבְרַיָּיא הֲווֹ אָמְרֵי, וַאֲנָא עִמְּהוֹן. הַשְׁתָּא אֵימָא אֲנָא בִּלְחוֹדָאי, וְכֻלְּהוּ צַיְיתִין לְמִלּוּלִי עִלָּאִין וְתַתָּאִין. זַכָּאָה חוּלָקִי יוֹמָא דֵּין.

30. RABBI SHIMON said, Here is Rav Hamnuna Saba, and around him seventy righteous people engraved with crowns, and shining each from the splendor of the radiance of the most concealed Atika Kadisha. He comes gladly to listen to the things I am saying. As he was sitting he said, since Rabbi Pinchas ben Yair is here, prepare his seat. The friends that were there trembled, rose and sat at the corners of the house, and Rabbi Elazar and Rabbi Aba remained before Rabbi Shimon. Rabbi Shimon said, In the Idra RABA the state was that all the friends were talking and I among them. Now I shall alone speak and everyone will listen to my words, higher and lower beings. Happy is my portion on this day.

31. פָּתַח ר״ש וְאָמַר, אֲנִי לְדוֹדִי וְעָלַי תְּשׁוּקָתוֹ. כָּל יוֹמִין דְּאִתְקְטַרְנָא בְּהַאי עָלְמָא, בְּחַד קְטִירָא אִתְקְטַרְנָא בֵּיהּ בְּקוּדְשָׁא בְּרִיךְ הוּא, ובג״כ הַשְׁתָּא וְעָלַי תְּשׁוּקָתוֹ. דְּהוּא וְכָל סִיעָתָא קַדִּישָׁא דִּילֵיהּ, אָתוּ לְמִשְׁמַע בְּחֶדְוָה, מִלִּין סְתִימִין, וּשְׁבָחָא דְּעַתִּיקָא קַדִּישָׁא, סְתִימָא דְּכָל סְתִימִין, פָּרִישׁ וְאִתְפְּרַשׁ מִכֹּלָּא, וְלָא פָּרִישׁ, דְּהָא כֹּלָּא בֵּיהּ מִתְדְּבַק, וְהוּא מִתְדְּבַק בְּכֹלָּא הוּא כֹּלָּא.

31. He opened with, "I am my beloved's, and his desire is towards me" (Shir Hashirim 7:11). All the days I was connected to this world, I was attached with one connection with the Holy One, blessed be He, and hence now, "His desire is towards me." For He and all His holy camp have come with joy to listen to hidden words and the praise of the most hidden Atika Kadisha, which is separated and divided, yet is not divided, since everything cleaves to Him and He cleaves to everything; He is everything.

7. Nine lights that glow with the establishments of Atika

A Synopsis

Rabbi Shimon talks about the most ancient among the ancient, Atika, saying that when it was established it produced nine lights or Sfirot. He tells us about the nature of Atika Kadisha and how it can be known by the lights that emanate from it.

32. עַתִּיקָא דְּכָל עַתִּיקִין, סְתִימָא דְּכָל סְתִימִין, אִתְתְּקַן וְלָא אִתְתְּקַן. אִתְתְּקַן, בְּגִין לְקַיְּימָא כֹּלָּא. וְלָא אִתְתְּקַן, בְּגִין דְּלָא שְׁכִיחַ.

32. The most ancient among the ancient, Atika, WHICH IS CALLED THE UNKNOWN HEAD, which is most concealed, was established yet not established. It was established in order to maintain everything, BUT FROM ITS OWN ASPECT it was not established, BECAUSE ITS OWN ESTABLISHMENTS REVEAL NOTHING OF ITS OWN NATURE, and it cannot be found, THAT IS, IT IS INCOMPREHENSIBLE.

33. כַּד אִתְתְּקַן, אַפִּיק ט' נְהוֹרִין, דְּלַהֲטִין מִנֵּיהּ, מִתִּקּוּנוֹי. וְאִינּוּן נְהוֹרִין מִנֵּיהּ, מִתְנַהֲרִין וּמִתְלַהֲטִין, וְאָזְלִין וּמִתְפַּשְּׁטִין לְכָל עִיבָר. כְּבוּצִינָא דְּאִתְפַּשְּׁטִין מִנֵּיהּ נְהוֹרִין לְכָל עִיבָר. וְאִינּוּן נְהוֹרִין דְּמִתְפַּשְּׁטִין, כַּד יִקְרְבוּן לְמִנְדַּע לוֹן, לָא שְׁכִיחַ אֶלָּא בּוּצִינָא בִּלְחוֹדוֹי. כַּךְ הוּא עַתִּיקָא קַדִּישָׁא, הוּא בּוּצִינָא עִלָּאָה, סְתִימָא דְּכָל סְתִימִין. וְלָא שְׁכִיחַ בַּר אִינּוּן נְהוֹרִין דְּמִתְפָּשְׁטָן, דְּמִתְגַּלְיָין, וּטְמִירָן. וְאִינּוּן אִקְרוּן שְׁמָא קַדִּישָׁא. ובג"כ כֹּלָּא חַד.

33. When it was established it produced nine lights, WHICH ARE THE NINE SFIROT KETER, CHOCHMAH, BINAH, CHESED, GVURAH, TIFERET, NETZACH, HOD AND YESOD OF ARICH ANPIN, THE GARMENTS OF WHICH ARE ABA AND IMA, MALE AND FEMALE, that glow from it, FROM THE UNKNOWN HEAD from its establishments. These NINE lights shine from it WITH CHASSADIM, glow from it WITH GVUROT, and spread in every direction BOTH TO CHOCHMAH AND TO CHASSADIM like a candle from which lights stream in every direction. When one approaches to observe the spreading lights, only the candle alone can be observed. THAT IS, THE

CANDLE AND THE LIGHTS STREAMING FROM THE CANDLE ARE NOT TWO THINGS, SINCE THE LIGHT SPREADING FROM IT HAS NO SELF-EXISTENCE OR POWER, BECAUSE ALL ITS EXISTENCE LIES WITHIN THAT CANDLE. IF YOU TAKE THE CANDLE TO A DIFFERENT PLACE, THE LIGHTS SHALL SPREAD IN A DIFFERENT PLACE AND NOTHING WILL REMAIN OF THEM IN THE FORMER PLACE. Such is Atika Kadisha. It is a lofty, most hidden candle, incomprehensible save for the lights spreading FROM IT, SOME OF WHICH ARE revealed and SOME OF WHICH ARE hidden. They are called the Holy Name. BUT THE LIGHTS SPREADING FROM ATIKA KADISHA HAVE NO SELF-EXISTENCE, HEAVEN FORBID, ALL THEIR EXISTENCE IS WITHIN ATIKA KADISHA, THOUGH THEY ARE COMPREHENSIBLE AND ATIKA KADISHA IS NOT, LIKE LIGHTS STREAMING FROM THE CANDLE. For that reason it is all one.

34. וּמַה דְּאַמְרֵי חַבְרָנָא בְּסִפְרֵי קַדְמָאֵי, דְּאִינּוּן דַּרְגִּין דְּאִתְבְּרִיאוּ, וְעַתִּיקָא קַדִּישָׁא אִתְגְּלֵי בְּהוּ, בְּכָל חַד וְחַד. מִשּׁוּם דְּאִינּוּן תִּקּוּנִין דְּעַתִּיקָא קַדִּישָׁא. לָאו הַשְׁתָּא עִידָנָא לְהָנֵי מִלִּין דְּהָא אֲמֵינָא לוֹן בְּאִדְּרָא קַדִּישָׁא. וַחֲמֵינָא מַה דְּלָא יְדַעְנָא הָכִי, וְעַד הַשְׁתָּא אַסְתִּים בְּלִבָּאִי מִלָּה. וְהַשְׁתָּא אֲנָא בִּלְחוֹדָאי אַסְהִידְנָא קַמֵּי מַלְכָּא קַדִּישָׁא, וְכָל הָנֵי זַכָּאֵי קְשׁוֹט דְּאָתוּ לְמִשְׁמַע מִלִּין אִלֵּין.

34. The friends have said in ancient books THAT THE CHANGES SPREADING FROM IT are created grades, THAT IS, THEY COME INTO BEING THROUGH THE ESTABLISHMENTS CREATED, and that Atika Kadisha is revealed through each of them, since they are the constructions of Atika Kadisha. THAT IS, THEY ARE TYPES OF COVERS OVER THE ILLUMINATION OF BLESSED THE ENDLESS LIGHT AND THROUGH THESE COVERS THE LOWER BEINGS ARE ABLE TO COMPREHEND IT. ITS CREATION IS IN RELATION TO PEOPLE, BUT IN THE LIGHT ITSELF THERE IS NO CHANGE, HEAVEN FORBID. THIS IS LIKE A MAN WHO PUTS ON CLOTHES TO APPEAR BEFORE HIS NEIGHBORS. THAT MAN IS NOT AFFECTED AT ALL BY THESE COVERS, THOUGH OTHERS ARE. This is not the time for these matters, because I have already spoken of them in the holy Idra. BUT NOW I realize what I have not known that well, which until now was hidden in my heart. Now I alone testify before the Holy King and BEFORE all the truly righteous who came to hear these matters.

8. The skull of Atika

A Synopsis

Here Rabbi Shimon talks about the skull of the head of Arich Anpin, and the flow that spreads and shines from it. We hear about the dew of plenty that drips every day to Zeir Anpin and with which the dead will be resurrected in the time to come. Within that head the supernal wisdom is hidden that is called the supernal brain; it can be comprehended only by itself.

35. גּוּלְגַּלְתָּא דְּרֵישָׁא חִוָּורָא, לָאו בֵּיהּ שֵׁירוּתָא וְסִיּוּמָא. קוּלְטְרָא דְּקִטְפּוֹי, אִתְפַּשָּׁט וְאִתְנְהִיר, וּמִנֵּיהּ יַרְתוּן צַדִּיקַיָּיא ד׳ מְאָה עָלְמִין דְּכִסּוּפִין לְעָלְמָא דְּאָתֵי. מֵהַאי קוּלְטְרָא דְּקִטְפָּא, דְּהִיא גּוּלְגַּלְתָּא חִוָּורָא, נָטִיף טַלָּא כָּל יוֹמָא, לְהַהוּא זְעֵיר אַנְפִּין, לַאֲתָר דְּאִתְקְרֵי שָׁמַיִם, וּבֵיהּ זְמִינִין מֵיתַיָּיא לַאֲחַיָּיא לְזִמְנָא דְּאָתֵי. דִּכְתִּיב וְיִתֶּן לְךָ הָאֱלֹהִים מִטַּל הַשָּׁמַיִם. וְאִתְמַלְיָיא רֵישֵׁיהּ וּמֵהַהוּא זְעֵיר אַפִּין, נָטִיף לַחֲקַל תַּפּוּחִין. וְכָל חֲקַל תַּפּוּחִין, נְהִירִין מֵהַהוּא טַלָּא.

35. The skull, NAMELY KETER, of the white head, NAMELY THE HEAD OF ARICH ANPIN, WHICH IS WHOLLY WHITE, THE SECRET OF THE REIGN OF CHESED, has neither beginning nor ending FOR REVEALING CHOCHMAH, THE SECRET OF SUPERNAL CHOCHMAH AND LOWER CHOCHMAH. FOR THE FLOW OF CHOCHMAH AND THE FLOW OF CHASSADIM ARE JOINED IN IT INTO ONE LIGHT OF CHASSADIM. Its joint flow spreads and shines FROM IT, and from it the righteous receive 400 desirable worlds for the World to Come. From the joint flow, which is the white head, dew drips, NAMELY PLENTY, daily to Zeir Anpin, which is a place called heaven. With it, THAT DEW, the dead shall be resurrected in the future to come, as written, "therefore Elohim give you of the dew of heaven" (Beresheet 27:28), NAMELY THE DEW OF ZEIR ANPIN THAT IS CALLED HEAVEN, and His head is filled. From Zeir Anpin it flows to the field of apple trees, WHICH IS MALCHUT, and the whole field of apple trees radiates with this dew.

36. הַאי עַתִּיקָא קַדִּישָׁא טָמִיר וְגָנִיז. וְחָכְמְתָא עִלָּאָה סְתִימָאָה, בְּהַהוּא גּוּלְגַּלְתָּא מִשְׁתְּכַח, וַדַּאי בְּהַאי עַתִּיקָא, לָא אִתְגַּלְיָיא אֶלָּא

רֵישָׁא בִּלְחוֹדוֹי, בְּגִין דְּאִיהוּ רֵישָׁא לְכָל רֵישָׁא. חָכְמְתָא עִלָּאָה, דְּאִיהִי רֵישָׁא, בֵּיהּ סָתִים, וְאִקְרֵי מוֹחָא עִלָּאָה. מוֹחָא סְתִימָא. מוֹחָא דְּשָׁכִיךְ וְשָׁקִיט. וְלֵית דְּיָדַע לֵיהּ, בַּר אִיהוּ.

36. This Atika Kadisha, WHICH IS ARICH ANPIN, is hidden and obscured, and concealed supernal Chochmah OF ARICH ANPIN is in that skull, WHICH IS KETER OF ARICH ANPIN. Surely only the head alone was exposed in that Atika, because it is the beginning (or: 'head') of every beginning. Supernal Chochmah, which is a head, is hidden within it, THE HEAD OF ARICH ANPIN, and is called the supernal brain, the covered brain, the subdued and quiet brain. None can comprehend it save it itself.

9. The three heads of Atika

A Synopsis

We learn about the three heads that are imprinted one inside another and one over another. One of these is concealed Chochmah, one is the most hidden Atika Kadisha and the third is absolutely incomprehensible. Rabbi Shimon talks about the hairs that come out of the skull of Arich Anpin; we learn that the hairs are all smooth and equal in weight. He says that Atika always abides in the thirteen attributes of Mercy.

37. תְּלַת רֵישִׁין אִתְגַּלְּפָן, דָּא, לְגוֹ מִן דָּא. וְדָא, לְעֵילָּא מִן דָּא. רֵישָׁא חֲדָא, חָכְמְתָא סְתִימָאָה, דְּאִתְכַּסְּיָיא, וְלָאו מִתְפַּתְּחָא. וְחָכְמְתָא דָּא סְתִימָאָה, רֵישָׁא לְכָל רֵישֵׁיהּ, דִּשְׁאַר חָכְמוֹת. רֵישָׁא עִלָּאָה, עַתִּיקָא קַדִּישָׁא, סְתִימָא דְּכָל סְתִימִין. רֵישָׁא דְּכָל רֵישָׁא, רֵישָׁא דְּלָאו רֵישָׁא. וְלֹא יָדַע, וְלָא אִתְיְדַע, מַה דַּהֲוֵי בְּרֵישָׁא דָּא, דְּלָא אִתְדְּבַק בְּחָכְמְתָא, וְלָא בְּסוּכְלְתָנוּ. וְעַל הַאי אִקְרֵי, בְּרַח לְךָ אֶל מְקוֹמֶךָ. וְהַחַיּוֹת רָצוֹא וָשׁוֹב.

37. Three heads were imprinted, one inside another, THAT IS, CONCEALED CHOCHMAH INSIDE THE SKULL and one over another, NAMELY THE UNKNOWN HEAD ABOVE THE SKULL. HE EXPLAINS, One head is concealed Chochmah, which is undisclosed and unopened. This concealed Chochmah is a beginning to every other beginning of other Chochmot. THIS IS THE FIRST HEAD FROM BELOW UPWARDS. THE SECOND HEAD is a supernal head, the most obscured Atika Kadisha, WHICH IS THE SKULL OF ARICH ANPIN. THE THIRD HEAD THAT IS LOFTY ABOVE EVERYTHING IS the head for every head, a head that is not a head, THAT IS, ITS BEING A HEAD INDICATES IT IS A BEGINNING OF EXPANSION AND COMPREHENSION, YET THIS HEAD IS ENTIRELY INCOMPREHENSIBLE because no one knows nor is it known what is in this head, because it is attached neither to Chochmah nor to Tevunah. It is therefore considered, "Therefore now flee to your place" (Bemidbar 24:11), "and the living creatures ran and returned" (Yechezkel 1:14), BECAUSE NO COMPREHENSION CAN APPLY THERE.

38. וּבְגִין כַּךְ עַתִּיקָא קַדִּישָׁא אִקְרֵי, אַיִן. דְּבֵיהּ תַּלְיָיא אַיִן. וְכָל אִינּוּן

שַׂעֲרֵי, וְכָל אִינּוּן נִימִין, מִמּוֹחָא סְתִימָאָה נָפְקִין. וְכֻלְּהוּ שְׁעִיעִין, בְּשִׁקּוּלָא. וְלָא אִתְחֲזֵי קְדָלָא.

38. For this reason Atika Kadisha, WHICH IS THE SKULL OF ARICH ANPIN is called naught, since naught derives from it, FROM THE UNKNOWN HEAD. THAT IS, SINCE THIS HEAD, THE SKULL, IS CLOSE TO THE UNKNOWN HEAD, WHICH IS UTTERLY INCOMPREHENSIBLE, IT TOO IS INCOMPREHENSIBLE, AND IS THEREFORE CALLED NAUGHT, WHICH INDICATES ITS COMPLETE INCOMPREHENSIBILITY. FOR THAT REASON all hairs and tiny hairs OVER THE SKULL DO NOT COME OUT OF THE SKULL BECAUSE NO JUDGMENTS ARE ATTACHED TO IT, BUT they come out of the concealed brain, WHICH IS THE BEGINNING OF THE EXPANSION OF CHOCHMAH. FOR SUPERNAL CHOCHMAH SPREADS FROM IT; THIS CHOCHMAH IS EVENTUALLY REVEALED IN MALCHUT WHERE THERE IS PLACE FOR JUDGMENTS. AND THE HAIRS ARE THE ROOT OF JUDGMENTS, AS IN, "FOR HE CRUSHES ME WITH A TEMPEST (OR: 'A HAIR')" (IYOV 9:17). HENCE THE HAIR OF THE HEAD AND BEARD COME OUT OF THE CONCEALED BRAIN, THOUGH IN THIS CASE THERE ARE NO JUDGMENTS IN THE HAIRS, BUT ROOTS ONLY. THEREFORE they are all smooth, THAT IS, SOFT WITHOUT JUDGMENT. AND THEY ARE ALL EQUAL in weight, BECAUSE EVERYTHING HERE IS OF THE SAME LIGHT OF MERCY and the back of the neck is invisible, WHICH INDICATES JUDGMENTS AND HIND PARTS, ACCORDING TO THE VERSE, "AND THEY HAVE TURNED THEIR BACK TO ME, AND NOT THEIR FACE" (YIRMEYAH 32:33).

39. כֹּלָּא הוּא, בְּגִין דְּהַאי עַתִּיקָא קַדִּישָׁא בְּחַד הֲוֵי. כֹּלָּא בְּחֵידוּ, וְלָא שַׁנְיָא מֵרַחֲמֵי לְעָלְמִין. בִּתְלַת עֲשַׂר מְכִילָן דְּרַחֲמִין אִשְׁתְּכַח. בְּגִין דְּהַאי חָכְמְתָא סְתִימָאָה דְּבֵיהּ, מִתְפָּרַשׁ תְּלַת זִמְנִין לְאַרְבַּע אַרְבַּע. וְהוּא עַתִּיקָא, כָּלִיל לוֹן, וְשַׁלִּיט עַל כֹּלָּא.

39. All this stems from the fact that this Atika is of the same LIGHT, NAMELY THE REIGN OF CHASSADIM, WHICH IS WHY THERE IS NO ROOM FOR JUDGMENT TO APPEAR. It is all in joy and never changes FROM THE ILLUMINATION of Mercy. THAT IS, THOUGH WE DISTINGUISH BETWEEN THREE COLUMNS, RIGHT, LEFT AND CENTRAL IN IT, IT NEVER STRAYS

FROM THE ASPECT OF THE RIGHT COLUMN, AND IS EVER OF MERCY AND CHASSADIM IN NATURE. It abides in the thirteen attributes of Mercy, because the hidden Chochmah in it divides three times into fours, WHICH IS TWELVE, and it, Atika ITSELF includes them and rules over everything. TOGETHER WITH IT, THERE ARE THIRTEEN ATTRIBUTES.

10. The path where the hairs split

A Synopsis

Rabbi Shimon says that the path that shines in the division of the hairs that come out of the hidden brain is the path of the righteous. He talks about the supernal Keter above that is a hidden and entirely unknown higher candle.

40. חַד אָרְחָא דְּנָהִיר בְּפַלְגּוּתָא דְּשַׂעְרֵי דְּנַפְקֵי מִמּוֹחָא, הוּא אָרְחָא דִּנְהִירִין בֵּיהּ צַדִּיקַיָּיא לְעָלְמָא דְּאָתֵי, דִּכְתִּיב וְאֹרַח צַדִּיקִים כְּאוֹר נוֹגַהּ וְגוֹ'. וע"ד כְּתִיב, אָז תִּתְעַנַּג עַל יְיָ'. וּמֵהַאי אָרְחָא מִתְנַהֲרִין כָּל שְׁאַר אָרְחִין, דְּתַלְיָין בִּזְעֵיר אַנְפִּין.

40. One path shines in THE MIDDLE OF the division of the hairs that come out of the CONCEALED brain, WHICH IS CONCEALED CHOCHMAH. It is the path where the righteous shine in the World to Come, as written, "But the path of just men is like the gleam of sunlight" (Mishlei 4:18), "then shall you delight yourself in Hashem…" (Yeshayah 58:14). From this path shine all other paths that derive from Zeir Anpin, WHICH ARE 613 PATHS.

41. הַאי עַתִּיקָא סָבָא דְּסָבִין, כִּתְרָא עִלָּאָה, לְעֵילָּא. דְּמִתְעַטְּרִין בֵּיהּ כָּל עִטְרִין, וְכִתְרִין, מִתְנַהֲרִין. וְכָל שְׁאַר בּוֹצִינִין מִנֵּיהּ מִתְלַהֲטִן וּמִתְנַהֲרָן. וְהוּא, הוּא בּוֹצִינָא עִלָּאָה, טְמִירָא דְּלָא אִתְיְדַע.

41. This Atika, WHICH IS ARICH ANPIN, the oldest among the old, FROM WHICH DERIVE SUPERNAL ABA AND IMA THAT ARE CONSIDERED OLD, is the supernal Keter above, NAMELY KETER OF ARICH ANPIN, with which all crowns are decorated, NAMELY ALL MOCHIN. FOR MOCHIN ARE CONSIDERED CROWNS, WHICH ARE THE SEVEN CHARACTERISTICS OF THE HEAD THAT SHALL BE EXPLAINED AND THE THIRTEEN CHARACTERISTICS OF THE BEARD. And the crowns shine FROM IT, WHICH ARE ABA AND IMA, and the other candles, NAMELY SEVEN LOWER SFIROT, WHICH CONTAIN JUDGMENTS, glow from it and shine. NEVERTHELESS, it ITSELF is a hidden supernal unknown candle.

11. Atika is present in three – in two it is one

A Synopsis

Rabbi Shimon tells us about the head that is high above the three heads of Arich Anpin. He says that Atika Kadisha is both the supernal Keter of all higher beings and also the head above it, the entirely unknown head. It is one, and everything is one.

42. הַאי עַתִּיקָא אִשְׁתְּכַח בִּתְלַת רֵישִׁין, וּכְלִילָן בְּחַד רֵישָׁא. וְהַהוּא רֵישָׁא עִלָּאָה, לְעֵילָּא לְעֵילָּא. וּבְגִין דְּעַתִּיקָא קַדִּישָׁא אִתְרְשִׁים בִּתְלַת, אוּף הָכִי כָּל שְׁאַר בּוּצִינִין דְּנַהֲרִין מִנֵּיהּ, כְּלִילָן בִּתְלַת. עוֹד, עַתִּיקָא אִתְרְשִׁים בִּתְרֵין. כְּלָלָא דְּעַתִּיקָא בִּתְרֵין. הוּא כִּתְרָא עִלָּאָה דְּכָל עִלָּאִין, רֵישָׁא דְּכָל רֵישֵׁי. וְהַהוּא דַּהֲוֵי לְעֵילָּא מִן דָּא, דְּלָא אִתְיְדַע. כַּךְ כָּל שְׁאַר בּוּצִינִין, סְתִימִין בִּתְרֵין. עוֹד עַתִּיקָא קַדִּישָׁא אִתְרְשִׁים וְאַסְתִּים בְּחַד, וְהוּא חַד, וְכֹלָּא הוּא חַד. כַּךְ כָּל שְׁאַר בּוּצִינִין, מִתְקַדְּשִׁין, מִתְקַשְּׁרִין, וּמִתְהַדְּרִין בְּחַד, וְאִינּוּן חַד.

42. This Atika, NAMELY ARICH ANPIN, is present in three heads included inside one head, AS TOGETHER THEY ARE ONE HEAD OF ARICH ANPIN, and that one higher head, NAMELY THE UNKNOWN HEAD, THE HEAD OF ATIKA, is high up, NAMELY, ABOVE THE THREE HEADS OF ARICH ANPIN. And since Atika Kadisha manifests in three HEADS, THE SECRET OF THE THREE COLUMNS, so do all the candles, NAMELY SFIROT, that radiate from it manifest in three. Moreover Atika Kadisha manifests in two, because Atik in all is in two: 1) it is the supernal Keter of all higher beings, the head of all heads; 2) and also that HEAD above it, NAMELY the unknown HEAD. So do all the candles manifest in two. Furthermore, Atika Kadisha both manifests and is hidden in one, THAT IS, ALL THE LIGHTS WITHIN IT ARE INCLUDED IN THE REIGN OF THE LIGHT OF CHASSADIM ALONE. It is one and everything is one. So are all the other candles sanctified and connected and revert to one, and are one.

12. The forehead of the will of Arich Anpin

A Synopsis

We learn that on Shabbat during the Minchah service the forehead of Atika Kadisha that is called 'will' is revealed, and at this time all judgments are subdued and there is mercy throughout all the worlds.

43. מִצְחָא דְּאִתְגַּלֵּי בְּעַתִּיקָא קַדִּישָׁא, רָצוֹן אִקְרֵי, דְּהָא רֵישָׁא עִלָּאָה דָּא סָתִים לְעֵילָּא, דְּלָא אִתְיְדַע פָּשִׁיט חַד טוּרְנָא בְּסִימָא, יָאָה, דְּאִתְכְּלִיל בְּמִצְחָא. וּבְגִין דְּהַהוּא רַעֲוָא דְּכָל רַעֲוִין, אִתְתְּקַן בְּמִצְחָא, וְאִתְגַּלְיָיא בְּבוּסִיטָא, הַאי מִצְחָא אִקְרֵי רָצוֹן.

43. The forehead that is revealed in Atika Kadisha, THAT IS, IN ARICH ANPIN, is called will. For this supernal head that is concealed above extends one force, mitigated and comely that is included in the forehead and revealed by reconciliation. HENCE this forehead is called will.

44. וְכַד רָצוֹן דָּא אִתְגַּלְיָיא, רַעֲוָא דְּרַעֲוִין אִשְׁתְּכַח בְּכֻלְּהוּ עָלְמִין, וְכָל צְלוֹתִין דִּלְתַּתָּא מִתְקַבְּלִין, וּמִתְנַהֲרִין אַנְפּוֹי דִּזְעֵיר אַנְפִּין, וְכֹלָּא בְּרַחֲמֵי אִשְׁתְּכַח, וְכָל דִּינִין אִתְטַמְּרָן וְאִתְכַּפְיָין.

44. When this will is exposed IN THE FOREHEAD, the Will of all wills is present throughout the worlds, THAT IS, THIS COMPLETE ILLUMINATION REACHES ALL WORLDS. All prayers below are accepted then, the face of Zeir Anpin shines, everything is in a state of Mercy and all Judgments hide and are subdued.

45. בְּשַׁבְּתָא בְּשַׁעֲתָא דִּצְלוֹתָא דְּמִנְחָה, דְּהוּא עִידָּן דְּכָל דִּינִין מִתְעָרִין, אִתְגַּלְיָיא הַאי מִצְחָא, וְאִתְכַּפְיָין כָּל דִּינִין, וְאִשְׁתְּכָחוּ רַחֲמִין בְּכֻלְּהוּ עָלְמִין. ובג"כ אִשְׁתְּכַח שַׁבָּת בְּלָא דִּינָא, לָא לְעֵילָּא וְלָא לְתַתָּא. וַאֲפִילּוּ אֶשָּׁא דְּגֵיהִנָּם אִשְׁתְּקַע בְּאַתְרֵיהּ, וְנַיְיחִין חַיָּיבַיָּא. וְעַל דָּא אִתּוֹסַף נִשְׁמְתָא דְּחֵדוּ בְּשַׁבְּתָא.

45. On Shabbat, during Minchah service, WHICH DURING WEEKDAYS is a time when all Judgments awaken, ON SHABBAT this forehead is revealed OF ARICH ANPIN AS THE DESIRE TO ILLUMINATE WITH CHASSADIM. All Judgments are subdued and Mercy abides throughout the worlds. Hence Shabbat is without Judgment above as well as below; even the fire of Gehenom sinks into its place and evil people take rest. Therefore an additional soul of joy is added on Shabbat.

13. The three meals of Shabbat

A Synopsis

Rabbi Shimon recalls that he has never neglected the three meals on Shabbat in his whole life. He says that the three meals are the meal of the Queen, the meal of the holy King, and the meal of the most hidden Atika Kadisha. In the world beyond one will be able to merit all these grades.

46. וּבָעֵי בַּר נָשׁ לְמֶחְדֵּי בִּתְלַת סְעוּדָתֵי דְּשַׁבְּתָא, דְּהָא כָּל מְהֵימְנוּתָא, וְכָל כְּלָלָא דִּמְהֵימְנוּתָא, בֵּיהּ אִשְׁתְּכַח, וּבָעֵי בַּר נָשׁ לְסַדְּרָא פָּתוֹרָא, וּלְמֵיכַל תְּלַת סְעוּדָתֵי דִּמְהֵימְנוּתָא, וּלְמֶחֱדֵי בְּהוּ.

46. One must rejoice in the three meals on Shabbat, for the whole Faith and the entirety of faith is present in it. And one must set his table, eat the three meals of faith and rejoice in them.

47. אָמַר רִבִּי שִׁמְעוֹן, אַסְהַדְנָא עָלַי לְכָל אִלֵּין דְּהָכָא, דְּהָא מִן יוֹמָאי לָא בָּטִילְנָא אִלֵּין ג׳ סְעוּדָתֵי, וּבְגִינֵיהוֹן לָא אִצְטְרִיכְנָא לְתַעֲנִיתָא בְּשַׁבְּתָא. וַאֲפִילוּ בְּיוֹמֵי אַחֲרִינֵי לָא אִצְטְרִיכְנָא, כ״ש בְּשַׁבְּתָא. דְּמַאן דְּזָכֵי בְּהוּ, זָכֵי לִמְהֵימְנוּתָא שְׁלֵימָתָא. חַד, סְעוּדָתָא דְּמַטְרוֹנִיתָא. וְחַד, סְעוּדָתָא דְּמַלְכָּא קַדִּישָׁא. וְחַד, סְעוּדָתָא דְּעַתִּיקָא קַדִּישָׁא, סְתִימָא דְּכָל סְתִימִין. וּבְהַהוּא עָלְמָא יִזְכֵּי בְּהוּ לְאִלֵּין. הַאי רָצוֹן כַּד אִתְגַּלְיָיא, כָּל דִּינִין אִתְכַּפְיָין מִשּׁוּלְשְׁלֵיהוֹן.

47. Rabbi Shimon said, I bring all those present here as witnesses that I have never neglected these three meals in my life. Due to their merit, I did not have to resort to fasting on Shabbat and even on other WEEK days I did not have to FAST, and all the more so on Shabbat. For whoever merits them, merits the entire faith. THEY ARE: one is the meal of the Queen, NAMELY ON SHABBAT EVE, BECAUSE NIGHT IS THE DOMAIN OF MALCHUT; one is the meal of the Holy King, WHO IS ZEIR ANPIN, THAT IS, DURING THE MEAL OF MINCHAH, WHEN ZEIR ANPIN RISES TO ATIKA KADISHA; and one is the meal of the most concealed Atika Kadisha AT THE MORNING MEAL. FOR ON SHABBAT ATIKA KADISHA IS SHINING BY MEANS OF SUPERNAL

ABA AND IMA, AND ZEIR ANPIN RECEIVES THE ILLUMINATION FROM THEM. BUT AT MINCHAH OF SHABBAT, ZEIR ANPIN HIMSELF ASCENDS TO ATIKA KADISHA AND RECEIVES HIS ILLUMINATION. HENCE THAT MEAL IS NAMED AFTER ZEIR ANPIN, AND THE MORNING MEAL AFTER ATIKA KADISHA. In that world, ONE can merit these GRADES. When this will IN THE FOREHEAD is revealed, all Judgments are subdued in their chains.

14. Concealed Chochmah of Arich Anpin and revealed Chochmah

A Synopsis

We are told that the establishment of Atika Kadisha is such that it is one structure that includes all others; it is supernal Chochmah that incorporates all the rest and is called supernal hidden Eden.

48. תִּקּוּנָא דְּעַתִּיקָא קַדִּישָׁא אִתְתְּקַן בְּתִקּוּנָא חַד, כְּלָלָא דְּכָל תִּקּוּנִין. וְהִיא חָכְמָה עִלָּאָה, סְתִימָאָה. כְּלָלָא דְּכָל שְׁאָר, וְהַאי אִקְרֵי עֵדֶן עִלָּאָה סְתִימָא. וְהוּא מוֹחָא דְּעַתִּיקָא קַדִּישָׁא. וְהַאי מוֹחָא אִתְפְּשַׁט לְכָל עִיבָר, מִנֵּיהּ אִתְפְּשַׁט עֵדֶן אַחֲרָא. וּמֵהַאי עֵדֶן אִתְגְּלַף.

48. The establishment of Atika Kadisha is such that it was established as one structure that includes all structures. It is supernal, hidden Chochmah, NAMELY, THE THIRD HEAD OF ARICH ANPIN, which incorporates all the rest, and is called supernal, hidden Eden. It is the brain of Atika Kadisha. This brain expands in every direction and from it spreads another Eden, SUPERNAL ABA AND IMA THAT ARE LOWER EDEN. From that Eden CHOCHMAH is engraved AND STARTS TO REVEAL ITSELF IN YISRAEL-SABA AND TEVUNAH, ZEIR ANPIN AND MALCHUT, WHICH IS THE SECRET OF LOWER CHOCHMAH, WHERE CHOCHMAH IS REVEALED.

15. The unknown head divested of a force that is contained in the forehead

A Synopsis

Rabbi Shimon explains the genesis of the beard of Arich Anpin that is called supernal Chesed; he says that this is the characteristic called "abundant in love."

49. וְהַהוּא רֵישָׁא סְתִימָא דִּבְרֵישָׁא דְּעַתִּיקָא דְּלָא אִתְיְדַע, כַּד פָּשִׁיט חַד טוּרְנָא, דַּהֲוָה מִתְתַּקַּן לְאִתְנַהֲרָא, בָּטַשׁ בְּהַאי מוֹחָא, וְאִתְגְּלַף, וְאִתְנְהִיר בְּכַמָּה נְהִירִין, וְאַפִּיק, וְאַרְשִׁים כְּבוֹסִיטָא דָא, בְּהַאי מִצְחָא. וְאִתְרְשִׁים בֵּיהּ חַד נְהוֹרָא, דְּאִקְרֵי רָצוֹן. וְהַאי רָצוֹן אִתְפְּשַׁט לְתַתָּא בְּדִיקְנָא, עַד הַהוּא אֲתָר דְּמִתְיַשְּׁבָא בְּדִיקְנָא, וְאִקְרֵי חֶסֶד עִלָּאָה. וְדָא אִיהוּ נוֹצֵר חֶסֶד. וּבְהַאי רָצוֹן כַּד אִתְגַּלְיָיא, מִסְתַּכְּלִין מָארֵי דְּדִינָא וּמִתְכַּפְיָין.

49. That hidden head in the head of Atika, which is unknown, NAMELY THE FIRST HEAD, when it extended a force constructed so as to illuminate, it struck THROUGH IT that brain, NAMELY THE CONCEALED CHOCHMAH OF ARICH ANPIN, became engraved and shone with many lights. CONCEALED CHOCHMAH produced ITS ILLUMINATION and marked a reconciliation, so to speak, in that forehead. Then a light, which is called will, was imprinted ON THAT FOREHEAD, which spread downwards through THE THIRTEEN CHARACTERISTICS OF the beard OF ARICH ANPIN down to the place where it settled in the beard called supernal Chesed. This is THE CHARACTERISTIC CALLED "abundant in Chesed," NAMELY THE EIGHTH OF THE THIRTEEN CHARACTERISTICS OF THE BEARD. When this will is revealed THROUGH THE CHARACTERISTIC OF "ABUNDANT IN LOVE," the prosecutors see it and surrender.

16. Opening the eyes

A Synopsis

We learn that the eyes of Atika Kadisha never sleep, and for that reason have neither eyebrows nor eyelids. Both these eyes are actually one. The brain is called the fountain of blessing, and since it glows with the three kinds of whiteness in the eyes then blessings come out of the eye. Rabbi Shimon says that the Concealed Book taught him that the letters Yud Hei Vav Hei derive from Atika in order to support those letters below; for that reason the Holy Name is both hidden and revealed – the hidden part corresponding to Atika Kadisha and the revealed part to Zeir Anpin. Thus all blessings should contain both the hidden and the revealed.

50. עֵינוֹי דְּרֵישָׁא דְּעַתִּיקָא קַדִּישָׁא, תְּרֵין בְּחַד שְׁקִילָן. דְּאַשְׁגְּחִין תָּדִירָא, וְלָא נָאִים. דִּכְתִּיב לֹא יָנוּם וְלֹא יִישָׁן שׁוֹמֵר יִשְׂרָאֵל, יִשְׂרָאֵל קַדִּישָׁא, בְּגִין כַּךְ לָא אִית לֵיהּ גְּבִינִין עַל עֵינָא, וְלָא כְּסוּתָא.

50. As for the eyes of the head of Atika Kadisha, WHICH IS ARICH ANPIN, both EYES are as one. They constantly observe and never sleep, as written, "Behold, He who keeps Yisrael shall neither slumber nor sleep" (Tehilim 121:4), which refers to holy Yisrael, ZEIR ANPIN. For that reason He has neither eyebrows nor eyelids.

51. הַהוּא מוֹחָא אִתְגְּלִיף וְנָהִר בִּתְלַת חִוָּורִין דְּעֵינָא, בְּחִוָּורָא חֲדָא מִסְתַּחְיָין עַיְינִין דִּזְעֵיר אַנְפִּין, דִּכְתִּיב רוֹחֲצוֹת בֶּחָלָב. דְּהוּא חִוָּורָא קַדְמָאָה. וּשְׁאַר חִוָּורִין אִסְתַּחְיָין וְנַהֲרִין לִשְׁאַר בּוֹצִינִין.

51. This brain, NAMELY, CONCEALED CHOCHMAH OF ARICH ANPIN, is engraved and shines with three types of whiteness in the eye. With one kind of whiteness in them, the eyes of Zeir Anpin wash in milk, as written, "washed with milk" (Shir Hashirim 5:12), WHICH IS CHESED CALLED MILK. It derives from the first kind of whiteness IN THE THREE TYPES OF WHITE IN THE EYES OF ARICH ANPIN, BEING THEIR RIGHT COLUMN. The other kinds of white wash and illuminate the other candles, NAMELY THE OTHER GRADES.

52. מוֹחָא אִקְרֵי נְבִיעָא דְּבִרְכָתָא, נְבִיעָא דְּכָל בִּרְכָאן מִנֵּיהּ אִשְׁתְּכָחוּ. וּבְגִין דְּהַאי מוֹחָא לָהִיט בְּג׳ חִוָּורִין דְּעֵינָא, בְּעֵינָא תלא בֵּיהּ בִּרְכָתָא, דִּכְתִּיב טוֹב עַיִן הוּא יְבוֹרָךְ, דְּהָא בְּמוֹחָא תַּלְיָין חִוָּורוּ דְּעֵינָא. הַאי עֵינָא כַּד אַשְׁגַּח בִּזְעֵיר אַנְפִּין, אַנְהֶרָן כֻּלְּהוּ בְּחֵדוּ. עֵינָא דָּא, הוּא כֹּלָּא יְמִינָא, לֵית בֵּיהּ שְׂמָאלָא. עַיְינִין דְּתַתָּא, יְמִינָא וּשְׂמָאלָא, תְּרֵי, בִּתְרֵי גַּוְונִין.

52. The brain, WHICH IS CONCEALED CHOCHMAH, is called the fountain of blessing, being the fountain whence all blessings flow. Since this brain glows with the three kinds of white in the eyes, THEN blessings come out of the eye, as written, "He that has a generous eye shall be blessed" (Mishlei 22:9), because the whiteness of the eye derives from the brain. When that eye observes Zeir Anpin, everyone shines joyfully. This eye, EVEN THOUGH IT HAS IN IT THE THREE COLUMNS, RIGHT, LEFT AND CENTRAL, is NEVERTHELESS all right and has no left in it. BUT the lower eyes, THOSE OF ZEIR ANPIN, are right and left, two that have two natures, THE RIGHT IS CHESED AND THE LEFT IS GVURAH OF THE ILLUMINATION OF CHOCHMAH.

53. בִּצְנִיעוּתָא דְּסִפְרָא אוֹלִיפְנָא, דְּהָא י׳ עִלָּאָה, י׳ תַּתָּאָה. ה׳ עִלָּאָה, ה׳ תַּתָּאָה. ו׳ עִלָּאָה, ו׳ תַּתָּאָה. כָּל אִלֵּין עִלָּאִין, בְּעַתִּיקָא תַּלְיָין. תַּתָּאִין, בִּזְעֵיר אַנְפִּין אִינּוּן. לָאו תַּלְיָין, אֶלָּא אִינּוּן מַמָּשׁ. וּבְעַתִּיקָא קַדִּישָׁא תַּלְיָין. דְּהָא שְׁמָא דְּעַתִּיקָא אִתְכַּסְיָיא מִכֹּלָּא, וְלָא אִשְׁתְּכַח. אֲבָל אִלֵּין אַתְוָון דְּתַלְיָין בְּעַתִּיקָא. בְּגִין דְּיִתְקַיְּימוּן אִינּוּן דִּלְתַתָּא. דְּאִי לָאו הָכִי לָא יִתְקַיְּימוּן.

53. We learned in Safra Detzniuta (the Concealed Book) that there is an upper Yud and a lower Yud, an upper Hei and a lower Hei, an upper Vav and a lower Vav. All the upper ones derive from Atika, and the lower ones are in Zeir Anpin. They do not derive from Him but are actually in Him, SINCE ZEIR ANPIN IS CALLED YUD HEI VAV HEI, AND THE SECRET OF THE LETTERS APPLIES TO HIM. But from Atika Kadisha THEY JUST derive, THAT IS, THE ROOTS OF THE FOUR LETTERS, YUD HEI VAV HEI, ARE IN

IT, BUT NOT THE ACTUAL LETTERS. For the name of Atika is hidden from all and is incomprehensible. But those letters YUD HEI VAV HEI derive from Atika in order to support those LETTERS BELOW, for otherwise THE LOWER ONES would not have survived.

54. וּבְגִין כַּךְ, שְׁמָא קַדִּישָׁא סָתִים וְגַלְיָא. הַהוּא דְּסָתִים לָקֳבְלֵיהּ דְּעַתִּיקָא קַדִּישָׁא, סְתִימָא דְּכֹלָּא. וְהַהוּא דְּאִתְגַּלְיָיא בִּזְעֵיר אַפִּין. וּבְגִין כַּךְ, כָּל בִּרְכָאן בַּעְיָין סָתִים וְגַלְיָיא. אִלֵּין אַתְוָון סְתִימָן דְּתַלְיָין בְּעַתִּיקָא קַדִּישָׁא.

54. For that reason the Holy Name is both hidden and revealed. The hidden part corresponds to the most hidden Atika Kadisha and the revealed part is in Zeir Anpin. Therefore all blessings should contain both the hidden and the revealed. THAT IS, THEY SHOULD CONTAIN THE SECOND, PRESENT PERSON, AS IN, 'BLESSED ARE YOU', AND THE THIRD, HIDDEN PERSON, 'WHO HAS SANCTIFIED US AND COMMANDED US', WHICH IS HIDDEN. IT IS HIDDEN TO CORRESPOND to the hidden letters that derive from Atika Kadisha, AND REVEALED TO CORRESPOND TO THE LETTERS IN ZEIR ANPIN.

17. The nose of Arich Anpin

A Synopsis

Rabbi Shimon reveals that it is by means of the spirit of life that emanates from the nose of Arich Anpin that people will gain wisdom during the time of King Messiah. He also says that anger comes mainly from the nose.

55. חוֹטָמָא, בְּהַאי חוֹטָמָא, בְּנוּקְבָא דְּפַרְדַּשְׁקָא דְּבֵיהּ, נָשִׁיב רוּחָא דְּחַיֵּי לִזְעֵיר אַפִּין. וּבְהַאי חוֹטָמָא, בְּנוּקְבָא דְּפַרְדַּשְׁקָא, תַּלְיָיא ה', לְקַיְּימָא ה' אַחֲרָא דִּלְתַתָּא. וְדָא רוּחָא נָפִיק מִמּוֹחָא סְתִימָאָה, וְאִקְרֵי רוּחָא דְּחַיֵּי. וּבְהַאי רוּחָא, זְמִינִין לְמִנְדַּע חָכְמְתָא, בִּזְמְנָא דְּמַלְכָּא מְשִׁיחָא. דִּכְתִּיב, וְנָחָה עָלָיו רוּחַ יְיָ' רוּחַ חָכְמָה וּבִינָה וְגוֹ'. הַאי חוֹטָמָא, חַיִּין מִכָּל סְטְרִין, חֵדוּ שְׁלֵימָא. נַחַת רוּחַ. אַסְוָותָא. בְּחוֹטָמָא דִּזְעֵיר אַנְפִּין כְּתִיב, עָלָה עָשָׁן בְּאַפּוֹ וְגוֹ'. וְהָכָא כְּתִיב וּתְהִלָּתִי אֶחֱטָם לָךְ.

55. The nose OF ARICH ANPIN: in this nose, within the window of its nostril the spirit (or: 'wind') of life blows on Zeir Anpin. Inside this nose, in the window of the nostril, Hei comes out to support another, lower Hei. This wind comes out from the concealed brain and is called the spirit of life. By means of that spirit people will gain wisdom during the time of King Messiah, as written, "and the spirit of Hashem shall rest upon him, the spirit of wisdom and understanding..." (Yeshayah 11:2). This nose is life from every aspect, complete joy, satisfaction and healing. Of the nose of Zeir Anpin it is written, "There went up a smoke out of His nostrils..." (II Shmuel 22:9). Here it is written, "and for My praise will I refrain (or: 'nose') for you" (Yeshayah 48:9).

56. וּבְסִפְרָא דְּאַגַּדְתָּא, דְּבֵי רַב יֵיבָא סָבָא, אוֹקִים, ה' בְּפוּמָא, וְהָכָא לָא מִתְקַיְּימָא הָכִי, וְלָא אִצְטָרְפָא, אע"ג דִּבְחַד סַלְקָא, אֶלָּא בְּהֵ' דִּינָא תַּלְיָא, וְדִינָא בְּחוֹטָמָא תַּלְיָא, דִּכְתִּיב עָלָה עָשָׁן בְּאַפּוֹ. וְאִי תֵּימָא, הָא כְּתִיב וְאֵשׁ מִפִּיו תֹּאכֵל. עִקָּרָא דְּרוּגְזָא בְּחוֹטָמָא תַּלְיָא.

56. In the Agadah book of the academy OF STUDY of Rav Yeba Saba, he interpreted the Hei AS MALCHUT THAT RECEIVES from the mouth OF ARICH ANPIN. But here, IN THIS MATTER, it does not work that way, and MALCHUT does not connect WITH THE MOUTH OF ARICH ANPIN, BUT WITH THE LEFT NOSTRIL OF THE NOSE. And even though it has the same meaning, many Judgments derive from Hei, while Judgment derives from the nose, as written, "There went up a smoke out of his nostrils." You may say it is written, "and fire out of His mouth" (II Shmuel 22:9), SO THERE ARE JUDGMENTS IN THE MOUTH AS WELL, TO WHICH HE ANSWERS, anger comes mainly from the nose.

18. The Chochmot, the concealed Chochmah and the revealed Chochmah

A Synopsis

We are told about the higher and lower Chochmah and about Hei which includes everything. From the Hei in Malchut below, Judgments stir, while from the Hei in the nose there is Mercy within Mercy.

57. כָּל תִּקּוּנִין דְּעַתִּיקָא קַדִּישָׁא, בְּמוֹחָא שָׁקִיט וְסָתִים מִתְתַּקְּנָן. וְכָל תִּקּוּנִין דִּזְעֵיר אַנְפִּין, בְּחָכְמָה תַּתָּאָה מִתְתַּקְּנָן. דִּכְתִּיב, כֻּלָּם בְּחָכְמָה עָשִׂיתָ וְה׳ כְּלָלָא דְּכֹלָּא וַדַּאי. מַה בֵּין ה׳ לְה׳. ה׳ דְּהָכָא, דִּינָא אִתְּעַר מִנָּהּ. וּדְהָכָא רַחֲמֵי גּוֹ רַחֲמֵי.

57. All the implements of Atika Kadisha are established in the concealed, quiet mind, THAT IS, IN CONCEALED CHOCHMAH. And all the implements within Zeir Anpin are established in lower Chochmah, as written, "in wisdom have You made them all" (Tehilim 104:24). And Hei, WHICH IS MALCHUT, surely includes everything. What is the difference between Hei, WHICH IS MALCHUT BELOW, and this Hei WITHIN THE LEFT NOSTRIL IN THE NOSE OF ZEIR ANPIN? From this Hei, IN MALCHUT BELOW, Judgments stir, while that Hei IN THE NOSE is Mercy within Mercy.

19. The hair on the beard of Arich Anpin

A Synopsis

Rabbi Shimon says that both the upper and lower beings all look to receive bounty from the Mazal that is the beard of Atika Kadisha, as all life derives from that Mazal; even heaven and earth and bountiful rains come from it. We learn about the thirteen streams of oil, or the thirteen attributes of mercy, that are derived from that beard and that come out to Zeir Anpin.

58. בְּדִיקְנָא דְעַתִּיקָא קַדִּישָׁא, תַּלְיָא כָּל יְקִירוּ דְּכֹלָּא. מַזָּלָא דְּכֹלָּא אִקְרֵי. מֵהַאי דִּיקְנָא, מַזָּלָא, יַקִּירוּתָא דְּכָל יַקִּירִין, מַזָּלֵי עִלָּאֵי וְתַתָּאֵי. כֻּלְּהוּ מַשְׁגִּיחִין לְהַהוּא מַזָּלָא. בְּהַאי מַזָּלָא תַּלְיָיא חַיֵּי דְּכֹלָּא, מְזוֹנֵי דְּכֹלָּא. בְּהַאי מַזָּלָא תַּלְיָין שְׁמַיָּא וְאַרְעָא. גִּשְׁמִין דְּרַעֲוָא. בְּהַאי מַזָּלָא, אַשְׁגָּחוּתָא דְּכֹלָּא. בְּהַאי מַזָּלָא תַּלְיָין כָּל חַיָּילִין עִלָּאִין וְתַתָּאִין.

58. Overall preciousness derives from the beard of Atika Kadisha, WHICH IS ARICH ANPIN. It is called general Mazal (Eng. 'luck'). From this beard, WHICH IS CALLED Mazal, which is most precious, the upper and lower beings became successful. They all look TO RECEIVE BOUNTY from that Mazal. All life derives from that Mazal, everyone's food. Heaven and earth, WHICH ARE ZEIR ANPIN AND MALCHUT, come from that Mazal, and bountiful rains. Everyone looks to that Mazal. The upper and lower hosts come out of that Mazal.

59. תְּלַת עֲשַׂר נְבִיעִין, דִּמְשְׁחָא דִּרְבוּתָא טָבָא, תַּלְיָין בְּדִיקְנָא דְּמַזָּלָא יַקִּירָא דָּא. וְכֻלְּהוּ נָפְקִין לִזְעֵיר אַנְפִּין. לָא תֵּימָא כֻּלְּהוּ, אֶלָּא תִּשְׁעָה מִנַּיְיהוּ, מִשְׁתַּכְּחָן בז"א, לְאַכְפְּיָיא דִּינִין.

59. There are thirteen streams of valuable goodly oil, NAMELY THE THIRTEEN ATTRIBUTES OF MERCY, derived from that beard, which is that precious Mazal. They all come out to Zeir Anpin. Do not say they all do, as nine of them are present in Zeir Anpin in order to subdue Judgments.

60. הַאי מַזָּלָא, תַּלְיָיא בְּשִׁקּוּלָא עַד טַבּוּרָא. כָּל קִדּוּשֵׁי קִדּוּשִׁין

דִקְדוּשָׁא בֵּיהּ תַּלְיָין. בְּהַאי מַזָּלָא, פָּשִׁיט פְּשִׁיטוּתָא דְקוּטְרָא עִלָּאָה. הַהוּא רֵישָׁא דְּכָל רֵישִׁין, דְּלָא אִתְיְדַע, וְלָא אִשְׁתְּמוֹדַע, וְלָא יַדְעִין עִלָּאִין וְתַתָּאִין. בְּגִין כַּךְ כֹּלָּא בְּהַאי מַזָּלָא תַּלְיָיא.

60. This Mazal goes down in equal measures to the middle. All the holiness of the Holy of Holies derive from this Mazal. Through this Mazal, the tangled supernal knot became untied from the head above all heads, which is unknown, not conceived or known to upper and lower beings. For that reason, everything derives from this Mazal.

61. בְּדִיקְנָא דָא, ג' רֵישִׁין דַּאֲמֵינָא, מִתְפַּשְּׁטָן. וְכֻלְּהוּ מִתְחַבְּרָן בְּהַאי מַזָּלָא, וּמִשְׁתַּכְחִין בֵּיהּ. וּבְגִין כַּךְ, כָּל יְקִירוּ דִּיַקִירוּתָא, בְּהַאי מַזָּלָא תַּלְיָיא. כָּל אִלֵּין אַתְוָון דְּתַלְיָין בְּהַאי עַתִּיקָא, כּוּלְהוּ תַּלְיָין בְּהַאי דִּיקְנָא, וּמִתְחַבְּרָן בְּהַאי מַזָּלָא, וְתַלְיָין בֵּיהּ, לְקַיְּימָא אַתְוָון אַחֲרָנִין. דְּאִלְמָלֵי לָא סְלִיק אִלֵּין אַתְוָון בְּעַתִּיקָא, לָא קַיְימִין אִלֵּין אַחֲרָנִין. וּבְגִין כַּךְ אָמַר מֹשֶׁה כַּד אִצְטְרִיךְ, יְיָ' יְיָ', תְּרֵי זִימְנָא, וּפָסִיק טַעֲמָא בְּגַוַּויְיהוּ. דְּהָא בְּמַזָּלָא תַּלְיָיא כֹּלָּא. מֵהַאי מַזָּלָא, מִתְכַּסְּפֵי עִלָּאֵי וְתַתָּאֵי, וּמִתְכַּפְיָין קַמֵּיהּ. זַכָּאָה חוּלָקֵיהּ מַאן דְּזָכֵי לְהַאי.

61. In this beard, the three heads I mentioned expand and they all connect to this Mazal and rest in it. For that reason all that is most precious derives from this Mazal. All the letters OF THE NAME YUD HEI VAV HEI that come out of Atika do so ONLY from the beard and connect to this Mazal and depend on it to support the other letters IN ZEIR ANPIN. And had not these letters gone up to Atik, NAMELY TO ITS BEARD, the others IN ZEIR ANPIN would not have survived. Hence Moses said, when it was needed, "Hashem, Hashem" (Shemot 34:6) twice, THE FIRST COMING FROM ARICH ANPIN AND THE SECOND FROM ZEIR ANPIN with a punctuation mark between them. Everything depends on Mazal AND NOT ON ARICH ANPIN ITSELF. The upper and lower beings shy away from this Mazal and are subdued before it.

20. How Chochmah of 32 paths emanated

A Synopsis

Rabbi Shimon tells of the supernal origin of the 32 paths of wisdom. He also explains what is included under the name Atika Kadisha, and we learn that the highest head is completely outside of the Sfirot, nor is it counted with them, even as their Keter. It is the place of the beginning.

.62 הַאי עַתִּיקָא קַדִּישָׁא, סְתִימָא דְּכָל סְתִימִין, לָא אַדְכַּר, וְלָא אִשְׁתְּכַח. וּבְגִין דְּאִיהוּ רֵישָׁא עִלָּאָה לְכָל עִלָּאִין, לָא אִדְכַּר, בַּר רֵישָׁא חֲדָא, בְּלָא גוּפָא, לְקַיְּימָא כֹּלָּא.

62. This most hidden Atika Kadisha is not mentioned IN THE TORAH, and is not present, since being a supernal head for all the upper beings, it is mentioned IN THE TORAH only as a bodiless head, THAT IS, "AND THE HAIR OF WHOSE HEAD WAS LIKE THE PURE WOOL" (DANIEL 7:9), THE TORSO, ARMS AND LEGS ARE NOT MENTIONED, LIKE THOSE OF ZEIR ANPIN MENTIONED IN SHIR HASHIRIM. The purpose is to support everything.

.63 וְהַאי טָמִיר וְסָתִים וְגָנִיז מִכֹּלָּא, תִּקּוּנוֹי אִתְתָּקְנָן, בְּהַהוּא מוֹחָא סְתִימָאָה דְּכֹלָּא, דְּאִתְפְּשַׁט וְאִתְתָּקַּן כֹּלָּא וְנָפִיק חֶסֶד עִלָּאָה, וְחֶסֶד עִלָּאָה אִתְפָּשַׁט וְאִתְתָּקַּן וְאִתְכְּלִיל כֹּלָּא בְּמוֹחָא סְתִימָאָה דָּא. כַּד אִתְתְּקַן חִוָּורָא דָּא בִּנְהִירוּ דָּא, בָּטַשׁ מַאן דְּבָטַשׁ, בְּהַאי מוֹחָא וְאִתְנְהִיר, וְתַלְיָיא מִמַּזָּלָא יַקִּירָא מוֹחָא אַחֲרָא, דְּאִתְפְּשַׁט וְנָהִיר לִתְלָתִין וּתְרֵין שְׁבִילִין. כַּד אִתְנְהִיר נָהִיר מִמַּזָּלָא יַקִּירָא. אִתְנְהִירוּ ג' רֵישִׁין עִלָּאִין, תְּרֵין רֵישִׁין, וְחַד דְּכָלִיל לוֹן. וּבְמַזָּלָא תַּלְיָין, וְאִתְכְּלִילָן בֵּיהּ.

63. The structures of the most hidden, concealed and treasured, KETER OF ARICH ANPIN, settled in the most hidden brain, WHICH IS CONCEALED CHOCHMAH. After it was wholly expanded and established, supernal Chesed came out OF KETER OF ARICH ANPIN. This supernal Chesed expanded and was established, and everything was incorporated in the concealed brain, WHICH IS CHOCHMAH OF ARICH ANPIN. When this whiteness was instituted within that light, someone, THAT IS, THE UNKNOWN HEAD, struck that brain, WHICH IS CONCEALED CHOCHMAH, shone and produced from the precious Mazal another brain, WHICH BRAIN expanded and shines upon 32 paths, WHICH ARE ABA AND IMA. When THIS BRAIN shines, it does so from the precious Mazal. Three lofty heads shone upon THAT BRAIN, two heads and one that incorporates them. THEY ARE CHOCHMAH AND BINAH, AND THE ONE THAT INCLUDES THEM IS THE BRAIN OF DA'AT. THESE CHOCHMAH, BINAH AND DA'AT derive from Mazal and are included in it.

64. מִכָּאן שָׁארִי לְאִתְגַּלְיָיא יָקִירוּ דְּדִיקְנָא, דְּאִיהוּ מַזָּלָא סְתִימָאָה. וְאִינּוּן מִתְתָּקְנָן, כְּמָה דְּעַתִּיקָא קַדִּישָׁא תְּלַת רֵישִׁין מִתְעַטְּרִין בֵּיהּ, הָכִי כֹּלָּא בִּתְלַת רֵישִׁין. וְכַד אִתְנָהֲרָן, תַּלְיָין כֻּלְּהוּ דָּא בְּדָא בִּתְלַת רֵישִׁין, תְּרֵין מִתְּרֵין סִטְרִין, וְחַד דְּכָלִיל לוֹן.

64. From here, THE BRAIN OF 32 PATHS, the preciousness of the beard, which is the concealed Mazal, begins to be revealed, BECAUSE FROM IT, THERE IS A FLOW ON EVERY GRADE. And when they are established THEY ARE ESTABLISHED THROUGHOUT THE GRADES, just as three heads are crowned with Atika Kadisha, so are all THE GRADES three headed. And when they shine, all THE GRADES derive each from the other with three heads, which are two from both sides, RIGHT AND LEFT, and one that includes them IN THEIR MIDDLE. THESE ARE THE THREE COLUMNS, RIGHT, LEFT AND CENTRAL PRESENT IN EVERY GRADE, THROUGH WHICH EACH GRADE FLOWS INTO A LOWER ONE.

65. וְאִי תֵּימָא, מַאן עַתִּיקָא קַדִּישָׁא. ת״ח, לְעֵילָּא לְעֵילָּא, אִית דְּלָא אִתְיְדַע, וְלָא אִשְׁתְּמוֹדַע, וְלָא אִתְרְשִׁים, וְהוּא כָּלִיל כֹּלָּא, וּתְרֵין רֵישִׁין בֵּיהּ כְּלִילָן. וּכְדֵין כֹּלָּא הָכִי אִתְתְּקַן. וְהַהוּא לָאו בְּמִנְיָינָא, וְלָא בִּכְלָלָא וְלָא בְּחוּשְׁבָּן אֶלָּא בִּרְעוּתָא דְּלִבָּא, עַל דָּא אִתְּמַר, אָמַרְתִּי אֶשְׁמְרָה דְרָכַי מֵחֲטֹא בִלְשׁוֹנִי.

65. You may ask who Atika Kadisha is, THAT IS, WHAT IS INCLUDED

UNDER THE NAME ATIKA KADISHA. HE ANSWERS, Come and see, high up there is the unknown, inconceivable and unmarked, WHICH IS THE UNKNOWN HEAD. It includes everything, and the two LOWER heads, THE SKULL AND THE CONCEALED BRAIN, TO THE RIGHT AND LEFT, are included within it, THAT IS, IT UNITES THEM. Everything is then established that way, THAT IS, IN THE MANNER OF TWO HEADS TO THE RIGHT AND LEFT AND ONE THAT INCORPORATES AND UNITES THE ONE WITH THE OTHER. It, THE UNKNOWN HEAD THAT INCLUDES TWO HEADS, is not counted WITH THE SFIROT nor is it part of them, NOT EVEN AS THEIR KETER. It is not part of the reckoning, NOT BEING OF THE ASPECT OF CHOCHMAH CALLED RECKONING, except through willingness. Hence it is said, "I said, I will take heed to my ways, that I sin not with my tongue" (Tehilim 39:2).

66. אֲתָר דְּשֵׁירוּתָא אִשְׁתְּכַח, מֵעַתִּיקָא קַדִּישָׁא, דְּאִתְנְהִיר מִמַּזָּלָא, הוּא נְהִירוּ דְּחָכְמְתָא, דְּאִתְפְּשַׁט לִתְלָתִין וּתְרֵין עִיבַר. וְנָפְקָא מֵהַהוּא מוֹחָא סְתִימָאָה, מִנְּהִירוּ דְּבֵיהּ. וּמַה דְּעַתִּיקָא קַדִּישָׁא נָהִיר בְּקַדְמֵיתָא, דָּא הִיא. וְשֵׁירוּתָא מִמָּה דְּאִתְגַּלְיָיא, וְאִתְעָבֵיד לִתְלַת רֵישִׁין, וְרֵישָׁא חֲדָא כָּלִיל לוֹן. וְאִלֵּין תְּלַת מִתְפַּשְּׁטָן לִזְעֵיר אַנְפִּין, וּמֵאִלֵּין נַהֲרִין כֹּלָּא.

66. The place where the beginning lies is from THE ILLUMINATION OF Atika Kadisha that illuminates from Mazal, which is the illumination of Chochmah that expands into 32 directions, THAT IS CHOCHMAH OF THE 32 PATHS, which comes out from the concealed brain when it illuminates. And as for Atika Kadisha shining in the beginning it is THE BRAIN OF 32 PATHS that is the beginning for what is revealed, which turns into three heads, THAT IS, TWO HEADS, CHOCHMAH AND BINAH, and one head including them, WHICH IS THE BRAIN OF DA'AT. And these three, CHOCHMAH, BINAH AND DA'AT, expand to Zeir Anpin and from them all GRADES illuminate AS SHALL BE EXPLAINED.

21. The expansion of Chochmah of 32 paths to the lower beings

A Synopsis

Rabbi Shimon goes on to explain how the two heads, Chochmah and Binah, and the one incorporating them expand from the brain of 32 paths to Zeir Anpin and then to the rest of the grades.

67. אִתְגְּלִיף הַאי חָכְמְתָא, וְאַפִּיק חַד נַהֲרָא, דְּנָגִיד, וְנָפִיק לְאַשְׁקָאָה גִּנְתָּא וְעָיֵיל בְּרֵישָׁא דִּזְעֵיר אַנְפִּין, וְאִתְעָבֵיד חַד מוֹחָא וּמִתַּמָּן אִתְמְשִׁיךְ וְנָגִיד בְּכָל גּוּפָא, וְאַשְׁקֵי כָּל אִינּוּן נְטִיעָאן. הה"ד, וְנָהָר יוֹצֵא מֵעֵדֶן לְהַשְׁקוֹת אֶת הַגָּן וְגוֹ'.

67. HE GOES ON TO EXPLAIN HOW THE TWO HEADS, CHOCHMAH AND BINAH, AND THE ONE INCORPORATING THEM, WHICH IS DA'AT, EXPAND FROM THE BRAIN OF 32 PATHS TO ZEIR ANPIN AND THE REST OF THE GRADES. HE SAYS, That Chochmah OF 32 PATHS was engraved and produced a river, WHICH IS BINAH, WHICH flows and comes out to water the garden THAT IS MALCHUT. It enters the head of Zeir Anpin and becomes a brain OF CHOCHMAH, whence it flows and goes into the whole body OF ZEIR ANPIN and waters all the plants. This is the secret of, "And a river went out of Eden to water the garden" (Beresheet 2:10).

68. תּוּ אִתְגְּלִיף הַאי חָכְמְתָא, וְאִתְמְשַׁךְ וְעָיֵיל בְּרֵישָׁא דִּזְעֵיר אַנְפִּין, וְאִתְעָבֵיד מוֹחָא אַחֲרָא. הַהוּא נְהִירוּ דְּאִתְמַשְׁכָא מִנֵּיהּ אִלֵּין תְּרֵין מְשִׁיכָן אִתְגְּלִיפוּ, מִתְחַבְּרָן בְּחַד רֵישָׁא דְּעָמִיקָא דְּבֵירָא, דִּכְתִּיב בְּדַעְתּוֹ תְּהוֹמוֹת נִבְקָעוּ. וְעָיֵיל בְּרֵישָׁא דִּזְעֵיר אַנְפִּין, וְאִתְעָבֵיד מוֹחָא אַחֲרָא, וּמִתַּמָּן אִתְמְשִׁיךְ וְעָיֵיל לְגוֹ גּוּפָא, וּמַלְיָיא כָּל אִינּוּן אִדָּרִין וְאַכְסַדְרִין דְּגוּפָא. הה"ד, וּבְדַעַת חֲדָרִים יִמָּלְאוּ.

68. This Chochmah OF 32 PATHS was also engraved, flowed and entered the head of Zeir Anpin, and another brain OF BINAH was made. LATER from that light two flows came out, were engraved and joined the one head of the depth of the pit, WHICH IS THE BRAIN OF DA'AT, as written, "By His knowledge the depths were broken up" (Mishlei 3:20). It entered the head of

Zeir Anpin and became another brain OF DA'AT, and from there it flowed and entered the whole body OF ZEIR ANPIN and filled all those chambers and halls. This is the meaning of, "and by knowledge are the chambers filled" (Mishlei 24:4).

69. וְאִלֵּין נַהֲרִין, מִנְּהִירוּ דְּהַהוּא מוֹחָא עִלָּאָה סְתִימָאָה, דְּנָהִיר בְּמַזָּלָא. וְכֹלָּא דָּא בְּדָא תַּלְיָין. וְאִתְקְשַׁר דָּא בְּדָא, וְדָא בְּדָא, עַד דְּיִשְׁתְּמוֹדַע דְּכֹלָּא חַד, וְכֹלָּא הוּא עַתִּיקָא, וְלָא אִתְפְּרַשׁ מִנֵּיהּ כְּלוּם. אִלֵּין תְּלַת נְהוֹרִין, נְהִרִין לִתְלַת אַחֲרָנִין, דְּאִקְרוּן אֲבָהָן. וְאִלֵּין נַהֲרִין לִבְנִין. וְכֹלָּא נָהִיר מֵאֲתָר חַד. כַּד אִתְגַּלְיָיא הַאי עַתִּיקָא, רַעֲוָא דְּרַעֲוִין, כֹּלָּא נָהִיר וְכֹלָּא אִשְׁתְּכַח בְּחֵדוּ שְׁלֵימָתָא.

69. These, CHOCHMAH, BINAH AND DA'AT OF ZEIR ANPIN, shine with the light of that supernal concealed brain that illuminates Mazal, and everything is interdependent and interconnected, to the point that it is known that it is all one, all is Atika, and nothing is separated from it. These three lights CHOCHMAH, BINAH AND DA'AT OF ZEIR ANPIN, shine to three others called fathers, CHESED, GVURAH AND TIFERET OF ZEIR ANPIN, which shine on the children, NETZACH, HOD AND YESOD OF ZEIR ANPIN. Everything shines from the same place, FROM THE CONCEALED BRAIN, WHICH IS ATIKA. And when Atika, the Will of all wills, is revealed, and everything shines, everything abides in perfect joy.

22. Supernal Eden and lower Eden

A Synopsis

Here we learn that Zeir Anpin is called 'You' because it is from Zeir Anpin that there is the beginning of revelation, but that Atika Kadisha, which is entirely concealed, is called 'He'.

70. הַאי חָכְמְתָא אִקְרֵי עֵדֶן, וְהַאי עֵדֶן אִתְמְשַׁךְ מֵעֵדֶן עִלָּאָה, סְתִימָאָה דְּכָל סְתִימִין. וּמֵהַאי עֵדֶן, אִקְרֵי שֵׁירוּתָא. דִּבְעַתִּיקָא לָא אִקְרֵי, וְלָא הֲוֵי שֵׁירוּתָא וְסִיּוּמָא. וּבְגִין דְּלָא הֲוֵי בֵּיהּ שֵׁירוּתָא וְסִיּוּמָא, לָא אִקְרֵי אַתָּה. בְּגִין דְּאִתְכַּסְיָיא וְלָא אִתְגַּלְיָיא. וְאִקְרֵי הוּא. וּמֵאֲתָר דְּשֵׁירוּתָא אִשְׁתְּכַח אִקְרֵי אַתָּה, וְאִקְרֵי אָב. דִּכְתִּיב, כִּי אַתָּה אָבִינוּ.

70. This Chochmah OF 32 PATHS is called Eden, and this Eden flows from the most hidden supernal Eden, WHICH IS THE CONCEALED BRAIN. From this Eden, WHICH IS CHOCHMAH OF 32 PATHS, it is considered a beginning OF SHINING UPON LOWER BEINGS, because in Atika, NAMELY IN THE CONCEALED BRAIN, neither beginning is indicated nor ending. Since IN ATIKA there is no beginning and no end, it is not called 'You', USING THE SECOND, PRESENT PERSON, because it is hidden and undisclosed, and is therefore called 'He' IN THE THIRD, HIDDEN PERSON. From where there is a beginning, NAMELY CHOCHMAH OF 32 PATHS, it is called 'You' and 'Father', as written, "You are our father" (Yeshayah 63:16).

71. בְּאַגַּדְתָּא דְּבֵי רַב יֵיבָא סָבָא, כְּלָלָא דְּכֹלָּא, זְעֵיר אַנְפִּין אִקְרֵי אַתָּה. עַתִּיקָא קַדִּישָׁא דְּאִתְכַּסְיָיא, אִקְרֵי הוּא. וְשַׁפִּיר. וְהַשְׁתָּא קָרֵינָן בַּאֲתָר דָּא דְּשֵׁירוּתָא אִשְׁתְּכַח, אַתָּה. אע"ג דְּאִתְכַּסְיָיא, מִנֵּיהּ הֲוֵי שֵׁירוּתָא, וְאִקְרֵי אָב. וְהוּא אָב, לַאֲבָהָן. וְהַאי אָב נָפִיק מֵעַתִּיקָא קַדִּישָׁא, דִּכְתִּיב וְהַחָכְמָה מֵאַיִן תִּמָּצֵא. ובג"כ לָא אִשְׁתְּמוֹדַע.

71. In the Agadah of Rav Yeba Saba HE SAYS, all in all Zeir Anpin is called 'You', BECAUSE IT IS REVEALED. Atika Kadisha, which is concealed, is called 'He'. This is correct. We now call this place where the beginning lies, WHICH IS THE BRAIN OF 32 PATHS, BY THE NAME 'You', for though it is

YET hidden, NEVERTHELESS the beginning OF REVELATION comes from it. HENCE IT IS CALLED 'YOU' AS WELL. It is called father and is a father to the fathers, CHESED, GVURAH AND TIFERET OF ZEIR ANPIN. And this father comes out of Atika Kadisha as written, "But where is wisdom to be found (or: 'wisdom is found from naught')" (Iyov 28:12), NAMELY FROM ATIKA KADISHA THAT IS CALLED NAUGHT, which is why it is unknown.

72. ת"ח, כְּתִיב אֱלֹהִים הֵבִין דַּרְכָּהּ, דַּרְכָּהּ מַמָּשׁ. אֲבָל וְהוּא יָדַע אֶת מְקוֹמָהּ, מְקוֹמָהּ מַמָּשׁ. וכ"ש הַהוּא חָכְמָה דִּסְתִּימָא בֵּיהּ בְּעַתִּיקָא קַדִּישָׁא.

72. Come and see, it is written, "Elohim understands its way" (Ibid. 23), actually its way, BECAUSE ELOHIM WHICH IS ZEIR ANPIN KNOWS THE WAY CHOCHMAH OF 32 PATHS EXPANDS TO LOWER CHOCHMAH, "and He," ATIKA KADISHA, "knows its place" (Ibid.), its very place, NAMELY THE ESSENCE OF SUPERNAL CHOCHMAH, WHICH IS ABA AND IMA, and naturally Chochmah concealed within Atika Kadisha, WHICH IS ITS OWN BRAIN.

23. Why Chochmah is considered to have 32 paths

A Synopsis

By saying that 32 paths expand from Chochmah, it means that the Torah, that is Zeir Anpin, is included in the 22 letters and the ten sayings. Rabbi Shimon also says that this Chochmah is a father to the fathers, and that in it there are a beginning and an ending.

73. הַאי חָכְמָה שֵׁירוּתָא דְּכֹלָּא, מִנֵּיהּ מִתְפַּשְּׁטָן תְּלָתִין וּתְרֵין שְׁבִילִין. וְאוֹרַיְיתָא בְּהוּ אִתְכְּלִילַת בְּעֶשְׂרִין וּתְרֵין אַתְוָון, וַעֲשַׂר אֲמִירָן. הַאי חָכְמָה אָב, לַאֲבָהָן. וּבְהַאי חָכְמָה, שֵׁירוּתָא וְסִיּוּמָא אִשְׁתְּכַח. ובג״ד, חָכְמָה עִלָּאָה חָכְמָה תַּתָּאָה. כַּד אִתְפְּשַׁט חָכְמָה, אִקְרֵי אָב לַאֲבָהָן. כֹּלָּא לָא אִתְכְּלִיל אֶלָּא בְּהַאי. דִּכְתִּיב כֻּלָּם בְּחָכְמָה עָשִׂיתָ.

73. This Chochmah OF 32 PATHS is the first beginning. From it 32 paths expand. THIS MEANS THAT the Torah, WHICH IS ZEIR ANPIN, is included in the 22 letters and the ten sayings. This Chochmah is a father to the fathers, CHESED, GVURAH AND TIFERET OF ZEIR ANPIN. In this Chochmah there are a beginning and an ending, WHICH ARE therefore CALLED upper Chochmah and lower Chochmah – THE FORMER IS THE BEGINNING AND THE LATTER THE ENDING. When Chochmah expanded TO ZEIR ANPIN it is called a father to fathers. Everything is included only in this CHOCHMAH, as written, "in wisdom have You made them all" (Tehilim 104:24).

24. Aba and Ima, which are Chochmah and Binah

A Synopsis

Rabbi Shimon tells the other rabbis that Atika Kadisha established everything as male and female, and that when Chochmah emerged and shone it shone only as male and female; Chochmah is a father and Binah a mother. When they joined they gave birth to Zeir Anpin and Malchut, and thus faith spread. Rabbi Shimon talks about the river that flows and that is called the World to Come, saying that this is the Eden of the righteous who will merit life in the World to Come. He now says explicitly what he has only hinted at throughout his life – that the Holy Name includes everything: it includes Chochmah, Binah, Zeir Anpin and Malchut. We also learn how Solomon interprets the two descriptions of the female – "my love" and "my bride" in Shir Hashirim – that are Ima and Malchut. Rabbi Shimon talks about the endless flow that emerges to the Garden that is Malchut. In another context he says that Binah is father, mother and son.

74. זָקַף ר״ש יְדוֹי, וְחַדֵי, אָמַר, וַדַּאי עִידָּן הוּא לְגַלָּאָה, וְכֹלָּא אִצְטְרִיךְ בְּשַׁעֲתָא דָא. תָּאנָא, בְּשַׁעֲתָא דְעַתִּיקָא קַדִּישָׁא, סְתִימָאָה דְּכָל סְתִימִין, בָּעָא לְאַתְקְנָא כֹּלָּא, אַתְקִין כְּעֵין דְּכַר וְנוּקְבָא. בַּאֲתָר דְאִתְכְּלִילוּ דְּכַר וְנוּקְבָא לָא אִתְקְיָימוּ, אֶלָּא בְּקִיּוּמָא אַחֲרָא דִדְכַר וְנוּקְבָא. וְהַאי חָכְמָה כְּלָלָא דְכֹלָּא, כַּד נָפְקָא וְאִתְנְהִיר מֵעַתִּיקָא קַדִּישָׁא, לָא אִתְנְהִיר אֶלָּא בִּדְכַר וְנוּקְבָא. דְּהַאי חָכְמָה אִתְפְּשַׁט, וְאַפִּיק מִינֵּיהּ בִּינָה, וְאִשְׁתְּכַח דְּכַר וְנוּקְבָא. הוּא, חָכְמָה אָב. בִּינָה אֵם. חָכְמָה וּבִינָה, בְּחַד מַתְקְלָא אִתְקָלוּ, דְּכַר וְנוּקְבָא. וּבְגִינַיְיהוּ כֹּלָּא אִתְקְיָים בִּדְכַר וְנוּקְבָא, דְּאִלְמָלֵא הַאי, לָא מִתְקַיְּימִין.

74. Rabbi Shimon lifted up his hands and was glad. He said, Surely it is a time of revelation, and there is a need for everything at such a time. We learned that when the most hidden Atika Kadisha wanted to prepare, He established everything as male and female. BUT where male and female were incorporated IN EVERY SFIRAH, they survived only by another existence of male and female. This Chochmah, which includes everything, NAMELY CHOCHMAH OF 32 PATHS, when it emerged and shone from Atika Kadisha, it shone only as male and female as Chochmah expanded and produced Binah from itself, and so there are male and female; Chochmah is a father and Binah a mother. Chochmah and Binah are weighed with the same measure, male and female, THAT IS, THEY ARE BOTH EQUAL. Because of them everything endured by means of male and female, for otherwise it would not have existed.

75. שֵׁירוּתָא דָּא אָב לְכֹלָּא, אָב לְכֻלְּהוּ אֲבָהָן, אִתְחַבָּרוּ דָּא בְּדָא, וּנְהִירוּ דָּא בְּדָא. כַּד אִתְחַבָּרוּ, אוֹלִידוּ, וְאִתְפַּשְׁטַת מְהֵימְנוּתָא. בְּאַגַּדְתָּא דְּבֵי רַב יֵיבָא סָבָא, הָכִי תָּאנֵי, מַהוּ בִּינָה. אֶלָּא כַּד אִתְחַבָּר דָּא בְּדָא, יוֹ״ד בְּהֵ״א, אִתְעַבְּרַת, וְאַפִּיקַת בֵּן, וְאוֹלִידַת, ובג״כ, בִּינָה אִקְרֵי, בֵּן יָ״הּ, שְׁלֵימוּתָא דְּכֹלָּא. אִשְׁתְּכָחוּ תַּרְוַויְיהוּ דְּמִתְחַבְּרָן, וּבֵן בְּגַוַּויְיהוּ. כְּלָלָא דְּכֹלָּא. בְּתִקּוּנַיְיהוּ אִשְׁתְּכַח שְׁלֵימוּתָא דְּכֹלָּא, אָב וָאֵם. בֵּן וּבַת.

75. This beginning, NAMELY, CHOCHMAH OF 32 PATHS, WHICH ARE ABA AND IMA, is a father to all, father to all fathers, WHO ARE CHOCHMAH, GVURAH AND TIFERET OF ZEIR ANPIN, AND CHOCHMAH AND BINAH, WHICH ARE ABA AND IMA, united with each other and shining into each other. When they joined they gave birth TO ZEIR ANPIN AND MALCHUT, and faith, WHICH IS MALCHUT CALLED FAITH, spread. In the Agadah of Rav Yeba Saba we learned it thus: what is Binah? When Yud and Hei joined each other, NAMELY CHOCHMAH AND BINAH, BINAH conceived, gave birth and produced a son, ZEIR ANPIN. Hence it is called Binah, for giving birth to the son (Heb. *ben*) of Yud Hei, AS BINAH IS SPELLED WITH 'BEN' AND THE LETTERS YUD HEI, which is overall perfection, for both CHOCHMAH AND BINAH join, and the son, ZEIR ANPIN, between them, which comprises everything. With their establishment, there is overall perfection, namely, everything, father and mother, CHOCHMAH AND BINAH, son and daughter, ZEIR ANPIN AND MALCHUT, WHICH ARE THE FOUR LETTERS YUD HEI VAV HEI, FROM WHICH ALL REALITY SPRINGS.

76. מִלִּין אִלֵּין, לָא אִתְיְיהִבוּ לְגַלָּאָה, בַּר לְקַדִּישֵׁי עֶלְיוֹנִין, דְּעָאלוּ וְנַפְקוּ, וְיַדְעִין אָרְחוֹי דְקוּדְשָׁא בְּרִיךְ הוּא, דְּלָא סָטָאן בְּהוּ לִימִינָא וְלִשְׂמָאלָא. דִּכְתִּיב, כִּי יְשָׁרִים דַּרְכֵי יְיָ׳ וְצַדִּיקִים יֵלְכוּ בָם וְגוֹ׳. זַכָּאָה

חוּלָקֵיהּ, דְּמַאן דְּזָכֵי לְמִנְדַּע אוֹרְחוֹי, וְלָא סָטֵי, וְלָא יִטְעֵי בְּהוּ. דְּמִלִּין אִלֵּין סְתִימִין אִינּוּן וְקַדִּישֵׁי עֶלְיוֹנִין נְהִירִין בְּהוּ, כְּמַאן דְּנָהִיר מִנְּהִירוּ דְבוּצִינָא. לָא אִתְמְסָרוּ מִלִּין אִלֵּין, אֶלָּא לְמַאן דְּעָאל וְנָפִיק. דְּמַאן דְּלָא עָאל וְנָפַק, טַב לֵיהּ דְּלָא אִבְרֵי. דְּהָא גַּלְיָא קַמֵּי עַתִּיקָא קַדִּישָׁא, סְתִימָא דְּכָל סְתִימִין, דְּמִלִּין אִלֵּין נְהִרִין בְּלִבָּאי, בְּאַשְׁלְמוּתָא דִּרְחִימוּתָא וּדְחִילוּ דְקוּדְשָׁא בְּרִיךְ הוּא. וְאִלֵּין בְּנֵי דְּהָכָא, יְדַעְנָא בְּהוּ דְּהָא עָאלוּ וְנָפְקוּ, וְאִתְנְהִירָן בְּאִלֵּין מִלִּין, וְלָא בְּכֻלְּהוּ. וְהַשְׁתָּא אִתְנְהִירוּ בִּשְׁלֵימוּתָא כְּמָה דְּאִצְטְרִיךְ. זַכָּאָה חוּלָקִי עִמְּהוֹן, בְּהַהוּא עָלְמָא.

76. Such things were not meant to be revealed except for lofty saints that entered INTO CHOCHMAH and came out from it IN PEACE, who know the ways of the Holy One, blessed be He, who never move from them right or left, as written, "for the ways of Hashem are right, and the just do walk in them…" (Hoshea 14:10). Blessed is the portion of he who merited knowing His ways and who does not stray nor is misled by them. For these matters are concealed, and the lofty saints shine upon them, as one shining with candlelight. These words were handed only to those who came INTO CHOCHMAH and came out. For whoever has not come in and out, it is better for him had he not been born. For it is known before the most hidden Atika Kadisha that these matters shine in my heart with the perfection of love and awe before the Holy One, blessed be He. And these my children in here, I know about them that they entered CHOCHMAH and came out of it IN PEACE, and they shone on these matters though not on them all. And now they shine fully, as befitting. Blessed is my portion with them in that world.

77. אָמַר ר' שִׁמְעוֹן, כָּל מַה דַּאֲמֵינָא דְּעַתִּיקָא קַדִּישָׁא. וְכָל מַה דַּאֲמֵינָא דִּזְעֵיר אַנְפִּין. כֹּלָּא חַד, כֹּלָּא הוּא חַד מִלָּה. לָא תַּלְיָיא בֵּיהּ פִּירוּדָא. בְּרִיךְ הוּא בְּרִיךְ שְׁמֵיהּ לְעָלַם וּלְעָלְמֵי עָלְמִין.

77. Rabbi Shimon said, All I said of Atika Kadisha and all I said of Zeir Anpin is all the same. It is the same matter without division in it. Blessed is He and blessed is His name forever and ever.

78. תָּ"ח, שֵׁירוּתָא דָּא דְּאִקְרֵי אָב, אִתְכְּלִיל בְּיוֹ"ד, דְּתַלְיָיא מִמַּזָּלָא קַדִּישָׁא. ובג"כ, יוֹ"ד כָּלִיל אַתְוָון אַחֲרָנִין. י' סְתִימָא דְּכָל אַתְוָון אַחֲרָן. י' רֵישָׁא וְסֵיפָא דְּכֹלָּא.

78. Come and see, this beginning that is called father is included within Yud that comes out AND SHINES FROM holy Mazal, WHICH IS THE BEARD. Yud therefore includes other letters, NAMELY VAV DALET, SINCE IT IS FULLY SPELLED YUD VAV DALET. Yud is the comprising of all other letters, AS EVERY LETTER BEGINS WITH A DOT, WHICH IS YUD. Yud is the beginning and ending of everything, AS SUPERNAL CHOCHMAH THAT IS THE BEGINNING OF EVERYTHING IS CALLED YUD, AND SO IS LOWER CHOCHMAH THE ENDING OF EVERYTHING, NAMELY MALCHUT.

79. וְהַהוּא נָהָר דְּנָגִיד וְנָפִיק, אִקְרֵי עָלְמָא דְּאָתֵי, דְּאָתֵי תָּדִיר וְלָא פָּסִיק. וְהַאי הוּא עִדּוּנָא דְּצַדִּיקַיָּא, לְזַכָּאָה לְהַאי עָלְמָא דְּאָתֵי, דְּאַשְׁקֵי תָּדִיר לְגִנְתָּא, וְלָא פָּסִיק. עָלֵיהּ כְּתִיב וּכְמוֹצָא מַיִם אֲשֶׁר לֹא יְכַזְּבוּ מֵימָיו. וְהַהוּא עָלְמָא דְּאָתֵי, אִבְרֵי בְּיוֹ"ד, הה"ד, וְנָהָר יוֹצֵא מֵעֵדֶן לְהַשְׁקוֹת אֶת הַגָּן. י' כָּלִיל תְּרֵין אַתְוָון ו"ד.

79. That river that comes out and flows, NAMELY BINAH THAT COMES OUT OF CHOCHMAH, is called the World to Come, BECAUSE it runs always and never stops. This is the Eden of the righteous who will merit life in that World to Come that constantly waters the Garden, NAMELY MALE AND FEMALE, and never stops. It says of it, "like a spring of water, whose waters fail not" (Yeshayah 58:11). That World to Come is created with Yud, THAT IS, BY CHOCHMAH THAT IS CALLED YUD. This is the meaning of, "And a river went out of Eden," THAT IS, BINAH COMING OUT OF CHOCHMAH THAT IS CALLED SUPERNAL EDEN, "to water the garden" (Beresheet 2:10), NAMELY TO WATER MALE AND FEMALE CALLED VAV DALET, since Yud FULLY SPELLED includes the two letters Vav Dalet, AS SHALL BE EXPLAINED.

80. בְּאַגַּדְתָּא דְּבֵי רַב יֵיבָא סָבָא תָּנֵינָן, אֲמַאי ו"ד כְּלִילָן בְּיוֹ"ד. אֶלָּא נְטִיעָה דְּגִנְתָּא דָּא, אִקְרֵי ו'. אִית גִּנְתָּא אַחֲרָא, דְּאִיהִי ד'. וּמֵהַאי ו',

אִשְׁתַּקְיָיא ד'. וְהַיְינוּ רָזָא דִּכְתִּיב, וְנָהָר יוֹצֵא מֵעֵדֶן וְגוֹ'. מַאי עֵדֶן. דָּא חָכְמָה עִלָּאָה, וְדָא י'. לְהַשְׁקוֹת. אֶת הַגָּן, דָּא הוּא ו'. וּמִשָּׁם יִפָּרֵד וְהָיָה לְאַרְבָּעָה רָאשִׁים, דָּא הוּא ד', וְכֹלָּא כָּלִיל בְּיוּ"ד.

80. In the book of Agadah of Rav Yeba Saba we learned why Vav Dalet are included within Yud. AND HE EXPLAINS, this planting of the Garden, WHICH IS ZEIR ANPIN, is called Vav. There is another Garden called Dalet. From this Vav, WHICH IS ZEIR ANPIN, Dalet is watered, WHICH IS MALCHUT. This is the secret of the words, "And a river went out of Eden to water the garden." Eden is supernal Chochmah, which is Yud. "To water the garden" refers to Vav, WHICH IS ZEIR ANPIN; "and from thence it was parted, and branched into four streams" (Ibid.) refers to Dalet, NAMELY MALCHUT. All that is included in Yud.

81. וּבְגִין כַּךְ, אִקְרֵי אָב לְכֹלָּא. אָב, לַאֲבָהָן. שֵׁירוּתָא דְּכֹלָּא, בֵּיתָא דְּכֹלָּא, דִּכְתִּיב בְּחָכְמָה יִבָּנֶה בָּיִת. וּכְתִיב, כֻּלָּם בְּחָכְמָה עָשִׂיתָ. בְּאַתְרֵיהּ, לָא אִתְגַּלְיָיא, וְלָא אִתְיְדַע. מִדְּאִתְחַבַּר בְּאִימָּא אִתְרְמִיז בְּאִימָּא ובג"כ אִימָּא כְּלָלָא דְּכֹלָּא, בָּהּ אִתְיְדַע, וּבָהּ אִתְרְמִיז, שֵׁירוּתָא וְסִיּוּמָא דְּכֹלָּא. דְּבָהּ סָתִים כֹּלָּא.

81. Because of that THAT EVERYTHING IS INCLUDED IN YUD, WHICH IS CHOCHMAH, CHOCHMAH is called a father to the fathers, WHO ARE CHESED, GVURAH AND TIFERET OF ZEIR ANPIN, a beginning to everything, a house to everything, as written, "Through wisdom a house is built" (Mishlei 24:3), and "in wisdom have You made them all" (Tehilim 104:24). CHOCHMAH in its place is neither revealed nor known. When it is united with Ima, WHICH IS BINAH, it is alluded to in Ima, and because of that Ima IS MADE all inclusive, in which the beginning and ending of everything is made known and indicated, NAMELY SUPERNAL CHOCHMAH AND LOWER CHOCHMAH, WHICH IS MALCHUT. For everything is hidden within it.

82. כְּלָלָא דְּכֹלָּא, שְׁמָא קַדִּישָׁא. עַד הַשְׁתָּא רְמִיזָא, וְלָא אֲמֵינָא כָּל אִלֵּין יוֹמִין. וְהָאִידָנָא מִתְגַּלְּפִין סִטְרִין, י', כָּלִיל בְּהַאי חָכְמָה. ה' דָּא

אִימָּא, וְקָרֵינָן בִּינָה. ו״ה, אִלֵּין תְּרֵין בְּנִין, דְּמִתְעַטְּרָן מֵאִימָּא. וְהָא תָּנֵינָן, דְּבִינָה אִתְכְּלִיל מִכֹּלָּא. יוּ״ד דְּמִתְחַבְּרָא בְּאִימָּא, וּמַפְּקִין בֵּ״ן. וְהַיְינוּ בִּינָה, אָ״ב וָאֵ״ם דְּאִינּוּן י״ה, בֵּן בְּגַוַּויְיהוּ.

82. What includes everything is the Holy Name. Up until now I have made allusions but have not said IT EXPLICITLY all these days. Now the aspects are imprinted; Yud OF YUD HEI VAV HEI includes this Chochmah, NAMELY CHOCHMAH OF 32 PATHS, WHICH IS ABA. Hei is Ima and is called Binah. Vav Hei are the two children, ZEIR ANPIN AND MALCHUT that are adorned by Ima. We have learned that Binah includes them all, because Yud, WHICH IS CHOCHMAH, is united with HEI, WHICH IS Ima, and they beget a son, WHICH IS ZEIR ANPIN. This is the meaning of THE LETTERS OF Binah: a father and mother, who are Yud Hei, with a son (Heb. *ben*) between them, BECAUSE BINAH IS THE LETTERS OF BEN YUD HEI.

83. הַשְׁתָּא אִית לְאִסְתַּכְּלָא, בִּינָה, וְאִקְרֵי תְּבוּנָה, אֲמַאי אִקְרֵי תְּבוּנָה, וְלָא בִּינָה. אֶלָּא תְּבוּנָה אִקְרֵי, בְּשַׁעֲתָא דְּיַנְקָא לִתְרֵין בְּנִין, בֵּ״ן וּבַ״ת, דְּאִינּוּן ו״ה, וְהַהִיא שַׁעֲתָא אִקְרֵי תְּבוּנָה. דְּכֹלָּא כָּלִיל בְּאִלֵּין אַתְוָון, בֵּ״ן וּבַ״ת, אִינּוּן ו״ה. וְכֹלָּא חַד כְּלָלָא, וְהַיְינוּ תְּבוּנָה.

83. We now have to examine: It is Binah, but it is called Tevunah. Why is it called Tevunah rather than Binah? AND HE ANSWERS, For IMA is called Tevunah when suckling the two children, a son and a daughter that are called Vav-Hei, NAMELY ZEIR ANPIN AND MALCHUT. At that time it is called Tevunah, since everything is included within those letters, *ben* (Eng. 'son') and *bat* (Eng. 'daughter'), who are Vav-Hei. THAT IS, TEVUNAH IS SPELLED WITH THE LETTERS OF ben and bat, Vav-Hei, and everything is one whole, namely Tevunah.

84. בְּסִפְרָא דְּרַב הַמְנוּנָא סָבָא אָמַר, דִּשְׁלֹמֹה מַלְכָּא, תִּקּוּנָא קַדְמָאָה דְּגַלֵּי וְאָמַר, הִנָּךְ יָפָה רַעְיָתִי מֵהַאי הוּא. וְתִקּוּנָא תִּנְיָינָא, אִקְרֵי כַּלָּה, דְּאִיהִי נוּקְבָּא דִּלְתַתָּא. וְאִינּוּן דְּאַמְרֵי, דְּתַרְוַויְיהוּ לְהַאי נוּקְבָּא דִּלְתַתָּא אִינּוּן, לָאו הָכִי. דְּהֵ״א קַדְמָאָה לָא אִקְרֵי כַּלָּה. וְהֵ״א בַּתְרָאָה,

אִקְרֵי כַּלָּה, לְזִמְנִין יְדִיעָן. דְּהָא זִמְנִין סַגִּיאִין אִינּוּן, דִּדְכוּרָא לָא אִתְחַבָּר עִמָּהּ, וְאִסְתַּלָּק מִינָּהּ, בְּהַהוּא זִמְנָא כְּתִיב, וְאֶל אִשָּׁה בְּנִדַּת טוּמְאָתָהּ לֹא תִקְרַב. בְּשַׁעֲתָא דְּאִתְדַּכְּאַת נוּקְבָּא, וּדְכוּרָא בָּעֵי לְאִתְחַבְּרָא עִמָּהּ, כְּדֵין אִקְרֵי כַּלָּ"ה. כְּכַלָּ"ה מַמָּשׁ אַתְיָיא.

84. In his book, Rav Hamnuna Saba said that the first description King Solomon revealed, when he said, "Behold, you are fair, my love" (Shir Hashirim 1:15), comes from it. THAT IS, IT RELATES TO IMA, WHOM ABA CALLS "MY LOVE." The second description HE MENTIONED, "COME WITH ME FROM LEBANON, MY BRIDE" (SHIR HASHIRIM 4:8) is considered a bride, who is the lower Nukva, NAMELY MALCHUT. As for those who say that both relate to the lower Nukva, MALCHUT, it is not so, because the first Hei OF YUD HEI VAV HEI is not considered a bride, BUT "MY LOVE," BECAUSE ABA AND IMA ARE CONSIDERED LOVERS. But last Hei is considered a bride at certain times, because on many occasions the male, ZEIR ANPIN, does not unite with her but leaves her. Of that time it is written, "Also you shall not approach to a woman in the impurity of her menstrual flow" (Vayikra 18:19). When the female is purified and the male wishes to unite with her, she is considered a bride, because she comes as a real bride.

85. אֲבָל הַאי אִימָּא, לָא אַפְסִיק רְעוּתָא דְּתַרְוַויְיהוּ לְעָלְמִין, בְּחַד נָפְקִין, בְּחַד שַׁרְיָין. לָא אַפְסִיק דָּא מִן דָּא, וְלָא אִסְתְּלַק דָּא מִן דָּא. ובג"כ כְּתִיב וְנָהָר יֹצֵא מֵעֵדֶן, יוֹצֵא תָּדִיר, וְלָא אַפְסִיק. הה"ד, וּכְמוֹצָא מַיִם אֲשֶׁר לֹא יְכַזְּבוּ מֵימָיו. ובג"כ כְּתִיב רַעְיָתִי, בִּרְעוּתָא דְּאַחְוָה שַׁרְיָין, בְּאַחֲדוּתָא שְׁלֵימוּתָא. אֲבָל הָכָא אִקְרֵי כַּלָּה, דְּכַד אָתָא דְּכוּרָא לְאִתְחַבְּרָא עִמָּהּ, הִיא כַּלָּה, כְּכַלָּה אִיהִי אַתְיָיא מַמָּשׁ.

85. But as for Ima, the desire of both ABA AND IMA never stops. They emerge as one and rest as one. The one does not stop flowing from the other, nor leaves the other. For that reason it is written, "And a river went out of Eden" (Beresheet 2:10). "went out" MEANS constantly, ceaselessly, as written, "like a spring of water, whose waters fail not" (Yeshayah 58:11). Hence it is written, "my love" ABOUT IMA, because they dwell with brotherly desire AND LOVE, with absolute unity. But here, IN MALCHUT, she is considered a bride, because when the male comes, WHO IS ZEIR ANPIN, to join her, she is a bride, and comes as an actual bride.

86. ובג״כ, תְּרֵי תִּקּוּנִין דְּנוּקְבֵי פָּרִישׁ שְׁלֹמֹה. תִּקּוּנָא דְּקַדְמֵיתָא, סְתִימָא, בְּגִין דְּאִיהִי סְתִימָא. וְתִקּוּנָא תִּנְיָינָא, פָּרִישׁ יַתִּיר, וְלָא סָתִים כּוּלֵּי הַאי. וּלְבָתַר תַּלְיָא כָּל שְׁבָחָא בְּהַהִיא דִּלְעֵילָּא. דִּכְתִּיב, אַחַת הִיא לְאִמָּהּ בָּרָה הִיא לְיוֹלַדְתָּהּ, וּבְגִין דְּאִיהִי אִימָּא מִתְעַטְּרָא בְּעִטְרָא דְּכַלָּה, וּרְעוּתָא דְּיוּ״ד לָא אַפְסִיק מִנָּהּ לְעָלְמִין, אִתְיְהִיב בִּרְשׁוּתָהּ כָּל חֵירוּ דְּעַבְדִין. כָּל חֵירוּ דְּכֹלָּא. כָּל חֵירוּ דְּחַיָּיבַיָּא, לְדַכָּאָה לְכֹלָּא. דִּכְתִּיב כִּי בַיּוֹם הַזֶּה יְכַפֵּר עֲלֵיכֶם. וּכְתִיב וְקִדַּשְׁתֶּם אֵת שְׁנַת הַחֲמִשִּׁים שָׁנָה יוֹבֵל הִיא. מַאי יוֹבֵל. כד״א וְעַל יוּבַל יְשַׁלַּח שָׁרָשָׁיו. מִשּׁוּם הַהוּא נָהָר דְּאָתֵי וְנָגִיד וְנָפִיק, וְאָתֵי תָּדִיר, וְלָא פָּסִיק.

86. For that reason, Solomon interprets the two descriptions of the female, IMA AND MALCHUT. The first description OF IMA is vague, because Ima is vague AND HIDDEN. The second description IN MALCHUT gives more explanation and is not so vague. Later, it applies all the value OF MALCHUT to the upper one, IMA, as written, "she is the only one of her mother, she is the choice one of her that bore her" (Shir Hashirim 6:9). And since Ima is bedecked with a bride's crown, and the desire of Yud, WHICH IS CHOCHMAH, towards her never stops, AND SHE IS ATTACHED TO BOTH THE UPPER AND LOWER BEINGS, THEREFORE the freedom of all slaves is under her jurisdiction to purify everything, as written, "for on that day will He forgive you" (Vayikra 16:30), and, "And you shall hallow the fiftieth year…it shall be a jubilee for you" (Vayikra 25:10). What is a Jubilee (Heb. *yovel*)? It accords with the words, "and that spreads out its roots by the river (Heb. *yuval*)" (Yirmeyah 17:8). FOR JUBILEE MEANS A RIVER after the river, WHICH IS IMA, that comes out, flows and emerges uninterruptedly TO THE GARDEN, WHICH IS MALCHUT.

87. כְּתִיב כִּי אִם לַבִּינָה תִקְרָא לַתְּבוּנָה תִּתֵּן קוֹלֶךָ. כֵּיוָן דְּאָמַר כִּי אִם לַבִּינָה תִּקְרָא, אֲמַאי לַתְּבוּנָה. אֶלָּא כֹּלָּא כְּמָה דַּאֲמֵינָא. הֵי מִנַּיְיהוּ עִלָּאָה. בִּינָה עִלָּאָה מִתְּבוּנָה. בִּינָה אָב וָאֵם וּבֵן. י״ה: אָב וָאֵם, וּבֵן

בְּגַוַּויְיהוּ. תְּבוּנָה: כֹּלָּא כְּלָלָא דִּבְנִין, בֵּן וּבַת, ו״ה. וְלָא אִשְׁתְּכַח אָב וָאֵם, אֶלָּא בְּבִינָה. וּבִתְבוּנָה וַדַּאי אִימָּא רְבִיעָא עָלַיְיהוּ, וְלָא אִתְגַּלְיָיא. אִשְׁתְּכַח, דִּכְלָלָא דִּתְרֵין בְּנִין, אִקְרֵי תְּבוּנָה. וּכְלָלָא דְּאָב אֵם וּבֵן, אִקְרֵי בִּינָה. וְכַד בָּעֵי לְאַכְלְלָא כֹּלָּא, בְּהַאי אִתְכְּלִיל.

87. It is written, “if (Heb. *im*) you cry after wisdom (Binah), and lift up your voice for understanding (Tevunah)” (Mishlei 2:3). HE ASKS, Once it said, “mother (Heb. *em*) you cry after Binah,” why ADD, “AND LIFT UP YOUR VOICE for Tevunah,” AND HE ANSWERS, Everything is as I said THAT WHEN BINAH SUCKLES THE SON AND DAUGHTER IT IS CALLED TEVUNAH. HE ASKS, Which one is superior, AND ANSWERS, Binah is superior to Tevunah. Binah is father, mother and son, SINCE Yud Hei are father and mother with a son between them, WHO IS VAV. THAT IS, BINAH IS SPELLED *BEN* (ENG. ‘SON OF’) YUD-HEI. All of Tevunah is entirely of children, AS IT IS SPELLED WITH THE LETTERS OF *ben* (Eng. ‘son’), *bat* (Eng. ‘daughter’), Vav-Hei. YUD-HEI ARE NOT MENTIONED IN IT. FROM THIS WE UNDERSTAND THAT BINAH IS SUPERIOR TO TEVUNAH, because father and mother, WHO ARE YUD-HEI, are only in Binah, but in Tevunah THERE IS NO YUD-HEI; surely the mother crouches over the children, VAV-HEI, WHILE THE MOTHER HERSELF does not appear THERE. HENCE TEVUNAH CONTAINS ONLY THE LETTERS OF BEN BAT VAV-HEI, BUT NOT YUD HEI. Thus the sum of all two children, ZEIR ANPIN AND MALCHUT, is called Tevunah, while the whole of the father, mother and son, WHO ARE CHOCHMAH, BINAH AND ZEIR ANPIN, is considered Binah, which, when wishing to include everything, YUD-HEI AS WELL, they are included IN BINAH.

25. Da'at, which is Zeir Anpin that unites Chochmah and Binah that are Aba and Ima

A Synopsis

Rabbi Shimon begins by saying that the father, mother and son are called Chochmah, Binah and Da'at, and he explains why this is so. He tells us that Da'at receives his father's and mother's inheritance.

88. וְהַאי אָב וָאֵם וּבֵן, אִקְרוּן חָכְמָה בִּינָה וָדַעַת. בְּגִין דְּהַאי בֵּן, נָטִיל סִימָנִין דַּאֲבוּי וְאִמֵּיהּ, אִקְרֵי דַּעַת, דְּהוּא סַהֲדוּתָא דְּתַרְוַויְיהוּ. וְהַאי בֵּן, אִקְרֵי בּוּכְרָא. דִּכְתִּיב, בְּנִי בְכוֹרִי יִשְׂרָאֵל. וּבְגִין דְּאִקְרֵי בּוּכְרָא, נָטִיל תְּרֵין חוּלָקִין. וְכַד אִתְרַבֵּי בְּעִטְרוֹי, נָטִיל תְּלַת חוּלָקִין. וּבֵין כַּךְ וּבֵין כַּךְ, תְּרֵין חוּלָקִין, וּתְלַת חוּלָקִין כֹּלָּא חַד מִלָּה. וְהַאי וְהַאי חַד הֲוֵי, יְרוּתָא דַּאֲבוּי וְאִמֵּיהּ יָרִית.

88. These father, mother and son are called Chochmah, Binah and Da'at. For when the son, ZEIR ANPIN, receives his father's and mother's tokens, THAT IS, WHEN HE TAKES AND INCLUDES WITHIN HIM CHOCHMAH AND BINAH OF ABA AND IMA, he is called Da'at, WHICH IS DERIVED FROM TESTIMONY (HEB. *EDUT*), because he bears testimony about both of them BY INCLUDING WITHIN HIM THE MOCHIN OF ABA AND IMA, AS DA'AT RECONCILES AND INCLUDES CHOCHMAH AND BINAH. This son, DA'AT, is called a firstborn SON, as written, "Yisrael is My son, My firstborn" (Shemot 4:22), SINCE ZEIR ANPIN, WHO IS DA'AT, IS CALLED YISRAEL, AND IT SAYS OF HIM, "YISRAEL IS MY SON, MY FIRSTBORN." Since he is considered a firstborn he receives two portions, A PORTION FROM ABA, WHO IS CHOCHMAH, AND A PORTION FROM IMA, BINAH. When he gets bigger with his crowns, he receives three portions, CHOCHMAH, BINAH AND DA'AT. In either case, two parts or three parts are all the same, SINCE DA'AT IS NO MORE THAN THE INCLUSION OF CHOCHMAH AND BINAH, IN SUCH A WAY THAT EVEN IN CHOCHMAH, BINAH AND DA'AT THERE ARE NO MORE THAN TWO, CHOCHMAH AND BINAH. Both are the same, BECAUSE DA'AT receives his father's and mother's inheritance, AND HENCE HAS ONLY CHOCHMAH AND BINAH LIKE HIS FATHER AND MOTHER, BUT NO MORE.

26. Inheritance and the two crowns in Chochmah, Binah and Da'at of Zeir Anpin

A Synopsis

Rabbi Shimon describes the nature of the inheritance that Zeir Anpin receives from Aba and Ima. We are led to understand that the son inherits everything and gives it to the daughter, Malchut, who is nourished from him.

89. מַאי יְרוּתָא דָּא. אַחֲסַנְתָּא דַּאֲבוֹי וְאִימֵּיהּ, וּתְרֵין עִטְרִין דַּהֲווֹ גְּנִיזִין בְּגַוַּויְיהוּ, וְאַחֲסִינוּ לְבֵן דָּא. מִסִּטְרָא דַּאֲבוֹי, הֲוָה גָּנִיז בְּגַוֵּויהּ חַד עִטְרָא, דְּאִקְרֵי חֶסֶד. וּמִסִּטְרָא דְּאִימָּא, חַד עִטְרָא, דְּאִקְרֵי גְּבוּרָה. וְכֻלְּהוּ מִתְעַטְּרִין בְּרֵישֵׁיהּ, וְאָחִיד לוֹן. וְכַד נַהֲרִין אִלֵּין אָב וָאֵם עָלֵיהּ, כֻּלְּהוּ אִקְרוּן תְּפִילִּין דְּרֵישָׁא. וְכֹלָּא נָטִיל בֵּן דָּא, וְיָרִית כֹּלָּא, וְאִתְפְּשַׁט בְּכָל גּוּפָא. וְהַאי בֵּן, יָהִיב לִבְרַתָּא. וּבְרַתָּא מִנֵּיהּ אִתְּזָן. ועכ"פ מִכָּאן, בְּרָא יָרִית, וְלָא בְּרַתָּא. בְּרָא יָרִית לַאֲבוּי וּלְאִמֵּיהּ, וְלָא בְּרַתָּא. וּמִנֵּיהּ אִתְּזָן בְּרַתָּא. כְּמָה דִּכְתִּיב וּמָזוֹן לְכֹלָּא בֵיהּ.

89. HE ASKS, What is this inheritance ZEIR ANPIN RECEIVES FROM ABA AND IMA, AND ANSWERS, It is his father and mother's inheritance, WHICH IS THEIR CHOCHMAH AND BINAH, and the two crowns hidden therein, which they bequeathed to that son, NAMELY THE TWO PARTS OF DA'AT THAT JOINS ABA AND IMA, SINCE ZEIR ANPIN INHERITS ALL THREE PARTS, CHOCHMAH, BINAH AND DA'AT FROM ABA AND IMA. For from his father's side a crown called Chesed was hidden within DA'AT and from his mother's side a crown called Gvurah. And all are crowned on the head OF ZEIR ANPIN and He holds to them. When Aba and Ima shine on Him BY MEANS OF THE INHERITANCE OF CHOCHMAH AND BINAH AND THE TWO PARTS OF DA'AT, they are all called the head Tefilin, THE SECRET OF THE FOUR PARAGRAPHS, SINCE THE INHERITANCE OF CHOCHMAH AND BINAH ARE, "SANCTIFY TO ME ALL THE FIRSTBORN (HEB. *KADESH LI*)" (SHEMOT 13:2), AND "AND IT SHALL BE, WHEN HASHEM YOUR ELOHIM SHALL BRING YOU (HEB. *VEHAYAH KI YEVIACHA*)" (DEVARIM 6:10); AND THE TWO PARTS OF DA'AT ARE, "HEAR O YISRAEL (HEB. *SH'MA YISRAEL*)" (DEVARIM 6:4), AND "AND IT SHALL COME TO PASS, IF YOU

HEARKEN (HEB. *VEHAYAH IM SHAMO'A*)." And this son takes and inherits everything, and it spreads within Him throughout the body. This son, ZEIR ANPIN, gives to the daughter, MALCHUT, who is fed from Him. In any case IT IS UNDERSTOOD from this that the son inherits rather than the daughter; the son inherits His father and mother, not the daughter, and the daughter is nourished by Him, as said ABOUT THE TREE THAT ALLUDES TO ZEIR ANPIN, "and on it was food for all" (Daniel 4:18).

90. הָנֵי אָב וָאֵם, כְּלִילָן וּמִתְחַבְּרָן דָּא בְּדָא. וְאָב טָמִיר יַתִּיר. וְכֹלָּא אָחִיד מֵעַתִּיקָא קַדִּישָׁא, וְתַלְיָא מִמַּזָּלָא קַדִּישָׁא, יָקִירוּ דְּכָל יַקִּירִין. וְאִלֵּין אָב וָאֵם, מְתַקְּנִין בֵּיתָא, כְּמָה דַּאֲמֵינָא דִּכְתִּיב, בְּחָכְמָה יִבָּנֶה בָּיִת וּבִתְבוּנָה יִתְכּוֹנָן וּבְדַעַת חֲדָרִים יִמָּלְאוּ כָּל הוֹן יָקָר וְנָעִים. וּכְתִיב כִּי נָעִים כִּי תִשְׁמְרֵם בְּבִטְנֶךָ.

90. These father and mother are included in and unite with each other, and Aba is more hidden THAN IMA. Everything is attached to Atika Kadisha, THAT IS, THE CONCEALED BRAIN, coming from the precious Mazal, which is most precious, SINCE THEY DO NOT RECEIVE STRAIGHT FROM ATIKA KADISHA BUT THROUGH THE BEARD CALLED MAZAL. The father and mother prepare the house, as I said regarding the secret of, "Through wisdom (Chochmah) a house is built; and by understanding (Tevunah) it is established; and by knowledge (Da'at) are the chambers filled with all precious and pleasant riches" (Mishlei 24:3), WHICH ARE CHOCHMAH, BINAH AND DA'AT OF ZEIR ANPIN. It is also written, "For it is a pleasant thing if you keep them within you" (Mishlei 22:18).

91. אר"ש, בְּאִדְּרָא לָא גָּלֵינָא כֹּלָּא. וְכָל הָנֵי מִלִּין, טְמִירִין בְּלִבָּאי הֲווֹ עַד הַשְׁתָּא, וּבָעֵינָא לְאַטְמְרָא לוֹן לְעָלְמָא דְּאָתֵי, מִשּׁוּם דְּתַמָּן שְׁאֶלְתָּא שָׁאִיל לָנָא, כְּמָה דִּכְתִּיב וְהָיָה אֱמוּנַת עִתֶּךָ חוֹסֶן יְשׁוּעוֹת חָכְמָה וָדָעַת וְגוֹ', וְחָכְמָה בַּעְיָין מִינִי, וְהַשְׁתָּא רְעוּתָא דְקוּדְשָׁא בְּרִיךְ הוּא בְּהַאי, הָא בְּלָא כְּסוּפָא אִיעוּל קַמֵּי פַּלְטְרוֹי.

91. Rabbi Shimon said, In the Idra RABA IN NASO I have not disclosed everything, and all these matters were hidden in my heart until this moment.

26. Inheritance and the two crowns in Chochmah, Binah and Da'at of Zeir Anpin

I wanted to conceal them for the World to Come, because there, IN THE WORLD TO COME, we are asked a question ABOUT WISDOM, as written, "And He shall be the stability of your times, a store of salvation, wisdom and knowledge…" (Yeshayah 33:6), since wisdom is asked of one. HE THEREFORE CONCEALED THESE MATTERS TO THE WORLD TO COME. Now I SEE that the Holy One, blessed be He, wishes it TO REVEAL THEM, in order that I shall come in without shame before His palaces.

27. Undisclosed Da'at, Da'at that is shining in the head, expanding Da'at

A Synopsis

Rabbi Shimon tells us about the three types of Da'at in Zeir Anpin, and he also talks about how God established a testimony in Jacob. Rabbi Shimon tells the other rabbis that he has known these matters for a long time but was afraid to reveal them, and now they are revealed. He laughs and weeps over what he is and is not allowed to reveal, and he says that he has only this one day at his disposal to tell what he wants to tell. And we find that he wants to reveal things so that he will not enter the World to Come in shame.

/

92. כְּתִיב כִּי אֵל דֵּעוֹת יְיָ׳. דֵּעוֹת וַדַּאי. הוּא הַדַּעַת, בְּדַעַת כָּל פַּלְטְרִי אִתְמַלְיָין, דִּכְתִּיב, וּבְדַעַת חֲדָרִים יִמָּלְאוּ. דַּעַת אַחֲרָא, לָא אִתְגַּלְיָא, דְּהָא טְמִירָא אָזִיל בְּגַוֵּויהּ, וְאִתְכְּלִיל בֵּיהּ. דַּעַת נָהִיר בְּמוֹחִין, וְאִתְפְּשַׁט בְּמוֹחָא כֹּלָּא.

92. It is written, "For Hashem is an El of knowledge (lit. 'knowledges')" (I Shmuel 2:3). Surely knowledges IN PLURAL, BECAUSE THERE ARE THREE TYPES OF DA'AT IN ZEIR ANPIN: 1) It is THE BRAIN OF Da'at, because through Da'at all palaces are filled, as written, "and by knowledge (Heb. *Da'at*) are the chambers filled with all precious and pleasant riches" (Mishlei 24:3); 2) Another Da'at CORRESPONDS TO THIS, which is not revealed but flows within it secretly and is included within it; 3) Da'at that shines into the parts of the brain and spreads throughout the brain BUT NOT INTO THE BODY.

93. בְּסִפְרָא דְּאַגַּדְתָּא תָּנֵינָן, כִּי אֵל דֵּעוֹת יְיָ׳, אַל תִּקְרֵי דֵּעוֹת, אֶלָּא עֵדוּת. דְּהוּא סַהֲדוּתָא דְּכֹלָּא, סַהֲדוּתָא דִּתְרֵין חוּלָקִין, כד״א וַיָּקֶם עֵדוּת בְּיַעֲקֹב. ואע״ג דְּהַאי מִלָּה, אוֹקְמוּהָ בְּסִפְרָא דִּצְנִיעוּתָא בְּגַוְונָא אַחֲרָא. הָתָם בְּאַתְרֵיהּ שְׁלִים, הָכָא כֹּלָּא שַׁפִּיר, וְכֹלָּא הֲוֵי, כַּד אַסְתִּים מִלָּה.

93. In the book of Agadah we studied, "Hashem is an El of knowledge (Heb. *de'ot*)." Do not pronounce 'de'ot' but '*edut* (Eng. 'testimony')', for it bears testimony about everything, the testimony of two portions, WHICH

MEANS IT INCLUDES WITHIN IT CHOCHMAH AND BINAH, WHICH ARE TWO PORTIONS, as written, "For He established a testimony in Jacob" (Tehilim 78:5), SINCE ZEIR ANPIN CALLED JACOB IS THE SECRET OF DA'AT THAT INCORPORATES CHOCHMAH AND BINAH. And though it has been explained differently in Safra Detzniuta (the CONCEALED Book), THAT CIRCUMCISION IS CALLED TESTIMONY, IT IS NOT IN THE CONCEALED BOOK IN OUR POSSESSION, BUT THEY HAD KABBALAH BOOKS THAT THEY CALLED SO. There, where it belongs THE EXPLANATION is complete, and ALSO here everything is correct. Everything should be EXPLAINED IN THE TEXT by concealing the matter BY HINTS.

94. הַאי אָב וָאֵם, כֻּלְּהוּ בְּהוּ כְּלִילָן, כֹּלָּא בְּהוּ סְתִימָן, וְאִינּוּן סְתִימָן בְּמַזָּלָא קַדִּישָׁא, עַתִּיקָא דְּכָל עַתִּיקִין. בֵּיהּ סְתִימָן. בֵּיהּ כְּלִילָן. כֹּלָּא הוּא, כֹּלָּא הֲוֵי. בְּרִיךְ הוּא, בְּרִיךְ שְׁמֵיהּ, לְעָלַם וּלְעָלְמֵי עָלְמִין.

94. Everything is included within these Aba and Ima, and everything is hidden within them. They are concealed AND ARE INCLUDED in the holy Mazal, NAMELY THE BEARD of the most ancient, ARICH ANPIN. They are concealed within it, incorporated in it. Everything is ATIKA, and ATIKA is everything. Blessed be He, and blessed be His name forever and ever.

95. כָּל מִלִּין דְּאִדְּרָא יָאוּת, וְכֻלְּהוּ מִלִּין קַדִּישִׁין, מִלִּין דְּלָא סָטָאן לִימִינָא וְלִשְׂמָאלָא, כֻּלְּהוּ מִלִּין דִּסְתִּימִין, וְאִתְגַּלְיָין לְאִינּוּן דְּעָאלוּ וְנַפְקוּ, וְכֹלָּא הָכִי הוּא. וְעַד הַשְׁתָּא הֲווֹ מִתְכַּסְיָין אִלֵּין מִלִּין, דְּדָחִילְנָא לְגַלָּאָה, וְהַשְׁתָּא אִתְגַּלְיָין. וְגַלֵּי קַמֵּי עַתִּיקָא קַדִּישָׁא, דְּהָא לָא לִיקָרָא דִּילִי, וּדְבֵית אַבָּא עֲבִידְנָא, אֶלָּא בְּגִין דְּלָא אִיעוּל בְּכִסּוּפָא קָמֵי פַּלְטְרוֹי עֲבִידְנָא. וְעוֹד, הָא חֲמֵינָא, דְקוּדְשָׁא בְּרִיךְ הוּא, וְכָל הָנֵי זַכָּאֵי קְשׁוֹט דְּהָכָא מִשְׁתַּכְּחָן, כֻּלְּהוּ מִסְתַּכְּמִין עַל יְדִי. דְּהָא חֲמֵינָא דְּכֻלְּהוּ חַדָּאן בְּהַאי הִלּוּלָא דִּילִי, וְכֻלְּהוּ זְמִינִין בְּהַהוּא עָלְמָא בְּהִילּוּלָא דִּילִי, זַכָּאָה חוּלָקִי.

95. All the matters in the Idra RABA are correct and they are all are holy matters, which stray neither right nor left. They are all hidden matters, revealed to those who entered WISDOM and came out OF IT COMPLETELY. All mysteries are in such a way THAT THEY ARE REVEALED SOLELY TO THOSE WHO CAME IN AND CAME OUT. Until now these matters, WHICH I HAVE DISCLOSED HERE, were hidden, because I was afraid to reveal them. Now they are revealed. It is known before Atika Kadisha that neither for my own glory nor for THE GLORY OF my father's house did I do this, but I did it so I would not enter shamefully before His palace. Moreover, I saw the Holy One, blessed be He, and all the truly righteous present here, all agreed with me THAT I SHOULD REVEAL THEM. For I have seen them all rejoicing in my joy, and that they are all invited to my feast in that world, happy is my portion.

96. א"ר אַבָּא, כַּד סַיֵּים מִלָּה דָּא בּוּצִינָא קַדִּישָׁא, בּוּצִינָא עִלָּאָה, אָרִים יְדוֹי, וּבָכָה וְחַיִיךְ. בָּעָא לְגַלָּאָה מִלָּה חֲדָא. אָמַר, בְּמִלָּה דָּא אִצְטָעַרְנָא כָּל יוֹמָאי, וְהַשְׁתָּא לָא יָהֲבִין לִי רְשׁוּתָא. אִתְתָּקַף, וְיָתִיב, וְרָחִישׁ בְּשִׂפְוָותֵיהּ, וְסָגִיד תְּלַת זִמְנִין, וְלָא הֲוָה יָכִיל ב"נ לְאִסְתַּכְּלָא בַּאֲתְרֵיהּ, כ"ש בֵּיהּ. אָמַר, פּוּמָא פּוּמָא, דְּזָכִית לְכָל הַאי, לָא אַנְגִּיבוּ מַבּוּעָךְ. מַבּוּעָךְ נָפִיק וְלָא פָּסַק. עֲלָךְ קָרֵינָן וְנָהָר יוֹצֵא מֵעֵדֶן. וּכְתִיב וּכְמוֹצָא מַיִם אֲשֶׁר לֹא יְכַזְּבוּ מֵימָיו.

96. Rabbi Aba said, When the Holy Luminary completed this word, the Supernal Luminary raised his hands, wept and laughed, because he wanted to reveal something. He said, All my life I was distressed about this matter TO REVEAL IT, but now I am not given permission. He drew strength and sat down and his lips were murmuring. He prostrated three times, and no one could look at where he was, let alone directly at him. He said, Mouth, mouth, you have merited all this and your streams have not dried up. Your stream gushes forth ceaselessly. We recite of you, "And a river went out of Eden" (Beresheet 2:10), and, "like a spring of water, whose waters fail not" (Yeshayah 58:11).

97. הָאִידָּנָא אַסְהַדְנָא עָלַי. דְּכָל יוֹמִין דְּקָאֵימְנָא, תָּאִיבְנָא לְמֶחֱמֵי יוֹמָא דָּא, וְלָא סָלִיק בִּידִי, בַּר הָאִידָּנָא, דְּהָא בְּעִטְרָא דָּא מִתְעֲטָּר הַאי יוֹמָא. וְהַשְׁתָּא בָּעֵינָא לְגַלָּאָה מִלִּין, קַמֵּיהּ דְּקוּדְשָׁא בְּרִיךְ הוּא, דְּהָא

27. Undisclosed Da'at, Da'at that is shining in the head, expanding Da'at

כֻּלְּהוּ מִתְעַטְּרִין בְּרֵישִׁי. וְהַאי יוֹמָא לָא יִתְרַחֵק לְמֵיעַל לְדוּכְתֵּיהּ, בְּיוֹמָא אַחֲרָא. דְּהָא כָּל יוֹמָא דָּא בִּרְשׁוּתִי קַיְּימָא. וְהַשְׁתָּא שָׁרֵינָא לְגַלָּאָה מִלִּין, בְּגִין דְּלָא אִיעוּל בְּכִסּוּפָא לְעָלְמָא דְּאָתֵי. וְהָא שָׁרֵינָא אֵימָא.

97. Now I testify about myself that all the days I lived IN THE WORLD I yearned to see this day, IN WHICH I WOULD HAVE PERMISSION TO REVEAL THESE SECRETS, but never succeeded, except for now because this day is crowned with this crown OF REVEALING SECRETS. And now I wish to reveal matters before the Holy One, blessed be He, because all THE SECRETS I REVEAL are crowned on my head. And this day will not be far from coming to its place IN THAT WORLD on another day. For all this day is at my disposal AND NO MORE. And now let me begin to reveal things so I should not enter with shame into the World to Come. Here, let me start speaking.

28. The union of Male and Female called Righteousness and Justice

A Synopsis

Rabbi Shimon tells how he sees that the illumination of all grades is joined in the one light and emanates ultimately from the hidden light within which dwells the Endless Light, that which can never be comprehended nor revealed. He talks about the perfect justice of God, saying that his judgments are always judgments of truth. We learn that there are two luminaries that establish the throne of God – these are called Righteousness and Justice. Everything is concealed in Justice, and Righteousness is nourished by this Justice. Rabbi Shimon talks about the state of mercy and perfection when male and female join and all the worlds are in a state of mercy and joy. And yet when the world is full of sin the male and female are separated and the serpent is aroused. At that time Severe Judgments prevail and many righteous people leave the world. When, however, there is a perfectly righteous person in the world who loves God, the world can still be saved for his sake. Rabbi Shimon tells us that before he sinned, King David was not afraid of any Judgment, not even of Righteousness, and yet after he sinned he was afraid even of Justice. Rabbi Shimon concludes that after he himself leaves the world there will not be any righteous people significant enough to protect the people of that generation.

98. כְּתִיב, צֶדֶק וּמִשְׁפָּט מְכוֹן כִּסְאֶךָ חֶסֶד וֶאֱמֶת יְקַדְּמוּ פָּנֶיךָ. מַאן חַכִּימָא, יִסְתָּכַּל בְּהַאי, לְמֶחֱמֵי אוֹרְחוֹי דְּקַדִּישָׁא עִלָּאָה, דִּינִין דִּקְשׁוֹט, דִּינִין דְּמִתְעַטְּרִין בְּכִתְרִי עִלָּאִין. דְּהָא חֲמֵינָא דְּכֻלְּהוּ בּוּצִינִין נַהֲרִין מִבּוּצִינָא עִלָּאָה, טְמִירָא דְּכָל טְמִירִין, כֻּלְּהוּ דַּרְגִּין לְאִתְנַהֲרָא. וּבְהַהוּא נְהוֹרָא דִּבְכָל דַּרְגָּא וְדַרְגָּא, אִתְגַּלְיָיא מַה דְּאִתְגַּלְיָיא, וְכֻלְּהוּ נְהוֹרִין אֲחִידָן, נְהוֹרָא דָּא בִּנְהוֹרָא דָּא, וּנְהוֹרָא דָּא, בִּנְהוֹרָא דָּא, וְנַהֲרִין דָּא בְּדָא, וְלָא מִתְפָּרְשָׁן דָּא מִן דָּא.

98. It is written, "Righteousness and justice are the foundation of Your throne; love and truth shall go before You" (Tehilim 89:15). Who is wise to observe this to see the ways of the Holy Supernal One, that they are judgments of truth, judgments adorned with supernal Sfirot. For I see all luminaries shine from the most hidden supernal luminary, WHICH IS ATIKA;

all GRADES are illuminated grades, AS EACH HAS ITS UNIQUE ILLUMINATION, and by the light within each and every grade something is revealed, NAMELY EACH HAS ITS OWN UNIQUE REVELATION. And all lights are attached to each other and shine into each other, not separating from each other.

99. נְהוֹרָא דְּכָל בּוּצִינָא וּבוּצִינָא, דְּאִקְרוּן תִּקּוּנֵי מַלְכָּא, כִּתְרֵי מַלְכָּא, כָּל חַד וְחַד, נָהִיר וְאָחִיד בְּהַהוּא נְהוֹרָא דִּלְגּוֹ לְגוֹ, וְלָא מִתְפְּרַשׁ לְבַר. ובג״כ כֹּלָּא בְּחַד דַּרְגָּא אִסְתְּלַק, וְכֹלָּא בְּחַד מִלָּה אִתְעֲטָר, וְלָא מִתְפְּרַשׁ דָּא מִן דָּא, אִיהוּ וּשְׁמֵיהּ חַד הוּא. נְהוֹרָא דְּאִתְגַּלְיָיא, אִקְרֵי לְבוּשָׁא דְּמַלְכָּא. נְהוֹרָא דִּלְגּוֹ לְגוֹ, נְהוֹרָא סָתִים, וּבֵיהּ שַׁרְיָא הַהוּא דְּלָא אִתְפְּרַשׁ וְלָא אִתְגַּלְיָיא.

99. The light within each of the luminaries that are called the King's characteristics, the King's Sfirot, each, NAMELY EACH LIGHT, shines and is attached to the light in the innermost. THAT IS, IT IS ABSOLUTELY INCONCEIVABLE. For that reason all amounts to the same grade, everything is adorned by the same thing and is inseparable from the other, He and His name are one. He, the revealed light, is called the King's garment. The light in the innermost OF ALL LIGHTS is a hidden light, within which dwells that which is neither explicable nor revealed, THE BLESSED THE ENDLESS LIGHT.

100. וְכֻלְּהוּ בּוּצִינֵי, וְכֻלְּהוּ נְהוֹרִין, נַהֲרִין מֵעַתִּיקָא קַדִּישָׁא סְתִימָא דְּכָל סְתִימִין, בּוּצִינָא עִלָּאָה. וְכַד מִסְתַּכְּלָן, כֻּלְּהוּ נְהוֹרִין דְּאִתְפַּשְּׁטָן. לָא אִשְׁתְּכַח בַּר בּוּצִינָא עִלָּאָה, דְּאַטְמָר וְלָא אִתְגַּלְיָיא.

100. All luminaries and all lights shine from the most concealed Atika Kadisha that is the supernal luminary. When observing, within all lights spreading FROM ATIKA there is only some of the hidden, non-revealed supernal light.

101. בְּאִינּוּן לְבוּשִׁין דִּיקַר, לְבוּשֵׁי קְשׁוֹט, תִּקּוּנֵי קְשׁוֹט, בּוּצִינֵי קְשׁוֹט,

אִשְׁתְּכָחוּ תְּרֵין בּוּצִינִין, תִּקּוּנָא דְּכוּרְסְיָיא דְּמַלְכָּא, וְאִקְרוּן צֶדֶק וּמִשְׁפָּט. וְאִינּוּן שֵׁירוּתָא, וּשְׁלֵימוּתָא, בְּכָל מְהֵימְנוּתָא. וּבְהָנֵי מִתְעַטְּרִין כָּל דִּינִין דִּלְעֵילָּא וְתַתָּא, וְכֹלָּא סָתִים בְּמִשְׁפָּט. וְצֶדֶק מֵהַאי מִשְׁפָּט אִתְּזָן. וּלְזִמְנִין קָרֵינָן לָהּ, וּמַלְכִּי צֶדֶק מֶלֶךְ שָׁלֵם.

101. Within these garments of glory, garments of truth, true establishments and true lights, there are two luminaries, which establish the King's throne, WHICH IS BINAH, and which are called Righteousness and Justice. THEY ARE ZEIR ANPIN THAT IS CALLED JUSTICE AND MALCHUT CALLED RIGHTEOUSNESS. They are the beginning and the completion in the whole faith, SINCE JUSTICE IS AT THE BEGINNING AND THE REVEALING OF PERFECTION WITHIN RIGHTEOUSNESS IS CALLED JUSTICE, and with these all Judgments above and below are adorned. Everything is concealed in Justice, WHICH IS ZEIR ANPIN, and Righteousness, WHICH IS MALCHUT, is nourished by this Justice, WHICH IS ZEIR ANPIN. And sometimes MALCHUT is called, "Melchizedek king of Salem" (Beresheet 14:18).

102. כַּד מִתְעָרִין דִּינִין מִמִּשְׁפָּט, כֻּלְּהוּ רַחֲמֵי, כֻּלְּהוּ בִּשְׁלִימוּ. דְּהַאי מְבַסֵּם לְהַאי צֶדֶק, וְדִינִין מִתְתַּקְּנִין, וְכֻלְּהוּ נַחְתִּין לְעָלְמָא בִּשְׁלִימוּ, בְּרַחֲמֵי. וּכְדֵין שַׁעֲתָא דְּמִתְחַבְּרָן דְּכַר וְנוּקְבָא, וְכָל עָלְמִין כֻּלְּהוּ בְּרַחֲמֵי, וּבְחֶדְוָותָא.

102. When Judgments are roused from Justice, they are all in a state of mercy and perfection. For this JUSTICE mitigates Righteousness, WHICH IS JUDGMENTS; Judgments are established and all descend into the world in perfection and mercy. It is then the time when male and female join and all worlds are in a state of mercy and joy.

103. וְכַד אַסְגִּיאוּ חוֹבֵי עָלְמָא, וְאִסְתַּאֲבַת מַקְדְּשָׁא, וּדְכוּרָא אִתְרְחַק מִן נוּקְבָא, וְחִוְיָא תַּקִּיפָא שַׁרְיָא לְאִתְעָרָא, וַוי לְעָלְמָא דְּמִתְּזָן בְּהַהוּא זִמְנָא מֵהַאי צֶדֶק. כַּמָּה חֲבִילֵי טְרִיקִין מִתְעָרִין בְּעָלְמָא, כַּמָּה זַכָּאִין מִסְתַּלְּקִין מֵעָלְמָא. וְכָל כַּךְ לָמָּה. בְּגִין דְּאִתְרְחַק דְּכוּרָא מִן נוּקְבָא, וּמִשְׁפָּט לָא קָרֵיב בְּצֶדֶק דָּא. וְעַל הַאי כְּתִיב, וְיֵשׁ נִסְפֶּה בְּלֹא מִשְׁפָּט,

דְּמִשְׁפָּט אִתְרְחַק מֵהַאי צֶדֶק, וְלָא אִתְבַּסְמָא, וְצֶדֶק יַנְקָא מֵאֲתָר אָחֳרָא.

103. When people's iniquities multiply and the Temple, MALCHUT, is defiled BY THEIR INIQUITIES, the male, ZEIR ANPIN, departs from the female, MALCHUT, and the fierce serpent begins to arouse. Woe to the world that is nourished at that time by righteousness, WHICH IS MALCHUT SEPARATED FROM ZEIR ANPIN THAT IS JUSTICE. Many legions of demons arouse in the world and many righteous people depart from the world. All this is because the male has left the female, and Justice does not approach this Righteousness. Of this it is written, "but sometimes ruin comes for want of judgment (Justice)" (Mishlei 13:23), WHICH MEANS THAT Justice, WHICH IS ZEIR ANPIN, departs from righteousness, and MALCHUT is not mitigated but Righteousness is fed from another place, NAMELY LEFT WITHOUT THE RIGHT, WHICH IS SEVERE JUDGMENTS.

104. וְעַ"ד אָמַר שְׁלֹמֹה מַלְכָּא, אֶת הַכֹּל רָאִיתִי בִּימֵי הֶבְלִי יֵשׁ צַדִּיק אוֹבֵד בְּצִדְקוֹ וְגוֹ', הָבֶל דָּא, הָבֶל חֲדָא, מֵהֲבָלִים דִּלְעֵילָּא, דְּאִקְרוֹן אַפֵּי מַלְכָּא, וְדָא אִיהוּ מַלְכוּתָא קַדִּישָׁא, דְּכַד הִיא מִתַּעְרָא בְּדִינוֹי, כְּתִיב יֵשׁ צַדִּיק אוֹבֵד בְּצִדְקוֹ. מ"ט. מִשּׁוּם דְּמִשְׁפָּט אִתְרְחַק מִצֶּדֶק. וּבְגִ"כ אִקְרֵי, וְיֵשׁ נִסְפֶּה בְּלֹא מִשְׁפָּט.

104. King Solomon said of this, "All things have I seen in the days of my vanity. There is a just man who perishes in his righteousness" (Kohelet 7:15). The reason is that Justice has departed from righteousness, AND MALCHUT REMAINS AS LEFT WITHOUT RIGHT. For that reason it is considered that "sometimes ruin comes for want of justice."

105. תָּ"ח, כַּד אִשְׁתְּכַח זַכָּאָה עִלָּאָה בְּעָלְמָא, רְחִימָא דְקוּדְשָׁא בְּרִיךְ הוּא, אֲפִילוּ כַּד אִתְּעַר צֶדֶק בִּלְחוֹדוֹי, יָכִיל עָלְמָא לְאִשְׁתְּזָבָא בְּגִינֵיהּ. וְקוּדְשָׁא בְּרִיךְ הוּא בָּעֵי בִּיקָרֵיהּ, וְלָא מִסְתָּפֵי מִן דִּינָא. וְכַד הַהוּא זַכָּאָה לָא קַיְימָא בְּקִיּוּמֵיהּ, מִסְתָּפֵי אֲפִילוּ מִמִּשְׁפָּט, וְלָא יָכִיל לְמֵיקָם בֵּיהּ. כ"ש בְּצֶדֶק.

105. Come and see, when there is a lofty righteous man in the world, loving the Holy One, blessed be He, even when Righteousness is roused on its own WITHOUT JUSTICE, the world can still be saved for his sake, for the Holy One, blessed be He, delights in his glory and he fears no Judgment. When this righteous man is not alive, people are afraid even of Justice and cannot handle it, not to mention righteousness.

106. דָּוִד מַלְכָּא, בְּקַדְמֵיתָא אָמַר, בְּחָנֵנִי יְיָ׳ וְנַסֵּנִי. דְּהָא אֲנָא לָא מִסְתַּפֵינָא מִכָּל דִּינִין, אֲפִילּוּ מֵהַאי צֶדֶק, וכ״ש דַּאֲחִידְנָא בֵּיהּ, מַה כְּתִיב. אֲנִי בְּצֶדֶק אֶחֱזֶה פָנֶיךָ, בְּצֶדֶק וַדַּאי. לָא מִסְתַּפֵינָא לְמֵיקָם בְּדִינוֹי. בָּתַר דְּחָב, אֲפִילּוּ מִמִּשְׁפָּט מִסְתָּפֵי, דִּכְתִּיב וְאַל תָּבֹא בְמִשְׁפָּט אֶת עַבְדֶּךָ. ת״ח, כַּד מִתְבַּסְמָא הַאי צֶדֶק מִמִּשְׁפָּט, כְּדֵין אִקְרֵי צְדָקָה. וְעָלְמָא מִתְבַּסְמָא בְּחֶסֶד, וְאִתְמַלְיָא מִנֵּיהּ. דִּכְתִּיב, אוֹהֵב צְדָקָה וּמִשְׁפָּט חֶסֶד יְיָ׳ מָלְאָה הָאָרֶץ.

106. At first, King David said, "Examine me, Hashem, and prove me" (Tehilim 26:2), for I am not afraid of any Judgment, not even of Righteousness. Moreover, I am attached to it, SINCE DAVID WAS A CHARIOT TO MALCHUT. It is written, "As for me, I will behold Your face in righteousness (Heb. *tzedek*)" (Tehilim 17:15), with Righteousness assuredly. I am not afraid to face its Judgments. After he sinned he was afraid even of Justice, as written, "And enter not into justice with Your servant" (Tehilim 143:2). Come and see, when this Righteousness (Heb. *tzedek*) is mitigated by Justice it is called Righteousness (Heb. *tzedakah*) WITH A FEMININE SUFFIX, BECAUSE IT BECOMES A FEMALE TO ZEIR ANPIN THAT IS CALLED JUSTICE, AND RECEIVES CHASSADIM FROM IT, the world is sweetened with Chesed and filled with it, as written, "He loves righteousness (Heb. *tzedakah*) and judgment. The earth is full of the goodness (Chesed) of Hashem" (Tehilim 33:5).

107. אַסְהַדְנָא עָלַי, דְּכָל יוֹמָאי הֲוֵינָא מִצְטַעֵר עַל עָלְמָא, דְּלָא יֶעֱרַע בְּדִינוֹי דְּצֶדֶק, וְלָא יוֹקִיד עָלְמָא בְּשַׁלְהוֹבוֹי. כְּמָה דִּכְתִּיב, אָכְלָה וּמָחֲתָה פִּיהָ. מִכָּאן וּלְהָלְאָה, כְּפוּם כָּל חַד, כְּפוּם בֵּירָא עִמְקָא, וְהָא בְּדָרָא דָּא אִית בֵּיהּ זַכָּאִין, וּזְעִירִין אִינּוּן דִּיקוּמוּן לְאַגָּנָא עַל עָלְמָא,

וְעַל עָאנָא, מֵאַרְבָעָה זִיוְיָן.

107. I bear testimony about myself that I was distressed about the world all my life lest it would meet the Judgments of Righteousness and be burned by its flames, as written, "she eats, and wipes her mouth" (Mishlei 30:20). From now on, AFTER MY DEMISE, THE WORLD WILL BEHAVE according to THE DEEDS OF everyone. As is the pit, SO IS its depth, THAT IS, DEEDS ARE REPAID MEASURE FOR MEASURE. In this generation there are righteous people but they are too insignificant to rise up and protect the people of the generation from the four directions OF THE WORLD.

29. Zeir Anpin

A Synopsis

Rabbi Shimon reveals some things about Zeir Anpin that were not revealed in the Idra Raba. He first repeats what the rabbis already know about how Zeir Anpin derives from Atika Kadisha. Next he talks about the kings of Edom who died because everything had not yet been properly established in Malchut. We learn that male and female cannot flourish without each other. Malchut is the daughter of both Chochmah and Binah and is fed from both aspects that radiate in two ways – with Chesed and with Judgments. Lastly Rabbi Shimon describes how the first worlds were destroyed like sparks that are extinguished immediately.

108. ע״כ אֲחִידָן מִלֵּי דָא בְּדָא, וּמִתְפָּרְשָׁן מִלִּין דִּסְתִימִין בְּעַתִּיקָא קַדִּישָׁא, סְתִימָא דְּכָל סְתִימִין, וְהֵיךְ אֲחִידָן אִלֵּין בְּאִלֵּין. מִכָּאן לְהָלְאָה, מִלִּין דִּזְעֵיר אַנְפִּין, אִינּוּן דְּלָא אִתְגַּלְיָין בְּאִדְרָא. אִינּוּן דַּהֲווֹ סְתִימִין בְּלִבָּאי, וְתַמָּן לָא אִתְקָנוּ. הַשְׁתָּא אִתְתְּקָנוּ וְאִתְגַּלְיָין, וְכֻלְּהוּ מִלִּין סְתִימִין, וּבְרִירִין כֻּלְּהוּ. זַכָּאָה חוּלָקִי, וְאִינּוּן דְּיָרְתוּ יְרוּתָא דָא, דִּכְתִּיב אַשְׁרֵי הָעָם שֶׁכָּכָה לוֹ וְגוֹ'.

108. Up until now my words were interconnected, and the concealed matters in the most hidden Atika Kadisha were explained, and how the ones are connected to the others, THAT IS, HOW THE THREE HEADS OF ATIKA ARE MUTUALLY ATTACHED, HOW THE BEARD IS ATTACHED TO ATIKA, AND HOW ABA AND IMA ARE CONNECTED TO THE BEARD. The following are matters that pertain to Zeir Anpin that were not revealed in the Idra RABA, those concealed in my heart, where they did not manifest. Now they are manifested and disclosed. All these matters are hidden yet clear. Blessed is my portion and that of those who receive this inheritance, as written, "Happy is the people, that is in such a case…" (Tehilim 144:15).

109. הַאי דְּאוּקִימְנָא, אָב וָאֵם בְּעַתִּיקָא אֲחִידָן, בְּתִיקּוּנוֹי, הָכִי הוּא. דְּהָא מִמּוֹחָא סְתִימָאָה דְּכָל סְתִימִין תַּלְיָין, וּמִתְאַחֲדָן בֵּיהּ. וְכַד יִסְתַּכְּלוּן מִלֵּי. כֹּלָּא הוּא עַתִּיקָא בִּלְחוּדוֹי, הוּא הֲוֵי, וְהוּא יְהֵא. וְכָל הָנֵי תִּקּוּנִין בֵּיהּ. אָ״ב וָאֵ״ם מֵהַאי מוֹחָא נַפְקוּ, אִתְכְּלִילוּ בְּמַזָּלָא, וּבֵיהּ

תַּלְיָין, וּבֵיהּ אֲחִידָן. זְעֵיר אַנְפִּין, בְּעַתִּיקָא קַדִּישָׁא תַּלְיָיא וְאָחִיד. וְהָא אוֹקִימְנָא מִלֵּי בְּאִדְּרָא. זַכָּאָה חוּלָקֵיהּ דְּמַאן דְּעָאל וְנָפִיק, וְיִנְדַּע אוֹרְחִין דְּלָא יִסְטֵי לִימִינָא וְלִשְׂמָאלָא. וּמַאן דְּלָא עָאל וְנָפַק, טַב לֵיהּ דְּלָא אִבְרֵי. וּכְתִיב כִּי יְשָׁרִים דַּרְכֵי יְיָ׳.

109. This we have explained, that Aba and Ima are attached to the manifestations of Atika, THAT IS, TO THE BEARD THAT MANIFESTED. It is so, because they derive from the most concealed brain and are attached to it. When they examine what I say THEY WILL SEE that everything is only Atika, that was, is and will be, and that all those manifestations are in it. Aba and Ima come out of this CONCEALED brain and are a part of Mazal. They derive from and are attached to it. Zeir Anpin derives from Atika Kadisha and is attached to it. We have already explained these issues in the Idra RABA. Blessed is the portion of he who came into WISDOM and came out IN PEACE, and who knows the paths not to deviate right or left BUT BE IN THE CENTRAL COLUMN. And whoever has not come in and out IN PEACE, it is better for him had he not been born, as it is also written, "for the ways of Hashem are right" (Hoshea 14:10).

110. אָמַר רִבִּי שִׁמְעוֹן, מִסְתַּכֵּל הֲוֵינָא כָּל יוֹמָא בְּהַאי קְרָא, דִּכְתִּיב, בַּיְיָ׳ תִּתְהַלֵּל נַפְשִׁי יִשְׁמְעוּ עֲנָוִים וְיִשְׂמָחוּ. וְהָאִידָּנָא אִתְקְיָים קְרָא כֹּלָּא. בַּיְיָ׳ תִּתְהַלֵּל נַפְשִׁי וַדַּאי, דְּהָא נִשְׁמָתִי בֵּיהּ אֲחִידָא, בֵּיהּ לַהֲטָא, בֵּיהּ אִתְדַּבְקַת וְאִשְׁתַּדְּלַת וּבְאִשְׁתַּדְּלוּתָא דָּא תִּסְתַּלַּק לְאַתְרָהָא. יִשְׁמְעוּ עֲנָוִים וְיִשְׂמָחוּ, כָּל הָנֵי צַדִּיקַיָּיא, וְכָל בְּנֵי מְתִיבְתָּא קַדִּישָׁא, וְזַכָּאִין דְּאַתְיָין הַשְׁתָּא עִם קוּדְשָׁא בְּרִיךְ הוּא, כֻּלְּהוּ שַׁמְעִין מִלַּי, וְחַדָּאן. בְּגִין כָּךְ, גַּדְּלוּ לַיְיָ׳ אִתִּי וּנְרוֹמְמָה שְׁמוֹ יַחְדָּיו.

110. Rabbi Shimon said, All my life I observed this verse that says, "My soul shall glory in Hashem; the humble shall hear of it, and be glad" (Tehilim 34:3), and now the whole verse is fulfilled. Surely "My soul shall glory in Hashem," because my soul is attached to Him, glows from Him, cleaves to Him and strives, through which striving it shall rise to its place. "the humble shall hear of it, and be glad" relates to all the righteous, the members of the holy Yeshivah, and the righteous who have come now with the Shechinah. They all listen to my words and rejoice. For that reason, "O magnify Hashem with me, and let us exalt His name together" (Ibid. 4).

111. פָּתַח וְאָמַר, כְּתִיב, וְאֵלֶּה הַמְּלָכִים אֲשֶׁר מָלְכוּ בְּאֶרֶץ אֱדוֹם. הה"ד, כִּי הִנֵּה הַמְּלָכִים נוֹעֲדוּ עָבְרוּ יַחְדָּיו. נוֹעֲדוּ, בְּאָן אֲתָר. בְּאֶרֶץ אֱדוֹם. בַּאֲתָר דְּדִינִין מִתְאַחֲדִין תַּמָּן. עָבְרוּ יַחְדָּיו, דִּכְתִּיב וַיָּמָת וַיִּמְלוֹךְ תַּחְתָּיו. הֵמָּה רָאוּ כֵּן תָּמָהוּ נִבְהֲלוּ נֶחְפָּזוּ, דְּלָא אִתְקַיָּימוּ בְּאַתְרַיְיהוּ, בְּגִין דְּתִקּוּנִין דְּמַלְכָּא לָא אִתְתָּקְנוּ, וְקַרְתָּא קַדִּישָׁא וְשׁוּרוֹי, לָא אִזְדַּמָּנוּ.

111. He opened with, "And these are the kings that reigned in the land of Edom" (Beresheet 36:31). This is the meaning of, "For, lo, great kings were assembled, they came (or: 'passed') on together" (Tehilim 48:5). Where were they assembled? In the land of Edom, which Judgments hold on to. "they passed on together," as written, "And…died…reigned in his place" (Beresheet 36:33-39). "As soon as they saw, they were astounded; they were affrighted; they rushed away" (Tehilim 48:6), because they were not settled BUT BROKE AND DIED, because the King's establishments had not yet set and the holy city, NAMELY MALCHUT, and its walls had not yet come to be.

112. הה"ד, כַּאֲשֶׁר שָׁמַעְנוּ כֵּן רָאִינוּ וְגוֹ', דְּהָא כֻּלְּהוּ לָא אִתְקַיָּימוּ, וְהִיא אִתְקַיְּימַת הַשְׁתָּא, בְּסִטְרָא דִּדְכוּרָא, דְּשַׁרְיָא עִמָּהּ. הה"ד, וַיִּמְלוֹךְ תַּחְתָּיו הֲדַר וְשֵׁם עִירוֹ פָּעוּ וְשֵׁם אִשְׁתּוֹ מְהֵיטַבְאֵל בַּת מַטְרֵד בַּת מֵי זָהָב. מֵי זָהָב וַדַּאי כְּמָה דְּאוּקִימְנָא בְּאִדְרָא.

112. This is the meaning of, "As we have heard, so have we seen…" (Ibid. 9), because none survived, but she, MALCHUT, survives now that the male dwelt with her, as written, "and Hadar reigned in his place, and the name of his city was Pa'u; and his wife's name was Mehitavel, daughter of Matred, daughter of Mezehab" (Beresheet 36:39); gold water certainly, as we explained in the Idra.

113. בְּסִפְרָא דְּאַגַּדְתָּא דְּרַב הַמְנוּנָא סָבָא אִתְּמַר, וַיִּמְלוֹךְ תַּחְתָּיו הֲדַר.

הֲדַר וַדַּאי, כד״א, פְּרִי עֵץ הָדָר. וְשֵׁם אִשְׁתּוֹ מְהֵיטַבְאֵל, כד״א כַּפּוֹת תְּמָרִים. וּכְתִיב, צַדִּיק כַּתָּמָר יִפְרָח, דְּאִיהִי דְּכַר וְנוּקְבָּא. הַאי אִתְקְרִיאַת בַּת מַטְרֵד, בַּת מֵהַהוּא אֲתָר דְּטַרְדִּין כֹּלָּא לְאִתְדַּבְּקָא, וְאִקְרֵי אָב. וּכְתִיב לֹא יָדַע אֱנוֹשׁ עֶרְכָּהּ וְלֹא תִּמָּצֵא בְּאֶרֶץ הַחַיִּים. ד״א, בַּת מֵאִימָּא, דְּמִסִּטְרָהָא מִתְאַחֲדִין דִּינִין, דְּטַרְדִין לְכֹלָּא. בַּת מֵי זָהָב, דְּיָנְקָא בִּתְרֵין אַנְפִּין, דְּנָהִירוּ בִּתְרֵין גַּוְונִין. בְּחֶסֶד וּבְדִינָא.

113. In the Agadah book of Rav Hamnuna Saba we learned that, "Hadar reigned in his place." Hadar surely, NAMELY YESOD THAT IS CALLED THE TREE HADAR, as written, "the fruit of the tree hadar" (Vayikra 23:40), IN WHICH MALCHUT IS CALLED FRUIT AND YESOD THE TREE HADAR; "and his wife's name was Mehitavel" as in "branches of palm trees" (Ibid.), WHICH IS YESOD AND WHICH IS NAMED IN THE PLURAL "PALM TREES" BECAUSE it is written, "The righteous man flourishes like the palm tree" (Tehilim 92:13), WHICH MEANS HE DOES NOT FLOURISH WITHOUT THE FEMALE, because THE PALM TREE is both male and female. HENCE IT SAYS OF HIM, "AND HIS WIFE'S NAME WAS MEHITAVEL." This MALCHUT is called "the daughter of Matred," WHICH MEANS SHE IS a daughter to that place everyone is busy (Heb. *trudim*) attaining, which is called a father, NAMELY CHOCHMAH. It is also written, "Man cannot know its price; nor is it found in the land of the living" (Iyov 28:13), SINCE EVERYONE IS BUSY ATTAINING IT. According to another explanation, she is a daughter to mother, WHO IS BINAH, from whose aspect Judgments rise that disturb (Heb. *matridim*) everyone. THIS IS WHY SHE IS CALLED "THE DAUGHTER OF MATRED." She is "the daughter of Mezehab (lit. 'gold water')," BECAUSE SHE is fed from both aspects that radiate in two manners, with Chesed and with Judgments, THAT IS, FROM RIGHT AND LEFT, THE RIGHT BEING CHESED AND CALLED WATER, AND LEFT THE SECRET OF CHOCHMAH CALLED GOLD. HENCE THE GOLD WATER.

114. עַד לָא אִבְרֵי עָלְמָא, לָא הֲווֹ מַשְׁגִּיחִין אַנְפִּין בְּאַנְפִּין, וּבְגִין כַּךְ, עָלְמִין קַדְמָאֵי אִתְחֲרָבוּ, וְעָלְמִין קַדְמָאֵי בְּלָא תִּקּוּנָא אִתְעֲבִידוּ. וְהַהוּא דְּלָא הֲוָה בְּתִקּוּנָא, אִקְרֵי זִיקִין נִצוֹצִין, כְּהַאי אוּמָּנָא, מַרְזַפְתָּא, כַּד אַכְתִּשׁ בְּמָנָא דְּפַרְזְלָא, אַפִּיק זִיקִין לְכָל עִיבָר, וְאִינּוּן זִיקִין דְּנָפְקִין,

נָפְקִין לְהִיטִין וּנְהִירִין, וְדַעֲכִין לְאַלְתָּר. וְאִלֵּין אִקְרוּן עָלְמִין קַדְמָאֵי. וּבְגִין כַּךְ אִתְחֲרָבוּ, וְלָא אִתְקְיָימוּ. עַד דְּאִתְתָּקַן עַתִּיקָא קַדִּישָׁא, וְנָפִיק אוּמָנָא לְאוּמָנוּתֵיהּ.

114. Before the world was created, they did not face and look at each other face to face, and because of that the earlier worlds were destroyed, BY BEING BROKEN AND DYING. The first worlds were formed but not fixed, and that KING that was not established was called glowing sparks, THAT IS, HIS KINGDOM AND REIGN WERE LIKE THE LIGHT OF A SPARK THAT IS IMMEDIATELY EXTINGUISHED AND DISAPPEARS. It is like a craftsman who strikes on an iron tool with a hammer, and produces sparks in every direction. These sparks come out glowing and shining but are extinguished at once. These are called the first worlds. For this reason they were destroyed and did not survive, until Atika Kadisha manifested and the craftsman began His work.

30. How Zeir Anpin emanated from Aba and Ima

A Synopsis

Rabbi Shimon recalls what the Baraitha says about the destruction of the first worlds and about how Atika Kadisha's craftsmanship later established everything as male and female. Then when Aba and Ima joined and were incorporated within each other, the head of Zeir Anpin emerged and expanded.

115. וְעַל הַאי תָּנֵינָא בְּמַתְנִיתָא דִּילָן, דְּבוּצִינָא אַפִּיק זִיקִין נִיצוֹצִין לִתְלַת מְאָה וְעֶשְׂרִין עִיבָר. וְאִינּוּן זִיקִין, עָלְמִין קַדְמָאֵי אִקְרוּן, וּמִיתוּ לְאַלְתָּר. לְבָתַר נָפִיק אוּמָנָא לְאוּמָנוּתֵיהּ, וְאִתְתְּקַן בִּדְכַר וְנוּקְבָא, וְהָנֵי זִיקִין דְּאִתְדַעֲכוּ וּמִיתוּ, הַשְׁתָּא אִתְקְיָים כֹּלָּא. מִבּוּצִינָא דְּקַרְדִינוּתָא, נָפַק נִיצוֹצָא, פַּטִּישָׁא תַּקִּיפָא, דְּבָטַשׁ, וְאַפִּיק זִיקִין עָלְמִין קַדְמָאֵי, וּמִתְעָרְבֵי בַּאֲוִירָא דַּכְיָא, וְאִתְבְּסָמוּ דָּא בְּדָא.

115. In regard to this we learned in our B'raita that the luminary scattered sparks and glitters to 320 sides, and that these sparks are called the first worlds, which died immediately. Afterwards, the craftsman, ATIKA KADISHA, went to do His craftsmanship, which was set as male and female, and the sparks that were extinguished and died became in existence now. For from the harsh candle a spark came out, which is the strong hammer that struck and produced sparks THAT WERE EXTINGUISHED IN the first worlds. It is mingled with pure air and they were sweetened by each other.

116. כַּד אִתְחַבָּר אַבָּ"א וְאִימָּ"א, וְהַהוּא אָב הוּא, מֵרוּחָא דְּגָנִיז בְּעַתִּיק יוֹמִין, בֵּיהּ אִתְגְּנִיז הַאי אֲוֵירָא, וְאַכְלִיל לְנִיצוֹצָא, דְּנָפִק מִבּוּצִינָא דְּקַרְדִּינוּתָא, דְּגָנִיז בְּמֵעוֹי דְּאִימָּא. וְכַד אִתְחַבָּרוּ תַּרְוַויְיהוּ, וְאִתְכְּלִילוּ דָּא בְּדָא. נָפִיק גּוּלְגַּלְתָּא חַד תַּקִּיפָא, וְאִתְפָּשַׁט בְּסִטְרוֹי, דָּא בְּסִטְרָא דָּא, וְדָא בְּסִטְרָא דָּא. כְּמָה דְּעַתִּיקָא קַדִּישָׁא תְּלַת רֵישִׁין אִשְׁתְּכָחוּ בְּחַד, כַּךְ כֹּלָּא אִזְדְּמַן בִּתְלַת רֵישִׁין, כְּמָה דַּאֲמֵינָא.

116. HE NOW EXPLAINS THE EMERGENCE OF ZEIR ANPIN FROM ABA AND IMA, SAYING: when Aba united with Ima, NAMELY MALE WITH

FEMALE, the PURE air, THE SECRET OF CHASSADIM, coming from the spirit hidden within Atik Yomin, was concealed within Aba and included the spark coming from the hard candle hidden within the belly of Ima, THAT IS, THE JUDGMENTS OF CHOCHMAH OF THE LEFT OF IMA. When the two joined and were incorporated within each other, CHOCHMAH OF IMA WITHIN THE CHASSADIM OF ABA AND VICE VERSA, a hard, strong skull, THE HEAD OF ZEIR ANPIN, emerged and expanded to the sides, one to one side and one to the other. Just like there are three heads together in Atika Kadisha, THE UNKNOWN HEAD, KETER AND CONCEALED CHOCHMAH, everything comes about through three heads as I said.

31. The skull of Zeir Anpin

A Synopsis

We read how dew drips from the skull of Arich Anpin to the skull of Zeir Anpin and from there to Malchut where it sustains everything. From this dew, manna is ground for the righteous in the World to Come, and through it the dead will be revived. Rabbi Shimon talks about how this dew dripped when Yisrael were wandering in the wilderness. As this event never happened at any other time in the world, we learn that children, length of life and sustenance depend not on merit but instead on Mazal. Lastly we hear that there is healing in the world only when Zeir Anpin and Atika Kadisha face each other; then everything is long-suffering.

117. בְּהַאי גּוּלְגַּלְתָּא דז״א, נָטִיף טַלָּא מֵרֵישָׁא חִוָּורָא, וְהַהוּא טַלָּא אִתְחֲזֵי בִּתְרֵי גְּוָונֵי. וּמִנֵּיהּ מִתְּזָן חַקְלָא דְתַפּוּחִין קַדִּישִׁין. וּמֵהַאי טַלָּא דְגוּלְגַּלְתָּא דָא, טַחֲנִין מָנָא לְצַדִּיקַיָּיא לְעָלְמָא דְאָתֵי, וּבֵיהּ זְמִינִין מֵתַיָּיא לְאַחֲיָיא. וְלָא אִזְדְּמַן מָנָא דְּנָפַל מֵהַאי טַלָּא, בַּר הַהוּא זִמְנָא בִּזְמְנָא דְאָזְלוּ יִשְׂרָאֵל בְּמַדְבְּרָא, וְזָן לְהוּ עַתִּיקָא דְכֹלָּא, מֵהַאי אֲתָר. מַה דְלָא אִשְׁתְּכַח לְבָתַר. הה״ד הִנְנִי מַמְטִיר לָכֶם לֶחֶם מִן הַשָּׁמָיִם. כד״א וְיִתֶּן לְךָ הָאֱלֹהִים מִטַּל הַשָּׁמַיִם וְגוֹ׳. הַאי בְּהַהוּא זִמְנָא. לְזִמְנָא אַחֲרָא תָּנֵינָן, קָשִׁים מְזוֹנוֹתָיו שֶׁל אָדָם קַמֵּי קוּדְשָׁא בְּרִיךְ הוּא. וְהָא בְּמַזָּלָא תַּלְיָיא בְּמַזָּלָא וַדַּאי. וע״כ בְּנֵי חַיֵּי וּמְזוֹנֵי, לָאו בִּזְכוּתָא תַּלְיָיא מִלְּתָא, אֶלָּא בְּמַזָּלָא תַּלְיָיא מִלְּתָא, וְכֹלָּא תַּלְיָין בְּהַאי מַזָּלָא, כְּמָה דְאוֹקִימְנָא.

117. In this skull of Zeir Anpin, dew drips from the white head, WHICH IS THE SKULL OF ARICH ANPIN, which appears in two colors, FOR THOUGH IT IS CHASSADIM THAT ARE CONSIDERED WHITE, NEVERTHELESS SOME REDNESS APPEARS IN IT, WHICH INDICATES THE INCLUSION OF CHOCHMAH, WHICH IS WHAT IS MEANT BY, "THE COLOR OF BDELLIUM" (BEMIDBAR 11:7). From Zeir Anpin the field of holy apple trees, WHICH IS MALCHUT, is sustained. From the dew in this skull, manna is ground for the righteous for the World to Come, and through it the dead shall be revived. This dew never dripped except when Yisrael wandered in the wilderness, sustained by the most ancient from that place, THE DEW ABOVE THE SKULL, and this never happened afterwards. This is the meaning of, "Behold, I will rain bread from heaven for you" (Shemot 16:4), as in, "therefore Elohim give you of the dew of heaven..." (Beresheet 27:28). FOR SOME OF THE DEW OF THE SKULL OF ARICH ANPIN DRIPS ON THE SKULL OF ZEIR ANPIN CALLED HEAVEN. This was at that time, WHEN THEY WERE FED BY THE DEW OF HEAVEN. Other times, we learned that man's sustenance is hard for the Holy One, blessed be He, because AT THAT TIME SUSTENANCE came from Mazal, Mazal certainly WHERE THERE ARE JUDGMENTS, AND NOT FROM THE DEW OF THE SKULL OF ARICH ANPIN, WHICH IS WHOLLY OF MERCY. Hence children, length of life and sustenance do not depend on merit, but on Mazal. Everything derives from that Mazal as we explained THAT IT IS THE BEARD OF ARICH ANPIN.

118. תִּשְׁעָה אַלְפִּין רִבּוֹא עָלְמִין, נַטְלִין וְסַמְכִין עַל הַאי גּוּלְגַּלְתָּא. וְהַאי אֲוִירָא דַּכְיָא אִתְכְּלִיל בְּכֹלָּא, כֵּיוָן דְּהוּא כָּלִיל מִכֹּלָּא וְכֹלָּא אִתְכְּלִיל בֵּיהּ, אִתְפְּשָׁטוּ אַנְפּוֹי לִתְרֵין סִטְרִין, בִּתְרֵי נְהוֹרִין כְּלִילָן מִכֹּלָּא. וְכַד אִסְתָּכָּלוּ אַנְפּוֹי, בְּאַנְפִּין דְּעַתִּיקָא קַדִּישָׁא, כֹּלָּא אֶרֶךְ אַפַּיִם אִקְרֵי. מַאי אֶרֶךְ אַפַּיִם. אֶלָּא הָכִי תָּנֵינָן, בְּגִין דְּאָרִיךְ אַפֵּיהּ לְחַיָּיבַיָּא. אֲבָל אֶרֶךְ אַפַּיִם, אַסְוָותָא דְּאַנְפִּין. דְּהָא לָא אִשְׁתְּכַח אַסְוָותָא בְּעָלְמָא, אֶלָּא בְּזִמְנָא דְּאַשְׁגְּחִין אַנְפִּין בְּאַנְפִּין.

118. 90,000,000 worlds journey and are supported by the skull. The pure air OF ABA is included within all GRADES OF ZEIR ANPIN, BOTH TO THE RIGHT AND TO THE LEFT, WHICH IS WHY THE FACE OF ZEIR ANPIN HAS EXPANDED to two sides, RIGHT AND LEFT, by two lights FROM CHASSADIM AND CHOCHMAH that include everything. When the face OF ZEIR ANPIN looks to the face of Atika Kadisha, everything, BOTH THE FACE OF ARICH ANPIN AND THE FACE OF ZEIR ANPIN, is called long-suffering. We learned that it is long-suffering because He is long-suffering to the wicked, but long- suffering MEANS healing come from the face, SINCE LONG (HEB. *AROCH*) MEANS HEALING, DERIVED FROM, "FOR I WILL RESTORE HEALTH (HEB. *ARUCHAH*) TO YOU" (YIRMEYAH 30:17), for there is healing in the world only when ZEIR ANPIN AND ATIKA KADISHA face each other.

32. Chochmah, Binah and Da'at of Zeir Anpin

A Synopsis

Rabbi Shimon tells us about the three lights that shine within the cavity of the skull, and about how these lights spread throughout the body. We learn about the perfection of Jacob, who drew Chochmah and bestowed it on Rachel and on Malchut. The Zohar says that Atika Kadisha is completely at one with the light of Chassadim alone, and the illumination of Chochmah has no power over it, and thus there is joy in it for everyone and life for everyone, and no Judgments extend from it.

119. בַּחֲלָלָא דְּגוּלְגַּלְתָּא, נְהִירִין תְּלַת נְהוֹרִין. וְאִי תֵּימָא תְּלַת, אַרְבַּע אִינּוּן, כְּמָה דַּאֲמֵינָא, אַחֲסַנְתֵּיהּ דַּאֲבוֹי וְאִמֵּיהּ, וּתְרֵין גְּנִיזִין דִּלְהוֹן, דְּמִתְעַטְּרָן כֻּלְּהוּ בְּרֵישֵׁיהּ, וְאִינּוּן תְּפִלִּין דְּרֵישָׁא. לְבָתַר מִתְחַבְּרָן בְּסִטְרוֹי, וְנַהֲרִין וְעָאלִין בִּתְלַת חֲלָלֵי דְּגוּלְגַּלְתָּא. נָפְקִין כָּל חַד בְּסִטְרוֹי, וּמִתְפַּשְׁטִין בְּכָל גּוּפָא.

119. Three lights shine within the cavity of the skull, NAMELY CHOCHMAH, BINAH AND DA'AT. You may argue, YOU SPEAK OF three, yet there are four, as I mentioned, which are the inheritance of His father and mother, NAMELY CHOCHMAH AND BINAH, THE ASPECT OF ABA AND IMA HE INHERITED and the two PARTS OF DA'AT hidden within them. They serve as crowns on the head OF ZEIR ANPIN as the head Tefilin. AND HE ANSWERS, AT FIRST THERE WERE FOUR LIGHTS, which later join at His sides, THAT IS, THE TWO PARTS OF DA'AT ARE JOINED IN HIM INTO ONE TO RECONCILE CHOCHMAH AND BINAH AND UNITE THEM WITH EACH OTHER, SO THEY BECOME THREE LIGHTS. They shine and enter the three cavities in the skull and come out each from its own side, ONE FROM THE RIGHT, ONE FROM THE LEFT AND ANOTHER FROM THE MIDDLE, and spread throughout the body.

120. וְאִלֵּין מִתְחַבְּרָן בִּתְרֵי מוֹחֵי. וּמוֹחָא תְּלִיתָאָה כָּלִיל לוֹן, וְאָחִיד בְּהַאי סִטְרָא וּבְהַאי סִטְרָא, וּמִתְפָּשַׁט בְּכָל גּוּפָא, וְאִתְעֲבֵיד מִנֵּיהּ תְּרֵי גְּוָונֵי כְּלִילָן כַּחֲדָא. וּמֵהַאי נָהִיר אַנְפּוֹי, וְאַסְהִיד בְּאַבָּא וְאִימָּא גְּוָונֵי

דְּאַנְפּוֹי. וְהוּא אִקְרֵי דַּעַת, בְּדַעַת כְּתִיב, כִּי אֵל דֵּעוֹת ה׳ וְגוֹ׳, בְּגִין דְּאִיהוּ בִּתְרֵי גְּוָונֵי לוֹ נִתְכְּנוּ עֲלִילוֹת. אֲבָל לְעַתִּיקָא קַדִּישָׁא סְתִימָאָה, לָא נִתְכְּנוּ. מ״ט נִתְכְּנוּ לְהַאי. בְּגִין דְּיָרִית תְּרֵין חוּלקי, וּכְתִיב עִם חָסִיד תִּתְחַסָּד וְגוֹ׳.

120. These FOUR LIGHTS join the two brain lobes CHOCHMAH AND BINAH and the third brain lobe that includes THE TWO LOBES and which is attached to this and that side, NAMELY TO THE RIGHT, WHICH IS CHOCHMAH, AND THE LEFT, WHICH IS BINAH, and spreads throughout the body and two colors are formed in Him blended into one, NAMELY THE RIGHT WITHIN IT, WHICH IS CHASSADIM AND THE LEFT WITHIN IT WHICH IS CHOCHMAH ARE INCORPORATED IN IT TOGETHER. This causes His face to shine, and the colors of His countenance testify about Aba and Ima. THAT IS, THEY SHINE WITH THE COLOR OF ABA, WHICH IS CHASSADIM, AND THE COLOR OF IMA, WHICH IS CHOCHMAH. And He is called Da'at, of which it is written, "For Hashem is an El of knowledge (lit. 'knowledges')" (I Shmuel 2:3), THAT IS, IN THE PLURAL, because He has two colors, CHOCHMAH AND CHASSADIM. Hence it is written, "With the merciful You will show Yourself merciful" (II Shmuel 22:26) BY SHINING CHASSADIM ON HIM, "AND WITH THE UPRIGHT MAN (HEB. *GIBOR*) YOU WILL SHOW YOURSELF UPRIGHT" (IBID.), BY SHINING GVUROT ON HIM, THAT IS, WITH THE ILLUMINATION OF CHOCHMAH, WHICH IS PERFECT, AS UPRIGHT MEANS PERFECT.

121. וְהָא בִּקְשׁוֹט אוֹקִימוּ חַבְרַיָּיא, דִּכְתִּיב, וַיַּגֵּד יַעֲקֹב לְרָחֵל כִּי אֲחִי אָבִיהָ הוּא. וַיַּגֵּד, הָא אוֹקְמוּהָ, דְּכֹלָּא רָזָא דְּחָכְמְתָא. וְכִי בֶּן רִבְקָה הוּא. בֶּן רִבְקָה, וְלָא כְּתִיב בֶּן יִצְחָק. רֶמֶז, וְכֹלָּא רְמִיזָא בְּחָכְמְתָא.

121. The friends explained it in truth, as written, "And Jacob told Rachel that he was her father's brother" (Beresheet 29:12). In relation to "told," it has been explained that everything is the secret of wisdom, WHICH MEANS THAT THE DRAWING OF CHOCHMAH IS CONSIDERED TELLING. "and that he was Rivka's son" (Ibid.): It is written, "Rivka's son" instead of, "Isaac's son," as an allusion, and everything is an allusion of wisdom.

122. וְעַל הַאי אִקְרֵי שְׁלִים בְּכֹלָּא. וּבֵיהּ אִתְחֲזֵי מְהֵימְנוּתָא. ובג"כ כְּתִיב, וַיַּגֵּד יַעֲקֹב, וְלָא כְּתִיב וַיֹּאמֶר.

122. For this JACOB is considered perfect in every respect, and faith is evident in him. THAT IS, HE BESTOWED CHOCHMAH ON MALCHUT CALLED BOTH RACHEL AND FAITH; THE BESTOWING OF CHOCHMAH IS CONSIDERED TELLING. Hence it is written, "And Jacob told Rachel," WHICH INDICATES THE BESTOWING OF CHOCHMAH, instead of 'said'.

123. הָנֵי גְּוָונֵי, כְּמָה דְנַהֲרִין בְּעִטְרָא דְרֵישָׁא, וְעָאלִין בַּחֲלָלֵי דְגוּלְגַּלְתָּא. הָכִי מִתְפַּשְּׁטִין בְּכָל גּוּפָא, וְגוּפָא אִתְאֲחִיד בְּהוּ. לְעַתִּיקָא קַדִּישָׁא סְתִימָא, לָא נִתְכְּנוּ, וְלָא יָאָן לֵיהּ, דְּהָא כֹּלָּא בְּחַד אִשְׁתְּכַח, חֵידוּ לְכֹלָּא, חַיִּים לְכֹלָּא. לָא תַּלְיָיא בֵּיהּ דִּינָא. אֲבָל בְּהַאי, לוֹ נִתְכְּנוּ עֲלִילוֹת וַדַּאי.

123. Just as these colors OF RIGHT AND LEFT IN DA'AT shine in the adornment of the head and enter the cavities of the skull, so they spread throughout the body and the body is attached to them, BUT for concealed Atika Kadisha "ACTIONS are not weighed" (I Shmuel 2:3), SINCE THERE IS NO CHOCHMAH IN IT and they are not suitable for it, because this ATIKA KADISHA is completely at one WITH THE LIGHT OF CHASSADIM ALONE, AND THE ILLUMINATION OF CHOCHMAH HAS NO POWER OVER IT, AND HENCE THERE IS joy IN IT for all, life for all, and no Judgments extend from it. But as for Him, ZEIR ANPIN, "by Him actions are weighed" (Ibid.), surely. HENCE THIS VERSE IS WRITTEN ONE WAY AND PRONOUNCED ANOTHER. IT IS WRITTEN "BY HIM (HEB. *LO, LAMED VAV*)," AND PRONOUNCED "NOT (HEB. *LO, LAMED ALEPH*)," ONE APPLYING TO ATIKA AND ONE TO ZEIR ANPIN.

33. Hairs, tresses and bristles on the head of Zeir Anpin

A Synopsis

Rabbi Shimon tells us about the locks of hair that hang from the head of Zeir Anpin and how they are intertwined with the supernal light from Aba and Ima. We hear about the lobes of the brain and how they encompass the laws and mysteries, the hidden and the disclosed. We also learn what should be done by a person who wants God to hear him.

124. בְּגוּלְגַּלְתָּא דְּרֵישָׁא, תַּלְיָין כָּל אִינּוּן רִבְּוָון וְאַלְפִין מְקוּצֵי דְּשַׂעֲרִין, דְּאִינּוּן אוּכָמִין. וּמִסְתַּבְּכִין דָּא בְּדָא, אֲחִידָן דָּא בְּדָא, דַּאֲחִידָן בִּנְהִירוּ עִלָּאָה דִּמְעַטֵּר בְּרֵישֵׁיהּ מֵאַבָּא, וּמִמּוֹחָא דְּאִתְנְהִיר מֵאַבָּא. לְבָתַר נָפְקִין נִימִין עַל נִימִין, מִנְּהִירוּ דְּמִתְעַטָּר בְּרֵישֵׁיהּ מֵאִימָּא, וּמִשְּׁאַר מוֹחֵי. וְכֻלְּהוּ אֲחִידָן, וּמִסְתַּבְּכֵי בְּאִינּוּן שַׂעֲרֵי דַּאֲחִידָן מֵאַבָּא, בְּגִין דְּאִינּוּן מִתְעָרְבִין דָּא בְּדָא, וּמִסְתַּבְּכִין דָּא בְּדָא,

124. From the skull of the head, WHICH IS KETER, tens of thousands of locks of hairs are hanging, which are black, entangled and intertwined in each other, since they are twined with the supernal light that adorns his head from Aba and from his brain that shines from the light of Aba. Then many tiny hairs come out of the light that adorns his head from Ima and from the other brain lobes, all connected and entangled in the hairs that hold to Aba, because they are disheveled and entangled in each other.

125. וְכֻלְּהוּ מוֹחֵי אֲחִידָן בְּגוּלְגּוּלְתָּא, בְּמוֹחָא עִלָּאָה. וְכֻלְּהוּ מְשִׁיכָן אִתְמַשְׁכָן מִתְּלַת חֲלָלֵי דְּמוֹחָא, אֲחִידָן בְּמוֹחֵי מִתְעָרְבָן דָּא בְּדָא, בְּדַכְיָא בִּמְסָאֲבָא. בְּכָל אִינּוּן טַעֲמִין, וְרָזִין, סְתִימִין וּמִתְגַּלְיָין. ובג״כ כֻּלְּהוּ מוֹחֵי רְמִיזֵי בְּאָנֹכִי יְיָ׳ אֱלֹהֶיךָ וְכוּ׳, כְּמָה דִּנְהוֹרִין בְּעִטְרָא דְּרֵישָׁא, וְעָאלִין בַּחֲלָלֵי דְּגוּלְגַּלְתָּא.

125. All the brain lobes ARE ATTACHED TO the skull, WHICH IS the supernal brain. And all the hairs flow from the three cavities of the brain that are attached to the SUPERNAL brain lobes and are intermixed in purity and impurity, WHICH ARE THE LAWS OF PURITY AND LOGIC BEHIND THE

WARNINGS CONCERNING IMPURITY, in all those laws and mysteries, the hidden and the disclosed. For that reason, all brain lobes are indicated in, "I am Hashem your Elohim" (Shemot 20:2). THEY ARE THE SECRET OF THE 248 POSITIVE AND THE 365 NEGATIVE PRECEPTS INCLUDED IN THAT VERSE, WHICH ARE ARRANGED as they shine in the head part, THAT IS, IN THE FOUR BRAIN LOBES IN THE SKULL, AND THEIR ILLUMINATION enters the THREE cavities of the skull INSIDE THE HEAD.

126. כָּל אִינּוּן קוֹצִין אוּכָּמִין, חַפְיָין וְתַלְיָין לְסִטְרָא דְּאוּדְנִין. וְהָא אוּקִימְנָא, דבג"כ כְּתִיב, הַטֵּה יְיָ' אָזְנְךָ וּשֲׁמָע. מִכָּאן אוּקִימְנָא, מַאן דְּבָעֵי דְּיַרְכִּין מַלְכָּא אוּדְנֵיהּ לָקֳבְלֵיהּ, יְסַלְסֵל בְּרֵישֵׁיהּ דְּמַלְכָּא, וְיִפְנֶה שַׂעֲרֵי מֵעַל אוּדְנוֹי, וְיִשְׁמַע לֵיהּ מַלְכָּא בְּכָל מַה דְּבָעֵי.

126. All the locks of black hair hang on and cover the ears, which is why we learned that it is written, "Hashem, bend Your ear, and hear" (II Melachim 19:16). From this we derive that whoever wishes the King to bend His ear to him should curl the hairs on the King's head, THAT IS, CONCENTRATE ON MITIGATING THE JUDGMENTS HANGING FROM THE HAIRS ON THE HEAD OF ZEIR ANPIN. He should also move the hair away from His ears SO THEY WOULD NOT OBSTRUCT THE HEARING OF PRAYER. Then the King will hear whatever He needs to.

34. The path that divides the hairs of Zeir Anpin

A Synopsis

We are told that wailers and moaners emerge from the rough hairs on the head of Zeir Anpin, and that they spread a trap for the wicked who are not familiar with the paths of the precepts of the Torah.

127. בְּפַלְגוּתָא דְּשַׂעֲרֵי, מִתְאַחֲדָא חַד אוֹרְחָא, בְּאָרְחָא דְּעַתִּיק יוֹמִין, וּמִתְפָּרְשָׁן מִנֵּיהּ כָּל אוֹרְחוֹי דְּפִקּוּדֵי אוֹרַיְיתָא, כָּל מָארֵיהוֹן דִּיבָבָא וִילָלָא תַּלְיָין בְּכָל קוֹצָא וְקוֹצָא, וְאִינּוּן מַפְרִשִׁין רִשְׁתָּא לְחַיָּיבַיָּא, דְּלָא יַדְעִין אִינּוּן אָרְחִין. הה"ד, דֶּרֶךְ רְשָׁעִים כָּאֲפֵלָה. וְכָל אִלֵּין תַּלְיָין בְּקוֹצִין תַּקִּיפִין, ובג"כ כֻּלְּהוּ תַּקִּיפִין. וְאוֹקִימְנָא בְּאִינּוּן שְׂעִיעָן אִתְאַחֲדָן מָארֵיהוֹן דְּמַתְקְלָא, דִּכְתִּיב, כָּל אָרְחוֹת יְיָ' חֶסֶד וֶאֱמֶת. וְכָל כַּךְ, בְּגִין דְּמַשְׁכִין מִמּוֹחִין סְתִימִין דִּרְהִיטֵי דְּמוֹחָא.

127. Where the hairs OF ZEIR ANPIN divide, a way joins the path of the Ancient of Days (Atik Yomin) WHERE THE HAIRS DIVIDE, THAT IS, IT RECEIVES BOUNTY FROM IT, and all the paths of the precepts of the Torah part from it. All the wailers and moaners come out from every rough hair IN THE HAIR and spread a trap for the wicked who are not familiar with these paths. This is the meaning of, "The way of the wicked is like darkness" (Mishlei 4:19). From the rough hairs those who are weighing come out, as written, "All the paths of Hashem are mercy and truth" (Tehilim 25:10). It is all this way because they emerge from the concealed brain lobes of THE LEFT, CALLED the strong lights of the brain.

35. The hair–tips in each of Chochmah, Binah and Da'at

A Synopsis

Rabbi Shimon clarifies the previous section and we learn that the wicked do not know that they are stumbling on harsh judgment.

128. ובג״כ מִשְׁתַּכְחֵי כָּל חַד כְּפוּם אוֹרְחוֹי, מֵחַד מוֹחָא בְּאִינּוּן קוֹצִין שְׁעִיעָן, אִתְמַשְׁכָן מָארֵיהוֹן דְּמַתְקְלָא, דִּכְתִּיב כָּל אָרְחוֹת יְיָ׳ חֶסֶד וֶאֱמֶת.

128. HE NOW EXPLAINS MATTERS MORE FULLY. For that reason, each OF THE HAIR-TIPS has its individual way, but from one brain lobe, THE MIDDLE ONE, WHICH IS DA'AT, weighing ones emerge from the smooth rough hair in it, OF WHOM it is written, "All the paths of Hashem are mercy and truth" (Tehilim 25:10).

129. מִמּוֹחָא תִּנְיָינָא, בְּאִינּוּן קוֹצִין תַּקִּיפִין, אִתְמַשְׁכָן וְתַלְיָין מָארֵיהוֹן דִּיבָבָא וִילָלָא דִּכְתִּיב בְּהוּ דֶּרֶךְ רְשָׁעִים כָּאֲפֵלָה לֹא יָדְעוּ בַּמֶּה יִכָּשֵׁלוּ. מַאי קָא מַיְירֵי. אֶלָּא לֹא יָדְעוּ, כְּלוֹמַר לָא יַדְעִין, וְלָא בָּעָאן לְמִנְדַּע, בַּמֶּה יִכָּשֵׁלוּ. אַל תִּקְרֵי בַּמֶּה, אֶלָּא בְּאִימָּא יִכָּשֵׁלוּ. בְּאִינּוּן דְּמִתְאַחֲדִין בִּסְטַר דְּאִימָּא. מַאי סִטְרָא דְּאִימָּא. גְּבוּרָה תַּקִּיפָא מִינַּהּ מִתְאַחֲדָן מָארֵיהוֹן דִּיבָבָא וִילָלָא.

129. From the second brain lobe, THE LEFT ONE, WHICH IS BINAH, THE SAID wailers and moaners come out from the rough hard hairs, of which it is written, "The way of the wicked is like darkness; they know not at what they stumble" (Mishlei 4:19). What does this mean? AND HE ANSWERS, they know not, namely they do not know nor wish to know at what they stumble. Do not pronounce it, "at what (Heb. *bemah*) they stumble," but rather, "on Ima (Heb. *be'ima*) they stumble," that is, on those attached TO THE SECOND BRAIN LOBE, WHICH IS BINAH of the aspect of Ima. The aspect of Ima is harsh Gvurah AT THE LEFT, from her are included the wailers and moaners.

130. מִמּוֹחָא תְּלִיתָאָה, בְּאִינּוּן קוֹצִין דְּאִינּוּן בְּאֶמְצָעִיתָא, אִתְמַשְׁכָן

וְתַלְיָין מָארֵיהוֹן דְּמִידִין. וְאִקְרוּן אַפִּין נְהִירִין וְלָא נְהִירִין. וּבְהָנֵי כְּתִיב פַּלֵּס מַעְגַּל רַגְלֶךָ. וְכֹלָּא אִשְׁתְּכַח בְּאִינּוּן קוֹצִין דְּשַׂעְרֵי דְּרֵישָׁא.

130. From the third brain lobe, from the rough hairs in the middle prosecutors come out and emerge. They are called shining countenances that are not yet shining. Of these it is written, "Make even the path of your foot" (Mishlei 4:26). Everything is in the rough hairs of the head.

36. The forehead of Zeir Anpin

A Synopsis

We are told that whenever it is exposed, the forehead of Zeir Anpin takes revenge on the wicked for their deeds. However, when the forehead of Atika is revealed within the forehead of Zeir Anpin it is a time of goodwill for everyone; this happens during the Minchah service on Shabbat. Rabbi Shimon explains why people are not punished by a celestial court until they are at least twenty years old.

131. מִצְחָא דְּגוּלְגַּלְתָּא, מִצְחָא לְאִתְפַּקְדָא חַיָּיבַיָּא עַל עוֹבָדֵיהוֹן. וְכַד הַאי מִצְחָא אִתְגַּלְיָיא, מִתְעָרִין מָארֵיהוֹן דְּדִינִין, לְאִינּוּן דְּלָא מִתְכַּסְפִין בְּעוֹבָדֵיהוֹן. הַאי מִצְחָא סוּמָקָא כְּוַורְדָא. וּבְשַׁעֲתָא דְּאִתְגַּלְיָיא מִצְחָא דְּעַתִּיקָא בְּהַאי מִצְחָא, אִתְהַדְּרַת חִוָּורָא כְּתַלְגָּא. וְהַהִיא שַׁעֲתָא, עֵת רָצוֹן אִקְרֵי לְכֹלָּא.

131. The forehead on the skull is a forehead that takes revenge on the wicked for their deeds. When this forehead is exposed, prosecutors are roused against those who are not ashamed of their actions. This forehead is as red as a rose. When the forehead of Atika is revealed within this forehead, it again becomes white as snow. That time is considered a time of goodwill for everyone.

132. בְּסִפְרָא דְּאַגַדְתָּא דְּבֵי רַב יֵיבָא סָבָא אָמַר, מֶצַח. זָכֵי מֶצַח, מִצְחָא דְּעַתִּיקָא. וְאִי לָאו, אַשְׁדֵי ח׳ בֵּין תְּרֵין אַתְוָון, כד״א וּמָחַץ פַּאֲתֵי מוֹאָב.

132. In the Agadah book of Rav Yeba Saba he spoke of the forehead (Heb. *metzach*, *Mem Tzadi Chet*). If people merit the forehead, it is the forehead of Atik, THAT IS, THE FOREHEAD OF GOODWILL. If they do not HAVE MERIT, Chet is placed between the two letters Mem and Tzadi, WHICH FORMS THE WORD '*MACHATZ*', as in, "and shall smite (Heb. *machatz*) the corners of Moab" (Bemidbar 24:17), WHICH MEANS THAT THE WICKED GET THEIR PUNISHMENT FROM IT.

133. וְאוֹקִימְנָא, דְּאִקְרֵי נֶצַח בְּאַתְוָון רְצוּפִין. וְכַמָּה נְצָחִים הֲווֹ. ואע״ג

דְּנֶצַח בְּאַתְרָא אָחֳרָא אִסְתְּלַק, וְאִית נְצָחִים אָחֳרָנִין דְּמִתְפַּשְּׁטִין בְּכָל גּוּפָא. וּבְגִין דְּשַׁבַּתָּא בְּשַׁעֲתָא דִּצְלוֹתָא דְּמִנְחָה, בְּגִין דְּלָא יִתְּעַר דִּינִין, גַּלְיָא עַתִּיקָא קַדִּישָׁא מִצְחָא דִּילֵיהּ, וְכָל דִּינִין אִתְכַּפְיָין וְאִשְׁתְּכָכוּ וְלָא אִתְעֲבִידוּ.

133. We explained that THE FOREHEAD (HEB. *METZACH*) is called Netzach using executive letters, CHANGING THE LETTER MEM WITH THE FOLLOWING IN ALPHABETICAL ORDER, NUN, WHICH INDICATES THAT THE LIGHT OF SUPERNAL NETZACH SHINES ON THE FOREHEAD. And even though Netzach rises to another place, THIS DOES NOT POSE ANY DIFFICULTIES, because other kinds of Netzach spread throughout the body. THE REASON THE FOREHEAD IS CALLED NETZACH IS THAT IT VANQUISHES (HEB. *NOTZE'ACH*) ALL JUDGMENTS, because on Shabbat during the Minchah service Atika Kadisha exposes its forehead so as not to arouse Judgments, and all Judgments are subdued and quieted and do not manifest.

134. בְּהַאי מִצְחָא תַּלְיָין כ"ד בָּתֵּי דִּינִין, לְכָל אִינּוּן דְּחַצִּיפִין בְּעוֹבָדֵיהוֹן. כְּמָה דִּכְתִּיב, וְאָמְרוּ אֵיכָה יָדַע אֵל וְיֵשׁ דֵּעָה בְּעֶלְיוֹן. וְהָא עֶשְׂרִים אִינּוּן, ד' לָמָּה. לָקֳבְלֵיהוֹן דְּד' מִיתוֹת בֵּית דִּינָא לְתַתָּא, דְּתַלְיָין מִלְעֵילָּא. וְאִשְׁתָּאֲרוּ עֶשְׂרִין. וּבג"כ לָא מַעֲנִישִׁין בֵּי דִּינָא עִלָּאָה, עַד דְּיַשְׁלִים וְסַלְקָא לְכ' שְׁנִין, לָקֳבְלֵיהוֹן דְּכ' בָּתֵּי דִּינָא. בְּמַתְנִיתָא סְתִימָאָה דִּילָן תָּנֵינָן, לָקֳבְלֵיהוֹן דְּכ"ד סְפָרִים דְּאִתְכְּלִילָן בְּאוֹרַיְיתָא.

134. 24 courthouses derive from the forehead for all those who are impudent in their actions, as in, "And they say, how does El know? And is there knowledge in the most High" (Tehilim 73:11). HE ASKS, Yet there are twenty courthouses, why add four to them, AND ANSWERS THAT four correspond to the four capital punishments allotted by the terrestrial courthouse that derive from up high, so only twenty COURTHOUSES remain. For that reason, one is not punished by a celestial court until he completes his twentieth year, which corresponds to the twenty courthouses. In our concealed B'raita we learned that they correspond to the four books in the Bible.

37. The eyes of Zeir Anpin

A Synopsis

Rabbi Shimon says that although the wicked think that the eyes of God are sleeping, they are not. We hear about the eyebrows and the eyelashes and eyelids of the eyes of Zeir Anpin, and we are told that when His eyes open they turn and see the open eye of Arich Anpin and they bathe in its whiteness – at this time all the prosecutors of Yisrael surrender. We learn about the four colors in the eyes of Zeir Anpin and we are told that the eyes supervise everyone in order to judge, that they generate mercy and goodness, and that they reveal man's actions as they are – good or bad. Rabbi Shimon talks again about the separation of Zeir Anpin and Malchut.

135. עַיְינִין דְּרֵישָׁא, אִינּוּן עַיְינִין דְּלָא מִסְתַּמְּרִין מִנַּיְיהוּ חַיָּיבַיָּא. עַיְינִין דְּנַיְימִין וְלָא נַיְימִין. ובג"כ אִקְרוּ עֵינָיו כְּיוֹנִים. מַאי יוֹנִים. כד"א, וְלֹא תוֹנוּ אִישׁ אֶת עֲמִיתוֹ. וע"ד כְּתִיב, וַיֹּאמְרוּ לֹא יִרְאֶה יָ"ה וְגוֹ'. וּכְתִיב הֲנוֹטַע אֹזֶן הֲלֹא יִשְׁמָע וְגוֹ'.

135. The eyes in the head OF ZEIR ANPIN are eyes from which the wicked are not guarded. They are eyes that sleep yet that do not sleep, THAT IS, THEY SOMETIMES SLEEP AND SOMETIMES DO NOT. For that reason they are called, "His eyes are like doves" (Shir Hashirim 5:12). What is meant by 'doves'? It is as in, "You shall not therefore defraud (Heb. *tonu*) one another" (Vayikra 25:17), DERIVED FROM FRAUD. FOR IT SEEMS TO THE WICKED THAT THEY ARE ASLEEP, THAT IS, NOT SUPERVISING THE WORLD. Hence it is written, "Yet they say, Hashem shall not see, nor shall the Elohim of Jacob regard it…" (Tehilim 94:7), and, "He that planted the ear, shall He not hear…" (Ibid. 9).

136. תִּקּוּנָא דְּעַל עֵינָא, שַׂעֲרֵי דְּמִתְּשַׁעְרָן בְּשִׁעוּרָא שְׁלִים. מֵאִינּוּן שַׂעֲרִין תַּלְיָין, אֲלַף וְז' מְאָה מָארֵי דְּאַשְׁגָּחוּתָא, לְאַגָּחָא קְרָבָא. וּכְדֵין קַיְימֵי כֻּלְּהוּ מִשּׁוּלְשְׁלֵיהוֹן וּמִתְפַּקְחִין עַיְינִין.

136. The characteristic above the eye is the hairs growing AT THE END OF THE FOREHEAD ABOVE THE EYES, in full measure. From these hairs 1,007 supervisors are ready to wage war, and then they stop from falling, THAT IS, STOP THEIR FALLING OVER THE EYES TO COVER THEM, BECAUSE THE HAIRS RISE ABOVE THE EYES and the eyes open.

137. כְּסוּתָא דְּעַל עַיְינִין, גְּבִינִין מִתְאַחֲדָן בְּהוּ. וַאֲלַף וְד׳ מְאָה רִבְּוָון מָארֵי תְּרִיסִין אִתְאַחֲדָן בְּהוּ, וְאִינּוּן אִקְרוּן כְּסוּתָא דְּעַיְינִין. וְכָל אִינּוּן דְּאִקְרוּן עֵינֵי יְיָ׳, לָא פַּקְחִין, וְלָא אִתְּעָרוּן, בַּר בְּזִמְנָא, דְּאִלֵּין כְּסוּתֵי דְּגְבִינִין, מִתְפָּרְשָׁן אִינּוּן תַּתָּאֵי מֵעִלָּאֵי. וּבְשַׁעֲתָא דְּאִתְפָּרְשָׁן גְּבִינֵי תַּתָּאֵי מֵעִלָּאֵי, וְיָהֲבִין אֲתַר לְאַשְׁגָּחָא מִתְפַּקְחִין עַיְינִין, וְאִתְחַזֵּי כְּמַאן דְּאִתְעַר מִשִּׁינְתֵיהּ. אִסְתַּחֲרוּ עַיְינִין וְחָמָא לְעֵינָא פְּקִיחָא, וְאִסְתָּחָן בְּחִוָּורָא דִּילֵיהּ. וְכַד אִסְתַּחְיָין, אִתְכַּפְיָין מָארֵיהוֹן דְּדִינִין לְיִשְׂרָאֵל. ובג״כ כְּתִיב, עוּרָה לָמָּה תִישַׁן יְיָ׳ הָקִיצָה וְגוֹ׳.

137. Eyelashes are attached to the eyelids, AND BOTH ARE CONSIDERED EYELIDS OR EYE COVERS. 14,000,000 protectors hold on to them, who are called eye covers. And all these are considered the eyes of Hashem. They never open or waken, except when the lower eyelids OVER THE EYES separate from the upper lids, THAT IS, THE LOWER PART IS SEPARATED FROM THE UPPER PART. And when the lower lids separate from the upper and make room for supervision, the eyes open and seem as one awakened from his sleep. The eyes turn and see the open eye OF ARICH ANPIN and bathe in its whiteness. When they wash IN WHITE all the prosecutors of Yisrael surrender. Hence it is written, "Awake, why sleep you, Adonai? Arise…" (Tehilim 44:24).

138. אַרְבַּע גַּוְונִין אִתְחַזְיָין בְּאִינּוּן עַיְינִין. מֵאִינּוּן נְהִירִין ד׳ בָּתֵּי דִּתְפִלִּין, דְּנַהֲרִין בִּרְהִיטֵי מוֹחָא. ז׳ דְּאִקְרוּן עֵינֵי ה׳. וְאַשְׁגָּחוּתָא נַפְקֵי, מִגְּוָון אוּכָמָא דְּעֵינָא. כְּמָה דְּאוֹקִימְנָא בְּאִדְרָא, דִּכְתִּיב עַל אֶבֶן אַחַת שִׁבְעָה עֵינָיִם. וְאִינּוּן גַּוְונִין מִתְלַהֲטִין בְּסִטְרַיְיהוּ.

138. Four colors can be seen in these eyes OF ZEIR ANPIN, WHITE, RED, GREEN AND BLACK. From them shine the four compartments of the Tefilin that illuminate the cavities of the brain. There are seven that are called the eyes of Hashem, THE SEVEN SFIROT, CHESED, GVURAH, TIFERET, NETZACH, HOD, YESOD AND MALCHUT IN THE EYE. WHITE IS CHESED, RED IS GVURAH, GREEN IS TIFERET THAT INCLUDES NETZACH, HOD AND YESOD, AND BLACK IS MALCHUT. Eyesight comes from the blackness in the eye, WHICH IS MALCHUT as we explained in the Idra RABA, as written, “upon one stone are seven facets (lit. ‘eyes’)” (Zecharyah 3:9), which are the colors that glow from their aspects.

139. מִסּוּמָּקָא, נָפְקִין אוּחֲרָנִין, מָארֵי דְּאַשְׁגָּחוּתָא לְדִינָא. וְאִינּוּן אִקְרוּן, עֵינֵי יְיָ׳ מְשׁוֹטְטוֹת בְּכָל הָאָרֶץ. מְשׁוֹטְטוֹת, וְלֹא מְשׁוֹטְטִים. בְּגִין דְּכֻלְּהוּ דִּינָא. מִירוֹקָא, נָפְקִין אוּחֲרָנִין, דְּקַיְימִין לְגַלָּאָה עוֹבָדִין, בֵּין טַב וּבֵין בִּישׁ. דִּכְתִיב כִּי עֵינָיו עַל דַּרְכֵי אִישׁ. וְאִלֵּין אִקְרוּן, עֵינֵי יְיָ׳ מְשׁוֹטְטִים. מְשׁוֹטְטִים, וְלֹא מְשׁוֹטְטוֹת. בְּגִין דְּאִינּוּן לִתְרֵין סִטְרִין, לְטָב וּלְבִישׁ. מֵחִוָּורָא, נָפְקִין כָּל אִינּוּן רַחֲמֵי, כָּל אִינּוּן טָבָאן, דְּמִשְׁתַּכְחֵי בְּעָלְמָא, לְאוֹטָבָא לְהוּ לְיִשְׂרָאֵל. וּכְדֵין אִסְתַּחְיָין כָּל אִינּוּן תְּלַת גְּוָונֵי, לְרַחֲמָא עָלַיְיהוּ.

139. From the red COLOR IN THE EYES come out SEVEN other EYES, which supervise to do Judgment, BECAUSE THE RED COLOR IS THE LEFT COLUMN THAT IS JUDGMENT. They are called, “the eyes of Hashem run to and fro throughout the whole earth” (II Divrei Hayamim 16:9). “run” IS WRITTEN AS FEMININE, instead of masculine, WHICH IS because they are all Judgment. From the green color IN THE EYE come out SEVEN other EYES, the purpose of which is to reveal MAN’S actions, both good or bad, as written, “For His eyes are upon the ways of man” (Iyov 34:21). These are called, “the eyes of Hashem, they rove to and fro” (Zecharyah 4:10), “rove” with a masculine suffix instead of the feminine, because they face both sides, the good as well as the bad, BECAUSE THE GREEN COLOR IS THE CENTRAL COLUMN THAT INCLUDES RIGHT AND LEFT, WHICH ARE CHESED AND JUDGMENT. HENCE IT IS IN THE MASCULINE, SINCE CHESED SHINES WITH THE MALE LIGHT. From the white COLOR IN THE EYE come out all the mercy and all the goodness that is present in the world to do good to Yisrael, for then the three colors, RED, GREEN AND BLACK, bathe IN THE WHITE COLOR, WHICH IS MERCY, in order to have mercy upon them.

140. אִלֵּין גַּוְונִין מִתְעָרְבִין דָּא בְּדָא, וְאִתְדַּבְּקָן דָּא בְּדָא. כָּל חַד אוֹזִיף לְחַבְרֵיהּ מִגְּוָונֵי דִּילֵיהּ, בַּר מֵחִוָּורָא, דְּכֻלְּהוּ כְּלִילָן בֵּיהּ כַּד אִצְטְרִיךְ, וְהוּא חָפֵי עַל כֹּלָּא. כָּל גַּוְונִין דִּלְתַתָּא, לָא יַכְלִין כָּל בְּנֵי עָלְמָא, לְאַסְחֲרָא לוֹן חִוָּורָא, לְאוּכָמָא לְסוּמָקָא וְלִירוֹקָא. וְהָכָא בְּאַשְׁגָּחוּתָא חַד, כֻּלְּהוּ אִתְאַחֲדָן וְאִסְתַּחְיָין בְּחִוָּורָא.

140. These four colors blend with each other and merge with each other, and each lends some of its color to its neighbor, except for the white color in which all are incorporated when IT is needed and when it covers everything. As for all the PHYSICAL colors below, no one can revert the black, red and green to look white. But here under the same supervision all THREE COLORS, BLACK, RED AND GREEN, join and bathe in the white color, THAT IS, THEY BECOME WHITE AGAIN, WHICH IS CHESED.

141. גְּבִינוֹי לָא מִשְׁתַּכְּבִין, בַּר כַּד בַּעְיָין גַּוְונִין דְּחִוָּורָא לְאַשְׁגָּחָא, בְּגִין דִּגְבִינִין יָהֲבִין אֲתַר לְאַשְׁגָּחָא, לְכֻלְּהוּ גְּוָונֵי. וְאִי אִינּוּן לָא יָהֲבִין אֲתַר, לָא יַכְלִין לְאַשְׁגְּחָא וּלְאִסְתַּכְּלָא. גְּבִינִין לָא קַיְימִין, וְלָא מִשְׁתַּכְּבִין שַׁעֲתָא חֲדָא שְׁלֵימוּתָא, אֶלָּא פַּקְחִין וְסַתְמִין, סַתְמִין וּפַקְחִין, מִשּׁוּם עֵינָא פְּקִיחָא דְּקָאֵי עֲלַיְיהוּ. וע״ד כְּתִיב, וְהַחַיּוֹת רָצוֹא וָשׁוֹב. וְהָא אוּקִימְנָא.

141. The eyebrows are never lying over the eyes except when the white colors wish to observe, because the eyebrows give all colors room to observe. If they do not, no COLOR can supervise and watch. The eyebrows do not stand IN ONE PLACE and never lie still for a whole hour, but open and close, close and open, since the observing eye is over them. Hence it is written, "And the living creatures ran and returned" (Yechezkel 1:14). I have already explained this.

142. כְּתִיב עֵינֶיךָ תִּרְאֶינָה יְרוּשָׁלַםִ נָוֶה שַׁאֲנָן, וּכְתִיב תָּמִיד עֵינֵי יְיָ׳ אֱלֹהֶיךָ בָּהּ מֵרֵשִׁית הַשָּׁנָה וְגוֹ׳. דְּהָא יְרוּשְׁלֵם בַּעְיָא כֵּן, דִּכְתִּיב, צֶדֶק יָלִין בָּהּ. ובג״כ יְרוּשָׁלַםִ, וְלָא צִיּוֹן. דִּכְתִיב, צִיּוֹן בְּמִשְׁפָּט תִּפָּדֶה וְגוֹ׳, דְּכֹלָּא רַחֲמֵי.

142. It is written, "your eyes shall see Jerusalem a quiet habitation" (Yeshayah 33:20), and, "the eyes of Hashem your Elohim are always upon it, from the beginning of the year…" (Devarim 11:12), because Jerusalem needs that. FOR JERUSALEM, WHICH IS MALCHUT, NEEDS TO HAVE THE EYES OF HASHEM, THE SECRET OF CHOCHMAH, IN IT, SINCE THE REVELATION OF CHOCHMAH IS IN MALCHUT CALLED LOWER CHOCHMAH. As written, "righteousness lodged in it" (Yeshayah 1:21), RIGHTEOUSNESS BEING THE SECRET OF THE JUDGMENTS THAT EMERGE FROM THE ILLUMINATION OF CHOCHMAH OF THE LEFT THAT SHINES IN MALCHUT. Hence it speaks of Jerusalem rather than Zion, WHICH IS THE INNER PART OF MALCHUT, THE SECRET OF THE ILLUMINATION OF CHASSADIM, as written, "Zion shall be redeemed with justice" (Ibid. 27), since all is Mercy, AS RIGHTEOUSNESS IS JUDGMENT OF THE LEFT AND APPLIES TO JERUSALEM, WHILE JUSTICE IS MERCY OF ZEIR ANPIN AND APPLIES TO ZION.

143. עֵינֶיךָ, עֵינְךָ כְּתִיב, עֵינָא דְּעַתִּיקָא קַדִּישָׁא, סְתִימָא דְּכֹלָּא. הַשְׁתָּא, עֵינֵי יְיָ׳ אֱלֹהֶיךָ בָּהּ, לְטָב וּלְבִישׁ, כְּמָה דְּאִתְחֲזֵי. בג״כ לָא אִתְקְיָימוּ בְּקִיּוּמָא תָּדִיר. וְהָתָם עֵינְךָ תִּרְאֶינָה יְרוּשְׁלַםִ, כֹּלָּא לְטָב, כֹּלָּא בְּרַחֲמֵי. דִּכְתִּיב, וּבְרַחֲמִים גְּדוֹלִים אֲקַבְּצֵךְ.

143. "your eyes SHALL SEE JERUSALEM" is spelled 'your eye' IN SINGULAR, WHICH INDICATES the eye of the most concealed Atika Kadisha, WHOSE TWO EYES BECOME ONE AGAIN, BEING WHITE WITHIN WHITE, WHICH WILL HAPPEN IN THE FUTURE. But for now it is written, "the eyes of Hashem your Elohim are always upon it," THAT IS, TWO EYES, which are for good and for evil as it should be. For that reason they do not exist always BUT IN THE FUTURE WILL AGAIN BE ONE EYE, SINCE there, "your eye shall see Jerusalem," NAMELY ONE EYE, which is all for good, all merciful, THAT IS, THE EYE OF ATIKA, as written, "but with great mercies will I gather you" (Yeshayah 54:7).

144. תָּמִיד עֵינֵי יְיָ׳ אֱלֹהֶיךָ בָּהּ מֵרֵשִׁית הַשָּׁנָה. מֵרֵשִׁית חָסֵר א׳ כְּתִיב, וְלָא רֵאשִׁית בְּאָלֶף. מַאן הִיא. הֵ״א דִּלְתַתָּא. וּלְעֵילָּא כְּתִיב, הִשְׁלִיךְ מִשָּׁמַיִם אֶרֶץ תִּפְאֶרֶת יִשְׂרָאֵל. מַאי טַעֲמָא הִשְׁלִיךְ מִשָּׁמַיִם אֶרֶץ. מִשּׁוּם דִּכְתִּיב אַלְבִּישׁ שָׁמַיִם קַדְרוּת, וְעַיְינִין בְּקַדְרוּתָא, בְּגַוְונָא אוּכָמָא אִתְחָפוּ.

144. "the eyes of Hashem your Elohim are always upon it, from the beginning (Heb. *resheet*) of the year." 'resheet' is defectively spelled without Aleph, instead of with it. What is THAT WHICH IS CALLED RESHEET WITHOUT ALEPH: it is lower Hei, NAMELY MALCHUT, SINCE RESHEET IS NAMED AFTER '*RASH* (ENG. 'POOR')'. Before that it is written, "and cast down from heaven (to) earth the beauty of Yisrael" (Eichah 2:1). What is the reason He "cast down from heaven earth," THAT IS, WHY WAS MALCHUT CALLED EARTH CAST DOWN FROM ZEIR ANPIN CALLED HEAVEN? AND HE ANSWERS, It is because it is written, "I clothe the heavens with blackness" (Yeshayah 50:3), WHICH MEANS the eyes are in blackness, that is, they are covered with blackness, SINCE THEN MALCHUT IS SEPARATED FROM ZEIR ANPIN AND HAS NOTHING TO RECEIVE FROM HIM.

145. מֵרֵשִׁית הַשָּׁנָה, מֵאָן אֲתָר מִסְתַּכְּלִין בִּירוּשְׁלֵם אִלֵּין עֵינֵי יְיָ׳, חָזַר וּפֵירַשׁ, מֵרֵשִׁית הַשָּׁנָה, דְּהוּא דִּינָא בְּלָא אָלֶף, וְדִינָא אִתְאֲחָד מִסִּטְרָהָא, אע״ג דְּלָאו הוּא דִּינָא מַמָּשׁ. וְעַד אַחֲרִית שָׁנָה, אַחֲרִית שָׁנָה וַדַּאי דִּינָא אִשְׁתְּכַח. דְּהָא כְּתִיב, צֶדֶק יָלִין בָּהּ, דְּהִיא אַחֲרִית הַשָּׁנָה.

145. "from the beginning of the year": namely whence do the eyes of Hashem behold Jerusalem? Again he explains, "from the beginning of the year," WHICH IS BINAH CALLED BEGINNING, spelled without Aleph because it is of Judgment, since Judgment is connected to its side, THAT IS, ITS LEFT SIDE. "to the end of the year" (Devarim 11:12): surely the end of the year is there, as it is written, "righteousness lodged in it," which is the end of the year, NAMELY MALCHUT.

146. ת״ח, א׳ בִּלְחוֹדוֹי אִקְרֵי רִאשׁוֹן, דְּכַר. בְּאָלֶף סָתִים וְגָנִיז מַה דְּלָא אִתְיְדַע. כַּד אִתְחַבָּר הַאי אָלֶף בַּאֲתָר אַחֲרָא, אִקְרֵי רֵאשִׁית. וְאִי תֵּימָא דְּאִתְחַבָּרָא. לָא. אֶלָּא אִתְגַּלְיָא בֵּיהּ, וְנָהִיר לֵיהּ, וּכְדֵין אִקְרֵי רֵאשִׁית. וַאֲפִילּוּ בְּהַאי רֵאשִׁית, לָא אַשְׁגַּח בִּירוּשְׁלֵם, דְּאִלְמָלֵא הֲוַת בְּהַאי, אִתְקַיְּימַת תָּדִירָא. אֲבָל מֵרֵשִׁית כְּתִיב. וּלְעָלְמָא דְּאָתֵי כְּתִיב, רִאשׁוֹן לְצִיּוֹן הִנֵּה הִנָּם וְגוֹ׳.

146. Come and see, Aleph on its own is called 'first', which is masculine, because that which is unknown is concealed and treasured in Aleph. When this Aleph is connected somewhere else, THE PLACE is called 'beginning'. You may argue it is connected to it, but it is not so. It is revealed in and shines on it, and then it is called beginning. Even in that beginning it does not observe Jerusalem, since had it received from this BEGINNING, it would have shone forever AND ITS UNION WOULD HAVE BEEN UNBROKEN. But 'beginning' is spelled without Aleph, AND HENCE ITS UNION IS INTERRUPTED. Of the World to Come it is written, "A harbinger (lit. 'first') for Zion will I give. Behold, behold them" (Yeshayah 41:27), WHERE ALEPH, WHICH IS CALLED FIRST WILL SHINE ON ZION, WHICH IS MALCHUT.

38. The nose of Zeir Anpin

A Synopsis

Rabbi Shimon tells us the difference between the nose of Atika Kadisha and the nose of Zeir Anpin. We learn that the nose of Zeir Anpin is of anger and judgment, yet that the judgment is mitigated by the sweet savor of the burnt offerings given by the children of Yisrael. The nose of Atika Kadisha is long-suffering, and it holds back the judgments of the short nose of Zeir Anpin.

147. חוּטְמָא דִּזְעֵיר אַנְפִּין, תִּקּוּנָא דְּפַרְצוּפָא. כָּל פַּרְצוּפָא בֵּיהּ אִשְׁתְּמוֹדַע. חוּטָמָא דָּא, לָאו כְּחוּטָמָא דְּעַתִּיקָא קַדִּישָׁא סְתִימָאָה דְּכָל סְתִימִין. דְּחוּטְמָא דְּעַתִּיקָא, חַיִּים דְּחַיִּים. דְּהָא מִתְּרֵין נוּקְבִין, נָפְקִין רוּחִין דְּחַיִּין, לְכֹלָּא. בְּהַאי זְעֵיר אַנְפִּין כְּתִיב, עָלָה עָשָׁן בְּאַפּוֹ וְגוֹ'.

147. The nose of Zeir Anpin characterizes the face, since the whole face is recognized by it. This nose is unlike the nose of the most concealed Atika Kadisha, since the nose of Atika is the life of life. For from the two nostrils OF THE NOSE come out spirits of life for everyone. Of Zeir Anpin it is written, "There went up a smoke out of His nostrils…" (II Shmuel 22:9).

148(1). בְּהַאי תְּנָנָא כָּל גְּוָונֵי אֲחִידָן בֵּיהּ, בְּכָל גְּוָונָא וּגְוָונָא, אֲחִידָן כַּמָּה מָארֵיהוֹן דְּדִינָא קַשְׁיָא. דַּאֲחִידָן בְּהַהוּא תְּנָנָא. וְלָא מִתְבַּסְּמִין כֻּלְּהוּ, אֶלָּא בִּתְנָנָא דְּמַדְבְּחָא דִּלְתַתָּא. וע"ד כְּתִיב, וַיָּרַח יְיָ' אֶת רֵיחַ הַנִּיחֹחַ. מַהוּ הַנִּיחֹחַ. אִתְבַּסְּמוּתָא דְּמָארֵי דִּינָא, נַחַת רוּחַ.

148.a All aspects hold on to the smoke IN THE NOSE, and in each class many harsh prosecutors hold on to that smoke. They are all sweetened only by the smoke on the altar below. Hence it is written, "And Hashem smelled the sweet savor" (Beresheet 8:21). The sweet savor is the mitigation of the prosecutors, NAMELY satisfaction.

148(2). וַיָּרַח יְיָ' אֶת רֵיחַ הַנִּיחֹחַ, אֶת רֵיחַ הַקָּרְבָּן לָא כְּתִיב, אֶלָּא אֶת רֵיחַ הַנִּיחֹחַ. דְּכֻלְּהוּ גְּבוּרָאן דַּאֲחִידָן בְּחוּטָמָא, וְכָל דְּאִתְאַחֲדָן בְּהוּ,

כָּלְהוּ מִתְבַּסְמָן. וְכַמָּה גְּבוּרָאן מִתְאַחֲדָן כַּחֲדָא, דִּכְתִּיב מִי יְמַלֵּל גְּבוּרוֹת יְיָ׳ יַשְׁמִיעַ כָּל תְּהִלָּתוֹ. וְהַאי חוֹטָמָא, מֵחַד נוּקְבָּא נָפַק אֶשָּׁא דְּאַכְלָא כָּל שְׁאַר אֶשִּׁין. בְּחַד נוּקְבָּא תְּנָנָא. וְהַאי וְהַאי אִשְׁתְּכַח בְּאֶשָּׁא וּתְנָנָא דְּמַדְבְּחָא. וְאִתְגַּלְיָיא הַאי עַתִּיקָא קַדִּישָׁא, וְאִשְׁתְּכַךְ כֹּלָּא. הַיְינוּ דְּאִתְּמַר וּתְהִלָּתִי אֶחֱטָם לָךְ.

148.b "And Hashem smelled the sweet savor." It does not speak of the smell of the sacrifice, but of the savory smell, because all the Gvurot are connected to the nose, and all Judgments that are connected TO THE NOSE are mitigated, and many Gvurot are joined together, as written, "Who can utter the mighty acts (Heb. *gvurot*) of Hashem? who can declare all His praise" (Tehilim 106:2). From one nostril of this nose (Heb. *chotem*) comes out fire that consumes all other fires, and from the other nostril comes out smoke. Both are MITIGATED by the fire and smoke of the altar. Atika Kadisha is uncovered WITH ITS CHASSADIM and all Judgments are quieted. This is the meaning of, "and for My praise will I refrain (Heb. *echetom*) for you" (Yeshayah 48:9), WHICH REFERS TO THE NOSE OF ATIKA.

149. חוֹטָמָא דְּעַתִּיקָא קַדִּישָׁא אָרִיךְ, וּמִתְפַּשַּׁט. וְאִקְרֵי אֶרֶךְ אַפַּיִם. וְהַאי חוֹטָמָא, זְעִיר. וְכַד תְּנָנָא שָׁרֵי נָפִיק בִּבְהִילוּ, וְאִתְעֲבֵיד דִּינָא. וּמַאן מְעַכֵּב לְהַאי. חוֹטָמָא דְּעַתִּיקָא. וְכֹלָּא כְּמָה דַּאֲמֵינָא בְּאִדְרָא, וְאִתְּעֲרוּ חַבְרַיָּיא.

149. The nose of Atika Kadisha is long and expansive, and is called long-suffering (lit. 'long nosed'). This nose OF ZEIR ANPIN is short. When smoke starts emerging in haste, Judgment is carried out. The nose of Atika detains it, NAMELY ITS CHASSADIM. All is as I said at the Idra RABA, where the friends have commented on it.

150. וּבְסִפְרָא דְּרַב הַמְנוּנָא סָבָא, אוֹקִים הָנֵי תְּרֵי נוּקְבֵי. מֵחַד תְּנָנָא וְאֶשָּׁא. וּמֵחַד נַיְיחָא וְרוּחָא טָבָא. דְּאִית בֵּיהּ יְמִינָא וּשְׂמָאלָא, וּכְתִיב וְרֵיחַ לוֹ כַּלְּבָנוֹן. וּבְנוּקְבָּא כְּתִיב, וְרֵיחַ אַפֵּךְ כַּתַּפּוּחִים. וּמַה בְּנוּקְבָּא הָכִי, כָּל שֶׁכֵּן בֵּיהּ. וְשַׁפִּיר קָאֲמַר.

150. In his book, Rav Hamnuna Saba explained about the two nostrils IN THE NOSE that from one there is smoke and fire and from another satisfaction and good spirit. Because it has in it right and left, FROM THE LEFT THERE IS SMOKE AND FIRE AND FROM THE RIGHT SATISFACTION AND GOODNESS OF SPIRIT, WHICH IS CHASSADIM INCLUDING CHOCHMAH. It is also written, "and his fragrance like the Lebanon" (Hoshea 14:7). Of the Nukva it is written, "the scent of your countenance (lit. 'nose') like apples" (Shir Hashirim 7:9), WHICH INDICATES THE ILLUMINATION OF CHOCHMAH CALLED SMELL. If this is true for the Nukva, it is all the more so FOR ZEIR ANPIN, WHICH SUSTAINS THE NUKVA. And he has spoken well.

151. וּמַה דְּאָמַר וַיָּרַח יְיָ׳ אֶת רֵיחַ הַנִּיחֹחַ. הַנִּיחֹחַ בִּתְרֵי סִטְרֵי, חַד נַיְיחָא, דְּאִתְגַּלְיָיא עַתִּיקָא קַדִּישָׁא סְתִימָא דְּכָל סְתִימִין, דְּהַאי הוּא נַיְיחָא וְאִתְבַּסְּמוּתָא לְכֹלָּא. וְחַד אִתְבַּסְּמוּתָא דִּלְתַּתָּא, בְּהַהוּא תְּנָנָא וְאֶשָּׁא דְּמַדְבְּחָא. וּבְגִין דְּאִיהוּ מִתְּרֵין סִטְרִין, כְּתִיב נִיחֹחַ. וְכֹלָּא בִּזְעֵיר אַנְפִּין אִתְּמַר.

151. As for the words, "And Hashem smelled the sweet savor (Heb. *nichoach*)," the sweet savor INDICATES DOUBLE SATISFACTION (HEB. *nachat)* on both sides RIGHT AND LEFT. The one ON THE RIGHT is satisfaction revealed from the most concealed Atika Kadisha, which brings pleasure and sweetening for everything, BOTH TO CHOCHMAH AND CHASSADIM. The one ON THE LEFT is sweetening coming from below with the smoke and fire on the altar. Since it is SWEETENED on both sides FROM ATIKA AND FROM BELOW, THEREFORE it is written, 'nichoach' WHICH INDICATES DOUBLE SATISFACTION. All this applies to Zeir Anpin.

39. The ears of Zeir Anpin

A Synopsis

We are told about the two ears that hear good and bad, and about the winged messengers who hear the prayers people say out loud and who carry those prayers up to the ears of God. Rabbi Shimon says it is important that the sound be 'tasted' for its quality, and that this be done slowly; he tells us that whatever happens too quickly does not possess complete wisdom. We hear about the cavities of the ears, eyes, mouth and nose, and about how the sound affects them. According to the sound, the eyes might cry and the mouth might speak words; the whole body might tremble. Therefore people must guard carefully what they say out loud. Rabbi Shimon goes on to say that supreme secrets originate from the ear of Zeir Anpin, and that those secrets are only revealed to those who walk the straight path. Wicked people are those who reveal secrets, and the righteous are those faithful spirits who conceal the secrets.

152. תְּרֵי אוּדְנִין, לְמִשְׁמַע טַב וּבִישׁ. וְתַרְוַויְיהוּ סַלְּקִין לְחַד. דִּכְתִיב, הַטֵּה יְיָ׳ אָזְנְךָ וּשֲׁמָע. אוּדְנָא לְגוֹ בְּגוֹ דִּילֵיהּ, תַּלְיָיא בִּרְשִׁימִין עַקִּימִין, בְּגִין דְּיִתְעַכָּב קָלָא לְאַעֲלָא בְּמוֹחָא, וְיַבְחִין בֵּיהּ מוֹחָא, וְלָא בִּבְהִילוּ, דְּכָל מִלָּה דַּהֲוֵי בִּבְהִילוּ, לָא הֲוָה בְּחָכְמְתָא שְׁלֵימָתָא.

152. There are two ears to hear good and bad, and both are considered one, as written, "Hashem, bend Your ear, and hear" (II Melachim 19:16). The innermost ear is formed of curved apertures so that the sound will be slowed down in entering the brain, the brain will be able to perceive it and it will not enter quickly, for whatever happens quickly does not possess complete wisdom.

153. מֵאוּדְנִין אִלֵּין תַּלְיָין כָּל מָארֵיהוֹן דְּגַדְפִין, דְּנַטְלִין קָלָא מֵעָלְמָא, וְכֻלְּהוּ הָכִי אִקְרוּן אָזְנֵי יְיָ׳, דִּכְתִּיב בְּהוּ, כִּי עוֹף הַשָּׁמַיִם יוֹלִיךְ אֶת הַקּוֹל וְגוֹ׳. כִּי עוֹף הַשָּׁמַיִם יוֹלִיךְ אֶת הַקּוֹל, הַאי קְרָא קַשְׁיָא, הַשְׁתָּא מַאי קוֹל אִיכָּא הָכָא, דְּהָא רֵישָׁא דִּקְרָא כְּתִיב גַּם בְּמַדָּעֲךָ מֶלֶךְ אַל תְּקַלֵּל, בְּמַדָּעֲךָ כְּתִיב, וּבְחַדְרֵי מִשְׁכָּבְךָ וְגוֹ׳. מַאי טַעֲמָא כִּי עוֹף הַשָּׁמַיִם יוֹלִיךְ אֶת הַקּוֹל, וְהָא לֵיכָּא הָכָא קָלָא.

153. From the ears originate all the winged creatures, who receive the sound from the world. They are all called 'the ears of Hashem', as it is written of them, "for a bird of the sky shall carry the sound..." (Kohelet 10:20). HE ASKS, This verse is difficult, for what sound is there here, if the beginning of the verse writes, "Do not curse the king, no, not even in your thought" (Ibid.). If it says, "in your thought...even in your bedchamber," THEN why the reasoning, "for a bird of the sky shall carry the sound," if there is no sound here BUT THOUGHT?

154. אֶלָּא וַדַּאי כָּל מַה דְּחָשִׁיב ב״נ, וְכָל מַה דְּיִסְתַּכַּל בְּלִבּוֹי, לָא עָבִיד מִלָּה, עַד דְּאַפִּיק לֵיהּ בְּשִׂפְוָותֵיהּ, וְהוּא לָא אִתְכַּוָּון בֵּיהּ. וְהַהִיא מִלָּה דְּאַפִּיק, מִתְבַּקְעָא בַּאֲוִירָא, וְאַזְלָא וְסַלְקָא וְטָסָא בְּעָלְמָא, וְאִתְעֲבִיד מִנֵּיהּ קָלָא. וְהַהוּא קָלָא נַטְלִין לֵיהּ מָארֵי דְּגַדְפִּין, וְסַלְקִין לֵיהּ לְמַלְכָּא, וְעָיֵיל בְּאוּדְנוֹי. הה״ד, וַיִּשְׁמַע יְיָ׳ אֶת קוֹל דִּבְרֵיכֶם. וַיִּשְׁמַע יְיָ׳ וַיִּחַר אַפּוֹ.

154. AND HE ANSWERS, Surely man does nothing with whatever he thinks or meditates on until he utters it with his lips, even if he does not mean to. The word he utters cleaves through the air, rises and flies in the world and turns into a sound. The winged ones take that sound; they raise it to the King and it enters His ears. This is the meaning of, "And Hashem heard the voice of your words" (Devarim 5:25), "and Hashem heard it; and His anger was kindled" (Bemidbar 11:1).

155. ובג״כ, כָּל צְלוֹתָא וּבָעוּתָא דְּבָעֵי ב״נ מִקַּמֵּי קוּדְשָׁא בְּרִיךְ הוּא, בָּעֵי לְאַפָּקָא מִלִּין בְּשִׂפְוָותֵיהּ, דְּאִי לָא אַפִּיק לוֹן, לָאו צְלוֹתֵיהּ צְלוֹתָא, וְלָאו בָּעוּתֵיהּ בָּעוּתָא. וְכֵיוָן דְּמִלִּין נָפְקִין, מִתְבַּקְעִין בַּאֲוִירָא, סַלְקִין וְטָסִין וְאִתְעֲבִידוּ קָלָא, וְנָטִיל לוֹן מַאן דְּנָטִיל, וְאָחִיד לוֹן לְאַתְרָא קַדִּישָׁא, בְּרֵישָׁא דְּמַלְכָּא.

155. Therefore, whatever the prayer or entreaty a man asks before the Holy One, blessed be He, he should utter the words with his lips, for if he does not utter them WITH HIS LIPS, his prayer is no prayer nor is his petition a real petition. Once the words are uttered and cleave the air, they rise and fly and become a sound that is taken by someone, who joins them in a holy place in the King's head.

156. מִתְּלַת חַלָלֵי דְּמוֹחֵי, נָטִיף נְטִיפָא לְאוּדְנִין, וְהַהוּא אִקְרֵי נַחַל כְּרִית. כד"א, נַחַל כְּרִית, כְּלוֹמַר, כְּרוּתָא דְּאוּדְנִין. וְקָלָא עַיֵּיל בְּהַהוּא עֲקִימָא, וְאִשְׁתְּאַב בְּהַהוּא נַהֲרָא, דְּהַהוּא נְטִיפָא. וּכְדֵין אִתְעַכָּב תַּמָּן, וְאִתְבְּחִין בֵּין טַב לְבִישׁ. הה"ד, כִּי אֹזֶן מִלִּין תִּבְחָן. ומ"ט אֹזֶן מִלִּין תִּבְחָן. מִשּׁוּם דְּאִתְעַכָּב קָלָא בְּהַהוּא נַהֲרָא דִּנְטִיפָא, בַּעֲקִימוּתָא דְּאוּדְנִין, וְלָא עַיֵּיל בִּבְהִילוּ. ובג"כ אִתְבְּחִין בֵּין טַב לְבִישׁ, וְחֵיךְ יִטְעַם לֶאֱכוֹל. מ"ט חֵיךְ יִטְעַם לֶאֱכוֹל. בְּגִין דְּיִתְעַכָּב תַּמָּן, וְלָא עַיֵּיל בִּבְהִילוּ בְּגוּפָא, וע"ד יִטְעַם וְיִתְבְּחָן, בֵּין מְתִיקָא לִמְרִירוּ.

156. From the three cavities of the brain, CHOCHMAH, BINAH AND DA'AT, a trickle drips to the ears; this trickle is called the stream of Kerit as in, "wadi Kerit" (I Melachim 17:3), that is, the cutting off (Heb. *keritah*) of the ears. The sound enters that place WITHIN THE EAR to be absorbed in the river of that trickle, where it is held and tested to see whether it is good or bad. This is the meaning of, "For the ear tries words" (Iyov 34:3). This is because the sound is slowed down in the river of that trickle in the curve of the ears and does not enter quickly. Then it is tested to see whether it is good or bad, LIKE "the palate tastes food" (Ibid.); this means that it is held in the palate and does not enter the body quickly, so it tastes and distinguishes between sweet and bitter.

157. בְּהַאי נוּקְבָא דְּאוּדְנִין, תַּלְיָין נוּקְבִין אוֹחֲרָנִין, נוּקְבָא דְּעַיְינִין. נוּקְבָא דְּפוּמָא. נוּקְבָא דְּחוֹטָמָא. מֵהַהוּא קָלָא דְּעַיֵּיל בְּנוּקְבָא דְּאוּדְנִין, אִי אִצְטְרִיךְ עַיֵּיל לְנוּקְבֵי דְּעַיְינִין, וְנַבְעִין דִּמְעִין. מֵהַהוּא קָלָא אִי אִצְטְרִיךְ, עַיֵּיל לְנוּקְבָא דְּחוֹטָמָא דְּפַרְדַּשְׁקָא, וּמַפְּקֵי תְּנָנָא וְאֶשָּׁא מֵהַהוּא קָלָא. הה"ד וַיִּשְׁמַע יְיָ' וַיִּחַר אַפּוֹ וַתִּבְעַר בָּם אֵשׁ יְיָ'. וְאִי אִצְטְרִיךְ, עַיֵּיל הַהוּא קָלָא לְנוּקְבָא דְּפוּמָא, וּמַלִּיל וְגָזַר מִלִּין מֵהַהוּא קָלָא. כֹּלָּא מֵהַהוּא קָלָא דְּאוּדְנִין. עַיֵּיל בְּכָל גּוּפָא וְאִתְרְגִישׁ מִנֵּיהּ

כֹּלָּא. כְּמָה תַּלְיָיא בְּהַאי אוּדְנָא. זַכָּאָה מַאן דְּנָטִיר מִלּוֹי. ע״ד כְּתִיב, נְצוֹר לְשׁוֹנְךָ מֵרָע וּשְׂפָתֶיךָ מִדַּבֵּר מִרְמָה.

157. From the ear cavity derive other cavities: the eye socket, the mouth cavity and the nostrils in the nose. From the sound that enters the ear cavities, if required it enters FROM THE EAR to the sockets of the eyes, and the eyes shed tears. From that sound, if required, it enters the nostrils of the opening in the nose and they bring forth smoke and fire from that sound. This is the meaning of, "and Hashem heard it; and His anger was kindled; and the fire of Hashem burned among them" (Bemidbar 11:1). If necessary, the sound enters the mouth cavity and it speaks and utters words from that sound. Everything is from the sound THAT ENTERS the ears; it enters the whole body and everything trembles from it. Much is derived from that ear. Blessed is he who guards what he says. Hence it is written, "Keep your tongue from evil, and your lips from speaking guile" (Tehilim 34:14).

158. הַאי אוּדְנָא קָרֵי בֵּיהּ שְׁמִיעָה. וּבִשְׁמִיעָה אִתְכְּלִילָן אִינּוּן מוֹחֵי. חָכְמָה אִתְכְּלִיל בֵּיהּ, דִּכְתִיב, וְנָתַתָּ לְעַבְדְּךָ לֵב שׁוֹמֵעַ. בִּינָה, כְּמָה דְּאַתְּ אָמֵר דַּבֵּר כִּי שׁוֹמֵעַ עַבְדֶּךָ. כִּי שׁוֹמְעִים אֲנָחְנוּ. דַּעַת, כד״א, שְׁמַע בְּנִי וְקַח אֲמָרָי. וּמִצְוֹתַי תִּצְפּוֹן אִתָּךְ. הָא כֹּלָּא תַּלְיָין בְּאוּדְנִין בְּהַאי אוּדְנָא תַּלְיָין, צְלוֹתִין וּבָעוּתִין, וּפְקִיחָא דְּעַיְינִין. הֲדָא הוּא דִּכְתִיב, הַטֵּה יְיָ׳ אָזְנְךָ וּשֲׁמָע פְּקַח עֵינֶיךָ וּרְאֵה. הָא כֹּלָּא בֵּיהּ תַּלְיָיא.

158. Hearing applies to this ear, NAMELY BINAH CALLED HEARING, and within the hearing are incorporated the brain lobes CHOCHMAH, BINAH AND DA'AT, SINCE CHOCHMAH IS REVEALED ONLY THROUGH BINAH. Chochmah is included in it, as written, "Give therefore your servant an understanding (lit. 'hearing') heart" (I Melachim 3:9), HEART (HEB. *LEV*, =32) BEING THE SECRET OF THE 32 PATHS OF WISDOM. Binah IS INCLUDED WITHIN IT, as written, "Speak, for your servant is listening" (I Shmuel 3:10), ALSO we are listening, WHICH MEANS WE UNDERSTAND. Da'at IS INCLUDED WITHIN IT, as written, "Hear, O my son, and receive my sayings" (Mishlei 4:10), "and treasure up My commandments with you" (Mishlei 2:1), IN WHICH HEAR MEANS KNOW. Thus everything derives from the ear. THE RECEPTION OF prayers and petitions depends on this ear, as well as the opening of eyes. This is the meaning of, "Hashem, bend Your ear, and hear; open, Hashem, Your eyes, and see" (II Melachim 19:16). Thus everything originates FROM THE EAR.

159. בְּהַאי אוּדְנָא, תַּלְיָין רָזִין עִלָּאִין, דְּלָא נָפְקִין לְבַר, בג״כ הִיא עֲקִימָא לְגוֹ. וְרָזָא דְּרָזִין סְתִימִין בֵּיהּ, וַוי לְהַהוּא מְגַלֶּה רָזִין. וּבְגִין דְּהַאי אוּדְנָא כָּנִישׁ רָזִין, וַעֲקִימוּתָא דִּלְגוֹ נָטִיל לוֹן, לָא גַּלֵּי רָזִין לְאִינּוּן דַּעֲקִימִין בְּאָרְחַיְיהוּ, אֶלָּא לְאִינּוּן דְּלָא עֲקִימִין. הה״ד סוֹד יְיָ׳ לִירֵאָיו וּבְרִיתוֹ לְהוֹדִיעָם, דְּנַטְלֵי אָרְחוֹי וְנַטְלֵי מִלִּין.

159. Supreme secrets, NAMELY CHOCHMAH, that do not go outside originate from that ear, which is why it is curved on the inside. The most secret among the secrets are hidden within it. Woe to him who reveals secrets. And when the ear gathers to itself the secrets and the inside curve receives them, it does not reveal secrets to those who follow crooked paths, but to those that walk the STRAIGHT path that is not crooked. This is the meaning of, "The counsel of Hashem is with them that fear Him; and He will reveal to them His covenant" (Tehilim 25:14), for they accept His way and HENCE accept His words.

160. וְאִינּוּן דַּעֲקִימִין בְּאָרְחַיְיהוּ, נַטְלֵי מִלִּין וְעַיְילִין לוֹן בִּבְהִילוּ, וְלֵית בְּהוּ אֲתָר לְאִתְעַכְּבָא. וְכָל נוּקְבִין אַחֲרָנִין, מִתְפַּתְּחִין בֵּיהּ, עַד דְּנָפְקִין מִלִּין בְּנוּקְבָּא דְּפוּמָא. וְאִלֵּין אִקְרוּ חַיָּיבֵי דָּרָא, שְׂנוּאֵי דְקוּדְשָׁא בְּרִיךְ הוּא, בְּמַתְנִיתָא דִּילָן תְּנָן, כְּאִילוּ קָטִיל גּוּבְרִין, וּכְאִלּוּ פָּלַח לע״ז. וְכֹלָּא בְּחַד קְרָא, דִּכְתִיב, לֹא תֵלֵךְ רָכִיל בְּעַמֶּךָ לֹא תַעֲמוֹד עַל דַּם רֵעֶךָ אֲנִי יְיָ׳. מַאן דְּעָבַר עַל הַאי רֵישָׁא דִּקְרָא, כְּאִילוּ עָבַר עַל כֹּלָּא.

160. Those whose path is crooked take matters and usher them in quickly, so they have no place to be detained. All the other cavities OF THE EYES AND NOSE open through it so the words come out through the mouth cavity. These are the wicked of the generation, hated by the Holy One, blessed be He. In our B'raita we learned THAT WHOEVER REVEALS SECRETS is as if he killed people and as if he worshiped idols. Everything is derived from the same verse, which says, "You shall not go up and down as a talebearer among your people; neither shall you stand aside when mischief befalls your neighbor," WHICH IS MURDER; and, "I am Hashem" (Vayikra 19:16), WHICH PROHIBITS IDOLATRY. Whoever transgresses the first part of the verse BY BEARING TALES AND REVEALING SECRETS, it is as if he transgressed them all, MURDER AND IDOLATRY.

161. זַכָּאָה חוּלָקֵיהוֹן דְּצַדִּיקַיָּיא, דְּעָלַיְיהוּ כְּתִיב, וְנֶאֱמַן רוּחַ מְכַסֶּה דָּבָר. נֶאֱמַן רוּחַ וַדַּאי, דְּהָא רוּחָא דִּלְהוֹן מֵאֲתַר עִלָּאָה קַדִּישָׁא אִשְׁתְּלִיף, ובג"כ נֶאֱמַן רוּחַ אִקְרוּן. וְסִימָן דָּא אוּקִימְנָא, הַהוּא דִּמְגַלֶּה רָזִין, בְּיָדוּעַ דִּנְשְׁמָתֵיהּ, לָאו אִיהוּ מִגּוּפָא דְּמַלְכָּא קַדִּישָׁא. ובג"כ לֵית בֵּיהּ רָזָא, וְלָא מֵאֲתָר דְּרָזָא הוּא. וְכַד תֵּיפּוּק נִשְׁמָתֵיהּ, לָא אִתְדַּבְקָא בְּגוּפָא דְּמַלְכָּא, דְּהָא לָא אַתְרֵיהּ הוּא. וַוי לְהַהוּא בַּר נָשׁ, וַוי לֵיהּ, וַוי לְנִשְׁמָתֵיהּ. זַכָּאָה חוּלָקֵיהוֹן דְּצַדִּיקַיָּיא, דִּמְכַסִּין רָזִין, כָּל שֶׁכֵּן רָזִין עִלָּאִין דְּקוּדְשָׁא בְּרִיךְ הוּא. עֲלַיְיהוּ כְּתִיב, וְעַמֵּךְ כּוּלָּם צַדִּיקִים לְעוֹלָם יִירְשׁוּ אָרֶץ.

161. Blessed is the portion of the righteous, of whom it is written, "but he that is of a faithful spirit conceals the matter" (Mishlei 11:13); surely they are of a faithful spirit, because their spirit is drawn from a supernal, holy place, THAT IS, FROM THE CENTRAL COLUMN. Hence they are considered to be of a faithful spirit. We have explained this sign. Whoever reveals secrets, it is known that his soul is not from the body of the Holy King ZEIR ANPIN, THAT IS, THE CENTRAL COLUMN. Hence there is no secret in him, nor is he from the area of secrets. When his soul leaves his body, it does not cleave to the body of the King, which is not its place. Woe to that man, woe to his soul. Blessed is the portion of the righteous, who conceal secrets, and more so supernal secrets of the Holy One, blessed be He. Of them it is written, "Your people also shall be all righteous; they will inherit the land" (Yeshayah 60:21).

40. The shining countenance of Zeir Anpin

A Synopsis

We hear about the two colors of the face of Zeir Anpin, red and white. When sins multiply on earth, the face illuminates in red and judgments prevail. When people are righteous then the white shines from Atika Kadisha, and everything is illuminated with mercy. We hear that all the angels assume the colors that this face assumes.

162. אַנְפּוֹי, כִּתְרֵין תַּקְרוֹבִין דְּבוּסְמָא. סַהֲדוּתָא עַל מַה דַּאֲמֵינָא, דְּהָא סַהֲדוּתָא בְּהוּ תַּלְיָא. וּבְכֹלָּא תַּלְיָא סַהֲדוּתָא. אֲבָל הָנֵי תַּקְרוֹבֵי דְּבוּסְמָא, חִוָּורָא וְסוּמָקָא, סַהֲדוּתָא לְאַבָּא וְאִימָּא. סַהֲדוּתָא לְאַחְסָנָא דְּיָרִית וְאָחִיד לוֹן. וְהָא בְּמַתְנִיתָא דִּילָן אוֹקִימְנָא, כַּמָּה פָּרְסֵי בֵּין חִוָּורָא לְסוּמָקָא, וְאִתְכְּלִילָן בֵּיהּ כַּחֲדָא בְּסִטְרָא דְּחִוָּורָא.

162. THE TWO APPLES OF the face OF ZEIR ANPIN ARE like two spice offerings, WHICH EMIT GOOD FRAGRANCE, THE SECRET OF THE ILLUMINATION OF CHOCHMAH FROM BELOW UPWARDS CALLED FRAGRANCE, AND THE SECRET MEANING OF, "A MAN'S WISDOM MAKES HIS FACE TO SHINE" (KOHELET 8:1). It is evidence of what I said ABOUT ABA AND IMA, for the WHOLE testimony OF READING THE FACE depends on it, ON THE FACE; yet evidence depends on the whole FACIAL EXPRESSION, THAT IS, ON THE FOREHEAD AND THE NOSE, AS HAS BEEN SAID THAT ONE TESTIFIES HE SAW A PERSON'S FACE ONLY WITH THE NOSE. But the two spice offerings, which are white and red, testify about Aba and Ima. They testify about the inheritance he received FROM ABA AND IMA and about his holding on to them. In our B'raita we explained the many differences between white and red, YET NEVERTHELESS they are included IN ZEIR ANPIN together on the white side, THAT IS, UNDER THE POWER OF WHITE, WHICH IS CHESED.

163. כַּד אִתְנְהִיר מִנְּהִירוּ דְּחִוָּורָא דְּעַתִּיקָא, חַפְיָיא הַהוּא חִוָּורָא עַל סוּמָקָא. וְכֻלְּהוּ בִּנְהִירוּ אִשְׁתְּכַח. וּכְדֵין כְּתִיב, יָאֵר יְיָ׳ פָּנָיו אֵלֶיךָ. וְכַד חַיָּיבִין סַגִּיאִין, תַּלְיָין דִּינִין בְּעָלְמָא, אִשְׁתְּכָחַת סְגִירוּתָא בְּכֹלָּא. וְסוּמָקָא אִתְפְּשַׁט בְּאַנְפִּין, וְחָפָא עַל חִוָּורָא. וּכְדֵין כֹּלָּא אִשְׁתְּכַח

בְּדִינָא. וּכְדֵין כְּתִיב פְּנֵי יְיָ' בְּעוֹשֵׂי רָע. וְכֹלָּא בְּהַאי תַּלְיָיא, וּבְגִין דָּא סַהֲדוּתָא הוּא בְּכֹלָּא.

163. WHEN THE FACE OF ZEIR ANPIN shines in white, THAT IS, WITH CHESED, from Atika, the white in it, WHICH IS CHESED, covers the red in it, THE SECRET OF CHOCHMAH OF THE LEFT, and everything is illuminated. Then it is written, "Hashem make His face shine upon you" (Bemidbar 6:25). When wicked people multiply and Judgments are suspended over the world, there is shutting off everywhere, THAT IS, ALL LIGHTS ARE SHUT AND DO NOT SHINE, and the red expands throughout the face, WHICH IS JUDGMENT, and covers the white, WHICH IS MERCY, and then everything is in a state of Judgment. Then it is written, "The face of Hashem is against those who do evil" (Tehilim 34:17). Everything depends on it and hence THE FACE indicates everything.

164. כַּמָּה וְכַמָּה מָארֵי תְּרִיסִין מְחַכָּאן לְהָנֵי גְּוָונֵי, מְצַפָּאן לְהָנֵי גְּוָונֵי. כַּד נְהִירִין גְּוָונֵי, כָּל עָלְמִין כֻּלְּהוּ בְּחֵדוּ. בְּזִמְנָא דְּנָהִיר חִוָּורָא, כֹּלָּא אִתְחָזוּ בְּהַהוּא גַּוְונָא. וְכַד אִתְחֲזֵי בְּסוּמָקָא כֹּלָּא הָכִי אִתְחָזוּ בְּהַהוּא גַּוְונָא.

164. There are many ANGELS with shields waiting for those FACIAL colors, WHITE AND RED, expecting those colors. When the colors shine, all the worlds are joyful. When the white shines, everything assumes this color THAT IS CHESED and when the red appears everything assumes that color THAT IS JUDGMENT.

41. The nine characteristics of the beard of Zeir Anpin

A Synopsis

Rabbi Shimon reveals that the valuable oil of the thirteen streams of the beard of Atika Kadisha illuminates the beard of Zeir Anpin. He says that the beginning of the beard is supernal Chesed, and that when the world is in need of mercy the holy Mazal appears from Arich Anpin; then all the characteristics of the beard of Zeir Anpin are in a state of mercy. Yet when the world is in need of judgment, judgment appears and God takes vengeance on the enemies of Yisrael. We hear that Moses spoke of the nine characteristics in order to revert them all to mercy.

165. בְּאִלֵּין תַּקְרוֹבִין דְּבוּסְמָא, שַׁארִי דִּיקְנָא לְאִתְחֲזָאָה, מֵרֵישָׁא דְּאוּדְנִין, וְנָחִית וְסַלִּיק בְּתַקְרוֹבָא דְּבוּסְמָא, שַׂעֲרִין אוּכָמִין דְּדִיקְנָא, בְּתִקּוּנָא יָאֶה שַׁפִּיר. כְּגִיבָּר תַּקִּיף, שַׁפִּיר. מִשְׁחָא דִּרְבוּת דְּדִיקְנָא עִלָּאָה דְּעַתִּיקָא, בְּהַאי דִּיקְנָא דִּזְעֵיר אַנְפִּין אִתְחֲזֵי, וְנָהִיר.

165. With these spice offerings, THAT IS, THE TWO APPLES OF THE FACE, the beard starts to appear at the beginning of the ears, falling and rising with the spice offering, NAMELY, IN THE FACE. The hair of the beard is black, which is a nice and handsome characteristic, like a courageous and strong handsome man. The valuable oil of the supernal beard of Atika appears and shines in the beard of Zeir Anpin.

166. שַׁפִּירוּ דְּהַאי דִּיקְנָא, בְּט׳ תִּקּוּנִין אִשְׁתְּכַח. וְכַד מִשְׁחָא דִּרְבוּת, דִּתְלַת עֲשַׂר נְבִיעִין דְּדִיקְנָא דְּעַתִּיקָא קַדִּישָׁא נָהִיר בְּהַאי דִּיקְנָא, אִשְׁתְּכָחוּ כ״ב תִּקּוּנִין. וּכְדֵין מִתְבָּרְכִין כֻּלְּהוּ. וְיִשְׂרָאֵל סָבָא מִתְבָּרְכָא בְּהַאי, וְסִימָן, בְּךָ יְבָרֵךְ יִשְׂרָאֵל. כָּל תִּקּוּנִין דְּדִיקְנָא דָּא, אוּקִימְנָא בְּאִדְרָא קַדִּישָׁא, דְּכֻלְּהוּ מִתִּיקּוּנִין דְּעַתִּיקָא קַדִּישָׁא אִתְקָנוּ. וְהָכָא בָּעֵינָא לְגַלָּאָה, מַה דְּלָא אִתְגְּלֵי תַּמָּן, בְּגִין לְמֵיעַל בְּלָא כִּסּוּפָא.

166. The beauty of this beard lies in nine characteristics. When the valuable oil of the thirteen streams of the beard of Atika Kadisha illuminates this beard OF ZEIR ANPIN, there are TOGETHER 22 characteristics. Then they are all blessed ABOVE AND BELOW. Yisrael Saba, WHICH IS ZEIR ANPIN, is blessed by it and it derives from, "By you (Heb. *becha*, = 22) shall Yisrael bless" (Beresheet 48:20), THAT IS, ZEIR ANPIN THAT IS CALLED YISRAEL BLESS WITH THE 22 CHARACTERISTICS. We explained all these characteristics in the holy Idra that they were all formed from the characteristics of Atika Kadisha. And here I wish to reveal what has not been revealed there in order to enter without shame THE WORLD TO COME.

167. שִׁיתָא אִינּוּן, ט' אִקְרוּן. תִּקּוּנָא קַדְמָאָה, נָפַק הַהוּא נִיצוֹצָא בּוֹצִינָא דְּקַרְדִינוּתָא, וּבָטַשׁ בִּתְחוֹת שַׂעֲרָא דְּרֵישָׁא, מִתְּחוֹת קוֹצִין דְּעַל אוּדְנִין, וְנָחִית מִקַּמֵּי פִּתְחָא דְּאוּדְנִין, עַד רֵישָׁא דְּפוּמָא, הָא תִּקּוּנָא דָּא מֵעַתִּיקָא קַדִּישָׁא לָא אִשְׁתְּכַח, אֶלָּא כַּד נָגִיד מַזָּלָא דְּעַתִּיקָא קַדִּישָׁא, וְתַלְיָיא מִנֵּיהּ הַהוּא מַבּוּעָא דְּחָכְמְתָא, כַּד אִימָּא אִתְמַשְׁכָא וְאִתְכְּלִילַת בַּאֲוִירָא דַּכְיָא, הַהוּא חִוָּורָא נָקִיט אִימָּא, וְנִיצוֹצָא עָאלַת וְנַפְקַת, וְאִתְאֲחָד דָּא בְּדָא, וְאִתְעֲבִידַת חַד תִּקּוּנָא.

167. There are six CHARACTERISTICS that are considered nine. The first characteristic is that the hard candle emerged and struck under the hairs of the head underneath the locks over the ears, going down starting in front of the opening of the ears to the top of the mouth. This characteristic does not originate from Atika Kadisha except when Mazal of Atika Kadisha flows, from which comes the fount of Chochmah. When Ima flows and is included in the pure air, Ima receives the whiteness. And the spark, THAT IS, THE HARD CANDLE, enters THE PURE AIR AND BECOMES A PART OF HER. THEN it emerges and they unite with each other, THAT IS, IT STRIKES THE LOCKS OF HAIRS OVER THE EARS, THE TWO JUDGMENTS JOIN EACH OTHER and become one characteristic.

168. וְכַד אִצְטְרִיךְ סַלְּקָא דָּא עַל דָּא, וְאִתְכַּסְּיָא חַד מִקַּמֵּי חֲדָא. ובג"כ כְּלָא אִצְטְרִיךְ, חַד לְמֶעְבַּד נוּקְמִין. וְחַד לְרַחֲמָא. וְעַל הַאי תָּאִיב לְהַאי דִּיקְנָא דָּוִד מַלְכָּא, כְּמָה דְּאוֹקִימְנָא.

168. When the need arises TO BESTOW CHESED OR JUDGMENTS, the one rises over the other, which is covered by it. THAT IS, WHEN THE TIME COMES TO BESTOW JUDGMENTS, CHESED IN THE BEARD IS COVERED AND JUDGMENT HAS SWAY. WHEN THE NEED ARISES TO BESTOW

CHESED, JUDGMENT IN THE BEARD IS COVERED AND CHESED RULES. And all is needed, BOTH THE FORCE OF CHESED AND THE FORCE OF JUDGMENT, one to take revenge ON THE ENEMIES OF YISRAEL and one to have mercy ON YISRAEL. For that reason David coveted this beard as we explained.

169. בְּהַאי דִּיקְנָא ט׳ תִּקּוּנִין אִשְׁתְּכָחוּ, שִׁיתָּא רִבְוָון דְּתַלְיָין בְּהוּ, וּמִתְפַּשְּׁטִין בְּכָל גּוּפָא. וְאִלֵּין שִׁיתָּא דְּתַלְיָין, תַּלְיָין בְּשַׂעֲרֵי דִּתְחוֹת תַּקְרוּבָא דְּבוּסְמִין. תְּלַת מֵהַאי סִטְרָא, וּתְלַת מֵהַאי סִטְרָא. וּבְיָקִירוּתָא דְּדִיקְנָא, תַּלְיָין תְּלַת אַחֲרָנִין. חַד לְעֵילָּא בְּשִׂפְוָון, וּתְרֵין בְּאִינּוּן שַׂעֲרִין דְּתַלְיָין עַד טַבּוּרָא. וְכָל הָנֵי שִׁיתָּא, ג׳ מִכָּאן וְג׳ מִכָּאן, אִתְמַשְׁכָן וְתַלְיָין כֻּלְּהוֹן, בְּאִינּוּן שַׂעֲרֵי דְּתַלְיָין וּמִתְפַּשְּׁטִין בְּכָל גּוּפָא.

169. There are nine characteristics to this beard, which are 60,000 HAIRS that come down from them and expand IN THEIR ILLUMINATION throughout the body. These six characteristics that come down do so from the hairs beneath the spice offering, THAT IS, BENEATH THE PART OF THE FACE CALLED SPICE OFFERING, three characteristics on the one side OF THE FACE and three characteristics on the other side OF THE FACE. From the preciousness of the beard, THAT IS, THE MOST VISIBLE PART OF THE BEARD THAT BEAUTIFIES THE FACE, come out three others, one above THE HAIRS over the lips, and two in the hair that hangs down to the navel. All the six, three on one side and three on the other, come down and hang with the hanging hairs and expand throughout the body.

170. וּבְגִין דְּהָנֵי תְּלָתָא אִינּוּן בְּיָקִירוּ דְּדִיקְנָא יַתִּיר מִכֻּלְּהוּ, כְּתִיב בְּהוּ שְׁמָא קַדִּישָׁא. דִּכְתִיב, מִן הַמֵּצַר קָרָאתִי יָּהּ, יְיָ׳ לִי לֹא אִירָא. וְהָא דְּאוּקִימְנָא בְּאִדְרָא, מִן הַמֵּצַר קָרָאתִי יָּהּ, מֵאֲתָר דְּשָׂרֵי דִּיקְנָא לְאִתְפַּשְּׁטָא, דְּהוּא אֲתָר דָּחִיק מִקַּמֵּי אוּדְנִין, שַׁפִּיר הוּא.

170. Since the three constitute the beauty of the beard more than the rest, BECAUSE THEY DECORATE AND BEAUTIFY THE FACE, the Holy Name is written regarding them, as written, “Out of my distress I called upon Yah; YAH ANSWERED ME WITH LIBERATION. Hashem is on my side” (Tehilim

118:5-6). In the Idra Raba we explained that, "Out of my distress I called upon Yah," WHICH IS THE FIRST CHARACTERISTIC, refers to the place where the beard starts to expand, where the place is narrow, THAT IS, WHERE THE EXPANSE OF HAIR IS NARROW RATHER THAN WIDE, in front of the ears. And this is well, THAT IT IS CONSIDERED "OUT OF MY DISTRESS (HEB. *METZAR*)" BECAUSE IT IS A NARROW (HEB. *TZAR*) SPACE. BUT HERE IT SAYS IT REFERS TO THE HAIRS ABOVE THE LIPS.

171. וּבְסִפְרָא דְּאַגַּדְתָּא דְּבֵי רַב יֵיבָא סָבָא, הָכִי אָמַר וְאוֹקִים, דְּשֵׁירוּתָא דְּדִיקְנָא מֵחֶסֶד עִלָּאָה, דִּכְתִּיב, לְךָ יְיָ׳ הַגְּדוּלָּה וְהַגְּבוּרָה וְהַתִּפְאֶרֶת וְגוֹ׳. וְכֹלָּא הוּא, וְהָכִי שָׁארֵי, וְתִשְׁעָה אִתְמַשְּׁכָן וְתַלְיָין בְּדִיקְנָא, וּמִקַּמֵּי אוּדְנִין, הָכִי שָׁארֵי, וְקִיּוּמָא לָא מִתְקַיְּימִין אֶלָּא בַּאֲתָר אָחֳרָא, כְּמָה דְּאוֹקִימְנָא.

171. HE FURTHER BUILDS UP HIS ARGUMENT. In the Agadah book of Rav Yeba Saba he so said and explained that the beginning of the beard STARTS with supernal Chesed, as written, "Yours, Hashem, is the greatness, and the power (Heb. *Gvurah*) and the glory (Heb. *Tiferet*)..." (I Divrei Hayamim 29:11). BUT everything IS IN THE BEARD because so does THE BEARD start TO COME OUT, AS RAV YEBA SABA SAID, and the nine characteristics come out from the beard and from before the ears, AS SAID IN THE IDRA RABA that THE BEARD begins TO SHOW this way, BUT they do not stay that way except in another place as I explained.

172. וְכַד אִצְטְרִיךְ עָלְמָא לְרַחֲמֵי, אִתְגַּלְיָיא מַזָּלָא קַדִּישָׁא. וְכָל הָנֵי תִּקּוּנִין דִּבְדִיקְנָא יַקִּירָא דִּזְעֵיר אַנְפִּין, כֻּלְּהוּ רַחֲמֵי מִשְׁתַּכְחֵי. וְכַד אִצְטְרִיךְ לְדִינָא, מִתְחַזְּיָיא דִּינָא, וּכְדֵין עַבְדִּין נוּקְמִין לְשַׂנְאֵיהוֹן דְּיִשְׂרָאֵל, לְאִינּוּן דְּעָקִין לְהוּ. כָּל יְקִירוּ דְּדִיקְנָא, בְּאִינּוּן שַׂעֲרֵי דְּתַלְיָין אִינְהוּ, מִשּׁוּם דְּכֹלָּא בְּהַאי תַּלְיָין.

172. When the world is in need of mercy, the holy Mazal appears, WHICH IS THE BEARD OF ARICH ANPIN, AND THEN all the characteristics of the precious beard of Zeir Anpin are in a state of mercy. When it is in need of

Judgment, Judgment appears, and then vengeance is wreaked on the enemies of Yisrael, those who distress YISRAEL. All the preciousness of the beard lies in those hanging hairs, THAT IS, THE VISIBLE EXPANSES OF THE BEARD, because everything emerges from them.

173. כָּל הָנֵי שַׂעֲרֵי דְּדִיקְנָא דִּזְעֵיר אַנְפִּין, כֻּלְּהוּ קַשִּׁישִׁין תַּקִּיפִין, מִשּׁוּם דְּכֻלְּהוּ אַכְפְּיָין לְדִינִין, בְּשַׁעֲתָא דְּמַזָּלָא קַדִּישָׁא אִתְגַּלֵּי. וְכַד בָּעָא לְאַגָּחָא קְרָבָא, בְּהַאי דִּיקְנָא אִתְחֲזֵי כְּגִבָּר תַּקִּיף, מָארֵי נַצְּחָן קְרָבַיָּא. וּכְדֵין מָרִיט מַאן דְּמָרִיט, וְאַגְלִישׁ מַאן דְּאַגְלִישׁ.

173. All the hairs of the beard of Zeir Anpin are coarse and strong, because they all compel Judgments when the holy Mazal appears. When it wishes to wage war, it appears by means of this beard as a strong mighty man victorious in war. Then some pluck the hair on the back of the head and some from the front of the head.

174. הָנֵי תִּשְׁעָה תִּקּוּנִין, אֲמָרָן מֹשֶׁה זִמְנָא תִּנְיָינָא, בְּשַׁעֲתָא דְּאִצְטְרִיךְ לְאַהַדְרָא לוֹן כֻּלְּהוּ רַחֲמֵי. דאע״ג דִּתְלֵיסַר תִּקּוּנִין לָא אֲמָרָן הַשְׁתָּא, בְּכַוָּונָא תַּלְיָיא מִלְּתָא, דְּהָא לָא יֵיעוּל בְּהָנֵי תִּקּוּנִין לְאַדְכְּרָא, אֶלָּא בְּמַזָּלָא אִתְכְּוָּון, וְאַדְכַּר לֵיהּ. הה״ד, עַתָּה יִגְדַּל נָא כֹּחַ יְיָ׳. מַאן כֹּחַ יְיָ׳. הַהוּא דְּאִקְרֵי מַזָּלָא קַדִּישָׁא, סְתִימָא דְּכָל סְתִימִין. דְּחֵילָא דָּא, וּנְהִירוּ דָּא, מִמַּזָּלָא תָּלֵי. וְכֵיוָן דְּאָמַר מֹשֶׁה דָּא, וְאַדְכַּר דָּא, וְאִתְכְּוָּון בֵּיהּ, אָמַר הָנֵי תִּשְׁעָה תִּקּוּנִין, דְּתַלְיָין בִּזְעֵיר אַנְפִּין. בְּגִין דְּיַנְהִירוּ כֻּלְּהוּ, וְלָא יִשְׁתְּכַח דִּינָא. וע״ד כֹּלָּא בְּמַזָּלָא תָּלֵי.

174. Moses said these nine characteristics a second time IN THE PORTION OF SHELACH when he had to revert them all to mercy. For though he did not now recite the thirteen characteristics AS IN THE PORTION OF TISA it all depends on intention. For he would not mention these characteristics OF ZEIR ANPIN THAT ARE NOT PURELY MERCY, but intended Mazal, NAMELY THE THIRTEEN CHARACTERISTICS OF THE BEARD OF ARICH ANPIN, and mentioned it, as written, "And now, I pray You, let the power of my Lord be great" (Bemidbar 14:17). What is "the power of Hashem"? It is that which is called the most concealed holy Mazal, THE BEARD OF ARICH ANPIN. The power and the light IN THE BEARD OF ZEIR ANPIN derive from Mazal. Once Moses said THE NINE CHARACTERISTICS OF ZEIR ANPIN and mentioned MAZAL CALLED THE POWER OF HASHEM, he spoke the nine characteristics deriving from Zeir Anpin so that they will all shine BY A DRAWING OF THE THIRTEEN OF ARICH ANPIN and there will be no Judgment evident, BECAUSE THE THIRTEEN OF ARICH ANPIN ARE WHOLLY OF MERCY. Hence everything depends on Mazal, WHICH IS THE BEARD OF ARICH ANPIN.

175. הַאי דִּיקְנָא כַּד שָׁרָאן שַׂעֲרֵי לְאִתְעָרָא, אִתְחֲזֵי כְּגִיבָּר תַּקִּיף כְּגִיבָּר מָארֵי נָצַח קְרָבִין. בְּהַאי דִּיקְנָא, נָגִיד מְשַׁח דִּרְבוּת מֵעַתִּיקָא סְתִימָאָה. כד"א, כַּשֶּׁמֶן הַטּוֹב עַל הָרֹאשׁ יוֹרֵד עַל הַזָּקָן זְקַן אַהֲרֹן.

175. At the beginning of the arising of the hairs, the beard looks like a strong mighty man, victorious in war TO TAKE REVENGE ON THE ENEMIES OF YISRAEL. The holy anointing oil flows on this beard from the concealed Atika Kadisha, as written, "It is like the precious ointment upon the head, running down upon the beard, the beard of Aaron" (Tehilim 133:2), THE SECRET OF THE BEARD OF ZEIR ANPIN.

42. The mouth of Zeir Anpin

A Synopsis

We read that good and evil and life and death depend on the lips of Zeir Anpin. When the lips speak all the watchers awaken to decree punishments. Rabbi Shimon explains what is meant by a 'watcher'. We learn that when words come out of the mouth of Zeir Anpin they illuminate 18,000 worlds.

176. אִלֵּין שַׂעְרֵי לָא חַפְיָין עַל שִׂפְוָון, וְשִׂפְוָון כֻּלְּהוּ סוּמָקִין כְּוַורְדָא. דִּכְתִּיב, שִׂפְתוֹתָיו שׁוֹשַׁנִּים. שִׂפְוָון מְרַחְשָׁן גְּבוּרָה, מְרַחְשָׁן חָכְמְתָא. בְּאִינּוּן שִׂפְוָון תַּלְיָין טַב וּבִישׁ, חַיֵּי וּמוֹתָא. מֵאִלֵּין שִׂפְוָון תַּלְיָין מָארֵיהוֹן דְּאַתְעָרוּתָא, דְּכַד מְרַחֲשִׁין אִלֵּין שִׂפְוָון, מִתְעָרִין כֻּלָּא לְמִגְזַר דִּינָא, בְּכָל בָּתֵּי דִּינִין, דְּאִקְרוּן עִירִין. דִּכְתִּיב, בִּגְזֵרַת עִירִין פִּתְגָּמָא וּבְמֵאמַר וְגוֹ'.

176. These hairs OF THE BEARD do not cover the lips, and the lips are wholly red as a lily, as written, "his lips like lilies" (Shir Hashirim 5:13). The lips whisper Gvurah and whisper Chochmah. Good and evil depend on these lips, and life and death. From these lips come out those who awaken, since when these lips whisper they all awaken to decree punishments throughout the courts that are called watchers, as written, "This matter is by the decree of the watchers, and the sentence…" (Daniel 4:14).

177. מַאי עִיר. בְּסִפְרָא דְּאַגַּדְתָּא, כד"א, וַיְהִי עָרֶךָ. דְּמִתְעֲרִין דִּינִין לְאִינּוּן דְּלָא אִתְרְחִימוּ לְעֵילָּא, בג"כ מִתְעָרִין אִלֵּין דְּאִינּוּן מָארֵי דְּבָבוּ, ועכ"ד בִּתְרֵי גְּוָונֵי בְּרַחֲמֵי וְדִינָא, וע"ד אִקְרוּן עִיר וְקַדִּישׁ דִּינָא וְרַחֲמֵי.

177. HE ASKS, What is a watcher (Heb. *ir*), AND ANSWERS, In the book of Agadah HE EXPLAINED that it is like in the words, "become your enemy (Heb. *ar*)" (I Shmuel 28:16). For Judgments rouse against those who are not beloved above, which is why those that arouse TO PUNISH are THEIR enemies, AND ARE CALLED 'WATCHERS'. Nevertheless, PUNISHMENT IS DECREED in two ways, with Mercy or with Judgment. They are therefore called a watcher (enemy) and a holy one, Judgment and Mercy, NAMELY, "THIS MATTER IS BY THE DECREE OF THE WATCHERS, AND THE SENTENCE BY THE WORDS OF THE HOLY ONES," WHERE A WATCHER ALLUDES TO JUDGMENT AND HOLY ONES TO MERCY.

178. וּבְאִלֵּין שִׂפְוָון, אִתְחֲזֵי פּוּמָא כַּד אִתְפְּתַח. רוּחָא דְּנָפִיק מִן פּוּמָא, בֵּיהּ מִתְלַבְּשִׁין כַּמָּה אֲלַף וְרִבְבָן. וְכַד אִתְפְּשַׁט, מִתְלַבְּשִׁין בֵּיהּ נְבִיאָן מְהֵימְנֵי. וְכֻלְּהוּ פֶּה יְיָ' אִקְרוּן. כַּד מִלִּין נָפְקִין מִן פּוּמָא, וּמִתְרַחֲשִׁין בְּשִׂפְוָון, מִתְנַהֲרִין לְכֻלְּהוּ תְּמָנֵי סָרֵי אַלְפִין עָלְמִין, עַד דְּמִתְקַטְּרִין כֻּלְּהוּ כַּחֲדָא, בִּתְמָנֵיסָר אוֹרְחִין וּשְׁבִילִין, דְּאִשְׁתְּמוֹדְעָן.

178. When the lips are open the mouth is seen. Thousands and tens of thousands are clothed in the air coming out of the mouth. When THE AIR expands, the faithful prophets are clothed in it and are all called 'the mouth of Hashem'. When words come out of the mouth, uttered by the lips, they illuminate together all of 18,000 worlds, until they all join together in 18 specific ways and paths.

179. וְכֹלָּא מְחַכָּאן לְפוּמָא דָּא, בְּלִישָׁן מְמַלֵּל רַבְרְבָן בְּקִיטְרָא דְּטִיהֲרָא בְּעוּטְרָא. וע"ד כְּתִיב, חִכּוֹ מַמְתַּקִּים, מַמְתַּקִּים וַדַּאי. מַאי חִכּוֹ. כד"א, וְחֵיךְ יִטְעַם לֶאֱכוֹל. וְכֻלּוֹ מַחֲמַדִּים, אֵשׁ וּמַיִם. אֶשָּׁא וּמַיָּא מִתְתַּקְּנָן, וְיָאָן בְּצִיּוּרוֹי, דְּהָא גְּוָונֵי מִתְחַבְּרָן כַּחֲדָא.

179. Everyone awaits this mouth with the great speaking tongue with the unification of polishing and adornment. Of this it is written, "His mouth (lit. 'palate') is most sweet" (Shir Hashirim 5:16). Surely it is most sweet. What is his palate? It is as in the verse, "the palate tastes food" (Iyov 34:3). "and he is altogether lovely" (Shir Hashirim 5:16), NAMELY fire and water. For water and fire are formed and are pretty AND LOVELY in their shape, THAT IS, THEY ARE LOVELY TO BEHOLD, because the colors RED AND WHITE join together, THAT IS, THE BEAUTY APPEARS FROM THE BLENDING OF WHITE AND RED TOGETHER.

43. Aleph, Chet, Hei, Ayin; Gimel, Yud, Caf, Kof

A Synopsis

Rabbi Shimon explains in detail how the four letters Aleph, Chet, Hei and Ayin are engraved on the throat and how those four are crowned with the four letters Gimel, Yud, Caf and Kof in the palate. We learn that the important thing is the balance of the three columns, and Rabbi Shimon says that throughout his whole life he was always careful never to receive the left column on its own except for a single instance, at which time he was warned not to do so by a flame of fire.

180. חִכּוֹ, בְּאַתְוָון רְשִׁימָן, דְּמִתְגַּלְּפָן בְּעִטְרוֹי גְּלִיפִין אחה״ע בַּגָּרוֹן. א׳, דְּטָרִיד מַלְכִּין, וּמְהַעְדֵּא מַלְכִּין, וּמְהָקֵם מַלְכִּין. ח׳, דְּטָרִיד וְנָחִית, וְסָלִיק וְעָטִיר, כָּבִישׁ בְּאֶשָּׁא גָּלִיף בְּרוּחָא. ה׳ יְנִיקָה דְּאִימָא, סָטִיר לְנוּקְבָא, אִתְפְּשַׁט לְנוּקְבָא רַבָּא, בְּתִיאוּבְתָא דְּקַרְתָּא קַדִּישָׁא, מִתְקַטְּרֵי אַתְרִין דָּא בְּדָא. כד״א, הַר הַמּוֹר גִּבְעַת הַלְּבוֹנָה. ע׳ טִיהֲרָא דְּטִיפְסָא, גְּלִיפָא בְּטִיפְסָא, רְהִיטִין דַּעֲנָפִין מִתְאַחֲדָן, לְסִטְרוֹי לְרוּחִין גְּלִיפִין.

180. "His mouth (lit. 'palate') IS MOST SWEET" (Shir Hashirim 5:16), because of the imprinted letters that are engraved on it with their crowns. THAT IS, THE SWEETNESS IN THE MOUTH COMES FROM THE FACT THAT THE LETTERS ARE ENGRAVED ON IT IN THE SEQUENCE OF THE THREE COLUMNS AND THE RECEIVING MALCHUT; THIS SEQUENCE ADORNS THEM WITH CROWNS. THE LETTERS Aleph, Chet, Hei and Ayin are engraved on the throat EACH WITH THREE COLUMNS. OF THE THREE COLUMNS OF Aleph, ITS RIGHT COLUMN drives kings away, THE LEFT COLUMN OF ALEPH deposes kings FROM THEIR KINGDOMS, AND THE CENTRAL COLUMN establishes kings. OF THE THREE COLUMNS OF Chet, ITS RIGHT COLUMN drives away and descends, THE LEFT COLUMN ascends and crowns, AND THE CENTRAL COLUMN conquers with fire and engraves with wind. OF THE THREE COLUMNS OF Hei THAT IS nourished from Ima, THAT IS, OF WHAT THE NUKVA RECEIVES FROM IMA, THE RIGHT COLUMN OF IMA strikes the Nukva; THROUGH THE LEFT COLUMN OF IMA, THE NUKVA spreads into a large Nukva; THE CENTRAL COLUMN OF IMA IS IN THAT, THAT through the desire of the holy city FOR CHASSADIM, IT IS CONNECTED WITH THE CENTRAL COLUMN. And the places OF RIGHT AND LEFT are interconnected, as it says, "the mountain of myrrh, and to the hill of frankincense" (Shir Hashirim 4:6). OF THE THREE COLUMNS OF Ayin, ITS RIGHT COLUMN IS the clarity of the shape of the grade; ITS LEFT COLUMN IS the engraved of the shape of the grade; ITS CENTRAL COLUMN IS when the running boughs join the engraved spirits at their sides.

181. וְהָא בְּרָזֵי דְּאַתְוָון דִּשְׁלֹמֹה מַלְכָּא, אִתְעַטְּרוּ אִלֵּין אַתְוָון ד׳, בד׳ גיכ״ק בַּחֵיךְ כד״א וְחֵיךְ יִטְעַם לֶאֱכוֹל, הֲיֵאָכֵל תָּפֵל מִבְּלִי מֶלַח וְגוֹ׳. וּכְתִיב וְהָיָה מַעֲשֵׂה הַצְּדָקָה שָׁלוֹם. הַנֶּחֱמָדִים מִזָּהָב וּמִפָּז רָב וּמְתוּקִים וְגוֹ׳. מְתוּקִים וַדַּאי.

181. And here, in the secret of the letters of King Solomon, HE SAYS that these four letters ALEPH, CHET, HEI AND AYIN, are crowned with the four LETTERS Gimel, Yud, Caf, Kof in the palate. HENCE THREE COLUMNS ARE INDICATED IN THE PALATE AS WELL. This is as in, "the palate tastes food" (Iyov 34:3), THE SECRET OF THE RIGHT COLUMN; "Can that which is unsavory be eaten without salt" (Iyov 6:6) REFERS TO THE LEFT COLUMN, WHICH, BEFORE IT IS JOINED WITH THE RIGHT, CANNOT BE ENJOYED LIKE UNSAVORY FOOD WITHOUT SALT. And the verse, "And the work of righteousness shall be peace" (Yeshayah 32:17) IS THE CENTRAL COLUMN THAT JOINS AND ESTABLISHES PEACE BETWEEN THE TWO COLUMNS, RIGHT AND LEFT. "More to be desired are they than gold, even much fine gold..." (Tehilim 19:11) REFERS TO MALCHUT THAT RECEIVES THE PLENTY OF THE THREE COLUMNS, which are surely very sweet.

182. דָּוִד מַלְכָּא אָמַר, גַּם עַבְדְּךָ נִזְהָר בָּהֶם וְגוֹ׳. אַסְהַדְנָא עָלַי דְּכָל יוֹמָאי אִזְדְּהַרְנָא בְּהוּ, דְּלָא לְאַטְעָאָה בְּהוּ, בַּר יוֹמָא חַד דְּעָטִירְנָא עִטְרֵי מַלְכָּא, בִּמְעַרְתָּא דְּמֵרוֹנְיָא, וַחֲמֵינָא בּוּצִינָא דְּאֶשָּׁא מִתְלַהֲטָא אַפּוּתְיָא דִּמְעַרְתָּא, וְאִזְדַּעֲזַעְנָא. מֵהַהוּא יוֹמָא אִזְדָּהַרְנָא בְּדַעְתָּאי בְּהוּ, וְלָא שָׁבִיקְנָא לוֹן כָּל יוֹמָאי. זַכָּאָה חוּלָקֵיהּ מַאן דְּאִזְדְּהַר בִּמְתִיקָא דְּמַלְכָּא, וְטָעִים בְּהוּ כִּדְחֲזֵי. עַל דָּא כְּתִיב, טַעֲמוּ וּרְאוּ כִּי טוֹב יְיָ׳ וְגוֹ׳. וּכְתִיב לְכוּ לַחֲמוּ בְּלַחְמִי וְגוֹ׳.

182. King David, AFTER THE WORDS, "MORE TO BE DESIRED..." THAT ALLUDE TO THE SWEET AND PRECIOUS BOUNTY OF THE THREE COLUMNS, CONCLUDES, "Moreover by them is Your servant enlightened (or: 'careful')..." (Ibid. 12), THAT IS, HE IS CAREFUL NOT TO RECEIVE FROM THE LEFT COLUMN WITHOUT THE RIGHT. RABBI SHIMON CONCLUDES, I testify about myself that throughout my life I was careful OF THE THREE COLUMNS not to mistake IN RECEIVING THE LEFT COLUMN ON ITS OWN, except for one day when I crowned the King in the cave of Meronia, WHEN HE WAS NOT CAREFUL TO HAVE THE LEFT UNITED WITH THE RIGHT. And I saw a flame of burning fire across the cave, THAT IS, HE SAW THE JUDGMENTS OF THE LEFT COLUMN WITHOUT THE RIGHT, WHICH IS A BURNING FIRE, and I trembled. Since that day I am careful in my mind TO RECEIVE ONLY FROM THE THREE COLUMNS TOGETHER and never left them throughout my life. Blessed is the portion of he that is careful with the sweets of the King and tastes of them judiciously. It says of this, "O taste and see that Hashem is good" (Tehilim 34:9), and, "Come, eat of my bread" (Mishlei 9:5).

44. Building the back part of the Nukva of Zeir Anpin

A Synopsis

Rabbi Shimon tells us how Malchut becomes attached to Zeir Anpin.

183. אִתְפְּשַׁט דְּכוּרָא בְּדַעַת, וְאִתְמַלְיָין אַכְסַדְרִין וְאִדָּרִין, מֵרֵישָׁא דְּגוּלְגַּלְתָּא שָׁרֵי, וְאִתְפְּשַׁט בְּכָל גּוּפָא, מְחַדוֹי וּדְרוֹעוֹי וּבְכֹלָּא. מֵאֲחוֹרוֹי, אִתְדְּבַק נִיצוֹצָא דְּבוּצִינָא דְּקַרְדִּינוּתָא, וְלַהֲטָא וְאַפִּיק גֻּלְגַּלְתָּא חֲדָא, סְתִימָא מִכָּל סִטְרוֹי, וּנְהִירוּ דִּתְרֵי מוֹחֵי גְּלִיפָן בָּהּ, וְאִתְדַּבְקַת בְּסִטְרוֹי דִּדְכוּרָא. בְּגִין כַּךְ אִתְקְרֵי יוֹנָתִי תַּמָּתִי, אַל תִּקְרֵי תַּמָּתִי אֶלָּא תְּאוֹמָתִי וַדַּאי.

183. The male, WHICH IS ZEIR ANPIN, spread into his brain lobe of Da'at and the corridors and chambers were filled, NAMELY NETZACH, HOD AND YESOD, AND CHESED, GVURAH AND TIFERET. DA'AT starts at the top of the head and spreads throughout the body in its chest, arms and the rest of it. Behind it, the spark is touched by the hard lamp, WHICH IS THE ILLUMINATION OF THE LEFT COLUMN OF BINAH, glows and produces one head blocked on all directions, with the illumination of the two brain lobes CHOCHMAH AND BINAH engraved in it. It is attached to the male side FROM THE BACK and hence is called, "my dove, my undefiled (Heb. *tamati*)" (Shir Hashirim 5:2). Do not pronounce it '*tamati*' but rather it is '*te'omati* (Eng. 'my twin sister')' for sure.

184. שַׂעֲרוֹי דְּנוּקְבָא כְּלִילָן בֵּיהּ גְּוָונֵי, כְּדִכְתִיב, וְדַלַּת רֹאשֵׁךְ כָּאַרְגָּמָן. אִתְקְטַר גְּבוּרָה בַּחֲמֵשׁ גְּבוּרָאן, וְאִתְפַּשְּׁטַת נוּקְבָא בְּסִטְרָהָא, וְאִתְדַּבְקַת בְּסִטְרוֹי דִּדְכוּרָא.

184. The hair of the Nukva, WHICH IS MALCHUT, includes the colors WHITE, RED, AND GREEN, AND IS CALLED PURPLE, as written, "and the hair of your head like purple" (Shir Hashirim 7:6). It is connected to five Gvurot. From her aspect OF GVURAH Malchut expands to become attached to the side of the male, ZEIR ANPIN, THAT IS, TO HIS BACK.

45. The formation of face to face of the Nukva of Zeir Anpin

A Synopsis

We are told that after Malchut separated from the sides of Zeir Anpin, she joined Him face to face. When they are joined they seem like one body, and all the worlds are joyful as on Shabbat when everything is under the influence of a whole body. From this idea Rabbi Shimon deduces that whoever does not exist as male and female receives no blessings and can not last. We learn that Malchut is considered a mother to all the lower beings of the three worlds. Rabbi Shimon speaks about the lower Chochmah and the supernal Chochmah.

185. עַד דְּאִתְפָּרְשָׁא מִסִּטְרוֹי. וְאָתִיאַת לְאִתְחַבְּרָא עִמֵּיהּ אַפִּין בְּאַפִּין. וְכַד מִתְחַבְּרָן מִתְחַזְיָין חַד גּוּפָא מַמָּשׁ. מֵהָכָא אוֹלִיפְנָא, דְּכַר בִּלְחוֹדוֹי, אִתְחֲזֵי פְּלַג גּוּפָא, וְכֻלְּהוּ רַחֲמֵי. וְכַךְ נוּקְבָא. וְכַד מִתְחַבְּרָן כַּחֲדָא, אִתְחֲזֵי כֹּלָּא חַד גּוּפָא מַמָּשׁ, וְהָכִי הוּא. אוּף הָכָא, כַּד דְּכַר אִתְחַבָּר בְּנוּקְבָא, כֹּלָּא הוּא חַד גּוּפָא, וְעָלְמִין כֻּלְּהוּ בְּחֵדוּ, דְּהָא כֻּלְּהוּ מִגּוּפָא שְׁלִים מִתְבָּרְכָן.

185. After MALCHUT separated from the sides OF ZEIR ANPIN, she joined Him face to face. When they are joined, they seem one body BECAUSE THEY ORIGINATE IN THE RIGHT AND LEFT SIDES OF THE SAME LEVEL. THUS, EVEN THOUGH THEY WERE DIVIDED AND FORMED AS TWO LEVELS, THEY REJOIN AS ONE BODY, AS THE RIGHT AND LEFT OF THE SAME LEVEL. The male by himself seems like half a body, THAT IS, THE RIGHT PART OF THE SOUL, which is wholly Chesed. So the female part OF THE SOUL IS THE LEFT PART AND IS WHOLLY GVURAH. When they join together it seems exactly like one body, BECAUSE THE TWO HALVES JOIN INTO ONE. And so it is TRULY. Here too, the male, WHICH IS ZEIR ANPIN, joined Malchut and everything is a single body. Then all the worlds are joyous, because they are blessed by a whole body.

186. וְהַיְינוּ רָזָא, עַל כֵּן בֵּרַךְ יְיָ׳ אֶת יוֹם הַשַּׁבָּת וַיְקַדְּשֵׁהוּ. דְּהָא אִשְׁתְּכַח כֹּלָּא בְּחַד גּוּפָא שְׁלִים, דְּהָא מַטְרוֹנִיתָא אִתְדַּבְּקַת בְּמַלְכָּא, וְאִשְׁתְּכַח גּוּפָא חַד. וְעַל כֵּן בִּרְכָאן מִשְׁתַּכְּחִין בְּהַאי יוֹמָא. וּמֵהָכָא,

מַאן דְּלָא אִשְׁתְּכַח דְּכַר וְנוּקְבָּא, אִקְרֵי פְּלַג גּוּפָא, וְלֵית בִּרְכָתָא שַׁרְיָא בְּמִלָּה פְּגִימָא וַחֲסֵירָא, אֶלָּא בַּאֲתָר שְׁלִים, בְּמִלָּה שְׁלִים, וְלָא בְּפַלְגוּת מִלָּה, וּפַלְגוּת מִלָּה לָא אִתְקַיָּים לְעָלְמִין, וְלָא אִתְבָּרְכָן לְעָלְמִין.

186. This is the secret of THE VERSE, "therefore Hashem blessed the Shabbat day, and hallowed it" (Shemot 20:11), since then everything is UNDER THE INFLUENCE OF a whole body, since Malchut cleaved to the King ON SHABBAT and they are as one body. Therefore there are blessings on that day. From this WE DEDUCED that whoever does not exist as male and female is considered a half body, and no blessings rest on a blemished and wanting thing, but on a whole place, a whole thing, not half a thing. And a half thing does not last and is never blessed.

187. נוֹי דְּנוּקְבָּא, כֹּלָּא מִנּוֹי דִּדְכוּרָא הוּא. וְהָא אוּקִימְנָא מִלֵּי, וְאִשְׁתְּמוֹדְעָן בֵּינֵי חַבְרַיָּיא. מֵהַאי נוּקְבָּא מִתְאַחֲדָן כָּל אִינּוּן דִּלְתַתָּא. מִנָּהּ יַנְקִין, וּבָהּ תָּבִין, וְהִיא אִתְקְרִיאַת אֵם לְכֻלְּהוּ. כְּמָה דְּאַחֲרָא אֵם לְגוּפָא, וְכָל גּוּפָא מִנָּהּ יַנְקָא. כַּךְ הַאי אֵם לְכֻלְּהוּ אַחֲרָנִין דִּלְתַתָּא.

187. All the beauty of the female comes from the beauty of the male. We have already established these matters and they are known to the friends. Through this Nukva, NAMELY FROM MALCHUT, all the lower beings OF THE THREE WORLDS OF BRIYAH, YETZIRAH AND ASIYAH are united. From here they are fed and to her they return BECAUSE MALCHUT IS THE ROOT FOR THE THREE WORLDS UNDER ATZILUT. She is considered a mother to them all, just like the other, BINAH, is a mother to the body, WHICH IS ZEIR ANPIN CALLED BODY, and the whole body is nourished by it, BY BINAH. So is MALCHUT a mother to all the others below IN BRIYAH, YETZIRAH AND ASIYAH.

188. כְּתִיב, אֱמוֹר לַחָכְמָה אֲחוֹתִי אָתְּ. אִית חָכְמָה וְאִית חָכְמָה, וְהַאי נוּקְבָּא, אִתְקְרֵי חָכְמָה זְעֵירָא לְגַבֵּי אַחֲרָא וע"ד כְּתִיב, אָחוֹת לָנוּ קְטַנָּה וְשָׁדַיִם אֵין לָהּ וְגוֹ'. דְּהָא דָּא בְּגָלוּתָא אִתְמְשַׁךְ. אָחוֹת לָנוּ קְטַנָּה, וַדַּאי קְטַנָּה אִתְחֲזֵי אֲבָל רַבְרְבָא הִיא, וְסַגִּיאָה הִיא, דְּהָא הִיא שְׁלִימוּ דְּנָטִיל

מִכֹּלָּא. כְּמָה דִכְתִּיב, אֲנִי חוֹמָה וְשָׁדַי כַּמִּגְדָּלוֹת. וְשָׁדַי, דְהָא מַלְיָין אִינּוּן לְיַנְקָא לְכֹלָּא. כַּמִּגְדָּלוֹת, דְאִינּוּן נַהֲרִין רַבְרְבִין דְנַפְקוּ מֵאִימָּא עִלָּאָה.

188. It is written, "Say to wisdom, you are my sister" (Mishlei 7:4). There is Chochmah and there is Chochmah, NAMELY SUPERNAL CHOCHMAH THAT IS ABA AND IMA AND LOWER CHOCHMAH THAT IS MALCHUT. This Nukva, NAMELY MALCHUT, is called small Chochmah in relation to the other, WHICH IS SUPERNAL CHOCHMAH. Hence it is written, "We have a little sister, and she has no breasts..." (Shir Hashirim 8:8). Since this CHOCHMAH flows in exile, IT THEREFORE HAS NO BREASTS TO FEED YISRAEL. "We have a little sister": certainly she seems little IN EXILE, but she is large and great, because she is perfection that receives from all SFIROT, WHEN YISRAEL ARE IN THEIR LAND, as written, "I was a wall, and my breasts were like towers" (Ibid. 10). They are my breasts when they are full to feed everyone; they are like towers, which are great rivers coming out of supernal Ima THAT ARE CALLED TOWERS.

46. The first three Sfirot of the lights and the Netzach, Hod and Yesod of the vessels of Chayah of Zeir Anpin

A Synopsis

Rabbi Shimon tells us about the great tree that is the whole body of Zeir Anpin, saying that this tree has food in it for everything. He outlines the Sfirot in terms of the positioning on the body, and says that in Yesod lies the whole desire of Zeir Anpin for Malchut. We are told that Zion is the covered place of Malchut, just like a woman's womb.

189. תּוּ אִתְפְּשַׁט דְּכוּרָא בִּימִינָא וּשְׂמָאלָא, בְּיָרוּתָא דְּאַחֲסָנָא. וְכַד גְּוָונֵי אִתְחַבְּרוּ, אִקְרֵי תִּפְאֶרֶת. וְאִתְתְּקַן כָּל גּוּפָא, וְאִתְעָבֵיד אִילָנָא רַבְרְבָא, וְתַקִּיף, שַׁפִּיר וְיָאֶה, תְּחוֹתוֹהִי תַּטְלֵל חֵיוַת בָּרָא, וּבְעַנְפּוֹהִי יְדוּרוּן עוֹפֵי שְׁמַיָּא, וּמָזוֹן לְכֹלָּא בֵּיהּ. דְּרוֹעוֹי יְמִינָא וּשְׂמָאלָא. בִּימִינָא חַיִּים וָחֶסֶד, בִּשְׂמָאלָא מִיתָה וּגְבוּרָה. מֵעוֹי, אִתְתָּקַן בְּדַעַת, וְאִתְמַלְיָין כָּל אַכְסַדְרִין וְאִדָּרִין, כְּמָה דַּאֲמֵינָא, דִּכְתִּיב, וּבְדַעַת חֲדָרִים יִמָּלְאוּ.

189. The male, WHICH IS ZEIR ANPIN, further expands to the right and left of the inheritance of the possession, NAMELY CHOCHMAH AND BINAH CALLED THE INHERITANCE OF ABA AND IMA. When the colors, RIGHT ON THE RIGHT AND RED ON THE LEFT join IN THE CENTRAL COLUMN, it is called Tiferet and the whole body is formed into a big and strong, comely and handsome tree. Underneath it wild animals, THE HOSTS OF BRIYAH, wander and in its boughs dwell the birds of the sky, WHICH ARE THE HOSTS OF YETZIRAH. In it is food for everything. Its arms are right and left, CHESED AND GVURAH, on the right ARE EXTENDED life and Chesed; on its left ARE EXTENDED death and Gvurah. Its bowels, THAT IS, ITS INNER ASPECT, is fixed with Da'at and fills all the corridors and all the chambers, WHICH ARE NETZACH, HOD AND YESOD AND CHESED, GVURAH AND TIFERET as I said, as written, "and by knowledge are the chambers filled" (Mishlei 24:4).

190. תּוּ אִתְפְּשָׁט גּוּפָא, בִּתְרֵין שׁוֹקִין. וּמִתְאַחֲדָן בֵּינַיְיהוּ תְּרֵין כּוּלְיָין, וּתְרֵין בֵּיעֵי דִּדְכוּרָא. דְּכָל מִשְׁחָא וּרְבוּת וְחֵילָא דְּכָל גּוּפָא, בְּהוּ אִתְכְּנַשׁ, דְּכָל חַיָּילִין דְּנָפִיק, מִנְּהוֹן נָפְקִין. וְשַׁרְיָין כֹּלָּא בְּפוּם

46. The first three Sfirot of the lights and the Netzach, Hod and Yesod of the vessels of Chayah of Zeir Anpin

אַמָּה. ובג״כ אִקְרוּן צְבָאוֹת, וְאִינּוּן נֶצַח וְהוֹד. תִּפְאֶרֶת, יְדֹוָ״ד. נֶצַח וְהוֹד, צְבָאוֹת. ובג״כ יְדֹוָ״ד צְבָאוֹת.

190. The body further expands to the two legs NETZACH AND HOD and between them unite two kidneys and two testicles of the male, WHICH ARE THE INTERNAL NETZACH AND HOD. FROM THE KIDNEY THE LIQUID REFUSE FLOWS TO THE EXTERNAL FORCES, AND FROM THE TESTICLES SEMEN FLOWS TO SOULS. For all oil, greatness, and the force of the whole body is gathered in them, IN THE TWO TESTICLES, as all the hosts that come out TO BRIYAH, YETZIRAH AND ASIYAH come out from them. They all dwell at the tip of the penis, which is why they are called hosts. And they are Netzach and Hod. Tiferet IS CALLED Yud Hei Vav Hei, and Netzach and Hod ARE CALLED hosts (Heb. *Tzva'ot*). Hence THEY ARE CALLED TOGETHER IN THE VERSE 'Hashem Tzva'ot'.

191. אַמָּה דִּדְכוּרָא, סִיּוּמָא דְּכָל גּוּפָא, וְאִקְרֵי יְסוֹד. וְדָא הוּא דַּרְגָּא דִּמְבַסֵּם לְנוּקְבָא. וְכָל תִּיאוּבְתָּא דִּדְכוּרָא לְגַבֵּי נוּקְבָא, בְּהַאי יְסוֹד עַיִּיל לְנוּקְבָא, לַאֲתָר דְּאִקְרֵי צִיּוֹן. דְּהָתָם הוּא אֲתָר כְּסוּתָא דְּנוּקְבָא, כְּבֵית רֶחֶם לְאִתְּתָא. ובג״כ, יְיָ׳ צְבָאוֹת אִקְרֵי יְסוֹד.

191. The virile member of the male is the ending of the whole body and is called Yesod. It is a grade that sweetens Malchut, IN WHICH LIES the whole desire of the male, WHO IS ZEIR ANPIN, to Malchut. In that Yesod it enters Malchut to the place called Zion, where the covered place of Malchut is like a womb is to a woman. For that reason Yesod is called Hashem Tzva'ot.

47. Face to face union of Male and Female principles

A Synopsis

In these last utterances of Rabbi Shimon he reminds the rabbis that when Zeir Anpin and Malchut are united all the worlds are blessed and are in a state of complete joy. He talks about the two grades above and below – Zion and Jerusalem – and says that no one is allowed into the holy of holies in this world except for the high priest that comes from the aspect of Chesed. We learn that Zion is Mercy and Jerusalem is Judgment. Rabbi Shimon says again that all the blessings flow from the brain of Zeir Anpin to all the body parts or Sfirot. He tells the rabbis that at the end Chesed enters the holy of holies, as written in, "for there Hashem has commanded the blessing, even life forever more".

192. כְּתִיב כִּי בָּחַר יְיָ׳ בְּצִיּוֹן אִוָּהּ לְמוֹשָׁב לוֹ. כַּד אִתְפָּרְשַׁת מַטְרוֹנִיתָא, וְאִתְחֲבְרַת בְּמַלְכָּא אַנְפִּין בְּאַנְפִּין, בְּמַעֲלֵי שַׁבְּתָא. אִתְעָבֵיד כֹּלָּא חַד גּוּפָא, וּכְדֵין יָתִיב קוּדְשָׁא בְּרִיךְ הוּא בְּכוּרְסְיֵיהּ. וְאִקְרֵי כֹּלָּא שְׁמָא שְׁלִים, שְׁמָא קַדִּישָׁא, בְּרִיךְ שְׁמֵיהּ לְעָלַם לְעָלְמֵי עָלְמִין. כָּל אִלֵּין מִלִּין סְלִיקְנָא עַד יוֹמָא דָא, דְּאִתְעַטָּר בְּהוּ לְעָלְמָא דְּאָתֵי, וְהַשְׁתָּא אִתְגַּלְיָין הָכָא, זַכָּאָה חוּלָקִי.

192. It is written, "For Hashem has chosen Zion; He has desired it for His habitation" (Tehilim 132:13), that is, after Malchut separated FROM CLEAVING TO HIS BACK and cleaved to the King face to face on Shabbat night and everything became a single body. Then the Holy One, blessed be He, sits on His throne, and everything is considered a whole Name, a Holy Name, blessed be it forever and ever. I have brought all these matters up on this day so they will adorn it to the World to Come, and now they have been revealed here. Blessed is my portion WITH THEM.

193. הַאי מַטְרוֹנִיתָא, כַּד אִתְחַבְּרַת עִם מַלְכָּא, כָּל עָלְמִין מִתְבָּרְכָן, וְאִשְׁתְּכָחוּ בְּחֶדְוָותָא דְּכֹלָּא. כְּמָה דִּדְכוּרָא כָּלִיל בִּתְלָתָא, וְשֵׁירוּתָא בִּתְלָתָא. כַּךְ כֹּלָּא הָכִי, וְסִיּוּמָא דְּכָל גּוּפָא הָכִי, וּמַטְרוֹנִיתָא לָא מִתְבָּרְכָא, אֶלָּא בִּכְלָלָא דִּתְלָתָא אִלֵּין, דְּאִינּוּן נֶצַח הוֹד יְסוֹד, וּמִתְבַּסְּמָא וּמִתְבָּרְכָא בַּאֲתָר דְּאִקְרֵי קֹדֶשׁ הַקֳּדָשִׁים דִּלְתַתָּא. דִּכְתִּיב,

כִּי שָׁם צִוָּה יְיָ׳ אֶת הַבְּרָכָה. דְּהָא תְּרֵין דַּרְגִּין אִינּוּן לְעֵילָּא וְתַתָּא.

193. When the Queen is united with the King, all the worlds are blessed and are in a state of complete joy. Just as the male is composed of three Columns, and the beginning is composed of three, NAMELY CHOCHMAH, BINAH AND DA'AT, so is everything, FOR THE BODY TOO IS COMPOSED OF THE TRIAD OF CHESED, GVURAH AND TIFERET, and the ending of the body, NETZACH, HOD AND YESOD. The Queen is blessed only from these three, Netzach, Hod and Yesod, and is sweetened and blessed from the place called the lower holy of holies, WHICH IS YESOD. FOR ARICH ANPIN AND ABA AND IMA ARE CALLED THE UPPER HOLY OF HOLIES, AND YESOD OF MALCHUT IS CALLED THE LOWER HOLY OF HOLIES, as written, "for there Hashem has commanded the blessing" (Tehilim 133:3), NAMELY IN ZION CALLED THE HOLY OF HOLIES. For there are two grades above and below, ZION AND JERUSALEM; YESOD OF MALCHUT IS CALLED ZION AND MALCHUT OF MALCHUT IS CALLED JERUSALEM, AND ZION IS CALLED THE HOLY OF HOLIES.

194. ובג״כ לֵית רְשׁוּתָא לְמֵיעַל תַּמָּן, בַּר כַּהֲנָא רַבָּא, דְּאָתֵי מִן סִטְרָא דְּחֶסֶד. בְּגִין דְּלָא עַיֵּיל לְהַהוּא אֲתָר דִּלְעֵילָּא, אֶלָּא הַהוּא דְּאִקְרֵי חֶסֶד, וְעַיֵּיל בְּקֹדֶשׁ הַקֳּדָשִׁים, וּמִתְבַּסְּמַת נוּקְבָּא. וּמִתְבָּרְכָא הַאי קֹדֶשׁ הַקֳּדָשִׁים בְּגוֹ לְגוֹ, אֲתָר דְּאִקְרֵי צִיּוֹן. צִיּוֹן וִירוּשְׁלֵם, תְּרֵין דַּרְגִּין אִינּוּן, חַד רַחֲמֵי, וְחַד דִּינָא. צִיּוֹן, דִּכְתִּיב צִיּוֹן בְּמִשְׁפָּט תִּפָּדֶה. יְרוּשְׁלַיִם, דִּכְתִּיב צֶדֶק יָלִין בָּהּ כְּמָה דְּאוֹקִימְנָא.

194. For that reason none is allowed into the holy of holies IN THIS WORLD except for the High Priest that comes from the aspect of Chesed, since no one enters that place above, THAT IS, YESOD OF MALCHUT CALLED ZION except that which is called Chesed OF ZEIR ANPIN, THE ASPECT OF THE HIGH PRIEST that enters the holy of holies. Malchut is mitigated and the holy of holies is blessed to its innermost, WHICH IS the place called Zion. Zion and Jerusalem are two grades, one Mercy and the other Judgment. Zion IS MERCY, as written, "Zion shall be redeemed with justice" (Yeshayah 1:27), JUSTICE BEING MERCY; Jerusalem IS JUDGMENT as written, "righteousness lodged in it" (Ibid. 21), RIGHTEOUSNESS BEING JUDGMENT as we explained.

195. וְכָל תִּיאוּבְתָּא דִּדְכוּרָא לְגַבֵּי נוּקְבָּא, הָכָא הוּא, וְקָרֵינָן לְהוּ בְּרָכָה, דְּמִתַּמָּן נַפְקֵי בִּרְכָּן לְכֻלְּהוּ עָלְמִין, וְכֻלְּהוּ מִתְבָּרְכָן. הַאי אֲתָר אִקְרֵי קֹדֶשׁ. וְכָל קֳדָשִׁים דִּדְכוּרָא עָיְילִין תַּמָּן, בְּהַהוּא דַּרְגָּא דַּאֲמֵינָא, וְכֻלְּהוּ אַתְיָין מֵרֵישָׁא עִלָּאָה דְּגוּלְגַּלְתָּא דִּדְכוּרָא, מִסִּטְרָא דְּמוֹחֵי עִלָּאֵי, דְּשַׁרְיָין בֵּיהּ, וְנָגִיד הַהִיא בְּרָכָה בְּכָל שַׁיְיפֵי גּוּפָא, עַד אִינּוּן דְּאִקְרוּן צְבָאוֹת. וְכָל הַהוּא נְגִידוּ דְּאִתְנְגִיד מִכָּל גּוּפָא, מִתְכַּנְּשֵׁי תַּמָּן, וע"ד אִקְרוּן צְבָאוֹת, דְּכָל צְבָאוֹת דְּעִלָּאִין וְתַתָּאִין תַּמָּן נָפְקִין. וְהַהוּא נְגִידוּ בָּתַר דְּאִתְכְּנִישׁ, תַּמָּן, שַׁרְיָין לֵיהּ בְּהַהוּא יְסוֹד קַדִּישָׁא, כֹּלָּא חִוָּורָא, בְּג"כ אִקְרֵי חֶסֶד. וְהַהוּא חֶסֶד עָיֵיל לְקֹדֶשׁ הַקֳּדָשִׁים, דִּכְתִּיב כִּי שָׁם צִוָּה יְיָ' אֶת הַבְּרָכָה חַיִּים עַד הָעוֹלָם.

195. The whole desire of the male, WHICH IS ZEIR ANPIN, towards Malchut is here IN ZION. It is called a blessing since from there blessings are issued to all the worlds and everyone is blessed. This place, ZION, is called holy, and all holies, NAMELY THE HOLY LIGHTS of the male, WHO IS ZEIR ANPIN, entered there the grade I mentioned, ZION, and all emerge from the supernal head of the skull of the male from the aspect of the lofty brain lobes that rest in it. That blessing flows FROM THE BRAIN LOBES to all the body parts, CHESED, GVURAH AND TIFERET, to those called hosts (Heb. *Tzva'ot*), NETZACH AND HOD, since all that plenty coming from the whole body is gathered there IN NETZACH AND HOD. Hence they are called hosts, since all the higher and lower hosts IN THE THREE WORLDS OF BRIYAH, YETZIRAH AND ASIYAH come out from them, FROM NETZACH AND HOD. And after that plenty gathers there IN NETZACH AND HOD it is placed in holy Yesod, which is entirely white, which is why it is called Chesed. That Chesed enters the holy of holies, as written, "for there Hashem has commanded the blessing, even life forever more."

48. The passing away of Rabbi Shimon ben Yochai

A Synopsis

Rabbi Aba recounts that after Rabbi Shimon uttered the word "life", all his words ceased. The light in the room was so great that Rabbi Aba could not look, and two voices were heard saying "For length of days, and long life", and then, "He asked life of You." We are told of the miraculous events that happened during the rest of that day.

196. א"ר אַבָּא, לָא סַיֵּים בּוּצִינָא קַדִּישָׁא לְמֵימַר חַיִּים, עַד דְּאִשְׁתְּכָכוּ מִלּוֹי, וַאֲנָא כָּתַבְנָא, סָבַרְנָא לְמִכְתַּב טְפֵי, וְלָא שְׁמַעְנָא. וְלָא זָקִיפְנָא רֵישָׁא, דִּנְהוֹרָא הֲוָה סַגִּי, וְלָא הֲוָה יָכִילְנָא לְאִסְתַּכְּלָא. אַדְּהָכִי אִזְדַּעֲזַעְנָא, שְׁמַעְנָא קָלָא דְּקָארֵי וְאָמַר אֹרֶךְ יָמִים וּשְׁנוֹת חַיִּים וְגוֹ'. שְׁמַעְנָא קָלָא אַחֲרָא, חַיִּים שָׁאַל מִמְּךָ וְגוֹ'.

196. Rabbi Aba said, the Holy Luminary barely finished uttering "life," when his words ceased. I was writing and was about to write more, yet heard nothing. I did not raise my head, because the light was great and I could not look. I then trembled and heard a voice calling and saying, "For length of days, and long life..." (Mishlei 3:2), AND THEN I heard another voice, "He asked life of You..." (Tehilim 21:5).

197. כֹּל הַהוּא יוֹמָא, לָא אַפְסִיק אֶשָּׁא מִן בֵּיתָא, וְלָא הֲוָה מַאן דְּמָטֵי לְגַבֵּיהּ, דְּלָא יָכִילוּ דִּנְהוֹרָא וְאֶשָּׁא הֲוָה בְּסוּחֲרָנֵיהּ. כָּל הַהוּא יוֹמָא נְפִילְנָא עַל אַרְעָא, וְגָעֵינָא. בָּתַר דְּאָזִיל אֶשָּׁא, חֲמֵינָא לְבוּצִינָא קַדִּישָׁא קֹדֶשׁ הַקֳּדָשִׁים, דְּאִסְתְּלַק מִן עָלְמָא, אִתְעֲטָף שָׁכִיב עַל יְמִינֵיהּ, וְאַנְפּוֹי חַיְיכִין.

197. All that day the fire did not cease from the house and no one reached him for they could not because of the light and fire that encircled him. I was prostrated all that day on the ground, crying loudly. After the fire was gone, I saw that the Holy Luminary, the holy of holies, was gone from the world, wrapped around and lying on his right side with a smiling face.

198. קָם רִבִּי אֶלְעָזָר בְּרֵיהּ, וְנָטִיל יְדוֹי וְנָשִׁיק לוֹן, וַאֲנָא לָחִיכְנָא עַפְרָא דִּתְחוֹת רַגְלוֹי. בָּעוּ חַבְרַיָּיא לְמִבְכֵּי, וְלָא יָכִילוּ לְמַלְּלָא. שָׁארוּ חַבְרַיָּיא בִּבְכִיָּה, וְרִבִּי אֶלְעָזָר בְּרֵיהּ נָפִיל תְּלַת זִמְנִין, וְלָא יָכִיל לְמִפְתַּח פּוּמֵיהּ. לְבָתַר פָּתַח וְאָמַר, אַבָּא אַבָּא. תְּלַת הֲווֹ, חַד אִתְחֲזָרוּ. הַשְׁתָּא תְּנוּד חֵיוָתָא, צִפֲּרָאן טָאסִין, מִשְׁתַּקְעָן בְּנוּקְבָּאן דְּיַמָּא רַבָּא, וְחַבְרַיָּיא כֻּלְּהוּ שַׁתְיָין דָּמָא.

198. Rabbi Elazar his son rose, took his hands and kissed them, while I licked the dirt under his feet. The friends started crying. Rabbi Elazar his son prostrated three times and could not open his mouth. He then started saying, Father, father, there were three that BECAME one again. THAT IS, THERE WERE THREE GREAT MEN IN THE LAND, RABBI ELAZAR, RABBI SHIMON BAR YOCHAI HIS FATHER AND HIS FATHER-IN-LAW RABBI PINCHAS BEN YAIR. NOW RABBI ELAZAR IS ORPHANED OF HIS FATHER-IN-LAW AND HIS FATHER RABBI SHIMON AND ONLY ONE REMAINS IN THE WORLD. NOW, AFTER THIS GREAT TREE IS GONE, UNDER WHICH THE BEASTS OF THE FIELD USED TO WALK AND IN WHICH BOUGHS DWELT THE BIRDS OF THE SKY AND WHICH HAD FOOD FOR EVERYONE, NOW the beasts will wander and the birds THAT USED TO DWELL IN ITS BOUGHS will sink into the chasm in the great sea, and the friends, INSTEAD OF THE FOOD THEY RECEIVED FROM IT will drink blood.

199. קָם רִבִּי חִיָּיא עַל רַגְלוֹי וְאָמַר, עַד הַשְׁתָּא בּוּצִינָא קַדִּישָׁא מִסְתַּכַּל עֲלָן. הַשְׁתָּא לָאו הוּא עִדָּן, אֶלָּא לְאִשְׁתַּדְּלָא בִּיקָרֵיהּ. קָם רִבִּי אֶלְעָזָר וְר' אַבָּא, נַטְלוּ לֵיהּ בְּטִיקְרָא דְּסִיקְלָא, מַאן חָמָא עִרְבּוּבְיָא דְּחַבְרַיָּיא, וְכָל בֵּיתָא הֲוָה סָלִיק רֵיחִין סְלִיקוּ בֵּיהּ בְּפוּרְיֵיהּ, וְלָא אִשְׁתַּמַּשׁ בֵּיהּ, אֶלָּא ר' אֶלְעָזָר וְר' אַבָּא.

199. Rabbi Chiya rose to his feet and said, Up until now the Holy Luminary used to protect us. Now is the time to strive to honor him. Rabbi Elazar and Rabbi Aba rose and took him FROM HIS PLACE to a bed made like a ladder IN ORDER TO RAISE HIM ON HIS BED. Who has ever seen such confusion of the friends! The whole house emitted good fragrances. They raised him on his bed, and none served him but Rabbi Elazar and Rabbi Aba.

200. אָתוּ טְרִיקִין, וּמָארֵי תְּרִיסִין דִּכְפַר צִפֳּרִי וְטַרְדָא בְּהוּ בְּנֵי מְרוֹנְיָא, צַוְוחִין בִּקְטִירִין, דְּחָשִׁיבוּ דְּלָא יִתְקְבַּר תַּמָּן. בָּתַר דְּנָפַק פּוּרְיָיא, הֲוָה סָלִיק בַּאֲוִירָא. וְאֶשָּׁא הֲוָה לָהִיט קַמֵּיהּ, שָׁמְעוּ קָלָא, עוּלוּ וְאָתוּ, וְאִתְכְּנָשׁוּ לְהִילוּלָא דְּרַבִּי שִׁמְעוֹן, יָבֹא שָׁלוֹם יָנוּחוּ עַל מִשְׁכְּבוֹתָם.

200. Bullies and armed people came from the village of Tzipori, WHO WANTED HIM TO BE BURIED THERE AND CAME TO TAKE HIM BY FORCE. The inhabitants of Meron drove them away and shouted at them in their multitudes, because they did not want him to be buried there BUT WHERE THEY THEMSELVES LIVED. After the bed left the house, it rose in the air and fire burned before it. They heard a voice, 'Come and gather to the feast of Rabbi Shimon. "shall enter in peace to them that rest in their graves"' (Yeshayah 57:2).

201. כַּד עָאל לִמְעַרְתָּא שָׁמְעוּ קָלָא בִּמְעַרְתָּא, זֶה הָאִישׁ מַרְעִישׁ הָאָרֶץ מַרְגִּיז מַמְלָכוֹת, כַּמָּה פַּטְרִין בִּרְקִיעָא מִשְׁתַּכְּכִין בְּיוֹמָא דֵּין בְּגִינָךְ, דְּנָא רשב״י, דְּמָארֵיהּ מִשְׁתְּבַּח בֵּיהּ בְּכָל יוֹמָא. זַכָּאָה חוּלָקֵיהּ לְעֵילָּא וְתַתָּא. כַּמָּה גְּנִיזִין עִלָּאִין מִסְתַּמְרָן לֵיהּ, עָלֵיהּ אִתְּמַר וְאַתָּה לֵךְ לַקֵּץ וְתָנוּחַ וְתַעֲמוֹד לְגוֹרָלְךָ לְקֵץ הַיָּמִין.

עַד כָּאן הַאִדְרָא קַדִּישָׁא זוּטָא

201. When he entered the cave they heard a voice inside the cave, 'This is the man who caused the earth to tremble, who provoked kingdoms. How many prosecutors in the firmament are quieted today for your sake. This is Rabbi Shimon bar Yochai, with whom his Master glorifies Himself daily. Blessed is his portion above and below. How many supernal treasures await him. Of him it says, "But go you your way till the end be, for you shall rest, and stand up for your allotted portion at the end of the days"' (Daniel 12:13).

End of the Idra Kadisa Zuta (the holy smaller assembly)

49. Holy, holiness, the holy of holies

A Synopsis

Rabbi Yosi and Rabbi Aba talk about the difference between "holy nation" and "holiness," and we hear about the connection of these terms with supernal wisdom.

202. אָמַר ר' יוֹסֵי, כַּמָּה חֲבִיבִין יִשְׂרָאֵל קַמֵּי קוּדְשָׁא בְּרִיךְ הוּא, בְּקַדְמֵיתָא קָרָא לוֹן גּוֹי קָדוֹשׁ, דִּכְתִּיב כִּי עַם קָדוֹשׁ אַתָּה וְגוֹ'. לְבָתַר קָרָא לוֹן קֹדֶשׁ, דִּכְתִּיב קֹדֶשׁ יִשְׂרָאֵל לַיְיָ' רֵאשִׁית תְּבוּאָתֹה. מַה בֵּין הַאי לְהַאי. א"ר אַבָּא, קֹדֶשׁ עִלָּאָה מִכֹּלָּא, דְּהָכִי תָּנֵינָן, כַּד אִתְחַבְּרָן כֻּלְּהוּ קְדוֹשֵׁי כַּחֲדָא, אִקְרוּן קָדוֹשׁ. וְכֻלְּהוּ סַלְּקִין וּמִתְכַּנְּשִׁין לְהַהוּא אֲתָר עִלָּאָה, דְּאִקְרֵי קֹדֶשׁ.

202. Rabbi Yosi said, How beloved are Yisrael before the Holy One, blessed be He, since at first He called them a holy nation, as written, "For you are a holy people" (Devarim 14:2). He then called them holiness, as written, "Yisrael is holiness to Hashem, the first fruits of His increase" (Yirmeyah 2:3). What is the difference between them, BETWEEN HOLY AND HOLINESS? Rabbi Aba said, Holiness is the highest, BEING CHOCHMAH, for so have we learned that when all sanctifications, WHICH ARE THE THREE COLUMNS, CHESED, GVURAH AND TIFERET, are joined together they are called holiness, BECAUSE THEN they rise and gather in the supernal place called holiness, NAMELY SUPERNAL CHOCHMAH.

203. ובג"כ ק' ק' ק', קֹדֶשׁ יִשְׂרָאֵל אִתְעֲבֵיד מִנַּיְיהוּ. וּבְגִין דְּיִשְׂרָאֵל בִּתְלַת דַּרְגִּין מִתְעַטְּרָן, כַּד אִתְחַבְּרָן כַּחֲדָא, אִקְרוּן קֹדֶשׁ יִשְׂרָאֵל לַיְיָ', דְּאִיהִי רֵאשִׁית. וְהָא אוֹקִימְנָא תְּבוּאָתֹה, בְּהֵ"א. כָּל אוֹכְלָיו יֶאְשָׁמוּ, מַאי כָּל אוֹכְלָיו יֶאְשָׁמוּ. א"ר אַבָּא, הָא אִתְּמַר, דִּכְתִּיב וְאִישׁ כִּי יֹאכַל קֹדֶשׁ בִּשְׁגָגָה. וּכְתִיב וְכָל זָר לֹא יֹאכַל קֹדֶשׁ, וְיִשְׂרָאֵל אִקְרוּן קֹדֶשׁ, בג"כ כָּל אוֹכְלָיו יֶאְשָׁמוּ.

203. Hence 'Holy, holy, holy', WHICH ARE CHESED, GVURAH AND TIFERET, THE SECRET OF THE PRIESTS, THE LEVITES AND YISRAEL, turn into "Yisrael is holiness." Since Yisrael are adorned with these three grades, when they join together they are called, "Yisrael is holiness (or: 'holy thing') to Hashem," which is first, SINCE THEN THEY RECEIVE FROM SUPERNAL CHOCHMAH CALLED FIRST (OR: 'BEGINNING'). We have explained that fruit is spelled with EXTRA Hei, WHICH INDICATES MALCHUT THAT IS CALLED HOLINESS WHEN RECEIVING FROM SUPERNAL CHOCHMAH. "all that devour him shall be held guilty" (Ibid.). What is meant by that? Rabbi Aba said, We have learned the verse, "And if a man eat of the holy thing unwittingly" (Vayikra 22:14), and, "No stranger shall eat of the holy thing" (Ibid. 10). Yisrael are considered a holy thing, and hence, "all that devour him shall be held guilty."

204. אר״א, שֵׁירוּתָא וְסִיּוּמָא דְכֹלָּא, אִתְכְּלִיל בְּקֹדֶשׁ. וְחָכְמָה עִלָּאָה קֹדֶשׁ אִקְרֵי, וְכַד נָהִיר דָּא חָכְמָה עִלָּאָה, חָכְמָה דִּשְׁלֹמֹה נָהִיר. כְּמָה דִּכְתִּיב, וַתֵּרֶב חָכְמַת שְׁלֹמֹה, דְּקַיְּימָא סִיהֲרָא בְּאַשְׁלְמוּתָא. וְהָא אוֹקִימְנָא. וְכַד אִתְבָּרְכָא מִיסוֹד, הָכִי קָרֵינָן לָהּ קֹדֶשׁ, דְּאִיהוּ אַנְהִיר בִּשְׁלִימוּ. וְכַד לָא אִתְנַהֲרָא מִתְעַטְּרָא בְּאַשְׁלְמוּתָא, קָרֵינָן לָהּ רוּחַ הַקֹּדֶשׁ, וְלָא אִתְקְרֵי קֹדֶשׁ כְּהַהוּא דִּלְעֵילָּא.

204. Rabbi Elazar said, The beginning, WHICH IS SUPERNAL CHOCHMAH, and the ending of everything, WHICH IS MALCHUT, are included in holiness, and supernal Chochmah is called holiness. And when supernal Chochmah shines, Solomon's wisdom shines AS WELL, WHICH IS MALCHUT, as written, "And Solomon's wisdom excelled" (I Melachim 5:10), when the moon, WHICH IS MALCHUT, stood in its fullness. This we have already explained. And when MALCHUT is blessed by Yesod, she is called holiness because she shines in her fullness. But when MALCHUT does not shine and is not perfectly adorned, she is called the Holy Spirit, she is not called holiness like the supernal CHOCHMAH.

205. וְכַד מִתְבָּרְכָא מֵהַאי יְסוֹד, וְיַנְקָא לְכָל אִינּוּן דִּלְתַתָּא, אִתְקְרֵי אֵם, כְּהַהִיא דִּלְעֵילָּא. וְקָרֵינָן לֵיהּ קֳדָשִׁים. וּכְדֵין קָרֵינָן לֵיהּ קֹדֶשׁ הַקֳּדָשִׁים, דְּבֵיהּ כַּלָּה דִּכְתִּיב אִתִּי מִלְּבָנוֹן כַּלָּה וְגוֹ׳. מַאי לְבָנוֹן. דָּא עֵדֶן, דְּאִתְלַבַּן מִכָּל סִטְרִין. וְעֵדֶן הָא יָדוּעַ לְגַבֵּי חַבְרַיָּיא.

205. When MALCHUT is blessed by Yesod and nourishes all the lower beings, she is called a mother like the one above, NAMELY LIKE BINAH CALLED A MOTHER. MALCHUT is THEN called holy things (or: 'holies'), and YESOD is then called holy of holies, since with it she is a bride. THAT IS, YESOD IS HOLINESS, AND TOGETHER WITH THE BRIDE THAT IS CALLED HOLIES, IT IS THE HOLY OF HOLIES, as written, "Come with me from Lebanon, my bride" (Shir Hashirim 4:8). What is Lebanon? Eden, NAMELY SUPERNAL CHOCHMAH. IT IS CALLED LEBANON because it became white (Heb. *nitlabnah*) in every direction, WHICH MEANS IT SHINES WITH CHESED, WHICH IS WHITE IN COLOR, BOTH FROM THE RIGHT AND LEFT SIDES. FOR IT IS THE SECRET OF SUPERNAL ABA AND IMA THAT ALWAYS HAVE THE MEANING OF, "BECAUSE HE DELIGHTS IN MERCY" (MICHAH 7:18), YET CHOCHMAH IS BESTOWED ON MALCHUT VIA THE RIVER THAT COMES OUT OF EDEN, WHICH IS BINAH. Eden is already known to the friends.

50. When the time comes for a righteous man to pass away, he should disclose wisdom

A Synopsis

We hear that when the time comes for a righteous man who is full of wisdom to die, he should reveal that wisdom to those who have the Holy Spirit among them.

206. תָּאנָא, כְּתִיב כִּי שֵׁם יְיָ׳ אֶקְרָא, מַאי כִּי שֵׁם יְיָ׳ אֶקְרָא. אר״ש, הָא כְּתִיב הָבוּ גוֹדֶל לֵאלֹהֵינוּ. א״ר אַבָּא, הָבוּ גוֹדֶל: דָּא גְּדוּלָּה: הַצּוּר תָּמִים פָּעֳלוֹ: דָּא גְּבוּרָה. כִּי כָל דְּרָכָיו מִשְׁפָּט: דָּא תִּפְאֶרֶת. אֵל אֱמוּנָה: דָּא נֶצַח. וְאֵין עָוֶל: דָּא הוֹד. צַדִּיק: דָּא יְסוֹד. וְיָשָׁר: דָּא צֶדֶק. הוּא כֹּלָּא שְׁמָא קַדִּישָׁא דְקוּדְשָׁא בְּרִיךְ הוּא, ובג״כ כִּי שֵׁם יְיָ׳ אֶקְרָא.

206. We learned that it is written, "because I will call on the name of Hashem" (Devarim 32:3). What is meant by that? Rabbi Shimon said, it is written, "ascribe greatness to our Elohim" (Ibid.). Rabbi Shimon said AS INTERPRETATION TO THE WORDS OF RABBI SHIMON, "ascribe greatness" refers to greatness, NAMELY CHESED. "He is the Rock, His work is perfect" (Ibid. 4) is Gvurah; "for all His ways are justice" (Ibid.) is Tiferet; "an El of truth" (Ibid.) is Netzach; "and without iniquity" is Hod. "just" is Yesod, "and right" is Righteousness, NAMELY MALCHUT. Thus everything is the Holy Name of the Holy One, blessed be He, NAMELY THE SEVEN SFIROT, CHESED, GVURAH, TIFERET, NETZACH, HOD, YESOD AND MALCHUT. This is why HE SAID, "because I will call on the name of Hashem."

207. א״ר יוֹסֵי, שֵׁם יְיָ׳ מַמָּשׁ. וּמֹשֶׁה בְּהַהִיא שַׁעֲתָא גַּלֵּי לְהוּ לְיִשְׂרָאֵל. דִּכְתִּיב, בֶּן מֵאָה וְעֶשְׂרִים שָׁנָה אָנֹכִי הַיּוֹם וְגוֹ׳. מִכָּאן אוֹלִיפְנָא, הַהוּא זַכָּאָה דְּחָכְמְתָא עִלָּאָה בֵּיהּ, כַּד מָטֵי יוֹמָא לְאִסְתַּלְּקָא מֵעָלְמָא, בָּעֵי לְגַלָּאָה הַהִיא חָכְמְתָא, לְאִינּוּן דִּי רוּחַ קַדִּישָׁא בֵּינַיְיהוּ. מְנָלָן. מִמֹּשֶׁה. דִּכְתִּיב בֶּן מֵאָה וְעֶשְׂרִים שָׁנָה אָנֹכִי הַיּוֹם. וּכְתִיב, וְעַתָּה כִּתְבוּ לָכֶם אֶת הַשִּׁירָה הַזֹּאת וְגוֹ׳.

207. Rabbi Yosi said, IT IS the very name of Hashem, which Moses revealed at that time to Yisrael, as written, "I am a hundred and twenty years old this day..." (Devarim 31:2), "NOW THEREFORE WRITE THIS POEM FOR YOURSELVES" (IBID. 19). From this we derive that when the time comes for a righteous man, in whom rests lofty wisdom, to pass away, he should reveal that wisdom to those who have the Holy Spirit among them. Whence do we know that? From Moses, as written, "I am a hundred and twenty years old this day...," WHICH MEANS HE REVEALED TO THEM WHAT HE HAD NOT REVEALED TO THEM UNTIL THEN.

208. וְאִם לָאו, עָלֵיהּ כְּתִיב, אַל תִּמְנַע טוֹב מִבְּעָלָיו. כד"א, כִּי לֶקַח טוֹב נָתַתִּי לָכֶם וְגוֹ'. בִּהְיוֹת לְאֵל יָדְךָ לַעֲשׂוֹת. עַד לָא תִּסְתָּלַּק מִן עָלְמָא, וְלָא אִתְיְיהִיב לָךְ רְשׁוּתָא לְגַלָּאָה.

208. If he does not REVEAL TO THEM THAT WISDOM, it says of him, "Withhold not good from those to whom it is due" (Mishlei 3:27), WHICH IS TORAH THAT IS CALLED GOOD, as written, "For I give you good doctrine" (Mishlei 4:2), "when it is in the power of your hand to do it" (Mishlei 3:27) before you pass away, BEFORE you will not have permission to disclose.

51. "because I will call on the name of Hashem"

A Synopsis

Rabbi Chiya makes it clear that God will only be close to those who call upon His name in truth. Part of this meaning is that God must be called upon with the quality of the Central Column, not from the aspect of the Left or Right.

209. א״ר חִיָּיא, הַאי קְרָא אוֹלִיפְנָא מִנֵּיהּ חָכְמְתָא עִלָּאָה, וְהָכִי הוּא. אֲבָל סֵיפֵיהּ דִּקְרָא, מְקַשֵּׁר קִשְׁרָא דִּמְהֵימְנוּתָא, בְּמַאי דִּכְתִּיב הוּא. כד״א, צַדִּיק וְיָשָׁר הוּא. כְּלוֹמַר הוּא כֹּלָּא. הוּא חַד בְּלָא פֵּרוּדָא. דְּאִי תֵּימָא כָּל הָנֵי סַגִּיאִין אִינּוּן, חָזַר וְאָמַר הוּא, כֻּלְּהוּ סַלְּקִין וּמִתְקַשְּׁרָן וּמִתְאַחֲדָן בְּחַד. וְכֹלָּא, הוּא הָיָה, וְהוּא הֹוֶה, וְהוּא יְהֵא. וְהוּא חַד. בְּרִיךְ שְׁמֵיהּ לְעָלַם וּלְעָלְמֵי עָלְמִין. ע״כ מִתְקַטְּרִין מִלִּין, וּמִתְאַחֲדִין מִלִּין קַדִּישִׁין, דִּשְׁמָא דְקוּדְשָׁא בְּרִיךְ הוּא.

209. Rabbi Chiya said, From this verse, "BECAUSE I WILL CALL ON THE NAME OF HASHEM" (DEVARIM 32:3), I have learned celestial wisdom and it is so. Yet the end of the verse connects the knot of faith with the word "He," as written, "just and right is He," which means He is everything, He is one without division. For if you say that all these NAMES IN THE VERSE are many, it says again, "He," as they all amount to and connect and join into one. And HE is everything; He was, He is and He will be and He is one. Blessed is His name forever and ever. Hence matters are connected and the holy matters of the name of the Holy One, blessed be He, are joined.

210. זַכָּאָה חוּלָקֵיהּ מַאן דְּקָרֵי לְמַלְכָּא, וְיִנְדַּע לְמִקְרֵי כַּדְקָא יָאוּת. וְאִי אִיהוּ קָרֵי וְלָא יְדַע לְמַאן קָרֵי, אִתְרְחִיק קוּדְשָׁא בְּרִיךְ הוּא מִנֵּיהּ, דִּכְתִּיב קָרוֹב יְיָ׳ לְכָל קוֹרְאָיו וְגוֹ׳. קָרוֹב יְיָ׳ לְכָל קוֹרְאָיו, לְמַאן קָרוֹב. חָזַר וְאָמַר, לְכֹל אֲשֶׁר יִקְרָאוּהוּ בֶאֱמֶת, וְכִי אִית מַאן דְּיִקְרֵי לֵיהּ בְּשִׁקְרָא. א״ר אַבָּא אִין, הַהוּא מַאן דְּקָרֵי וְלָא יְדַע לְמַאן דְּקָרֵי. מְנָלָן. דִּכְתִּיב לְכֹל אֲשֶׁר יִקְרָאוּהוּ בֶאֱמֶת. מַאי בֶאֱמֶת. בְּחוֹתָמָא דְגוּשְׁפַּנְקָא דְּמַלְכָּא, דְּהוּא שְׁלִימוּ דְּכֹלָּא. הה״ד, תִּתֵּן אֱמֶת לְיַעֲקֹב חֶסֶד לְאַבְרָהָם.

ובג״כ לְכֹל אֲשֶׁר יִקְרָאוּהוּ בֶאֱמֶת כְּתִיב. זַכָּאָה חוּלָקֵיהּ דְּמַאן דְּעָאל, וְנָפַק לְמִנְדַּע אָרְחוֹי דְּקוּדְשָׁא בְּרִיךְ הוּא. וע״ד כְּתִיב, וְאֹרַח צַדִּיקִים כְּאוֹר נוֹגַהּ וְגוֹ׳. וּכְתִיב וְעַמֵּךְ כֻּלָּם צַדִּיקִים וְגוֹ׳.

210. Happy is the portion of he who calls the King and knows how to call Him properly. If he calls yet knows not upon whom he called, the Holy One, blessed be He, keeps away from him, as written, "Hashem is near to all those who call upon Him" (Tehilim 145:18). To whom is He near? It says again, "to all who call upon Him in truth" (Ibid.). Is there anyone who calls upon Him falsely? Rabbi Aba said, Yes; it is he who calls yet knows not upon whom he calls. Whence do we know that? From the words, "to all who call upon Him in truth." What is "in truth"? It is the seal of the King's ring, WHICH IS THE SECRET OF THE CENTRAL COLUMN THAT SEALS THE MOCHIN TOGETHER WITH MALCHUT THAT IS CALLED THE KING'S RING, which is overall perfection. This is the meaning of, "You will show truth to Jacob, loyal love to Abraham" (Michah 7:20), NAMELY ZEIR ANPIN THAT IS THE CENTRAL COLUMN CALLED JACOB, AS TRUTH WAS BESTOWED ON THE CENTRAL COLUMN. This is why it is written, "to all who call upon Him in truth." AND WHOEVER KNOWS NOT TO CALL UPON HIM WITH THE QUALITY OF THE CENTRAL COLUMN, BUT TENDS TO THE LEFT COLUMN OR THE RIGHT COLUMN, THE HOLY ONE, BLESSED BE HE, DRAWS AWAY FROM HIM. Happy is the portion of whoever entered WISDOM and came out whole, to know the ways of the Holy One, blessed be He. Hence it is written, "But the path of just men is like the gleam of sunlight" (Mishlei 4:18), and, "Your people also shall be all righteous…" (Yeshayah 60:21).

52. The wicked cause a damage, so to speak, above

A Synopsis

Rabbi Aba recalls that Rabbi Yitzchak said that all the structures devised in order to bestow blessings upon people cannot be effective because they are marred by the deeds of the wicked. Rabbi Yosi says that when the wicked sin below the patriarchs above cannot receive their supply of blessings either.

211. תַּנְיָא א״ר יִצְחָק, כָּל הָנֵי תִּקּוּנִין, וְכָל הָנֵי מִלֵּי, לִמְחַצְדֵי חַקְלָא אִתְמַסְרָן. וְתָנֵינָן, חַיָּיבִין כִּבְיָכוֹל עַבְדִּין פְּגִימוּתָא לְעֵילָּא. מַאי פְּגִימוּתָא. כְּמָה דִּכְתִּיב, שִׁחֵת לוֹ לֹא בָּנָיו מוּמָם דְּהָא כָּל הָנֵי תִּקּוּנִין לָא מִשְׁתַּכְּחֵי כַּדְקָא יָאוּת. כָּתוּב אֶחָד אוֹמֵר, וַיִּלְבַּשׁ צְדָקָה כַּשִּׁרְיָן, וְכָתוּב אֶחָד אוֹמֵר וַיִּלְבַּשׁ בִּגְדֵי נָקָם תִּלְבּוֹשֶׁת. אֶלָּא א״ר יִצְחָק, וַיִּלְבַּשׁ צְדָקָה, בִּזְמְנָא דְּיִשְׂרָאֵל זַכָּאן. לֹא זָכוּ, וַיִּלְבַּשׁ בִּגְדֵי נָקָם וְגוֹ׳.

211. We learned that Rabbi Yitzchak said, All these structures and these matters were given to the reapers of the field, NAMELY TO THOSE WHO HAVE ALREADY FINISHED THE WORK OF HOLINESS AND PURIFICATION, AND HAVE ALREADY MERITED TO BEHOLD THE FRUIT OF THEIR WORK. We learned that the wicked cause, so to speak, blemish above. The blemish accords with the verse, "Not His the corruption, but the blemish of His sons" (Devarim 32:5); THE DAMAGE IS ONLY IN RELATION TO THE SONS, WHO CANNOT RECEIVE THEIR PLENTY, because all these structures DEVISED IN ORDER TO BESTOW UPON THE LOWER BEINGS are not properly settled, BECAUSE OF THE DEEDS OF THE WICKED. THIS IS THE MEANING OF, "THE BLEMISH OF HIS SONS." One verse says, "For He put on righteousness as a breastplate" (Yeshayah 59:17), and another verse says, "and He put on the garments of vengeance for clothing" (Ibid.). Yet, says Rabbi Yitzchak, "He put on righteousness" when Yisrael are worthy. When they have no merit, "He put on the garments of vengeance..." THIS IS THE BLEMISH THE WICKED CREATE IN THE SUPERNAL STRUCTURES, SO HE TAKES OFF, SO TO SPEAK, THE GARMENT OF RIGHTEOUSNESS AND WEARS GARMENTS OF VENGEANCE.

212. א״ר יוֹסֵי מַאי פְּגִימוּתָא. כְּמָה דְּתָנֵינָן, דַּאֲבָהָן לָא מִסְתַּפְּקִין

לְאִתְבָּרְכָא מֵהַהוּא שַׁקְיוּ דְּנַחֲלָא. כ״ש בְּנִין. כד״א, שִׁחֵת לוֹ לֹא בָּנָיו מוּמָם. מַאי לוֹ לֹא תְּרֵי זִמְנֵי. אֶלָּא חַד לְעֵילָּא, וְחַד לְתַתָּא.

212. Rabbi Yosi said, What is the blemish THE WICKED DO WITH THEIR ACTIONS ABOVE? It is as we learned that the patriarchs, WHO ARE CHESED, GVURAH AND TIFERET, do not receive supply to be blessed from the flow of the river, WHICH IS THE PLENTY OF BINAH, and even less so do their children. FOR SINCE THEY DO NOT RECEIVE PLENTY FOR THE LOWER BEINGS, A BLEMISH AND DAMAGE ARE MADE BELOW, as written, "Not (Heb. *lo*) His (Heb. *lo*) the corruption, but the blemish of His sons." Why 'lo' twice? ONE COULD HAVE SUFFICED IN SAYING 'IT IS HIS SONS' BLEMISH'. Yet one is above, AS A BLEMISH WAS CREATED ABOVE, BECAUSE THEY DO NOT RECEIVE BLESSINGS, FOR WHICH IT SAYS, "HIS THE CORRUPTION," and one below, BECAUSE THEY ARE WANTING IN EVERY RESPECT, WHICH IS WHY IT SAYS, "THE BLEMISH OF HIS SONS." MEANING, IT IS NOT CONSIDERED A BLEMISH IN RELATION TO THE HIGHER BUT ONLY IN RELATION TO THE CHILDREN, WHO ARE YISRAEL.

213. וְהַיְינוּ דאר״ש, כָּל זִמְנָא דְּחַיָּיבַיָּא סַגִּיאוּ בְּעָלְמָא, כִּבְיָכוֹל שְׁמָא קַדִּישָׁא לָא מִתְבָּרַךְ בְּעָלְמָא. וְכָל זִמְנָא דְּחַיָּיבַיָּא לָא סַגִּיאוּ בְּעָלְמָא, שְׁמָא קַדִּישָׁא מִתְבָּרַךְ בְּעָלְמָא. הה״ד, יִתַּמּוּ חַטָּאִים וְגוֹ׳, בָּרְכִי נַפְשִׁי אֶת יְיָ׳ הַלְלוּיָהּ. א״ר אַבָּא, מִקְרָא זֶה מַמָּשׁ הוּא, דִּכְתִּיב שִׁחֵת לוֹ לֹא בָּנָיו מוּמָם. מַאן גָּרִים לְחַבְלוּתָא דָּא. דּוֹר עִקֵּשׁ וּפְתַלְתּוֹל, בְּגִין דְּאִינּוּן חַיָּיבַיָּא וְדָרָא אִשְׁתְּכַח הָכִי.

213. This is the meaning of the words of Rabbi Shimon that as long as there are many wicked men in the world, the Holy Name is not blessed, so to speak, in the world. And as long as there are not many wicked in the world, the Holy Name is blessed in the world. This is the meaning of, "The sinners will be consumed…Bless you Hashem, O my soul. Haleluyah" (Tehilim 104:35). Rabbi Aba said, This verse is certainly precise, which says, "Not His the corruption, but the blemish of His sons." Who brought that blemish about? "a perverse and crooked generation" (Devarim 32:5), because the evil people and that generation are in such a state.

214. בג"כ בָּתַר דְּאָמַר מֹשֶׁה כָּל הָנֵי מִלִּין, וְאַדְכַּר שְׁמָא קַדִּישָׁא כַּדְקָא יָאוּת, אָמַר וַדַּאי צַדִּיק וְיָשָׁר הוּא, מִלָּה בְּתִקּוּנֵיהּ. אֲבָל שִׁחֵת לוֹ לֹא בָּנָיו מוּמָם. מ"ט הָכִי. מִשּׁוּם דְּאִינּוּן דּוֹר עִקֵּשׁ וּפְתַלְתּוֹל. א"ר יְהוּדָה, לוֹ לֹא, כְּלוֹמַר לְגַרְמַיְיהוּ עַבְדִּין דָּא חַיָּיבִין, דְּגַרְמִין לְאִסְתַּלְּקָא בִּרְכָאן מֵעָלְמָא. א"ר אַבָּא, לוֹ לֹא, הָא אוֹקִימְנָא וְהָכִי הוּא. מַה כְּתִיב בַּתְרֵיהּ. הַלַיְיָ' תִּגְמְלוּ זֹאת, לְשַׁלָּמָא גְּמוּל דָּא לְקוּדְשָׁא בְּרִיךְ הוּא, עַל כָּל אִינּוּן טָבָאן דְּגָרִים לָךְ, וְעָבֵיד לְקַבְלָךְ.

214. This is why after Moses said all these things, and properly invoked the Holy Name, he said, surely, "just and right is He" (Ibid. 4), when things are as they should be, but "Not His the corruption, but the blemish of His sons." The reason it is so is that "they are a perverse and crooked generation." Rabbi Yehuda said, "not His" means that the wicked bring it upon themselves, causing blessings to be missing from the world. Rabbi Aba said, "not His" was explained and it is so. The following verse says, "Do you thus requite Hashem" (Ibid. 6), THAT IS, YOU reward this way the Holy One, blessed be He, for all the good things He brought on you and performed before you.

53. "And yet for all that, when they are in the land of their enemies" – "Do you thus requite Hashem"

A Synopsis

Rabbi Aba says that even though Yisrael sinned and went into exile, God and His Shechinah are always with them. Rabbi Yehuda wonders how Yisrael could repay God for His goodness by sinning and thus sending the Shechinah into exile.

215. ר"א פָּתַח, וְאַף גַּם זֹאת בִּהְיוֹתָם בְּאֶרֶץ אוֹיְבֵיהֶם וְגוֹ'. זַכָּאִין אִינּוּן יִשְׂרָאֵל, עַל כָּל עַמִּין עכו"ם, דאע"ג דְּאַרְגִּיזוּ קָמֵי מָארֵיהוֹן, קוּדְשָׁא בְּרִיךְ הוּא לָא בָּעֵי לְשַׁבְקָא לוֹן. דִּבְכָל אֲתָר דְּגָלוּ בֵּינֵי עַמְמַיָּא, קוּדְשָׁא בְּרִיךְ הוּא עִמְּהוֹן בְּגָלוּתָא. הה"ד וְאַף גַּם זֹאת בִּהְיוֹתָם בְּאֶרֶץ אוֹיְבֵיהֶם וְגוֹ'.

215. Rabbi Aba opened with, "And yet for all that, when they are in the land of their enemies..." (Vayikra 26:44). Yisrael are blessed above all other idolatrous nations, since even though they have angered their Master, the Holy One, blessed be He, does not want to leave them, as wherever they are exiled among the nations the Holy One, blessed be He, is with them in exile. This is the meaning of, "And yet for all that, when they are in the land of their enemies..."

216. ר' אַבָּא אָמַר, וְאַף גַּם זֹאת בִּהְיוֹתָם. ת"ח, כַּמָּה חֲבִיבוּתָא דְקוּדְשָׁא בְּרִיךְ הוּא לְגַבֵּיהוֹן דְּיִשְׂרָאֵל, דאע"ג דְּגַרְמִין לְמִגְלֵי בֵּינֵי עַמְמַיָּא, שְׁכִינְתָּא לָא אִתְעֲדִיאַת מִנְּהוֹן לְעָלְמִין. דְּלָא תֵּימָא דְּאִינּוּן בִּלְחוֹדַיְיהוּ בְּגָלוּתָא מִשְׁתַּכְּחִין. אֶלָּא וְאַף גַּם זֹאת עִמְּהוֹן מִשְׁתַּכְּחִין. הה"ד וְאַף גַּם זֹאת בִּהְיוֹתָם בְּאֶרֶץ אוֹיְבֵיהֶם וְגוֹ'.

216. Rabbi Aba said, "And yet for all that, when they are." Come and see how great is the love of the Holy One, blessed be He, for Yisrael. Even though they caused themselves to be in exile among the nations, the Shechinah never removed Herself from them. Do not say that they are in exile alone, but, "And yet for all that (Heb. *zot*)," AS THE SHECHINAH CALLED 'ZOT' is with them. This is the meaning of, "And yet for all that, when they are in the land of their enemies…"

217. לְמַלְכָּא דְּאַרְגִּיז עַל בְּרֵיהּ, גָּזַר עָלֵיהּ עוֹנְשָׁא לְאִתְרַחֲקָא מִנֵּיהּ, וּלְמֵיזַל לְאַרְעָא רְחִיקָא. שְׁמָעָה מַטְרוֹנִיתָא וְאָמְרָה, הוֹאִיל וּבְרִי אָזִיל לְאַרְעָא רְחִיקָא, וְשַׁדֵּי לֵיהּ מַלְכָּא מֵהֵיכָלֵיהּ, אֲנָא לָא אֶשְׁבּוֹק לֵיהּ, אוֹ תַּרְוָונָא כַּחֲדָא נֵיתוּב לְהֵיכָלָא דְּמַלְכָּא אוֹ תַּרְוָונָא כַּחֲדָא נֵיתִיב בְּאַרְעָא אַחֲרָא. לִזְמְנִין, פָּקִיד מַלְכָּא עַל מַטְרוֹנִיתָא, לָא אַשְׁכְּחָהּ. דַּהֲוַות אַזְלַת עִם בְּרֵיהּ, אָמַר הוֹאִיל וּמַטְרוֹנִיתָא תַּמָּן תַּרְוַויְהוּ יְתוּבוּן.

217. It is like a king who was angry with his son and decreed that as punishment he should go away from him into a faraway land. The queen heard it and said, Since my son is going to a faraway land and the king threw him out of his palace, I shall not leave him. The two of us shall either return to the king's palace or together dwell in another land. After a few days the king visited the queen but did not find her because she left with his son. He said, Since the queen is there, let both of them return.

218. וּבְזִמְנָא דְּפָקִיד קוּדְשָׁא בְּרִיךְ הוּא לְמַטְרוֹנִיתָא, פָּקִיד לָהּ בְּקַדְמֵיתָא, וּבְגִינָהּ פָּקִיד לִבְנוֹי. הה״ד, וְגַם אֲנִי שָׁמַעְתִּי אֶת נַאֲקַת בְּנֵי יִשְׂרָאֵל וְגוֹ׳. מַאן גָּרִים דַּאֲנָא שְׁמַעְנָא עֲקַתְהוֹן. כִּבְיָכוֹל, מַטְרוֹנִיתָא. דִּדְכַרְנָא לָהּ. הה״ד, וָאֶזְכּוֹר אֶת בְּרִיתִי. וּכְתִיב וַיִּזְכּוֹר אֱלֹהִים אֶת בְּרִיתוֹ. וְכַד קוּדְשָׁא בְּרִיךְ הוּא יֶהְדַּר לְיִשְׂרָאֵל מִן גָּלוּתָא, מַה כְּתִיב. וְשָׁב יְיָ׳ אֱלֹהֶיךָ אֶת שְׁבוּתְךָ וְרִחֲמֶךָ, דָּא מַטְרוֹנִיתָא. וְעוֹד כְּתִיב, רָצִיתָ יְיָ׳ אַרְצֶךָ שַׁבְתָּ שְׁבוּת יַעֲקֹב.

218. It will happen the same way when the Holy One, blessed be He, will visit the Shechinah. He shall visit Her first and for Her sake visit His children. This is the meaning of, "And I have also heard the groaning of the children of Yisrael…" (Shemot 6:5). Who brought it about that "I have also heard the groaning"? It is as if the Shechinah HAS CAUSED IT that I remembered Her. This is the meaning of, "and I have remembered My covenant" (Ibid.), THAT IS, THE SHECHINAH CALLED COVENANT. It is also written, "and Elohim remembered His covenant" (Shemot 2:24). AND WHEN THE HOLY ONE, BLESSED BE HE, WILL BRING YISRAEL BACK FROM EXILE IT IS WRITTEN, "Hashem your Elohim will turn your captivity, and have compassion upon you" (Devarim 30:3). It is the Shechinah, OF WHOM IT SAYS, "WILL TURN YOUR CAPTIVITY." It is also written, "Hashem, You have been favorable to Your land; You have brought back the captivity of Jacob" (Tehilim 85:2), NAMELY THE SHECHINAH CALLED LAND.

219. א״ר יְהוּדָה, הַלַיְיָ׳ תִּגְמְלוּ זֹאת, בְּגִין דְּאַתּוּן דוֹר עִקֵּשׁ וּפְתַלְתּוֹל, אַתּוּן הֲוֵיתוּן גַּרְמִין דְּתִגְלֵי זֹאת בְּגָלוּתָא. הַלַיְיָ׳ תִּגְמְלוּ זֹאת. דָּא הוּא גְּמוּל דְּעָבֵיד עִמְּכוֹן, בְּכָל אִינּוּן נִימוּסִין דְּמִצְרַיִם, בְּכָל אִינּוּן אַתְוָון דְּעָבֵד לְכוּ, דָּא הוּא גְּמוּל דְּאַתּוּן שָׁלְמִין לְהַאי זֹאת. מַאן גָּרַם לְכוֹן דָּא. בְּגִין דְּאַתּוּן עַם נָבָל וְלֹא חָכָם, וְלָא מִסְתַּכְּלִין בְּכָל אִינּוּן טָבָן דְּעָבֵד לְכוּ עַד הַשְׁתָּא.

219. Rabbi Yehuda said, "Do you thus (Heb. *zot*) requite Hashem" (Devarim 32:6), you are, "a perverse and crooked generation" (Ibid. 5). You cause 'zot' to go into exile. "Do you thus (Heb. *zot*) requite Hashem"? Is this how you requite Him for all that He did to you, for all those signs He performed for you. Is this the reward you pay to 'zot'? Who brought it upon you? It is because you are a "foolish people and unwise" (Ibid.), not looking at all the good He did for you until now.

54. Hei of Behibar'am

A Synopsis

Rabbi Yitzchak and Rabbi Chiya discuss how God went with Yisrael into exile because if He had not done so the people would not have been able to bear it. God never forgot His covenant with them. We also hear a discussion of the generations of the heaven and of the earth, and we learn that the three worlds were created both from Zeir Anpin and Malchut. The World to Come, Binah, is created with Chochmah. We hear again about the flow from Chochmah that finally gathers in the great sea that is Malchut. From there the generations come out to all the worlds.

220. הַלְיָיָ' תִּגְמְלוּ זֹאת, דָּא שְׁכִינְתָּא. וְהָא אוֹקִימְנָא מִלֵּי, דְּתַנִינָן, הֵ"א דִּבְהִבָּרְאָם, זְעֵירָא. הֵ"א דִּבְהַלְיָיָ' רַבְרְבָא. וְהָא אִתְּמַר דְּתַנְיָא, א"ר יְהוּדָה, הֵ"א דִּבְכָל אֲתָר קוּדְשָׁא בְּרִיךְ הוּא, וְאִקְרֵי אֵם. וּתְרֵי עָלְמִין נִינְהוּ, דִּכְתִּיב מִן הָעוֹלָם וְעַד הָעוֹלָם. וְהָא תָּנֵינָן בְּרָזָא דִּקְרָא, בְּשֶׁמֶן כָּתִית רְבִיעִית הַהִין.

220. "Do you thus (Heb. *zot*) requite Hashem" (Devarim 32:6): ZOT is the Shechinah. We have explained this issue that we learned that Hei of "when they were created (Heb. *behibar'am*)" (Beresheet 2:4) is small, ALLUDING TO MALCHUT. Hei in "Do you (Heb. *ha*)," is large, ALLUDING TO BINAH. It has been said that we learned what Rabbi Yehuda said: Hei always ALLUDES TO the Holy One, blessed be He, and is called a mother. There are two worlds, BINAH AND MALCHUT, of which it is written, "from everlasting (lit. 'world') to everlasting" (Tehilim 106:48), THAT IS, FROM BINAH TO MALCHUT. We have learned this in regard to the meaning of the words, "mingled with the fourth part of a hin of beaten oil" (Bemidbar 28:5), WHICH MEANS THAT YESOD OF ZEIR ANPIN DRAWS OIL FROM THE SUPERNAL WORLD TO THE LOWER WORLD, WHICH IS MALCHUT. THIS IS THE MEANING OF, "DO YOU THUS REQUITE HASHEM," WHICH COMBINES TOGETHER THREE GRADES, WHICH ARE THE UPPER WORLD, WHICH IS THE LARGE HEI OF "DO YOU," YUD HEI VAV HEI ITSELF, WHICH IS ZEIR ANPIN THAT DRAWS PLENTY FROM IT TO 'ZOT', WHICH IS THE SHECHINAH.

221. תַּנְיָא ר' יְהוּדָה אוֹמֵר, בְּכַמָּה אַתְרֵי אִסְתַּכַּלְנָא, דְקוּדְשָׁא בְּרִיךְ

הוּא לָא אַעֲדֵי רְחִימוּתָא מִנַּיְיהוּ דְּיִשְׂרָאֵל, דִּבְכָל אֲתָר דְּאִינּוּן הֲווֹ, קוּדְשָׁא בְּרִיךְ הוּא בֵּינַיְיהוּ. דִּכְתִּיב לֹא מְאַסְתִּים וְלֹא גְעַלְתִּים לְכַלּוֹתָם לְהָפֵר בְּרִיתִי אִתָּם. דַּיְיקָא אִתָּם, בֵּינַיְיהוּ עִמְּהוֹן לָא אַעֲדֵי מִנַּיְיהוּ לְעָלְמִין.

221. We learned that Rabbi Yehuda said, I have looked in several places that the Holy One, blessed be He, did not withdraw His love from Yisrael. For wherever they were, the Holy One, blessed be He, was among them, as written, "I will not cast them away, nor will I abhor them, to destroy them utterly, and to break My covenant with them" (Vayikra 26:44). "with them" is exact, WHICH MEANS THAT THE HOLY ONE, BLESSED BE HE, IS among them and never left them.

222. ר׳ יִצְחָק הֲוָה אָזִיל בְּאָרְחָא, וּפָגַע בֵּיהּ ר׳ חִיָּיא, א״ל חֲמֵינָא בְּאַנְפָּךְ, דְּהָא בְּמָדוֹרָא דִּשְׁכִינְתָּא מָדוֹרָךְ. מַאי כְּתִיב. וָאֵרֵד לְהַצִּילוֹ מִיַּד מִצְרַיִם. וָאֵרֵד, אֵרֵד מִבָּעֵי לֵיהּ. וָאֵרֵד בְּקַדְמֵיתָא. אֵימָתַי. כַּד נָחַת יַעֲקֹב לְמִצְרַיִם. וְלָמָּה. לְהַצִּילוֹ מִיַּד מִצְרַיִם. דְּאִלְמָלֵא לָא הֲוָה בֵּינַיְיהוּ, לָא יַכְלִין לְמִסְבַּל גָּלוּתָא. כד״א עִמּוֹ אָנֹכִי בְצָרָה אֲחַלְּצֵהוּ וַאֲכַבְּדֵהוּ.

222. Rabbi Yitzchak was walking along the way when Rabbi Chiya came across him. He said to him, I see in your face that you dwell in the dwelling of the Shechinah. It is written, "and I am come down to deliver them out of the hand of Egypt" (Shemot 3:8). IT IS WRITTEN, "and (Heb. *Vav*) I am come down," yet it should have been "I am come down," SO VAV IS REDUNDANT. HE ANSWERS, "and I am come down," means beforehand, SINCE THE VAV IS THE PREFIX OF THE PAST TENSE. When is that? When Jacob went down to Egypt, THE HOLY ONE, BLESSED BE HE, WENT DOWN WITH HIM. Why DID HE COME DOWN? "to deliver them out of the hand of Egypt." For had He not been among them, they would not have been able to tolerate the exile, as written, "I will be with him in trouble; I will deliver him, and honor him" (Tehilim 91:15).

223. א״ל, וַדַּאי בְּכָל אֲתָר דְּיִשְׂרָאֵל שַׁרְיָין, קוּדְשָׁא בְּרִיךְ הוּא בֵּינַיְיהוּ. וְכָל אֲתָר דְּחַכִּימֵי דָּרָא אַזְלִין, קוּדְשָׁא בְּרִיךְ הוּא אָזִיל עִמְּהוֹן, דִּכְתִּיב

כִּי מַלְאָכָיו יְצַוֶּה לָךְ וְגוֹ'. מְנָלָן דִּכְתִּיב, וְיַעֲקֹב הָלַךְ לְדַרְכּוֹ וְגוֹ', וַיֹּאמֶר יַעֲקֹב כַּאֲשֶׁר רָאָם מַחֲנֵה אֱלֹהִים זֶה. הַשְׁתָּא נִשְׁתַּתֵּף כַּחֲדָא, וְנֵיזִיל בְּאָרְחָא, דְּהָא יְדַעְנָא דִּלְאֲתָר חַד אַזְלֵינָן, לְקַבְּלָא אַנְפּוֹי דִּשְׁכִינְתָּא. א"ל, וַדַּאי. א"ר יִצְחָק, תָּנֵינָן, שְׁלוּחֵי מִצְוָה אֵינָן נִיזוֹקִין, לָא בַּהֲלִיכָתָן וְלָא בַּחֲזָרָתָן. וַאֲנָן לְאִתְחֲזָאָה קַמֵּי קוּדְשָׁא בְּרִיךְ הוּא אַזְלֵינָן, וְלָא דְּחִילְנָא.

223. He said to him, Surely wherever Yisrael dwell, the Holy One, blessed be He, is among them. And wherever the sages of the generation go, the Holy One, blessed be He, goes with them, as written, "For He shall give His angels charge over you" (Tehilim 91:11). We derive it from the verse, "And Jacob went on his way…And when Jacob saw them, he said, This is Elohim's camp" (Beresheet 32:2-3) surely. Let us now join together and walk the path I know as we are walking to a certain place to welcome the Shechinah, NAMELY TO RABBI SHIMON BAR YOCHAI. He said to him, IT IS certainly SO. Rabbi Yitzchak said, We have learned that those who act as messengers to perform a good deed are harmed neither in their going nor in returning; and we are going to be seen before the Holy One, blessed be He, so we are not afraid.

224. עַד דַּהֲווּ אָזְלֵי, א"ר חִיָּיא, כְּתִיב אֵלֶּה תוֹלְדוֹת הַשָּׁמַיִם וְהָאָרֶץ. הַשָּׁמַיִם, לְאַכְלְלָא קוּדְשָׁא בְּרִיךְ הוּא. וְהָאָרֶץ, לְאַכְלְלָא קוּדְשָׁא בְּרִיךְ הוּא וְכָל מַה דִּלְתַתָּא, אִינּוּן אִקְרוּן תוֹלְדוֹת הַשָּׁמַיִם מִנַּיְיהוּ.

224. While they were walking Rabbi Chiya said, It is written, "These are the generations of the heaven and of the earth" (Beresheet 2:4). The heaven comes to include the Holy One, blessed be He, NAMELY ZEIR ANPIN CALLED HEAVEN; and the earth comes to include the Holy One, blessed be He, WHO IS MALCHUT CALLED EARTH. And all that is below ATZILUT, NAMELY THE THREE WORLDS, BRIYAH, YETZIRAH AND ASIYAH, are called the generations of heaven and of earth, from which THEY WERE BROUGHT FORTH, NAMELY FROM ZEIR ANPIN AND MALCHUT.

225. א"ל אִי הָכִי מַהוּ בְּהִבָּרְאָם, וְאִתְּמַר בְּה' בְּרָאָם. א"ל כֹּלָּא חַד

מִלָּה, כַּד שָׁמַיִם אִתְחַבָּרוּ, הַאי ה' אַפִּיקַת תּוֹלְדוֹת, וְאִינּוּן אִקְרוּן, תּוֹלְדוֹת הַשָּׁמַיִם וְהָאָרֶץ. א"ל אִי הָכִי, בְּמַאי אוֹקִימְנָא בְּה' בְּרָאָם, בְּאַבְרָהָם. א"ל כֹּלָּא חַד מִלָּה הוּא, בְּאַבְרָהָם, הַיְינוּ הַשָּׁמַיִם, דְּמִתַּמָּן שַׁרְיָין לְאִתְפַּשְׁטָא. בְּה' בְּרָאָם, הַיְינוּ וְהָאָרֶץ, וְכֹלָּא חַד מִלָּה.

225. He said to him, In that case, what is, "when they were created (Heb. *behibar'am*)" (Ibid.)? We learned that *beHei bra'am* (Eng. 'with Hei He created them'), NAMELY WITH MALCHUT. YET YOU SAY THEY ARE THE GENERATIONS OF HEAVEN AND EARTH, NAMELY FROM ZEIR ANPIN AS WELL. He said to him, It is all the same thing, since when heaven, WHICH IS ZEIR ANPIN, joined WITH MALCHUT, then this Hei, WHICH IS MALCHUT, produced generations, which are called "the generations of the heaven and of the earth." He said to him, If that is so, why have we explained that *behibar'am* means *beAbraham* (Eng. 'with Abraham'), WHICH IS SPELLED WITH THE SAME LETTERS? HOW IS ABRAHAM CONNECTED WITH THIS? He said to him, It is all the same; *beAbraham* IS CHESED OF ZEIR ANPIN THAT IS CALLED ABRAHAM, that is, he is the heaven THAT IS ZEIR ANPIN. For from there, FROM THE SFIRAH OF CHESED, ZEIR ANPIN begins to spread. THAT IS, THE FIRST SFIRAH OF ZEIR ANPIN IS CHESED, AND SO THE NAME ABRAHAM ALSO ALLUDES TO ZEIR ANPIN LIKE THE NAME HEAVEN. AS FOR WHAT HAS BEEN SAID IS THAT *beHei bra'am* is the earth, WHICH IS MALCHUT. THUS HEAVEN AND EARTH ARE INDICATED IN THE WORD *BEHIBAR'AM*. And all this is the same issue.

226. א"ל, וַדַּאי הָכִי הוּא, וְהָא אוֹלִיפְנָא, דִּכְתִּיב, אֵלֶּה תוֹלְדוֹת הַשָּׁמַיִם וְהָאָרֶץ. וְתָנֵינָן, הָעוֹלָם הַזֶּה נִבְרָא בְּה', דִּכְתִּיב בְּהִבָּרְאָם. וְהָעוֹלָם הַבָּא, נִבְרָא בְּי', דִּכְתִּיב, וְנָהָר יוֹצֵא מֵעֵדֶן לְהַשְׁקוֹת אֶת הַגָּן. לְאַכְלְלָא הַשָּׁמַיִם. אֶת הַגָּן, לְאַכְלְלָא אֶת הָאָרֶץ.

226. He said to him, It is surely so. I have learned that it is written, "These are the generations of the heaven and of the earth," and we have learned that this world was created with Hei, WHICH IS MALCHUT, as written, "*behibar'am*," NAMELY *BEHEI BRA'AM* (ENG. 'HE CREATED THEM WITH HEI'). The World to Come, WHICH IS BINAH, is created with Yud, WHICH IS CHOCHMAH, as written, "And a river went out of Eden to water the garden" (Beresheet 2:10). THE RIVER, WHICH IS BINAH, GOES OUT OF EDEN, CHOCHMAH, TO WATER THE GARDEN, NAMELY ZEIR ANPIN. HE ALSO SAYS THAT A RIVER THAT WENT OUT OF EDEN incorporates the heaven, WHICH IS ZEIR ANPIN THAT IS ALSO CALLED A RIVER. The Garden incorporates the earth, WHICH IS MALCHUT. THUS THE EXPLANATION ALSO SAYS THAT ZEIR ANPIN GOES OUT OF CHOCHMAH AND BINAH THAT ARE BOTH CALLED EDEN, AND WATERS MALCHUT, THE SECRET OF THE GARDEN.

227. וְהָא אוֹקִימְנָא, דִּכְתִּיב, מַעְיַן גַּנִּים, דָּא הִיא הַשָּׁמַיִם, בְּאֵר מַיִם חַיִּים, דִּכְתִּיב וַיִּכְרוּ שָׁם עַבְדֵי יִצְחָק בְּאֵר, דִּכְתִיב וַיַּעְתֵּק מִשָּׁם וַיַּחְפּוֹר בְּאֵר אַחֶרֶת וְגוֹ'. וְנוֹזְלִין מִן לְבָנוֹן, דְּאִינּוּן מִתְעַטְּרִין לְעֵילָּא, וְסַלְּקִין בְּרֵישָׁא דְּמַלְכָּא. דִּכְתִּיב, כִּי גָּדוֹל מֵעַל שָׁמַיִם חַסְדֶּךָ.

227. For we have explained that the words, "a fountain of gardens" (Shir Hashirim 4:15) refer to the heaven, WHICH IS ZEIR ANPIN THAT IS CALLED RIVER AS MENTIONED. It is a well of living water, as written, "and there Isaac's servants dug a well" (Beresheet 26:25), and, "And he removed from there, and dug another well" (Ibid. 22). "and streams from Lebanon" (Shir Hashirim 4:15), NAMELY FROM CHOCHMAH THAT IS CALLED LEBANON, AS THE STREAMS are adorned above WITH CHOCHMAH and rise to the head of the King, NAMELY TO THE THREE FIRST SFIROT OF ZEIR ANPIN, as written, "For Your steadfast love (Chesed) is great above the heavens" (Tehilim 108:5), SINCE THEY ARE DRAWN FROM CHOCHMAH, WHICH IS ABOVE ZEIR ANPIN CALLED HEAVEN SINCE THEY ARE DRAWN FROM CHOCHMAH, WHICH IS ABOVE ZEIR ANPIN CALLED HEAVEN.

228. מִן לְבָנוֹן, מִתַּמָּן נָפְקִין לְבִינָה. וְנָגִיד וְאִתְמְשַׁךְ לְכָל זִוְויָין, עַד דְּנַגְדִּין אִינּוּן מַבּוּעִין, וְנַחְתִּין לְאִתְכַּנְּשָׁא לַאֲתַר דְּאִקְרֵי יַמָּא רַבָּא. דִּכְתִּיב כָּל הַנְּחָלִים הוֹלְכִים אֶל הַיָּם וְגוֹ'. וּכְתִיב, הַבִּיטוּ אֶל צוּר חוּצַּבְתֶּם וְגוֹ'. לְבָתַר כְּתִיב, גַּן נָעוּל אֲחוֹתִי כַלָּה וְגוֹ'. וּמִכָּאן, נְפִיקוּ תּוֹלְדוֹת לְכֹלָּא. דִּכְתִּיב, בְּהִבָּרְאָם, בְּה' בְּרָאָם מַמָּשׁ, בְּאַבְרָהָם. א"ר יִצְחָק, וַאֲפִילוּ בְּיַעֲקֹב מַמָּשׁ. וְכֹלָּא חַד מִלָּה.

228. HE EXPLAINS HIS WORDS: "from Lebanon," WHICH IS CHOCHMAH, come out STREAMS, NAMELY PLENTY to Binah, and flow and are drawn to all corners, NAMELY, TO THE FOUR WINDS, CHESED AND GVURAH, TIFERET AND MALCHUT OF ZEIR ANPIN until those founts stream and come down to gather in that place called the great sea, NAMELY MALCHUT, as written, "All the rivers run into the sea" (Kohelet 1:7), WHICH MEANS THAT THE STREAMS OF CHESED AND GVURAH, TIFERET AND MALCHUT OF ZEIR ANPIN RUN TO MALCHUT THAT IS CALLED SEA. It is also written, "look to the rock whence you are hewn" (Yeshayah 51:1), WHICH IS ABRAHAM, NAMELY CHESED OF ZEIR ANPIN. Following "AND STREAMS FROM LEBANON" it is written, "A garden enclosed is my sister, my bride" (Shir Hashirim 4:12), WHICH IS MALCHUT THAT RECEIVES THE STREAMS FROM ZEIR ANPIN. From it, FROM MALCHUT, generations came out to all WORLDS, as written, "when they were created (Heb. *behibar'am*)" – He created them with Hei (Heb. *behei bra'am*), WHICH IS MALCHUT, THAT IS, actually with Abraham, WHO IS CHESED OF ZEIR ANPIN THE SECRET OF THE STREAMS THAT FLOW FROM SUPERNAL CHOCHMAH THAT IS CALLED LEBANON TO ZEIR ANPIN, AND FROM ZEIR ANPIN TO MALCHUT, AND FROM THEM TO ALL THE GENERATIONS IN BRIYAH, YETZIRAH AND ASIYAH. Rabbi Yitzchak said, Even with Jacob himself, WHO IS TIFERET OF ZEIR ANPIN, SINCE TIFERET INCLUDES WITHIN IT CHESED AND GVURAH. It is all the same issue.

55. “Can a woman forget her sucking child”

A Synopsis

Rabbi Chiya has received a spirit message about the title verse that he does not understand, and so he is going to see Rabbi Shimon for an interpretation. Rabbi Yitzchak remembers that Rabbi Elazar explained in the name of his father that Yisrael are God’s children and so they cannot possibly be forgotten. God can no more forget His children than He can forget His own Name, because they are attached to His Name.

229. א״ר יִצְחָק, כַּד אֲנָן יָתְבִין לְקַמֵּיהּ דר״ש, כֹּלָּא אִתְּמַר קַמֵּיהּ בְּאִתְגַּלְיָא, וְלָא אִצְטְרִיכְנָא לְכָל הַאי. א״ל, לָאו ר״ש כִּשְׁאָר בְּנֵי נָשָׁא, דְּכֻלְּהוּ קַמֵּיהּ, כִּשְׁאַר נְבִיאֵי לְקַמֵּי מֹשֶׁה. עַד דַּהֲווֹ אָזְלֵי, א״ר חִיָּיא, כְּתִיב, הֲתִשְׁכַּח אִשָּׁה עוּלָהּ מֵרַחֵם בֶּן בִּטְנָהּ וְגו׳. הַאי קְרָא אוֹקְמוּהָ, וְהָכָא מַאי קָא מַיְירֵי. א״ר יִצְחָק, אִי בְּקִטּוּרָא דְּחַבְרַיָּיא, סְמִיכָא לָא אַסְמַכְנָא, אֲנָן מַה נֵימָא.

229. Rabbi Yitzchak said, When we sit before Rabbi Shimon, everything is said openly before him and we have no need for all this, THAT IS, THEY DO NOT NEED TO CONCEAL ANYTHING THERE UNDER NAMES AND TERMS. He said to him, Rabbi Shimon is not like other men, who are all before him like the other prophets before Moses. While they were walking Rabbi Chiya said, It is written, “Can a woman forget her sucking child, that she should not have compassion on the son of her womb?” (Yeshayah 49:15). This verse has been explained. Yet here, IN AN INNER SENSE, what does it mean? He said to him, If in the gathering of the friends we were not supported IN INTERPRETING THIS VERSE, what could we say?

230. א״ל, דְּהָא קָלָא דִּרְמִיזָא חַד, שְׁמַעְנָא יוֹמָא חַד, כַּד הֲוָה אֲזִילְנָא בְּאָרְחָא, וְלָא יְדַעְנָא מַאן אָמַר, וְלָא יְדַעְנָא מִלָּה. ות״ח, ז׳ יוֹמִין הֲווֹ דַּחֲלִישְׁנָא ע״ד, וְלָא טְעִימְנָא מִדִּי. וְהַשְׁתָּא אֲזִלְנָא לְגַבֵּיהּ דְּבוּצִינָא קַדִּישָׁא, דְּלֵימָא לִי דִּילְמָא אַדְכַּר. א״ל, דִּילְמָא הַהוּא יוֹמָא דַּהֲוָה אָזִיל ר׳ אֶלְעָזָר לְגַבֵּיהּ דְּחָמוּי, וְהַהוּא יוֹמָא אֲזִילְנָא עִמֵּיהּ, וְהָא אַדְכַּרְנָא מִלָּה.

230. He said to him, I have heard a voice that hinted to me about the interpretation of the verse, one day, when I was walking on the way. But I knew not who said it, and I do not understand it. Come and see, for seven days I have been ill because of that and ate nothing. Now that I am going to the Holy Luminary so he will tell me, I may remember. RABBI YITZCHAK said to him, It could have been on the very day Rabbi Elazar was going to his father-in-law. I accompanied him that day, and now have remembered it.

231. ת"ח, הָכִי א"ר אֶלְעָזָר מִשְּׁמֵיהּ דַּאֲבוּי, אָמְרוּ יִשְׂרָאֵל קָמֵי קוּדְשָׁא בְּרִיךְ הוּא, מִיּוֹמָא דְּנָפַלְנָא בְּגָלוּתָא, קוּדְשָׁא בְּרִיךְ הוּא שָׁבִיק לָן בְּגָלוּתָא, וְאַנְשֵׁי לָן. הֲדָא הוּא דִּכְתִּיב, וַתֹּאמֶר צִיּוֹן עֲזָבַנִי יְיָ' וַיְיָ' שְׁכֵחָנִי. אָמְרָה שְׁכִינְתָּא, הֲתִשְׁכַּח אִשָּׁה עוּלָהּ, וְכִי יִשְׂרָאֵל דְּאִקְרוּן בְּנִין, כְּמָה דְּאַתְּ אָמֵר, בָּנִים אַתֶּם לַיְיָ' אֱלֹהֵיכֶם. מֵרַחֵם בֶּן בִּטְנָהּ, כד"א, וְאָנֹכִי נְטַעְתִּיךְ שׂוֹרֵק כֻּלֹּה זֶרַע אֱמֶת. גַּם אֵלֶּה תִשְׁכַּחְנָה, דִּכְתִּיב, אֵלֶּה תוֹלְדוֹת הַשָּׁמַיִם וְהָאָרֶץ. וְאָנֹכִי לֹא אֶשְׁכָּחֵךְ, מִכָּאן, דְּקוּדְשָׁא בְּרִיךְ הוּא לָא שָׁבִיק לוֹן לְיִשְׂרָאֵל לְעָלְמִין.

231. Come and see, thus said Rabbi Elazar in the name of his father. Yisrael said before the Holy One, blessed be He, ever since we fell into exile, the Holy One, blessed be He, left us in exile and forgot us. This is the meaning of, "But Zion said, Hashem has forsaken me, and my Lord has forgotten me" (Ibid. 14). The Shechinah said, "Can a woman forget her sucking child." For Yisrael are considered children, as written, "You are the children of Hashem your Elohim"(Devarim 14:1), AND HOW COULD THEY BE FORGOTTEN. "that she should not have compassion on the son of her womb" resembles, "And I have planted you a noble vine, an entirely right seed" (Yirmeyah 2:21). "even these may forget" (Yeshayah 49:15), as in, "These are the generations of the heaven and of the earth" (Beresheet 2:4), "yet I will not forget you" (Yeshayah 49:15). From this we derive that the Holy One, blessed be He, never leaves Yisrael.

232. תּוּ אָמַר, הֲתִשְׁכַּח אִשָּׁה עוּלָהּ מֵרַחֵם בֶּן בִּטְנָהּ. דָּא הוּא רָזָא עִלָּאָה, דְּאָמַר קוּדְשָׁא בְּרִיךְ הוּא, הָא מִלִּין אִלֵּין בִּשְׁמֵיהּ אֲחִידָן, כְּמָה דְקוּדְשָׁא בְּרִיךְ הוּא לָא אַנְשֵׁי שְׁמֵיהּ, דְּהָא הוּא כֹּלָּא. כַּךְ קוּדְשָׁא בְּרִיךְ

הוּא לָא אַנְשֵׁי לוֹן לְיִשְׂרָאֵל דְּאִינּוּן אֲחִידָן בִּשְׁמֵיהּ מַמָּשׁ. אִתְרְגִּישׁ ר׳ חִיָּיא, אָמַר וַדַּאי דָּא הִיא מִלָּה. בְּרִיךְ יְהֵא קוּדְשָׁא בְּרִיךְ הוּא דְּאַעַרְעְנָא לָךְ, וְיָדַעְנָא מִלָּה. וְיָדַעְנָא מַאן הַהוּא דְּשָׁמַעְנָא מִנֵּיהּ.

232. He also says that, "Can a woman forget her sucking child, that she should not have compassion on the son of her womb?" is a lofty secret, that the Holy One, blessed be He, said, 'These things are connected with My name'. Just as the Holy One, blessed be He, does not forget His name, which is everything, so does the Holy One, blessed be He, not forget Yisrael, because they are truly attached to His name. Rabbi Chiya trembled and said, Surely these are the words I HEARD BUT FORGOT. Blessed be the Holy One, blessed be He, that I have met you and knew it, and also knew from whom I heard it.

233. ות״ח, דְּהַהוּא יוֹמָא דְּרָהִיטְנָא ד׳ מִילִין, וְלָא אַשְׁכַּחְנָא מַאן הֲוָה. א״ל, בְּגִין דְּעָאלְנָא בְּחַד מְעַרְתָּא דר׳ אֶלְעָזָר נָפִישׁ שַׁעֲתָא חֲדָא. קָרֵי עָלֵיהּ רִבִּי חִיָּיא הָנֵי קְרָאֵי, אָז יִבָּקַע כַּשַּׁחַר אוֹרֶךָ וְגוֹ׳. אָז תִּקְרָא וַיְיָ׳ יַעֲנֶה וְגוֹ׳ אָז תִּתְעַנַּג עַל יְיָ׳ וְגוֹ׳.

233. Come and see, on the same day I HEARD THIS VOICE THAT INDICATED TO ME THIS EXPLANATION, I ran four miles but didn't find who SAID IT. RABBI YITZCHAK said to him, This is because we went into a cave and Rabbi Elazar rested there an hour. Rabbi Chiya recited about him these verses, NAMELY, OF THE TIME HE MERITED TO BE WITH RABBI ELAZAR IN THE CAVE, "Then shall your light break forth like the morning…Then shall you call, and Hashem shall answer" (Yeshayah 58:8-9), "then shall you delight yourself in Hashem…" (Ibid. 14).

56. "Remember the days of old, consider the years of many generations..."

A Synopsis

Rabbi Aba says that the days of the world are the six days with which God created the world, and that these six days are the Sfirot Chesed, Gvurah, Tiferet, Netzach, Hod and Yesod. When the six days created the world they did it for the sake of the children of Yisrael, so that they would come and study the Torah. If they did not the world would return to chaos.

234. זְכוֹר יְמוֹת עוֹלָם בִּינוּ שְׁנוֹת דוֹר וָדוֹר וְגוֹ׳. זְכוֹר יְמוֹת עוֹלָם, ר׳ אַבָּא אָמַר, מַאן יְמוֹת עוֹלָם. אִינּוּן שִׁיתָּא יוֹמִין, דְּעָבֵד קוּדְשָׁא בְּרִיךְ הוּא עָלְמָא בְּהוּ. דִּכְתִּיב, כִּי שֵׁשֶׁת יָמִים עָשָׂה יְיָ׳ וְגוֹ׳. שֵׁשֶׁת יָמִים, וְלָא בְּשֵׁשֶׁת יָמִים, וְהָא אוּקִימְנָא. בִּינוּ שְׁנוֹת דוֹר וָדוֹר. כְּלוֹמַר, אִינּוּן יְמוֹת עוֹלָם, יָדְעוּ וְיִשְׁתְּמוֹדְעוּ כָּל אִינּוּן שְׁנִין וְיוֹמִין, וְכָל דָּרָא וְדָרָא, עַד דָּרָא דָּא דְּאַתּוּן קַיְימִין.

234. "Remember the days of old, consider the years of many generations..." (Devarim 32:7). "Remember the days of old (lit. 'world')": Rabbi Aba said, What are the days of the world? They are the six days with which the Holy One, blessed be He, created the world, as written, "for six days Hashem made heaven and earth" (Shemot 31:17), rather than "in six days," BECAUSE THEY ARE THE SIX SFIROT, CHESED, GVURAH, TIFERET, NETZACH, HOD AND YESOD THAT CREATED THE WORLD. We have already explained it. "consider the years of many generations" means that the days of the world, CHESED, GVURAH, TIFERET, NETZACH, HOD AND YESOD, will be known and acknowledged by all these years and days, and each and every generation to the generation in which you live.

235. שְׁאַל אָבִיךָ וְיַגֵּדְךָ, דָּא קוּדְשָׁא בְּרִיךְ הוּא. הה״ד, הֲלֹא הוּא אָבִיךָ קָּנֶךָ. וְיַגֵּדְךָ, וְהוּא יְגַלֶּה עוּמְקָא דְּחָכְמְתָא. וּמַאי הִיא. אֶלָּא כַּד אִינּוּן שִׁיתָּא יוֹמִין שַׁכְלֵילוּ עָלְמָא, לָא שַׁכְלֵילוּ לֵיהּ, אֶלָּא בְּגִינָךְ, דְּתֵיתֵי אַנְתְּ וּתְקַיֵּים אוֹרַיְיתָא. דְּתָנֵינָן, כָּל מַה דְּעֲבַד קוּדְשָׁא בְּרִיךְ הוּא, עַל תְּנַאי עֲבַד, דִּכַד יֵיתוּן יִשְׂרָאֵל, אִי יְקַבְּלוּן אוֹרַיְיתָא יָאוּת, וְאִי לָא

דְיִהֲדַר לֵיהּ לְתֹהוּ וָבֹהוּ. ובג"כ, אִינּוּן יְמוֹת עוֹלָם יָדְעוּ וְאִשְׁתְּמוֹדְעָן כֹּלָּא.

235. "ask your father, and he will recount it to you" (Devarim 32:7) is the Holy One, blessed be He. This is the meaning of, "is not He your father that bought you?" (Ibid. 6). "and he will recount it to you" means that He will disclose to you depth of wisdom. What is it? When the six days, CHESED, GVURAH, TIFERET, NETZACH, HOD AND YESOD, comprehended the world, they did so only for your sake that you will come and be occupied in Torah. As we have learned, whatever the Holy One, blessed be He, did, He did on condition that Yisrael will appear. If they will receive the Torah, good. Otherwise, THE WORLD will return to chaos. For this reason, the days of the world knew and realized everything.

236. וְהָא תָּנֵינָן, הַנְהוּ עַנְפֵּי דְּאִילָנָא, הֵיךְ מִתְאַחֲדָן בְּגוֹ אִילָנָא, וְהָא אוֹקִימְנָא, כְּדֵין קוּדְשָׁא בְּרִיךְ הוּא בָּרֵר לוֹן, לְמְמָנָן תְּרִיסִין, עַל שְׁאַר עַמִּין, וְאַתּוּן מַה כְּתִיב. כִּי חֵלֶק יְיָ' עַמּוֹ יַעֲקֹב חֶבֶל נַחֲלָתוֹ, דְּלָא יָהַב לְהוּ לְרַבְרְבָא, וְלָא לְמַלְאָכָא, וְלָא לְמְמָנָא אַחֲרָא, וְהַאי עַמָּא דְקוּדְשָׁא בְּרִיךְ הוּא נָסַב לְחוּלָקֵיהּ.

236. We have learned how the boughs of the tree, NAMELY THE SEVENTY MINISTERS OF THE NATIONS, are connected within the tree, WHICH IS ZEIR ANPIN. We have explained that the Holy One, blessed be He, then split the seventy ministers into officers and protectors over the rest of the nations. And of you YISRAEL, it is written, "For Hashem's portion is His people; Jacob is the lot of His inheritance" (Devarim 32:9), since He gave them not to a minister, an angel or any other officer, as He took as His portion this nation of the Holy One, blessed be He.

237. בְּאָן אֲתַר אַשְׁכַּח לֵיהּ. יִמְצָאֵהוּ בְּאֶרֶץ מִדְבָּר וּבְתֹהוּ יְלֵל יְשִׁימוֹן וְגוֹ'. דִּכְתִּיב, תֶּרַח אֲבִי אַבְרָהָם וְגוֹ'. וָאֶקַּח אֶת אֲבִיכֶם אֶת אַבְרָהָם וְגוֹ'. וּמֵהָכָא דָּבַר לְהוּ לְיִשְׂרָאֵל בְּכָל דָּרָא וְדָרָא, וְלָא אִתְפְּרַשׁ מִנַּיְיהוּ,

וְדָבַר לְהוּ בְּרַחֲמֵי, הה"ד כְּנֶשֶׁר יָעִיר קִנּוֹ וְגוֹ'.

237. Where did He find them? It is written, "He found him in a desert land, and in the waste howling wilderness" (Ibid. 10), "Terah, the father of Abraham…And I took your father Abraham" (Yehoshua 24:2-3). Since then He guided Yisrael in every generation and did not separate from them, and led them with compassion, as it says, "As an eagle stirs up her nest" (Devarim 32:11).

57. "As an eagle stirs up its nest"

A Synopsis

Rabbi Yosi talks about the compassion that an eagle has for its children, and he derives part of the meaning from Jacob's role as representative of the Central Column. The eagle is merciful toward its own children yet harsh toward others; this is the way that God guides His own children.

238. כְּנֶשֶׁר יָעִיר קִנּוֹ. א״ר יוֹסֵי, לָא אַשְׁכַּחְנָא מַאן דְּחָיֵיס עַל בְּנוֹי, כְּהַאי נִשְׁרָא. ועיד תָּנֵינָן, כְּתִיב, וּפְנֵי אַרְיֵה אֶל הַיָּמִין וּפְנֵי שׁוֹר מֵהַשְּׂמֹאל. נֶשֶׁר בְּאָן דּוּכְתֵּיהּ. בַּאֲתָר דְּיַעֲקֹב קָאִים. הה״ד, דֶּרֶךְ הַנֶּשֶׁר בַּשָּׁמַיִם. בְּהַהוּא אֲתָר מַמָּשׁ. מ״ט. בְּגִין דְּאִיהוּ רַחֲמֵי עַל בְּנוֹי, וְדִינָא לְגַבֵּי אַחֲרָנִין. כַּךְ קוּדְשָׁא בְּרִיךְ הוּא, דָּבַר לִבְנוֹי כְּנֶשֶׁר דָּא.

238. "As an eagle stirs up her nest" (Devarim 32:11). Rabbi Yosi said, We have found no one that has compassion over his children like this eagle. Hence we learned the verse, "the face of a lion, on the right side; and they four had the face of an ox on the left side" (Yechezkel 1:10). Where is the place of the eagle? In the place where Jacob is situated, NAMELY IN THE CENTRAL COLUMN THAT INCLUDES RIGHT AND LEFT. This is the meaning of, "the way of the vultures in the air" (Mishlei 30:19), in that very place, NAMELY IN ZEIR ANPIN THAT IS CALLED HEAVEN, WHICH IS THE CENTRAL COLUMN. The reason is that it is merciful towards its children, and harsh towards others. So does the Holy One, blessed be He, WHO INCLUDES RIGHT AND LEFT, WHICH IS CHESED AND JUDGMENT, guide His children like the eagle.

239. מַה כְּתִיב יְיָ׳ בָּדָד יַנְחֶנּוּ וְאֵין עִמּוֹ אֵל נֵכָר. הוּא בִּלְחוֹדוֹי, דִּכְתִּיב וַיְיָ׳ הוֹלֵךְ לִפְנֵיהֶם וְגוֹ׳. וְאֵין עִמּוֹ אֵל נֵכָר, דְּלָא דָּבַר לְהוּ לְיִשְׂרָאֵל לָא מַלְאָכָא, וְלָא מְמָנָא אַחֲרָא, דְּאִינּוּן אִקְרוּן אֵל נֵכָר. וְדָא הוּא דְּאָמַר מֹשֶׁה, אִם אֵין פָּנֶיךָ הוֹלְכִים אַל תַּעֲלֵנוּ מִזֶּה. הֲדָא הוּא דִּכְתִּיב, יְיָ׳ בָּדָד יַנְחֶנּוּ. הוּא בִּלְחוֹדוֹי, וְאֵין עִמּוֹ אֵל נֵכָר.

239. It is written, "So Hashem alone did lead him, and there was no strange El with Him" (Devarim 32:12), that is, none guides Yisrael, neither an angel nor another officer that are called a strange El. This is the meaning of Moses' words, "If Your presence go not with me carry us not up from here" (Shemot 33:15). This is the meaning of, "So Hashem alone did lead him," He alone, "and there was no strange El with him."

240. זַכָּאָה חוּלָקֵהוֹן דְּיִשְׂרָאֵל, דְּקוּדְשָׁא בְּרִיךְ הוּא דָּבַר עִמְּהוֹן, הָכִי עֲלַיְיהוּ כְּתִיב, כִּי יַעֲקֹב בָּחַר לוֹ יָהּ יִשְׂרָאֵל לִסְגוּלָּתוֹ, וּכְתִיב, כִּי לֹא יִטּוֹשׁ יְיָ' אֶת עַמּוֹ וְגוֹ'. מ"ט לֹא יִטּוֹשׁ ה' אֶת עַמּוֹ. בַּעֲבוּר שְׁמוֹ הַגָּדוֹל, בְּגִין דְּהַאי בְּהַאי אִתְדְּבַק. וע"ד לָא יִשְׁבּוֹק לוֹן קוּדְשָׁא בְּרִיךְ הוּא, דִּבְכָל אֲתַר דְּאִינּוּן שַׁרְיָין, קוּדְשָׁא בְּרִיךְ הוּא עִמְּהוֹן כְּמָה דְּאוֹקִימְנָא.

240. Happy is the portion of Yisrael that the Holy One, blessed be He, guides them thus, that it is thus written of them: "For Hashem has chosen Jacob to Himself" (Tehilim 135:4), and, "For Hashem will not abandon His people," THAT IS, "for His great name's sake" (I Shmuel 12:22), since they are mutually attached, AS YISRAEL CLEAVED TO HIS GREAT NAME. Hence the Holy One, blessed be He, will not leave them, and wherever they dwell the Holy One, blessed be He, is with them, as we explained.

58. "O that they were wise, that they understood this"

A Synopsis

The rabbis speak about the admonishments that Moses made to Yisrael before he died, and how they were all connected to the Holy Name. Rabbi Aba says that the whole Torah is the Name of God. We hear that if Yisrael keep the commandments then Malchut will take revenge on their enemies. Rabbi Yehuda says that Abraham said Yisrael should be forced into exile rather than go to Gehenom because they could not bear both the years of exile and Gehenom too. God agreed that as long as Yisrael sinned they would fall into exile and be enslaved by their enemies.

241. לוּ חָכְמוּ יַשְׂכִּילוּ זֹאת. א״ר יוֹסֵי, כָּל הָנֵי קְרָאֵי דְּהָכָא, אוֹכָחֵי אִינּוּן, דְּאוֹכַח לְהוּ מֹשֶׁה לְיִשְׂרָאֵל, בַּר הַהוּא שְׁמָא קַדִּישָׁא, דְּגַלֵּי בְּשֵׁירוּתָא דְּמִלּוֹי. א״ר אַבָּא, וַאֲפִילוּ מַה דְּאוֹכַח לְיִשְׂרָאֵל, בִּכְלָלָא דִּשְׁמָא קַדִּישָׁא הוּא, דְּלֵית מִלָּה בְּאוֹרַיְיתָא דְּנָפִיק מִכְּלָלָא דִּשְׁמָא קַדִּישָׁא. דְּאוֹרַיְיתָא כֹּלָּא שְׁמָא דְּקוּדְשָׁא בְּרִיךְ הוּא אִינּוּן.

241. "O that they were wise, that they understood this" (Devarim 32:29). Rabbi Yosi said, All the verses here are reproofs with which Moses admonished Yisrael, except for the Holy Name he disclosed at the beginning of his words, NAMELY, "BECAUSE I WILL CALL ON THE NAME OF HASHEM..." (IBID. 3), WHICH ARE THE SECRET OF CHESED, GVURAH, TIFERET, NETZACH, HOD AND YESOD. Rabbi Aba said, Even the verses in which he admonished Yisrael are part of the Holy Name, because there is nothing in the Torah that is excluded from the Holy Name, as the whole Torah is the name of the Holy One, blessed be He.

242. וְהָנֵי קְרָאֵי יְדִיעָאן אִינּוּן. אֲבָל בְּגִין דִּשְׁמָא דְקוּדְשָׁא בְּרִיךְ הוּא רָשִׁים בְּהַאי פַּרְשְׁתָּא, אִצְטְרִיכְנָא עַד הַשְׁתָּא. וְהָכָא הָא כְּתִיב, לוּ חָכְמוּ יַשְׂכִּילוּ זֹאת, זֹאת וַדַּאי, וְהָא בְּכַמָּה אֲתָר אוֹקִימְנָא הַאי, דְּאִי יִשְׂרָאֵל יִנְדְּעוּן הַאי, אֵיךְ זֹאת אֲחִידָא בְּדִינוֹי לְאִתְפָּרְעָא מִן חַיָּיבַיָּא, יָבִינוּ לְאַחֲרִיתָם, וְיִסְתָּמְרוּ לְמֶהֱוֵי בָּהּ. כְּמָה דִּכְתִיב, וְאֶרֶץ מִתְקוֹמָמָה לוֹ.

242. The verses WE HAVE EXPLAINED SO FAR are known TO EVERYONE, but since the name of the Holy One, blessed be He, is mentioned in this portion, we had TO EXPLAIN THEM until now. But here it is written, "O that they were wise, that they understood this (Heb. *zot*)," assuredly zot, WHO IS MALCHUT. We have explained it in several places that if Yisrael knew how zot held to its punishments to take revenge on the wicked, "they would consider their latter end" (Devarim 32:29), and take care to be in it, THAT IS, TO KEEP ITS COMMANDMENTS, as written, "the earth," WHICH IS MALCHUT, "shall rise up against him" (Iyov 20:27).

243. ד"א לוּ חָכְמוּ יַשְׂכִּילוּ זֹאת. דְּאִיהִי מִתְקַשְׁרָא בְּהוּ בְּיִשְׂרָאֵל, כַּד נַטְרִין פִּקּוּדֵי אוֹרַיְיתָא, וְיַתְבִין עִמָּהּ בִּשְׁלָם, יִנְדְּעוּן דִּסְיַיעְתָּא דְּהַאי זֹאת עִמְּהוֹן, לְאִתְפָּרְעָא מִשַּׂנְאֵיהוֹן. וְיִשְׂרָאֵל דְּאִינּוּן זְעִירִין בֵּינֵי עַמְמַיָּא, יִנְדְּעוּן, אֵיכָה יִרְדּוֹף אֶחָד אֶלֶף וּשְׁנַיִם יָנִיסוּ רְבָבָה. וּמַאן גָּרִים לְהוּ. הַאי זֹאת, דַּהֲוָה בְּהוּ בִּשְׁלָם, כַּד עַבְדִּין פִּקּוּדֵי אוֹרַיְיתָא. וּלְעָלְמִין לָא אִתְעֲדֵי מִנַּיְיהוּ, לְמֶעְבַּד לְהוּ נוּקְמִין.

243. Another explanation for, "O that they were wise, that they understood this (Heb. ZOT)" is that when zot is attached to Yisrael, THAT IS, WHEN they keep the commandments of the Torah and dwell with it wholly, they shall know they have with them the help of zot in taking revenge on their enemies. And Yisrael, who are a minority among the nations shall know, "How should one man chase a thousand, and two put ten thousand to flight" (Devarim 32:30). Who brought it about? Zot, which was wholly in them when they performed the commandments of the Torah. And it will never leave them, or leave wreaking vengeance for them ON THEIR ENEMIES.

244. אִם לֹא כִּי צוּרָם מְכָרָם וַיְיָ' הִסְגִּירָם. מ"ט כִּי צוּרָם מְכָרָם. בְּגִין צוּר יְלָדְךָ תֶּשִׁי, דְּתִקּוּנִין לָא שָׁרָאן כַּדְקָא יָאוּת בְּאַתְרַיְיהוּ. אִם לָא כִּי צוּרָם מְכָרָם. א"ר יְהוּדָה דָּא אַבְרָהָם, כְּמָה דְּאוֹקִימְנָא, דְּאָמַר אַבְרָהָם יִתְחַיְּיבוּן יִשְׂרָאֵל בְּגָלוּתָא, וְלָא יֵיעֲלוּן בַּגֵּיהִנָּם דִּתְרֵין אִלֵּין גָּלוּתָא וְגֵיהִנָּם, לָא יִסְבְּלוּן יִשְׂרָאֵל. וְקוּדְשָׁא בְּרִיךְ הוּא אִסְתְּכַם עַל יְדוֹי, דְּכָל זִמְנָא דִּי יְחוּבוּן יִשְׂרָאֵל, יִפְּלוּן בְּגָלוּתָא, וְיִשְׁתַּעְבְּדוּן בְּהוּ שַׂנְאֵיהוֹן. וּבג"כ, צוּרָם מְכָרָם וַדַּאי, וַיְיָ' הִסְגִּירָם, וְאִסְתְּכַם עַל יְדוֹי.

244. "unless their Rock had sold them, and Hashem had shut them up" (Ibid.). What is the reason "their Rock had sold them"? It is because, "Of the Rock that begot you you are unmindful" (Ibid. 18), as these structures do not properly rest in their place. "their Rock had sold them": Rabbi Yehuda said, This is Abraham, as we explained that Abraham said, Let Yisrael be forced into exile rather than go to Gehenom, because Yisrael cannot bear these years of exile and Gehenom. And the Holy One, blessed be He, agreed with him that as long as Yisrael sin they will fall into exile and their enemies will enslave them. For that reason, that "their Rock had sold them," surely, NAMELY ABRAHAM WHO DELIVERED THEM INTO EXILE, "and Hashem had shut them up," since He agreed with him.

59. The reason Moses admonished them

A Synopsis

Rabbi Yehuda and Rabbi Yitzchak talk about why Moses admonished them with his poem when they were about to enter the promised land.

245. תַּנְיָא, א"ר יְהוּדָה, מ"ט אוֹכַח לְהוּ מֹשֶׁה בְּהַאי שִׁירָה הָכִי, בְּגִין דְּאִינְהוּ זְמִינִין לְמֵיעַל לְאַרְעָא, ולאשרי בֵּינַיְיהוּ שְׁכִינְתָּא, ובג"כ אוֹכַח לְהוּ עַל הַאי.

245. We learned, Rabbi Yehuda said, What is the reason Moses admonished them in this poem? It is that they were about to enter the land of Yisrael and the Shechinah was about to rest among them. For that reason He admonished them about that.

246. ר' יִצְחָק אָמַר, בִּתְרֵי אַתְרֵי קוּדְשָׁא בְּרִיךְ הוּא זַמִּין לְאוֹכָחָא לְהוּ לְיִשְׂרָאֵל, וְחָדָאן אוּמּוֹת הָעוֹלָם. חַד דִּכְתִּיב, וְרִיב לַיְיָ' עִם יְהוּדָה וְלִפְקוֹד עַל יַעֲקֹב כִּדְרָכָיו וְגוֹ'. שַׁמְעִין אוּמּוֹת הָעוֹלָם חָדָאן, אַמְרֵי, הַשְׁתָּא יִשְׁתֵּצוּן מֵעָלְמָא, כַּד חָמֵי קוּדְשָׁא בְּרִיךְ הוּא דְּאִינּוּן חַדָאן, מַה כְּתִיב בַּתְרֵיהּ. בַּבֶּטֶן עָקַב אֶת אָחִיו וְגוֹ'. כַּד שַׁמְעִין, אַמְרִין דָּא הוּא תְּשׁוּבָה.

246. Rabbi Yitzchak said, The Holy One, blessed be He, will admonish Yisrael in two places and the nations in the world will rejoice. The first is as written, "Hashem has also a controversy with Judah, and will punish Jacob according to his ways" (Hoshea 12:3). The nations of the world hear and rejoice. They say, Now these will be wiped away from the world. But when the Holy One, blessed be He, saw them rejoicing, it is then written, "He took his brother by the heel in the womb…" (Ibid. 4). When they heard that, they said, This means repentance FOR THE INIQUITIES OF YISRAEL.

247. לְאִתְּתָא דַּהֲוָה לָהּ קְטָטָה בִּבְרָהּ, אַזְלַת לְמִקְבִּיל עָלֵיהּ דִּינָא, חָמַאת לְדַיָּינָא דְּאִין נַפְשִׁין. מְנַּיְיהוּ לְאַלְקָאָה, לְצַלְבָא, לְאוֹקְדָא,

אָמְרָה וַיְיָ מַה אַעֲבִיד מִן בְּרָא. כַּד סַיֵּים דִּינָא, אָמַר לְהַהִיא אִינְתּוּ, אִימָּא, מַה אַעֲבִיד לָךְ בְּרִיךְ, אָמְרָה קוֹבְלַנִי עכ"מ.

247. THIS IS like a woman who had a quarrel with her son. She went to cry out and sue him. When she saw the judge judging criminal laws, sentencing some to whipping, and some to hanging or burning, she said, Woe if I shall do so to my son. THAT IS, SHE BEGAN TO FEAR LEST HE WILL SENTENCE HER SON TOO TO ONE OF THESE PUNISHMENTS. When the judge finished the trial, he said to that woman, Tell me what your son did. She said to him, I complain (THE END IS MISSING). ACCORDING TO THIS IT SEEMS THAT SHE SAID SHE COMPLAINED THAT HE PAINED HER IN HER WOMB, WHEN SHE WAS PREGNANT WITH HIM. OF COURSE, THE JUDGE DID NOTHING TO HIM FOR THAT.

60. From the book of physician Kartana

A Synopsis

We learn about the things written in the book of a physician called Kartana, who wrote about the care a wise physician needed to take of people who were sick. A correspondence is made between sick people and those who are ill in the sense that they cannot worship God. God wishes there to be a wise physician who can help people to get well, that is, to repent and atone for their sins. If the physician can administer medicine for the body, it is well, but otherwise he should give a person healing for his soul. God will bless such a physician in this world and in the World to Come. We hear that some of the remedies in the book of Kartana were permitted to use and some were forbidden. Rabbi Elazar had had the book in his possession for twelve months, and learned many mysteries from it, but eventually he was told in a dream that he should not use the book, so he gave it away to Rabbi Yosi. Rabbi Elazar concludes Ha'azinu by blessing God for abolishing witchcraft from the world.

248. יִמְצָאֵהוּ בְּאֶרֶץ מִדְבָּר וּבְתֹהוּ, וַדַּאי לְבָתַר עָבֵד לְכָל אִינּוּן קְלִיפִּין, דִּיהוֹן כֻּלְּהוּ מִשְׁתַּעְבְּדִין לֵיהּ. עַד הָכָא הֲוָה כְּתִיב בְּהַהוּא סִפְרָא, דְּקַרְטָנָא אַסְיָא לְבָתַר הֲוָה רָשִׁים בְּהַאי קְרָא, כָּל נְטוּרָא דְּאִצְטְרִיךְ אַסְיָא חַכִּים לְמֶעְבַּד לִמְרַע דְּשָׁכִיב בְּבֵי מַרְעֵיהּ, בֵּי אֲסִירֵי דְּמַלְכָּא, לְמִפְלַח לְמָארֵי עָלְמָא.

248. "He found him in a desert land, and in the waste" (Devarim 32:10): Surely he afterwards caused all these Klipot IN THE WILDERNESS AND IN THE DESERT to be all enslaved TO YISRAEL. THE VERSES heretofore were written in the book of a physician called Kartana. He used to write under this verse all the care a wise physician needs to take of the sick in their bed. THAT IS, IT IS THE CUSTOM OF THE PHYSICIAN TO FIRST WRITE DOWN BEFORE HIM THE STATE HE FOUND THE PATIENT IN, AND THEN TO PRESCRIBE MEDICINE. IN THIS ORDER THESE VERSES WERE ARRANGED HERE IN THAT BOOK. AT FIRST THE BOOK MENTIONED THE VERSES, "HE FOUND HIM IN A DESERT LAND...," NAMELY THE STATE IN WHICH HE FOUND THE PATIENT. THEN HE USED TO WRITE THE NEXT VERSE, IN WHICH IS WRITTEN ALL THE CARE A WISE PHYSICIAN HAS TO TAKE OF A

SICK MAN LYING IN BED, in the prison of the prisoners of the King, THAT IS, THEY ARE ILL IN THE SENSE THAT they CANNOT worship the Master of the universe.

249. דְּכַד אָזִיל אַסְיָא חַכִּים לְגַבֵּיהּ, יִמְצָאֵהוּ בְּאֶרֶץ מִדְבָּר וּבְתֹהוּ יְלֵיל יְשִׁימוֹן, מַרְעִין דְּשַׁרְיָין עָלֵיהּ, אַשְׁכַּח לֵיהּ בַּאֲסִירוּ דְּמַלְכָּא. אִי תֵּימָא הוֹאִיל וְקוּדְשָׁא בְּרִיךְ הוּא פָּקִיד לְתַפְשָׂא לֵיהּ, דְּלָא יִשְׁתְּדַל בַּר נָשׁ אֲבַתְרֵיהּ. לָאו הָכִי, דְּהָא דָּוִד אָמַר, אַשְׁרֵי מַשְׂכִּיל אֶל דָּל וְגוֹ', דָּל הַהוּא דְּשָׁכִיב בְּבֵי מַרְעֵיהּ. וְאִי אַסְיָא חַכִּים הוּא, קוּדְשָׁא בְּרִיךְ הוּא יָהִיב לֵיהּ בִּרְכָאן, לְהַהוּא דְּיִשְׁתְּדַל בֵּיהּ.

249. THIS IS WHAT HE WROTE IN THAT BOOK: when a wise physician visited a sick man, "He found him in a desert land, and in the waste howling wilderness," that is, since illnesses rest on him, he is placed in the King's jail, IN A WASTE WILDERNESS. You may say that since the Holy One, blessed be He, ordered to detain him in jail, one must not try for his sake TO CAUSE HIM TO REPENT. This is not so, as David said, "Blessed is he who considers the poor…" (Tehilim 41:2). That SICK MAN who lies on his bed is poor. If HIS NEIGHBOR is a wise physician, the Holy One, blessed be He, blessed whoever strives for his sake.

250. וְהַהוּא אַסְיָא, יִמְצָאֵהוּ בְּאֶרֶץ מִדְבָּר, בְּבֵי מַרְעֵיהּ שְׁכִיב. וּבְתֹהוּ יְלֵיל יְשִׁימוֹן, דְּאִינּוּן מַרְעִין דַּחֲקִין לֵיהּ. מַאי אִצְטְרִיךְ לֵיהּ לְמֶעְבַּד. יְסוֹבְבֶנְהוּ: יְסוֹבֵב סִבּוֹת, וְיֵיתֵי עִלּוֹת, בְּגִין דְּיִמְנַע מִנֵּיהּ אִינּוּן מִלִּין דְּנַזְקִין לֵיהּ. יַקִּיז לֵיהּ, וְיַפִּיק מִנֵּיהּ דָּמָא בִּישָׁא. יְבוֹנְנֵהוּ: יִסְתְּכַּל וְיָבִין הַהוּא מַרְעָא מִמָּה הֲוֵי, וְיִסְתְּכַּל בְּגִין דְּלָא יִתְרַבֵּי עֲלוֹי, וְיַמְאִךְ לֵיהּ. לְבָתַר יִצְּרֶנְהוּ כְּאִישׁוֹן עֵינוֹ, בְּגִין דִּיְהֵא נָטִיר כַּדְקָא יָאוּת, בְּאִינּוּן מַשְׁקֵי, בְּאִינּוּן אַסְוָותָא דְּאִצְטְרִיכוּ לֵיהּ, וְלָא יִטְעֵי בֵּינַיְיהוּ. דְּאִלְמָלֵי יִטְעֵי, אֲפִילוּ בְּמִלָּה חַד, קוּדְשָׁא בְּרִיךְ הוּא חָשִׁיב עַל הַהוּא אַסְיָא, כְּאִלּוּ שָׁפִיךְ דָּמָא וְקַטְלֵיהּ.

250. HE EXPLAINS HIS WORDS, That physician "found him in a desert land," namely lying on his sickbed; "and in the waste howling wilderness," beset by illnesses. What should he do? "he led him about" (Devarim 32:10), to bring about reasons AND EXCUSES to withhold from him what is harmful to him, to let HIS BLOOD, and take out of him the evil blood; "he instructed him" – he should observe and understand the origin of the disease, and make sure the disease will not spread but diminish. Then, "he kept him as the apple of his eye" (Ibid.), so that he will be properly kept in regard to the drinks and the medicines he needs, and not get confused between them. For if he confuses even one thing AND DIES, the Holy One, blessed be He, considers that doctor as if he shed blood and killed him.

251. בְּגִין דְקוּדְשָׁא בְּרִיךְ הוּא בָּעֵי, דאע"ג דְּהַהוּא בַּר נַשׁ אִיהוּ בְּבֵי אֲסִירֵי דְּמַלְכָּא, וְאִיהוּ אָסִיר בְּבֵי אֲסִירֵי, דְּיִשְׁתְּדַל בַּר נַשׁ עָלֵיהּ, וִיסַיֵּיעַ לֵיהּ לְאַפָּקָא לֵיהּ מִבֵּי אֲסִירֵי. וַהֲוָה אָמַר הָכִי. קוּדְשָׁא בְּרִיךְ הוּא דָּן דִּינִין דִּבְנֵי עָלְמָא לְעֵילָּא, הֵן לַמָּוֶת הֵן לְשָׁרוּשֵׁי, הֵן לַעֲקוֹר, הֵן לַעֲנוֹשׁ נִכְסִין, וּלְאָסוּרִין. מַאן דְּאִתְחֲזֵי לַעֲנוֹשׁ נִכְסִין, נָפַל בְּבֵי מַרְעֵיהּ, וְלָא יִתְסֵי, עַד דְּיִתֵּן כָּל מַה דְּאִתְגְּזַר עָלֵיהּ. כֵּיוָן דְּאִתְעֲנָשׁ בְּמָמוֹנֵיהּ, וְיָהִיב כָּל מַה דְּאִתְגְּזַר עָלֵיהּ, אִתְסֵי, וְנָפַק מִבֵּי אֲסִירֵי. וע"ד אִצְטְרִיךְ לְאִשְׁתַּדְּלָא עָלֵיהּ דְּיִתֵּן עוֹנְשֵׁיהּ וְיִפּוּק.

251. For the Holy One, blessed be He, wishes it that although that person is in the King's prison and is imprisoned there, UNABLE TO FREE HIMSELF, someone will make an effort for him and help him get out of jail. And he used to say: The Holy One, blessed be He above sentences the people in the world either to death, to be uprooted from the root BOTH ONE AND ONE'S CHILDREN, to be punished in property, or to be put in jail. Whoever is sentenced to a punishment regarding his property falls ill and is not healed until he pays whatever he was sentenced to. After being punished in his money and having given whatever he was sentenced to, he is healed and leaves prison. This is why one must persuade him to serve his penalty and leave prison.

252. מַאן דְּיִתְחֲזֵי לְשָׁרוּשֵׁי, יִתְפְּסוּן לֵיהּ, וְיָהֲבֵי לֵיהּ בְּבֵי אֲסִירֵי, עַד דְּיִשְׁתְּרַשׁ מִכֹּלָּא. וּלְזִמְנִין דְּיִשְׁתְּרַשׁ מִשַּׁיְיפֵי, אוֹ מֵחַד מִנַּיְיהוּ, וּלְבָתַר יַפְּקוּן לֵיהּ מִבֵּי אֲסִירֵי. מַאן דְּיִתְחֲזֵי לַמָּוֶת, הָכִי הוּא, דְּאִילּוּ יִתֵּן כָּל

כּוּפְרָא, וְכָל מָמוֹנָא דְעָלְמָא לָא יִשְׁתְּזִיב.

252. Whoever is sentenced to uprooting, he is seized and put in prison until he is uprooted in every sense, THAT IS, UNTIL HE AND HIS CHILDREN DIE. Sometimes he is uprooted in limbs or in one of them. Whoever is sentenced to death, it so happens THAT HE DIES. And even if he gives as ransom all the money in the world, he cannot be saved.

253. וְעַל דָּא אִצְטְרִיךְ לְאַסְיָא חַכִּים, לְאִשְׁתַּדְּלָא עֲלֵיהּ, אִי יָכִיל לְמֵיהַב לֵיהּ אַסְוָותָא מִן גּוּפָא, יָאוּת. וְאִי לָאו, יִתֵּן לֵיהּ אַסְוָותָא לְנִשְׁמָתֵיהּ, וְיִשְׁתְּדַל עַל אַסְוָותָא דְּנִשְׁמְתָא. וְדָא הוּא אַסְיָא דְּקוּדְשָׁא בְּרִיךְ הוּא יִשְׁתְּדַל עָלֵיהּ בְּהַאי עָלְמָא וּבְעָלְמָא דְּאָתֵי.

253. A wise physician is therefore needed to make efforts for him. If he can administer bodily medicine, it is well. Otherwise, he should give him healing for his soul, and strive for healing for the soul. The Holy One, blessed be He, will strive TO BLESS such a physician in this world and in the World to Come. (UNTIL HERE THE WORDS OF THE BOOK OF THE PHYSICIAN KARTANA).

254. א״ר אֶלְעָזָר, עַד הַשְׁתָּא לָא שְׁמַעְנָא מֵאַסְיָא דָּא, וּמִסִּפְרָא דָּא. בַּר מִזִּמְנָא חֲדָא, דְּאָמַר לִי טַיְּיעָא חֲדָא, דְּשָׁמַע לַאֲבוֹי, דְּאַסְיָא חַד הֲוָה בְּיוֹמוֹי, דְּכַד הֲוָה מִסְתַּכַּל בב״נ, כַּד אִיהוּ בְּבֵי מַרְעֵיהּ, הֲוָה אָמַר, דָּא חַי וְדָא מֵת. וַהֲווּ אַמְרִין עָלֵיהּ דְּהוּא זַכָּאָה קְשׁוֹט, דְּחִיל חַטָּאָה. וְכָל מַה דְּלָא יָכִיל לְמִדְבַּק מַה דְּאִצְטְרִיךְ, אִיהוּ הֲוָה קָנֵי, וְיָהִיב מִדִּילֵיהּ. הֲוָה אַמְרִין, דְּלֵית חַכִּים בְּעָלְמָא כְּגִינֵיהּ. וּבִצְלוֹתֵיהּ הֲוָה עָבֵיד יַתִּיר, מִמַּה דַּהֲוָה עָבֵיד בִּידוֹי. וּכְדִדְמֵי לָן, דָּא הֲוָה הַהוּא אַסְיָא.

254. Rabbi Elazar said, I have never heard until now of this doctor KARTANA, and of this book, except once when a merchant told me he heard from his father that there used to be a doctor in his time, who, when he would look at a person in his bed, he would pronounce, this one shall live, that one shall die. They say about him that he was a truly righteous who feared sin. Whatever the patient had to get but could not afford, he used to buy and give of his own. They say there was none as wise in the world as he. He used to do more in his prayer than what he would do with his hands. It seems to us it is the same doctor KARTANA.

255. אָמַר הַהוּא טַיְּיעָא, וַדַּאי סִפְרָא דִּילֵיהּ בִּידִי אִיהוּ, דְּקָא יָרִיתְנָא מֵאָבִי אַבָּא, וְכָל מִלּוֹי דְּהַהוּא סִפְרָא, כֻּלְּהוּ אִתְיַיסְּדוּן עַל רָזִין דְּאוֹרַיְיתָא, וְרָזִין סְתִימִין אַשְׁכַּחְנָא בֵּיהּ, וּמִלִּין דְּאַסְוָותָא סַגִּיאִין, דְּאִיהוּ אָמַר דְּלָא יָאוּת לְמִפְעַל לוֹן, בַּר אִי אִיהוּ דְּחִיל חַטָּאָה.

255. That merchant said, Surely his book, OF THAT DOCTOR, is in my possession. I inherited it from my father's father. All the subjects of that book were based on secrets of the Torah. I have found in it hidden mysteries and many medical instructions, OF WHICH he said one may not use unless he is sin-fearing.

256. וְאִינּוּן מִמַּה דַּהֲוָה עָבִיד בִּלְעָם, דַּהֲוָה לָחִישׁ לְחִישִׁין עַל מְרַע, וַהֲוָה אָמַר בְּפוּמוֹי וְאִתְסֵי מִיַּד. וְכֻלְּהוּ בָּרִיר לוֹן בְּהַהוּא סִפְרָא. וְאָמַר, דָּא אָסוּר, וְדָא מוּתָּר לְמַאן דִּדְחִיל חַטָּאָה. בְּגִין דְּמַרְעִין סַגִּיאִין אָמַר, דְּתַלְיָיא אַסְוָותָא דִּלְהוֹן, בִּלְחִישׁוּ דְּפוּמָא. וְאִינּוּן מִסִּטְרָא דְּנָחָשׁ, וּמִנְּהוֹן מִסִּטְרָא דְּקֶסֶם. וְכָל אִינּוּן דְּאָסוּר לוֹמַר בְּפוּמָא, וְאָסוּר לְמֶעְבַּד בְּעוֹבָדָא, הֲוָה אָמַר. עַד דְּאַשְׁכַּחְנָא עַל מַרְעִין יְדִיעָאן דְּאִצְטְרִיךְ לוֹמַר כָּךְ. וּלְנַדּוּיֵי בְּנִדּוּי וּבְשַׁמְתָּא, עַל הַהוּא מְרַע. וְאִיהוּ תַּוָּוהָא סַגֵּי לְגַבָּן.

256. They, THE REMEDIES WRITTEN DOWN THERE, come from what Bilaam used to do. He used to whisper incantations over the disease and utter with his mouth, and he would be instantly healed. They are all explained in that book. He said that this one is forbidden for whoever fears sin TO USE and that one is permitted TO USE. For there are many diseases, he said, which medicine derives from whispering with the mouth. Some come from the aspect of enchantment and others from the aspect of divination. He stated THERE all those it is forbidden to utter and forbidden to act. I even found what should be said in cases of certain diseases to eradicate the diseases. This amazed us greatly.

257. חַדֵי ר׳ אֶלְעָזָר, וְחַדוּ חַבְרַיָּיא. א״ר אֶלְעָזָר, אִי הַהוּא סִפְרָא הֲוָה לְגַבָּן נֶחְמֵי מַה אִיהוּ אָמַר. אֲנָא אִמְסַר בִּמְסִירָה, עַל מְנַת לְאַחֲזָאָה לְבוּצִינָא קַדִּישָׁא. וְתָנֵינָן, א״ר אֶלְעָזָר, הַהוּא סִפְרָא הֲוָה בִּידִי תְּרֵיסָר יַרְחֵי, וְאַשְׁכַּחְנָא בֵּיהּ נְהוֹרִין עִלָּאִין וְיַקִּירִין. כַּד מָטֵינָא לְאִינּוּן רָזִין דַּהֲוָה מִבִּלְעָם תַּוַּוהְנָא.

257. Rabbi Elazar rejoiced and so did the friends. Rabbi Elazar said, If we have that book we will know what it says. And I shall deliver it, THAT IS, HE WILL GIVE A PROMISE to show it to the Holy Luminary, HIS FATHER RABBI SHIMON. We learned that Rabbi Elazar said, That book was in my possession twelve months, and I have found in it supernal precious mysteries. When I reached the secrets that came from Bilaam I was amazed.

258. יוֹמָא חַד לָחִישְׁנָא בַּאֲתָר חַד, וַהֲווֹ אַתְוָון סַלְקָן וְנַחְתָּן. עַד דַּחֲמֵינָא בְּחֶלְמָא, וְאָמַר לִי מַה לָּךְ לְמֵיעַל בִּתְחוּמָא דְּלָא דִּילָךְ, וְלָא אִצְטְרִיךְ לָךְ. אִתְּעַרְנָא, וְאַבְאִישׁ קַמָּאי, עַל רָזִין סְתִימִין דַּהֲווֹ תַּמָּן. שָׁדַרְנָא לְהַהוּא יוּדָאִי, וְר׳ יוֹסֵי בַּר׳ יְהוּדָה שְׁמֵיהּ, וְיָהִיבְנָא לֵיהּ סִפְרָא.

258. One day I made an incantation in a certain place and the letters went up and down, until I saw him in my dream telling me, It is not your business going into a field that is not your own; you do not need it. And I woke up. It was difficult for me TO PART WITH THIS BOOK, because it contained concealed mysteries. I sent it to that Jew, Rabbi Yosi son of Rabbi Yehuda by name, and gave him that book.

259. וּבְרָזִין דְּבִלְעָם אַשְׁכַּחְנָא, מֵאִינּוּן שְׁמָהָן דְּמַלְאָכִין דְּשָׁדַר לֵיהּ בָּלָק, וְלָא הֲווֹ מִסְתַּדְּרָן עַל תִּקּוּנַיְיהוּ כַּדְקָא יָאוּת. אֲבָל כַּמָּה זִינֵי אַסְוָותָא אַשְׁכַּחְנָא בֵּיהּ, דְּקָא מִתְתַּקְּנֵי עַל תִּקּוּנֵי אוֹרַיְיתָא, וְרָזִין סְתִימִין דִּילָהּ. וַחֲמֵינָא דְּאִינּוּן בַּחֲסִידוּתָא. וּצְלוֹתִין וּבָעוּתִין לְקוּדְשָׁא בְּרִיךְ הוּא. וְאִי תֵּימָא, דַּהֲוָה עָבֵיד אַסְוָותָא בִּפְסוּקֵי אוֹרַיְיתָא, אוֹ בְּרָזִין דְּאוֹרַיְיתָא. ח״ו. אֶלָּא הֲוָה אָמַר רָזִין דְּאוֹרַיְיתָא, וְעַל הַהוּא רָזָא אַפִּיק רָזִין דְּאַסְוָותָא, דְּלָא חֲמֵינָא כְּהַהוּא גַּוְונָא לְעָלְמִין. אֲמֵינָא בְּרִיךְ

רַחֲמָנָא, דְּאַחְכִּים לִבְנֵי נָשָׁא מֵחָכְמְתָא דִּלְעֵילָּא.

259. In the secrets of Bilaam I found some of the names of the angels Balak sent to him, but they were not properly arranged. But I have found different kinds of medicines in it, IN THAT BOOK, based on the structures of the Torah and its hidden mysteries, and saw they are founded on piety, prayers and petitions to the Holy One, blessed be He. If you argue that he used to practice medicine using words of Torah or the secrets of the Torah, heaven forbid, because it is forbidden to do so. But he would speak secrets of the Torah, and based on that secret he would invent medical secrets such as I have never seen. I said, blessed is the Merciful who made people wise with celestial wisdom.

260. וּמֵאִינּוּן מִלִּין דְּבִלְעָם נָסִיבְנָא, וַחֲמֵינָא בְּהוּ דְּלָא הֲוָה בְּעָלְמָא חַכִּים בַּחֲרָשִׁין כְּגִינֵיהּ. אֲמֵינָא, בְּרִיךְ רַחֲמָנָא דְּבִטֵּל מֵעָלְמָא חַרְשִׁין, דְּלָא יִטְעוּן בְּנֵי נָשָׁא מִבָּתַר דַּחַלְתָּא דְקוּדְשָׁא בְּרִיךְ הוּא יִת' וְיִת' שְׁמוֹ אָמֵן. ע"ב.

260. From the words of Bilaam I received, and saw from them that there was no one in the world as knowledgeable in witchcraft as he. I said, blessed is the Merciful, who abolished witchcraft FROM THE WORLD, so they will not mislead and remove people from fearing the Holy One, blessed be He, may His name be exalted and blessed, amen.

בָּרוּךְ יְיָ' לְעוֹלָם אָמֵן וְאָמֵן יִמְלוֹךְ יְיָ' לְעוֹלָם אָמֵן וְאָמֵן.

Blessed is Hashem forever Amen and Amen. May Hashem reign forever, amen and amen.

NOTES